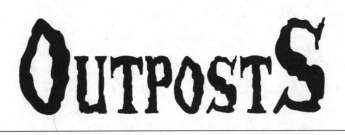

# OUTPOSTS

## A CATALOG OF RARE AND DISTURBING
## ALTERNATIVE INFORMATION

# OUTPOSTS

## BY RUSS KICK

## A CATALOG OF RARE AND DISTURBING ALTERNATIVE INFORMATION

CARROLL & GRAF PUBLISHERS
A RICHARD KASAK BOOK
NEW YORK

First Carroll & Graf/A Richard Kasak Book Edition 1995

First Printing May 1995

ISBN 0-7867-0202-8

Cover Art © 1995 Robert Therrien, Jr.

Cover Design by Kurt Griffith

Series Editor: Jennifer Reut

Manufactured in the United States of America

Published by Carroll & Graf
260 Fifth Avenue
New York, NY 10001

*To my parents, who taught me that it's OK to be strange.*

## TABLE OF CONTENTS

| | |
|---|---|
| Introduction | 1 |
| How to Use This Book | 5 |
| Freedom | 7 |
| Conspiracies, Cover-ups, and Hidden Information | 33 |
| Drugs | 59 |
| Sex | 73 |
| Alternative Culture | 121 |
| Cyberculture | 127 |
| Extremism | 133 |
| Merry Mischief | 143 |
| The Body | 151 |
| The Mind | 167 |
| Beliefs | 175 |
| The Unexplained | 183 |
| Comix | 193 |
| Art | 199 |
| Fiction | 213 |
| Grab Bag | 231 |
| Appendix A: General Book Catalogs | 243 |
| Appendix B: Publishers' Addresses | 247 |

## AN UNFORTUNATELY NECESSARY DISCLAIMER, BECAUSE WE ARE LIVING IN A LITIGATION-HAPPY SOCIETY

*Outposts* reviews material that may discuss activities that are illegal, quasi-legal, and/or risky. The author, the publisher, and all other parties involved with this book are merely presenting this information. They are not giving legal, financial, medical, or any other type of advice. They are not saying that you should do these things.

Look, what it boils down to is this: The people of *Outposts*—as well as everybody else in the world—cannot and will not be held responsible for your actions. Your actions are yours and yours alone. (Kinda scary, ain't it?)

## ACKNOWLEDGMENTS

Many people helped make *Outposts* possible. First of all, I'd like to thank my parents. They let me live at home and write this book, without ever once even dropping a hint that I should get a "real job." Without their support, I wouldn't have been able to complete this book in even twice the time it took me. Big thanks also to Richard Kasak at Masquerade for believing in my ideas and abilities. *Outposts* was the easiest sell in the history of publishing. I also appreciate the tireless efforts of everybody at Masquerade who made this unwieldy beast of a book the best that it could be.

Thank you, Seth Friedman for letting me do reviews for the legendary *Factsheet Five* and not complaining when my book consumed all my time. Thanks, Barry Hoffman, for allowing me to be *Gauntlet's* resident non-fiction reviewer.

Most of all, I'd like to thank all the publishers and writers who spend their energy, money, and time to bring their visions into the world.

# INTRODUCTION

## OR THE OUTPOSTS MANIFESTO

### OR HOW TO TELL CONSENSUS REALITY TO KISS YOUR ASS, AND LIVE HAPPILY EVER AFTER

> In a world of hypocrites and false prophets,
> it's the outlaws who know where the spirit resides.
>
> —Paul Monette

We live in a collective delusion. To make this scary and confusing world a little more bearable, we humans have created an artificial, arbitrary set of rules and regulations that we expect ourselves and others to follow. These rules may be official laws (if you ingest certain substances, you will go to prison) or unofficial mores (if a woman enjoys sex, she is a slut). These rules, regulations, laws, mores, codes, guidelines, and standard operating procedures don't have to make sense, they don't have to be fair, and they don't have to be applied equally to all people in all situations. They are, however, in place, and anyone who disobeys them is asking for trouble.

Fortunately, there are many people who ask for trouble. They raise their finger to society. They give a big "FUCK YOU!" to governments, religions, corporations, the media, the education system, the medical and scientific establishments, and any other institutions that try to ram their conformist messages down our throats. These rebels and rabble-rousers have identified and short-circuited the tricks and traps that society uses to silence dissenters.

## TRICKS AND TRAPS

The previously named institutions will try any number of insidious methods to get people to accept unquestioningly the oppressive conditions they live under. The most obvious method is active suppression. Declaring the zine *Boiled Angel* to be "obscene" and arresting its publisher, comix artist Mike Diana, is a perfect example. As always, Christian fundamentalists are continuing to get books banned from school and public libraries. Also, Canada often will not allow sadomasochistic and homoerotic material into its borders.

Using dirty tricks to disrupt publication and distribution of books is another way of suppressing ideas and information. This is what the FBI did to the publishers of *Ecodefense: A Field Guide to Monkeywrenching*. The FBI and one of its agents did fancy legal maneuvering to keep *In the Spirit of Crazy Horse*, which tells the real story of the war against the American Indian Movement, off the shelves. It worked for a while—the book was unavailable for almost a decade—but now it's out again. Which just proves the cyberpunk maxim: Information wants to be free. Although this saying originally meant "free" as in "no cost," "free" has achieved the broader meaning of "without restrictions and limitations." In other words, the authorities can try all they want to quash ideas and facts, but such tactics will never completely work. Information will always escape and reach people who want and need it.

A related method of suppressing information is through intimidation and threats. Among those who know this well are the Holocaust revisionists, who say that the Nazi program of genocide against Jewish people never occurred. This idea is inflammatory, and it's easy to see why so many people are infuriated by it, but that doesn't justify the Gestapo-like tactics of terror, violence, and destruction that are used against the Holocaust revisionists. The forces of suppression have even gone so far as to burn down the offices of the leading publisher of such material.

Intimidation also occurs in the legal arena. When *Adbusters* magazine ran a parody of the Absolut vodka ads, Absolut threatened the publication with legal action. *Adbusters* responded by running another Absolut parody. The proposed Victims of Pornography legislation would shift blame for rapes from the rapist to the people who produce and distribute pornography. Under this legislation, victims of rape would be able to sue pornographers if they can somehow prove that the porn "made" the rapist commit the act. (For decades, rape was blamed on the victim. Now rape is being blamed on an uninvolved third party. When will the responsibility for rape finally be put squarely on the shoulders of the actual criminal?)

The third way of making sure people aren't exposed to nonconformist ideas is to ignore such information. The mainstream news media are masters of this. Despite rhetoric to the contrary, the media are not liberal. Nor are they conservative. They are pitifully status quo oriented. With few exceptions, the last thing the mainstream media want to do is rock the boat. Tobacco-driven magazines are scared to run articles about the deadly effects of and despicable advertising campaigns for Jesse Helms's favorite addictive drug. CNN would rather run "hard-hitting exposés" on alternative health practitioners who are obviously charlatans instead of telling the world about truly life-saving alternative treatments for cancer, AIDS, and other diseases. The media will gladly report on Senator Alfonse D'Amato (R-NY) leveling charge after well-deserved charge against President Clinton based on Whitewater, but do you ever hear reports on D'Amato's own supremely sleazy dealings?

The fourth tactic takes a different approach than the previous three. Instead of trying to prevent you from getting "dangerous" information, society makes you afraid of such information. If people learn how to grow their own marijuana, we'll have a nation of potheads. If people read a book on how to kill people, they'll go out and do it. If children are exposed to pro-gay literature, they'll grow up homosexual. These real-life idiocies are all examples of "infophobia," the fear of information. Books, magazines, art, movies, music, etc. cannot hurt you. Moreover, these things cannot "make" you or anyone else do anything. You must realize that if someone has the desire and inclination to kill someone, whether or not they read a book isn't going to make a damn bit of difference. The reverse is also true. I could read books on killing people night and day for the rest of my life, and I would still never harm a living soul (except in the case of self-defense).

A variation of the "be afraid—be very afraid tactic" is the "ridicule tactic." Those in power will make fun of information in order to make the rest of us think that such ideas and facts are worthless. This is what the medical establishment does to alternative medicine. Chiropractic, vitamins, oxygen therapy, unorthodox theories about AIDS, etc. are all laughed at, and practitioners are made out to be quacks, charlatans, and garden variety idiots. Although some of these people are no doubt bogus (people like that exist in every field), there are many practitioners who have had amazing successes with nontraditional methods. People are being denied chances to receive life-saving cures because the medical establishment, on the whole, is as rigid and narrow-minded as any organized religion you could name.

Finally, besides ridiculing information, society will make fun of *you* if you are interested in things or hold opinions that aren't deemed appropriate. Examples abound. Conspiracy theorists are "paranoid." People interested in sex are "perverts." People interested in drugs are "junkies." If you are fascinated by death, you're a morbid "ghoul." If you honestly examine whether there are differences among people based on race, gender, or other characteristics, you're "racist, sexist, politically incorrect."

## THE METHOD TO MY MADNESS

Much of the material in *Outposts* is extraordinarily provocative. Being familiar with the fate of people who question things, I can see the reactions now. Even a lot of people who are open-minded and progressive in their thinking will no doubt be upset by what I've included in this book. Good. As speculative fiction writer Harlan Ellison has said, "I'm not here to reaffirm your concretized myths and provincial prejudices. I make your nose run and your eyes water." I want to push your buttons and piss you off. "That's great, Mr. Tough Guy," I can hear people saying, "but how would you like that done to you?" I love it! I routinely read things I don't agree with. Reading only stuff that supports your beliefs gets you nowhere. You're just a member of a congregation listening to the preacher. I read things that upset me because I want to know what other people have to say. I want them to present theories and facts that I may never otherwise be exposed to. If I still don't agree with them, at least I know where they're coming from. And sometimes they'll point something out or unleash an explosive fact that will cause me to rethink my own precious beliefs. Some people might argue that if my opinions can be swayed, then they aren't very strong to begin with. I would have to counter with a quote I picked up somewhere along the way: "If you can't change your mind, are you sure you still have one?"

## MY BIAS

I've tried not to take sides in my reviews. I've tried *so* hard not to make smart-ass comments (although a few did creep in—to thyself be true). Being neutral is an especially hard thing to do when you're discussing things you don't agree with, but my main goal in this book is to present you with a rainbow of radical ideas and let you make up your own mind. The only bias I show—you'll have no trouble spotting it on every page—is against authority and for freedom. This world would be so much nicer if everybody would leave everyone else the hell alone. So you'll notice me lashing out at manipulative institutions and people who would deny us the freedom to write what we want, think what we want, have sex with whom we want, ad nauseam. I believe hatred for authority is the only healthy kind of hatred there is.

## AUTHORITY'S CROTCH

Understanding the traps that society has laid out for people who question the way things are is an important part of the battle to be free, to think for yourself. Deciding to defy these bogus traps is the next step, and the most important one. Actually forming your own opinions requires listening to what everybody has to say. You already know what mainstream society and the bastions of authority have to say—all of us practically drown in their ridiculous messages every day. The key is getting access to ideas outside the norm. You need information that has run the gauntlet of suppression, intimidation, ridicule, and being ignored. That's where *Outposts* comes in.

No doubt many of you are already familiar with much of the material in this book. Hopefully, there are some of you who are being exposed to it for the first time. You're taking your first steps into new, unfamiliar territory. No matter what level you're at, I hope *Outposts* will expose you to new ideas, new sources of information, and new doors to walk through.

I've always questioned the way things are because my parents taught me to think for myself (although I've taken their basic philosophy to levels I'm sure they never dreamed of). But it wasn't until several years ago that I became seriously immersed in all facets of underground, alternative, and independent thinking. I learned a lot while developing my own radical views and an unquenchable interest in everybody else's radical views. Even so, the six short months during which I wrote *Outposts* formed the most intense period of my life. Every single day I was bombarded from all directions by so much mind-blowing, reality-challenging information that it changed me radically. I've developed new ideas, questioned old beliefs, and become much more uncompromising in my rejection of all forms of limitations and restraints. In fact, I like to think of *Outposts* as a direct kick to authority's crotch. I strongly encourage you to do some kicking of your own.

# HOW TO USE THIS BOOK

*Outposts* contains more than seven hundred reviews of books, zines, newsletters, and catalogs, plus a few videocassettes, and a CD-ROM. Chapters divide the material into broad categories, and subheads further classify the material. Deciding where to put various items was a chore at times. The "tyranny of categories" forced me to place everything somewhere, so I did the best I could. You may not agree with where I put everything, but remember, I may not agree with where I put everything either.

Every item is listed because I thought it deserved attention and that you'd like to know about it. Publishers did not pay to be in this book, and I refused to accept bribes (mainly because no one offered any).

The end of each review contains information about that item. Zines and newsletters are listed with their addresses, single-issue prices, and subscription prices. Not all periodicals offer you the chance to buy a single issue through the mail. If you don't see a price listed for just one issue, you might try writing and pleading with the publisher. Each catalog review contains the appropriate address and price.

Entries on books include a bit more information:

•The publisher's name. Refer to Appendix B, "Publishers' Addresses," to find the address, phone number, shipping charges, etc., of a particular publisher. If a publisher's name is followed by another name in parentheses, for example, "Basic Books (HarperCollins Publishers)," the first name is an imprint or subcompany of the second name. The second name is the one you'll find listed in Appendix B.

•Price. Prices are given in U.S. dollars, except where noted. When something is published outside the United States, I've also given the U.S. price when the publisher has set one. Otherwise, consult your bank or tune into CNN for current exchange rates, and then get an international money order at a post office.

•Publication date. I've given the original publication dates (as opposed to reprint dates) for books. When a book is a second edition, revised edition, etc., I've given the date for that edition.

•Format. The format of a book can change. A hardcover that I've reviewed may be out in a cheaper softcover version by the time you read the review. Large publishers and university presses almost always release softcover versions of their hardcover books. Small presses sometimes do, but it's not as often.

•Page count. What can I tell ya?

## GETTING THESE PUBLICATIONS

I hope that after reading these reviews you're going to want some of this stuff. If you're interested in buying, check the bookstores in your area first. Also check the various catalogs listed throughout the chapters and in Appendix A, "General Book Catalogs." I suggest you get at least get two or three catalogs, if not all of them.

If you can't find the book or zine, or you're too embarrassed to buy it in a store, you can always order it from the publisher. As mentioned, book publishers' addresses are in Appendix B. The addresses of zines, newsletters, and catalogs are given right after the review. Note that the name of a publisher or business isn't always the same as the name of its publication. For example, when ordering an issue of *Nude and Natural*, you'd write to The Naturists, Inc. You also should make all checks and money orders payable to the business or individual listed in the address.

When ordering a zine, the general rule is to send cash. I know that's not how you were brought up, but the zine world is an exception. Many publishers don't have business accounts in their zine's name. If you do send cash, however, realize that the publisher isn't responsible if it gets lost.

If you order directly from the publisher, please mention that you saw their book, zine, etc. in *Outposts*. Publishers like to know where you found out about their products, and they'll know that being included in my book helped them gain exposure.

If lack of money is the problem, check public and university libraries. You might not think of libraries as a place to load up on strange and subversive reading material, but you'd be surprised. You might find what you're looking for. If not, don't forget to try interlibrary loan. Just be prepared for some strange looks (I've certainly received my fair share).

## GLOSSARY FOR THE SUBCULTURALLY IMPAIRED

I really hope that many people will get their first taste of underground/independent thought from *Outposts*. It is for these people that I offer this short glossary of frequently used terms. For the rest of you, it will seem hopelessly elementary, but don't forget that we all had to learn this somewhere.

**pomo:** short for postmodern. Postmodernism is a somewhat vague concept that applies to art, literature, philosophy, your basic attitude, and more. Basically, it means that reality is up for grabs. Everything is relative, there are no absolutes, linear thought is just one option, and rules are for sissies. In its more specific sense, postmodernism refers to the brain-crushing lines of thought being presented by (mainly French) philosophers such as Jacques Derrida and Jean Baudrillard.

**SM:** short for sadomasochism. Often abbreviated by outsiders as S&M. You'll also see it referred to as S/M. No matter how you abbreviate it, SM refers to a wide variety of erotic activities that involve the *voluntary* giving and receiving of pain and/or humiliation for fulfillment. These activities may or may not involve sexual penetration and orgasms.

**zine:** "Zine" was originally short for "fanzine," which was in turn short for "fan magazine," although it now refers to any amateur periodical. Zines are usually put out by one or two people as a labor of love, not to make money. There are many arguments about what makes a publication a zine as opposed to a full-fledged magazine. Is it attitude, circulation, production values, the number of people who work on it, or some other factors that define a zine? I've chosen to use the term "zine" in the loosest sense, meaning any periodical with an independent attitude and a blatant disregard for commercialism and mass appeal.

Zines cover every subject you could ever imagine. It's been estimated that at any point in time, there are 10,000 zines in existence. Most zines last one issue, although there are many—such as the ones I list—that have proved their staying power.

# FREEDOM

## FREE SPEECH

### BANNED IN THE U.S.A.:
#### A REFERENCE GUIDE TO BOOK CENSORSHIP IN SCHOOLS AND PUBLIC LIBRARIES
#### by Herbert N. Foerstel

Schools and public libraries being forced to remove controversial books has become a familiar event. Guardians of purity step in to yank any book that doesn't give children a candy-coated, sissified view of the real world. The author does a great job chronicling this phenomenon in a number of ways.

Chapter 1 presents some major book-banning incidents from 1973 to 1992. In West Virginia, a school board member, who also happened to be a preacher's wife, charged that textbooks under consideration for use were "filthy, disgusting trash, unpatriotic, and unduly favoring blacks." Furthermore, the PTA charged, "Several passages are extremely sexually explicit." Fliers were passed around that contained sexually explicit passages from other books, but it was claimed that they came from the textbooks. When parents actually read the textbooks, of course, they couldn't find the offending passages, so—get this—they actually accused the administration of hiding the books with the "filthy" passages. The school board adopted all but eleven of the books, and all hell broke loose. Of the county's forty-five thousand school kids, nine thousand were kept home by their parents, and practically the whole county went on strike. In a beautiful, brotherly move, "The Reverend Charles Quigley shocked the county by asking Christians to pray that God would kill the three board members who voted to keep the books." Also, "A *Charleston Gazette* article revealed: 'A few extremists among the churchmen who wanted 'godless' textbooks removed from the schools became so fanatical they discussed bombing carloads of children whose parents were driving them to school in defiance of a boycott called by the book protestors.'" In fact, one school was dynamited and another was firebombed, school buses were shot at, and homes of children who attended school were stoned.

The textbook committee met again, deciding to keep almost all the textbooks but giving parents the right to refuse to have their children taught from them. A lot of good that did. Violence got worse, and two police cars escorting a school bus were fired on. By the next school year, new, bland books were approved, and some schools even went back to textbooks they used in the 1940s.

Chapter 2 examines all of the Supreme Court cases relevant to the freedom of schools to use books. Chapter 3 contains the author's discussions with several of the most banned authors, including Judy Blume, Robert Cormier (author of *I Am the Cheese*), and Jan Slepian (*The Alfred Summer*). The final chapter lists the fifty most banned books of the 1990s, with a short history of the battles surrounding each one.

Greenwood Publishing Group; $45
1994; hardcover; 231 pp.

### CENSORSHIP NEWS

Put out five times a year by the National Coalition Against Censorship, this four-page newsletter is my assurance that I will get pissed off at least once every two or so months (actually, I get pissed off a lot more than that). Issue #57 brings word of a case of censorship so ludicrous that it defies explanation. It is almost beneath contempt, but I'm going to show contempt anyway. Here's the deal—the boneheaded vice squad of Cincinnati, the city that brought you the Mapplethorpe case, arrested the owner, manager, and clerk of a gay/lesbian bookstore for "pandering obscenity." Their horrendous crime? An undercover vice officer rented from them Pier Paolo Pasolini's film *Salò*. This twenty-year-old movie about Fascists who sexually degrade a group of teenagers and young adults is without a doubt disturbing. But for

something to be declared obscene, it must be shown to have no "literary, artistic, political, or scientific value." Pasolini is considered one of the greatest directors in the history of cinema, and he's also a well-respected poet and novelist. *Salò* has undisputed artistic and political value, so there is no way in hell that it will ever be ruled obscene. I can't help but wonder what's next on the Cincinnati vice squad's seizure list. Michelangelo's *David*? The *Venus de Milo*?

This and other issues regularly contain articles about library censorship, radical feminists attacking "porn," textbook challenges, and loads of other topics.

NCAC/275 Seventh Avenue/New York, NY 10001
By donating at least thirty dollars you get five issues of *Censorship News* and access to other NCAC publications.

### 50 WAYS TO FIGHT CENSORSHIP:
#### AND IMPORTANT FACTS TO KNOW ABOUT THE CENSORS
#### by Dave Marsh

A manual of ways to individually or collectively fight the suppression of ideas. Some of the ideas are more do-able than others, and some seem more likely to accomplish something than others, but at least you can get some good starting points here. Some of the activities include voting, writing Congress, getting involved with your library, writing a letter to your local paper, buying banned records, "write movie moguls and tell them to eliminate the MPAA system," joining the ACLU, running for office, organizing a voter registration drive, petitioning, starting a newsletter, "make sure local schools have a course on freedom of speech" (yeah, I can see *that* happening), picketing the censors, sue, etc.

*50 Ways* also contains addresses and information about anti-censorship and procensorship organizations.

Thunder's Mouth Press; $5.95
1991; softcover; 128 pp.

### FORBIDDEN 3-D

A 3-D comic book that details the national hysteria over comics in America in the late 1940s through the mid-1950s. During this time many self-appointed guardians of purity, most notably children's book author Sterling North and psychiatrist Fredric Wertham, attacked comic books, saying that they were corrupting the nation's children, turning them into rebellious, violent, and even homicidal delinquents. Parents went out of their minds in terror and many comic book burnings took place. Congress even held hearings on comics and juvenile delinquency, placing incredible pressure on the comic industry. To defuse the witch hunt, the comic publishers agreed to set up the censorious Comics Code Authority, which effectively ended the Golden Age of comics.

The whole brouhaha over comics is being exactly paralleled today by the attack on video games and TV violence. As always, our nation's leaders are willing to attack fictional representations of violence instead of addressing its true causes. Some things never change. (Note: 3-D glasses are included with this comic.)

The 3-D Zone; $3.95
1993; comic book format; 24 pp.

*Girls Lean Back Everywhere* ➤ by Edward de Grazia
(See page 10)

*Censorship and the First Amendment.*

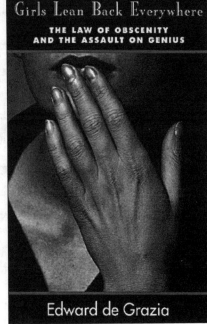

Girls Lean Back Everywhere
THE LAW OF OBSCENITY AND THE ASSAULT ON GENIUS

Edward de Grazia

## THE FREE SPEECH MOVEMENT:
### COMING OF AGE IN THE 1960s
### by David Lance Goines

This book takes us back to the roots of the Free Speech Movement, which was a major turning point in the history of the First Amendment. The author was part of this movement. It was he and some other University of California at Berkeley students who set up a table on campus offering literature. In September of 1964, the University of California declared, "University facilities may not, of course, be used to support or advocate off-campus political or social action." Later that month, Goines and some fellow students set up a table to distribute political literature. They were suspended. The next day another student set up another table and this time was arrested. In a totally unplanned move, for thirty-two hours 3,000 students blocked the police car that was hauling off the student.

The Free Speech Movement had started. In December students organized a strike and sit-in at Sproul Hall. California's largest mass arrest in history resulted, with more than eight hundred people going to the klink. The movement spread out and helped to change obscenity laws and sexual attitudes. From there, leaders of the movement went on to become guiding lights of the civil rights, anti–Vietnam War, and farm workers' movements.

But this book is much more than a firsthand account of the movement. It's an encyclopedia containing a plethora of information and source documents: accounts from other movement insiders, more than two hundred photos, a list of all eight hundred or so people who were arrested and the results of their trials, a glossary of organizations and terms, a forty-four-page chronology of the movement and related events, a reprint of *The Free Speech Songbook*, and even more.

Put simply, if you're into First Amendment issues, you must have this book. Period.

Ten Speed Press; $27.95
1993; hardcover; 767 pp.

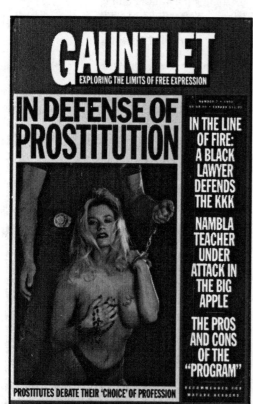

*Gauntlet*

*Free speech,
from down in
the trenches.*

## GAUNTLET:
### EXPLORING THE LIMITS OF FREE EXPRESSION

*Gauntlet* is a thick semi-annual magabook devoted to exploring free speech issues, not from a bland, academic viewpoint but from down in the trenches. Not only does *Gauntlet* look at the most controversial issues of the day, it also reprints censored material.

Each issue contains a theme that runs through anywhere from eight to thirty articles. Themes have included political incorrectness, media manipulation, pornography, black racism, and prostitution. Other hot potato subjects *Gauntlet* has dealt with are an African American lawyer who defended the KKK, a member of the North American Man/Boy Love Association who's teaching at a New York high school, pot legalization, hate-crime legislation, adoptee rights, and more.

What pushes *Gauntlet* over the edge is that in addition to tackling inflammatory topics, it reprints inflammatory images. Artists such as Andres Serrano, David Wojnarowicz, Robert Williams, Clive Barker, and John Rousso have had their work shown in *Gauntlet*. Issue #6 contained an article on the iconoclastic lesbian magazine *On Our Backs*. It seems that *OOB* planned to run three photos that their printer found objectionable, and for a while no one was sure if the issue was going to get printed at all.

Eventually, *OOB* replaced the photos in question, but *Gauntlet* printed all three photos, including one of a white woman licking a black dildo, which evidently sent the printers into shock. That same issue of *Gauntlet* also reprinted drawings by Mike Diana that had led in part to Diana's arrest and conviction on obscenity charges.

The major chain bookstores refuse to carry *Gauntlet,* and it's had trouble getting into Canada and prisons, all because it frankly examines the exercise of free expression. Highly recommended.

Gauntlet/309 Powell Road/Springfield, PA 19064
Single issue: $11.95; Canada: $13.95; foreign: $16.95
One-year sub (2 issues): $22; Canada: $28; foreign: $34

## THE BEST OF GAUNTLET:
### EXPLORING THE LIMITS OF FREE EXPRESSION
### edited by Barry Hoffman

This book presents twenty-eight of the best articles dealing with sex and gay and lesbian issues from the first seven issues of *Gauntlet*. Several of the articles deal with adult comix—*Cherry*, *Raw*, *Hot Box*, and Mike Diana's work. Others deal with pornography, including Phyllis Schlafly's antiporn piece "Pornography's Victims." Sex-positive role models Annie Sprinkle and Candida Royalle are interviewed. Other articles deal with the media's treatment of the queer community, controversial art, and prostitution.

Unfortunately, this book isn't illustrated, which is a terrible drawback considering that so much of *Gauntlet*'s reputation is built on its willingness to show what others are afraid to.

A Richard Kasak Book (Masquerade Books); $12.95
1994; softcover; 226 pp.

## HATE SPEECH:
### THE HISTORY OF AN AMERICAN CONTROVERSY
### by Samuel Walker

One of the stickiest First Amendment issues—one that troubles even some free speech advocates—is the use of hate speech. "Difficult though the question might be, the United States has fashioned a clear and coherent answer. As a matter of law and national policy, hate speech is protected by the First Amendment." This book deals with the question of how that commitment to protecting hate speech developed.

To answer that question, the author goes back to the 1920s, when groups persecuted on racial and religious grounds began organizing and demanding their rights. One of their battles was against hate speech. On the other side was the American Civil Liberties Union. These battles marked the first time the issues surrounding hate speech were raised. However, these struggles didn't rise to national attention and were soon forgotten.

In the 1930s, with the Nazis' rise to power in Germany, fascist groups began appearing in the United States, sparking debates that raised the issue of hate speech to a national level. In the 1940s the Supreme Court began to put together a coherent policy on free speech, including the protection of inflammatory speech directed at specific groups. The culmination of this policy, as the author sees it, was the Supreme Court's decision in 1978 to let a neo-Nazi group march in Skokie, Illinois.

But things changed in the 1980s. Campuses nationwide began instituting speech codes that prohibited language deemed offensive to various minorities and women. The Supreme Court, however, did strike down the campus speech codes at two major universities. It also ruled that a St. Paul ordinance against hateful symbols (e.g., burning crosses, swastikas) was unconstitutional. Even without free speech advocate Justice Earl Warren, the Supreme Court still protects the most extreme forms of speech.

*Hate Speech* provides vital information on perhaps the most emotionally charged of First Amendment issues.

University of Nebraska Press; $11.95
1994; softcover; 217 pp.

## NEWSLETTER OF INTELLECTUAL FREEDOM

If you want the up-to-the-minute score on the battle between the thought police and people who want to think for themselves, you can't do better than the *Newsletter of Intellectual Freedom*, put out by the American Library Association. The bimonthly, thirty-two-page newsletter reports from all fronts. It contains dozens of short articles on censorship occurring in cities across the United States and other countries—instances involving libraries, schools, student publications, periodicals, theaters, television, music, art, and more. There are also reports on court decisions regarding schools, broadcasting, commercial speech, etc. The section "Is It Legal?" reports on actions across the country that either possibly or definitely violate the First Amendment and related laws. For example, the March 1994 issue reports on a school district in Pennsylvania where students and teachers publicly read Bible verses, in direct opposition to a 1963 Supreme Court ruling that expressly outlawed such action.

Just when everything locks hopeless, just when you're ready to bang your head against the wall repeatedly because all is lost, you get to the newsletter's final section, "Success Stories." The March 1994 issue reports on public libraries all over the United States that refused to yank controversial material, such as *Rolling Stone*, historical romances, *Heather Has Two Mommies*, *Halloween ABC*, *Do or Die*, and others.

Each issue also contains longer articles on topics including gangsta rap, Christian college libraries, freedom of the press in Eastern Europe, censorship surveys, etc. The last page of each issue contains a bibliography of recent articles and books relating to free speech. The newsletter is an invaluable guide, easily worth its price.

Newsletter of Intellectual Freedom/American Library Association/50 E. Huron Street/Chicago, IL 60611
Single issue: $8
One-year sub (6 issues and annual index): $40

## WAR OF WORDS:
### The Censorship Debate
### edited by George Beahm

A collection of interviews, speeches, essays, and source documents concerning free speech and censorship. Although the book is obviously weighted toward free speech, much space is given to those with opposing viewpoints. Among the people and groups sounding off are Kurt Vonnegut, James Michener, Art Buchwald, Salman Rushdie, former NEA chairman John Frohnmeyer, Jesse Helms, Pat Robertson, Phyllis Schlafly, Isaac Asimov, the American Library Association, Frank Zappa, Morality in the Media, and Anne Rice.

Many interesting documents are included, too. The position statement of Waldenbooks proclaims, "The shelves of our 1,150 stores hold a wide array of titles containing ideas as diverse as the world in which we live." Yeah, just try to find something by Pat Califia, Louis Farrakhan, or RE/Search Publications at your local mall bookstore. The Comics Code of the Comics Magazine Association of America, Inc., is interesting: "Policemen, judges, government officials, and respected institutions shall never be presented in a way as to create disrespect for established authority.... Females shall be drawn realistically without exaggeration of any physical qualities [Am I to understand that the seven-foot, green-skinned She-Hulk is a realistically drawn female?].... Seduction and rape shall never be shown or suggested [interesting how this sentence implies that seduction and rape are equivalent]." The list of programs attacked by Rev. Donald Wildmon, founder of the American Family Association, is a revelation. Although I can understand why a Puritan would object to *The Golden Girls*, *Cheers*, and *Three's Company*, why does the list also contain *World of Disney*, *20/20*, and *Let's Make a Deal*?

Andrews and McMeel; $12.95
1993; softcover; 430 pp.

## WHAT JOHNNY SHOULDN'T READ:
### Textbook Censorship in America
### by John Delfattore

The author first became concerned about textbook censorship when he was teaching a summer class in literature for teachers. The class was studying *Romeo and Juliet*. Two of the teachers were using high school literature anthologies that contained the play; the other teachers used paperback versions. It turns out that the anthologies had cut three hundred lines from Shakespeare's play, and, what's more, they made no mention of this fact. All sexual references (including "bosom" and "maidenhood") had been excised, as had lines that characterized religion as harsh and judgmental.

The author's quest to see what else our children were being denied led him to censors on both sides of the political fence. Conservative Christians want to do away with textbooks that deal with reason or creative thinking because these are both acts of rebellion against God. Liberal censors demand that textbooks only show women in nontraditional roles, denying the fact that many women actually do stay home and make tea and cookies.

It is the Christian fundamentalists, though, who do the bulk of censoring, and all six federal cases described in this book are the work of fundies, including the rancorous *Mozert* v. *Hawkin County Public Schools*, a four-and-a-half-year battle to get Holt readers out of classrooms, which is described in detail. The author also looks at the tactics used to have the teaching of evolution stopped and to ban works of literature from being taught in school.

The most disturbing parts of the book are the final two chapters, which show the chilling effects this controversy has had on textbook publishers. A spokesman from publishing giant Holt, Rinehart and Winston summed it up: "When you're publishing a book, if there's something that is controversial, it's better to take it out." Some publishers include Martin Luther King Jr.'s "I Have a Dream Speech" in textbooks, but they remove its references to racism in southern states. The states of California and Texas, the two most lucrative textbook markets in the country, have the clout to force publishers to change their books, from deleting entire selections to making line-by-line changes.

Yale University Press; $12
1992; softcover; 209 pp.

# ARTISTIC FREEDOM

## THE BODY IN QUESTION
### (Aperture #121)

My hat is off to *Aperture* for creating one of the gutsiest, most confrontational anticensorship publications ever produced. The images they present are so controversial that it is highly possible that even possessing this issue could get you in hot water. But let me back up. *Aperture* is one of the world's leading magazines on photography (they also publish highly respected books and monographs). Although *Aperture* is a "magazine," each issue is more like an oversized, high-quality book with no ads (kind of like the *RE/Search* series, except not as thick). *Aperture* is concerned with photography as art. And as we all know, art has come under intense fire in the last few years, with photography being one of the hardest hit areas.

This issue of *Aperture* examines several aspects of the debate by looking at how the body is portrayed in photography, which leads to discussions of gender, AIDS, domestic violence, sex, and naked children. "The Mirrors of Christer Strömholm" presents that artist's photos of the prostitutes and transsexuals of Paris's red-light district. "The Doll" is a disturbing short story about incest by Patrick McGrath. Karen Finley turns in a poem about abortion. Four of David Wojnarowicz's most controversial works are reprinted along with an essay by the artist. "Sex Workers" reprints several artists' pictures of prostitutes.

By far the most controversial article is "The Right to Depict Children in the Nude," written by Allen Ginsberg and Joseph

Richey, and accompanied by photographs of naked children by Sally Mann, Robert Mapplethorpe, and others. "National hysteria over sexual exploitation cases has created an environment in which the police surveillance extends its bounds to enter the art world, guns drawn, handcuffs ready.... Professional photographers, family album compilers, and shutterbugs alike now need to know when a photo has crossed a fine line in the police mindset to become 'child pornography.'" We hear the horror stories of three artists (all of whom have pictures in this issue) who were busted. The artists' homes and studios were raided, their lives' works were confiscated, and they were prosecuted (persecuted). Steve Miles was threatened with life in prison, but he was able to cop a plea, something he was forced to do because defending himself would have ruined him financially. Alice Sims had her children taken away from her for twenty-four hours, and the Department of Social Services tried to nail her as an "unfit mother." Because of the ludicrousness of the case, the government dropped charges before they embarrassed themselves further. Jock Sturges, the third artist/victim, sums it up this way: "There is no harm or crime in my work—just innocence. When innocence is judged obscene, the obscenity is in the eye of the beholder—*is* the eye of the beholder."

Aperture; $19.95
1990; oversize softcover; 79 pp.

## CULTURE WARS:
### DOCUMENTS FROM THE RECENT CONTROVERSIES IN THE ARTS
### edited by Richard Bolton

A well-rounded collection of documents concerning the controversy triggered by the government's funding of art considered obscene by some. Documents include newspaper columns, speeches to Congress, laws, transcripts of debates, direct mailings, letters, essays from mainstream and alternative press magazines. Among the contributors are Jesse Helms, Patrick Buchanan, National Association of Artists' Organization, Allen Ginsberg, Karen Finley, David Wojnarowicz, Garrison Keillor, former NEA chairman John Frohnmeyer, and a host of other government officials, organizations, artists, and conservative and liberal social commentators.

As you can imagine, tempers flare and opinions are fierce in much of this anthology. In a direct mail piece from Pat Robertson's Christian Coalition about Robert Mapplethorpe's photographs, we find this: "So they're [the ACLU and liberal Democrats] calling anyone who attacks this garbage 'censors' and they're hiding behind 'free speech' and 'freedom of expression' as a reason to continue funding this pornographic filth." In a *Washington Times* column, Richard Grenier says, "I'm just imagining Mr. Mapplethorpe's dead body lying around someplace, and me seized with a desire to express myself.... So I think I'd sprinkle him with kerosene and burn him up."

Allen Ginsberg counters: "This arts censorship rot-gut originated in the beer-soaked bucks of Joseph Coors, was moonshined in Heritage Foundation think-tanks, and is peddled nationwide by notorious tobacco-cult Senator Jesse Helms. These alcohol-nicotine kingpins have the insolence to appoint themselves arbiters of Public Morality." Robert Hughes, art critic for *Time*,

writes, "One of Serrano's pieces [*Piss Christ*] was a photo of a plastic crucifix submersed in the artist's urine—a fairly conventional piece of postsurrealist blasphemy, which, though likely to have less effect on established religion than a horsefly on a tank, was bound to irk some people."

Besides having about one hundred written pieces, *Culture Wars* also reprints many controversial works of art, including *Piss Christ* and several of Mapplethorpe's SM photographs.

The New Press; $19.95
1992; softcover; 363 pp.

## GIRLS LEAN BACK EVERYWHERE:
### THE LAW OF OBSCENITY AND THE ASSAULT ON GENIUS
### by Edward de Grazia

It's only within this century that artistic expression has been recognized as protected under the First Amendment. One of the people who has helped bring that about happens to be the author of this book, defense attorney Edward de Grazia. De Grazia gives a detailed account of the court battles and political wranglings over dozens of books and other art—James Joyce's *Ulysses*, Radclyffe Hall's *The Well of Loneliness*, Henry Miller's *Tropic of Cancer*, Vladimir Nabokov's *Lolita*, William Burroughs's *Naked Lunch*, Allen Ginsberg's *Howl*, Holly Hughes's performance art, Robert Mapplethorpe's photographs, Lenny Bruce's monologues, 2 Live Crew's songs (OK, so they're not exactly in the same league as everything else on this list), and more.

De Grazia approaches the subject in a unique way. His own narrative is interspersed with hundreds upon hundreds of quotes, many quite lengthy, from the people involved—authors, artists, publishers, judges, censors, etc.—and from the books involved. The quotes are well picked, shedding light on the matter at hand. For example, De Grazia quotes Henry Miller's description of his own book *Tropic of Cancer*: "This then? This is not a book. This is libel, slander, defamation of character...a prolonged insult, a gob of spit in the face of Art, a kick in the pants to God, Man, Destiny, Time, Love, Beauty..."

By combining his own commentary with choice source material, De Grazia has created an epic depicting the struggle for artists to create what they want to create and people to read what they want to read.

Vintage Books (Random House); $17
1992; softcover; 814 pp.

## SEX, SIN, AND BLASPHEMY:
### A GUIDE TO AMERICA'S CENSORSHIP WARS
### by Marjorie Heins

This book takes a look at the stifling of free expression that is occurring in a large number of areas: movie ratings systems, censorship of certain plays and dances, the photographing of nude children, gangsta rap, flag art, blasphemous art, pornography, performance art, and more. Heins tells of the movement by Tipper Gore et al. to label records: "The hearing became a kind of media circus in which Senator Ernest Hollings attacked rock as 'outrageous filth' that he would ban completely if he could. Sixties musical legend Frank Zappa described the perils of labeling, recounting how one music store had labeled his album, *Jazz from Hell*—even though it was entirely instrumental." Long live rock!

This book also covers the ways in which censorship is performed—through the idiotic notion of "obscenity" (if authorities get something labeled obscene, it can no longer be legally sold or purchased by *anyone*), veiled and outright threats by government officials to make trouble if certain movies or records are not taken off store shelves, slapping the word *pornography* on any work of art that deals with sex or even contains nudity, Christian groups pressuring gutless corporations into withdrawing their ads from certain "subversive" shows, only allowing government funding based on a set of criteria (à la the NEA), and even the newest weapon of closed minds, political correctness. "In late 1991 a female professor at Pennsylvania State University's Schuylkill

*Culture Wars*
edited by
**Richard Bolton**

*Guerrilla Girls bite back on behalf of artists everywhere.*

campus complained that the display on a classroom wall of Francisco de Goya's classic *Nude Maja* constituted sexual harassment.... She was supported by the university's Commission for Women, and the reproduction was taken down."

The New Press; $11.95
1993; softcover; 210 pp.

# RELIGION

## BLASPHEMY:
### VERBAL OFFENSE AGAINST THE SACRED FROM MOSES TO SALMAN RUSHDIE
### by Leonard W. Levy

When I found out that a history of sacrilegious writing and speech was coming out, I was excited by the prospects of finding out all about this explosive topic. When I found out that it was going to be put out by a major publisher, I got worried. Would it be sanitized? Would they ask their author, a First Amendment scholar, to tone things down? Then when I saw the cover, I realized I didn't have to worry. It's a full-page reproduction of Andres Serrano's infamous photograph *Piss Christ*. But what's really interesting is that in the book itself, the author refers to this picture, and a collage by David Wojnarowicz that contains an image of Jesus shooting up, as "scum" and implies that they are "garbage." Luckily he holds the civil libertarian view that even scum and garbage are protected by the First Amendment. "The use of the criminal law to assuage affronted religious feelings imperils liberty—not greatly, to be sure, because blasphemy laws have become legal relics in the Anglo-American world. But they are reminders that a special legal preference for religion in general, or for Christianity in particular, violates the Constitution."

This history of blasphemy begins thirty-three centuries ago, when the Christians believe, God told Moses that blasphemers should be put to death, setting in motion the rich Judeo-Christian tradition of killing people with different beliefs. Other early beliefs were uptight about slandering the sacred, too. Anaxagoras, the first Athenian philosopher, was persecuted and nearly killed for espousing monotheism. Only Pericles' silver tongue saved Anax from getting the ax.

The author continues his detailed trip through two millennia of history with examinations of Jesus' trial for heresy, early Christian heresy, Christian treatment of Jews, Protestantism's love affair with blasphemy, Anabaptists, Unitarians, Ranters, Diggers, Quakers, Deists, atheists, colonial America, Thomas Paine, blasphemy and obscenity, America and England in the 1800s, Bible burning, and modern blasphemy cases such as the prosecution of the *Gay News* for publishing a poem, and the death threats given to Salman Rushdie for writing the *Satanic Verses*.

The book concludes on the ominous note that it's still possible—though unlikely—to be prosecuted for blasphemy in the United States. The Supreme Court has never ruled that any blasphemy law is unconstitutional. Also, there are still blasphemy laws on the books in some states. "When the right occasion and the right prosecutor happen to coincide and a jury does its duty towards religion, someone might be convicted."

Alfred A. Knopf; $35
1993; hardcover; 688 pp.

## CASTING THE FIRST STONE:
### THE HYPOCRISY OF RELIGIOUS FUNDAMENTALISM AND ITS THREAT TO SOCIETY
### by R.A. Gilbert

A penetrating look at the goals, tactics, and successes of the Religious Right. The author contends that the RR stands for intolerance, against freedom, and wants to impose its minority viewpoint on all of society. He does a great job of showing exactly what the RR is saying in its attacks on the New Age so-called cults, Catholicism, Freemasonry, rock and roll, environmentalism, and alternative health, among other targets.

The RR's propaganda against cults, legal moves to curtail religious freedom, twisting of scientific arguments, and spreading of satanic panic are all examined.

One of the best aspects of the book is that it exposes the lunacy of some of the claims being made by the RR. Appendix 3 reprints partial lists of areas "that could open the door to the occult" from Ron Livesy's book *Understanding the New Age*. Under the heading "Occult," items include hypnosis, Taoism, karate, mascots, Freud, and Indian elephants (what?). A list of cults includes Marxism, Roman Catholicism, Islam, Hinduism, and Buddhism (in other words, any religion except Christianity is a cult). Livesy also believes that "Holistic Healing" is a path to the devil, and lists such culprits as acupuncture, placebo, interpersonal relationships, and positive thinking (are you as confused as I am at this point?).

Element Books; $12.95
1993; softcover; 184 pp.

## CHURCH & STATE

Founded in 1947, Americans United for Separation of Church and State uses advocacy, education, and litigation to protect the wall between religion and government. They fight against mandatory prayer in school, tax money for parochial schools, the Religious Right's attempt to create a theocracy, and the government's meddling in religious affairs. Their monthly newsletter *Church & State* reports from the front lines of the battles.

The July/August 1994 issue reported on a victory—the U.S. Supreme Court overturned a New York court's decision that set up a separate public school district for ultra-Orthodox Hasidic Jewish children. The cover article discusses the Religious Right's growing power in the GOP at state and national levels. Most observers now think that the RR has control of the Republican party in seven states: Virginia, Minnesota, Texas, Oregon, Iowa, South Carolina, and Washington. Some districts in the Lone Star State have passed resolutions saying that abortion is "the shedding of innocent blood which will surely bring God's judgment upon our nation." Lately I'm having trouble remembering if we're living in Iran or the United States.

This issue contains numerous smaller articles covering Louisiana parochial schools losing some federal aid, President Clinton's meeting with the Pope, the possible violation of federal law by Jesse Helms during his 1992 senatorial campaign, a federal court ruling that says closing Illinois public schools on Friday is unconstitutional, and more.

AUSCS/8120 Fenton Street/Silver Spring, MD 20910
Single copy: $2
One-year sub (11 issues): $18

## THE FAMILY AND THE NEW RIGHT
### by Pamela Abbott and Claire Wallace

This dry book examines the philosophy of the New Right, especially as it pertains to the family and related issues—women's rights, sexual orientation, welfare, etc. The authors hit the nail right on the head when they say, "The appeal of the New Right is one of nostalgia—for a lost past when children respected parents, the crime rate was low, marriage was for life and the streets were safe for everyone to walk in. What is concealed when this image of the past is invoked is that it was never a reality but an ideal, a middle-class dream."

The authors dissect and counter (this isn't an objective book) the ideas of the New Right, especially as they are presented by Roger Scruton and Ferdinand Mount in Britain and George Gilder, Charles Murray, et al. in the United States. They also examine the social policies enacted by the best friends the New Right ever had—President Reagan and Prime Minister Thatcher.

Pluto Press; $17.95
1992; softcover; 155 pp.

## SCHOOL PRAYER:
### THE COURT, THE CONGRESS, AND THE FIRST AMENDMENT
### by Robert S. Alley

School prayer is as hot an issue now as it ever was. To make sense of it all, this book begins at the beginning, with James Madison, the "architect" of the religion clauses of the First Amendment. Madison's struggle to phrase and introduce the clauses into the Constitution is a lesson in courage and patience. The author pays particular attention to the second half of this century, covering in great detail presidential pronouncements, congressional struggles, and Supreme Court decisions. Lengthy arguments from all sides are reproduced and commented on. The issue isn't as simple as no prayer in school vs. prayer in school. There are many factors that complicate things. If there is prayer in school, who will create the prayers and who will lead? What about non-Christians? What about voluntary prayer and Bible reading? This book doesn't shy away from the tough gray areas.

Prometheus Books; $27.95
1994; hardcover; 273 pp.

# TAXATION

## THE BIGGEST TAX CHEAT IN AMERICA IS THE IRS
### by Carl Japikse

In a friendly, conversational manner the author shows us how we are being shafted right up the keester by the IRS. He demonstrates how the tax system is used for social engineering; how the system puts the burden of collection on us, forcing us to become intimately familiar with thousands of pages of tax codes or face severe penalties; how you are guilty until proven innocent in IRS court; how you can be audited twice for the same deduction from the same year and have it disallowed the second time even though it was cleared the first time; how the system ruins (and ends) people's lives; and how arrogant the IRS can be. In the end, the author suggests ways to change the IRS for the better and how you can try to make a difference (to tell you the truth, there ain't a whole lot you can do).

Like so many other books I review in this book, this one will make you hopping mad. Don't read it if you have high blood pressure.

Ariel Press; $7.95
1992; softcover; 126 pp.

## COSTLY RETURNS:
### THE BURDENS OF THE U.S. TAX SYSTEM
### by James L. Payne

This book is the first to look at the hidden costs of the U.S. tax system. While the party line is that the IRS is an efficient organization and that running it only costs 1% of the taxes it brings in, looking at all the costs tells a different story. For every dollar we pay in taxes, we pay sixty-five cents in other costs!

What are these other costs? First is the burden of just having to file the damn returns. Keeping records, filling out forms, and hiring tax preparers costs almost a fourth as much as the taxes collected. Second, there are the costs of participating in audits, litigation, and collections. The third cost is the economic disincentive our tax system creates. Taxes discourage investing and working by taking away rewards. Fourth, the cost of avoiding and evading taxes adds to the bill. Finally, there is the relatively low cost of running the IRS. The author also discusses, but doesn't factor into the equation, moral and ethical costs, such as sweating bullets that you're going to get audited and the massive destruction of civil liberties perpe-

trated by the IRS. The author devotes at least a chapter to each cost, conclusively showing that the tax system is more of a burden than anyone has realized.

ICS Press; $14.95
1993; softcover; 264 pp.

## THE FEDERAL MAFIA:
### HOW IT ILLEGALLY IMPOSES AND UNLAWFULLY COLLECTS INCOME TAXES AND HOW AMERICANS CAN FIGHT BACK (SECOND EDITION)
### by Irwin Schiff

Let me preface this review by saying that becoming a tax protester is a good way to get yourself in a world of trouble with a quickness. There are lots of ways that have been developed to get around paying taxes. Most of them will get your ass in a sling. You can go to jail, have all your property stripped from you, and your wages can be garnished for the rest of your life (unless you're Willie Nelson, in which case the IRS will forgive half of your $6 million debt). They don't call the IRS the American Gestapo and the Federal Mafia for nothing, you know.

However, there are some methods that are meeting with some success. People who declare themselves citizens of the sovereign state in which they live seem to be winning the battle not to pay federal income tax. Of course, no matter what approach you take, you damn well better research your heart out and know *exactly* what you're doing. One wrong move, and you're history.

I'm not vouching for the system this book outlines. As always, I'm merely presenting you with an interesting idea. What you do with it is up to you. Irwin Schiff says that paying federal income tax is voluntary. "This is because a compulsory income tax would violate the Constitution's *three taxing clauses*, the Bill of Rights, and the 16th Amendment—all of which impose *restrictions on the government's power and ability* to tax income in ways few Americans understand. So, in order for income tax **not to be unconstitutional** it had to be written on a *non-compulsory basis*." (Sorry about all the italics and bold, but that's how the man writes.) He reproduces many IRS documents stating that compliance in paying taxes is voluntary. He also shows how the IRS and federal courts have manipulated and obscured the truth, so that taxes appear mandatory.

In an interesting point, Schiff notes that no law has ever defined what "income" is. The Supreme Court has ruled that income is corporate profit. Since no individual can earn "corporate profit," there is nothing that can be taxed.

Schiff goes on to explain that since you don't have to pay taxes, every IRS seizure, lien, imprisonment, and so on is illegal. He shows the tricky ways in which the IRS makes such actions look kosher. He also exposes the IRS courts as phony bureaucratic star chambers with no legitimate power.

After presenting his arguments, Schiff gets down to the nitty-gritty. He tells how anyone can stop paying his/her taxes, including how to get your employer to stop withholding taxes and how to prevent withholdings on interest and dividends. He also delves into avoiding IRS audits and summonses, suing the government, suing federal judges personally, government dirty tricks, and more.

Of course, things aren't as simple as they may appear. Schiff has gotten into hot water over his failure to pay taxes and has done time in the klink *twice*. Now, he says he wasn't guilty, and that very well may be the case, but the court system is heavily rigged in favor of the IRS. So even if you're in the right, you can still come out on the short end of the stick. To his credit, Schiff openly admits the troubles he's seen, and he spends much of the book detailing governmental attacks and his counterattacks.

Even if you're not planning to try this stunt yourself, *The Federal Mafia* is a great book to have because it so plainly outlines the reasons that taxes are voluntary and backs it up with IRS codes, Treasury Department documents, and more.

Freedom Books; $23
1990, 1992; oversize softcover; 304 pp.

## AGIT-PROP

### WAR TAX RESISTANCE:
#### A GUIDE TO WITHHOLDING YOUR SUPPORT FROM THE MILITARY (FOURTH EDITION)
#### by the War Resisters League

When you pay your taxes, you are supporting the killing of fellow human beings. In this latest version of the classic guide to tax protest, you'll learn how to withhold your contribution to the war machine. The initial chapters talk about why to resist, the philosophical and moral questions, and how much the United States spends on defense. The chapter "How to Resist" gets down to brass tacks. Not paying your phone tax is one way to resist, but the most effective and prominent way is through income taxes. You can file your tax return like normal, but not pay what you owe. Or you can not file at all. This has an added risk because, "If you don't file, the IRS may invent a ridiculously high income for those years. Another option is to live so that your taxable income is below the level required for filing. Of course, many people have employers who automatically withhold part of their income for tax. This chapter lists six ways to get around this inconvenience."

OK, so you've withheld your money—what do you do when the IRS tries to crucify you? Three chapters deal with the audit and appeals process, collections methods used by the IRS, and how to resist collections. The rest of the book covers the history of war tax resistance, resisting in other countries (Britain, Canada, Germany, Japan, Palestine, and others), personal histories of seventeen resisters, legal resistance (paying under protest, like the woman who gave the IRS a legal, cashable check written on a coffin lid!), and resources for resisters.

New Society Publishers; $14.95
1992; oversize softcover; 131 pp.

### WHO PAY$, WHO PROFIT$?:
#### THE TRUTH ABOUT THE AMERICAN TAX SYSTEM
#### by Ralph Estes

This book uses a unique format to get its ideas across. It's set up as a dialog between an accounting professor at the American University in Washington, D.C., and Rip van Winkle VIII, who's been asleep since 1972. When the professor wakes him up, their discussion turns to taxes, and ol' Rip is in for some rude awakenings. For example, when they discuss taxes on interest payments, the prof says that interest payments on home mortgages are deductible. Rip replies, "Thanks a lot—I don't even have a house mortgage, because I don't have a house. At best I'll be renting an apartment. What interest can I deduct there?" "None." "Well, let's see now. A corporation borrows money to build my apartment building. It gets to deduct the interest?" "Yes." "Some rich dude living in a fancy mansion gets to deduct the mortgage interest on that mansion?" "Right, although it's subject to a maximum limit." "Big deal. Same person borrows money to invest, and gets to deduct the interest." "Yeah." "I'm a poor working stiff renting an apartment, I don't get to deduct any interest?" "Sorry."

In this relatively painless format, the author discusses all kinds of taxes and deductions, pointing out their inherent unfairness. He ends with a vision of how a good tax system would work. There are no IRS horror stories here, just an examination of how the tax system screws the little guy. Essential for understanding how things really work.

Institute for Policy Studies; $8.95
1993; softcover; 147 pp.

### ACT LIKE NOTHING'S WRONG:
#### THE MONTAGE ART OF WINSTON SMITH
#### by Winston Smith

Smith is best known as the visual mastermind behind the Dead Kennedys' album covers, inserts, logo, etc. This book collects his collages, the majority of which subvert those hokey illustrations from ads in 1950s *Life* magazines and *Saturday Evening Posts*. You know the kind—the happy white family sitting around the dinner table or good ol' Mom vacuuming the family room. The perfect example is "Nuclear Family": Mom and Dad are happy and smiling; Junior is jumping for joy. The only problem is Mom has two pupils in one eye, Dad has two ears on one side of his head, and Junior is the worst off—he's got twelve fingers, three ears, and an upside-down eye. Obviously our cheerful suburbanites live in Three Mile Island.

*Act Like Nothing's Wrong* by Winston Smith

*"I love the bomb."*

Other works include Jesus crucified on a cross of dollar bills ("Idol"), a mother cradling her babe, feeding him with a U.S. bomber instead of a bottle ("Force-Fed War"), and a fetus wielding a pistol ("Fetal Attraction"). "We Don't Care. We Don't Have to" shows a corporate room filled with rich, smug executives, while in the foreground two starving children hold up empty bowls.

Last Gasp; $24.95
1993; oversize softcover; 96 pp.

### AIDS DEMO GRAPHICS
#### by Douglas Crimp with Adam Rolston

A collection of written and visual protest from the AIDS Coalition to Unleash Power (ACT UP), an uncompromising, confrontational, activist group that demands that something be done about AIDS. They are not afraid to place blame squarely on the shoulders of profiteering pharmaceutical companies, spineless politicians, the FDA, church leaders, the *New York Times*, and anyone else who, because of greed, hatred, fear, or stupidity, is allowing people to die of AIDS.

ACT UP has created some powerful agit-prop that is reproduced throughout this book. Their most famous work is the minimalist pink triangle with the words "Silence = Death" on a black background. Also powerful is the collage of New York City mayor Ed Koch in a field of tombstones. The headline reads: "What does Koch plan to do about AIDS? Invest in marble and granite."

The bulk of the book is text about ACT UP's numerous protests, demonstrations, disruptions, kiss-ins, and similar events, accompanied by many photographs. The facts and demands presented in ACT UP's fliers and fact sheets are also reproduced. A classic book for anyone involved with the AIDS battle or anyone interested in the methods of powerful protest.

Bay Press; $13.95
1990; softcover; 141 pp.

## FLYPOSTER FRENZY:
### POSTERS FROM THE ANTICOPYRIGHT NETWORK

The Anticopyright Network is a loose coalition of anti-authoritarians who develop and distribute subversive posters. You're encouraged to photocopy these posters and glue them where you think they would do the most good—bus stops, telephone poles, construction sites, etc.

One of the posters shows a person snoozing away happily in bed. The caption says, "I DIDN'T GO TO WORK TODAY...I DON'T THINK I'LL GO TOMORROW. Let's take control of our lives and live for pleasure not pain." Another shows a picture of a riot cop aiming a gun at a protester. The words read "Plastic bullets KILL." Another poster has a woodcutlike illustration of a woman and says, "DEFEND WOMEN'S HEALTH CLINICS." One particularly powerful poster shows a knife stuck through a swastika. The headline screams, "THE ONLY GOOD FASCIST IS A DEAD ONE."

Other posters are pro-labor, pro-queer, anti-rich, anti-consumerism, anti-military, etc. Most of the posters are grainy and amateurish, giving them that real revolutionary, underground-on-a-shoestring feel.

Available from AK Distribution; $12
1992; oversize softcover; 97 pp.

## GRAPHIC AGITATION:
### SOCIAL AND POLITICAL GRAPHICS SINCE THE SIXTIES
#### by Liz McQuiston

Words cannot convey what a work of art this magnificent book is. Inside the huge (10" by 11³/⁴") covers, printed on thick, semiglossy paper, we are treated to a beautifully assembled collection of thousands of posters, T-shirts, billboards, magazines, album covers, and more. All are "weapons of protest and propaganda, shock and subversion" meant to "arrest, accuse, provoke, and plead." All are printed in color (except the black-and-white ones), and the captions and text are extremely informative.

The introductory material presents a brief history of propaganda and protest graphics, including two surprisingly tame etchings from Goya's series *The Disasters of War* and Montgomery Flagg's iconic "I Want You" Uncle Sam poster. Chapter 1 looks at politics. It contains everything from JFK's and LBJ's political posters to Robbie Conal's "art attacks" on Reagan and Bush and the infamous "Fuck the Draft" card-burning poster. The United States, France, Britain, Germany, Japan, Cuba, Central and Eastern Europe, USSR, China, and South Africa are among the nations surveyed.

The chapter on global issues features angry graphics concerning peace, Hiroshima, human rights, apartheid, solidarity, wealth and power, anti-fascism, and more. Chapter 4 is "Shocks to the System: Alternative, Anti-Establishment, and

*Graphic Agitation* by Liz McQuiston

*Anger* and *art from ACT UP.*

Liberation Movements." Graphics in this section include underground comix, the back cover of John Lennon and Yoko Ono's *Two Virgins* (but why not the much more revealing front cover?), the cover of "God Save the Queen" by the Sex Pistols, Black Panther posters, and other stuff dealing with women's lib, the sexual revolution, obscenity, lesbian and gay pride, etc.

"The Caring Society" shows powerful social messages about smoking (including the packaging for Britain's infamous Death cigarettes), drugs, AIDS, alcohol, nutrition and health, gun control, the environment, animal welfare (including stills from the in-your-face, blood-drenched anti-fur commercial from Lynx, a Greenpeace splinter group), and other causes.

In short, this book has got it all. If you're into propaganda and other revolutionary tactics, you simply must dig down deep in your pockets and get this book. It will be the centerpiece of your collection.

Chronicle Books; $49.95
1993; oversize hardcover; 240 pp.

## STEALWORKS:
### THE GRAPHIC DETAILS OF JOHN YATES
#### by John Yates

John Yates has described himself as a "visual media mechanic, image manipulator, and graphic surgeon." He takes images of war, hatred, and stupidity, combines them with a pithy caption, and voila!—instant subversion. This book collects Yates's work from his zine *Punchline*, as well as other publications, T-shirts, album covers, and more.

The work on the book's cover is a good example to start with—it's a grainy picture of a roomful of coffins, each covered in an American flag. At the top in large letters: "Mom, We're Home!" Here are a few other choice examples:

• "Police brutality is a myth. Where's your proof?" The picture is a night shot on a street. A fat, cigarette-smoking cop just a couple of feet away is rearing back with his nightstick, apparently about to knock the shit out of the photographer.

• Remember the famous picture of the South Vietnamese colonel shooting his Viet Cong prisoner in the head, execution style? That picture is reproduced here, except instead of a prisoner, the officer is blowing the Statue of Liberty's head off.

• A picture of two Native Americans huddled in blankets in a rundown wooden building. The captions say: "Amerika—Make Your Reservations Early" and "A White Man's Country—By Invitation Only."

AK Press; $11.95
1994; oversize softcover; 129 pp.

# MEDIAWRENCHING/ CULTURE JAMMING

The idea behind mediawrenching (aka culture jamming) is to beat the media at its own game, to turn the words and images of those who would manipulate us (the news media, corporations, the government) back against them or to offer alternatives to them. Methods include parody advertisements, billboard modification, guerrilla postering of public places, pirate TV and radio, camcorder surveillance, community access television, media pranks, disrupting live media events, and appropriating bits of media into new forms.

## ADBUSTERS QUARTERLY

*Adbusters* is the brainchild of a group of former advertising executives who got fed up with manipulating people. They started *Adbusters* as a way to show how advertising mindfucks the population and encourages mass consumption that destroys the environment. Their most hated targets are those peddlers of poison—alcohol and tobacco companies.

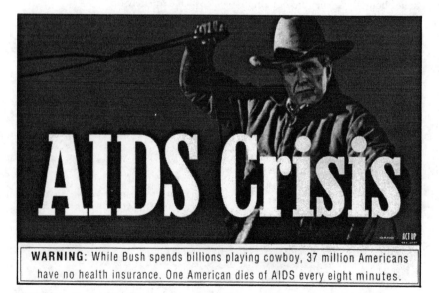

**AIDS Crisis**

**WARNING:** While Bush spends billions playing cowboy, 37 million Americans have no health insurance. One American dies of AIDS every eight minutes.

*Adbusters*'s most famous technique is satirizing famous ads. Their dead-on parody of Absolut vodka ("Absolut Hangover") triggered outrage and legal threats from that company. These enfants terribles of the ad age have also slammed Benetton ("The United Color of Money"), McDonald's, and Calvin Klein (their parody of Obsession, called "Obsessed," shows a very dramatic, tinted shot of a young woman kneeling in front of a toilet bowl, a position familiar to anorexics).

*Adbusters* covers a lot of ground in its quest to help us all take back control of our brains. For example, the winter 1994 issue talked about baby bottles designed to look like Pepsi and 7-Up bottles, a critique of the commercial for the 1994 Honda Accord, genetic manipulation as a future way of changing one's appearance to something more "desirable," Joey Skaggs's latest media prank, ecoforestry, the effects of cyberspace on human interaction, the Cultural Environmental Movement, cigarette advertising, the commodification of Generation X™, and a history lesson called "From Advertising to Subvertising." This magazine is essential reading.

Media Foundation/1243 W Seventh Avenue/Vancouver, BC V6H 1B7/CANADA
Four-issue sub: $18; overseas: $40

## THE COMPLETE MANUAL OF PIRATE RADIO
### by Zeke Teflon

Relatively inexpensive and accessible technology is decentralizing the media. Like camcorders, copy machines, and home computers, pirate radio is another way of using technology to get your message out. Sure, your little pirate radio station may not reach as many people as National Public Radio, but at least you're getting your voice out there.

This booklet gives you all the goods on how to set up your own station by someone who's been there and done it. In a clear, direct manner, Zeke tells you what you need to know about broadcasting on different bands, getting away with radio piracy, buying and building equipment (schematics are included), finding parts, and more. You'll need a basic understanding of electronics to make use of this information. If you're electronically illiterate, Zeke has some suggestions for your education.

See Sharp Press; $5
1993; softcover; 47 pp.

## THE CULTURE JAMMER'S VIDEO

From the Media Foundation, the same pissed-off group of ex-advertising execs who produce *Adbusters*, comes this video of anti-commercials and messages. One shows a slack-jawed couch potato watching TV. The voice-over asks, "Do you spend more time watching nature TV than experiencing the real thing?... More time watching TV sex than making love yourself?" (Do I really have to answer that last question?) Another anti-ad shows a young man eating junk food and watching the tube. The voice-over says, "Your living room is the factory. The product being manufactured is you." The camera travels around the dude and shows a UPC bar code at the base of his neck.

The "American Excess" uncommercial shows the North American continent as a fat, oinking pig. The narrator informs us that 5 percent of the world's population uses one-third of its resources and produces almost half of its nonorganic waste. That small percentage of people are North Americans.

Other messages focus on TV violence, cars, tree farms, and apathy. You can get broadcast-quality copies of these anti-ads for free from the Media Foundation. They can be aired after midnight pretty cheaply. One imaginative *Adbusters* reader suggested copying the messages from this tape over the commercials and coming attractions at the beginning of videos you rent. Do whatever it takes to spread the word.

Media Foundation; $25
1993; VHS videocassette; 12 min

## CULTURE JAMMING:
### CULTURE JAMMING, HACKING, SLASHING, AND SNIPING IN THE EMPIRE OF SIGNS
### by Mark Dery

This pamphlet first examines the "empire of signs" in which we live, filled with "Hollywood blockbusters, television sitcoms, catchphrases, jingles, buzzwords, images, one-minute megatrends, financial transactions flickering through fiberoptic bundles. Our wars are Nintendo wars, fought with camera-equipped smart bombs that marry cinema and weaponry in a television that kills." Dery then examines the more common forms of cultural jamming: subvertising, creating anti-ads or ad parodies; media hoaxing, getting the media to cover a bogus event; audio agit-prop, such as Chris Burke's "Oil War," a montage of presidential speeches; and billboard banditry, such as changing the message "Hits Happen. New X-100" into "Shit Happens—New Exxon." The final section is on the promises and perils of cyberspace.

Open Magazine Pamphlet Series #25; $4
1993; long thin pamphlet; 18 pp.

◄ *Adbusters Quarterly*

*"From Advertising to Subvertising" by those who would know.*

## RADIOTEXT(E)
### (SEMIOTEXT(E) #16)
### edited by Neil Strauss

A big, eclectic anthology devoted to that underrated communication medium, radio. More than sixty essays cover radio's beginnings, important personalities, hidden history, famous broadcasts, listeners, control of radio, pirate broadcasting, paranormal and extraterrestrial aspects of radio, and more.

"Lives of Great DJ's" pays tribute to the pioneer of border radio: "Born in North Carolina, 1895, John Romulus Brinkley was the first gringo to flee across the border for the practically unregulated Mexican airwaves. He beamed his message back to the USA at a whopping million watts in order to lure suckers into one of his medical clinics. The good doctor specialized in implanting goat gonads into the human scrotum for the purpose of a longer-lasting existence." "FM: Frequency Modulation or Fallen Man" tells the distressing story of Edward Armstrong, inventor of FM radio, who was driven to suicide because the FCC and AM broadcasters did everything they could to destroy FM, and then RCA and NBC attempted to skirt Armstrong's patent by developing what they claimed was a different form of FM. The lengthy trial drained him financially, physically, and emotionally. His life's work had been alternately suppressed, belittled, and stolen.

"Pirate Radio Pirates" gives the history of literal pirate radio, that is, unlicensed radio stations operating on ships anchored in international waters. Among the transcribed broadcasts printed in *Radiotext(e)* is "America Was Promises" by poet, anti-Semite, and fascist symp Ezra Pound. Old Ezra should've just stuck to writing verse, because in 1941 on Rome Radio he boldly stated that, "ALL thought of America going to war is bunkum, it is hogwash, bugwash, unmitigated b.b.b...." (Don't ask me what "b.b.b." stands for. I have no earthly idea.)

"The Ergonomy of Music" is an enlightening piece of corporate propaganda from Muzak. "In a slaughterhouse recently...they were having problems. The animals' blood would clot. They say the blood flows freely now. The music relaxes them as they die." If you're worried that WWIII might put an end to Muzak, you can relax: "In the event of nuclear war, Muzak has its own power

*Animal Scam* ➤
by Kathleen
Marquardt

*People for
the Ethical
Treatment
of People.*

generators to ensure no failure of the Basic Program to those facilities still functioning and able to receive our transmission."

Radio's alleged inventor, Guglielmo Marconi, and its actual inventor, Nikola Tesla, both believed that the dead can be heard through radio. This belief is taken to heart by the one hundred members of the American Association of Broadcast Voice Phenomena, one of whom wrote the article "Radio from Beyond the Grave." Members turn their radios (AM, FM, or short-wave) to an unoccupied frequency, adjust the volume so the static is barely audible, turn on a tape recorder, and ask an entity to speak. Hitler, Jung, George Washington, Plato, Descartes, and thousands of other famous people have allegedly been recorded broadcasting from the Great Beyond. One association member, a composer, has recorded messages from famous musicians. "Mozart, reportedly, is a big fan of rap music, Chopin can't stand it, and Beethoven hasn't heard it."

Autonomedia; $12
1993; softcover; 350 pp.

## CONTRARY OPINIONS

I wasn't sure where to put this section, but I think it seems appropriate for "Freedom," since it's because of freedom that people can air these controversial opinions.

### THE AMERICAN HERETIC'S DICTIONARY

#### by Chaz Bufe, illustrated by J.R. Swanson

A bitter, cynical sequel to Ambrose Bierce's bitter, cynical *Devil's Dictionary*, which was filled with "definitions" that skewered the powers that be and the absurdities of life. Bufe has decided to pen a modern-day version of the dictionary, and he has done an admirable job. Below are a few examples:

"COMMODITY, n. In the United States, a synonym for 'person.'

"FRIEND, n. A person with whom we can share the enjoyment of another's misfortune.

"MONOGAMY, n. A common misspelling. See 'Monotony.'

"MORMON, n. A common misspelling. Only one 'm' is necessary.

"RELIABLE SOURCE, n. A journalistic term referring to a politician or political appointee with an interest in seeing certain 'facts' in print.

"SUICIDE: Doing one's bit for the environment."

See Sharp Press; $7.95
1992; softcover; 85 pp.

### ANIMALSCAM:
#### THE BEASTLY ABUSE OF HUMAN RIGHTS
#### by Kathleen Marquardt

The premise of this book is that the animal rights movement, as exemplified by People for the Ethical Treatment of Animals, is aimed at destroying the rights of humans by eliminating clothing, food, animal companions and entertainment, and animal research that provides important medicines, such as insulin and vaccines. The author says that the animal rights movement is a misanthropic menace that routinely alters or ignores facts that don't support its cause.

In the chapter on fur, the author claims that the photos of mangled animals in leghold traps are mostly fakes featuring road-kill. That animals don't really gnaw off their legs to get free. That leghold traps don't hurt very much (to demonstrate, she stuck her hand in one: "...causes a sting but certainly not major pain.") These are interesting points, but sometimes the author strays into irrelevance: "People have used traps to catch animals for the past twenty-five thousand years.... From prehistoric times to the present, every continent shows evidence of traps...." So what? Much of the time the author sounds like an apologist mindlessly repeating the party line. She says that the way fur-bearing animals are killed causes unfounded outrage. "The only methods of killing *certified by the Fur Farm Animal Welfare Coalition* are those approved by the American Veterinary Medical Association—pure carbon monoxide, dioxide bottled gas, or lethal injection—the same means used at animal shelters" [emphasis mine]. All she has told us are the methods approved by a certain group. What about the extent of unapproved methods of killing? How many places use anal electrocution, for example? The author doesn't even bring up the subject in her effort to gloss over all the facts.

The book looks at the results of the animal rights movement. Animal overpopulation leading to starvation and outbreaks of diseases like rabies. A cutback in the amount of life-saving biomedical work being done. Animal researchers living in as much fear as abortion clinic workers. This last point I found extremely interesting. The things that are done by animal rights activists are identical to the tactics used by some right-to-lifers—mail bombs, graphic death threats, threats against family members, firebombings of buildings, etc. So far as I know, though, no animal rights militant has pumped hot lead into a defenseless animal experimenter.

The author takes exceptional issue with the movement's hatred of humans and their belief that an animal life is just as important as a human life. She quotes Michael W. Fox, the VP of the Humane Society: "Man is the most dangerous, destructive, selfish, and unethical animal on earth." Personally, I find that one a little hard to argue with. After all, dolphins haven't killed millions of other dolphins in the name of God, and it wasn't the chipmunks who created the nuclear bomb. Among the other quotes offered is Chris DeRose's (director of Last Chance for Animals) assertion: "If the death of one rat cured all diseases, it wouldn't make any difference to me."

Regnery Publishing; $24
1993; hardcover; 221 pp.

### ECOSCAM:
#### THE FALSE PROPHETS OF ECOLOGICAL APOCALYPSE
#### by Ronald Bailey

On the back of the very first page of this book, published by St. Martin's Press, is the inscription "A Cato Institute Book." The Cato Institute is a famous right-wing think tank, so their attack on environmentalism comes as no surprise. But remember, we shouldn't automatically approve or disapprove of a book just because it comes from a certain publisher or group. We need to listen to all sides, and the voices that say we're nowhere near killing the earth are alone in the wilderness. This book is one of the few salvos to come from that side of the debate.

Ronald Bailey compares people forecasting dire consequences for the earth to apocalyptic demagogues. They are in the same league as Christian fundamentalists and others who believe in millennial, end-of-the-world myths. They "declare that humanity can only avert total ruin if society repents and quickly adopts their sweeping proposals for radical social restructuring and economic redistribution." Bailey then proceeds to dismantle the common wisdom, scare tactics, and unfulfilled prophecies regarding nuclear war, population explosions, the depletion of natural resources, global climate changes (a new ice age and global warming), nuclear winter, biotechnology, and the hole in the ozone.

Not all of Bailey's counterarguments will sway you, but he does do a lot to promote a balanced, reasonable assessment of our planet's condition.

St. Martin's Press; $10.95
1993; softcover; 228 pp.

## THE HERETIC'S HANDBOOK OF QUOTATIONS:
### CUTTING COMMENTS ON BURNING ISSUES (EXPANDED EDITION)
### edited by Charles Bufe

This book is *Bartlett's Quotations* for subversives. It's packed full of contrary opinions, dissenting views, and just plain venom from hundreds of nonconformists, including Ambrose Bierce, Noam Chomsky, Emma Goldman, Thomas Jefferson, Jack London, Karl Marx, John Stuart Mill, Friedrich Nietzsche, Henry David Thoreau, Mark Twain, and hundreds of others. But besides quoting radical freedom-lovers, Bufe also includes scary material from the other end of the spectrum—the likes of St. Augustine, Adolf Hitler, Benito Mussolini, Joseph Stalin, and Mao Tse-tung.

Here are some thought-provoking quotes I ran across. The Law: "The law, in its majestic equality, forbids the rich as well as the poor to sleep under bridges, to beg in the streets, and to steal bread."—Anatole France. Politics: "A man like me cares nothing for the lives of millions."—Napoleon Bonaparte. Revolution: "The first duty of any revolutionary is to get away with it."— Abbie Hoffman. Property: "Sell a country! Why not sell the air, the clouds, and the great sea as well as the earth?"—Tecumseh. Misogyny: "When you see a woman, consider that you face not a human being, but the devil himself. The woman's voice is the hiss of the snake."—St. Anthony. Sex: "Chastity: the most unnatural of the sexual perversions."—Aldous Huxley. Christianity: "The Christian God is a being of terrific character—cruel, vindictive, capricious, and unjust."—Thomas Jefferson.

Rounding out this treasury of heresy are numerous cartoons and illustrations and a special section containing atrocities and contradictions from the Bible. A must-have.

See Sharp Press; $14.95
1992; oversize softcover; 237 pp.

## THE SOUTH WAS RIGHT!
### by James Ronald Kennedy and Walter Donald Kennedy

Following Napoleon's truism that history is written by the victors, the Kennedy brothers argue that the truth about the Civil War (or, as they refer to it, the War for Southern Independence) has been suppressed. They intend to correct this.

They present evidence that the South seceded fair and square. Based on recognized international precedents, Dixie was indeed an independent nation. Even the United States seems to have recognized this. Official papers prepared by the United States right after the Civil War list the combatants as the United States and the Confederate States—two separate nations. (This explains why the brothers shun the term "Civil War." A civil war is one in which two factions fight for control of a government. In this case, one nation was at war with another to preserve its newly declared independence.)

The authors write, "Southern history, as taught in our public and private schools today, is nothing more than a recitation of the North's justification for invasion, conquest, and oppression of the Southern people." They proceed to demolish the myths

around Abraham Lincoln. Using Abe's own words from debates with Stephen A. Douglas, the authors show that Lincoln did not believe in the equality of the races and wanted to separate blacks and whites. The famed Emancipation Proclamation, according to the Kennedys, was only a thin pretext for war. The Proclamation only freed slaves in those states that had already seceded. The slaves in areas under Northern control were *not* freed. In fact, West Virginia and the six parishes of Louisiana under Yankee control were specifically excluded from the Proclamation. And to top it off, Ulysses S. Grant's wife had slaves at the beginning of the war. These and other pieces of evidence persuasively suggest that slavery was not the cause of the Civil War.

The North invaded the South not to preserve the Union but to create a colonial empire. "This empire was built upon the ashes of our Southern nation, our freedom, our economic security, and our well-being as a people." To this day, it is argued, the North continues to exploit the South economically and politically, leaving its people to a large extent in poverty, unfairly governing it, and trying to wipe out its symbols and heritage.

The Kennedys spend a lot of time being rightfully upset about the federal government's abuses of power. Our Founders believed that the states should be free, sovereign entities, and that the federal government should be an equal partner with the states and not a supreme entity. The federal government, in reality, is a domineering bully that has stripped the states of the their rights and is therefore "an illegal and illegitimate governmental force." The southern people should demand a return to our Founders' vision or, if that fails, they should again declare themselves a free nation, according to the Kennedys. They call on "Unreconstructed Southerners" (also called "Southern Nationalists") to lead the charge.

Pelican Publishing Co; $22.50
1991; hardcover; 431 pp.

# THE WAR ON "SUBVERSIVES"

## AGENTS OF REPRESSION:
### THE FBI'S SECRET WARS AGAINST THE BLACK PANTHER PARTY AND THE AMERICAN INDIAN MOVEMENT
### by Ward Churchill and Jim Vander Wall

A well-documented, thorough examination of the FBI's harassment and attempted destruction of the Black Panther Party and the American Indian Movement (AIM). This book presents an extraordinarily detailed account of the Feds' use of groundless arrests, smear campaigns, fake letters, informants, and the orchestration of assassinations in their quest to destroy these two dissident groups. William O'Neal, an FBI infiltrator, gave police a detailed floorplan of Panther leader Fred Hampton's apartment, which they later used to storm Hampton's pad and kill him. It is alleged that O'Neal drugged Hampton before the slaying and that police wounded Hampton while he slept, then put two bullets in his head execution style.

On the Pine Ridge reservation, the FBI armed and equipped the pro-government, anti-AIM vigilantes known as GOONs. As a result, the GOONs wantonly killed and attacked AIM members for two and a half years. For example, "On September 10, 1975, Jim Little, an AIM supporter and former Tribal Council member (aligned with Severt Young Bear), was stomped to death by four GOONs; although the incident occurred less than two miles from the Pine Ridge hospital, it took nearly an hour for an ambulance (driven by more known GOONs) to arrive."

The author also gives a much briefer look at the FBI's targeting of the Puerto Rican independence movement and Central American activists. The text is supported by an unbelievable eighty pages of endnotes and hundreds of visuals, including the actual FBI-produced cartoons used to create animosity between the Panthers and another radical black group, the United Slaves. Also enlightening is the map showing how U.S. corporations (including Shell, Exxon, and Mobil) had divided up the Sioux Nation like a great big pie.

South End Press; $16
1990; softcover; 509 pp.

## ALIEN INK:
### THE FBI'S WAR ON FREEDOM OF EXPRESSION
### by Natalie Robins

Using the files gained through the Freedom of Information Act, Natalie Robins has uncovered the FBI's widespread habit of keeping files on, harassing, and spying on American writers. Starting in 1911, the FBI kept track of writers who joined or expressed sympathy for communist or socialist causes, who were active in antiwar and civil rights causes in the 1960s, or who expressed "un-American" or anti-FBI sentiments in their writings. The list of people the Feds considered dangerous is about 150 names long and contains such luminaries as Truman Capote, e.e. cummings, William Faulkner, Allen Ginsberg, Ernest Hemingway, Langston Hughes, Jack London, Carson McCullers, Arthur Miller, John Steinbeck, and Tennessee Williams.

Faulkner first earned a spot in the Bureau's files in 1939 when "agents found his name on the list of writers asking that the embargo on the Spanish Republic be lifted." His file also claims that "the Civil Rights Congress had 'procured' a statement from Faulkner on behalf of Willie McGee, the black man accused of raping a white woman in Laurel, Mississippi, in 1945."

Ginsberg's file, which runs over nine hundred pages, contains reference to only one crime—a theft committed by one of Ginsberg's friends, for which Ginsberg himself was never convicted. The rest of the file is devoted to his antiwar sentiments, a visit to Cuba to judge a poetry contest, his "obscene" poems, and his role as a primary member of the Beat movement. Robins reports, "Not only was Ginsberg unceasingly watched by the FBI ('He was met at the airport by three "hippie type" individuals'), but his writing and lecturing were obstructed, his mail was opened, his passport questioned, and he was often detained for rude interrogations.... Ginsberg not only has an FBI file, but a record at fifteen other agencies, including the CIA, Defense Department, the U.S. Postal Service, the Treasury Department, and the Drug Enforcement Agency."

All of this paranoid silliness makes me wonder—should I save the FBI some trouble and just send them a copy of my book for their file on me? I might be wasting my time since the FBI now claims that it doesn't keep files on subversive writers and their work. Unfortunately, that sounds a lot like J. Edgar Hoover's statement that the FBI didn't have a file on John Steinbeck, when in fact it did have a file 139 pages long.

Rutgers University Press; $14.95
1992; softcover; 495 pp.

*Alien Ink*
by Natalie
Robins

*The intelligence
war on the
intelligencia.*

## BLACK AMERICANS:
### THE FBI FILES
### by Kenneth O'Reilly, edited by David Gallen

The FBI was dead set against the civil rights movement in the 1960s. "Hoover maintained that black leadership had to be destroyed. Despite Malcolm's [X] angry stance and his bloody death, physical violence (as opposed to the rhetoric of violence) was never more than a peripheral part of the struggle for racial justice. However, political violence was a central part of the FBI's response to that struggle." The author angrily notes that "although

Bureau agents in the 1930s walked through Thompson submachine gun firestorms when going after John Dillinger, agents in the 1960s would not take a baseball bat away from a Klansman even as the bat turned red with the blood of the person being beaten." He continues, "If the FBI began the 1960s by passively observing racist violence against civil rights workers, it ended the decade by egging on the racists."

The first sixty-five pages of this book document the FBI's war against civil rights. The rest of the book contains primary source material—the actual files the FBI kept on James Baldwin, W.E.B. Du Bois, Medgar Evers, Marcus Garvey, Fanny Lou Hamer, Martin Luther King Jr., Adam Clayton Powell Jr., A. Philip Randolph, Paul Robeson, Bayard Rustin, Roy Wilkins, and Malcolm X. Interesting material abounds. An FBI report about writer and NAACP cofounder W.E.B. Du Bois says "...[Du Bois] had stated in a speech made while in Japan that the Japanese were to be complimented on their progress and especially upon their military prowess. Further, that in the Japanese he saw the liberation of the Negroes in America, and that when the time came for them to take over the United States, they would find they would have help from the Negroes in the United States."

An FBI report on Malcolm X entitled "Contact with the KKK" states the following: "[Bureau deletion] advised on January 30, 1961, that certain Klan officials met with leaders of the NOI [Nation of Islam] on the night of January 28, 1961, in Atlanta, Georgia. One of these NOI leaders identified himself as Malcolm X of New York, and it was the source's understanding that Malcolm X claimed to have a hundred seventy-five thousand followers who were complete separationists, were interested in land and were soliciting the aid of the Klan to obtain land."

Carroll & Graf; $14.95
1994; softcover; 518 pp.

## FBI ON TRIAL:
### THE VICTORY IN THE SOCIALIST WORKERS PARTY SUIT
### AGAINST GOVERNMENT SPYING
### edited by Margaret Jayko

In 1973 the Socialist Workers Party (SWP) filed suit against the FBI for the Bureau's harassment, infiltration, and disruption of the SWP and another communist group, the Young Socialist Alliance. Over the previous thirty or more years, the FBI, by its own admission, had gathered more than five million pages of files on the two groups. The SWP managed to obtain hundreds of thousands of these documents for the trial.

Thirteen years after the suit was filed, the judge handed down a historic decision, reprinted in full in this book. He ruled, "There can be no doubt that these disruption operations were patently unconstitutional and violated the SWP's First Amendment rights of free speech and assembly. Moreover there was no statutory or regulatory authority for the FBI to disrupt the SWP's lawful political activities." On top of that, the judge ruled that the mere presence of informants violated members' right to privacy.

The judge's ruling detailed the FBI's poison-pen letters, media manipulation, harassment, and disruption. "It enumerates 20,000 days of wiretaps and 12,000 days of listening 'bugs' between 1943 and 1963. It documents 208 FBI burglaries of offices and homes of the SWP and its members, resulting in the theft or photographing of 9,864 private documents."

The judge awarded the SWP $264,000, which didn't even come close to the over one and a half million dollars the group spent during the lengthy trial. In another historic move, one year later, he issued an injunction telling the FBI that it could no longer use any of the illegally obtained information on the SWP or the YSA in its files.

*FBI on Trial* contains introductory essays, the complete decision and injunction, transcripts of testimony, the Justice Department's brief and affidavits, and other material. This crucial trial is a major victory for the rights of any group or individual holding unpopular views.

Pathfinder Press; $16.95
1988; softcover; 260 pp.

## HAULING UP THE MORNING:
### WRITINGS AND ART BY POLITICAL PRISONERS AND PRISONERS OF WAR IN THE U.S.
### edited by Tim Blunk and Raymond Luc Levasseur

American prisons contain almost 200 political prisoners, people who are in the klink for their protests against racism and injustice. Granted, some of these protests were armed, but some were not, and some of the prisoners were framed. They are members of the Black Panthers, the Weather Underground, the American Indian Movement, the IRA, the New Afrika movement, and other groups the government hates. An amazing number of them are in jail, not for any specific act, but for the easiest "crime" in the world to "prove"—conspiracy.

This book contains poems, essays, drawings, and paintings by these individuals. The fact that political prisoners exist in America is shameful. The fact that we can hear what they have to say in this book is wonderful.

> Red Sea Press; $15.95
> 1990; softcover; 408 pp.

## IT DID HAPPEN HERE:
### RECOLLECTIONS OF POLITICAL REPRESSION IN AMERICA
### by Bud Schultz and Ruth Schultz

This book collects oral histories from thirty-one Americans who have been persecuted, prosecuted, fired, harassed, and/or beaten for their political views. Some of them have even seen their compatriots killed because of their beliefs.

Famed child psychologist Dr. Benjamin Spock tells of his conviction on conspiracy charges to aid, counsel, and abet draft resisters. Under the Selective Service Act of 1948, doing such things is illegal. But Spock wasn't accused of doing them—he was accused of conspiring to do them. "The lawyers explained to us that the conspiracy indictment makes the prosecutors' job easier. They don't have to prove that there was counseling, aiding, or abetting. They only have to show that there was an 'agreement' to do that. And, it turned out, the agreement didn't have to be among people who planned anything together or even knew each other. It didn't have to be secret or include illegal acts. As the judge made it clear the first day of the trial, conspiracy only means going on a parallel course." The evidence against Spock and the four other defendants was their making public speeches denouncing the war, turning in hundreds of draft cards, and signing the Call to Resist Illegitimate Authority. The judge was against them from day one, and the trial ended with guilty verdicts for four of them, including Spock. Luckily, a year later, an appeals court overturned the conviction.

The Kent State massacre, in which National Guardsmen opened fire on unarmed student protesters, is a well-known event. But two years earlier the same thing had happened at South Carolina State College, an integrated university in Orangeburg. Cleveland Sellers, a civil rights worker who was a student a SCSC, tells about that night. During the previous week, students had tried to force their way into the whites-only bowling alley. Police showed up, and the whole thing got ugly. The next day, the university administration told students not to leave campus. The National Guard set up shop nearby. On February 8, 1968, Sellers awoke to shouting and went outside. Something was burning down the street, and a group of students were standing in the middle of the campus. State troopers opened fire at the students, who started running immediately. "At least ninety percent of the kids were shot either in the back of the head, the back, the back of the leg, or the bottom of their feet." Three students died and twenty-seven, including Sellers, were wounded.

*It Did Happen Here* also chronicles the repression of unionists, communist sympathizers, other leftists, immigrants, and other "subversives."

> University of California Press; $14.95
> 1989; softcover; 427 pp.

## SPYING ON AMERICA:
### THE FBI's DOMESTIC COUNTERINTELLIGENCE PROGRAM
### by James Kirkpatrick Davis

◄ *Hauling Up the Morning* **edited by Tim Blunk & Raymond Luc Levasseur**

*The art of defiance from U.S. political prisoners.*

From 1956 to 1971 the FBI conducted operations under the name COINTELPRO that surveilled, infiltrated, disrupted, and tried to destroy several domestic groups of a radical political/social nature: the Communist Party USA, the Socialist Workers Party, white hate groups, Black nationalist hate groups, and the New Left. This book covers all five operations in detail—wiretaps, blackmail, threats, fake letters designed to sow dissension, agents provocateurs, and more. One of the techniques the Bureau used on the Klan was to send members postcards saying, "Klansman, trying to hide behind your sheets? You received this and someone knows who you are!" To disrupt the Black Panthers, rumors were circulated that some loyal members were actually police informants, probably resulting in many unpleasant situations for the targets of this method. The FBI's tactics were successful overall, helping to destroy many of the groups or group chapters. Of course, civil liberties were trashed, lives were ruined, and many deaths resulted, but in the end the Feds got what they wanted.

Needless to say, no one knew that any of this was going on at the time. COINTELPRO only became public when a group calling itself the Citizen's Commission to Investigate the FBI broke into an FBI office in Pennsylvania, snatched about 1,000 classified documents, and began releasing them to the media. Thus, the program officially ended, but such tactics are still being carried out today.

*Spying on America* is a great record on this shameful episode in intelligence history.

> Greenwood Publishing Group; $35
> 1992; hardcover; 192 pp.

## THE TRIAL OF LEONARD PELTIER
### by Jim Messerschmidt

In the summer of 1975 things were awfully tense on the Pine Ridge Reservation in South Dakota. A reign of terror and murder had been led by tribal leader Dick Wilson and his personal vigilantes, known as the GOONs, against the American Indian Movement. Wilson was a government stooge who let government and personal interests rather than Native American interests motivate his decisions. The AIM was a group of traditionalists who wanted an end to government exploitation of their people. The GOONs used strong-arm, death-squad tactics to terrorize the traditionalists, actually murdering dozens of them.

Into this pressure cooker rode two plainclothes FBI agents in an unmarked car, allegedly chasing a man with an outstanding warrant against him for stealing cowboy boots. They opened fire on a house, and AIM members, thinking they were under yet another GOON attack, fired back and killed the agents. Joe Stuntz of the Lakota tribe was also killed.

AIM members escaped into the forest, and many were

captured by the FBI. Four were charged with killing the agents. One of them was Leonard Peltier, an AIM leader whom the FBI had previously targeted. He had escaped to Canada, but was illegally extradited on the grounds of three conflicting affidavits signed by a woman said to be Peltier's girlfriend (though they didn't even know each other) and said to be a witness to the murder (though she wasn't even at the shoot-out). She later recanted her testimony, saying the FBI had threatened to kill her and her daughter.

Things only went downhill from there. While the other three defendants got off the hook, Peltier was convicted and sentenced to two consecutive life sentences. This book gives a detailed account of the trial and events surrounding it, showing that the FBI withheld evidence of Peltier's innocence and manufactured evidence of his guilt. The contradictions and physical impossibilities in the FBI's versions of events are plainly shown. In short, it's one of the most blatant examples of injustice in America's history, and this book exposes every dirty facet of it.

The evidence of Peltier's being railroaded is so convincing that members of the House and Senate, other prominent political individuals, and *fourteen million* people have signed petitions and otherwise demanded that Peltier be given a retrial—a fair one this time. So far, the courts have refused to grant a new trial or parole for Peltier.

> South End Press; $14
> 1983; softcover; 198 pp.

## IN THE SPIRIT OF CRAZY HORSE
### by Peter Mathiessen

For those of you who want a more in-depth treatment of Leonard Peltier's trial and the FBI's war on the American Indian Movement in general, this classic account is just the ticket. The author discusses the Oglala Lakotas' plight, starting in 1835, through the formation of the AIM, the Wounded Knee massacre, the U.S. puppet government of Dick Wilson, and the shoot-out at Pine Ridge. More than 350 pages are devoted to the shoot-out and the events that it triggered. One chapter, appropriately titled "Forked Tongues," reveals crucial withheld evidence uncovered years later under the Freedom of Information Act. The rest of the book discusses what has happened to the Lakota and AIM since the trial.

Although this book was published in 1983, it only became available again a few years ago (1991) because lawsuits by public officials stopped further publication. *In the Spirit of Crazy Horse* was the subject of one of the longest and bitterest court battles in the history of publishing. Its reprinting "is a defeat for former South Dakota Governor William Janklow, for the Federal Bureau of Investigation, and for FBI Special Agent David Price, all of whom tried to stop this book by filing suits in three states, waging an eight-year litigation, and calling and threatening booksellers and bookbuyers." The whole disgraceful matter is discussed in detail in the book's new afterword.

> Penguin Books; $15
> 1983 (1991); softcover; 646 pp.

# PRIVACY AND SURVEILLANCE

## APPLIED CRYPTOGRAPHY:
### PROTOCOLS, ALGORITHMS, AND SOURCE CODE IN C
### by Bruce Schneier

The rise of information stored and transmitted digitally has led to the problem of security and privacy. In the face of an overwhelming need to protect data, cryptography has become a hot topic. Once reserved for governments only, the ability to encrypt messages so that only the recipient can read them is now in the hands of private citizens, and the government is *mucho* pissed. The government's official stance is that individuals have no right to unbreakable cryptography. In other words, what they are claiming is that their ability to read your documents is guaranteed by the Constitution. Sure.

One of the things that has the spooks running scared is a freeware program called PGP (Pretty Good Privacy), which provides encryption that is for all practical purposes unbreakable. It is widely available on the Internet. Another blow to the government's monopoly on cryptography is Schneier's book, which the National Security Agency tried to block. The author throws down the gauntlet in the opening paragraph: "There are two kinds of cryptography in this world: cryptography that will stop your kid sister from reading your files, and cryptography that will stop major governments from reading your files. This book is about the latter."

*Applied Cryptography* is a big lug of a book that is obviously intended for programmers, not for someone wanting a popular treatment of the subject. Part One examines encryption protocols—how they work and how they can be defeated, if possible. Protocols include key exchange, timestamping services, undeniable digital signatures, flipping a coin fairly over a modem, secure elections, certified mail, digital cash, and more. Part Two discusses handling keys and using algorithms. Part Three is a technical discussion of dozens of algorithms. Part Four looks at the real world—legal issues, government organizations, patents, and actual examples of implementation. Part Five lists 113 pages of source code for several algorithms.

A two-disk set containing source code for more than forty algorithms is available from the author (details are on the last page of the book).

> John Wiley & Sons; $44.95
> 1994; softcover; 618 pp.

## FULL DISCLOSURE

*Full Disclosure* is a surveillance/privacy tabloid that gives the inside dirt on such hot topics as credit reporting companies, telephone secrets, caller ID, satellite interception, forgery, voice mail, computer security, government fascism, and Social Security numbers. One of *Full Disclosure*'s main themes is electronic surveillance, and they regularly offer articles on the latest high-tech spy gadgets whose very existence is supposed to be known to "law enforcement agencies only." An article on one such device, for intercepting cellular phone calls, brought the threat of a lawsuit from the device's manufacturer. Issue #29 had an article on "purchase orders and bid[s] requested by various public bodies for surveillance-related equipment." In it we learn that the IRS is buying some disguised antennas and transmitters and the FDA is looking to buy a lamp and picture frame that conceal cameras and microphones. Do I even have to tell you that *Full Disclosure* is on the government's shit list?

Issue #30 has one of the best articles on the Waco tragedy that I've ever seen. Did you realize that during the siege, the BATF tried to kill Wayne Martin, the respected lawyer who was negotiating for the Branch Davidians? After Martin told an agent over the phone that he was at the south wall of the building, the BATF fired into the south wall with machine guns for a minute. Issue #27 confirmed a suspicion I had when it revealed that when you call an 800 phone number, the party you're calling automatically gets your phone number. So take precautions if you want to remain anonymous when calling toll-free numbers.

> First Amendment Press
> 8129 N. Thirty-Fifth Avenue, Suite 134
> Phoenix, AZ 85051
> Twelve-issue sub: $29.95; Canada: $44.95; foreign: $54.95

## HOW TO GET ANYTHING ON ANYBODY 2:
### THE ENCYCLOPEDIA OF PERSONAL SURVEILLANCE
### by Lee Lapin

Other books may promise dirt, but this one delivers. Page after page of down-and-dirty, detailed info on bugs, wiretaps, hidden cameras, night vision, scramblers, countersurveillance, etc. In a conversational, humorous style, the author shows us how these things work, gives names of actual models, and tells where to get them. There are also specific instructions on intercepting cellular phones, faxes, and pagers; hacking answering machines; cracking computers; tailing people; accessing databases; and other fun activities. You can get in on the action with a twenty-two-page listing of mainly mail-order outfits that actually sell this stuff. Personally, I have my eye on the teddy bear with a hidden video camera inside from Spytech....

Paladin Press; $35
1991; oversize softcover; 223 pp.

## THE NAKED CONSUMER:
### HOW OUR PRIVATE LIVES BECOME PUBLIC COMMODITIES
### by Erik Larson

Big Brother *is* watching you. But he doesn't care what you're thinking, only what you're buying. Perhaps the most insidious invaders of our privacy are marketing firms and the corporations who hire them. People have become "consuming units" in the all-important quest to get you to buy buy buy. Erik Larson became so intrigued (and disturbed) by the faceless megacorporations that knew all about him and his family that he embarked "on what soon became a rather spooky journey among a little-seen but hugely influential legion of marketers obsessed with capturing, quantifying, and ultimately distilling the soul of the American consumer. With a little help from their enthusiastic allies—census bureaucrats, demographers, postal officials, ex–military surveillance experts—the marketers have built a vast intelligence network containing the names, addresses, and personal records of virtually every consumer in America, all for the lofty goal of finding more irresistible ways to sell us soaps, laxatives, and detergents."

Larson posed as the CEO of a fictitious direct-mail firm interested in gaining as much knowledge as possible about consumers. He takes us on a name-naming journey into this shadowy world where nothing is sacred—not your political affiliation, not your sexual orientation, and not even whether or not you are able to have children. Since we're all consumers, this book should be read by everyone. You'll never look at your "junk" mail the same way again.

Penguin; $10.95
1992; softcover; 275 pp.

## OUR VANISHING PRIVACY:
### AND WHAT YOU CAN DO TO PROTECT YOURS
### by Robert Ellis Smith

Smith is the publisher of the *Privacy Journal*. In this book he goes on a roller-coaster ride through 1984-Land. "Are Your Papers in Order?" looks at the government's new demands that you always have identification on you. "An innocent black man is stopped and arrested fifteen times in two years while walking in a white neighborhood, merely because he does not produce 'bona fide identification.'" Another chapter looks at how marketers invade our lives: "Kids and adults who ordered the Cap'n Crunch Dick Tracy Wrist Watch Radio through a Quaker Oats offer in cereal boxes were sent an intrusive questionnaire that asked about these three political issues [drug testing, school prayer, and gun control], plus street addresses, income, what credit cards the family uses, the names, ages, and preferences of smokers in the family, and who has what diseases in the family."

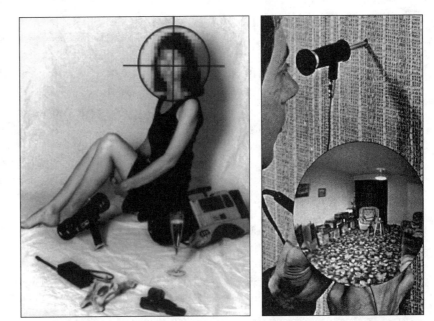

◄ *How to Get Anything On Anybody 2 by Lee Lapin*

*Snooping is fun!*

Other chapters deal with the intrusiveness of caller-ID, the ease with which medical records can be gotten, your Social Security number as national identification number, polygraph, urine, and blood tests, how the press invades privacy, taxes on periodicals (which amount to "a state issued-license to publish..."), and the "let's do it till we get caught" attitude of the three major credit bureaus.

The book ends with a crash course on the laws that protect our privacy and on the twenty principles of information privacy. In all, *Our Vanishing Privacy* offers a wide array of ways in which our privacy is going up in smoke. Unfortunately, it does not live up to its subtitle, only presenting ways to protect your Social Security Number and get around caller-ID.

Loompanics Unlimited; $12.95
1993; softcover; 132 pp.

## PRIVACY JOURNAL:
### AN INDEPENDENT MONTHLY ON PRIVACY IN A COMPUTER AGE

One of the most respected privacy publications you can get, the *Privacy Journal* reports on news items, legislation, conferences, and articles and reports that relate to privacy. The April 1994 issue covers the ACLU's survey that finds most Americans are tolerant of private conduct, health record legislation, and caller-ID; Equifax's little-known database that contains info on millions of property and auto insurance claims; upcoming conferences on cryptography and crime; and a synopsis of the proceedings of the Conference on Computers, Freedom, and Privacy, which contains the following tidbit: "As the attendees departed, one hacker boasted that over the weekend he broke into the Palmer House hotel computer system by finding a terminal in an unlocked business-service center. He said he found there a collection of blank hotel room card keys that he easily could have encoded for entry into rooms."

Privacy Journal/PO Box 28577/Providence, RI 02908
One-year sub (12 issues): $35

# MISCELLANEOUS

## AIN'T NOBODY'S BUSINESS IF YOU DO:
### THE ABSURDITY OF CONSENSUAL CRIMES IN A FREE SOCIETY
### by Peter McWilliams

A "consensual crime," also known as a victimless crime, is defined as "any activity—currently illegal—in which we, as adults, choose to participate that does not physically harm the person or property of another." Examples of consensual crimes include drug use, prostitution, gambling, oral sex, anal sex, adultery, fornication (sex between unmarried, consenting adults), polygamy, and cohabitation ("shacking up"). These acts have been outlawed in at least some states, not because they hurt other people, but because lawmakers don't think we should be allowed to do them for moral reasons, safety reasons, or both. Our puritanical government officials think that we shouldn't be allowed to do anything that they profess to find immoral or offensive (even though these hypocrites do many of these things themselves). They often justify these violations of our freedoms by saying that they're saving us from ourselves. If you can't gamble, you can't lose your money. If you can't have sex outside marriage, your marriage will (supposedly) stay together. The author quotes singer Billie Holliday's response to this mind-set: "I never hurt nobody but myself and that's nobody's business but my own."

*Ain't Nobody's Business* contains some of the best-thought-out, best-written defenses of freedom and attacks on oppression that I've read. McWilliams presents his ideas in a straightforward, conversational style, and he's obviously given the subject a lot of thought. He stands fully and completely on the side of freedom. "The one idea behind this book is this: *You should be allowed to do whatever you want with your own person and property, as long as you don't physically harm the person or property of another.*" AMEN! If I didn't know better, I'd swear I wrote that myself.

McWilliams lays bare the absolute stupidity, arrogance, and pigheadedness of anyone who would limit our freedoms. He writes, "...the consensual crimes that seem the *silliest* to me are the ones directed against homosexuality. Why should anyone care about who other people love, feel affection for, date, live with, marry, or have sex with? I just don't get it." (This ties in with my personal philosophy: "Screw and let screw." You have sex with whomever you want, let everyone else have sex with whomever they want, and this will be a much better world.) As for gambling: "Neither church nor state can, without transparent hypocrisy (neither minds hypocrisy, mind you, but that *transparent* hypocrisy might cause trouble), strongly oppose gambling—church and state both rely on gambling as a source of income....With the exception of Nevada, Atlantic City, and a handful of cities that allow poker clubs, church and state have a monopoly on gambling, and they're not about to give it up."

He criticizes the media's watered-down presentations of violence. In most cases, people who are shot get little red holes on their bodies and die instantly. "The day after a severe beating, our hero has a few red marks, a little white tape, and that's about it." If the entertainment media would portray violence realistically, in all its stomach-churning messiness, the author predicts: "Far fewer people would watch violent programs" and "People would be less likely to take part in violence."

McWilliams looks at the real effects of laws against adultery, fornication, cohabitation, and similar sexual practices: "In their attempts to preserve the 'American family,' fundamentalists are, in fact, destroying the institution of marriage. Lifelong, monogamous marriage is a relationship that a great many people are naturally drawn to. But when society programs those *not* drawn—for what-

*Are You Still a Slave?* ➤ by Shahrazad Ali

*More than a metaphor.*

ever reason—to that particular relationship to believe that they *should* or even *must* get married, people who have no business being in that relationship muck it up for those who want to be."

Besides being fascistic and counterproductive, outlawing consensual activities is destroying society. Allow me to crib some statistics:

•There are more than 350,000 people in jail right now for consensual crimes, and another 1,500,000 are out on parole or probation.

•This year more than 4,000,000 people will be arrested for consensual crimes.

•The United States will spend $50,000,000,000 (fifty billion) this year to punish people for consensual crimes. At the same time, we will lose $150,000,000,000 in tax revenue from people who could have been working instead of going to jail.

If we just legalized all of these "crimes" that don't harm anyone or anything else, we would solve many of this country's worst problems. We would free the authorities to capture *real* criminals—murderers, rapists, robbers, etc. We would free up our overburdened court system and double available jail space, which would stop the practice of letting violent criminals back on the streets because "there just isn't enough room in our prisons."

*Ain't Nobody's Business* is one of best books on freedom you could possibly get.

Prelude Press; $22.95
1993; hardcover; 815 pp.; illus.

## AMERICAN OPINION BOOK SERVICES BOOK LIST

The catalog of the John Birch Society. Contains books and videos from an anticommunist, Christian, right-wing perspective. They sell about two dozen books from their own press, Western Island Books, including *The Blue Book of the John Birch Society, Conspiracy Against God and Man, The Establishment's Man* (i.e., George Bush), *Teddy Bare: The Last of the Kennedy Clan, and The United Nations Conspiracy.* The bulk of the catalog contains books and videos from other publishers: *America: To Pray or Not to Pray, Immigration Time Bomb, Kinsey: Sex and Fraud, Legal Terrorism: The Truth About the Christic Institute, Red Cocaine, That Every Man Be Armed, America's Godly Heritage* (video), and *Anarchy, USA in the Name of Civil Rights* (video). They also sell some bumper stickers, T-shirts, and other paraphernalia.

American Opinion Book Services
PO Box 8040/Appleton, WI 54913
Catalog: $2

## AMERICAN UTOPIAS
### by Charles Nordhoff

*American Utopias* is a firsthand account of some of the most successful collective communities (now usually referred to as intentional communities) in the United States. First published in 1875, it was written by a journalist/author who actually traveled to the major communities while they were still thriving. He writes of the histories, principles, and daily lives of the members of the Amana Society, the Harmonists, the Separatists of Zoar, the Shakers, the Perfectionists, the Icarians, the Social Freedom Community, and several others.

The most fascinating aspects of this book are the two recurring subtexts of conformity and persecution. Almost all of these communes were based on strict principles, usually religious, and the people led simple, homogeneous lives with little room for deviation. Time and time again, these people faced unbelievable persecution for their different ways. Some wouldn't send their children to public schools, let their young men serve in the armed forces, or attend the dominant church of the area. For a book written well over a century ago, *American Utopias* reads remarkably smoothly, although it is a bit dry.

Berkshire House Publishers; $14.95
1875 (1993); softcover; 449 pp.

## ANARCHY:
### A JOURNAL OF DESIRE ARMED

*Anarchy* stands for freedom—complete and total freedom of speech, beliefs, sexuality, etc. Don't get this type of anarchy confused with the word *anarchy* as it is usually used, to denote total chaos, confusion, and perhaps violence. Anarchy as envisioned here means everybody doing what brings them joy and voluntarily cooperating with and helping each other. Hey, it's a long shot, but if it ever comes to pass, it'll be great.

Each issue of *Anarchy* features lots of reviews, a round-up of international anarchist happenings, and an incredible thirty pages of letters. Issue #38 has articles on the Branch Davidians, "a critique of half-assed radicalism," "survival sickness," memoirs of an anarchist family fleeing from Spanish fascist Francisco Franco, an interview with two squatters, and more.

B.A.L. Press/P.O. Box 2647/New York, NY 10009
Single issue: $3.50 One-year sub: $12;
Canada and Mexico: $15; elsewhere by surface mail: $18;
elsewhere by airmail: $32

## ARE YOU STILL A SLAVE?
### by Shahrazad Ali

This book is based on the premise that many of the things African Americans do and feel are actually holdovers from the days of slavery. "We cannot hope to solve our problems until we accurately itemize and dissect the routine daily events that existed during slavery which have a prolonged effect on our personalities." To do this, Ali has created a fifty-question "Freedom I.Q. Test" with long, explanatory answers.

At first I assumed that Ali was approaching the subject from a metaphorical standpoint. That is, many African Americans are still acting like slaves, kowtowing to white people. This is a large part of Ali's argument, but he also presents a strange, Lamarckian theory that says that somehow today's African Americans have physically and psychologically inherited slave memories from their ancestors. "We are all unconsciously and subconsciously plagued with repressed past memories which repeatedly control our destiny and, unless resolved, they will continue to be genetically transmitted from one generation to another." This line of thinking is central to question #12, which asks about various aches and pains that seem to have no discernible physical causes. These, Ali says, are "body memories," caused by "the physical brutality our ancestors endured during slavery." Body memories can include chest pain, dizziness, nausea, amnesia, genital ache, vomiting, and back pain.

Question #3 asks: "Is it okay to laugh when a Caucasian tells a joke, as long as it is not racially offensive in nature?" The correct answer is "false." Slaves were expected to laugh on cue at their masters' jokes, and continuing to laugh at white peoples' jokes is a form of slavery. Another question asks if it's all right to report criminal activity to authorities. It's not. This smacks of the days when slaves would snitch to their masters about things other slaves were doing. Ali implies—but never directly says—that the proper way to take care of such situations is for African Americans to handle them on their own.

Sections in the back of the book cover "Inherited Post-Traumatic Stress Syndrome," genocide of African Americans, and jewelry styles and foods that have been inherited from slavery. The "General Slave Profile" lists twenty-six characteristics of people who are still slaves, including: "Wears brand-name clothes so the designer's name is clearly visible," "Consults the Holy Bible daily or weekly and defends Christianity," and "Has parties and invites Black and white guests."

Civilized Publications; $10
1994; softcover; 158 pp.

## BEYOND BLADE RUNNER:
### URBAN CONTROL–THE ECOLOGY OF FEAR
### by Mike Davis

Cities are turning into fortresses where fear, crime, surveillance, and the loss of civil liberties go hand in hand. The author looks in particular at the present and future Los Angeles as an example of this "urban control." Cameras in buildings and on the street, gratings, cages, bulletproof glass, and private armed mercenaries are becoming accepted parts of the militarized city. Davis describes one such "goon squad": "Led by a six-foot-three, 280-pound 'soldier of fortune' named David Roybal, this security squad is renowned among landlords for its efficient brutality. Suspected drug dealers and their customers, as well as mere deadbeats and other landlord irritants, are physically driven from the building at gunpoint. Those who resist or even complain are beaten mercilessly."

Where is all this headed? The author paints a grim picture of a police state dystopia, complete with a map, of the possible future of L.A. and other cities. He sees containment zones for the homeless and drug users, armed response units, and a ring of gated affluent suburbs, all surrounded by a toxic rim of landfills and hazardous waste dumps. Of course, the way out of this scenario is to address the root problems of crime and violence, but it's much easier just to keep dealing with these problems in a superficial way. The future Davis envisions is not that far off.

I highly recommend this scary look at an important but underrecognized topic.

Open Magazine Pamphlet Series #23; $4
1992; long thin pamphlet; 22 pp.

## THE BUM'S RUSH–
### PHRASES AND FALLACIES
### OF RUSH LIMBAUGH: THE SELLING
### OF ENVIRONMENTAL BACKLASH
### by Don Trent Jacobs

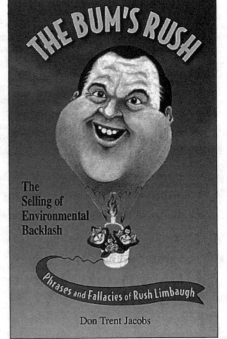

*The Bum's Rush by Don Trent Jacobs*

*Propaganda for beginners.*

Despite his claims of being a "truth detector," it should be readily apparent to any halfway knowledgeable human being that Rush Limbaugh is a brilliant propagandist. His politics are simplistic. He only presents those facts that support his rhetoric and he ignores or twists those that don't. If the truth happens to be on his side, then he will speak it. If it's not on his side, he buries it. This is opinion-shaping of the highest order. Joseph Goebbels would be jealous.

This book specifically counters the claims Limbaugh has made regarding animals and the environment. The first part of the book is a primer in persuasion, defining and giving examples from Limbaugh of twenty-nine tactics used by propagandists, including metaphors, emotional words, loaded questions, circular reasoning, personal attack, ignoring the issue, and intimidation. Part Two looks at many of the things Limbaugh has written and said, shows how they use several of the twenty-nine techniques, and counters them. Several times Limbaugh has misrepresented other people's ideas and pronouncements. When speaking of Paul Ehrlich's book *The Population Bomb,* he says: "Almost nothing he predicted came to pass. The book bombed, so to speak, in terms of accuracy." The author shows that many of Ehrlich's prophecies have indeed come true.

In one of Limbaugh's most ludicrous moments, he actually claims that white people have never committed genocide on Native Americans. To support this airhead concept, Limbaugh says that "there are more American Indians alive today than there were when Columbus arrived or at any other time in history." This is true. The statistics tell us that in 1492 there were a minimum of 1.1 million Native Americans, and in 1992 there were almost 2 million. But what Limbaugh conveniently leaves out—the fact that utterly destroys his argument—is that in 1870 there were not even 26,000 Native Americans in North America.

As long as we're on the topic, I may as well tell you what bugs the hell out of me about Limbaugh. Even more than his fascistic ideas, I'm upset by the colossal waste of talent and influence he represents. With his hugely popular radio and TV shows, his number one best-selling books, and his newsletter, he is in an extraordinary position to tell people the truth. He could expose the fact that everyone lies like dogs, everyone is corrupt—Democrats *and* Republicans, liberals *and* conservatives, Clinton *and* Bush. Instead he vilifies everybody of one political persuasion and white-washes everybody of the other. Instead of shining a light and exposing the truth no matter whom it hurts, he's content to present a one-sided view of the world, and his brain-dead zombie followers are content to lap it up. What a waste.

Legendary Publishing; $12
1994; softcover; 165 pp.

## A CALL FOR HAWAIIAN SOVEREIGNTY
### by Michael Kioni Dudley
### and Keoni Kealoha Agard

A movement to give Hawai'i back to the Hawaiians is well under way. Thousands of native Hawaiians belong to sovereignty groups, and there have even been two Constitutional Conventions that created a Constitution for a free Hawai'i (incidentally, this is how the purists spell it).

Until 1893 Hawai'i was a sovereign nation with a reigning monarch. Through a series of intrigues described thoroughly in this book, it came to pass that, in the words of President Grover Cleveland, "...Hawaii was taken possession of by the United States forces without consent or wish of the government of the islands, or of anybody else so far as shown, except the United States Minister [of Hawai'i]." A provisional government took over and refused President Cleveland's request that they restore Queen Lili'uokalani to power. Grover then turned to Congress for a solution, with predictable results. "When Congress was pressed for a decision, they opted for inaction. Despite the clear case presented by the President of immoral and illegal wrongdoing by the United States in the setting up of this hollow, non-representative government, now that the situation was so favorable to American interests, Congress conveniently decided they should follow the precept of international law and not interfere in the 'internal affairs' of the 'sovereign government' of Hawai'i." In 1897, when William McKinley became president, the alleged government of Hawai'i worked up an annexation treaty, which was narrowly approved by Congress.

In a replay of what happened to Native Americans, the Hawaiian language was outlawed. Hawaiian culture was replaced by American culture. Children went to American schools where they were taught the conqueror's version of history. "Hawaiian children were taught that their people were lazy, stupid, and worthless, and that they should turn against their culture and make themselves into Yankee adults."

*Hawaiian Sovereignty* looks at the history and present state of the sovereignty movement and the groups and individuals that constitute it. It discusses the two basic forms of sovereignty that have been tabled—the "nation within a nation" setup used by Native American tribes, and the movement to become a complete sovereign nation again. The only way the book suggests doing this is through an agreement with the United States, not by force.

"Hawaiian and non-Hawaiian leaders have suggested the hundredth anniversary of the overthrow, January 17, 1993, as the target date for restoration of Hawaiian sovereignty." Obviously they missed that goal, but it can be hoped that in the not-too-distant future Hawai'i will once again be under the control of Hawaiians.

Na Kane O Ka Malo Press; $12.95
1990; softcover; 162 pp.

## CONQUEST AND CAPITALISM, 1492–1992
### by Steve Brouwer

A leftist look at capitalism's success, the road to which has been paved with genocide, slavery, military coercion, suppression of organized labor, environmental destruction, and so on. The author takes a hard look at Columbus, the decimation of Native Americans, the slavery of Africans, the exploitation of Central America, the Industrial Revolution, the New World Order, Amazon rain forests, the Third World, and more. "The people of the North must remember that their traditions of equality and freedom also originated in the long struggles of common people to limit arbitrary power and safeguard the general welfare. If they can identify with the common destiny of the people of the South, resist the temptations of racism and consumerism, and reinvigorate their own traditions of democratic socialism, then there is some hope for the world."

Big Picture Books; $10
1992; oversize softcover; 116 pp.

## THE DECLINE AND FALL
## OF THE AMERICAN EMPIRE
### by Gore Vidal

Vidal is one of America's foremost leftist social observers. In this slim book of slightly modified essays that appeared in *The Nation*, Vidal slams Christianity, Pat Buchanan, the media, and intelligence agencies and calls for a new Constitutional Convention to remake a country that no longer works. Vidal is fun to read because you have to wonder how someone whose attacks are so extreme could become so well known and respected. "I do not accept the authority of any state—much less one founded as was ours upon the free fulfillment of each citizen—to forbid me, or anyone, the use of drugs, cigarettes, alcohol, sex with a consenting partner or, if one is a woman, the right to an abortion. I take these rights to be absolute, and should the few persist in their efforts to dominate the private lives of the many, I recommend force as a means of changing their minds."

Odonian Press; $5
1992; paperback; 95 pp.

## FIFTH ESTATE

A long-running, thick, anarchist tabloid with page after page of news and views that haven't been watered down. These people hate authority in all its trappings—they are hostile toward the right and the left. "From time to time readers...question why we are so hostile to the Left in our pages. It's not just our philosophical and theoretical differences with socialists and communists, but that when their ideas are translated into reality—such as at Kronstadt [in Russia]—they are murderous. Each leninoid sectlet adulates some mass murderer—Lenin, Trotsky, Mao, Stalin, etc.— who built state capitalism and a dictatorship on the bones of millions of workers."

Issue #344 (I told you they were long-running) has articles about the Zapatista revolution in Mexico, the role of guns in the United States, remembering the atrocities of Vietnam, nature's weather assault on the human race, interviews with Noam Chomsky and Hopi documentary filmmaker Godfrey Reggio, anarchist/antifascist happenings around the world, and more. This issue also contains a bonus—they've inserted the first issue of the Detroit anarchist paper *Daily Barbarian* to be published in almost nine years.

Fifth Estate/4632 Second Avenue/Detroit MI 48201
Single issue: $1.50
One-year sub (4 issues): $6; foreign: $8

## FREE IRELAND:
### TOWARDS A LASTING PEACE
### by Gerry Adams

Gerry Adams is the president of Sinn Féin, the Irish political party that calls for an end to British rule and a return to a united Ireland. Sinn Féin is generally regarded as the political arm of the Irish Republican Army, although Adams denies this. The lengths to which the British government have gone to silence Adams are incredible. In 1972 he was held in an internment ship where he was tortured so brutally that he still suffers today. He was imprisoned for four years without a trial. He is the leader of a legitimate political party and has twice been elected to Parliament, yet he is not allowed to travel to other parts of Great Britain. In one of the most absurd examples of government idiocy I've run across, the Brits won't allow Adams's voice to be transmitted on TV or radio, although his face can be shown. "This leads the British media to the unfortunate device of having an actor read his exact words as he mouths them."

In this book Adams tells about growing up in Northern Ireland and his involvement with the republican struggle. He recounts the manipulation and atrocities committed by both sides and looks at the toll that has been exacted: 3,290 people have died, and the British government has the worst human rights record in all of Europe. The British occupation employs more than 35,000 people and costs £1.2 billion (about $3 billion U.S.) per year, about as much as the North's education budget. Adams also outlines his peace plan and discusses the impact of his trip to the United States in early 1994.

Roberts Rinehart Publishers; $11.95
1994; softcover; 224 pp.

## GONE TO CROATAN:
### ORIGINS OF NORTH AMERICAN DROPOUT CULTURE
### edited by Ron Sakolsky and James Koehnline

Americans have been "dropping out" since long before Timothy Leary urged the hippies to do so. The very first instance took place in early colonial times. The famed "vanished colony" of Roanoake, Virginia, had disappeared off the face of the earth when Sir Walter Raleigh & Co. returned from England. The only clue as to what happened was the name "Croatoan" inscribed in the bark of a tree. The settlers had ditched "civilization" and taken up residence with a Native American tribe called the Croatoan (also spelled "Croatan"). This mingling produced a group of gray-eyed Indians who are still around today.

*Gone to Croatan* is a collection of articles documenting the hidden history of groups who simply said "to hell with it" and went native. One such group was the Tribe of Ishmael, also known as Ishmaelites, a quasi-nomadic community consisting of escaped slaves, "free" Blacks, Native Americans, and escaped indentured white servants. From 1785 till 1905, when outside pressures forced them to disperse, the Ishmaelites settled in the deep Kentucky woods, moved to Ohio, and finally settled down in "Indian Country" in Indiana.

A similar group known as the Maroons established communities all over the colonies, the largest and most militant being in North Carolina. The Maroons were escaped slaves and indentured servants, Native Americans, South American Indian slaves, Irish and British convicts, and other people outside the mainstream, dominant culture. The Maroons made raids in which they freed slaves, and they fought in the Revolution and the Civil War.

Other articles deal with America's first communal experiment, multiracial workers' rebellions, anarchy and the American Revolution, the outlaw vagabond Henry Tufts, Shay's Rebellion, the Whiskey Rebellion, pan-Indian resistance, the Iroquois influence on women's rights, and much more.

History has ignored the Ishmaelites, Maroons, and others who "went to Croatan." By leaving mainstream society, they also left the history books. *Gone to Croatan* presents an alternative history of America. Most highly recommended.

Autonomedia/AK Press; $12
1993; softcover; 382 pp.

## HOW TO LIE WITH STATISTICS
### by Darrell Huff, illustrated by Irving Geis

*How to Lie with Statistics* is a classic look at the deceptive uses of numbers. Published in 1954, it has lost none of its relevance in the intervening forty years. Some of the specific examples may be a little dated, but the techniques of deception haven't changed. Lying never goes out of style.

In the introduction, the author lays the truth bare: "The secret language of statistics, so appealing in a fact-minded culture, is employed to sensationalize, inflate, confuse, and oversimplify." One statistical warper is the method of sampling a population in a poll. Huff shows how pollsters can pick a biased population that throws off the results.

The word *average* is meaningless, since it can refer to the mean, the median, or the mode. These three processes all come up with an "average," but they can be extremely far apart. Other chicanery Huff investigates includes using a small group to get a statistically significant result, using maps and line graphs to mislead, quoting irrelevant statistics, implying causality, using decimals to give an air of precision, adding up percentages, and more. Besides giving you all this great ammo with which to confront the rising infotide, this edition of the book retains all the quaint, if slightly dorky, *Saturday Evening Post*–style cartoons from the original edition.

W.W. Norton & Co/$4.95
1954; paperback; 142 pp.

## THE HUNGER ARTISTS:
### STARVING, WRITING, AND IMPRISONMENT
### by Maud Ellmann

Hunger strikes are a powerful, time-honored method of protest. But why? In this book the author attempts to answer the following questions: "What is a hunger strike? Why is it that prisoners so often turn to this self-lacerating form of protest? Is it possible that they are gripped by a compulsion similar to that of anorexia? Do they lose their appetite for food once they have feasted on the void and thus become 'inebriate of air,' as Emily Dickinson describes the jouissance of self-starvation? Is their protest merely an excuse to justify the ecstasy of disembodiment?"

To answer these questions, Ellmann looks at two vastly different cases of self-starvation—the Irish Hunger Strike of 1981 and the violated heroine of Samuel Richardson's eighteenth-century novel *Clarissa*. Although one of these cases is real and one is fictive, "nonetheless, the drama of starvation unsettles the dichotomy between the fictive and the real, between the world of language and the world of violence.... The starving body is itself a text, the living dossier of its discontents, for the injustices of power are encoded in the savage hieroglyphics of its sufferings." Heavy stuff.

Harvard University Press; $19.95
1993; hardcover; 136 pp.

## INDIAN ROOTS OF
## AMERICAN DEMOCRACY
### edited by José Barreiro

The Constitution of the United States, and thus the American system of democracy, is based in large part on the Iroquois Great Law of Peace, an oral set of rules that five Indian nations used as a guide to government, peace, war, and diplomacy. Benjamin Franklin and many of the other Founders greatly admired this system and incorporated its principles and symbols into the creation of the United States.

This book is a collection of articles on the Great Law of Peace and its legacy from a conference held at Cornell University in 1987. The authors discuss in detail what the Great Law was all about and how it was incorporated into the government, as well as its effect on town meetings and women's rights.

From "Land of the Free, Home of the Brave" by Oren Lyons: "Sovereigns and sovereignty as understood by the Europeans related to the power of kings and queens, of royalty to rule men as they saw fit, to enslave human beings and control in total the lives and property of their subjects. Strange indeed it must have been for these immigrants to find a land with nothing but free people and free nations."

The Akwe:kon Press; $12
1988; softcover; 209 pp.

## THE IRRATIONAL IN POLITICS:
### SEXUAL REPRESSION AND AUTHORITARIAN CONDITIONING
### by Maurice Brinton

This slim essay examines how individuals are conditioned to accept their mindless slavery and unquestioningly become a part of an authoritarian, hierarchical society. Sexual repression plays a huge role in this process. Parents suppress every sexual instinct and action they observe in their child. They fill their child full of anxieties about sexual needs. Somehow, the author believes, this sexual repression generalizes so that any thoughts of rebellion against parental authority trigger anxiety. Thus, the child has become afraid of his or her own needs and desires, and to reduce anxiety, he or she becomes a bootlicking, kowtowing wimp.

By creating automatons who crave authority and can't think for themselves, the family also perpetuates itself. By discouraging sexual freedom, parents help to ensure that their kids will grow up and enter into a nice monogamous relationship of their own. Then they can create their own kids, whom they will infect with their anxieties and fears. The process repeats itself.

This booklet presents an interesting theory about how so many people can be turned into obedient sheep. Its Marxist and Freudian aspects can be annoying, though. So much of this essay is based on the ideas of radical psychoanalyst and scientist Wilhelm Reich that it could almost be considered a Reichean primer.

See Sharp Press; $5.95
1993; softcover; 52 pp.

The Last Great American Hobo photos by Michael Williamson

From "hobo" to "homeless" in fifty years.

## THE LAST GREAT AMERICAN HOBO
### photographs by Michael Williamson, essay by Dale Maharidge

"Montana Blackie" is probably the last of the Depression-era hobos. He started hopping trains as a teenager in 1928, and sixty years later he was still leading the nomadic existence. Things had changed, though. He had gone from being a "hobo" to being "homeless." Cities were cracking down on transients, and Blackie got chased out of one city after another. Finally, he settled down deep in the brush along the east bank of the Sacramento River. He built a posh (by hobo standards) shack for himself and put out the call to other hobos to create a semipermanent "city" in the area.

In the spring of 1989, the cops moved in and chased away Blackie, Shorty, Woody, Luke, and the others. Everybody relocated to the west bank of the river, but in December the sweeps happened again (Merry Christmas!). This time, Blackie and his friends decided to fight. They demanded a jury trial, where they

planned to use a necessity defense to allow them to keep their camp. Their court-appointed lawyer wasn't a big help, and when they learned that their case would take months of legal maneuvers and they'd probably get shafted in the end anyway, they decided to give up the good fight. They copped a plea, and the judge gave them one month to scram. Blackie stayed with some friends at the dumpiest motel you've ever seen. But the road called to him, and he split. No one knows where he went or even if he's still alive.

Blackie's story is told through text and pictures. A seventy-four-page essay relates his adventures, his genteel hobo philosophy, the changes in the hobo scene over the decades, and the problems he faced. The one hundred black-and-white photographs are powerful examples of photojournalism. *Washington Post* photographer Michael Williamson records life at Blackie's camp, Blackie's friends and pets, the police sweeps, the court battle, and what became of the camp after it was abandoned.

*Hobo* is a valuable document of a man who lived by his own rules for more than half a century.

Prima Publishing; $24.95
1993; hardcover; 278 pp.

## LIBERTYTREE REVIEW AND CATALOGUE

A catalog of libertarian books, tapes, and paraphernalia. All selections reflect the libertarian motto "Free minds and free markets." Books you can get include *Our Enemy the State, Common Sense by Thomas Paine, Capitalism and Freedom, Economic Liberties and the Constitution, The Roots of the Bill of Rights, Jefferson and Civil Liberties: The Darker Side, The Rights of Gun Owners, The Iran-Contra Connection, Defending the Undefendable, Home Schooling for Excellence,* and *The Great Income Tax Hoax.*

You can get the catalog as part of joining the LibertyTree. You also receive a 10 percent discount on all purchases and a gift (right now it's a choice of two posters, but you may want to write to see what their latest incentive is). Still, the price seems a little bit steep.

LibertyTree/Independent Institute
134 Ninety-Eighth Avenue/Oakland, CA 94603
One-year membership: $25
Catalog: Send a few bucks to get on their list

## LOST RIGHTS:
### THE DESTRUCTION OF AMERICAN LIBERTY
### by James Bovard

It seems like something terrible is happening in America. We are constantly hearing reports of police seizing property without due process just because they think the owner might be selling drugs, of the IRS terrorizing citizens in special IRS courts where the defendant is guilty until proven innocent, of corporations suing citizens who protest environmental destruction. And then there are the big events, such as the Waco massacre, that show unjustifiable abuse of power. Wouldn't it be nice if someone did a detailed study of all these abuses and many others? Wouldn't it be nice if someone put the scattered pieces of the puzzle into a coherent whole that shows that we truly are living in a borderline police state? And wouldn't it be great if this person wrote about all this with cynical wit fueled by mistrust of authority? Well, someone has.

Journalist James Bovard has assembled an extremely damaging document that needs to be read by everyone in America, because every one of us is affected. Bovard covers so much ground and shows so many civil liberties going up in smoke that my mind reels. In discussing the laws that destroy rights in the name of the War on (Some) Drugs, the author says, "Today, because some people grow marijuana, government officials must effectively have unlimited power to trespass on almost all private land.... Because some teenagers hide tiny bags of drugs in their underwear, government officials must be allowed to closely inspect schoolchildren's crotches. The government vigorously prosecutes dancers for indecent exposure for getting naked in front of willing viewers—but it is supposedly okay for school officials to forcibly strip a person."

The chapter "Spiking Speech, Bankrupting Newspapers, and Jamming Broadcasts" covers censorship. When trying to get material declared obscene and therefore illegal, "...prosecutors go out and commandeer the most revolting material, put twelve people in a government courtroom, show it to them while declaiming how horrible it is, and then seek to use that small group to restrict what everyone else in the community can see." Censorship is also occurring through libel suits, using the RICO act to utterly destroy small-time pornographers, and not allowing alcohol to be sold simply because of its name (i.e., PowerMaster malt liquor and Black Death vodka).

Among the many other subjects dealt with are seizure laws, declaring old, privately owned homes as historic sites and depriving their owners of their rights, harassing people who modify their property if it is considered "wetlands," the FDA's endless red tape for new drugs ("The FDA sometimes manipulates test results, or forces drug companies to use weaker doses of a drug in tests, and then pronounces the drugs to be ineffective"), the Post Office's monopoly on mail, ridiculous child labor laws, the subjugation of students by public schools, the Americans with Disabilities Act ("one of the worst written, most morally pretentious laws of the modern era"), the assault on the right to bear arms, the IRS's war on self-employed people—the list goes on and on. I've really only scratched the surface of what this book has to offer.

*Lost Rights* is one of the most important books to come out in a long time. No one can afford to be without it.

St. Martin's Press; $24.95
1994; hardcover; 408 pp.

# THE MAKING OF A FRINGE CANDIDATE 1992
## by Lenora B. Fulani

In the 1992 election Dr. Lenora Fulani of the New Alliance Party received more than 200,000 votes nationwide, coming in fifth (behind Ross Perot and the Libertarian Party). In this book Fulani discusses her political career, paying special attention to the last presidential election. She describes her struggles for oppressed people and the resistance that she met from a large number of people and organizations who didn't want her to be heard —Bill Clinton, Jesse Jackson, Black revolutionaries, *The Nation*, the FBI, the Anti-Defamation League, and members of the Communist Party USA.

The book is a fascinating case study of an outsider trying to break into the establishment while at the same time playing by her own rules and refusing to compromise. Fulani brooks no crapola. "I have the distinction of being one of the two Black leaders to have received the support of Louis Farrakhan in a run for national office. But unlike the other one, Jesse Jackson, I didn't turn around and kick the Minister in the teeth." "Jesse's 'Hymietown' remark reflected the fact that Blacks and Jews in the Democratic Party hate each other; the way the party has historically organized that relationship sparks this kind of antagonism." "Independent Black leaders have always been regarded by the powers-that-be as a particular threat: Malcolm X, Dr. Martin Luther King, Jr., the Black Panther Party. (Those who resisted co-optation in life are sometimes more 'cooperative' dead; once buried, they may be safely resurrected as monuments—and lucrative ones, at that.)"

Castillo International; $11.95
1992; softcover; 241 pp.

# MOUTH:
### THE VOICE OF DISABILITY RIGHTS

*Mouth* is a radical disability rights zine. Their motto: "Piss on pity!" All they want—make that, all they *demand*—is that the disabled have the same access to buildings, to vehicles, jobs, etc. as the nondisabled. They don't want favoritism, they don't want condescension, and they sure as hell don't want pity.

*Mouth* doesn't pull any punches. In much the same way that gays and lesbians have reclaimed the word "queer" and African Americans sometimes refer to themselves as "niggers," *Mouth* uses the word "crip." *Mouth* was instrumental in the much-publicized slagging that Jerry Lewis and his telethons have taken in recent years for parading people with MS around like pitiful sideshow attractions. Clearly, the *Mouth*sters aren't screwing around.

This fact is nowhere more evident than in their "Charity Biz" issue (September/October 1993), which put the screws to alleged charities. The article "Murder by Charity" directly blames the National Hemophilia Foundation (NHF) and plasma product manufacturers for the fact that 10,000 hemophiliacs have contracted HIV from tainted plasma products, which assist in blood clotting. Almost all the manufacturers refused to modify their donor selection process or use antiviral methods on their products after AIDS entered the scene. The NHF constantly downplayed dangers and sometimes "Urged the continued use of the deadly clotting factor compound." Federal income tax records for 1989 show that plasma manufacturers donated almost one million dollars to the NHF that year. Now 10,000 people, including many children, are infected with HIV. The issue also reprints an eye-opening chart showing the salary and benefits of the top two officials in a number of large nonprofit charities. Some interesting stats: In the fiscal year ending June 30, 1992, Planned Parenthood Federation had an income of $43,842,766. Its president got $234,672 in wages and benefits and its executive vice president got $163,177. Not a bad haul. The Association for Retarded Citizens took in a paltry $4,805,521 as of fiscal March 31, 1992. Their two highest-paid execs raked in a total of $218,589.

The next issue reported this tidbit: "Upon his retirement, the head of the Spastic Society of Britain was asked if he could envision the day when a person with spasticity would head that charity. 'That'd be like putting dogs and cats in charge of the Humane Society,' he quipped."

Besides exposing fraud, corruption, and incompetence at charities, rehab centers, and other places, *Mouth* prints pieces in which disabled people chronicle the frustration in their lives. The photo-essay "Curb Cuts from Hell" shows curb cuts in New York that make accessibility for people in wheelchairs impossible, like the one that is totally covered in trash three feet high.

Every issue of *Mouth* is controversial, but in their May/June 1994 issue, they upped the ante. That issue was devoted to sex. As the writers point out, disabled people are seen as asexual by society at large. The idea that they are still sexual beings with wants, needs, and hangups is enough to fry people's brains. Johnny Crescendo's poem "Say It Now" cuts right to the heart of the matter: "Disabled people are allowed to say/victim/brave/helpless/special/little/severely/chronically/profoundly/and vegetable/but they're not allowed to say fuck."

Although discussing sex and the disabled is undoubtedly going to cause 99 percent of the nondisabled to freak out, a surprising number of disabled people and sympathizers were evidently horrified by *Mouth*'s up-front approach to the topic. For months after the issue appeared, subscription cancellations and outraged letters poured in. The bluenoses are everywhere.

*Mouth* is loud, angry, defiant, and utterly unafraid to point fingers and name names. In short, it's everything a zine should be. *Get it.*

Mouth/61 Brighton Street/Rochester, NY 14607
Single issue: $3
One-year sub (6 issues): $24; person with disability: $12
(There are several other rates, including a hardship sub and a professional sub)

## NIGHTMARE ABROAD
### by Peter Laufer

The most famous recent case of an American getting fucked over in another country is that of Michael Fay in Singapore. I know I shouldn't have even brought this up, because every time I do, I go into a rant. I scream about the fact that Fay wasn't actually caught vandalizing. The kid who *was* caught was given clemency for ratfinking on his supposed accomplices, and Fay was one of the kids he named. I scream about how Fay's confession was beaten out of him. I scream about the fact that the law under which he was brutally punished calls for caning only when the graffiti are *anti-governmental* in nature. Fay was charged with simply painting orange stripes on cars. I scream about the fact that another kid who was indicted as one of the vandals was allowed to cop a plea and just pay a fine. This kid was Malaysian. Fay, of course, is American, which was actually his only real "crime." I say we nuke Singapore.

OK, I've ranted. I feel a little better. Now, about this book. It shows that Fay's case is nothing new. Americans have been getting in deep doo-doo in other countries for a long time. Sometimes an American is definitely trying to pull something off and gets caught, but often a person is incarcerated for a misunderstanding, an accident, or just plain being in the wrong place at the wrong time. If you drive in Mexico, you'd better be extremely careful. In 1991, sixty-four people were arrested South of the Border for traffic violations. And Mexican jails aren't the funnest places to be in. Some poor sap maxed out his credit card in Greece and spent a week in the klink. In 1980 a reporter was arrested in Bolivia for "spreading lies" about that country in her stories for the *Economist* and other magazines. During her interrogation, her life was threatened repeatedly, and she spent six days locked in a closet.

What makes the situations even worse is that in most countries, when a person is arrested, bail is difficult or impossible to attain, so many people spend six months to a year in jail before their trial. At their trial, they are usually considered guilty until proven innocent. Asking the U.S. government for help doesn't work because the government can't get Americans out of foreign jails, and they almost never want to risk screwing up foreign relations by trying to convince the foreign government to ease up.

Take my advice. Stay in the United States. It's not perfect, but at least you've got some recourse.

Mercury House; $20
1993; hardcover; 193 pp.

*NRA*
*by Josh Sugarmann*

*Disillusioned Lifetime NRA members in happier times.*

## NRA:
### NATIONAL RIFLE ASSOCIATION: MONEY–FIREPOWER–FEAR
### by Josh Sugarmann

This exposé of the National Rifle Association presents some unpleasant facts about America's largest pro-gun organization. It shows the remarkable political power that comes through money and intimidation. The NRA's political action committee, the Political Victory Fund, has given hundreds of thousands of dollars to members of Congress. As of *NRA*'s writing, the Federal Election Commission had brought suit against the NRA five times.

The author looks at the changing role of the NRA. Founded in 1871, the group originally focused on marksmanship skills. After World War II, it incorporated hunter safety into its agenda. In the mid-1970s things changed. The NRA became overridingly political and dominated

by what the author calls "Second Amendment fundamentalists," who see every gun control measure as a personal attack on their liberty and, perhaps, their lives. NRA mass mailings took on a near-hysterical tone that whipped members into a frenzy. Death threats, physical intimidation, and vandalism against gun control politicians began occurring.

The NRA's current situation is said to be bleak. Membership is down. The NRA has lost the support of its main ally, the police, not to mention millions of other gun owners, because of its defense of the right to bear armor-piercing "cop killer" bullets, handguns made mostly out of plastic resin, and military-style assault weapons. The author thinks that the passage of the Brady Bill shows that the NRA might be on the ropes. It looks as if he might be right. With public anger and fear over crime at an all-time fever pitch, talking about gun control has gone from being political suicide to being politically correct.

National Press Books; $19.95
1992; hardcover; 285 pp.

## OPEN FIRE:
### THE OPEN MAGAZINE PAMPHLET SERIES ANTHOLOGY
### edited by Greg Ruggiero and Stuart Sahulka

The Open Magazine Pamphlets are a series of short, radical, and incisive pamphlets addressing some of the major concerns of our day. They have helped reinvigorate the art of pamphleteering as social/political commentary. Here then are the best pamphlets from the first two years of the series (1991–1993):
- *How Mr. Bush Got His War* by Michael Emery
- *Reproductive Freedom* by Marlene Fried and Loretta Ross
- *ACT UP, the AIDS War, and Activism* by George Carter
- *U.S. Politics and Global Warming* by Tom Athanasiou
- *Los Angeles Was Just the Beginning* by Mike Davis
- *Media Control* by Noam Chomsky and seven others. Three pamphlets published after this anthology came out are reviewed elsewhere in this book ("Culture Jamming," "Beyond Blade Runner," and "Zapatistas"). I should also mention that you can subscribe to the Open Pamphlet Series. Look them up in the publisher listing for complete info.

The Free Press; $12.95
1993; softcover; 300 pp.

## THE PATRIOT REVIEW

Tabloid-size periodical from a white Christian right-wing perspective. The March 1993 issue contains articles on the limits of presidential power (and how they are violated), debunking global warming, how to fight seizure of your property, the real story of the government's attack on Randy Weaver and his family, "foreign" U.N. troops on American soil, and similar topics. (See also: CPA Book Publisher catalog in the chapter on extremism.)

The Patriot Review/PO Box 905/Sandy, OR 97055
Single issue: $2
One-year sub (12 issues): $24

## POLITICS AT THE PERIPHERY:
### THIRD PARTIES IN TWO-PARTY AMERICA
### by J. David Gillespie

For all practical purposes, the United States is a two-party country. There's no law against third parties, of course, it's just that the political machinery has evolved in a way that forces any third party to climb a long, hard road. That sure hasn't stopped people from trying, though. Ross Perot's run for president in 1992, covered in this book, showed that maybe outsiders do have a prayer after all (especially if they're multimillionaires).

Gillespie's study of third parties in American history is comprehensive and, perhaps more importantly, a fascinating read. He covers the defunct third parties, most of which are from the 1800s and early 1900s: Southern Democrats, Dixiecrats, Bull

Moose Party, Anti-Masonic Party, Liberty Party, Free Soil Party, the Know-Nothings, Greenback Party, and Progressive Party.

Next come the parties that are still around: All-African People's Revolutionary Party, American Nazi Party, Anti-Lawyer Party, Black Panther Party, Communist Party USA, Expansionist Party, Fourth International Tendency, Green Party, Libertarian Party, Natural Law Party, Prohibition Party, Youth International Party (Yippies), and dozens more. Gillespie examines the history, performance, philosophy, and candidates of these parties in a thorough fashion, including many tables indicating election returns. There are also several sidebars highlighting particularly interesting candidates, such as Lyndon LaRouche, George Wallace, Martin Kerr of the National Socialist White People's Party, and Belva Ann Lockwood, who ran under the Equal Rights Party in 1884, becoming the first female candidate for president. She received 4,149 votes, all from men, since women were not yet allowed to vote.

University of South Carolina Press; $14.95
1993; softcover; 334 pp.

## PRANKS!
### (RE/SEARCH #11)

"Society imposes a grid of habit-forming pathways on its denizens to 'produce results' without lateral detouring.... Pranks blast the rigidified politeness and behavior patterns which bespeak sleepwalkers acting on automatic pilot.... Pranks challenge all aspects of the 'social contract' which have been ossified." With these words, the RE/Search gang launches into an exploration of those acts that shake up the status quo and subvert authority's power.

Mark Pauline of Survival Research Laboratories talks about his billboard modifications and machine performances. Joey Skaggs tells of his elaborate pranks, such as pretending to run a whorehouse for dogs. As a result the ASPCA sent armed investigators after him, and the attorney general subpoenaed him. He also pretended to be a Gypsy protesting against the name "gypsy moth," and the *New York Times* fell for it, running a story on him. Jello Biafra offers the following prank: "Rent yourself a safety deposit box, insert a little package of frozen dead fish, and never return! Slowly but surely the decomposing fish will stink up the entire vault, but by law the bank is forbidden to go through all the boxes to see where it might be coming from!"

Abbie Hoffman reminisces about his countercultural pranks. Among the many revelations Hoffman offers is that he wrote a sequel to *Steal This Book*. It was "the definitive work on counterfeiting, jewel smuggling—you name it," but he submitted his only copy to a publisher who went bankrupt and lost the 500-page manuscript! Paul Krassner discusses his classic prankzine, *The Realist*, and its most famous moment, when Krassner printed a fake article that said Lyndon Johnson had sex with JFK's throat wound aboard Air Force One. The kicker is that a lot of people actually believed it. Other pranksters who are interviewed include Timothy Leary, Karen Finley, Joe Coleman, Earth First!, Jon Waters, and over two dozen others.

RE/Search Publications; $17.99
1987; oversize softcover; 233 pp.

## THE PROSPEROUS FEW
## AND THE RESTLESS MANY
### by Noam Chomsky

More interviews in which Chomsky spills the beans on a whole lot of things no one wants you to know—Somalia, the former Yugoslavia, Israel, India, racism, American fascism, NAFTA, and class struggle. About NAFTA, Chomsky says, "As you'd expect, this whole structure of decision making answers basically to the transnational corporations, international banks, etc. It's also an effective blow against democracy. All these structures raise decision making to the executive level, leaving what's

called a 'democratic deficit'—parliaments and populations with less influence.... That's a real success in depriving formal democratic structures of any process."

Odonian Press; $5
1993; paperback; 95 pp.

◄ *Pranks!*

*Legendary trickster Boyd Rice thinking up more kooky antics.*

## QUARTERLY REVIEW
## OF DOUBLESPEAK

Don't let the fact that this newsletter is put out by the National Council of Teachers of English scare you away. Trust me, if English class were this interesting you may have actually looked forward to it. The *Quarterly Review of Doublespeak* is devoted to uncovering instances where language has purposely been twisted to obscure its true meaning. For example, the military's use of the word *incapacitate* instead of kill.

The January 1994 issue contained the Doublespeak Awards for 1993. The winner was the Department of Defense for consistently using doublespeak, among other unsavory tactics, during the 1980s to convince Congress to appropriate hundreds of billions of dollars for new weapons systems. One example of this occurred during the DoD's capability tests of the Star Wars system. In three consecutive tests a heat-seeking missile failed to intercept its target. Knowing that the success of the fourth test was absolutely crucial for funding, "a target missile was artificially heated to make it appear ten times bigger to the heat-seeking interceptor missile." This didn't mean that the test was rigged, though. A project official said that the target missile had merely been "enhanced."

Second prize went to George Bush for pardoning his Iran-Contra buddies who had secretly engaged in acts specifically forbidden by law, including dealing in arms with a terrorist state, failure to obtain congressional approval for arms sales to another state, and transferring arms to the Nicaraguan Contras. After these illegal acts were exposed, some of these officials lied under oath and destroyed evidence of their crimes. "In his pardon, President Bush called the people who committed these crimes 'patriots' and said their legal troubles were simply a matter of a 'criminalization of policy differences.'"

Third prize went to President Clinton for referring to a tax increase of 35 percent on Social Security benefits as a "spending cut"; for referring to a tax to raise money for his health care plan as a "wage-based premium"; and for constantly substituting the word *investment* for the word *spending*.

Nominees for the award included PBS, which refers to the corporate commercials at the beginning of their programs as "enhanced underwriter acknowledgments." A Post Office official, when told by Congress that almost one-fourth of "Priority Two-Day Mail" takes three days to reach its destination, said, "I would call Priority Mail a delivery commitment, but not a guarantee." Television stations are supposed to carry a certain amount of programming that "serves the educational and informational needs of children" as mandated by the 1990 Children's Television Act. When the FCC asked stations for reports of their compliancy, many cited *The Jetsons*, *The Flintstones*, *G.I. Joe,* and *Super Mario Brothers* as fulfilling their requirements because these shows address "issues of social consciousness and responsibilities."

In addition to articles dissecting the deceptive use language, the *Review* also runs book reviews, book excerpts, and other material. May I suggest that you exchange monetary units for the privilege of being shipped subsequent printings of this periodical? (Translation: buy a subscription to this newsletter.)

NCTE/1111 W Kenyon Road/Urbana, IL 61801-1096
One-year sub (4 issues): $10

## THE SACRAMENT OF ABORTION
### by Ginette Paris

This book is basically an extended meditation on the pro-choice slogan "Every child a wanted child." The author contends that women who get abortions do so because they know that bringing an unwanted child into this world condemns it to a "living death." Thus, a life must be wanted or it should not exist.

The author sees abortion as a sacrifice to Greek goddess Artemis, who does not want to give life unless it is pure. "This little book develops the idea that abortion is a sacred act, that it is an expression of maternal responsibility and not a failure of maternal love." Radical stuff.

Spring Publications; $12
1992; softcover; 113 pp.

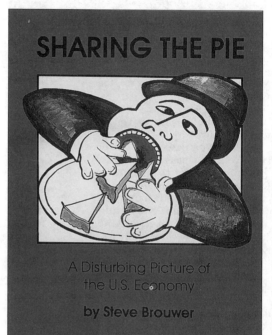

*Sharing the Pie*
*by Steve Brouwer*

*The ABCs*
*of the GNP.*

## SHARING THE PIE:
### A DISTURBING PICTURE OF THE U.S. ECONOMY
### by Steve Brouwer

A large-format, easy-to-understand guide to the true nature of our economy. The author explains why the gulf between the haves and the have-nots is widening, why education spending is going down while military spending is going up, why corporations get special treatment at everybody else's expense, control of politics by the corporate rich, unemployment, health care, and the disappearing middle class. "We live by patterns of capital accumulation and political influence that originated in the era of the nineteenth-century 'Robber Barons'; these patterns are not only antiquated and anti-democratic, but they prevent American society from functioning as well and as fairly as other advanced industrial societies."

Big Picture Books; $8
1992; oversize softcover; 84 pp.

## SURVEILLANCE IN THE STACKS:
### THE FBI'S LIBRARY AWARENESS PROGRAM
### by Herbert N. Foerstel

Since the 1970s, the FBI has been using libraries as a way to monitor "subversives," which basically means anybody from the Middle East or the Soviet Union. They have attempted, and often succeeded, to access library records of who has checked out which books. They have also recruited librarians to be permanent stool pigeons, reporting on certain people who borrow books or magazines that are for, in the FBI's words, "loyal Americans only."

The FBI is interested in who checks out material on terrorism, explosives, engineering, and anything else that could be considered dangerous if you're paranoid enough. For example, at the University of Cincinnati Library in 1985, the FBI "requested records of library use by a Soviet citizen. An FBI agent claimed that the Soviet's proper field of interest should have been mining engineering, but he had instead borrowed books on robotics." At the University of Michigan Library "agents expressed concern that a visiting Russian mathematics professor who specialized in graph theory was spending a suspicious amount of time at the photocopy machines."

To their credit, the vast majority of librarians approached by the Feds refused to grant them access to library records, although they were sometimes forced by court orders to comply. Chapter 3 is, in fact, devoted to the role of librarians in this program. The final chapter deals with privacy, confidentiality, and intellectual freedom issues as they relate to the FBI's book-snooping.

Greenwood Publishing Group; $49.95
1991; hardcover; 171 pp.

## T.A.Z.:
### THE TEMPORARY AUTONOMOUS ZONE, ONTOLOGICAL ANARCHY, POETIC TERRORISM
### by Hakim Bey

*T.A.Z.* is a collection of essays from guerrilla reality engineer Hakim Bey. It contains the complete Broadsheets of Ontological Anarchism, all the communiqués of the Association for Ontological Anarchy, and the new essay "The Temporary Autonomous Zone." Bey's hallucinatory prose defiantly tears away at all of society's ways of keeping you down, in the hopes that you'll experience true freedom, even if it's only for one brief, glorious moment.

According to Bey, chaos is alive and well and is the key to our freedom. "Avatars of chaos act as spies, saboteurs, criminals of *amour fou*, neither selfless nor selfish, accessible as children, mannered as barbarians, chafed with obsessions, unemployed, sensually deranged, wolfangels, mirrors for contemplation, eyes like flowers, pirates of signs & meanings." As an agent of chaos, Bey says, "I am awake only in what I love & desire to the point of terror—everything else is just shrouded furniture, quotidian anesthesia, shit-for-brains, sub-reptilian ennui of totalitarian regimes, banal censorship & useless pain."

They key to chaos and liberation is to be true to yourself. "First murder the IDEA—blow up the monument inside us—& then perhaps…the balance of power will shift. When the last cop in our brain is gunned down by the last unfulfilled desire—perhaps even the landscape around us will begin to change." Bey gives some concrete actions you can take in order to break the chains that bind you. "Poetic Terrorism," a classic essay in underground circles, is full of ideas, such as, "Kidnap someone & make them happy." "Art Sabotage" suggests a hands-on approach to getting rid of "aesthetic blight": "Don't picket—vandalize. Don't protest—deface. When ugliness, poor design & stupid waste are forced upon you, turn Luddite, throw your shoe in the works, retaliate. Smash the symbols of the Empire in the name of nothing but the heart's longing for grace."

The long essay "The Temporary Autonomous Zone" (T.A.Z.) is a study of little-known anarchist utopias in which people enjoyed complete freedom. But besides being a lesson in hidden history, "T.A.Z." discusses the possibility of setting up an actual temporary autonomous zone today.

Autonomedia; $7
1985, 1991; paperback; 141 pp.

## UNEQUAL JUSTICE:
### WAYNE DUMOND, BILL CLINTON, AND THE POLITICS OF RAPE IN ARKANSAS
### by Guy Reel

*Unequal Justice* is a sickening tale of rape, vigilantism, and political cowardice. In 1984, a seventeen-year-old girl was raped in a small town in Arkansas. Her father was a prominent businessman, friend of the sheriff, and fraternity brother of the assistant prosecutor. This girl originally fingered a man who turned out to have an airtight alibi. Later, she saw Wayne Dumond, a handyman, driving around town and turned him in as the rapist. Brought in to pick her attacker out of a lineup, she couldn't at first. Some people say that she left the room with her father and the police chief, and when she came back, she picked Dumond.

After Dumond was released on bond, two men broke into his home and castrated him. At the scene later, the sheriff took the testicles, put them in formaldehyde, and showed them off to his friend, the victim's father. Dumond was later convicted and sentenced to life for the rape. But then DNA tests proved conclusively that Dumond's semen didn't match that found on the rape victim; he was not the rapist.

And where does Bill Clinton fit into all of this? He was governor of Arkansas at the time, and he refused to grant clemency for Dumond when the tests showed Dumond wasn't the rapist. Oh yeah, he's also a second cousin of the girl who was raped.

Prometheus Books; $22.95
1993; hardcover; 261 pp.

## WHAT UNCLE SAM REALLY WANTS
### by Noam Chomsky

Chomsky is probably the best-known liberal political commentator of our time. His efforts to reveal the true workings of the media and U.S. foreign policy in particular have opened cans of worms that can never again be shut. The essays in this book (taken from interviews and speeches) focus on these two areas. Chomsky looks at what the United States has done to El Salvador, Nicaragua, Guatemala, Panama, Southeast Asia, Eastern Europe, and other countries. "Now, when some client state complains that the U.S. government isn't sending us enough money, they no longer say, 'we need it to stop the Russians'—rather, 'we need it to stop drug trafficking.' Like the Soviet threat, this enemy provides a good excuse for a U.S. military presence where there's rebel activity or other unrest." Chomsky also looks at the way we are duped in this country by media and government doublespeak.

Odonian Press; $5
1992; paperback; 111 pp.

## WORKERS VANGUARD

The biweekly tabloid newspaper of the Spartacist League, one of the most prominent communist organizations in the United States. *Workers Vanguard* is a top-notch source of information about labor struggles, police atrocities, racism, military aggressiveness, and American political prisoners. As with all publications, even if you don't agree with *WV*'s political stance, you can still learn valuable things from it.

The July 8, 1994, issue has an article on South Africa asserting that even though Nelson Mandela has become president, the machinery of white domination is still in place and will be until it is overthrown by the Black working class. Another article deals with the despicable way Keith McHenry, co-founder of Food Not Bombs, is being harassed by San Francisco's government. McHenry is allegedly being targeted because he gives food to starving people instead of trying to drive them away as the government does. In a textbook case of "No good deed goes unpunished," McHenry has been arrested ninety-two times, assaulted by officials twice, and was left to bleed for more than six hours without medical attention from a severed artery he sustained during an arrest. Several other articles deal with Haiti, the draconian sentences given to surviving Branch Davidians, the imprisonment of former Black Panther Mumia Abu-Jamal, and more. There's also a picture of police spraying pepper spray point-blank into the eyes of kneeling unionists engaged in civil disobedience.

Subscriptions to *Workers Vanguard* also include *Spartacist*, "Organ of the International Executive Committee of the International Communist League."
One-year sub (22 issues): $10 (U.S. & Canada);
foreign surface: $7; foreign airmail: $25

*Workers Vanguard*

*Vive la revolution!*

# CONSPIRACIES, COVER-UPS, AND HIDDEN INFORMATION

## JFK

### THE ASSASSINATION OF JOHN F. KENNEDY:
#### A COMPLETE BOOK OF FACTS
#### by James P. Duffy and Vincent L. Ricci

This mammoth book supposedly catalogs "every person, place, object, event, and theory connected in any way with the president's death." Of course, the book can't actually live up to this hype, but it does do an admirable job of presenting a ton of information in an accessible encyclopedia format. The approximately one thousand entries include the "Babushka Lady," Bethesda Naval Hospital, *Crossfire*, Fair Play for Cuba Committee, E. Howard Hunt, Office of Naval Intelligence, Dan Rather, sniper's nest, temple wound controversy, windshield damage, and Zapruder film.

One area in which this book shines is its impressive logging of people connected to the assassination. For example, the entry for Dennis "Peanuts" McGuire informs us: "An employee of Oneal's Funeral Home, McGuire helped place the president's body inside the coffin at Parkland Memorial Hospital." Herbert Orth was the photo chief at *Life* who edited the Zapruder film for publication. James Simmons was a railroad worker and one of many people who said that shots came from the grassy knoll.

Of course, I do have some quibbles with the book, such as not including anything about Aristotle Onassis or not mentioning that the three "hoboes" picked up by police near the scene were clean-shaven and wearing unwrinkled suits and highly shined shoes. Overall, though, there don't seem to be any glaring omissions or seriously malnourished entries, making this a valuable reference for conspiracy researchers.

Thunder's Mouth Press; $14.95
1992; softcover; 538 pp.; illus.

### CASE CLOSED:
#### LEE HARVEY OSWALD AND THE ASSASSINATION OF JFK
#### by Gerald Posner

*Case Closed* is a massive attempt to show that Oswald did indeed act alone when he killed Kennedy. Gerald Posner uses new interviews, previously unseen documents, and computer enhancement of photos and films of the assassination to make his point. He brings up evidence that Oswald was a very good marksman, that he had time to fire three shots, that Oswald was not in the depository lunch room during the assassination, that he did kill Officer Tippit, that JFK's wounds were indicative of the official version of events, that JFK's body couldn't have been tampered with, that the "pristine" bullet could do all the damage it's said to have done, that the backyard photos of Oswald weren't faked, that Jack Ruby acted alone, and much, much more.

Posner attempts to dismantle every major point brought up by conspiracy researchers. Sometimes he succeeds, and sometimes he doesn't. He does a great job, for example, of demolishing

the testimony of Jean Hill, who now claims to have seen a second assassin fire from behind a fence on the grassy knoll. But when she was interviewed by a news crew a half hour after the assassination, they asked her if she had seen anybody unusual. She said no. Later that day, she testified at the sheriff's office that there was a shaggy white dog in between Kennedy and his wife. When she found out there was no dog, she said it must have been the white roses they had. The roses were red. She also said she saw a man running across the street toward the other side of the plaza. She claimed to have run across the street after him, nearly being hit by a police motorcycle. Photographs of the scene show that after the motorcade had passed, Hill was standing still in her initial spot. Later on she would add to her story that the man left behind a trail of blood. Police reports at the time show no blood was found.

Posner's explanation of the "Umbrella Man," though, is utterly unconvincing. In the Zapruder film a man is seen opening and closing his umbrella, even though it was a sunny day, as the shots started ringing out. Some have said that he fired a poisoned dart at Kennedy, and others think he was giving some sort of signal to the gunmen. During the House Select Committee's investigation into the matter, Louie Witt came forward claiming that he was the Umbrella Man. He said that he was heckling the president. Case closed? Hardly.

*Case Closed* is absolute heresy to JFK and other conspiracy researchers. However, when considering every scenario, the "conspiracy of one" theory must be examined, too. Even if there was a conspiracy, *Case Closed* helps by calling into question a lot of evidence, making certain theories more plausible than others.

Random House; $14.95
1993; softcover; 607 pp.; illus.

◄ *Case Closed*
by Gerald
Posner

*Absolute
heresy?*

### THE FOURTH DECADE:
#### A JOURNAL OF RESEARCH ON THE
#### JOHN F. KENNEDY ASSASSINATION

For more than ten years, *The Fourth Decade* (formerly titled *The Third Decade*) has presented a wide array of opinions, facts, and theories about Kennedy's assassination. Every conceivable aspect of the case is microscopically analyzed. For example, "Closing Arguments" by Jerry Organ discusses the "Umbrella Man," Louie Witt. When Witt presented the umbrella he claimed he had been holding on Dealey Plaza, it had ten ribs. "[Researcher

Gary] Mack alleges Witt's umbrella 'had a different number of "ribs" than the one in the Zapruder film.' Relying on the Willis 5 slide, Robert Cutler purports the umbrella at Dealey Plaza had eight ribs whereas Witt's has ten. But Zapruder frames 221–231 disclose not quite half of a side of the umbrella to the right of the Stemmons sign. Two and a half 'webs' are visible in that quadrant, which can be doubled to five per half, making *ten* total." And that's just the tip of the iceberg.

Obviously *The Fourth Decade* isn't for the casually interested, but if you're a hard-core JFK researcher, it's indispensable.

The Fourth Decade
State University College/Fredonia, NY 14063
Single issue: $4
One-year sub (6 issues): $20; Canada: $25;
foreign surface: $25; foreign airmail: $38

## JFK:
### FIRST DAY EVIDENCE
#### by Gary Savage

Now that enough books, articles, and monographs on the assassination have been written to fill a school book depository, you may be saying, "Can anybody really say anything new at this point?" The answer is a resounding "yes." R.W. "Rusty" Livingston was a Crime Lab Detective for the Dallas Police who was working when Kennedy was shot. He made personal copies of much of the evidence surrounding the murder, including documents and photos. For the first time we get to see very clear, uncropped, first-generation reproductions of the photos, instead of the second- and third-generation photos we're used to seeing. (This entire book is printed on slick, heavy paper—the kind reserved for "photo inserts" in normal books—so all 144 reproductions look as sharp as possible.)

Livingston and many of his fellow detectives who were interviewed for this book recount what happened in the crime lab during the hours and days immediately following the shooting. There are chapters devoted to Oswald's finger- and palm prints, the infamous backyard photographs of Oswald, the sixth floor of the book depository (with scads of photographs), Jack Ruby, and the Minox spy camera that the FBI denied existed (accompanied by a previously unpublished photo of the camera).

Also reproduced are the Dallas arrest reports of Oswald and Ruby, the homicide reports of Kennedy and Oswald, a scale drawing of the sixth floor, fake ID found on Oswald, and more. Finally, there's a reprint of a scarce document by a former Dallas Police supervisor rebutting the acoustical evidence theory of the House Select Committee.

The Shoppe Press; $25
1993; hardcover; 416 pp.; illus.

## JFK ASSASSINATION:
### A VISUAL INVESTIGATION (CD-ROM)

This CD-ROM has all kinds of goodies related to Kennedy's assassination. The "Overview" portion of the disk contains dozens of screens of photos and text covering Kennedy's early life, the motorcade route, Secret Service reaction, the Babushka Lady, the sniper's nest, the grassy knoll, possible groups behind the assassination, autopsy findings, Officer Tippit's murder, Jack Ruby, the Warren Commission, and many other topics. Cross-referenced words in the text are highlighted. Clicking on them takes you to the appropriate entry in *The Assassination of John F. Kennedy: A Book of Facts*. The "Go Xfire" button at the top of the screen will take you to the corresponding section of *Crossfire* by Jim Marrs.

The "Dealey Plaza" portion has three maps. The witness map shows the location of various bystanders—John Chism, Jean Hill, and so on. Click on their location and a picture of the witness appears along with text and narration about him or her. A larger map of Dealey Plaza shows all the surrounding buildings and structures. Clicking on one of them will bring up info on how it relates to the assassination. The final map shows the location of

people who captured the crime on videotape or still pictures.

"Analysis" allows you to choose various reconstructions of the shooting done using computer animation. You can select different vantage points (the grassy knoll, sniper's nest, etc.) and different theories (Warren Commission, second gunman, etc.).

This CD also contains the complete text of the single-volume version of the Warren Commission's report, *Crossfire*, and *The Assassination of John F. Kennedy* (reviewed above). You can do keyword searches through the last two books and the photo library (described below).

The real pièce de resistance, in my opinion, is the inclusion of four—count 'em, four—videos of the assassination. Of course the famous Zapruder film is here, as are the Nix, Muchmore, and Hughes films. All of them except the last one capture the actual shots hitting Kennedy. You can view these films in normal speed, slow-motion, frame by frame, full screen, and full screen slo-mo. The Zapruder film offers options to focus in on the running little girl or JFK. Or you can view a close-up of JFK frame by frame, which gives you a great view of his exploding head.

There's also a photo library with pictures of the magic bullet, the president's coat, the limousine, the rifle, the funeral, Oswald captured by police, David Ferrie, Jim Garrison, limo driver William Greer, and various mobsters, autopsy photos, X rays, the backyard photos of Oswald, Oswald's mugshot, and so on.

*JFK Assassination* is a powerful resource, To run it you'll need a PC with a 486SX or higher microprocessor, 4 MB of RAM, 4 MB of hard disk space, a CD-ROM drive, VGA or better display with 256 color support, and Microsoft Windows 3.1 or later. It's strongly recommended that you have an audio board with speakers and a mouse.

Medio Multimedia; $59.95
1993; CD-ROM

## PROJECT SEEK:
### ONASSIS, KENNEDY AND THE GEMSTONE THESIS
#### by Gerald A. Carroll

Around 1973 a strange photocopied document surfaced. Copied innumerable times and passed from person to person, the *Skeleton Key to the Gemstone Files* claimed to expose who killed JFK, among other controversial revelations. This twenty-two-page report was a summary of a one thousand-page document written by Bruce Roberts, who supposedly had intelligence connections.

*Project Seek* reprints the entire *Skeleton Key*, including the names of individuals, and dissects the document to see what can be confirmed and what can't. The basic gist of the *Gemstone Files* is that Aristotle Onassis pulled the plug on JFK and RFK. The reason is that Onassis and the Kennedy brothers' father, Joseph Kennedy, were in business (illegal and legal) together and made a fortune. John and Robert uncovered the details of their father's and Onassis's doings and for some reason decided to make life rough for the Greek billionaire. They arrested many of Onassis's Mafia pals, including Jimmy Hoffa. Onassis struck back first by wooing Jacqueline Kennedy (the *Gemstone Files* allege they were romantically involved before the assassination). When Castro came to power he seized money from Mafia casinos in Cuba. Onassis was enraged and organized Castro's assassination, which narrowly failed. After JFK made a half-hearted invasion attempt at the Bay of Pigs, Onassis had him snuffed. He also had Robert killed when the attorney general wouldn't stop hounding him.

Although that's the meat of the *Skeleton Key*, it does contain numerous other allegations. For example, President Nixon believed that the Democrats had files on the Kennedy-Onassis connection, so he had the same guys who handled the Bay of Pigs and JFK's assassination break into their headquarters. Also, in 1957 Onassis kidnapped Howard Hughes, replaced him with a double, and kept the real Hughes prisoner on a remote island. The motive was to gain control of Hughes's defense and aviation empire and all of the politicians Hughes had bought (including Vice President Nixon).

America West Publishers; $16.95
1994; softcover; 388 pp.; illus.

## WHO KILLED JFK?
### by Carl Oglesby

This slim little book covers some of the very basics of the conspiracy to kill President Kennedy. The first chapter examines some of the people who hated Kennedy, including the CIA, militant racists, anti-Castro Cubans, and the Mafia. The next chapter presents the two official versions of what happened, as told by the Warren Commission and the House Select Committee on Assassinations. The third chapter shows some of the evidence for a conspiracy. The official version of the actual shooting is disputed by eyewitness testimony, medical evidence, acoustical evidence, and the Zapruder film. The author also presents evidence that Oswald was framed, that he didn't kill Officer Tippit, and that he had ties to U.S. intelligence. The final chapter looks at the strong and weak points concerning several theories about who was behind the assassination.

For those who just want an introduction to JFK conspiracy theory without getting bogged down in dozens of eight-hundred-page books, this paperback is the ticket.

Odonian Press; $5
1992; softcover; 95 pp.; illus.

## WHO SHOT JFK?:
### A GUIDE TO THE MAJOR CONSPIRACY THEORIES

### by Bob Callahan, illustrated by Mark Zingarelli

With a funky design and tons of noir illustrations from artist and underground comics creator Mark Zingarelli, *Who Shot JFK?* romps through the major (and some minor) conspiracy theories and controversies surrounding the assassination.

Thirty-eight short, punchy chapters and nearly one hundred sidebars cover a huge number of topics: Mark Lane's first salvo against the "lone nut" theory, Mr. X, the John Birch Society, David Ferrie, Jim Garrison, Jack Ruby's sanity, the single bullet controversy, Oswald's marksmanship, the friendly fire theory, Gerald Ford's biography of Oswald, the FBI's autopsy report, the grassy knoll, the "three tramps," the Dallas-Cuba connection, the "conspiracies don't happen in the United States" mentality, *Life* magazine's botched reporting of the Zapruder film, Dan Rather's botched reporting of the Zapruder film, the head snap controversy, the crossfire theory, the possible CIA-Mafia alliance, associates of Jack Ruby who died strange, violent deaths, Dallas police, Marilyn Monroe, Oliver Stone, novels based on the assassination, and on and on.

Besides hitting the major theories, the author throws in some of the loopier ones just for fun. For example, there's the "gay thrill kill" theory, which claims that Oswald, Ruby, David Ferrie, and Clay Shaw snuffed JFK for kicks (which would make the Zapruder film the most widely seen snuff flick of all time). Then there's the "mother of all conspiracy theories": "The honorary leader of the truly apocryphal branch of the Conspiracy Movement would have to be George C. Thomson, a Southern California swimming pool engineer who has written that twenty-two shots were fired at President Kennedy in Dealey Plaza. Five people were killed in the fusillade, including Officer J.D. Tippit, who was riding in the presidential limousine, impersonating JFK. According to Thomson, Kennedy actually escaped, and was seen more than a year later attending a private birthday party for New York author Truman Capote."

With so many books on JFK out there, it's dangerous to make such a bold statement, but I'd have to say that this book is the best introduction/overview of the assassination available.

Fireside (Simon & Schuster); $12
1993; oversize softcover; 159 pp.; illus.

# OTHER ASSASSINATIONS

## THE ASSASSINATION OF LINCOLN:
### HISTORY AND MYTH

### by Lloyd Lewis

This really isn't a conspiracy book in the strictest sense. First published in 1929 as *Myths After Lincoln*, it chronicles the strange myths and legends and even stranger facts regarding Lincoln's death. Lloyd Lewis shows John Wilkes Booth to have been an extremely charismatic, egocentric actor who built up a following of lowly men and one woman to help him assassinate the president. Lewis rejects the notion that Wilkes was a madman. "As Lincoln's saintliness became more and more apparent with each day's passing, so did it become clear to many Americans that no one but a mad man could have killed him. It became easier and easier to dismiss J. Wilkes Booth with a shake of the head and a sighing explanation, 'He was crazy, that was all.'" (Quite fortuitous words. This explanation is now given for why Oswald, Sirhan, Ray, Hinckley, and others are officially considered "lone nuts.")

The prosecution's tactic, however, was to paint Booth & Co. as part of a conspiracy fomented by the South, perhaps even Jefferson Davis. Lewis discounts this, too. He shows that the "Radical Republicans," hard-line members of Lincoln's party, were upset with Lincoln for his forgiveness towards the South. He stops short of saying that it was a plot by this faction, but his implication was the impetus for later researchers who came right out and said it.

Lewis faults the way Secretary of War Stanton ordered Booth's body immediately destroyed after soldiers had shot the assassin. Stanton's rationale was that he didn't want any remains to become a "holy relic" for the South to rally around. However, by getting rid of the body, Stanton gave credence to rumors that authorities had killed the wrong man and Booth had gotten away.

Besides the conspiracy around Lincoln's death, other revelations in this book are fascinating examples of hidden history. Lewis details the almost-successful plot to steal Lincoln's corpse. In 1876 a group of counterfeiters planned to snatch Lincoln's remains and ransom them for the release of one of their comrades, a platemaker of the first degree. Luckily, the government had planted a mole in the group, but the authorities' botched attempt to catch the graverobbers red-handed allowed the men to get away. They had even managed to get Lincoln's body halfway out of the coffin. Days later they were arrested at a relative's house.

Rumors flew that the "resurrectionists" had really succeeded and that Lincoln's marble sarcophagus, visited by hundreds of thousands of people every year, contained an empty coffin. The funny thing is, the rumor was partially right. Seven days after the incident, the small group in charge of Lincoln's memorial was so worried about a repeat attempt at corpsenapping that they secretly moved Lincoln's body and coffin to the catacombs underneath the memorial, where it stayed for eleven years. A new, stronger tomb was built, and Lincoln's remains were again where they were supposed to be.

Eighteen people who knew Lincoln examined the body before reburial to make sure it was really him. Incredibly, though he had been killed twenty-two years earlier, his corpse was still intact. His face was "...darker, somewhat, more like the bronze face of the statue that stood on the monument above, yet still the same gaunt, strange features..."

A Bison Book (University of Nebraska Press); $12.95
1929; softcover; 367 pp.

◄ *Who Shot JFK?* by Bob Callahan

*The illustrated conspiracist.*

## THE ASSASSINATION OF MALCOLM X
### by George Breitman, Herman Porter, and Baxter Smith

This book has two basic purposes. First and foremost, it examines the evidence of a conspiracy, perhaps with FBI backing, in the killing of Malcolm X. Second, it presents a sympathetic account of Malcolm's teachings. "It aims to stimulate the study of his views and a recognition of their importance for effective political action against racism, war, the oppression of women, and the exploitation of working people the world over."

Strange events surround Malcolm's death. Most large morning newspapers print two editions per day—a morning edition prepared during the night and an afternoon edition prepared during the day. All three New York morning newspapers, in their first edition on the morning after the shooting, had headlines proclaiming that police had nabbed two suspects at Audubon Ballroom, the site of the assassination. But in their afternoon editions, all three papers had headlines stating that the police had captured *one* suspect. The *Herald Tribune* deleted all references in the story to a second suspect. The *Times*, however, left the information in both editions. They said that this second mystery suspect, whose name wasn't given, was rescued from the angry crowd by Patrolman Thomas Hoy, who reported taking him to the Wadsworth Precinct station. This is the last time a second suspect being arrested at the scene is ever mentioned. The official version of the story still states that only one suspect was apprehended. Who was this mystery man? The author speculates he may have been a member of the police's red squad.

Three men ended up standing trial for the crime, including Talmadge Hayer, who was the "one" suspect caught at the scene. All three were convicted even though there was no material evidence linking the other two with the shooting, and the prosecution couldn't even prove that they were at the crime scene that night. Also, during the trial, Hayer admitted his role in the killing, but said that his two co-defendants were completely innocent.

This book provides several disquieting revelations, but it could have been much more exhaustive in its approach.

Pathfinder Press; $13.95
1976, 1991; softcover; 196 pp.; illus.

go back to his room after the shooting to retrieve it—a sequence which would add to the time needed for a clean escape..."

Piece by piece, the official version of events is broken down and Melanson draws the conclusion that rogue intelligence agents were behind the murder. The arguments are precisely detailed and backed up by twenty pages of notes.

Shapolsky Publishers, Inc; $12.95
1991; softcover; 232 pp.; lightly illus.

## THE ROBERT F. KENNEDY ASSASSINATION:
### NEW REVELATIONS ON THE CONSPIRACY AND COVER-UP, 1968–1991
### by Philip H. Melanson, Ph.D.

Melanson is the director of the RFK Assassination Archives at Southeastern Massachusetts University. As such, he has had access to an incredible amount of material surrounding the assassination. He has also *not* had access to an incredible amount of material surrounding the assassination. Why? Because it's gone. The Los Angeles Police Department incinerated 2,400 photographs, including three rolls of film that were shot right as Kennedy was being assassinated! As if that isn't enough of a travesty, of the 3,470 interviews conducted by the LAPD and FBI, only 301 have survived, and none of them are the 51 interviews that the FBI considered the most crucial. There is also much physical evidence, including the left sleeve of RFK's shirt and jacket, that is missing.

Melanson and his staff did have access to 82,000 pages of information, though. Melanson interviewed witnesses and other key individuals, as well as examining evidence himself. He concludes that there were two, maybe even three, gunmen firing and that the point-blank shots that caused RFK to shuffle off this mortal coil couldn't have come from Sirhan Sirhan. He shows that there was a massive cover-up of the evidence and harassment of witnesses. Melanson doesn't engage in speculation about who did kill Kennedy, but he does show that Sirhan couldn't have acted alone.

Shapolsky Publishers; $19.95
1991; hardcover; 362 pp.; illus.

*The Martin Luther King Assassination by Dr. Philip H. Melanson*

*James Earl at home— not guilty or under orders?*

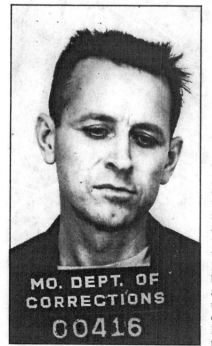

MO. DEPT. OF CORRECTIONS 00416

## THE MARTIN LUTHER KING ASSASSINATION:
### NEW REVELATIONS ON THE CONSPIRACY AND COVER-UP, 1968–1991
### by Philip H. Melanson, Ph.D.

This book is a classic, thorough examination of the conspiracy to kill Martin Luther King Jr. The author tracked down and interviewed several key players in the assassination: a high-ranking ex-CIA agent, "the fat man" who delivered a mysterious envelope to Ray after the assassination, and a man who looks like Ray, who was even questioned as a suspect.

"There is no indication that any official investigators, from 1968 to the present, bothered to attempt any systematic, logical reconstruction of Ray's alleged time and motion." The author presents such an analysis and finds that it points away from the official version of events. "If Ray was surveilling from his room [in the boarding house], then, at the moment King appeared, Ray had to gather up the bundle containing the radio, beer cans, and cartridges, add the binoculars, and go up the hall to bathroom, hoping that none of the thirteen tenants was occupying it. If Ray did not take the bundle with him into the bathroom, then presumably he had to

## WHO KILLED MARTIN LUTHER KING?:
### THE TRUE STORY BY THE ALLEGED ASSASSIN
### by James Earl Ray

James Earl Ray is generally believed to be the lone nut who killed Martin Luther King Jr. It didn't help that Ray pleaded guilty to the assassination when he was extradited from England a year later, but there lies a major portion of Ray's story. Researching and writing from a tiny concrete cubical, Ray has assembled his claims and objective evidence to prove that he didn't commit the crime and that he was coerced into admitting guilt. Ray says that he was subjected to sensory deprivation and blinding lights twenty-four hours a day to get him to admit guilt. The Feds also threatened to arrest his elderly father. On top of that, he says his lawyer was a money-hungry shark who wanted to avoid a trial and get on with writing a book about the case. Apparently the government wanted to avoid a trial, too, since the evidence against Ray is minimal at best.

The two key witnesses are husband and wife Charles and Grace Stephens. On April 4, 1968, Charles was drunk. He pounded on the boardinghouse's bathroom, where the shot that killed King was alleged to have been fired. When nobody opened the door, he went outside to take a leak in the bushes. Then there was a shot. Grace came out of her room to see a man carrying a package walk out of the bathroom and leave. When shown a picture of Ray by the authorities, she stated that he was definitely not the man she saw. Despite being offered a reward and then threatened, Grace wouldn't finger Ray. She was then mysteriously locked away in a mental institution for ten years, even though she had no history of mental illness.

Charles, being shitfaced at the time of the shooting, signed a statement declaring that Ray had been the man in the bathroom. Chas did this after the FBI told him he could collect a $100,000 reward. (Later, when shown a picture of Ray, he said that he wasn't the man he saw.) This deposition was the sole piece of evidence used to extradite Ray from England. Incidentally, after signing the statement, Charles was immediately arrested for allegedly being drunk. He was thrown in jail and isolated from outside contact.

Other evidence Ray presents certainly makes you wonder: FBI head J. Edgar Hoover, who hated King with a passion, called in a memo for harassment and "removal" of King from the scene; the director of Memphis's police and fire departments, a close associate of Hoover's for twenty-five years, removed two Black firemen and one Black policeman from their posts, where they could have seen the assassination, the day before the shooting; Ray, who was made out to be a violent racist, had absolutely no connections to racist groups and had never been arrested for a violent crime; the FBI never ran ballistics tests on the fatal bullet of the alleged murder weapon. Ray's book may not convince you that he's innocent, but it does make a strong case for giving him a trial to air some of this dirty laundry.

National Press Books; $12.95
1992; softcover; 285 pp.; illus.

## WHO KILLED ROBERT KENNEDY?
### by Philip Melanson

A small book that gives an intro to the murky circumstances surrounding Robert Kennedy's death. On June 5, 1968, just a few minutes after midnight, Kennedy made a victory speech concerning his nomination as Democratic candidate for president. After finishing the speech in the ballroom of the Ambassador Hotel, Kennedy and his entourage took the back way out, heading down a narrow corridor to the hotel's pantry area. A young man named Sirhan Sirhan came toward Kennedy, fired some shots at him, and was wrestled to the ground. While being disarmed, he still managed to squeeze off the rest of his ammo.

The LAPD handled the investigation, and almost from the word go, they decided that Sirhan was a lone nut. Any evidence to the contrary was ignored, discredited, or destroyed. This book examines three main areas of evidence. First, it looks at the autopsy and ballistics findings indicating that there had to be another gunman, because Sirhan's shots couldn't have killed Kennedy. Sirhan rushed Kennedy from the front and only got within two to four feet of him. But the three bullets that hit Kennedy all came from behind him, and the fatal head wound was fired at point-blank range, anywhere from one and half inches to actual contact, according to medical testimony.

Second, there's the weird case of the woman in the polka-dot dress. This woman was seen by several people in the company of Sirhan Sirhan in the weeks before the shooting. She was also seen at the ballroom during the assassination—wearing a polka-dot dress—with a tall man in a light blue jacket. Witness accounts differ as to whether she left the building right after the shooting or stuck around. A married couple known only as the Bernsteins claimed that a woman in a polka-dot dress and a man ran past them toward the exit stairs. The woman was repeatedly saying, "We shot him. We shot him." One of the Bernsteins asked whom she had shot, and she said, "Senator Kennedy." They went to a nearby police officer and told him what happened. The cop put out an APB on the suspects, which was mysteriously canceled a short time later. The couple was never interviewed, and the police report containing their names and address disappeared.

Finally, the book shows how lame the official version of Sirhan's motivation is. Supposedly, RFK's support for Israel was what triggered Sirhan. However, the evidence is that Sirhan really didn't care about politics, and, even if he did, why single out RFK when the other major contenders for the presidency also supported Israel? Sirhan claims that he doesn't even remember shooting RFK or writing anti-RFK slogans in a notebook of his, leading to the theory that he was programmed to

kill Kennedy. The author examines who may have programmed Sirhan and why.

Like *Who Killed JFK?* (above), this is a quick, bare-bones introduction to a very sticky subject.

Odonian Press; $5
1993; paperback; 94 pp.; illus.

# POWS/MIAS

## THE BAMBOO CAGE:
### THE TRUE STORY OF AMERICAN P.O.W.S IN VIETNAM
### by Nigel Cawthorne

The author spent three years tracking down American POWs, talking to people and examining documents in the United States, Southeast Asia, and Australia. He found National Security Agency documents of intercepts of Vietnamese radio signals reporting captured pilots or ground troops on days when the Pentagon says no Americans became missing. Other intelligence reports and eyewitness accounts all give the impression that many, many, more soldiers were captured than the United States ever admitted. Cawthorne also relates the ways in which the Nixon administration and all subsequent administrations covered up the truth about POWs still in Vietnam. A new afterword discusses the controversial POW picture that came to national attention in 1991 and the struggle to interest U.S. publishers in publishing this book.

The only problem I have with the book is the author's hatred of Vietnamese people. At one point he writes, "Okay, so you can't trust the dinks. These little slant-eyed gooks are all lying sons-of-bitches." Is this an exposé or hate literature?

Shapolsky Publishers; $5.99
1991; paperback; 345 pp.

## THE MEN WE LEFT BEHIND:
### HENRY KISSINGER, THE POLITICS OF DECEIT, AND THE TRAGIC FATE OF POWS AFTER THE VIETNAM WAR
### by Mark Sauter and Jim Sanders

The U.S. government will never admit that there is evidence of American POWs still being held in other countries, because if they admitted that there is evidence, they would be forced to do something about it. Therefore, all evidence is officially referred to simply as "information." The system guarantees there can be no evidence: "Remarkably, the Pentagon's filing system for POW reports, which includes categories for 'fabrications' and reports of Soviets mistaken for American prisoners, has no category for U.S. POWs actually held after the [Vietnam] war."

In this book, the authors present the evidence—excuse me, the information—that Vietnam offered to give back American POWs for ransom. In 1966 and 1967 the Soviet Union and East Germany offered to swap the American POWs from Vietnam that they were holding for Soviet spies held by the United States. What follows is a complicated game in which the North Vietnamese demand ransom, the United States agrees, then backs out. The Ford and Carter administrations apparently refused to play ball. Reagan refused, too, but changed his mind in 1984. Hundreds of millions of dollars and other goodies were put on the table to have American POWs repatriated "sensitively and quietly," which was Secretary of State George Schultz's double-speak for secretly.

At this point things get downright bizarre. The authors claim that there is evidence, but no unquestionable proof, that POWs from 'Nam have been secretly brought back to the United States since the 1970s. They cite the story of a distinguished, well-known Green Beret who claims that in 1982 he received a call from "an old friend." The friend turned out to be a comrade from his combat control unit, a man still listed as MIA. He claimed to have been shuffled around various prisons and then moved to Bangkok, where he and some others met U.S. officials and were quietly brought back to the United States. Other people have similar stories. A woman in Pennsylvania got a call from a man asking if she was Linda Pepper and if she had been married to a Vietnam vet. She said that that was her name, but that he had the wrong Linda Pepper. He explained that he was a POW who had been secretly released, and he was calling Linda Peppers, hoping to find his wife.

*The Men We Left Behind* and the authors' other book, *Soldiers of Misfortune* (below), stand as towering testaments to the plight of soldiers whose country turned its back on them in the name of politics.

National Press Books; $23.95
1993; hardcover; 394 pp.; illus.

## SOLDIERS OF MISFORTUNE:
### WASHINGTON'S SECRET BETRAYAL OF AMERICAN POWs IN THE SOVIET UNION
### by James D. Sanders, Mark A. Sauter, and R. Cort Kirkwood

This book demonstrates that thousands of American POWs have been and probably still are held in Russian gulags. The authors shows that 23,500 soldiers being held in areas under control of the Soviet Union never returned after World War II. After that war, Stalin demanded the return of anti-communist prisoners. The United States and Britain didn't comply, so the USSR kept the American and British POWs as slave labor and political bargaining chips.

During the Korean War, from 800 to 1,200 men were shipped on crowded cattle trains from Korea to Siberia. Colonel Philip Corso, a former intelligence officer, contacted the authors and admitted that he had personally told President Eisenhower in 1955 of this situation. He and Eisenhower agreed to abandon the POWs and lie about their existence. Pentagon officials who talked to the authors said that American POWs survived in Soviet prisons until at least 1989, and there's a good chance some of them are still there.

As for the Vietnam War, the Pentagon officially says that there is "no evidence" that American soldiers were transferred from jails in Indochina to jails in the Soviet Union. Former U.S. intelligence officials the authors talked to, however, tell a different story. They say that as many as three hundred POWs were sent to gulags. The authors actually examined a *still-classified* CIA report that confirms that figure.

During the cold war, hundreds of pilots on peacetime reconnaissance missions were shot down and captured, and many American citizens were snatched off the streets of Europe. According to eyewitnesses and government reports, many of these people ended up in Soviet prisons.

The authors also show the string of bald-faced lies that the government, including every president since FDR, has foisted on

*Disposable Patriot* ➤
by Jack Terrell

*The all-female company of the Mon National Liberation Army of Burma.*

the American people. The government still doesn't want you to know the truth—National Security Advisor Brent Scowcroft personally intervened to prevent the authors from getting documents from the National Archives. Now you can read what your own government doesn't want you to know.

National Press Books; $23.95
1992; hardcover; 352 pp.; illus.

# REAGAN/BUSH SHENANIGANS

## THE CRIMES OF A PRESIDENT:
### NEW REVELATIONS ON CONSPIRACY AND COVER-UP IN THE BUSH AND REAGAN ADMINISTRATIONS
### by Joel Bainerman

Investigative reporter Joel Bainerman brings under one roof most of the deceit, crimes, covert activities, and secret agendas of Presidents Reagan and Bush, with the main emphasis on Bush. Some of the activities are well-known scandals, such as the Iran-Contra affair. Bush claims to have been "out of the loop" until the end of 1986, but Bainerman presents many documents—Oliver North's notebooks, a memo from North, a memo from National Security Advisor Donald Gregg to Bush, notes taken by Bush's aide Craig Fuller, and others—that show Bush was actively involved in the secret operations as early as 1983.

Some of the incidents are not widely known. In December 1985 at Gander, Canada, a U.S. military plane crashed, killing 248 soldiers. It was "the tenth worst disaster in military aviation history, the worst ever in Canadian history, and the tenth worst in the world." Yet you may never have heard of it because the government swept it under the rug as quickly as possible. Terrorist fear was at a frenzy level, but U.S. officials were declaring the crash was an accident before the wreckage had even been examined. It turns out that there is evidence that the plane was hauling arms, possibly for the Contras, which is why the United States wanted to write it off. It also might have been the retaliation the Iranians had secretly promised Reagan because the United States had ripped off Iran by selling them substandard TOW missiles.

The author provides a full accounting of the United States' arming of Iraq, beginning in 1982 and continuing right until Iraq invaded Kuwait. He also examines the Justice Department's theft of the PROMIS software, government drug trafficking, hanky-panky with Israel, the bombing of Pan Am 103, the secret reasons for the Persian Gulf War, the looting of the S&Ls, the use of disinformation, and more. This book is the definitive account of the Reagan-Bush years.

Shapolsky Publishers; $5.99
1992; paperback; 324 pp.

## DISPOSABLE PATRIOT:
### REVELATIONS OF A SOLDIER IN AMERICA'S SECRET WARS
### by Jack Terrell with Ron Martz

Jack Terrell grew up in Alabama patriotic, ultraconservative, and commie-hating. He turned to a life of crime, but upon getting out of jail, went "straight" for a while. Taking part in a program for former inmates, he was introduced to the world of intelligence by Washington businessman Milton Nottingham.

Soon Terrell joined the Civilian Military Assistance (CMA), an Alabama-based group of ragtag mercenaries and misfits taking part in the Contra cause. With his high IQ and extensive reading in military and intelligence subjects, Terrell rose to a prominent position in the CMA. One day he was called by someone claiming to be Donald Fortier, third in position at the National Security Council, who convinced Terrell to spy on the CMA.

Terrell went with his men to Nicaragua but was disap-

pointed when they weren't allowed to fight. He realized they were just there to assure the Contras of continued financial and material assistance from the United States. Much of this assistance was embezzled by the Contra leaders and never made its way to the frontline soldiers. Terrell was further disillusioned by the drug smuggling and assassination plots that were occurring. He eventually took sides with the Miskito Indians, who were being treated terribly by the Contras and the Sandinistas.

Terrell was forced out of Nicaragua at gunpoint under orders of Oliver North. When he got back to the United States, he received calls from renegade intelligence agents who were upset by the Reagan administration's unconstitutional, shadow government determining and carrying out foreign policy. They used Terrell to leak extremely sensitive information. It was Terrell who blew the lid off "Contra-gate" five weeks before Attorney General Edwin Meese admitted that funds had been diverted from arms sales to the Contras. This endeared Terrell to the superpatriot crowd even less than his turning against the Contras, and Oliver North succeeded in destroying his credibility by painting him as a terrorist who was plotting to assassinate President Reagan. Terrell disproved all allegations against him in court, and even managed to bring damaging evidence against the government to light. In a landmark decision the federal judge revealed that the United States had combat troops deployed inside Nicaragua.

National Press Books; $24.95
1992; hardcover; 480 pp.; illus.

# THE IMMACULATE DECEPTION:
## THE BUSH CRIME FAMILY EXPOSED
### by Russell S. Bowen

Retired Brigadier General Russell Bowen, who has taken part in some unsavory secret government operations, has penned this book about what snakes in the grass George Bush & family are. Believing that Bush is just another branch in a rotten family tree, Bowen starts by showing how George's dad, Prescott Bush, and his associates helped fund Nazi Germany *and* the Soviet Union. Prescott's morals were handed down to George, who, as this book demonstrates, has aided his pals Saddam Hussein and Manuel Noriega.

Other Bush escapades covered in this book include his possible role in covering up the JFK assassination, his fishy oil business, his stint as director of the CIA during which he got Congress off the Agency's back so they could return to business as usual, his association with anti-Semites, Nazi sympathizers, and fascists (including several on his election staff), his miserable tenure as Drug Czar during which the amount of cocaine smuggled into the United States doubled, his role in the October Surprise, his key role in the Iran-Contra scandal, and his use of the Bank of Commerce and Credit International (BCCI) to funnel money for his misdeeds.

The last chapter of the book is about the shady dealings of other Bushes—brother Prescott Jr. and sons George Jr., Jeb, and Neil. Neil, as it turns out, was on the board of Silverado S&L, one of the biggest, most costly of the failed S&Ls. Two of Neil's business partners borrowed a total of $143 million from Silverado, and Neil voted to approve every one of their loans. Now they claim to be broke and won't be able to pay back the money.

Although this book contains some footnotes, it doesn't do an adequate job referencing its claims. For example, Bowen writes, "Did Congress realize that Nixon and Bush had openly discussed killing JFK for stopping the air cover for the Bay of Pigs invasion of Cuba?" But he doesn't tell where this startling accusation comes from. *The Immaculate Deception* is good, but *The Crimes of a President*, because of its scrupulous documentation and use of a large number of sources, is a much more persuasive book.

America West Publishers; $12.95
1991; softcover; 210 pp.

# THE IRAN-CONTRA SCANDAL:
## THE DECLASSIFIED HISTORY
### edited by Peter Kornbluh and Malcolm Byrne

The Iran-Contra scandal is one of the biggest political debacles in the history of the United States. More than eight years after the story broke, there are still many unanswered questions. Pieces of the puzzle are still well hidden, but a lot of the pieces that are available have been collected in this massive book.

The National Security Archive is an organization that files tens of thousands of Freedom of Information suits each year to obtain declassified government documents, which they then make available to researchers, reporters, etc. This book reprints 101 of the most important revelatory documents on the Iran-Contra affair. Included are a memorandum from William Casey to Robert McFarlane, "Supplemental Assistance to Nicaragua program"; a memo from Oliver North to Robert McFarlane, "Assistance for the Nicaraguan Resistance"; John Poindexter's memo for the president, "Covert Action Finding Regarding Iran"; Craig Fuller's memo detailing Bush's meeting with chief Israeli intermediary Amiram Nir, who explained to Bush all of Israel's arms-for-hostages negotiations on behalf of the United States; Richard Secord's message to North regarding a meeting with Iranians in Brussels ("I told them all things negotiable if we can clear the hostage matter quickly"), several entries from Oliver North's notebooks, the indictment of Caspar Weinberger for withholding evidence from Congress, and Bush's pardon of Weinberger and six others.

The New Press; $24.95
1993; oversize softcover; 412 pp.

# THE MAFIA, CIA, AND GEORGE BUSH:
## THE UNTOLD STORY OF
## AMERICA'S GREATEST FINANCIAL DEBACLE
### by Pete Brewton

During the S&L scandal, a crucial element of the story went unreported and for the most part undiscovered. There was a small group of Texas businessmen, including George Bush and Senator Lloyd Bentsen, who used the S&L situation to their advantage with the help of two shadowy organizations: the CIA and the Mafia. The author shows how these partners in crime milked the S&Ls and ran away with the money. The trail is a dark, complex one that the author navigates as best he can. To give you some idea of how complicated this web becomes, this book has a listing of major players in the front with brief descriptions in case you forget who is who. This list is almost ten pages long.

Within this labyrinth of deception, counterdeception, and countercounterdeception are buried some frightening revelations. One of President Bush's close associates helped a CIA agent/money launderer obtain an S&L, which he promptly bankrupted. The Justice Department was pressured by the CIA not to prosecute a CIA agent who defrauded an S&L. This same agent and his partner also did business with Bush's son Jeb. Mysteriously, the fraud indictment against the agent was dropped. The owner of one of the worst S&L failures happened to be a close associate of James Baker. Baker's former law firm led the investigation into this S&L's failure and in the end they didn't do a damn thing.

Again and again, we learn that Mafia figures and CIA "assets" looted the S&Ls, either by owning them, borrowing from them and never paying back, or receiving S&L money borrowed by a go-between. Much of the missing S&L money (that we taxpayers are having to foot the bill for) went to fund the CIA's black projects, according to Brewton. The long tentacles of the Texas businessmen are almost always somehow wrapped up in the thick of things.

Shapolsky Publishers; $22.95
1992; hardcover; 418 pp.; illus.

## TRICK OR TREASON:
### THE OCTOBER SURPRISE MYSTERY
### by Robert Parry

Just when you thought the October Surprise had been debunked, along comes Robert Parry to show you that that's what the powers-that-be would love you to believe, but it just ain't so. October Surprise is the name given to the operation in which William Casey, George Bush, and associates got the Iranian government to hold the American hostages until after the 1980 election. It was feared that if the hostages were released under Carter's watch, particularly toward the end of his term, he would get reelected. Holding the hostages would help assure a Reagan victory.

In 1990, the PBS documentary series *Frontline* asked Parry to look into the October Surprise. Even mentioning the October Surprise had been dubbed professional suicide for anyone in the Washington press, but Parry was sick of his colleagues' timidity and herd mentality. He accepted the assignment and began to dig. Two years later, Parry had interviewed arms dealers, intelligence agency operatives, Iranian ex-officials, and the biographer of the French spymaster Count Alexandre de Marenches (the count has said off the record that the October Surprise did occur). In the end, Parry admits that there still is no smoking gun proving that the deal happened. You'll have to arrive at your own conclusions based on the evidence he presents.

Sheridan Square Press; $24.95
1993; hardcover; 350 pp.

# MILITARY SECRETS

## "AREA 51" VIEWER'S GUIDE
### by Glen Campbell

Area 51 is the name given to a military test site in Nevada. (Area 51, as far as anyone can tell, technically refers to the facility at Groom Lake, while the facility at Papoose Lake, immediately to the south, is called Area S-4. However, when speaking informally, Area 51 refers to both areas.) In the past couple of years, Area 51 has become a mecca for ufologists and people keeping tabs on the government's secret technology. That supersecret stuff is going on in the area is undeniable, but exactly what it is, no one knows for sure. The facility definitely is used to test ultrasecret planes, such as the Stealth fighter and the fabled Aurora, supposedly capable of speeds of Mach 5 to Mach 8. Bob Lazar, who claims to be a privately employed physicist sent to work in Area S-4, has said that the government is holding several extraterrestrial saucers at the facility. The government has been emulating this alien technology, and it is these craft that people are seeing. Whatever the case, weird things are going on, and many people have seen strange lights and, rarely, the actual craft during daylight hours.

This book is a manual for those who want to check this place out themselves. Although Area 51 is of course off-limits, there are several places in the surrounding mountains that are public property and offer views of the facility. The author tells you *exactly* how to get to these spots (detailed maps are in the back of the book). He also provides numerous valuable tips about what not to do, where not to go, what supplies you'll need, handling security guards, scanner frequencies, safety, etc. Plenty of maps are included.

For your further edification, the author includes a detailed account of all the strange objects he has seen in the area and a large reference section. If you want to make a full vacation out of your trip, you'll appreciate the sections on other interesting sites near Area 51 and the nongambler's guide to Las Vegas.

Secrecy Oversight Council; $15
1994; oversize spiral-bound softcover; 115 pp.; illus.

## THE COMPREHENSIVE GUIDE TO MILITARY MONITORING
### by Steven A. Douglass

It's surprisingly easy and inexpensive to become a monitor (a person who listens in on military communications over the radio spectrum). The author starts with a straightforward explanation of the different bands in the spectrum and who uses them. He tells exactly what to look for when buying equipment, even rating several specific receivers and antennae.

Once you're set up, the rest of the book will serve you well as a veritable telephone book of military frequencies. Do you want to hear the president making calls (often personal ones) from Air Force One? Try 407 to 416 MHz on the UHF band. Or you can listen in on fighter pilots, aircraft carriers, army bases, the Secret Service, the Coast Guard, and more. There are almost 200 big pages of frequency listings and glossaries of terms you'll hear used by the military. There are even maps of the layout of every major air force base in the country. A final chapter deals with monitoring "black projects," top-secret airplanes in development.

Universal Electronics; $19.95
1994; oversize softcover; 279 pp.; illus.

## THE DEFENSE MONITOR

The Center for Defense Information is an independent monitor of the military. Founded in 1972 by Admiral Gene R. La Rocque, today "CDI is the foremost research organization in the country analyzing military spending, policies, and weapons systems." The CDI's philosophy is as follows: "The CDI believes that strong social, economic, political, and military components and a healthy environment all contribute equally to the nation's security. CDI opposes excessive expenditures for weapons and policies that increase the danger of war." The Center has the largest military library outside of the Department of Defense and answers information requests from the media, including NBC, ABC, CBS, CNN, and others.

CDI publishes an influential monthly newsletter that presents an unbiased picture of the military. The third issue of 1994 looked at the United States, the United Nations, and policing the world. Among the *Defense Monitor*'s conclusions: "Most of the $280 billion annual U.S. military budget goes to preparing for the self-appointed role of world policeman." And, "The U.N. is overextended, with eighteen underfunded military missions. It often lacks the means to enforce Security Council decisions." Finally, "Military intervention, whether by the U.S. or the U.N., is seldom the wisest course."

The next issue offered a savage account of how Americans perceive war. "Post-World War II Americans, who grew up with film and television, developed the expectation that the cavalry, western lawmen, and combat heroes always 'win.' Violence by 'good' Americans was always portrayed as producing positive results." But fictional presentations of war aren't the only problems: "In modern war the military creates and manages the film images the public sees. Such control can make war seem precise and largely bloodless." The *Defense Monitor* concludes, "We have been so heavily bombarded with images depicting war as a positive part of our history that we no longer see war for the horror it is."

CDI
1500 Massachusetts Avenue NW/Washington, DC 20005
Single issue: $1, One-year sub (12 issues): $25, not illus.

## THE FIRE THIS TIME:
### U.S. WAR CRIMES IN THE GULF
### by Ramsey Clark

Former U.S. Attorney General Ramsey Clark has written a devastating account of atrocities committed by U.S. forces against the people of Iraq. Clark was a firsthand witness to Operation Desert Storm and its aftermath. These observations, along with reports from other witnesses, form the basis of this book.

Among Clark's many charges: The war was a turkey shoot—125,000 to 150,000 Iraqi soldiers were killed; 148 American soldiers were killed, at least 37 by friendly fire. Scores of premature infants died when power to run their incubators was knocked out. U.S. forces buried Iraqi troops alive by using tanks to bulldoze dirt over bunkers and trenches. Iraqi troops were killed by gunfire and explosives while retreating or surrendering. 110,000 sorties dropped 88,000 tons of explosives on Iraq, much of it falling on civilian populations. Among the explosives the United States used were napalm bombs, cluster bombs, and fuel-air explosives (FAEs), devastating "devices of near-nuclear power." (In 1990, the *Los Angeles Times* claimed the United States didn't have FAEs, even though we've been stockpiling them since Vietnam. Later, Michael Kinsley would say that the United States was just using them to clear out minefields. Actually, they were being dropped on Iraqi troops.) The infrastructure of the country was destroyed to "inflict maximum hardship on the Iraqi people." The Amariyah civilian bomb shelter was bombed, killing 1,500 people, mostly women and children.

Clark contends that the United States alleged reason for Desert Storm—the liberation of Kuwait—is a total lie. "The U.S. government used the Kuwaiti royal family to provoke an Iraqi invasion that would justify a massive assault on Iraq to establish U.S. dominion in the Gulf." In the end, Clark sums it up: "There was no war. There was only a premeditated, calculated slaughter of civilian life and defenseless soldiers."

Thunder's Mouth Press; $13.95
1992; softcover; 325 pp.; illus.

## THE GRAND DECEPTION:
### UFOs, Area 51, and the U.S. Government (video)
### by Norio Hayakawa

Norio Hayakawa, founder and director of the Civilian Intelligence Network, gives a lecture explaining his ideas concerning upcoming apocalyptic events. He foresees a Russia-backed Arab confederacy invading Israel, triggering the New World Order that will last seven years. Meanwhile numerous earthquakes will be rocking the world. Undesirables will be herded into remote camps, and mind control will relax the populace into an unquestioning state. A charismatic leader from the European Community will head the New World Order. He will claim that aliens were the ones responsible for deporting undesirables. Faced with this external threat, people will come together.

Hayakawa also believes that there really are aliens on earth. Interdimensional serpentine aliens are swapping technology and information with us. Developments based on this alien technology are being created at Area 51 and at the supersecret research centers of McDonnell-Douglas and Lockheed. The video presents aerial photos of these sites, revealing strangely shaped hangars, short runways, and no aboveground planes or activity.

Hayakawa's predictions are full of holes and most of his information regarding Area 51 isn't new. The most worthwhile part of this video is the footage of Hayakawa and his companions being chased by a helicopter while they were driving in the public lands surrounding Area 51.

Lightworks Audio and Video; $29.95
1992; VHS videocassette; 100 min.

# INTELLIGENCE AGENCIES

## THE CIA'S GREATEST HITS
### by Mark Zepezaur

Ah yes, where would America be without the CIA and its band of merrymakers? Now you can relive forty-eight great moments, from all-time classics to the CIA's latest operations. These two-page chapters, each with a cartoon, will transport you to the wonderful world of assassinations, rigged elections, and

genocide. Who could ever forget the bloody deaths of JFK, RFK, Martin Luther King, Malcolm X, and exiled Chilean diplomat Orlando Letelier? And what about the MK-ULTRA mind-control experiments, the Bay of Pigs, Watergate, Iran/Contra, Pan Am Flight 103, and massive drug trafficking? They're all here!

But wait, there's more! You also get to revel in the sights and sounds of exotic foreign lands. Watch as the CIA puts the kibosh on democracy in Italy, Guatemala, Chile, and many other countries. Lean back and relax as you hear about the agency's support of leaders who censor, suppress, torture, and commit genocide on their enemies.

You get all this and more for the low, low price of six dollars. There is no better quick guide to the fantastic career of "the Company" than *The CIA's Greatest Hits*. Order yours today!

Odonian Press; $6
1994; paperback; 95 pp.; heavily illus.

## THE INTELLIGENCE GAME:
### The Illusions and Delusions of International Espionage
### by James Rushbridger

This highly critical examination of intelligence agencies (primarily the CIA, the KGB, Britain's MI5 and MI6, and Israel's Mossad) declares that such organizations are self-serving, abusive, unethical, and inefficient. "Neither terrorism nor espionage is as widespread and important as the security services would have us believe, nor are they particularly good at preventing either. In the post-war years Britain's security service has seldom caught a spy or traitor on its own, while the IRA is no nearer defeat after twenty years of intensive security operations that have turned much of Britain into an armed fortress. On the basis of this very typical record, intelligence agencies cannot possibly justify their hugely expensive peacetime organizations and their extensive files that poke into people's private lives."

To justify their existence and keep their budgets growing, agencies must keep creating enemies. Besides wild-eyed foreign crazies, agencies can find an endless supply of radicals and subversives in their home countries. "Because politicians suffer from even worse paranoia than those who work in intelligence, it is not hard to create this aura of suspicion...." Intelligence agencies also release bogus stories in which they claim to have foiled plots that turn out to be nonexistent. For example, British agencies claimed that they foiled a planned IRA attack on the wedding of Prince Andrew and Fergie. There was no such plot.

*The Intelligence Game* contains a lot of embarrassing information. The author has gathered hundreds of instances of agencies dropping the ball, being duped, sitting on their hands, creating lies, breaking laws, trampling on rights, and so on. It is a damaging book that ties together scores of incidents that I have never before seen together under one cover.

New Amsterdam Books; $24.95
1989; hardcover; 294 pp.; illus.

## THE OFFICIAL KGB HANDBOOK

This is an English translation of the instruction book for rank-and-file members of the Soviet Union's intelligence/secret police agency, the KGB. It contains instructions for external surveillance, combating profiteering, conducting internal intelligence, conducting inquiries, and being an obedient little spy. "It is a bad servant who does not carry out the orders of his master. Agents should be devoted to the party and remember one thing at all times: that they are combating their most bitter enemies whom they should not pity."

The *Handbook* provides a useful look at the Soviet mind-set, but it isn't electrifying reading. Most of the instructions are routine and boring: "In memorising [sic] the description of personal characteristics one should be guided by the table of characteristics here attached and turn one's attention to those which cannot be changed at will of the observed person, such as height, eyes, nose, limp, etc." And don't expect this to be a torture manual, either. This guidebook whitewashes the KGB: "To incline the accused to confession is a difficult matter and demands great agility and skill from the person conducting the inquiry. In the Middle Ages inquisitional method permitted torture. Now that type of torture is not permitted."

Interspersed throughout the book are comments by the publisher describing the *real* workings of the KGB or explaining certain terms.

Autonomedia; $10
No date; softcover; 127 pp.; illus.

## SILENT WARFARE:
### UNDERSTANDING THE WORLD OF INTELLIGENCE (REVISED EDITION)
### by Abram N. Shulsky, revised by Gary Schmitt

This book is a nonjudgmental primer on the world of intelligence and is often used as a college textbook. It's a good introduction to the basic concepts and terms behind intelligence. It doesn't have any explosive information, just a general framework on which to build your own study of intelligence agencies.

*Silent Warfare* starts with a look at what intelligence is—what activities and information do and don't constitute intelligence. The next four chapters deal with the four basic elements of intelligence: collection, which is the element most closely associated with intelligence by the public; analysis, putting the information together, interpreting it, and making predictions; covert action, taking a hands-on approach to directly influence political events; and counterintelligence, preventing foreign agents from gathering intelligence.

"Guarding the Guardians" looks at questions of governmental or public oversight, political influence on intelligence agencies, and the doctrine of plausible denial, which allows a government's leader to deny knowledge of covert action. The last two chapters examine two views of intelligence and try to build a theoretical basis.

Brassey's (USA); $20
1993; hardcover; 285 pp.; illus.

*Silent Warfare by Abram N. Shulsky*

*The text book for the science of secrecy.*

# SECRET SOCIETIES AND THE HIDDEN GLOBAL ELITE

## MULTINATIONAL MONITOR

In a classic case of David against the Goliath(s), there is one magazine out there keeping tabs on the unsavory tactics of the multinationals and, risking tons of ungrounded lawsuits, reporting them to us. Since 1980 *Multinational Monitor* has been letting us know what's going on with tobacco companies, logging industries, toxic waste dumpers, nuclear facilities, chemical manufacturers, unbelievable loopholes for multinationals, grassroots resistance, etc.

The December 1993 issue listed the top ten in the corporate hall of shame. Among the inductees were Dow Corning for their breast implants, Du Pont for a "fungicide that caused what the customers claim was the worst human-made agricultural disaster in history," Jack in the Box for their tainted burgers, and RJR

Nabisco for their continued use of "drug pusher extraordinaire" Joe Camel.

Multinational Monitor
PO Box 19405/Washington, DC 20036
Single issue: $3, 10-issue sub (one year): $25;
Canada and Mexico: $35; foreign: $40

## THE SECRET EMPIRE:
### HOW 25 MULTINATIONALS RULE THE WORLD
### by Janet Lowe

Multinational corporations are giant, hulking corporate beasts that operate in several countries. Many of them break laws, violate safety codes, kill and injure workers, and get away with it. How? Because of the tricky laws governing multinationals' behavior and because of the enormous financial/political power they wield. The top multinationals, which the author calls meganationals, have the power to "wrest control away from governments, manipulate the flow of currency, set prices, sway political policy, and change the fundamental nature of the countries in which they do business."

How can this happen? While looking at the Persian Gulf War and the failed coup in Russia, Lowe points out, "Both Sadam Hussein and the USSR 'emergency committee' were working against a wave that was sweeping the world. The old world believed in political ideology; the new world believes in economics. The new theology is capitalism, and the high priests of the religion are the multinational corporations."

Some of the meganationals are Dai-Ichi Kangyo Bank (with assets of $470.2 billion), Mitsubishi Bank, Citicorp, Exxon, General Motors, IBM, General Electric, Hitachi, Philip Morris, AT&T, Coca-Cola, and Nestlé. The author looks at the mergers and takeovers that have created these giants, meganationals vs. government, environmental and cultural effects of these corporations, employees of multinationals, the good things that the multinationals do, and what the future holds. Keep in mind that this book was written by a business journalist and published by a respected publisher of management and business books, so there is no wild speculation, just cold, hard facts.

Irwin Professional Publishing; $27.50
1992; hardcover; 245 pp.

## TRILATERALISM:
### THE TRILATERAL COMMISSION AND ELITE PLANNING FOR WORLD MANAGEMENT
### edited by Holly Sklar

The definitive statement on the Trilateral Commission, a behind-closed-doors organization made up of the world's most powerful people—politicians (including U.S. presidents), scientists, heads of corporations, media moguls, and top bankers. Presidents Carter, Bush, and Clinton were or are members.

"The Commission's purpose is to engineer an enduring partnership among the ruling classes of North America, Western Europe, and Japan—hence the term 'trilateral'—in order to safeguard the interests of Western capitalism in an explosive world. The private Trilateral Commission is attempting to mold public policy and construct a framework for international stability in the coming decades."

The TLC, as it is ironically called, believes that the will of individuals and even whole nations should be subservient to the interests of multinational corporations and banks. They are scared of true democracy, as evidenced by a TLC report that says the biggest threat to democratic governments comes not from external enemies but "from the internal dynamics of democracy itself in a highly educated, mobilized, and participant society." In other words, democracies work best when the people are uneducated and apathetic.

The TLC's ideas have a lot of pull in the United States. In 1976, Richard Ullman, then-director of the Council on Foreign Relations said, "In the U.S.—among elites, at any rate—trilateralism has become almost the consensus position on foreign policy." Upon being elected, Jimmy Carter appointed twenty-five fellow Trilats, including his national security advisor, secretary of state, secretary of defense, ambassador to the United Nations, and chairman of the Federal Reserve Board. Carter's VP, Walter Mondale, was also a Trilateralist. Because this book came out in 1980, there's no information on how many TLC-ers Bush and Clinton brought aboard.

The articles in this collection approach the TLC from a variety of angles—the founding of the Commission, a selection of Commission documents, a listing of members, conflict in the TLC, Jimmy Carter, Saudi Arabia, apartheid, the Caribbean, the International Monetary Fund, world hunger, labor, energy, and much more.

*Trilateralism* is the best peek you can get into the workings of this shadowy group of the world's most powerful men. I would give anything to see an updated edition covering their exploits of the last fifteen years.

South End Press; $20
1980; softcover; 604 pp.; illus.

# HUMAN GUINEA PIGS

### ATOMIC HARVEST:
### HANFORD AND THE LETHAL TOLL OF
### AMERICA'S NUCLEAR ARSENAL
### by Michael D'Antonio

Built beside the Columbia River during the early 1940s, the Hanford Nuclear Reservation, along with the adjoining town of Richland, Washington, has become the most polluted place in the Western world. Try to imagine a lake of liquid radioactive waste forty feet deep covering the area of Manhattan. Imagine that beside it are 177 steel tanks, each containing more than a million gallons of nuclear waste. Half the tanks are leaking, and some are in danger of exploding. Imagine that this facility has leaked more than one million curies of radiation (by contrast, Three Mile Island leaked seventeen curies). You have just imagined the reality of Richland.

The government always said that the Hanford facility was safe, but when deformed animals became a frequent occurrence and whole families developed cancer, farmer Tom Bailie broke the town's uneasy silence and began asking questions. His struggle for answers and justice is the focal point of the book. At the same time Bailie and others were fighting for some truth despite fierce opposition and death threats, Casey Ruud, an inspector at Hanford, came forward with troubling revelations. The facility was improperly dumping nuclear waste, the design of the facilities was flawed, safety and security regulations were violated, and radiation was leaking. Deliberate experimentation on townspeople was also uncovered. The articles based on Ruud's whistleblowing that ran in the *Seattle Times* caused the Hanford site to be closed down within days.

For forty years the government had lied about Hanford. It knew that massive amounts of radiation were escaping and that people in nearby towns—even as far away as Spokane, 125 miles to the east—were being bombarded. These findings were always kept quiet.

As bad as Richland is, there are many other sites that are almost as polluted, including Rocky Flats, Colorado, and Savannah River, South Carolina, and ten sites that have lesser but still substantial problems. The cleanup estimate ranges from $200 billion to $1 trillion. "It is certain, whatever the final amount, that cleaning up the nuclear complex will cost more than the savings-and-loan scandal of the 1980s, more than the cost of the entire Vietnam War."

Crown Publishers; $22.50
1993; hardcover; 304 pp.; illus.

### CLOUDS OF SECRECY:
### THE ARMY'S GERM WARFARE TESTS
### OVER POPULATED AREAS
### by Leonard A. Cole

Using army reports, congressional hearings, and testimony given in court as evidence, Cole shows that the military has been coating civilian and military populations in the United States with biological weapons for decades. You want smoking guns? They're here, pal. The Department of Defense issued a report in 1986 to the House Appropriations Committee titled "Biological Defense Program." In it the army revealed that open air testing was taking place in Utah when the report was issued.

In 1977 a Senate subcommittee held hearings in which "Army spokesmen acknowledged that 239 populated areas from coast to coast had been blanketed with bacteria between 1949 and 1969. Tests involved covering areas of Alaska and Hawaii and the cities of San Francisco and Washington, D.C., Key West, and Panama City in Florida. Some tests were more focused, such as those in which bacteria were sprayed onto the Pennsylvania Turnpike or into the New York City subway system."

Perhaps the scariest part of the whole thing is the unrepentant attitude of so many involved. In a 1981 trial concerning the bacterial spraying of San Francisco in 1950, "Former military and scientific officials who had administered the testing program testified that they would be spraying today if still in charge."

The next time some government-believing simp says to you, "Prove it!" whip out this book and make 'em read every word.

University Press of America; $14.95
1989; softcover; 188 pp.; illus.

*Atomic Harvest*
◄ *by Michael*
*D'Antonio*

*The Bailies:*
*One of America's*
*most irradiated*
*families.*

## THE MANIPULATED MIND
### by Denise Winn

This classic work on brainwashing shows not only how it is done in its most extreme cases, as with American POWs in Korea, but also how it occurs to all of us, more slowly, in the course of everyday life.

One of the keys to brainwashing is undermining the unquestioned beliefs of the individual. Most people cling tenaciously to their belief system, whatever it may be. They've never really thought about why they believe what they believe (other than that's how Mommy and Daddy raised them). They can't conceive of any other belief system being right, and the world has to appear in black and white with no shades of gray. When people like this are forced to question their belief system for the first time, it can severely damage their faith and their entire view of the world. People who question their own beliefs and know why they believe what they do are less susceptible to this tactic.

Conditioning is another brainwashing tactic. Sex roles are one of society's most pervasive forms of conditioning. Parents and other caregivers reward or support their children when they display sex-appropriate behavior and punish or scold them when they display sex-inappropriate behavior. This helps to ensure that the children will grow up to accept unquestioningly the roles of he-man breadwinner or obedient little homemaker.

Humans appear to have an inborn need to conform, to follow the group path, seeking approval and affection from those around them. Brainwashers play on this need to be like everybody else. They also give approval when a person acts the way the manipulator approves of. You may not agree with the manipulator but as long as he, she, or it is giving you approval, you'll go along.

The author discusses several other methods of manipulation, including playing on fears, not letting people make decisions, inducing guilt, and not allowing authority to be questioned. Besides showing how intense, malevolent brainwashing works, this book earns kudos for its examination of conformity and the mechanisms by which it is induced in the population at large.

ISHK Book Services; $25
1983; hardcover; 217 pp.; illus.

## PSYCHIATRY AND THE CIA:
### VICTIMS OF MIND CONTROL
### by Harvey M. Weinstein

This remarkable book presents us with the human side of the CIA's MKULTRA mind control experiments. The author's father was one of the guinea pigs. Harvey Weinstein, now a psychiatrist, relates his happy childhood with his father, Lou. During an examination for kidney stones, Lou felt as though he was choking. This feeling of choking and of not being able to breathe continued and became so persistent that Lou sought psychiatric help. He was referred to one of North America's preeminent psychiatrists, Dr. Ewen Cameron at the Allan Memorial Institute in Montreal. Little did he realize that Cameron was a Nazi-wannabe running a subprogram of MKULTRA under direction of the CIA and the Canadian government.

Harvey's descriptions of what his father was put through are a litany of horrors—multiple electroshocks, ingesting psychedelic drugs including LSD, prolonged sensory deprivation, forced sleep for weeks at a time, induced insulin comas, and psychic driving. The latter technique involves listening to a recorded message over and over for days. It was instrumental in "depatterning" Lou so that he could no longer "think, talk, or act in any way like a human being."

During a two-month stay, Lou was first kept asleep for two weeks with barbiturates and chlorpromazine and was given ten shock treatments. However, according to the resident doctor's records, "He is beginning to be oriented, and no longer incontinent." To remedy this they gave him an intensive form of shock therapy called Page-Russell, even after he had developed pneumonia. After forty-four days the forced sleep was discontinued. Lou was put in sensory isolation and psychic driving was performed for five days. Afterward, Cameron made some half-hearted attempts at therapy and soon discharged Lou, who had become incompetent, helpless, and aggressive.

Lou went to Cameron repeatedly for the next five years and proceeded to become little more than a vegetable. Once, Lou's wife called the resident doctor to complain that her husband was deteriorating, not getting better. "He informed her that she should not question the treatment, that if she wanted to help her husband she should just encourage him to go along with what they prescribed."

Lou gradually broke connections with Allan Memorial, but he was left with permanent psychic scars, including losing his personal hygiene, becoming unaware of others, humming constantly, limited conversational ability, and periods of depression.

The rest of the book concerns Harvey's research about Dr. Cameron, MKULTRA, and human experimentation. He also writes about the grueling lawsuit he and the relatives of other guinea pigs brought against the CIA. Eventually the CIA settled out of court, paying each victim $100,000 (Canadian).

American Psychiatric Press; $30
1990; hardcover; 312 pp.; illus.

# MEDIA MANIPULATION

## CENSORED–THE NEWS THAT DIDN'T MAKE THE NEWS AND WHY:
### THE 1994 PROJECT CENSORED YEARBOOK
### by Carl Jensen and Project Censored

Once again Project Censored has produced an invaluable guide to the true sociopolitical landscape of the United States and the world. Every year the project's team of muckrakers and media critics identify the twenty-five most important stories of the previous year that the news media underreported, slanted, or—most likely—just plain ignored. In the 1994 Yearbook the number one story is the fact that "The U.S. Is Killing Its Young." A U.N. report found that of all the kids murdered in the industrialized nations (United States, Canada, France, Japan, etc.), nine out of ten of them are killed in the United States.

The number two story reveals the real reason we went to Somalia. I sure hope you didn't swallow that humanitarian mission bullshit. When's the last time the government spent billions of dollars and lost American lives out of the goodness of its heart? Actually, back before Somalia's pro-U.S. government was overthrown, our government had divided up Somalia among four American oil companies. They were given exclusive rights to exploit their share of the Somalia pie.

Other revelations: the U.S. Army has quietly started testing bio-warfare weapons after a ten-year hiatus; selenium runoff from California and thirteen other states is an environmental nightmare worse than the *Exxon Valdez* oil spill; 5 to 10 percent of doctors are dangerous to your health due to their alcoholism, drug addiction, senility, gross incompetence, etc.; the existence of Silicon Valley sweatshops; and the fact that the DARE antidrug program aimed at schoolkids doesn't work.

Censored also contains a chronology of censorship, a resource listing, a writer's market listing for the alternative press, reprints of the articles that originally reported the top ten censored stories, and more. This is a vital yearly addition to your library.

Four Walls Eight Windows; $14.95
1994; softcover; 318 pp.; illus.

## EXTRA!

Published by Fairness and Accuracy in Reporting (FAIR), *Extra!* is a media watchdog with a left-wing slant, meaning it focuses on ways in which the media gives short shrift to minorities and consumers and plays kissie-face with corporations. Their classic Special Issue 1992 examined the roles (or lack thereof) of women in the media. The media were lambasted for their reporting on Clarence Thomas, William Kennedy Smith, battered women, acquaintance rape, welfare mothers, abortion, and women's sports. *Extra!* also looked at how the media handle corporate manipulation of women (e.g, silicone breast implants and tobacco companies).

FAIR/Extra! Subscription Service
PO Box 911/Pearl River, NY 10965-0911
One-year sub (6 issues): $30; Students, seniors,
low income: $20; foreign: $40

## LIES OF OUR TIMES:
### A MAGAZINE TO CORRECT THE RECORD

*Lies of Our Times* is a monthly magazine devoted to uncovering the lies, slants, omissions, and hypocrisy of the "newspaper of record," the *New York Times*. The *Times* doesn't like *LOOT* one bit, which means that the magazine is doing a good job. Although the *Times* is *LOOT*'s main focus, it does slam other members of the mainstream media as well.

The June 1994 issue attacks the *Times* and the *Washington*

*Post* for claiming that the mainstream press went doggedly after the Iran-Contra story. It also catches the *Wall Street Journal* reporting a supposedly false story about L.J. Davis, a reporter for the *New Republic* who did a story on the Rose Law Firm. He returned to his hotel room at 6:30 and woke up four hours later. Four important pages from his diary were said to be missing, and it was claimed that he came back with a bump on his head. However, the *New York Observer* reports that he had been drinking that night. The *Arkansas Democratic Gazette* quoted the hotel's bartender as saying that Davis was at the bar during the entire four hours he claimed to have been knocked out. Finally, Davis himself admitted that the crucial four pages weren't missing but merely torn.

Other articles look at the media's sloppy job reporting election irregularities in the El Salvador election, Clinton's "invisible labor policy," an error-filled, apologetic article on Grenada in the *Times*, the media's quest for violence during the South African elections, the *Times*'s downplaying of white violence in South Africa, and more. Since the *Times* reports on so much national and international news, this magazine is worth getting even if you don't live in the Big Apple.

Sheridan Square Press
145 W. Fourth Street/New York, NY 10012-1054
One-year sub (10 issues): $28;
Canada & Mexico: $36; others: $40

## MEDIA CIRCUS:
### THE TROUBLE WITH TODAY'S NEWSPAPERS
### by Howard Kurtz

Howard Kurtz is the press critic for the *Washington Post*, but despite working for a mainstream newspaper, he manages to kick some tails. He has harsh words for reporters of the 1990s: "Today's scribe is a well-tailored, well-educated, health-conscious baby boomer who travels with a cellular phone and Toshiba laptop and speaks the language of political image makers. The new zeitgeist is one of cool detachment, of moving with the media mob from one mega-event to the next, scribbling down the details that CNN might miss. Passion is noticeably absent, lest it be confused with partisanship."

He lambastes the media, including himself, for the oceans of ink that were wasted on Donald Trump. "It is a bit embarrassing to recall how wild we all went over The Donald, how eagerly we gushed over his antics, and how utterly inconsequential it all seems now."

The media also missed the boat on the problems of urban squalor and racism until after the L.A. riots threw these issues in our faces. "Where had the press been all along? Why was the anguish of big-city poverty and the ugliness of racial hatred suddenly page-one news?" The press also did a horrible job covering the Persian Gulf War. When it came down to a question of the press versus the military, "The press got its butt kicked."

Kurtz also roasts the media, again often including himself, for its terrible job of covering the S&L debacle, the HUD scandals, and Al Sharpton. He examines the problems of invasion of privacy, rumors, trash journalism, plagiarism, conflicts of interest, and kowtowing to advertisers.

Times Books (Simon & Schuster); $14
1993; softcover; 434 pp.

## THE MEDIA MONOPOLY
### (FOURTH EDITION)
### by Ben H. Bagdikian

When the first edition of this now-classic book was published in 1983, fifty corporations owned most outlets of news and entertainment media. Now that power is concentrated in the hands of twenty corporations. In the earlier editions, Ben Bagdikian predicted that more media would be run by fewer corporations and that this oligarchy would have detrimental effects. "It would bring even greater uniformity of content in the country's dominant mass publications. It would further increase corporate pressures to emphasize events, policies, and politicians favored by media owners. And it would add to the existing power of media owners to bend government policy to their collective will." He was right.

"In any field, whether the media or detergents, when most of the business is dominated by a few firms and the remainder of the field is left to a scattering of dozens or hundreds of smaller firms, it is the few dominant ones that control the market. With detergents it means higher prices and lowered choice. With the media it means the same thing for public news, information, ideas, and popular culture." Fourteen corporations now control the newspaper market; three control the magazine market; three control TV; six control the book industry; four control movies.

Information that is unflattering to a media outlet's parent corporation is often deep-sixed. In 1979 investigative reporter Mark Dowie had written a book called *Corporate Murder*, about corporations that let their products kill people because adding safety features would cut into profits. He brought the manuscript to Simon & Schuster, whose editor and staff absolutely loved it. Simon & Schuster is owned by Gulf + Western, one of the biggest conglomerates in existence. Simon & Schuster's president rejected the book.

*The Media Monopoly* is filled with stories of censorship, self-serving news stories, subservient politicians (including Richard Nixon), and pissed-off advertisers. You'll never read another news story or watch another movie without wondering what was compromised just so it could see the light of day.

Beacon Press; $14
1993; softcover; 288 pp.

## MUCKRAKER:
### JOURNAL OF THE CENTER FOR INVESTIGATIVE REPORTING

The Center for Investigative Reporting is one group of reporters that isn't afraid to get its hands dirty. Its magazine, *Muckraker*, prints about two major stories of their own and reprints about three from other periodicals. The winter 1994 issue has original articles on GM's business dealings with Iraq and the saga of Trader's, a major California gun seller that the Feds couldn't shut down despite evidence of numerous violations of gun sale laws. The reprints deal with "financial service" businesses that shaft their poor clients, the white supremacist Church of the Creator, and the "wholesome" corporations, such as Procter & Gamble and Kodak, who either make or just recently stopped making products used in cigarettes.

CIR Publications and Videos
568 Howard Street, 5th Floor/San Francisco, CA 94105-3008
Single issue: $5, One-year sub (4 issues): $20;
student/low income: $15; foreign: $30

# BIG SECRETS

## BIG SECRETS
### by William Poundstone

The original, groundbreaking book that exposes "the uncensored truth about all sorts of stuff you are never supposed to know." As with all the *Big Secrets* books, there is a lot of material on food. One of the biggest culinary secrets Poundstone attempts to reveal is the formula for Coca-Cola. Supposedly only two people know the complete ingredients for Coke, and their identities are secret. Based on a court case, books by insiders, and other sources, Poundstone makes some guesses about Coke's ingredients. He also shows that Coke still must contain a minute amount of cocaine. Coca-Cola "decocanizes" the coca leaves used in its drink. However, that process cannot remove every last bit of cocaine, so there may be the tiniest trace amounts (measured in molecules) left behind. This isn't enough to have any physiological effects. Still, Poundstone claims, it's surely there.

*Big Secrets* also clears the air about perfumes. One ingredient that's used in some perfumes is ambergris, a waxy substance that floats in tropical seas. For years its exact nature was a mystery, but now scientists know what it is. Sperm whales eat squid, which have indigestible "beaks." These beaks irritate the whales' intestines, which then secrete ambergris. Only slightly more disgusting is civet, "a thick, yellowish secretion of the anal glands of the civet cat of Asia and Africa." Chanel No. 5 is among the many perfumes that use this substance.

If you've ever wondered what psychologists think they know about you based on your answers to the Rorschach inkblot test, wonder no more. *Big Secrets* reproduces the outlines of the ten inkblots used in the test and tells what your interpretations supposedly mean. Blot number five is very obviously a batlike shape. "It is a bat or a butterfly, period. You don't want to mention anything else. Seeing the projections on the ends of the bat wings as crocodile heads signifies hostility. Seeing the paired butterfly antennae or feet as scissors or pliers signifies a castration complex." Every one of the blots contains at least one shape designed to look like a penis, vagina, and/or breasts.

Other chapters cover the number 372 hidden on the U.S. $5 bill, credit card numbers, UPC codes, how playing cards are marked, the Drano sex-prediction test, how to beat a lie detector, secrets of the Freemasons, secret radio frequencies, whether Walt Disney is in cryonic suspension, how the Amazing Kreskin performs ESP tricks, and tons more cool information.

Quill; $10
1983; softcover; 228 pp.; illus.

**80 | BIG SECRETS**

**How to Crack the Universal Product Code**

 U U 1 2 3 4 5   6 7 8 9 0 U U
 A B  C     D    E

**A** Two thin "guard bars" don't mean anything; they frame the real message. Repeated in middle and at other end of bar pattern.

**B** Wide space, bar, narrow space, thin bar encode the 0 at left of symbol. 0 means it's regular groceries. 3 is for drugs.

**C** Ten spaces and ten bars encode the 12345 at bottom, which identifies the manufacturer. 21000 would be Kraft, etc.

**D** Encodes the 67890, which identifies the product, including size of package. Price is not encoded.

**E** A secret "check digit" (here 5) to catch any error or tampering. If someone widens a bar with a felt-tip pen, the check digit helps the scanner detect it.

▲
*Big Secrets*
**by William Poundstone**

*Decoding the Codes.*

### BIGGER SECRETS
### by William Poundstone

The "food" section of the second volume of secrets provides a lab analysis and an educated guess at the recipe of the most jealously guarded secret in gourmet dining—Oysters Rockefeller at Antoine's in New Orleans. Moving down the food chain a bit, Poundstone also blows the whistle on Twinkies, White Castle ham-burgers, Oreos, Moon Pies, red velvet cake, and other junk food. In a section that may ruin your appetite, you can read for yourself the FDA's guidelines concerning acceptable amounts of foreign matter in food. "As many as 10% of the beans in a sample of coffee can be infested or damaged by insects.... Frozen Brussels sprouts can have 40 aphids or thrips per 100 grams. That amounts to about 200 vermin in a 1-pound package."

Poundstone reveals what you can expect when you become a member of strange groups like the Rosicrucians, Knights of Columbus, Odd Fellows, and the Church of Scientology. "When you join the Rosicrucians, you get a membership packet, which includes instructions for an 'experiment' you're supposed to do: Stare at someone who is not looking at you and see if you can get his attention just by concentrating on him."

Not even amusement parks are safe from Poundstone's scrutiny. He exposes the secrets of Disney World's Haunted Mansion and Coney Island's Hell Hole. Disneyland has a secret, exclusive, unbelievably posh restaurant called Club 33 on its premises. It's located near the Pirates of the Caribbean, to the right of the Blue Bayou Restaurant. The only indication it exists is a door with "33" inscribed on a plaque. To get in, you talk into an inter-com and are "buzzed in," to where you take an elevator to the second floor. Of course, you have to be a member to get in. Membership is $10,000. "The menu has entrees such as Steak Diane for a fixed price of $25.... When you get up from the table

(there is a good view of the fireworks), you return to find a new napkin, freshly folded.... At each table is a matchbook engraved with the name of the guest.... The women's room has wicker toilets."

Among the many other topics covered: secret rites of fraternities; the Mount Weather complex, which will house the U.S. government in the event of nuclear war; cocaine in U.S. money; telephone company secrets; what your answers to psychological tests reveal; baseball cheating; Life Saver sparks; Mae West's portrait allegedly hidden on Camel cigarette packs; the secrets behind magic tricks, including David Copperfield's "disappearing" Statue of Liberty stunt; backward messages in records; and subliminal shots in movies.

Houghton-Mifflin; $8.95
1986; softcover; 244 pp.; illus.

### BIGGEST SECRETS
### by William Poundstone

It took seven years for this third volume to come out, but it was worth the wait. Through diligent detective work, Poundstone has found out the real or probable ages of many stars, including Frank Sinatra, Joan Rivers, Nancy Reagan, and Zsa Zsa Gabor (most likely born in 1917). The section "Secret Identities" unmasks (or attempts to) the real authors of the Hardy Boys/Nancy Drew mysteries, the Guerrilla Girls, the Residents, and *New York* magazine restaurant critic Gael Greene, and examines whether Thomas Pynchon and J.D. Salinger are the same writer.

Secret recipes that are unlocked in this volume include Mrs. Field's cookies, Kellogg's Frosted Flakes, and Grey Poupon. "Fakes" blows the whistle on Trump Tower (which claims to be sixty-eight stories but is really fifty-eight), estimates of crowd sizes, copyright traps in maps, bogus people listed in *Who's Who*, and fake autographs.

We all know that many famous actors and actresses posed for nude pictures early in their careers, but what about starring in full-blown porno movies? Joan Crawford has been rumored for decades to have made such a film, but Poundstone was unable to track it down. He did get his hands on a grainy fifteen-minute porn short featuring a woman who looks uncannily like Barbara Streisand having sex with a man. However, he hasn't been able to verify that it was indeed Yentl. One hard-core movie whose star is undeniably a famous person is *A Party at Kitty and Stud's*, featuring Sylvester Stallone.

Other cool stuff unearthed in *Biggest Secrets* includes how they get a ship in a bottle, the Capitol's secret conference room, what gang graffiti means, hidden images in paintings by the Masters, the 1989 Fleer baseball card that contains the phrase "Fuck Face" on Bill Ripken's bat, escaping from a straitjacket, Siegfried and Roy's white tigers, Ingmar Bergman's soap commercials, more backward messages on records (including the heavy metal albums alleged to incite suicide) and subliminal shots in movies, humiliating ordeals of the Boy Scouts, and the home movie JFK made in which he dies.

William Morrow & Co; $20
1993; hardcover; 272 pp.; illus.

## MISCELLANEOUS

### A-ALBIONIC RESEARCH

A-albionic is a multifaceted operation providing information for conspiracy researchers. Their current predominant theory is that "the overt and covert organs of the Vatican and Neo-British empires are locked in mortal combat for control of the world." Their basic underlying theory is that there are an elite few who have manipulated history.

A-a's most valuable function is providing conspiracy books that cover a wide range of political/religious views. Their Regular Catalog contains more than 450 in-print and out-of-print books, pamphlets, tapes, and videos, most of which are briefly described.

Titles include *Gang and Governments: The Human Predicament, The Secret Teachings of All Ages, Born in Blood: The Lost Secrets of Freemasonry, Henry Kissinger: Soviet Agent, The Treachery of Thomas Jefferson, The Federal Reserve Conspiracy, Secret: FBI Documents Link Bill and Hillary Clinton to Marxist-Terrorist Network, Blue Book of the John Birch Society, The Man Who Invented "Genocide," How We Are Being Brainwashed, The Nazis and the Occult, The Ruses for War, Rockefeller Internationalist: The Man Who Misrules the World, The Vatican Empire,* and *The Great AIDS Hoax.* They also have a Super Catalog that contains more than 3,000 items, and they will do book searches for you.

A-a publishes a newsletter, *The Project,* that contains the newest findings of researchers studying the controlling elite. More than thirty back issues are available. These are all described in the catalogs, or you can get a separate, smaller catalog describing just the back issues for $2.

A-a also provides custom database research and back issues of the defunct *Conspiracy Digest.*

A-albionic Research/PO Box 20273/Ferndale, MI 48220
Single issue of *The Project*: $4.75
One-year sub (4 issues) to *The Project*: $30;
outside United States and Canada: $45
(various levels of subscription are offered)
Regular catalog: $10; not illus.
Super catalog: $20; not illus.

# BEHOLD A PALE HORSE
## by William Cooper

William Cooper claims to have been a member of the U.S. Naval Intelligence Briefing Team and to have seen many top secret documents. In this book he purports to spill the beans on the workings of the Secret Government. To say that Cooper is a controversial character in conspiracy circles would be a major understatement. Many researchers claim that his stories keep changing and that his pronouncements are an unlikely mix of various conspiracy theories that are already floating around. Still, he has his adherents.

This book is a mishmash presentation of Cooper's writings, other people's writings, and source documents. Cooper presents some truly funky accusations. Among them: It was the driver of JFK's limo who shot the president. Kennedy was killed because he threatened to "clean up" the government's drug-running activities and tell the American people about the presence of space aliens. Secretary of Defense James Forrestal was killed because he, too, threatened to expose the aliens. He was also one of the first UFO abductees. There is already an earth colony on Mars. *UFO* magazine is financially backed and controlled by the CIA.

Cooper says that there is a plan by the Secret Government to take control of the United States, and one of the first steps will be to round up and detain all "patriots." This will probably happen on Thanksgiving night, when people are most likely to be home, stuffed with turkey, and contented. Cooper writes: "MY RECOMMENDATION IS THAT NO PATRIOT SHOULD EVER BE AT HOME OR AT THE HOME OF ANY FAMILY MEMBER ON ANY HOLIDAY EVER AGAIN UNTIL THE TRAITORS HAVE BEEN HUNG AND THE CONSTITUTION RESTORED AS THE SUPREME LAW OF THE LAND."

While Cooper may have some seemingly far-fetched ideas, he does expose some areas that are definitely genuine causes for concern: National Security Directives, the Federal Emergency Management Agency (whose chief can declare martial law without the president's approval), the Anti-Drug Abuse Act of 1988, and the Federal Reserve.

One of the conspiracy documents that Cooper reprints is "Silent Weapons for Quiet Wars," allegedly a plan for global domination written by the Bilderberg Group. It's said to have been discovered in a copier purchased at a surplus sale. The authors of the document have decided that it is in the world's best interest that wealth and natural resources be shifted from the many to the few, and the best way to do this is to set up a manipulatable, predictable economy. "In order to achieve a totally predictable economy, the low-class elements of the society must be brought under total control, i.e., must be housebroken,

trained, and assigned a yoke and long-term social duties from a very early age, before they have an opportunity to question the propriety of the matter."

Cooper also reprints the infamous forgery "Protocols of the Elders of Zion." This is allegedly a document produced by the Jewish group that runs the world in which they outline their methods. The common wisdom now says that it was created by the Russian Czarist secret police to sow anti-Semitism. Cooper implies that it was written by the real conspirators (the Illuminati) as a red herring to shift suspicion from them onto the Jews.

Light Technology Publishing; $20
1991; softcover; 500 pp.; lightly illus.

# THE BIG WHITE LIE:
## THE CIA AND THE COCAINE/CRACK EPIDEMIC
## by Michael Levine with Laura Kavanau-Levine

Michael Levine was a DEA agent for twenty-five years and took part in some of the biggest sting operations in the agency's history. During his career as a drug-bustin' good guy, he came to the sickening realization that he had met the enemy and he is us (or should I say "U.S."?). Levine chronicles the role the CIA has played in smuggling cocaine and crack into the United States. Among the revelations he offers: how the CIA protects drug dealers and murderers; how the CIA protected and otherwise aided a South American woman known as the "Queen of Cocaine" while she imported huge amounts of coke; how the only Bolivian government that ever wanted to help the DEA was overthrown by CIA-sponsored terrorists led by Nazi Klaus Barbie (they engaged in "the worst torture and killing spree in Bolivia's history"); how the CIA helped drug kingpins and Nazis set up *La Corporación*, "the General Motors of Cocaine," which supplied 50 to 90 percent of the world's cocaine through the 1980s.

Like *Compromised* and *Disposable Patriot*, this is a book by an insider who has the unbelievable courage to step forward and tell what he knows about the way the government really works, no matter how ugly or unbelievable the truth may be.

Thunder's Mouth Press; $22.95
1993; hardcover; 472 pp.; illus.

# COMPROMISED:
## CLINTON, BUSH, AND THE CIA
## by Terry Reed and John Cummings

If you're like me, you were grudgingly relieved by Clinton's election victory. He may not be a political messiah, but at least he's not a guns-for-hostages-swapping, Contra-funding, October-Surprising, Iraq-arming, Noriega-loving, drug-smuggling, blood-for-oil-trading, Skull-and-Bones-joining, Halcion-addicted ex-CIA assassin. Not so fast. Clinton may not be as bad as Bush yet, but he does have some major skeletons in his closet. I'm not talking about piddling Whitewater molehills but Iran-Contra mountains. It seems that when our man in the White House was governor of Arkansas, he let his state be used for Contra-related operations, including the manufacture of untraceable weapons, money laundering, and training Contra fighter pilots.

This information comes to us courtesy of Terry Reed, an eight-year Air Force Intelligence veteran and a former CIA asset. He was assigned by Oliver North to train Contra pilots in Mena, Arkansas. But when he learned that the CIA was smuggling cocaine into the country, Reed could no longer justify being a party to these obscene operations. He left this unholy alliance of superpatriot dirtbags only to run cross-country as his former pals tried to kill him. When snuffing didn't work, the government slapped trumped-up federal charges on Reed, of which he was found not guilty. To top it off, when Reed told his story, *Time* magazine ran a slanted, error-filled attack piece on him, which indicates to me that he was pretty close to the truth.

George Bush is indicted as a co-conspirator, which shows that he and Clinton are just two peas in the same corrupt pod.

Shapolsky Publishers; $23.95
1994; hardcover; 556 pp.; illus.

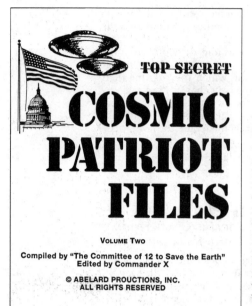

TOP SECRET

# COSMIC PATRIOT FILES

## VOLUME TWO

Compiled by "The Committee of 12 to Save the Earth"
Edited by Commander X

© ABELARD PROUCTIONS, INC.
ALL RIGHTS RESERVED

*Cosmic Patriot Files edited by Commander X*

*Mind candy for the paranoid.*

## COSMIC PATRIOT FILES

### compiled by "The Committee of 12 to Save the Earth," edited by Commander X

Conspiracy books can generally be divided into two categories, although there are many shades of gray in between. At one extreme, you have scrupulously documented books that use credible eyewitnesses, government documents, congressional testimony, diary entries, court cases, etc., to show that something rotten is happening. Then you have books like this that are filled with incredible, far-out theories (which we must remember may actually be true) and no proof or documentation except for other books that promote the same theories. This book surely won't convince anyone that any conspiracies exist, but it does have value as mind candy. It's a fun read that sets off ideas in your head: "What if this is true...?"

This book was edited by Commander X (see his other books in the "Unexplained" chapter). His stream-of-consciousness, non sequitur style of writing also shows up in full force in his editing. *The Cosmic Patriot* Files is a mélange of theories, ideas, and excerpts that cover every theory on the map from a decidedly right-wing patriotic view, which is out of character for this book's publisher. To present a coherent overview of these two volumes would be impossible, so I will simply list some of the hundreds of topics that are covered scattershot in this strange work: the Illuminati, Freemasonry, the New World Order, underground UFO bases, the Inslaw software piracy scandal, government development of alien technology, alien abduction, the divine truth of the Bible, hidden messages in the Bible, the government's clandestine space program, cold fusion, John Lear's UFO revelations, the Men in Black, the Philadelphia experiment, mind control, Satanic cults, the multiple deaths of scientists working on the Star Wars project, the secret symbolism of Washington D.C.'s design, and tons more. Volume One also contains thirty pages describing hundreds of books and tapes available from several mail order outfits, particularly A-albionic Research and the Christian Patriot Association. This is really quite a waste of space considering most of the descriptions were lifted verbatim from these catalogs.

Inner Light Publications; $39.95
No copyright date; two oversize softcovers; 75 pp. and 147 pp.

## COVERT ACTION QUARTERLY

*CAQ* looks at the hidden machinations of governments all over the world, especially the United States. Issue #49 has an article on Vladimiro Montesinos, "traitor, narco-lawyer, convict, human-rights violator, CIA-linked spy, mastermind behind the Fujimori 'self-coup' and possibly the most powerful person in Peru." Montesinos, with the help of drug-trafficking organizations and the CIA (is that redundant?), wormed his way into behind-the-scenes power and engineered elected President Fujimori's claim to dictatorial powers. Another article uncovers "Gladio," the United States' fifty-year program to interfere in Italy's politics to prevent left-wing elements from taking control. Tactics included forging alliances with the Mafia and right-wing factions in the Vatican and training Mussolini's ex-police to perform terrorist acts that were then blamed on the left.

Other articles deal with the United States' radiation experiments on unwitting citizens, Sudan's extremist Islamic government, the uphill battle South Africa still faces, and El Salvador's attempts at creating the illusion of democracy.

Covert Action Quarterly
1500 Massachusetts Ave. NW #732/Washington, DC 20005
Single issue: $8
One-year sub (4 issues): $22; Canada and Mexico: $27;
Latin America and Europe: $33; others: $35

## COVERT INTELLIGENCE NEWSLETTER

A monthly one-pager (front and back) with short pieces on terrorism, mercenary activity, paramilitary operations, etc. The issues I saw had articles on the possible funders of the Chiapas revolution in Mexico, the arrest of Iranians who bought plutonium, gunrunning in Central America, terrorists gathering information in the United States, the continuing menace of the KGB, and more. Details are sometimes sketchy, but it is a cheap source of hard-to-find info.

Horizone/PO Box 67/St Charles, MO 63302
Single issue: $2
One-year sub (12 months): $15; foreign: $19

## CRIMINAL POLITICS

An oversized magazine exploring governmental conspiracies from a right-wing Christian perspective, which means there's lots of material here against the "Jewish conspiracy," the Anti-Defamation League, the ACLU, and the "gay agenda." But let me say one more time—even if you don't agree with a publication's politics, you can still learn a lot from it. This is the case with *Criminal Politics*. In just one issue (April 1994) there were articles on the Tyson Foods/Clinton connection, the Clintons' tax cheating, scary aspects of the crime bill before Congress (which has since passed), how we're slowly getting drawn into a war in Bosnia, government drug running, Alan Greenspan's constant jacking up of interest rates, and the doozy of them all: The man who allegedly discovered the body of Clinton pal/White House counsel Vince Foster has come forward to say that there was no gun on the scene, meaning the official suicide explanation is a lie.

A lot of the politics in *Criminal Politics* will no doubt offend people, but try to think of the magazine as a recommended but prohibitively expensive part of a balanced conspiracy reading list.

Criminal Politics/PO Box 37432/Cincinnati OH 45222
Single issue: $15 (United States and overseas)
Six-month sub (6 issues): $95; overseas: $107
One-year sub (12 issues), special introductory offer: $79;
overseas: $199.50

## THE DAVE EMORY ARCHIVE CASSETTE CATALOG

Dave Emory hosts a San Francisco radio show that focuses on conspiracies. This catalog contains more than 100 of his shows on audiocassette. Among the topics available are the assassination of JFK, mind control, the history of fascist groups in America, the World Anti-Communist League, AIDS as a military product, the Vatican's ties with fascists, CIA drug running, Iran-Contra, Pan Am 103, the CIA-Jonestown connection, the Knights of Malta, Satanic cults as fronts for intelligence agencies, George Bush's possible role in the shooting of Ronald Reagan, Nazi spy Errol Flynn, the "Rex '84" plan to institute martial law in the United States, the U.S. invasion of Panama, the secret origins of the Vietnam War, and much, much more.

Most of the programs are on one to four 90-minute tapes, with prices ranging from $4 to $14.

Archives on Audio
PO Box 170023/San Francisco, CA 94117-0023
Catalog: $3

## DEFRAUDING AMERICA:
### A PATTERN OF RELATED SCANDALS (SECOND EDITION)
### by Rodney Stich

Rodney Stich is a former federal investigator. Together with a group of highly-placed CIA whistleblowers, he has put together a mountainous book detailing a host of scandals. He shows how the S&Ls were looted. One tactic was "land flips": "Selling lands several times over in fraudulent sales, showing a continuing higher 'purchase' price, and then obtaining a loan based on the latest purchase price, which could be five or more times the actual market value. No payments would be made on the loan after receiving the loan proceeds, and the property was allowed to go into foreclosure." Despite official claims to the contrary, much of the stolen S&L money can be traced, and the author tells where some of it is.

Stich also reveals a previously hidden aspect of the Iran-Contra scandal. When caught, Oliver North tried to put a humanitarian spin on the funding of the Contra rebels, saying that the United States was helping them fight communism. Actually, North and friends were supplying *both* sides—the Contras and the Sandinistas. The author writes, "One CIA operative stated to me, 'How else could we keep the fighting going!'"

Chapter 11 bankruptcy courts are a "multi-billion-dollar-a-year" racketeering organization, according to Stich. The Justice Department forces, or crooked attorneys persuade, organizations and individuals with multimillions to declare bankruptcy. The judges then force the parties into liquidation and court-appointed trustees steal millions of dollars. This system is protected by federal courts, which refuse to do anything about such corrupt acts.

Some of Stich's more startling accusations are that the CIA and the Mossad planned to assassinate candidate Bill Clinton in the summer of 1992, and that Pepsico played a role in the October Surprise. Strangely, Stich also makes a passing reference to Pepsico's "drug processing laboratories in foreign countries" but doesn't follow up on it.

Other areas that are investigated include the PROMIS software piracy, the criminal acts and air safety violations associated with a series of airplane crashes, media cowardice, drug trafficking by the CIA, DEA, Customs Department, and Department of Justice, and loads more.

Diablo Western Press; $25
1994; softcover; 654 pp.; lightly illus.

## DISHONORED GAMES:
### CORRUPTION, MONEY & GREED AT THE OLYMPICS
### by Vyv Simson and Andrew Jennings

When you think of the Olympics, you think of the best athletes in the world coming together in harmony, deciding who's best through clean, healthy competition, right? 'Fraid not. The authors of this book paint a dismal portrait of the International Olympic Committee (IOC). It is a picture filled with bribes, drugs, cheating, racketeering, greed, and arrogance. The authors, who have written books or made documentaries exposing the Mafia, terrorism, and corruption in Scotland Yard, say that this is the hardest book they've ever written. The fortress surrounding the IOC and international sports in general is almost impenetrable. As soon as the book came out, the IOC slapped the authors and publisher with a criminal libel suit.

Members of the IOC live an extravagant lifestyle, paid for largely by host cities or cities wanting to become hosts. "All Olympic gatherings are a constant and glittering round of first-class travel, five-star hotels, champagne receptions, extravagant banquets, mountains of gifts and lavish entertainments. And frequently, there's not even an athlete in sight."

The IOC's president, Juan Antonio Samaranch, has an unsavory past. For some reason IOC propaganda and the media never mention that for almost forty years Samaranch was a true-blue fascist. From the time he was a teenager until Franco's fascist regime in Spain died in the late 1970s, Juan was active in Spanish politics, serving as president of the Catalan Regional Council and as sports minister. "Even after he had risen to become IOC vice

president, touring the world as the guardian of the Olympic ideal, Samaranch continued to lift his right arm in the fascist salute at political gatherings in Spain."

The authors also chart how the Olympics have become a corporate whore. Multinationals each cough up millions, or even tens of millions, to become "the official _____ of the Olympics" and print the Olympic rings on their packages. Just a quarter of a century ago that was blasphemy to the IOC. It formed a Committee for the Protection of the Olympic Emblems to safeguard against their commercial use. The IOC also forbade competitors to wear any clothing that displayed a logo.

In another sordid chapter of Olympic history, Korea was held financial hostage during the days before the 1988 Games. The problem was that if the Olympics finals were held in the evenings in Seoul, they would be reaching America in the wee morning hours, meaning major losses in advertising revenue. Changing competition times is at the discretion of the federation for each type of sport (e.g., gymnastics). Dr. Primo Nebiolo was the president of the crucial track and field federation. If he didn't move the finals to the morning or early afternoon, Korea was screwed. Sensing that he had Korea by the short hairs, Nebiolo held out until the host country was on its knees. Then he asked for $20 million, which he got. As the authors put it, "He held the Games of 1988 to ransom...."

*Dishonored Games* contains many other bothersome revelations. It shows that the principles outlined in the Olympic Charter have been broken more often than world records.

Shapolsky Publishers; $19.95
1992; hardcover; 291 pp.; illus.

*Dishonored Games*
by Vyv Simson and Andrew Jennings

*IOC president Samaranch had a healthy regard for fascism.*

## THE GREENPEACE GUIDE TO ANTI-ENVIRONMENTAL ORGANIZATIONS
### by Carl Deal

Most Americans are concerned about the environment, and to capitalize on this sentiment, many earth-killing industries have set up "green facades"—organizations that sound like they are for the environment but are actually helping to destroy it. This book helps you cut through the greenwashing and find out whom you're really giving money to, or, if you're an activist, whom you're really fighting.

The almost sixty groups listed here fall into eight categories: public relations firms, corporate front groups, think tanks, legal foundations, endowments and charities, and wise use and share groups. The Alliance for a Responsible CFC Policy, for example, "was founded in 1981 by more than 400 CFC [chlorofluorocarbons] manufacturers, distributors and other companies to influence government regulation of CFCs... Despite 'responsible' in its name, the Alliance's real goal is to slow down the timetable for phasing out CFCs." A partial list of funders includes ARCO Chemical, Dow Chemical, E.I. Du Pont, GTE, Texaco Chemical, and 3M.

The American Freedom Coalition is a political offshoot of the Unification Church (Moonies). It is attempting to become a third party, and the "policies it endorses are decidedly anti-environmental, anti-feminist, and homophobic." The National Wetlands Coalition was actually started by a group of utility companies, miners, and real estate developers to get the government to ease up on restrictions of industrial use of wetlands. They helped get Dan Quayle's Council on Competitiveness to propose a new definition of wetlands that removed 50 percent of wetlands from protection. Bush accepted this new definition, but the head of the EPA overturned it. The coalition is funded in part by Amoco Production Co., Chevron, Exxon, Shell Oil, and Texaco.

This guide is a much-needed resource. My hat is off to Odonian Press, a David taking on Goliaths and risking numerous harassment-style lawsuits by telling you what multibillion-dollar megacorporations are up to.

Odonian Press; $5
1993; paperback; 110 pp.

## THE HIDDEN SIGNALS ON SATELLITE TV
### (THIRD EDITION)
### by Thomas P. Harrington

Your satellite dish is good for more than just getting cricket matches from Britain and porno movies from New York. There's a hidden world of nonvideo (i.e., audio and text) services out there just waiting to be explored. This is the first book to tell you how to access all these signals. Some of the necessary equipment is inexpensive and relatively easy to use, and some is costly and more advanced.

After discussing the basics, the author jumps right into instructions for getting world news services (including Reuters, AP, and UPI), stock market and commodity reports, weather reports, radio stations, private telephone calls (!), teletext, a service that reads popular periodicals for the sight-impaired, and more. Be warned—this is technical stuff, so it ain't for sissies. But if you can handle it, you'll have a whole new world of information at your disposal.

Universal Electronics; $19.95
1992; oversize softcover; 238 pp.; illus.

## INSIDE ISRAEL

As Israel's only investigative news source, *Inside Israel* is the source for getting the real story about America's biggest beneficiary. One article in the June 1994 issue examined the continuing fallout over Israel's hideous baby-selling operations. "Between 1948 and 1956, the highest echelons of the Israeli government and the Jewish Agency participated in the ugliest crime of the country's history. During that period, 4,500 infants and young children, all immigrants, most from Yemen, were kidnapped and sold to adoptive parents abroad." For decades anyone attempting to expose this travesty was treated brutally. The latest victim is Rabbi Uzi Meshulum, who has been railroaded into jail for speaking out and attempting to track down the now-adult children.

Other articles dealt with the strange hanging death of antiterrorism expert Jennifer May, a swindle that caused Israel to pay a billion dollars too much for fighter planes, the 50 percent increase in car theft in Israel since the Palestinians were given limited autonomy (thieves take stolen cars to the West Bank), and more. A unique source of information.

Inside Israel/PO Box 489/Breit Shemesh/ISRAEL
U.S. address: Inside Israel
1456 Second Avenue, Suite 142/New York, NY 10021
Single issue: free
One-year sub (12 issues): $98

## THE LAST HURRAH BOOKSHOP

The catalog from Last Hurrah offers more than one thousand titles—most secondhand, some currently in print—dealing with assassinations and conspiracies. The lion's share of these books, magazines, audiocassettes, CD-ROMS, and photocopied articles deal with JFK's assassination. Almost every conceivable angle, every theory is represented. The other items deal with RFK's assassination, other assassinations and suspicious deaths, intelligence operations, Nazis, terrorism, and related topics. Most items are accompanied by an extremely brief description. This is a powerful research tool.

The Last Hurrah Bookshop
937 Memorial Avenue/Williamsport, PA 17701
Catalog: $4 for one-year sub (2 catalogs)

## THE LEADING EDGE

*The Leading Edge* is a monthly document that seems almost too good to be true. Each photocopied, stapled issue contains around 120 pages of reprints of all kinds of bizarre information, from tiny articles to five-page newsletters, from mainstream newspaper articles to the most obscure, unusual publications in the world. The information presented has to do with government conspiracies, UFOs, suppressed health information, etc.

Let's look at the contents of just one issue (#69): an interview with David Bohm on the implicate order and reality, religious abuse and addiction, healing at the cellular level, Monarch mind control methods, *The Cosmic Awareness Newsletter,* self-organization in living cells, a constitutional amendment that was ratified but has since been ignored and no longer appears in the Constitution (although it appeared from 1819 to 1876), the real meaning of the Second Amendment, weather control by the Knights of Malta, New World Order activities, vaccinations, the Cult Awareness Network, homeschooling, the Crime Control Act, and loads more cool topics.

Leading Edge Research also has a lengthy back-issues catalog that lists the major articles in all sixty-something issues of this publication. Almost half of the articles are briefly described.

Leading Edge Research/PO Box 481-MU58/Yelm, WA 98597
Single issue: $12
Three-issue sub: $36
Catalog: $8

## LYING EYES:
### THE TRUTH BEHIND THE CORRUPTION AND BRUTALITY OF THE LAPD AND THE BEATING OF RODNEY KING
### by Tom Owens with Rod Browning

Tom Owens served in the marines for six years, doing four tours of duty in Vietnam, and served in the Los Angeles Police Department for twelve years. He started his own private investigation firm that handled a lot of police brutality cases that no one else would touch. Rodney King's lawyer hired him as the primary investigator into King's beating by L.A. police officers.

As a cop himself, Owens understood the necessity of using force to arrest some suspects. He admits several times that he had occasionally crossed the line into excessive force and had seen other officers cross that line. But, he says, "In all my years on the department, I hadn't seen that kind of officer-inflicted violence."

Defenders of the LAPD say that we have only seen twenty seconds of the infamous video of King being beaten. That scene of him lying helpless on the ground getting the living shit beaten out of him might have been taken out of context. If we could see the whole video, the argument goes, we'd get a different picture. Owens has seen the whole video, and, yes, it does present a different picture. The LAPD said the beating lasted eighty-one seconds. It actually lasted almost three minutes. The LAPD said that King received fifty-four baton blows. Yeah, but if you add in the kicks, punches, and stomps, it comes out to ninety-one separate strikes. The LAPD said that they thought King was on PCP and therefore immune to pain. King's screams can be heard throughout the video. One particularly bloodcurdling scream occurs when King's leg is broken with a baton blow.

Owens gives an exciting narrative of his investigation—tracking down witnesses, getting a copy of the beating video, investigating the officers' backgrounds, obtaining witnesses' statements from insiders, etc. He found that the LAPD hadn't changed since he worked for them; racism, brutality, and the code of silence are still built into the police force. As to how the jury in the criminal trial could watch the tape and still hand down a not-guilty verdict, Owens blames it on desensitization. He says that the defense purposely wanted the film shown repeatedly, in slow-motion, freeze-framed, and so on, until it stopped shocking the jurors and they became numb to it. It worked.

Thunder's Mouth Press; $22.95
1994; hardcover; 282 pp.; illus.

## THE NEW WORLD ORDER
### by A. Ralph Epperson

An excellent primer on the right-wing Christian take on the New World Order. The author believes that the New World Order is a plot to destroy all nations and religions, bringing about a global tyranny. Among the changes that will be wrought are: "...parents will not be allowed to raise their children (the state will); all women will be employed by the state and not allowed to be 'homemakers';...the private ownership of property will be outlawed; religion will be outlawed and believers will be either eliminated or imprisoned; there will be a new religion: the worship of man and his mind..." This plan will be brought about slowly, so that most people won't realize what is happening. The author boldly predicts that the New World Order will be fully in place by 1999.

Epperson takes a wide-ranging look at those responsible for bringing about the New World Order, implicating the Illuminati, communism, humanism, Freemasonry, the New Age "religion," and other forms of Lucifer worship. In Chapter 16 we are told about Karl Marx: "Marx had first been brought to the ideas of socialism by Moses Hess when he was twenty-three. But the most important influence in his young life was the worship of Satan." The author also reveals the nefarious meanings behind the Great Seal and looks at the current attacks on religion, education, property, and nationalism that herald the coming of the New World Order.

Publius Press; $15.95
1990; softcover; 357 pp.

## NEXUS:
### NEW TIMES

*Nexus* is a heady mix of conspiracy theory, suppressed health information, and fringe science. Conspiracy topics that have been dealt with include the coming cashless society, NASA's efforts to conceal the Mars monuments, the Federal Reserve, ID cards, Interpol, mind control, nonlethal weapons, suitcase nuclear bombs, the Federal Emergency Management Agency, and the global oil conspiracy. Health topics addressed by *Nexus* include suppressed cancer cures, the nonconnection between HIV and AIDS, vaccinations, fluoride, oxygen therapies, ELF waves and heart problems, healing with magnets, and healing with electricity. Fringe science topics that have been covered include free energy, hydrogen-powered cars, orgone energy, giant human fossils, hollow earth, energy grids, and teleportation.

Coming from Australia, *Nexus* doesn't appear to have caught on in America yet, which is a shame. It's a valuable source of all kinds of hidden information.

Nexus Magazine/PO Box 177/Kempton, IL 60946-0177
Single issue: $5
One-year sub (6 issues): $25; Canada: $30; Europe: $40

## PARANOIA:
### THE CONSPIRACY READER

The magazine for "hip paranoids" is definitely one to put on your wish list. The topics are deadly serious, but *Paranoia* still retains a sense of humor. Using an attractive layout, they reprint well-written articles from a variety of sources. Articles have covered Leonard Peltier, KAL 007, Jonestown and Martin Luther King Jr, the Federal Emergency Management Agency, AIDS, John Lennon's murder, and the trafficking of children's organs (I used to think this was just a rumor, but after reading this article, I think it may be true).

The "Paranotes" section is one of the best parts of *Paranoia*. I learned, for instance, that the U.S. military is calling into question the alleged "suicides" of forty soldiers at military bases around the world. Also, the head of the secessionist Alaskan Independence Party has been missing since the summer of 1993. The Reverend Joseph Chambers has published a booklet called "Purple Messiah" in which he claims that Barney the Dinosaur is a Satanic cult leader who works against family values and leads children into the occult.

*Paranoia*
Magazine

*Reading for hip paranoids.*

*Paranoia* also contains valuable reviews and resources. Issue #4 even has a picture of Henry Kissinger picking his nose. What a find!

Paranoia/PO Box 3540/Cranston, RI 02910
Single issue: $4; foreign: $6
One-year sub (4 issues): $12; international: $24

## PROFITS OF WAR:
### INSIDE THE SECRET U.S.-ISRAELI ARMS NETWORK
### by Ari Ben-Menashe

Ari Ben-Menashe worked at the highest levels of Israeli intelligence, playing major roles in the dirty deeds of his country and the United States. When it got out that Prime Minister Yitzhak Shamir had been secretly communicating with the PLO, the government needed a fall guy, so Ben-Menashe was jailed in America for selling transport planes to Iran. He was furious at his betrayal and decided to spill the beans in this book.

He tells about his role in funneling billions of dollars of weapons to Iran. "Under the noses of the American people, 4,000 TOW missiles were flown out of Marana Base in Arizona to Guatemala and were shipped through Australia, where they were temporarily parked in the western part of that country." He also helped in the purchase of U.S. electronics that were shipped to Israel and then illegally flown to Iran. In 1981 he and ex–CIA director Robert Gates arranged the transfer of $52 million to Iran. In 1986 Ben-Menashe briefed Vice-President Bush completely on Israel's arms sales to Iran.

It wasn't Ben-Menashe's first encounter with Bush, though. In one of the book's most controversial claims, the Israeli says he was part of the negotiations in which Bush and others convinced the Iranians to hold U.S. hostages until after the 1980 election, an event referred to as the October Surprise.

More allegations and intrigue follow—Margaret Thatcher's son is an arms dealer, the Israeli government sponsors terrorist acts, Israel and the United States blocked attempts at Middle East peace. *Profits of War* lays bare some of the most insidious events of the 1980s. It's no wonder that the Israeli government and the CIA both tried to prevent this book from coming out.

Sheridan Square Press; $24.95
1992; hardcover; 394 pp.

## THE SCIENCE OF CHRISTIAN ECONOMY:
### AND OTHER PRISON WRITINGS
### by Lyndon H. LaRouche Jr.

Lyndon LaRouche is one of the most controversial figures in politics. In the 1960s he was a radical leftist, but during the 1970s he swung over to what is often labeled an extreme right-wing position, although it's different from what most people think of as the radical right. One book on LaRouche has labeled his ideas "the New American Fascism," and a report on his tactics was titled "Right Woos Left." LaRouche himself discounts the whole left-right system of thinking and refuses to be labeled.

LaRouche has assembled perhaps the most successful private intelligence network in the world. He has met with Ronald Reagan and the CIA to share information. (This is all detailed in Jonathan Vankin's great book, *Conspiracies, Cover-Ups, and Crimes,* which is currently out of print.) LaRouche has written that Henry Kissinger is a pawn of Britain, and he has uncovered information on drug smuggling by the governments of the United States and Britain. It appears that the government launched a campaign to nail LaRouche, and eventually he was sentenced to federal prison on financial fraud charges that may have been trumped up. He was paroled in January 1994.

Anyway, LaRouche's books are hard to come by, and I was excited when I was able to get my hands on *The Science of Christian Economy.* I was expecting some juicy conspiracy theories and controversial opinions. Unfortunately, these three writings, which LaRouche penned while in the pen, are about his overarching philosophy. They constitute a very dense, hard-to-follow mixture of traditional philosophy, mathematics, physics, economics, and music theory (?!). Check out this passage: "The easiest argument defining the indivisible unity of any truly *transfinite* conception, is the deductive case. For example, the 'hereditary principle' specific to any deductive theorem-lattice is related to the associated, integral set of (inseparable) variously stated and implied axioms and postulates, and also to each and all subsumed theorems." Not all of the book is that impenetrable, but it's pretty darn close.

If you want read about political criminals, look elsewhere, but if you want to hear some of LaRouche's more esoteric ideas explained by the man himself, and not mangled by a third party, get this book.

Schiller Institute; $15
1991; softcover; 506 pp.; illus.

## SECRECY & GOVERNMENT BULLETIN

This one-page, double-sided, legal-sized newsletter was created "to challenge excessive government secrecy and to promote public oversight and free exchange in science, technology, defense, and intelligence." Issue #32 reported that while the common wisdom is that classified documents become less sensitive over time (which is why they are eventually released after decades), the CIA, in a court case involving its experiments on humans, has refused to release documents from 1952 on the grounds that they may have become *more* sensitive over time. Another story told of a man who was visited by the FBI because he filed a Freedom of Information request.

Issue #34 contains an article about a new Executive Order on classification stating that, beginning after a four-year waiting period, all documents twenty-five years or older will automatically be declassified, whether or not they've been reviewed. There is, of course, an allowance for exceptions. But at least there's a tiny glint of hope of piercing the massive armor of government secrecy.

Federation of American Scientists
307 Massachusetts Avenue NE/Washington, DC 20002
Sample issue: free
One-year sub (6 issues): $20

## SECRET AND SUPPRESSED:
### BANNED IDEAS AND HIDDEN HISTORY
### edited by Jim Keith

Edited by Jim Keith (of *Dharma Combat* fame), this anthology could be considered a companion piece to another one of the publisher's books, *Apocalypse Culture.* Like that strange tome, *Secret and Suppressed* sails the backwaters of society's consciousness, but this time the focus is completely on conspiracies and cover-ups. We're treated to a host of articles covering mind control technology, subliminal messages in *JFK,* the "death" of Jim Morrison, the Jonestown slaughter, the Waco slaughter, *The Anarchist Cookbook* as dangerous disinformation, AIDS as biological warfare, the current international Nazi network, and more. Among the great source documents here are Jim Jones's last testament and "My Father Is a Clone." This document, you may recall, was read by consumer reporter David Horowitz in 1987, when a man burst in on his live telecast and held a gun on him while he read the message. But the true coup is the reprint of reporter Danny Casolaro's proposal for a book exposing the "Octopus," the vast conspiracy that grips Amerika. (Unfortunately, Casolaro was "suicided" in a hotel room, and the notes for his book, which he had with him, mysteriously disappeared.) From beginning to end, *Secret and Suppressed* is required reading for the well-informed thought criminal.

Feral House; $12.95
1993; softcover; 309 pp.; illus.

## THE SECRET HISTORY OF THE NEW WORLD ORDER
### by Herbert G. Dorsey III

Presented here is a synthesis of the Freemason/Illuminati branch of conspiracy theory. The Knights Templar, the secret military arm of the Vatican, were outlawed in 1307 under pressure from King Philip IV of France. They fled to other parts of Europe and formed the basis of a new secret society, the Freemasons, who were instrumental in the birth of Protestantism. The Freemasons also orchestrated Adam Weishaupt's founding of the Illuminati.

"The United States of America is the result of centuries of work, mostly in secret, of the Freemasons. The American Revolution was secretly organized and led by Freemasons. The Constitution was written by Freemasons. About one-third of United States Presidents have been Freemasons. Freemasons are also well represented in Congress and the Senate."

Forming an interlocking, overlapping conspiracy with the Freemasons and Illuminati are the Skull and Bones Society at Yale, the Council on Foreign Relations, and the Committee of 300. These groups have been instrumental in the formation of the Federal Reserve, World War II, the creation of Israel, the assassination of JFK, Iran-Contra, and government drug trafficking—all of which are covered in this book.

The Secret Information Network; $10
1992, 1993; oversize, spiral-bound softcover; 81 pp.

## THE SECRET SPACE PROGRAM
### by Herbert G. Dorsey III

This book is a mixture of conspiracy theory, ufology, and fringe science, but mainly it's a retread of other right-wing UFO conspiracy books, especially *Behold a Pale Horse* by William Cooper (above). Owing to the fact that it rambles as it makes its many points, I'll just offer up a list of some of its more interesting proclamations.

•In 1947, President Truman convinced John von Neumann to head Project Phoenix, a research program that developed time travel, teleportation, and "throughportation," a technology that moves objects, including humans, through solid matter.

•The Nazis had their own alien technology research programs. They actually developed a working flying disk.

•President Truman met with different groups of extraterrestrials. He eventually formed a treaty with the malevolent beings from the Betelgeuse solar system. The aliens get to study our genetics and run several underground bases, and in return, they give us advanced technology.

•A joint U.S.-Soviet program in the 1960s established bases on Mars and the moon. The bases are manned by slaves, who are "missing persons" here on Earth.

•The Mars probe that NASA "lost contact" with in August 1993 was actually sabotaged and is still capable of sending back information to the saboteurs.

•Spaceships accompanied all the rockets in the *Apollo* missions.

•"There are areas on the moon where plant life grows and even changes color with the seasons." (This sentence was lifted verbatim from page 221 of *Behold a Pale Horse*.)

•NASA was created as a smokescreen to cover the real space program.

The Secret Information Network; $10
1992, 1993; oversize, spiral-bound softcover; 71 pp.; illus.

## SENATOR POTHOLE:
### THE UNAUTHORIZED BIOGRAPHY OF AL D'AMATO
### by Leonard Lurie

Alfonse D'Amato, the Republican senator from New York, led the Republican charge against President Clinton during the first Whitewater investigation (and it's likely he'll head any further investigations). Every night he had his soundbite on the news, leveling charge after charge against Clinton. Of course, Clinton deserved every bit of it (and more), but if there was ever a textbook example of the pot calling the kettle black, that was it.

You'd never know it, though, if you depended on the mainstream media for your news. Almost nobody has had the guts to expose just how sleazy D'Amato is. In *Senator Pothole*, Leonard Lurie unveils the truth. He describes D'Amato as "probably the most corrupt member of Congress of our day." Knowing the current state of the legislature, being the most corrupt member is no small task, yet D'Amato has managed.

Consider this: D'Amato's early political career took place in the incredibly corrupt area of Hempstead/Nassau County. In 1975 there was a huge trial concerning this widespread moral bankruptcy. Specifically, prosecutors were interested in the fact that government employees were forced to pay 1 percent of their salaries to the Republican Party. In front of a grand jury, D'Amato was asked if he had ever put pressure on anyone to pay this kickback. He said, "No." "In reality, D'Amato, in his role as executive leader of the Island Park Republican Club, had been forcing such payments from the easily coerced and the more reluctantly giving for at least ten years. His circle of extortion had widened during his two years as receiver of taxes, riding herd over hundreds of docile civil servants. Each year, he assigned section enforcers to collect the 1 percent from intimidated workers and ordered punishment for the tardy." Hundreds of people testified to this fact. There was even a letter in the prosecution's possession from D'Amato that spelled out this extortion, although at the time no one realized that it was buried among thousands of other documents. To spell it out very plainly: *Senator D'Amato committed perjury before a grand jury.* What makes it even more infuriating is that in another trial ten years later, after the statute of limitations had run out, he changed his story, admitting that he had pressured people into paying.

But perjury is just the beginning. The Bronx defense contractor, Wedtech, gave D'Amato "large, illegal 'contributions'" for the senator's vigorous role in getting Wedtech lucrative contracts with the Defense Department. In 1985, D'Amato approached his friend Rudolph Giuliani, then a U.S. attorney, about dropping murder charges against godfather Paul Castellano, head of the Gambino crime family and considered the most powerful criminal in America by the FBI. And how about the savings and loan disaster? "D'Amato's role in the S&L debacle was larger and more significant than any of the Keating Five's. As Chairman of the Banking Security Subcommittee, D'Amato, at the behest of his contributor Drexel Burnham Lambert, blocked

the Senate's moves to ban the S&Ls from trafficking in risky junk bonds."

And still the abuses don't stop: unbridled influence peddling, milking HUD, intimidating accusers, dirty election tricks, sabotaging the Senate Ethics Committee's investigation of him, ad nauseam. If it weren't for the fact that it's true, you'd swear D'Amato was a fictional character created by a modern-day Mark Twain who vehemently hates politicians.

Backed up by court records and transcripts, interviews with family and associates, and massive quantities of other documentation, *Senator Pothole* will stand as one of the most damning political exposés ever written.

Birch Lane Press (Carol Publishing Group); $24.95
1994; hardcover; 546 pp.; illus.

## SHEIKH ABDEL RAHMAN, THE WORLD TRADE CENTER BOMBING AND THE CIA
### by Robert I. Friedman

This pamphlet claims that the invective blind Muslim cleric, Sheikh Abdel Omar Rahman, was a CIA asset in the Afghan War. Rahman, who openly calls for a jihad (holy war) to forcibly create an Islamic world, met in 1990 with the Afghan mujahedeen. This group trained Rahman's terrorist organization for their attempted overthrow of the Egyptian government. The mujahedeen received their aid and training from the CIA for their efforts to expel the Soviets from Afghanistan. When he moved to Brooklyn in May 1990, Rahman helped the CIA move guns and money to the mujahedeen. Once the Soviets left Afghanistan, the CIA kept up its supply network to topple the Afghan government, but stopped several months later. This didn't sit well with Rahman and the mujahedeen, and so it is alleged the cleric had his followers bomb the World Trade Center. The CIA is now sweating bullets because it's afraid that a trial will bring to light its cozy relationship with the sheikh.

Open Magazine Pamphlet Series; $4
1993; long, thin pamphlet; 16 pp.; illus.

## "SLICK WILLIE" II:
### WHY AMERICA STILL CANNOT TRUST BILL CLINTON
### by Deborah J. Stone and Christopher Manion

In *"Slick Willie,"* released just before the 1992 presidential elections, the authors gave a rundown of all the questionable issues surrounding candidate Clinton—smoking pot, dodging the draft, deflowering Gennifer Flowers, raising taxes in Arkansas, etc. Less than a year and a half into Clinton's term, the authors give a rundown of all the questionable issues surrounding President Clinton—Nannygate, Travelgate, Clinton's alleged "uncontrolled promiscuity and adultery," the Waco massacre, tampering with investigations and trials of fellow Democrats, coddling terrorists, empty threats against the Serbs in Bosnia, Somalia, and, of course, Whitewater.

*Slick Willie* II ventures into conspiracy territory in its chapter on the death of Deputy White House Counsel Vincent Foster. Foster, a boyhood friend of Clinton, was a partner at Arkansas' Rose law firm when Clinton appointed him to be the number two White House lawyer. He also continued to be the Clintons' private lawyer. On July 20, 1993, Foster's body was found by an unknown person in the Fort Marcy Park. Because the body was on a piece of federal land, Park Police had jurisdiction and they investigated the death.

The police immediately called it "an apparent suicide" and that's what the official conclusion remained. The investigation, however, was seriously flawed. The Clintons were never interviewed, although they had been in close business and personal contact with Foster. President Clinton repeatedly denied to the media that he had spoken with Foster soon before his death. Suddenly, he admitted that he talked to Foster the night before his death. Investigators also failed to interview the emergency medical personnel on the scene. The *New York Post* did, though, and the emergency worker they talked to said that Foster's body was laid out neatly, "as if in a coffin." He was still holding the gun, which is almost unheard of in a suicide. Also, there was very little blood or gore. Considering Foster was shot in the mouth, it should have been a mess. The investigators also "failed to conduct footprint tests in the area around Foster's body, failed to take an official crime scene photo, and failed to conduct 'fiber sweeps of Foster's clothes and car.'"

There are other strange aspects to the case. The investigating police were denied access to Foster's office. The official search of the office was performed by White House Counsel Bernard Nussbaum, who took documents that FBI and Justice Department officials who were monitoring the search were not allowed to see. On July 29 the White House announced that on July 26 an associate White House counsel had found a "suicide note" in Foster's briefcase. The note, for some reason, had been torn into twenty-eight pieces—twenty-seven pieces were recovered. The missing piece was the lower right corner, where one might expect a signature. There were no fingerprints on the note.

Besides exposing unethical, illegal, and incompetent actions of Clinton, the authors, obviously conservatives, make the mistake of trashing Clinton because of his political views. Injecting this dose of ideological bitching into an otherwise politically neutral exposé of the president's misdeeds threatens to undermine the whole book in the eyes of many people, who can claim that it's merely a conservative attack. The authors are upset over Clinton's views regarding safe sex, gay rights, gun control, health care, and his appointment of such controversial figures as Surgeon General Joycelyn Elders and assistant HUD secretary Roberta Achtenberg.

Other than this drawback, "Slick Willie" II makes a fine introduction to the dark side of the first year and a half of the Clinton presidency.

Annapolis-Washington Book Publishers; $9.95
1994; softcover; 263 pp.; illus.

---

**The Splendid Blond Beast** by Christopher Simpson

*Genocide: Who pays, who profits.*

# THE SPLENDID BLOND BEAST:
## MONEY, LAW, AND GENOCIDE IN THE TWENTIETH CENTURY
### by Christopher Simpson

Genocide doesn't just happen—it has to be allowed to happen. Who has profited from genocide in the twentieth century and who turns a blind eye to it are the subjects of this book. "Most genocides of this century have been perpetrated upon nation states upon ethnic minorities living within the states' own borders; most of the victims have been children. The people responsible for mass murder have by and large gotten away with what they've done. Most have succeeded in keeping wealth that they looted from their victims; most have never faced trial."

Having control of a country and hating an ethnic group are not enough to commit genocide. The whole nation has to be mobilized into the process of obliterating an entire group of people. How is this done? "Put bluntly, the Nazis succeeded in genocide in part through offering bystanders money, property, status, and other rewards for their active or tacit complicity in the crime." The Nazis set up Aryanization laws that made it profitable for banks and other businesses to seize Jewish property and businesses. Hundreds of industrial companies, including Daimler Benz, BMW, and Siemens, were able to cut costs by using slave labor from concentration camps.

Similar circumstances surround the Ittihad government's genocide of the Armenians in Turkey, 1915–1918. The property of deported, imprisoned, or murdered Armenians was declared "abandoned," and those who participated were allowed to seize and liquidate Armenian businesses, property, stocks, and other holdings.

One reason why many perpetrators of genocide are never brought to justice is that the very basic institutions of society took part in the mass killings. Even when the killing stops and the government is overthrown, these institutions are still in place. Sometimes certain factions of the new power structure see an opportunity for added power by aligning themselves with these institutions. They then protect the perpetrators. Also, in the case of Turkey, after the Ittihad government was overthrown and members were being tried, a strong nationalist movement sprang up that protected the Ittihad, obstructed justice, and rallied popular opinion.

International law is actually a hindrance to preventing and punishing genocide, because it "obstructed bystanders from rescuing victims of mass crimes and, in some cases, from punishing the perpetrators. The biases in international law that favored the powerful and prosperous also tended to protect and encourage persecutors, especially when these groups intertwined or overlapped."

*The Splendid Blond Beast* is an essential tool in understanding how economics and politics are bedfellows of genocide. Its importance is as critical now as ever, since genocide, far from being a ghost from the past, is a very real presence in today's world.

Grove Press; $24.95
1993; hardcover; 399 pp.

---

# STEAMSHOVEL PRESS

*Steamshovel Press*, along with *Paranoia*, has become required reading for conspiracy lovers of all stripes. *Steamshovel* addresses so many conspiracies from so many angles, each issue becomes a treasure trove of hidden information. Issue #8 contains articles on Philip K. Dick's encounters with the Illuminati, the Secret Service files on conspiracy queen Mae Brussell, "folkloristic and Oriental clues to the Medieval origins of Rosicrucianism," the Shroud of Turin, Sean Morton on Area 51, Lars Hansson on J. Edgar Hoover, and more.

Issue #9 plums the beginning of the U.S. bio-warfare program, Lyndon LaRouche, Ezra Pound, Nazi UFOs, the FBI's files on cattle mutilations, Bob Dylan's sympathy for Lee Harvey Oswald, Waco, the Anti-Defamation League, the "Green conspiracy," and part one of the story of Mary Meyer, one of JFK's mistresses, who might have introduced him to LSD.

Issue #10 contains an interview with Dave Emory, a damning review of the JFK book *Case Closed*, mind control and false memory syndrome, the destruction of history's greatest libraries, the Scientology underpinnings of *The Gods of Eden* (reviewed in the "Unexplained" chapter), conspiracy theorist and acknowledged mentor of President Clinton, Carroll Quigley, unreported happenings in South and Central America, and more.

Steamshovel Press/PO Box 23715/St Louis, MO 63121
Single issue: $5
Four-issue sub: $20; foreign: $26

---

# STOLEN FOR PROFIT:
## HOW THE MEDICAL ESTABLISHMENT IS FUNDING A NATIONAL PET THEFT CONSPIRACY
### by Judith Reitman

This shocking book uncovers a conspiracy that I had never previously even heard of. Medical research facilities are supposed to buy animals for experimentation purposes only from USDA-certified animal dealers. These dealers, in turn, are only supposed to sell animals that they have bred or that they have bought from authorized pounds and animal shelters. That isn't the way it works, though. Many suppliers steal unattended dogs and cats right off the street and out of peoples' yards. Others answer those "Free to a Good Home" classified ads.

"Each year as many as two million family pets are stolen and sold into a gulag of a nightmare that trades them into a black market for pet stores, puppy mills, dog-fighting rings, and satanic cults. But by far the most valued and reliable buyer for these animals is the medical research industry, which can pay premium tax dollars for preferred laboratory subjects: family pets, no questions asked." Once inside the labs, they will be subjected to a well-publicized battery of torture—radiation, shooting, burning, addiction, poisoning, etc.

This loosely organized pet-theft syndicate is nationwide. "Nowhere is the scope of this network more visible than at dog auctions in the Midwest, where dealer and buncher [people who steal animals and sell them to dealers] trucks from virtually every state in the Union converge to swap stolen dogs and cats, switch license plates and cab loads at state borders, phoney-up paperwork, and fill orders from nearly all the universities, hospitals, product-testing companies, even military bases in the country that conduct research using dogs and cats. Many of these institutions send their own trucks to the auctions."

It's easy to tell where the theft ring is operating at a particular time—pets end up missing in large numbers. One thousand dogs and cats went missing in one month in Indianapolis; twenty big dogs disappeared within a week in Bristol, Tennessee; and 10,000 dogs and cats were reported missing in a six-month period in Rochester, New York.

So why doesn't someone stop this organized crime? Why doesn't the Department of Agriculture, the huge agency in charge of enforcing the Animal Welfare Act, do something? Because of the huge power of the multibillion-dollar medical research industry. If the USDA were to start actually enforcing the law and putting the bunchers and dealers out of business, the industry would make sure that heads roll. According to USDA employees who dared to speak, the top brass ensures that nothing is done about the problem. Anyone who rocks the boat is out in a hurry. Plus, the USDA has a lucrative setup going. When inspectors find that a supplier is housing animals in inhumane conditions (which is almost always the case), the supplier can simply pay a fee (i.e., a bribe) to avoid a court case. The suppliers don't even have to improve the conditions for the animals—they can just pay another "fee" the next time they get inspected. This way, the suppliers buy the USDA's silence, and the agency makes a tidy sum of money.

*Stolen for Profit* focuses on the victims—pets and their owners—of the "Dog Mafia" and looks at the courageous people who run the gauntlet of physical violence, death threats, and frivolous lawsuits by fighting these human scum. It also gives advice for pet owners who want to protect their nonhuman family members. The most fundamental action you can take is this: "Never leave your dog or cat out alone where it may be seen or taken."

Pharos Books; $19.95
1992; hardcover; 258 pp.; illus.

## TERROR ON RUBY RIDGE:
### THE RANDY WEAVER STORY
### by Len Martin

On August 21, 1992, federal marshals began a siege of Randy Weaver's cabin in Ruby Ridge, Idaho. The marshals ended up killing, in order, the Weavers' dog Striker, Weaver's fourteen-year old son Sammy, and Weaver's wife, Vicki. Family friend Kevin Harris and Weaver himself were wounded. Weaver's daughters—Sara, sixteen, Rachel, eleven, and Elisheba, ten months—came through physically unharmed. During the standoff after the deaths and woundings occurred, around 400 marshals, police, SWAT members, and National Guardsmen, all armed to the teeth, were on the scene. Luckily, Colonel Bo Gritz, who knew Weaver, helped convince Weaver and the others to come out of the cabin before anybody else was killed.

Why were so many people so anxious to kill Weaver and his loved ones? The official story is that Weaver was wanted for selling a sawed-off shotgun to BATF officials. For some reason the BATF waited a year after the alleged incident to indict Weaver. It

was another year before they arrested him, and then, when they had him, they let him go the very next day. Eighteen months later, federal marshals went to storm Weaver's cabin, ostensibly to apprehend him for the arms violation. But the author says the real reason Weaver was attacked is that he is a Christian Patriot and, as such, believes in the separation of the races and the illegality of income tax. His treatment sent a message to all the other people who go to remote areas of Idaho and the Northwest to escape the government's iron fist.

There's much more to the story than I've related, and it makes for fascinating and infuriating reading. Since this book is put out by a Christian Patriot publisher, it is very sympathetic to Weaver and is loaded down with the usual anti-Jewish, Christianity-is-under-attack baggage. Still, this is a very important incident that reveals the government's flagrant abuse of power.

CPA Book Publisher; $4
1993; saddle-stitched softcover; 62 pp.

## THE UNFRIENDLY SKIES:
### SAGA OF CORRUPTION (THIRD EDITION)
### by Rodney Stich

Rodney Stich has been a pilot (navy, airline, Federal Aviation Administration) for fifty years. He was also an investigator for the FAA. In this book he documents the scandalous factors that are behind airplane crashes. "The primary direct cause of airline crashes has been blamed on pilot error, and this is correct, with an important qualifying statement almost always omitted. The pilot error is usually a result of money-saving inadequate training, the risks of which are known to the airlines responsible for the shortcoming, and to the FAA who knows of its existence."

One of the main problems is the FAA itself. Charged with regulating airlines and making sure of safety, the FAA routinely overlooks problems with "preferred" carriers. This may be because FAA officials expect cushy jobs in the airline industry when they leave the government, or members of Congress may block actions against certain airlines. There's also the possibility of old-fashioned bribery.

Stich reports that when he was an FAA inspector, he investigated an engine flameout aboard a United DC-8. He reported that the incident occurred due to the engineer's error, which in turn was due to United's inadequate training. Stich was told to change his report, blaming the engineer but not mentioning the bad training. Stich refused, so his report was illegally removed from the government files.

Stich attempted to blow the whistle on FAA corruption several times but ran into members of Congress, the Justice Department, and the FBI, who wanted nothing more than to cover up the truth.

*Unfriendly Skies* also looks at the effects of air traffic control, alcohol and drugs, sabotage, design, aging, deregulation, and a worthless system of checks and balances. Stich chronicles a disturbing array of crashes and the preventable factors behind them. This is an impressive and scary book.

Diablo West Press; $25
1990; softcover; 656 pp.; illus.

## THE UNSEEN HAND:
### AN INTRODUCTION TO THE
### CONSPIRATORIAL VIEW OF HISTORY
### by A. Ralph Epperson

The "accidental view" of history is the dominant paradigm for understanding the past. It says that "historical events occur by accident, for no apparent reason. Governmental rulers are powerless to prevent the event from happening." The "conspiratorial view" of history, on the other hand, claims that "historical events occur by design, for reasons that are not made known to the people." *The Unseen Hand* presents the conspiratorial view as it applies to the United States from the Revolution onward, the Russian Revolution, communism, economics, and education.

Actually, I should say that it presents *a* conspiratorial view, since there are many competing views on who's conspiring and who's responsible for which historical events. This book comes from a right-wing direction, laying blame on the Illuminati, the Freemasons, the Council on Foreign Relations, communists, international bankers, etc.

All of these groups, however, are either branches of or under the control of the central group of men who run the show. "The Conspiracy's one unchanging purpose has been to destroy all religion, all existing governments, and all traditional human institutions, and to build a new world order...upon the wreckage they have created."

War is a prominent tool of the Conspiracy. By keeping nations at war with each other (and within themselves, as in civil wars), the conspirators keep themselves rich. The American Civil War was orchestrated by European bankers, most of whom were members of the Conspiracy. The bankers wanted to establish a central bank under their control in the United States. They instigated the Civil War so that the North would have to borrow money, leaving itself ripe for the picking. But instead of borrowing money or creating a national bank, Lincoln issued the debt-free Greenback. This enraged the conspirators and led to his assassination.

The Conspiracy also uses nonviolent means to achieve its ends. Groups such as the Bilderbergers, the Institute of Pacific Relations, and the World Council of Churches are all internationalist organizations working for the destruction of nations. Rock and roll is another tool of the Conspiracy. The author points his finger at John Lennon's "Imagine" and states as fact the ridiculous rumor that KISS is an acronym for Knights in Service to Satan.

Other topics covered include World Wars I and II, the Cuban Revolution, the Korean War, the Monroe Doctrine, the Federal Reserve, income tax, population control, the Trilateral Commission, the atomic bomb, humanism, education, abortion, suppressed cancer treatments, and much more.

This conspiratorial view of history does have some flaws in it, especially in the way it views the function of wars. Far from destroying governments and other institutions, war strengthens them. It keeps people patriotic, nationalistic, and jingoistic. The author even admits that wars keep nations strong by giving governments a raison d'être. War keeps people divided instead of bringing them together in a "one-world government," which is supposedly the Conspiracy's ultimate goal. This fundamental flaw undermines the book's main tenet, but there are still thought-provoking subtopics that deserve a look.

*Votescam*
*by James M.*
*and Kenneth F.*
*Collier*

*Making*
*every vote*
*count?*

Publius Press; $13.95
1985; softcover; 488 pp.; illus.

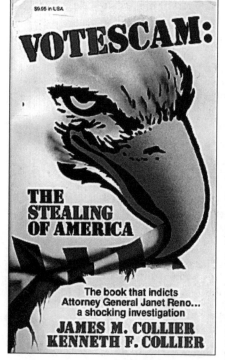

## VOTESCAM:
### THE STEALING OF AMERICA
**James M. Collier**
**and Kenneth F. Collier**

The authors proclaim that "...one of the most mysterious, low-profile, covert, shadowy, questionable mechanisms in American democracy is the American vote count." Although the Constitution says that only the Senate can tally the votes, election outcomes are actually tabulated by computers owned by a private corporation, News Election Service (NES), which is a consortium of the three major networks, CNN, UPI, AP, the *New York Times*, and others.

NES feeds election results to the media almost instantly, so they can bring you up-to-the-second results on the nightly news. *This is where all the media get their election results.* Even if there's no plot to rig elections, this fact alone is highly disturbing. When NES

president Robert Flaherty was asked exactly how his system works, he said, "This is not a proper area of inquiry." When asked if the way election results are determined is something that shouldn't be discussed, he replied, "Yes, that is a proprietary matter not open to the public."

The use of computerized voting is what allows the cheating. Each vote is no longer recorded on a piece of paper that can be physically verified. "The instant after a voter chooses his or her ballot selection on a computer, the electronic impulse that is triggered either records that vote or it does not. Either way, the computer program immediately erases all record of the transaction except for the result, which is subject to an infinite variety of switching, column jumping, multiplication, division, subtraction, addition and erasure."

The authors relate the ways in which vote-counting computers are tampered with and how it has affected various elections, including the crucial 1988 New Hampshire Republican primary where Bush won by eight points even though every poll showed him losing by nine points.

Victoria House Press; $9.95
1992; paperback; 394 pp.; illus.

## WACO:
### THE BIG LIE (VHS VIDEO)

Rarely have I seen such a devastating document. Using actual video footage of the siege of the Mount Carmel compound, Linda D. Thompson and the American Justice Federation trash the government's version of the story and show that the Branch Davidians were murdered.

In a straightforward style with clear narration, the video first gives some background on the Davidians. Their troubles started when self-professed prophet Marc Breault joined the group. He tried to usurp power from David Koresh and was asked to leave. Upset by this, he started to make trouble for the Davidians by spreading stories of multiple wives, sexual abuse of children, and stockpiling of guns. He found a willing ally in the infamous Cult Awareness Network, which helped spread his allegations.

According to sources other than this video, the Bureau of Alcohol, Tobacco, and Firearms' budget was coming up for approval soon, and they wanted a grand show of force to prove what a great job they were doing. The "kooky" Davidians seemed like an easy target, so, as the video shows, the BATF trumped up some excuses for a raid. *Waco* dissects the search warrant mercilessly. Among the reasons given in the warrant are the allegations of child abuse and polygamy among the Davidians. In fact, the BATF has absolutely no jurisdiction over such cases. It handles cases involving—what else—alcohol, tobacco, and firearms, not child abuse and marital violations. What's more, the Sheriff's Department and the Texas Welfare Department—which did have jurisdiction—had both investigated these claims in 1991 and 1992 and found them baseless.

The warrant also relates that neighbors had complained of machine-gun fire coming from the compound. What the warrant fails to mention is that the sheriff had also investigated this claim and found that Koresh was using a *legal* device called a hellfire trigger that creates small bursts from semi-automatic guns. In Texas, it is legal to own a machine gun if you pay a $200 tax on it. There is no record of the Davidians paying that tax, so the BATF groundlessly concluded that they must have had machine guns they hadn't paid taxes on.

The BATF agent who wrote the warrant claims in that document to be familiar with federal firearms law, but this is obviously not the case. He repeatedly misuses the terms "machine gun," "destructive device," "explosive," and "explosive device," all of which have specific, distinct definitions in federal law.

Now the most revealing parts of the video begin. Using actual feed footage that was supplied to the networks, but which the networks only showed tiny portions of, *Waco* shows something quite incredible. Four agents are seen going up a ladder onto the first-level roof of the compound. They bust out a window on the next story, and three of them enter through it while the fourth covers them. Once the three are inside, the fourth agent goes to the window, throws something inside the room his comrades just entered, and fires his machine gun into the room! All three of those agents were killed. Strangely, all three of them had been Clinton's bodyguards during the 1992 election.

On the final day of the siege, when the compound and its residents went up in flames, the footage shows what really happened. Many of the Davidians were holed up in two underground bunkers under the lawn. The only entrance was a trapdoor just outside one of the buildings. At 6:10 A.M. smoke is seen pouring from the underground bunkers. Just before that, footage shows a tank equipped with a battering ram demolishing the side of the building by the trapdoor. The resulting debris buried the only exit from the bunkers just as they began to burn. Despite what the FBI, and thus the media, told us, this was the first fire at the compound.

The second fire was the one that destroyed the compound itself. Tales are told of accidentally ignited tear gas, knocked-over lanterns, and mass suicide by fire, but one piece of footage shows that all of that is a crock. This footage is literally the smoking gun. As we see a tank (different from the battering ram tank) repeatedly smashing into the front of the house, backing up, and going into the house again, *there are flames coming out of the tank's barrel.* This tank is actually a rolling flamethrower, and it is caught in the act of torching the compound. This footage alone shows that the Davidians were murdered.

Further footage shows the tanks methodically pushing debris from the compound into the fire to destroy all evidence of what really happened. Later, agents can be seen walking and standing right outside the smoldering remnants of the buildings, which wouldn't be advisable if there were truly millions of rounds of ammunition waiting to explode from the flames and heat.

*Waco* exposes even more lies and atrocities than these, but suffice it to say that it is the most damning thing I've seen dealing with the Waco massacre. I cannot recommend it highly enough.

American Justice Federation; $19.95
1993; VHS videocassette; 32 min.


# WAR OF NUMBERS:
## AN INTELLIGENCE MEMOIR
### by Sam Adams

During the Vietnam War, Sam Adams was a midlevel CIA bureaucrat involved in the gathering of intelligence about enemy troop strength in Vietnam. He held the belief that the purpose of government intelligence is to gather the truth, not manipulate the truth (i.e., lie) for political reasons. He knew that military brass, top government officials, and higher-ups in intelligence agencies were lying about the strength of communist forces in 'Nam. They deliberately underestimated the number of troops and inflated body counts to make it look as if the United States was winning the war. By Adams's accounting, the government's estimates of enemy troop strength was only half of what it should have been. About 300,000 communist soldiers were mysteriously written out of the equation.

This chicanery may have been political fun and games to those involved but to the officers and grunts on the ground, it was life and death. A commander expecting 100 enemy troops would suddenly be confronted with 1,000.

Adams had the documents to back up his claims, and he approached his boss, CIA director Richard Helms, about setting up an official inquiry into the matter. Getting nowhere by that route, he also approached the Nixon administration and Congress, again to no avail. Adams's information was brought to light in CBS's documentary *The Uncounted Enemy: A Vietnam Deception.* This show triggered a libel suit by General William Westmoreland, and during the trial hundreds of thousands of pages of documents were declassified, and military officials testified under oath. Adams's accusations were supported.

In *War of Numbers* Adams shows who cooked the books and why they did it. He also reveals the struggles he had to overcome during his valiant fight to bring the matter to light.

Steerforth Press; $22
1994; hardcover; 251 pp.

# DRUGS

## PSYCHEDELICS

### THE ENTHEOGEN REVIEW:
#### A Quarterly Ethnobotanical Update

A reader-based zine concerned mainly with the nuts and bolts of using psychedelic plants. The editor and readers discuss the best ways to grow, prepare, and ingest such substances. Volume 3, #1 has info on getting smokable DMT from plants, simplified column chromatography, and experimenting with *Acorus calamus, Justica pectoralis,* ayahuasca, toad venom, etc. There is also an interview with Thomas Lyttle (editor of *Psychedelic Monographs and Essays*) and news about legalities and religious freedom. This publication is essential if you're planning on actually using any plants of the gods.

Entheogen Review/PO Box 778/El Rito, NM 87530
Single issue: $5
One-year sub (4 issues): $20; foreign: $25

### LYSERGIC WORLD/MONDO LYSERGICA

A probable one-shot publication that celebrates the fiftieth anniversary of LSD's creation. Although no second issue is imminent, *Lysergic World* #1 is a self-contained tabloid that offers the acid-head some groovy info. It contains the first publication of Albert Hofmann's look at his most famous creation on its fiftieth birthday: "I had planned in my prolific endeavor to create a stimulant for the blood circulation when I synthesized lysergic acid diethylamide (LysergSaure-Diathylamid), but this self-willed child decided to become a stimulant for the psyche."

There's also an LSD chronology, ninety important LSD books, twenty LSD movies, the stupid laws surrounding LSD ("An LSD defendant who received twenty years in prison for selling 12,000 doses of LSD received the same amount of time as someone selling one-to-two million doses of heroin and four-to-five million doses of cocaine."), an LSD crossword puzzle, acid and religion, the CIA and LSD, a satirical piece called "My 24-Hour Orgasm Under LSD" by Madonna, a comparison of the art of 1960s concerts and 1990s raves, and more.

A loving tribute to a chemical that changed the world.

L-World/40 Fourth Street, Suite 260/Petaluma, CA 94952
Single issue: $5; Foreign: $7

### THE PEYOTE CULT
#### (FIFTH EDITION)
### by Weston La Barre

This book is considered the definitive book on peyote, and it's easy to see why. First published in 1938, it has been updated four times and contains a wealth of information about everybody's favorite cactus. The author covers peyote's botanical properties and chemistry, how peyote affects a user, several ritual and nonritual uses of peyote, the psychological aspects of peyotism, the spread of peyotism, Christian elements in the peyote cult, the struggles of the Native American Church and other sects that use peyote for religious purposes, peyote in art and literature, Timothy Leary, Carlos Castaneda, and more. This edition also contains an unbelievable fifty-four-page bibliography jam-packed with everything ever written about peyote (at least it seems that way).

If you only get one book on the cactus of the gods, make sure it's this one.

University of Oklahoma Press; $15.95
1989; softcover; 334 pp.

### PEYOTE RELIGION:
#### A History
### by Omer C. Stewart

While the *Peyote Cult* (above) is concerned with all aspects of peyote and peyotism, this book concentrates on the history of peyote use by Native Americans. By focusing on this aspect, it gives a richly detailed chronicle of the early uses of peyote (starting with pre-Columbian Mexico), its spread among tribes such as the Comanche, Kiowa, Caddo, and Navajo, the formation of the Native American Church, and the struggles for legalization of ritual peyote use. Along the way we meet a large number of individuals who were willing to risk their freedom and their lives to practice the religion of their choice. Why all this fuss over a cactus? The author summarizes the beliefs of two major peyote theologies: "Peyote is good; peyote comes from God; peyote heals. Peyote teaches one to think good thoughts; it teaches one to know good from evil. It can cure anything, if one is sincere, if one concentrates, if one is full of devotion."

This book also contains the church canons for the Native American Church of South Dakota, 1948, and a forty-seven-page bibliography.

University of Oklahoma Press; $15.95
1987; softcover; 454 pp.

### PIHKAL:
#### A Chemical Love Story
### by Alexander and Ann Shulgin

Every once in a while a book comes along that is so monumentally important that everyone who reads it recognizes its greatness. This newly published book can't help but become one of the towering classics of its field.

In *Pihkal*, psychopharmacologist Alexander Shulgin and his wife, Ann, a writer and researcher, explore the nature and effects of phenethylamines (PIHKAL is an acronym for Phenethylamines I Have Known And Loved). Book One: "The Love Story" is a slightly fictionalized tale of a psychopharmacologist and his wife who explore life, love, and altered states of consciousness. In Part One, psychopharmacologist "Dr. Borodin," writing in the first person, tells of his life and his experiences with morphine, mescaline, TMA, ecstasy, and the strangest of all drugs, love. He also relates how he synthesized several drugs, including MMDA and DOM (known on the street as STP). Part Two is told by "Alice," who relates her drug experiments, her life-threatening miscarriage, and how she met, fell in love with, and married Dr. Borodin. Part Three, told in alternating voices, focuses on the drug experiences of the Borodins and their close circle of friends. Exploring the mind's hidden regions isn't always a barrel of laughs, as Alice finds out after taking forty milligrams of DESOXY, a drug her husband created: "I see me—a sort of twisted, squashed version of me—it's hard to see what its shape is—have to focus. Yes. Oh, Christ. Looks like a slimy little pink maggot. Dirty. Disgusting. The maggot feels the hate-contempt and knows it deserves it." Then again, it can be a beautiful experience, as experienced by a friend called Dante who took 2C-T-7: "Suddenly I am completely pierced, down to the core of my being, by what feels like the penetration of the Finger of God. It seems to be a female source that reaches me and touches. I am totally undone by this deep touching, and sob uncontrollably for several minutes, crying out all my pains and fears, and feeling sheer ecstasy."

Book Two: "The Chemical Story" is a treasure trove of arcane psychedelic knowledge. In it Dr. Shulgin gives the exact recipes for 179 phenethylamines he has created. Of course, these highly technical instructions aren't of much use to anyone but other psychopharmacologists, both professional and amateur. But the rest of us can still enjoy this chapter because each recipe is accompanied by a firsthand account of the drug's effects and a commentary on these effects.

*PIHKAL* is an awesome testament to the age-old drive to

explore the mind through chemical catalysts. In the book's introduction, Dr. Shulgin gives a succinct and eloquent reason for his quest: "I am completely convinced that there is a wealth of information built into us, with miles of intuitive knowledge tucked away in the genetic material of every one of our cells. Something akin to a library containing uncountable reference volumes, but without any obvious route of entry.... The psychedelic drugs allow exploration of this interior world, and insights into its nature."

Transform Press; $18.95
1992; softcover; 978 pp.

*Plants of
the Gods
by Richard
Evan Schultes
& Albert
Hofmann*

*A yarn painting
by Ruturi
depicting the
powers of the
plant world.*

## PLANTS OF THE GODS:
### THEIR SACRED, HEALING, AND HALLUCINOGENIC POWERS
### by Richard Evans Schultes and Albert Hofmann

A classic addition to the literature of psychedelic drugs, this book provides detailed information on 91 of the 140 or so known plants with psychoactive powers. "The Plant Lexicon" provides color illustrations of and botanical information on these plants, each one representing a different genus. Following the lexicon is a thirteen-page chart that gives a comparative overview of usage by region, preparation, uses, chemical components, and effects of all the plants.

Further chapters discuss fourteen of the plants in detail. Among them are fly agaric, marijuana, ergot, ayahuasca, and peyote. The authors also present an overview of the plant kingdom, where hallucinogens fit into the scheme of things, the chemical structure of hallucinogens, etc.

Besides being rich in detail, *Plants of the Gods* is rich in illustration. There have got to be at least one thousand photos, drawings, diagrams, and works of art in these pages, with more than a hundred in color. Many of the pictures of indigenous peoples and their ritual uses of plants are published here for the first time.

Healing Arts Press (Inner Traditions International); $19.95
1979 (1992); oversize softcover; 192 pp.

## PSILOCYBIN:
### MAGIC MUSHROOM GROWER'S GUIDE
### by O.T. Oss and O.N. Oeric

Terence McKenna's classic instruction book for growing 'shrooms. "The sections which follow give precise, no-fail instructions for growing and preserving the magic mushroom. We have made these instructions as clear and direct as possible;

what is described is only slightly more complicated than canning or making jelly. These instructions can be adapted to undertakings of any size, from a few jars to thousands."

The painfully explicit instructions for indoor growing are accompanied by lots of diagrams and step-by-step photographs.

Quick Trading Company; $16.95
1976 (1986); softcover; 81 pp.

## PSYCHEDELICS:
### A COLLECTION OF THE MOST EXCITING NEW MATERIAL ON PSYCHEDELIC DRUGS
### edited by Thomas Lyttle

Thomas Lyttle, the creator of the indispensable journal *Psychedelic Monographs & Essays*, has assembled an anthology of writings that explore the cutting edge of thought on psychedelic drugs and related topics. A couple of the essays look at the use of hallucinogens in lucid dreaming. A.S. Kay proposes that psychedelics, lucid dreams, meditation, near-death experiences, and out-of-body experiences are all doorways to other worlds, different paths to the same destination. Joel Bartlett's article is much more informal, recounting some of his more memorable lucid dreams that were aided by an LSD-like compound. "...I was stargazing through the branches of a birch tree. After a while, the branches stirring in the breeze took on the form of a bubbling fountain of giant spiders, their jointed legs clicking and chirring as they fell about me and scurried away. Then, bored with it, I conjured up a tank truck shifting gears as it pulled into the driveway. On the side of the tank was emblazoned the word 'RAID.' A man got out of the cab, wearing yellow neoprene rubber gloves, and said, 'You the guy who ordered ten thousand gallons of RAID?'..."

Another article examines the seven deadly sins of media hype, specifically as they relate to the media's coverage of MDMA (ecstasy). Sins include one-upmanship, sensationalism, false objectivity, and careless and deliberate distortions. Thomas Lyttle contributes an important article on U4Euh (also known as intellex and ice), a drug that has not yet received much coverage.

In a creative article, Thomas B. Roberts interprets *Snow White and the Seven Dwarfs* on several levels—the dwarfs representing the seven chakras, the various characters as Jungian archetypes, and the whole story as a parallel to Stanislav Grof's model of human consciousness. Interesting factoid: those red-capped mushrooms with white dots that appear throughout the movie are amanita, a psychedelic variety of 'shroom.

Barricade Books; $14.95
1994; softcover; 254 pp.

## PSYCHEDELIC ILLUMINATIONS

A professionally produced magazine "exploring the world of visionary plants and their impact on humans." Issue #5, the Special LSD Fiftieth Anniversary Edition, is quite impressive. It contains articles on California's Hemp Initiative, the liberating potential of personal computers, drugs and spirituality, the Hoasca Project, the "plant mind," rain-forest news, a simple method of raising magic mushrooms, a global review of psychedelic research in 1994, the global celebrations on "Bicycle Day" (LSD's fiftieth anniversary), psychedelics as tools in psychiatry, identifying 'shrooms, an interview with Timothy Leary, "How LSD Originated" by Albert Hofmann, and loads more. They also have a great events section listing conferences, seminars, retreats, fairs, radio programs, and other noteworthy events relating to psychedelic/cyberdelic culture.

*PI* regularly publishes contributions from the biggest names in psychedelia, including Leary, Hofmann, Terence McKenna, Alexander Shulgin, Robert Anton Wilson, Jonathan Ott, etc. Quite an impressive publication.

Psychedelic Illuminations Magazine
PO Box 3186/Fullerton, CA 92634
Four-issue sub: $28; Canada/Mexico: $40

## PSYCHEDELIC MONOGRAPHS AND ESSAYS #6
### edited by Thomas Lyttle

Thomas Lyttle has a great idea. About once a year, put out a collection of articles about psychedelic drugs. Have everyone from underground experimenters to laboratory scientists to anthropologists write the articles, and cover every aspect of hallucinogens, from their chemical structures to their spiritual effects. The result, *Psychedelic Monographs and Essays*, has become one of the leading documents on mind-expanding drugs.

In the sixth issue, PM&E's 214 pages contain "The Spiritual View of Psychedelics" by Sufi wiseman Meher Baba, a look at the uses of ibogain in psychotherapy and drug treatment, how philosopher Walter Benjamin's theory of "divine language" might present a way to describe drug experiences, a research effort aimed at creating tryptamine-based hallucinogens that can be taken orally, an examination of how psilocybin mushrooms create their "magic ingredient," and an article by an American psychologist concerning his experiences with ayahuasca while training with a Peruvian shaman.

"The Rescue of Psychedelics from Psychiatry" by Bartlett J. Ridge tells about the *DSM* Reform Initiative. *The Diagnostic and Statistical Manual* is the bible of psychiatry and other mental health fields. It classifies and gives the symptomology of every mental disorder recognized by psychiatry. Mental health workers all over the world use it to label and compartmentalize their patients. What's got people so pissed off is that the current Third Edition (Revised) of the *DSM* classifies as mentally ill anyone who uses pot or psychedelics for any reason (except medical). At one time psychiatry classified homosexuality as a pathological disorder, but intense pressure got this changed. Now the *DSM* only recognizes same-sex attraction as a disorder when the person doesn't want to be gay but can't help experiencing the feelings. Well, the brand-new *DSM-IV* has come just out and, unfortunately, the drug initiative failed. Psychiatry still stigmatizes pot smokers and peyote eaters as pathological weirdos in need of help.

PM&E Publishing Group; $20
1993; softcover; 214 pp.

## PSYCHEDELIC SHAMANISM:
### THE CULTIVATION, PREPARATION, AND SHAMANIC USE OF PSYCHOTROPIC PLANTS
### by Jim DeKorne

A hands-on guide for the exploration of other levels of reality through psychedelic plants. In Part One the author discusses his own experiences and those of others using plants of the gods. He tells about his own trips to heaven and hell and outside the body, the teleportation of material objects, an encounter with a voice, strange marks in the snow, and other unusual events (some of which did occur using LSD, not natural psychedelics). He relates the idea of the existence of many dimensions and parallel worlds and devotes two chapters to encounters with beings in these other levels of existence: "...voices heard by schizophrenics are often indistinguishable in tone and content from those evoked by psychedelic plants."

Part Two is devoted to the nitty-gritty details of raising, preparing, and using the belladonna alkaloids, morning glory seeds, peyote, ayahuasca and DMT, coleus, fly agaric mushrooms, and other good stuff. The instructions on cultivation are very basic, but there are many other books that go into great detail about that aspect. What is more crucial in this book are the methods of ingesting the plants: what form to use, how much to take, what the good and bad effects will be, and so on. The author also includes what may be the first printed instructions on getting smokable DMT from reed canary grass.

If you're serious about using hallucinogenic plants for exploring your mind and reality, you need this book. Think of it as a road atlas for your head.

Loompanics Unlimited; $19.95
1994; oversize softcover; 155 pp.

## PSYCHEDELICS ENCYCLOPEDIA
### (THIRD EDITION)
### by Peter Stafford

This book is the standard reference work on hallucinogenic drugs. Culled from scientific literature, popular literature, and personal accounts, the valuable information it contains covers all aspects of psychedelics—from chemistry and botany to preparation and use to effects and social history. What else would you want to know?

The author covers the nine "true" psychedelic compound-clusters: LSD, happy cactus, magic mushrooms, pot and hash, nutmeg and MDA, short-acting tryptamines (DMT, DET, etc.), ayahuasca and friends, iboga and ibogaine, and fly agaric, panther caps, and soma. The final section covers five substances that are often considered hallucinogenic, including kava-kava and nitrous oxide.

Besides being an unparalleled reference work, the *Psychedelics Encyclopedia* is a fascinating read. Peter Stafford has brought together loads of scattered information under one cover. The reaction of Zen master Alan Watts to LSD is interesting: "I was amazed and somewhat embarrassed to find myself going through states of consciousness that corresponded precisely with every description of major mystical experiences I had ever read." An unidentified user had this to say about tripping on DMT: "I took a puff—and then my arms and legs fell off...and the garden of God opened up."

This edition of the *Encyclopedia* also contains short biographies of psychedelic pioneers, a guide to organizations and publications, themes and trends in psychedelia, and a section on ecstasy.

Ronin Publishing; $24.95
1992; softcover; 420 pp.

## THE SACRED MUSHROOM SEEKER:
### ESSAYS FOR R. GORDON WASSON
### edited by Thomas J. Riedlinger

photo: Allan B. Richardson

The late R. Gordon Wasson was a businessman (vice president of J.P. Morgan & Co.) and amateur mycologist (studier of mushrooms) who, with his wife until her death in 1958, developed the field of ethnomycology through the study of sacred psychedelic mushrooms. He and his wife, Valentina, visited the indigenous Mexicans, and Wasson became the first outsider to partake of the divine 'shroom during a sacred ritual. In 1959 *Life* magazine reported on the Wassons' adventures, and the existence of magic mushrooms was revealed to the world at large. Gordon and Valentina wrote the massive *Mushrooms, Russia, and History*, and on his own he wrote *Soma: Divine Mushroom of Immortality*, *The Wondrous Mushroom*, and *Persephone's Quest: Entheogens and the Origins of Religion*.

Wasson's contribution to the study of psychedelics cannot be overstated. In this book, friends, colleagues, disciples, and his daughter write essays in tribute to him. Many contributors reminisce about the man behind the mushrooms. Keewaydinoquay, a member of the Ojibway tribe, tells of her tribe's first meeting with Wasson, who proudly proclaimed, "I am a friend of Claude Lévi-Strauss!" Nobody had any idea what the hell he was talking about, but everyone figured that it must be a good thing because Wasson was so obviously proud of the fact.

Other essays examine Wasson's work and the effects it had. Still other essays branch off in different directions. Terence McKenna looks at Wasson's precursors, including Lewis Carroll. Robert DeMarest looks at the beautiful first editions of Wasson's books, which are now highly sought after by bibliophiles.

This book also contains a massive Wasson bibliography and more than ninety photos, including thirty-nine in color. Wasson may have gone to the Big Toadstool in the Sky, but his work and his memory live on.

Timber Press, Inc.; $37.95
1990; oversize hardcover; 283 pp.

*The Sacred Mushroom Seeker edited by Thomas J. Riedlinger*

*The seeker and ethnomycologist.*

## ROSETTA

Offers a vast wealth of information you ain't gonna get anywhere else, period. Rosetta's folios contain photocopies of articles from scholarly journals, small-circulation newsletters, and other sources unavailable to the average armchair ethnobotanist. Here's a small sampling of their folios:

•San Pedro Cactus: History, Care, Propagation, and Shamanic Use. Five articles including "Space and Ritual Time in a Peruvian Healing Ceremony" and "Alkaloids of Trichocereus Species and Other Cacti"

•Sociology: Drugs and Contemporary Culture. Six articles including "Drug-based Religions and Contemporary Drug Taking" and "Psychedelic Agents in Creative Problem Solving"

•Folio H1-6: Six articles including "A Partial List of Legal Plants That Contain Controlled Substances" and "How Hallucinogenic Drugs Work"

•Folio V1-2+: Three articles including "The Basic Constituents of Toad Venom" and "The Magic Toads of Cozumel"

•Folio TRY6-7: Two articles—"A Multidisciplinary Overview of Intoxicating Enema Rituals in the Western Hemisphere" and "A Multidisciplinary Overview of Intoxicating Snuff Rituals in the Western Hemisphere"

Rosetta also carries many independently published books, facsimile editions of out-of-print magazines (*The Psychedelic Review, The Psychozoic Press*, etc.), monographs (sets of articles and a print of indigenous drug art), T-shirts of such art, and ethnobotanical teas. Put this catalog on your "To get immediately" list.

Rosetta/PO Box 4611/Berkeley, CA 94704
Catalog: $1

# TERENCE MCKENNA

*Food of the Gods*
*by Terence*
*McKenna*

*La Morphiniste*
*(1893), Eugene*
*Gassett's*
*strangely*
*contemporary*
*addict.*

## FOOD OF THE GODS:
### THE SEARCH FOR THE ORIGINAL TREE OF KNOWLEDGE— A RADICAL HISTORY OF PLANTS, DRUGS, AND HUMAN EVOLUTION
### by Terence McKenna

In the book that catapulted him to psychedelic stardom, McKenna provides a revisionist look at the human race's relationship with drugs. He believes that food, plants, drugs, and spices have played crucial roles in our evolution. The most important role occurred early on. McKenna thinks that it was the presence of hallucinogenic substances in early humanoid diets that allowed the brain's information-processing capabilities to be rewired, leading to self-awareness, language, art, culture—in short, everything that makes us human.

From there we are treated to a history of the human race as it revolves around soma, alcohol, cannabis, sugar, coffee, chocolate, opium, tobacco, heroin, television, and other drugs.

McKenna thinks that our next step in evolution must involve hallucinogens. "Implicit in the ending of profane and secular history is the notion of our involvement with the reemergence of the vegetable mind. That same mind that coaxed us into self-reflecting

language now offers us the boundless landscapes of the imagination." Later, McKenna says, "We need to think back to the last sane moment that we, as a species, ever knew and then act from the premises that were in place at that moment.... This shift in viewpoint would enable us to see plants as more than food, shelter, clothing, or even sources of education and religion; they would become models of process."

Bantam Doubleday Dell Publishing Group; $14.95
1992; softcover; 311 pp.

## THE INVISIBLE LANDSCAPE:
### MIND, HALLUCINOGENS, AND THE I CHING
### by Terence McKenna and Dennis McKenna

When Terence and his brother Dennis, who has a Ph.D. in psychopharmacology, were still in their early twenties, they went sailing down the Amazon to experiment with ayahuasca and other drugs. They never completed their journey as planned, but they did find some mushrooms that opened up new doors of perception for them. Terence's book *True Hallucinations* looks back on that journey, but this book was written shortly after their trip, providing an unfiltered, raw examination of what they experienced. Originally published in 1975, and unavailable for many years, *The Invisible Landscape* is a seminal piece of psychedelic literature. Terence has said that it is his and Dennis's magnum opus.

The goal of the McKennas' book is nothing less than the explanation of reality itself. As they admit in their new foreword, they may not have always hit the nail on the head but they did make some pretty worthy attempts. They emphasize that you should take the book for what it is: "[the effort of] two individuals struggling to come to grips with a deluge of ideas triggered by a very personal and idiosyncratic experience."

In the first chapters, the brothers explain the nature of shamanism, its relationship to schizophrenia, and the holographic theory of the mind. Next comes a dense, technical speculation concerning exactly how they think molecules interact with the mind to bring about changes in consciousness. The McKennas discuss their personal psychedelic experiences. "We could feel the presence of some invisible hyperspatial entity, an ally, which seemed to be observing and sometimes exerting influence on the situation to keep us moving gently toward an experimental resolution of the ideas we were generating.... We were led to speculate that the role of the presence was somehow like that of an anthropologist, come to give humanity the keys to galactarian citizenship."

If you think this is a heavy book, you ain't seen nothin' yet. Part Two examines the ancient divinitory system, the *I Ching*, in relation to the mind, reality, and hallucinogens. "The *I Ching*, through its concern with detailing the dynamics of change and process, may hold the key to modeling the temporal dimension that metabolism creates for organisms, the temporal dimension without which mind could not exist." And that's just for starters!

HarperSanFrancisco; $14
1975 (1994); softcover; 229 pp.

## ALIEN DREAMTIME
### (VHS VIDEO)

On February 26 and 27, 1993, Terence McKenna and a group of artists and musicians put on a multimedia show designed to express cyberdelic concepts through sight, sound, and words. McKenna talked about the end of history, which is occurring because "the dominator culture has led the human species into a blind alley." We've become entrapped by capitalism, monotheism, monogamy, and monotonism. Psychedelics are a key to the next step in evolution, where we will lose our egos and go back to the good ol' days 15,000 to 20,000 years ago on the African plains, back when we weren't the victims of divisiveness, hatred, guilt, and consumer fetishism. By making this leap forward into the past, we will once again celebrate love, sex, and play. Hey, I'm sold. When do we leave?

While McKenna is relating his ideas of psychedelic utopia and speaking in "DMT tongues," we are treated to a visual kaleidoscope on screen, courtesy of the Rose•X group. Colorful undulating mandalas form the basis, while primal imagery weaves in and out—flowers, fire, space, penises, fetuses, topless dancers, jellyfish, UFOs, and more. Every so often, we see McKenna in the mix, his image distorted with posterization, reversal, and other tricks. Technomusic ranging from a background drone to a funky, get-up-and-dance beat plays under McKenna's speech, coming to the fore during the two intermissions. Accompanying this music by Space Time Continuum is the Australian Aboriginal didgeridoo played by Stephen Kent.

*Alien Dreamtime* can serve a variety of purposes, ranging from a serious introduction to Terence McKenna's ideas to a great companion for your next trip.

City of Tribes Communications; $19.95
1993; VHS videocassette; 60 min.

# ETHNOBOTANICALS BY MAIL

## HORUS BOTANICALS

Horus has an amazing selection of about three hundred psychedelics, poisons, herbs, spices, and other plants. They've recently started selling heirloom food plant cultivars. Most seed companies cater to huge agribusinesses that want a hybrid seed that produces fruits and veggies that are nice-looking, tough, etc. (but not necessarily tasty). Therefore, seeds of different strains are getting scarcer. Horus is helping to keep biodiversity alive by selling seeds of onion, okra, peanuts, tabasco pepper, watermelon, tomatoes, etc.

They also carry wolfsbane, sweet flag, *Hikuli sunami*, mugwort, absinthe, yage, nightshade, frankincense, coffee, poppies, mandrake, San Pedro cactus, and much, much more. They mainly sell seeds, but for some plants they have dried cuttings, tincture, or the plant itself.

Horus Botanicals/HCR 82 Box 29/Salem, AK 72576
Catalog: $2

## JLF

JLF sells several variations of the *Amanita muscaria* mushroom, either in 'shroom form or as extract and resin. They also have seeds, extracts, and/or cuttings of belladonna, caapi, hemlock, yohimbe, toloache, morning glory, sneezeweed, white water lily, opium poppy, mescal bean, Japanese yew tree, San Pedro cactus, periwinkle, and others. Coming soon, we are promised, is cobra venom.

JLF/PO Box 184/Elizabethtown, IN 47232
Catalog: $2

## L.E.R.

Legendary Ethnobotanical Resources sells all kinds of goodies. They have seeds/plants for wadalee gum, cat's-eye, calamus, chocolate vine, mugwort, ayahuasca/yage, Aztec tobacco, mescal bean, etc. You can also get oils, essences, organic coffees, smoke blends, herbal teas, gums and resins, herbs and spices, posters, cookbooks, pill-making supplies, and more. To keep up with their constant new offerings, subscribe to L.E.R.'s supplement/newsletter, published every six to ten weeks.

L.E.R./PO Box 1676/Coconut Grove, FL 33233
Catalog: $3

## ...OF THE JUNGLE

This business sells seeds and botanical products year round, and live plants and cuttings are available from April/May through October/November. These plants come from all over the world and many are quite rare. You can get plants and/or seeds for calamus root, chicalote, Atropa belladonna, ayahuasca/yage, khat, chile habañero, Jimson weed, purple coneflower, California poppy, gotu kola, coyote tobacco, various cacti, henbane, mescal bean, and dozens more. Botanical products include absinthe herb (the key ingredient in the notorious drink), guarana extract, amber essence, Montezuma's Secret (an Aztec aphrodisiac), kola nut powder, reishi mushroom tincture, and various stimulant herbal mixes. Finally, ...of the jungle sells flower essences.

...of the jungle/PO Box 1801/Sebastopol, CA 95473
Catalog: $2

# MARIJUANA

## HEMP TODAY
### edited by Ed Rosenthal

The first in a planned series of yearly editions, *Hemp Today* is a collection of articles on the many uses of hemp and the positive economic, environmental, and medicinal effects that would result from widespread use. Cannabis is one of the most useful plants in existence—it can provide us with paper, clothing, food, building supplies, fuel, and medicine, which are often more economical and better for the planet than what we're currently using.

The first part of the book examines hemp's history in the United States. You'll learn many interesting facts:

—Hemp was grown by Thomas Jefferson and George Washington, who said, "Make the most of hemp seed. Sow it everywhere."

—Hemp was used for the currency in colonial times.

—"The USS *Constitution* used sixty tons of hemp in its riggings and sails."

—"Tariffs protecting the hemp industry were passed in 1789, 1816, and 1861."

—"Henry Ford, an avid chemurgist [someone who finds industrial uses for crops], formed a car body of plastic reinforced with hemp fiber."

—"A *Popular Mechanics* article in 1938 raved hemp as the source for 50,000 products, essentially plastics, and called it the 'Billion Dollar Crop.'"

The reason that hemp has been outlawed is not because its almost identical twin, marijuana, makes you feel good when you smoke it (something pleasure-hating politicians simply cannot allow). Although that was definitely a factor in rousing public fears, hemp was outlawed because of a complex battle—called the "Fiber Wars"—between hemp, flax, cotton, synthetics, and other fibers that was fought by powerful special interests, corporations, government industries, and farmers. Hemp and flax got the short end of the stick.

The book's next section takes a realistic, balanced look at hemp's potential. The authors may disagree on the extent of hemp's usefulness, but they all feel that it is a very important plant that should be used in at least some industries.

Hemp use is definitely on the upswing worldwide, as the articles in Section Three indicate. Australia, China, England, Holland, Hungary, the Ukraine, the United States, and other countries are producing and/or using hemp. Just a few years ago, things looked gloomy for cannabis. Now, "...the industry is rebounding with increased acreage, new production facilities producing new products, and most importantly, it has a new set of customers and end users."

The book's final section looks at the economics of cannabis legalization. Dr. Dale Gieringer provides some eye-opening figures. Since statistics on pot use are far from certain and it's hard to predict how much legalized pot will cost, Gieringer's estimates cover a wide range, but are impressive nonetheless. Excise tax on marijuana would raise $2.2 to $6.4 billion annually, and sales tax would bring in an additional $200 million to $1.3 billion. Savings to law enforcement would be on the order of $6 to $9 billion. On a related note, spin-off industries, such as coffeehouses and paraphernalia, could result in 60,000 retailers and 100,000 jobs.

The appendix contains a wealth of source documents on hemp that would be worth the price of the book by themselves. Included are a 1913 article from the Department of Agriculture, *USDA Bulletin #404*, a 1921 *Scientific American* article, the previously mentioned *Popular Mechanics* article, a transcript of the government-produced documentary *Hemp for Victory,* and more.

The end of the book has listings and ads for almost one hundred pro-legalization groups and businesses selling hemp products (clothes, purses, paper, twine, etc.).

Quick American Archives; $19.95
1994; softcover; 459 pp.; illus.

## GROW YER OWN STONE
### by Alexander Sumach

This an almost exact reproduction of the classic 1973 guide to growing pot. The only differences are this edition has a new cover and one of the illustrations (on the third page) is covered up with a sticky square of paper, evidently to prevent massive lawsuits from corporate goons who don't believe the First Amendment covers the right to parody. If you *gently* and *slowly* peel this sticker off, you can uncensor the original drawing (but you didn't hear it from me).

The book is handwritten (in a neat, legible style) and contains lots of pictures, drawings, and hand-drawn headline typefaces. The whole thing has a very homey, underground feel to it. Humor is abundant. When considering options other than smoking the wacky tobaccy, the author plays with the idea of giving up cannabis and switching to a less safe intoxicant. He says, "Alcohol is fun" as a caption to a picture of a man holding a knife to a woman's throat; "Find yourself with acid" next to a picture of Charles Manson; and "The joys of tobacco" next to a picture of a cell labeled "Cancer cell from a lung."

What follows is a down-to-earth guide to planting, raising, harvesting, storing, and enjoying your weed. This book was written in Canada for people trying to grow in a cold, hostile climate, as opposed to the sunny climate of California, which is what other books cover. Among the valuable tips to remember: Forget cops, the weather, and bugs, "Your worst enemies by far are fellow dope smokers. A nice, friendly head is transformed into a fiend at the site of an undefended plot of cannabis." This book is good as either a practical instruction manual for Canadian stoners or a teary-eyed memento of your hippie days, before you became a Republican.

Quick Trading Company; $12.95
1973 (1992); softcover; 96 pp.

*Grow Yer Own Stone by Alexander Sumach*

*The classic (handwritten) 1973 guide to growing pot.*

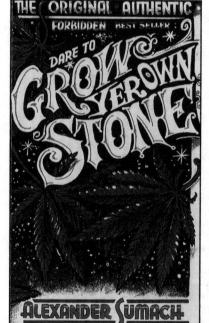

## MARIHUANA RECONSIDERED:
### THE MOST THOROUGH EVALUATION OF THE BENEFITS AND DANGERS OF CANNABIS
### by Lester Grinspoon, M.D.

In the 1960s Harvard psychiatrist Lester Grinspoon was convinced that marijuana was a dangerous, terrible substance, so he set out to write a book that would alert the world, especially the hippies, to the horrors of pot. "But as I reviewed the scientific, medical, and lay literature, my views began to change. I came to understand that I, like so many other people in this country, had been misinformed and misled." Grinspoon realized that the risks were minimal and that pot had many medical benefits.

Les was so convinced that this information would change things, he predicted when his book was originally published in 1971 that pot use for adults would be legalized within ten years. As he says now: "I had not yet learned that there is something peculiar about illicit drugs: if they don't always make the drug user behave irrationally, they certainly cause many nonusers to behave that way." Indeed, the opposite has happened; we are now under "a climate of psychopharmacological McCarthyism."

In this groundbreaking book, Grinspoon smashes many widely accepted notions about Mary Jane. He states unequivocally that it is not addictive, although it may be psychologically addictive to those people who are so messed up anyway that they'd become addicted to anything that helped them escape the pain of their crummy lives. Also, the idea that pot is a "stepping stone" to harder drugs is shown to be false. Grinspoon doesn't completely debunk the idea of "pot psychosis" because, while there's little evidence that it exists, "it seems clear that the drug may precipitate in susceptible people one of several types of mental dysfunction."

The author closely examines what users feel when they get high and why pot often has no effect on a first-time smoker. Further chapters look at the medical uses of weed, the campaign against pot, and the issues involved in legalization.

Quick Trading Company; $16.95
1971 (1994); softcover; 474 pp.

## MARIHUANA:
### THE FORBIDDEN MEDICINE
### by Lester Grinspoon, M.D., and James B. Bakalar

More than twenty years after writing *Marihuana Reconsidered*, Dr. Grinspoon decided to take an in-depth look at a benefit of pot that was only given a chapter in his first book. In *Marihuana*, Grinspoon presents the testimony of numerous individuals who used marijuana to reduce or rid themselves of the symptoms of chemotherapy, glaucoma, epilepsy, multiple sclerosis, paralysis, chronic pain, migraine, menstrual pain, depression, chronic itching, and AZT treatment.

Pot's effects are almost miraculous. A man with MS describes what smoking daily did for him: "Within a few weeks I was able to walk again unaided. I was soon walking half a block alone with some effort. I regained strength as I got more exercise, and my eyesight returned to normal. After six months all my symptoms had improved greatly. The spasms had vanished and I regained the ability to read, write, and walk." This man then did something that is fairly common among the people in this book. He simply couldn't believe that a simple and allegedly evil plant could make such a difference, so, as an experiment, he stopped smoking. "Within a few weeks I needed a cane and then a walker. Eventually I was bedridden again." He resumed smoking after four months, and his symptoms once again went away.

Pot helps glaucoma by relieving the intraocular pressure associated with the disorder. One woman who ate marijuana brownies saw her eye pressure go literally overnight from the upper forties to fourteen and sixteen, which are normal, healthy pressures. A man with glaucoma reported that after smoking he would watch as the tricolored halos and white-blindness that filled his vision simply disappeared.

Cancer patients report how Mary Jane nullifies the side effects of chemotherapy. People who used to puke their lungs up and dry heave for days after a round of chemo would smoke some pot before treatment and would actually be hungry immediately afterward. The parents of one boy voiced a sentiment that was echoed throughout the book: "Marihuana was the safest, most benign drug he received in the course of his battle against cancer."

Reading this book is incredibly frustrating. Here we have a natural plant that has wonderful health effects on people. It keeps them from going blind, helps them to walk, stops spasms, controls nausea, gets rid of unbearable pain, and much more, yet because it has the side effect of intoxication, our posturing, fascist government has decided that people can't have it. In July

1994, pot-smoker President Clinton once again refused to lift the medicinal ban on marijuana, and therefore forced tens of thousands of people to suffer needlessly or risk imprisonment for growing or buying a drug that helps them.

Yale University Press; $22.50
1993; hardcover; 184 pp.

# THE ALLIANCE FOR CANNABIS THERAPEUTICS

The Alliance for Cannabis Therapeutics is a patients' rights organization that pushes for the prescription use of marijuana. Its founder and president, R.C. Randall, is one of only ten or so people in the country who have gone through the red tape nightmare, and he is currently receiving government-approved pot for his glaucoma. Randall has edited five books that stand as massive testaments to the healing power of cannabis.

## MARIJUANA, MEDICINE AND THE LAW, VOLUME 1
### edited by R.C. Randall

In 1987 the Drug Enforcement Administration held historic hearings aimed at the possible rescheduling of marijuana, which was and still is laughably designated as a Schedule I drug, along with heroin and cocaine. These hearings focused on marijuana's medical benefits. This first volume contains loads of direct testimony, both for and against the medicinal use of cannabis, from medical authorities, patients, and families of patients. Witnesses for the Alliance for Cannabis Therapeutics (ACT) testified specifically on cancer, glaucoma, chronic pain, skin disorders, and spasticity. Witnesses for the National Organization to Reform Marijuana Laws (NORML) testified on the psychological effects of pot and its use for various conditions. The witnesses for the DEA sounded much more reserved notes, saying that marijuana hasn't been shown to be *that* effective in reducing nausea, it might have bad long-term effects, and so on. Interestingly, all of the DEA's witnesses were ivory tower intellectuals and none of them ever had a horrible disease and thanked God for marijuana. Finally, there is a rebuttal to the DEA's arguments by witnesses for ACT and NORML.

Galen Press; $29.95
1988; softcover; 502 pp.

## MARIJUANA, MEDICINE AND THE LAW, VOLUME 2
### edited by R.C. Randall

This volume contains the legal arguments presented by all parties concerning the rescheduling of marijuana. The ACT, NORML, and the Cannabis Corporation of America, which wants to make a natural "pot pill," present arguments for rescheduling. The DEA and the National Federation of Parents for Drug-Free Youth argue against rescheduling. The first three organizations then present rebuttals.

Next, a transcript of an oral debate between both sides is presented. It makes for particularly interesting reading. Charlotte Mapes, a mouthpiece for the DEA, inadvertently shows that agency's true, condescending, elitist colors when she says, "I think that the Agency certainly believes that the acceptance of the medical community is a very important factor in determining marijuana's accepted medical use, but I don't think there is anything in the legislative history, in the Statute, in any of the background that would support acceptance by the public as determining medical use.... *It is not the patients that determine the drugs that they are going to take*" (emphasis definitely mine). When asked if a patient's report of how she feels after taking a drug

should affect the doctor, Mapes says yes, "but I also think it's the physician's evaluation of the patient's use, not the patient's evaluation of the drug, that is important here."

Finally, the decision of the judge ruling over the proceedings is given. Hold your breath, kiddies, as I cut right to the chase: "The judge recommends that the Administrator [of the DEA] transfer marijuana from Schedule I to Schedule II." Are you as amazed as I am? What's not amazing is that the judge's decision was ignored; marijuana remains a Schedule I drug. Which begs the question, what was the point of having the hearings if the DEA was just going to sweep the decision under the rug?

The one good thing that came from the proceedings is the massive amount of testimony and research for pot's medicinal value that was presented. That wealth of material, presented in these two volumes, is a gold mine for doctors, healers, activists, and people with AIDS, cancer, glaucoma, and other diseases.

Galen Press; $25.95
1989; softcover; 484 pp.

## CANCER TREATMENT AND MARIJUANA THERAPY
### (MARIJUANA, MEDICINE AND THE LAW SERIES, VOLUME 3)
### edited by R.C. Randall

This volume presents testimony from the DEA hearings that specifically shows marijuana's positive benefits in reducing or eliminating nausea and vomiting caused by chemotherapy, and in stimulating appetite. Cancer patients, parents of children with cancer, oncologists, and other authorities and researchers (including Lester Grinspoon, author of two books reviewed above) testified on behalf of Mary Jane's strong powers of relief. Dr. Ivan Silverberg, an oncologist in San Francisco, testified that "...there has evolved an unwritten but accepted standard of treatment within the oncologic community which readily accepts marijuana's use."

Also included are two legal briefs from the Alliance for Cannabis Therapeutics and the National Organization for the Reform of Marijuana Laws. There are several appendixes and, of course, the ruling of the DEA administrative judge who oversaw the procedures: "The overwhelming preponderance of the evidence in this record establishes that marijuana has a currently accepted medical use in treatment in the United States for nausea and vomiting resulting from chemotherapy treatments in some cancer patients. To conclude otherwise, on this record, would be unreasonable, arbitrary, and capricious." [Note: All of the material in this book is contained in *Marijuana, Medicine and the Law*, Volumes 1 and 2, above.]

Galen Press; $23.95
1990; softcover; 365 pp.

## MUSCLE SPASM, PAIN AND MARIJUANA THERAPY
### (MARIJUANA, MEDICINE AND THE LAW SERIES, VOLUME 4)
### edited by R.C. Randall

This volume contains mostly testimony and legal briefings that were given at the DEA hearings regarding pot's ability to reduce or eliminate muscle spasms and chronic pain associated with various conditions such as paralysis, multiple sclerosis, and arthritis. Some of the book, about thirty-five pages, is testimony from an Idaho court case in which Lynn Hastings was arrested for growing marijuana to treat her rheumatoid arthritis. The Idaho Supreme Court ruled that Hastings had shown that marijuana was a necessity for helping her condition. The prosecutor dropped all charges. [Note: All of the material in this book, except that related to the Hastings case, is contained in *Marijuana, Medicine and the Law*, Volumes 1 and 2, above.]

Galen Press; $14.95
1991; softcover; 237 pp.

## MARIJUANA & AIDS:
### POT, POLITICS & PWAS IN AMERICA
### written and compiled by R.C. Randall

Pot's ability to eliminate nausea and vomiting, stimulate appetite, and control pain and spasms without causing a drug stupor (or worse side effects) makes it perfect for people with AIDS (PWAs). In this book Randall looks at the movement to gain access to marijuana, which has been kicked into overdrive by PWAs. We learn of Steve, who was the first PWA to get legal access to marijuana; Danny, who was the second such person; Barbara and Kenny Jenks, an HIV-positive couple who were arrested for possessing pot; and Ivan Silverberg, a San Francisco oncologist who is one of the few doctors with the guts to call for legalized medicinal marijuana. Steve's comment on the situation crystallizes the cruelty of the authorities: "The people who discriminate against marijuana are not sick and don't have as much to lose as I do."

Marijuana's effects on the immune system have been hotly debated and are of obvious importance to PWAs. They obviously wouldn't want to smoke anything that would weaken their defenses further. Dr. Leo Hollister provides a comprehensive overview of the contradictory and flawed research on immuno-suppression and pot.

The author also discusses Marinol, the "pot pill," which is a synthesized version of marijuana's psychoactive ingredient, THC. Marinol is available by prescription. The only problem is that it sucks. Its effects are not nearly as powerful as pot's and it has nasty side effects like anxiety, disorientation, and edginess. As one PWA put it: "From my experience the choice between Marinol and marijuana is clear—flush the Marinol down the toilet and have a smoke."

Part Four of the book is the most important. It gives you all the forms and instructions you need to apply for the government's kind permission to legally obtain pot for AIDS.

Galen Press; $12.95
1991; softcover; 183 pp.

*Our Right to Drugs by Thomas Szasz*

*Drug laws that treat us like children...*

## LEGALIZATION

## OUR RIGHT TO DRUGS:
### THE CASE FOR A FREE MARKET
### by Thomas Szasz

Szasz, the leading light of the anti-psychiatry movement, turns his attention to the area of drugs, both illegal and prescription. He feels that the government is treating us like children with its drug laws, which deny us the right to decide what we put into our own bodies. But drugs are harmful, right? So why not let other people make decisions for us? Szasz puts it this way: "We want drugs to relieve our pains, cure our diseases, enhance our endurance, change our moods, put us to sleep, or simply make us feel better—just as we want bicycles and cars, trucks and tractors, ladders and chain saws, skis and hang gliders to make our lives more productive and more pleasant. Each year tens of people are killed and injured with the use of such artifacts. Why do we not speak of 'ski abuse' or a 'chain saw problem'?" The answer is that we expect people who use things to know how to use them properly and safely.

Szasz argues that drug laws have denied us our constitutional right to property and have deprived us of control of our own bodies. He points out that, ironically, most Americans now believe in "the right to die," but few people think they have a right to drugs.

This book includes a history of the War on Drugs, which really started in 1906 with the passage of the Food and Drugs Act. Szasz also looks at drugs as scapegoats, drug education (which encourages children to turn in their parents for doing something the government thinks they shouldn't, à la the Hitler Youth Corps), drug legalization, the War on Drugs as a war on African Americans, and more. *Our Right to Drugs* is a powerful stand on a highly controversial topic—the right to control our own bodies. Szasz's arguments are bold and convincing. As he puts it so well, "Drug censorship, like book censorship, is an attack on capitalism and freedom."

Greenwood Publishing Group; $19.95
1992; hardcover; 199 pp.

## AMERICA'S LONGEST WAR:
### RETHINKING OUR TRAGIC CRUSADE AGAINST DRUGS
### by Steven B. Duke and Albert C. Gross

A distinguished Yale law professor and an attorney show that the War on (Some) Drugs is an utter failure and always will be. "The major accomplishments of our war on drugs have been to squander literally hundreds of billions of dollars, flood our streets with guns and gangsters, rack up record levels of crime, corrupt the police, logjam the courts, overwhelm the penal system, and produce widespread and costly health care problems. And what is equally devastating to the common good, the entire spectrum of constitutionally guaranteed rights and liberties has been eroded in the name of drug war necessity."

The authors take a wonderfully methodical approach to the subject. First they attempt to identify the "enemy." Words like *drug* and *abuse* have very slippery meanings. Next the authors look at our most harmful drugs and our most popular illegal drugs: tobacco, alcohol, marijuana, cocaine, and heroin. They present the research of James Ostrowski of the Cato Institute, who attempted to calculate drug-fatality rates of legal and illegal drugs. He concluded, "Thus, for every death caused by the intrinsic effects of cocaine, heroin kills 20, alcohol kills 37 and tobacco kills 132." Marijuana is so benign, it didn't even rank.

A quick look at the politically motivated history of drug regulation and prohibition follows. The authors then identify the nine crime waves that have followed in the wake of drug prohibition: direct violations of prohibition, crimes to get drug money, systemic violence, proliferation of deadly weapons, corruption of the criminal justice system, undercover crime, police perjury and obstructions of justice, vigilantism, and social deterioration.

The next four chapters look at the freedom costs, autonomy costs, social costs, and health and safety costs of the drug war. After examining how damaging this exercise in stupidity is, the authors show why the creation of "a drug-free America" can never, ever, be achieved. The only logical answer is legalization, so the authors look at the benefits and costs of lifting the ban on drugs. They conclude that the benefits far, far outweigh the risks. Finally, they present a variety of approaches to legalization, as well as concurrent education and treatment programs.

*America's Longest War* is a persuasively argued book, but then again, in my case the authors are preaching to the converted. I hope that this book would help those who aren't convinced see the sanity of legalization, but I'm afraid there are too many ideologues whose minds are cemented shut.

Jeremy P. Tarcher/Putnam; $26.95
1993; hardcover; 348 pp.

## THE ENTHEOGEN LAW REPORTER

This newsletter doesn't actually argue for legalization, but it does keep you informed about exactly what hallucinogenic substances are and are not legal. It's the only periodical that keeps tabs on all the legalities concerning 'shrooms, khat, peyote, psychedelic toads, and so on. The Summer 1994 issue contains an overview of court cases concerning magic mushrooms, a report of an Alaska business that was raided for selling *Psilocybe cubensis* mushroom-growing kits, the first known court case involving possession of toad venom, the growing war on drug paraphernalia, and the use of the Religious Freedom Restoration Act in a peyote case. One article explained that the Ninth Circuit Court of Appeals has set a scary precedent by saying that customs officials have "just cause" to open your mail if it meets two conditions: It's from a country known as a "common source of drugs" and it's addressed to a post office box. Those are it! That's the only requirements that have to be met for some bureaucrat to tear into your mail.

*The Entheogen Law Reporter* is full of frightening news, but it also offers ways to defend yourself if you're ever caught with the goods. Nobody who partakes of psychedelics can afford to be without it.

The Entheogen Law Reporter
PO Box 73481/Davis, CA 95617-3481
One-year sub (4 issues): $25

## NEW AGE PATRIOT

A magazine for people and groups taking an active role in trying to re-legalize marijuana. The term "re-legalize" is an important part of the *Patriot*'s stance, since it reminds people that marijuana was legal until the late 1930s. They are simply fighting for an end to the idiotic prohibition that has been imposed.

"Hemp is actually more accurately perceived as a 'universal commodity' that can be used to produce an incredible diversity of products, ranging from paper, to textiles, to car fuel, to food...to over 50,000 different products. In 1938 *Popular Mechanics* was so impressed with the potential of hemp that they predicted that it would become the first 'billion-dollar' agricultural crop in U.S. history. And it actually has exceeded this billion-dollar mark even though its use has been restricted to that of a psychotropic drug in an illicit market. It is hard to imagine how many billions of dollars it would generate and how many American jobs it might produce if only it were legal" (Spring 1994).

But the *Patriot* does more than just bemoan pot's outlaw status; it reports on initiatives, petitions, marches, picnics, rallies, and other events designed to raise public consciousness or change the laws surrounding the personal, medicinal, and industrial uses of Mary Jane. This is definitely a hands-on group of activists.

New Age Patriot/PO Box 419/Dearborn Heights, MI 48127
Single issue: $2.50
One-year sub (4 issues): $15

# SMART DRUGS AND NUTRIENTS

## SMART DRUGS AND NUTRIENTS:
### How to Improve Your Memory and Increase Your Intelligence Using the Latest Discoveries in Neuroscience

### by Ward Dean, M.D., and John Morgenthaler

The book that galvanized the smart drugs movement. In 1990 word was getting around that there were substances, often developed for people with Alzheimer's, that could soup up your brain. Then *Smart Drugs and Nutrients* came out, showing that you could indeed get a better memory, become more creative and mentally alert, and even boost your intelligence through chemicals.

The authors give us the lowdown on a large number of

cognitive enhancers: piracetam, fipexide, oxiracetam, ginkgo bilboa, vasopressin, and vitamins. Most of these substances work by affecting your neurotransmitters and receptors. They either increase transmitter production, slow transmitter breakdown, or increase the number of receptor areas. Others increase oxygen and blood flow. The authors explain exactly how each substance works, results of research, dosages, and precautions. They are careful to emphasize the fact that smart drugs work differently on different people. The active amount can vary by a factor of hundreds from person to person. Taking too much is as bad as taking too little. Therefore, you have to experiment to find just the right amount to help you.

Since smart drugs are only available by prescription—and then only for the treatment of Alzheimer's, Parkinson's, etc.— you have to order them in small amounts from other countries. The addresses of foreign sources in this book are outdated, but the authors are offering a monthly updated list for a small price (see *Smart Drugs II*, below).

B&J Publications; $12.95
1990; softcover; 222 pp.

*Smart Nutrients*
by Dr. Abram
Hoffer & Dr.
Morton Walker
(See page 68)▼

## SMART DRUGS II:
### The Next Generation

### by Ward Dean, M.D., John Morgenthaler, and Steven Wm. Folkes

*Play Beat the Clock with your body and win?*

A look at the next wave of smart drugs plus new info on your old favorites. Among the cognitive enhancers covered are Deprenyl, Melatonin, Milacemide, Nimodipine, Piracetam, and vitamins. Besides improving memory, creativity, and clarity of mind, some of these substances may combat depression and enhance sexual performance. The authors explain what these drugs can do for you, how they work, what the recommended dosages are, and what, if any, side effects exist. Since smart drugs first arrived on the scene, many studies have been performed on healthy humans, the results of which are included here.

The second major section of the book contains testimonials from people who souped up their noggins with smart drugs. An airline pilot, movie producer, professor, stroke victim, alcoholic, and dozens of other people share their successes. The final major section contains seventy pages of questions from readers, with answers from the authors. People have written to the authors' *Smart Drugs Newsletter* with questions about dosages, combinations, government policy, research, etc. The answers provide some much-needed information and addressed many of my personal concerns.

The appendix offers addresses and phone/fax numbers of domestic smart nutrient suppliers. Smart drug suppliers aren't listed, though, mainly because the FDA is getting bitchy and detaining shipments from several suppliers. Also, suppliers change addresses and go out of business, while new ones start up, making any listing very time-sensitive. To solve this problem, the authors offer a monthly listing of suppliers and sympathetic physicians. To get the latest listing, send them $2 and a self-addressed stamped envelope.

Health Freedom Press; $14.95
1993; softcover; 286 pp.

## BRAIN BOOSTERS:
### FOOD AND DRUGS THAT MAKE YOU SMARTER
### by Beverly Potter and Sebastian Orfali

A complete overview of the whole smart drugs and nutrients issue. The first chapter examines the different groups who are integral parts of the smart scene: the cyberdelic counterculture that goes to raves, stressed-out yuppies looking for an edge, and old people with memory loss. From there the authors move into a primer on how the brain works and what happens to it as it ages.

The whole smart drug/nutrient phenomenon has been controversial. The authors look at the cottage industry that has developed around these substances and the FDA's reactionary reaction to it.

The second half of the book contains the more practical material. It examines the usage and effects of nootropics and other brain-cell rejuvenators, including Deprenyl, DMAE, and K.H.3. If you'd rather go natural, there is information on vitamins (B1, B3, C), nutrients (lecithin, selenium, royal jelly), and herbs and foods (ginseng, gotu-kola, and chocolate) that can help get the juices flowing in your melon.

Finally, two appendixes give addresses for smart-substance suppliers and a state-by-state directory of life-extension physicians.

> Ronin Publishing; $12.95
> 1993; softcover; 257 pp.

## SMART NUTRIENTS:
### A GUIDE TO NUTRIENTS THAT CAN PREVENT AND REVERSE SENILITY
### by Dr. Abram Hoffer and Dr. Morton Walker

The main focus of this book is not on boosting your already significant brain power but on preventing and treating senility through the use of natural substances. The authors state: "Aging is inevitable and so is death. The rate at which aging occurs, however, is not highly correlated with age itself as measured in years. It is this flexible relationship—inevitable aging at variable rates of time—that makes this book possible and necessary."

The docs discuss the physical and mental effects of aging. No one is sure of the actual physical causes of senility, so the authors present several hypotheses, including their own. They believe that senility occurs when the brain's cells lose their ability to process oxygen adequately. But why does this inability to utilize oxygen happen? Our crummy diets that put us in a state of "subtle, chronic malnutrition" are the main reason. The processed food we eat has been leached of nutrients and filled with impurities, so that it slowly poisons us. Other factors contributing to senility are stress, a weakened immune system, and hypoglycemia (chronic low blood-sugar levels).

The authors tell what nutrients are the best for staving off senility or treating it if it has already occurred. Vitamins B1, B3, C, and E, pantothenic acid, calcium, magnesium, and zinc are among the most crucial weapons in the anti-aging arsenal. The doctors tell how these and other substances can help, list which foods have the highest nutrient contents, and give dietary and exercise tips.

> Avery Publishing Group; $9.95
> 1994; softcover; 200 pp.

*Absinthe
by Barnaby
Conrad III ➤*

*Albert
Maignan's* The
Green Muse *celebrating the
green hour.*

# MISCELLANEOUS

## ABSINTHE:
### HISTORY IN A BOTTLE
### by Barnaby Conrad III

Absinthe is a forbidden green liquor that tastes exactly like licorice and provides a pleasant, subtle high owing to its active ingredient, the herb wormwood. It's been around since ancient times, when absinthe was the name given to any wine or spirit that had wormwood in it. Modern absinthe was supposedly invented by a French doctor in 1872, who passed the recipe on to other people. It eventually wound up in the hands of Henri-Louis Pernod, who made it famous worldwide, although it was most popular in Switzerland, New Orleans, and France, where happy hour was referred to as "green hour."

Absinthe has more of a mystique surrounding it than any other alcoholic beverage. One reason is because it became the favorite drink of a bunch of decadent writers and artists, including Toulouse-Lautrec, Van Gogh, Manet, Picasso, Degas, Oscar Wilde, Verlaine, Rimbaud, Edgar Allan Poe (who drank it mixed with whiskey), and others. They produced much of their creative output while under the influence of the Green Fairy (as absinthe was called) and actually immortalized her in many poems and paintings. Wilde described the effects of drinking absinthe: "The first stage is like ordinary drinking, the second when you begin to see monstrous and cruel things, but if you can persevere you will enter in upon the third stage where you see things that you *want* to see, wonderful curious things."

Absinthe's alleged effects have also been responsible for its outlaw image. Common wisdom is that if you drink enough over a long period of time, you'll go insane. This is a myth, although wormwood may have some unpleasant side effects. Unfortunately, the evidence is inconclusive, but high enough doses of wormwood may cause epileptic-type seizures. The author does a good job covering the ambiguous evidence.

In the late 1800s, in a familiar turn of events, a movement developed to outlaw absinthe. Anti-alcohol sentiment was sweeping many countries, and absinthe bore the brunt of the attack. Pleasure-hating alarmists blamed practically all of society's ills on the Green Fairy, and it was eventually outlawed all over the world except in Spain, where it's still being made and sold.

*Absinthe* does an incredible job examining the Emerald Enchantress, and it's a good thing, because it's the only available book on the subject. It has more than one hundred illustrations (many in color) showing absinthe in paintings and advertisements, and anti-absinthe propaganda. It deserves a special place on your drug bookshelf.

Should you want to make absinthe yourself, fear not, for I will now impart some forbidden knowledge not contained in the book. Although absinthe is illegal, absinthe minus the wormwood is not. It's called Pernod, and it's available in the United States at larger liquor stores. Wormwood by itself is also legal. You can buy it from some of the businesses listed in the "Mail Order Ethnobotanicals" section of this chapter. Simply add one teaspoon of wormwood for every cup of Pernod Fils (this is the traditional ratio) and let sit for two days. Then strain out the wormwood. Voilà, you've got absinthe! (Just remember, the jury is still out on wormwood's effects.)

> Chronicle Books; $19.95
> 1988; oversize softcover; 160 pp.; heavily illus.

## ALCOHOLICS ANONYMOUS:
### CULT OR CURE?
### by Charles Bufe

Bufe takes a critical look at the tactics of Alcoholics Anonymous. He points out that AA evolved from an aggressive evangelical organization known as the Oxford Group Movement. Most of this group's beliefs were codified in the Twelve Steps of Alcoholics Anonymous, which are highly religious. Bufe points out that "*religion* is presented as a cure for what is commonly considered a *disease*." He is disturbed by the overt religiosity of the Twelve Steps and the fact that it drives away many people who come looking for help. Conversely, many of the people who are in Alcoholics Anonymous are convinced that the Twelve Steps is the only path to recovery, and they get a smug satisfaction out of watching non-AA members drink themselves to death.

Bufe is also concerned that the Twelve Steps, starting with the very first step, tells followers that they are powerless, that they have no control over their own lives. This can only contribute to low self-esteem, which the majority of alcoholics already have.

In determining if AA is a cult, as some have charged, Bufe comes to the conclusion that it is not, although it does have some cultlike tendencies. "The ideological system of AA is that of a cult: AA is religiously oriented, self-absorbed, irrational, dogmatic, insists on the submission of the individual to the will of God, and views itself as the exclusive holder of truth (at least in regard to the treatment of alcoholism). AA, however, has neither a charismatic leader nor an authoritarian hierarchy. It doesn't economically exploit its members. It doesn't employ mind-control techniques...."

On the plus side, Bufe does think that AA has helped many people, even though it's not terribly effective, and he does admire its noncoercive, anarchic structure. Two appendixes discuss secular alternatives to AA and the Twelve Steps.

See Sharp Press; $9.95
1991; softcover; 158 pp.

## AMERICA'S FAVORITE DRUG:
### COFFEE AND YOUR HEALTH
### by Bonnie Edwards, RN

A short book that sums up the health effects—negative and positive—of coffee. "Americans drink more than 400 million cups of coffee daily. Over half the population drinks at least two cups a day. 25% of coffee drinkers consume about five cups daily, and another 25% drink ten or more cups a day.... But coffee isn't just a drink—it's a drug." Research findings are presented in easy-to-consume bite-size chunks covering anxiety, blood pressure, cancer, exercise, the heart, PMS, sleep disturbance, etc. Each chapter also tells you what you can do to minimize coffee's effects on you.

Here are some cappuccino factoids. Surprisingly, coffee can actually help asthma sufferers. Three cups can be enough to stop an attack. Also, a strong cup of coffee drunk early enough may stave off a migraine. Pesticides that have been banned in the United States have been found in imported coffee beans. Caffeine can make PMS worse. Women who drink coffee during pregnancy can have caffeine-addicted babies. Pregnant women who down more than five cups of joe a day have more breech births. Also, caffeine is a mutagen—a substance that can screw up genes. To put it simply, if you're preggers, stay away from the Maxwell House! The book ends with tips on how to cut back or quit drinking coffee.

Odonian Press; $5
1992; paperback; 111 pp.

## CRACK WARS:
### LITERATURE—ADDICTION—MANIA
### by Avital Ronell

With a writing style so thick and dense you need a machete to make your way through it, pomo philosopher Avital Ronell approaches addiction from a somewhat metaphysical standpoint. She argues that addiction is not an aberration but an inborn part of the human race. Drugs, then, "do not close forces with an external enemy (the easy way out) but have a secret communications network with the internalized demon. Something is beaming out signals, calling drugs home." In her quest to understand addiction and drugs, Ronell examines Heidegger, Freud, Baudelaire, William Burroughs, and others. About half the book is a "narcoanalysis" of Flaubert's novel *Madame Bovary*.

Ronell chose to use crack in the title of this book because crack marked a turning point in the history of drugs, addiction, and law: "In an altogether uncanny manner, the polemics surrounding drugs historically became a War only when crack emerged. At this moment drugs acquired the character of political question.... Security was upped; civil liberties went down."

*Crack Wars* is a demanding book, but anything that attempts to remap the language of addiction and shed new light on drugs is worth the struggle.

University of Nebraska Press; $9.95
1992; softcover; 175 pp.

## THE DRUG USER:
### DOCUMENTS 1840–1960
### edited by John Strausbaugh and Donald Blaise

An impressive collection of firsthand accounts of drug use from before the 1960s chemical renaissance. There are many famous names here—Baudelaire, Artaud, John (Fire) Lame Deer, R. Gordon Wasson, Albert Hofmann, Anaïs Nin, Freud, Cocteau, and Huxley. Mark Twain is present, too, but his essay is not, unfortunately, about taking drugs. Instead, he relates that at one time he had intended to go to the Amazon to set up a coca shipping empire but his funds never allowed it.

The other essays present a rich tapestry showing the many facets of drug use. I was amazed at James Lee's ability to introduce drug on top of drug into his body. Lee was a British libertine and iconoclast who ran a mining operation in northern India. While there, he was introduced to many marvelous new drugs, which he proceeded to mix and match with reckless abandon. "Had I a headache on some rare occasion? I removed it at once with a mixture of morphia [morphine] and cocaine." "Morphine and brandy together will produce a voracious appetite..." "I was now using fairly large quantities of cocaine, often tempered with morphia, and smoking a little opium every night." Add to the mix hashish and unnamed drugs that Lee discovered during jungle expeditions, and you've got one daring experimenter.

In 1857 Fitz Hugh Ludlow published *The Hasheesh Eater*, an account of his experiences with hash. Many of his visions were indescribably beautiful, but he warns do not ever take any hash while you are still under the effects of a previous dose or "such agony will inevitably ensue as will make the soul shudder at its own possibility of endurance without annihilation." Poor Fitz found out the hard way. After doing hash on top of hash, he was visited by two demons. "Suddenly the nearest fiend, snatching up a pitchfork (also of white-hot iron), thrust it into my writhing side, and hurled me shrieking into the fiery cradle.... Through increasing grades of agony I lay unconsumed, tossing from side to side with the rocking of the dreadful engine, and still above me peeled the chant of blasphemy, and the eyes of demoniac sarcasm smiled at me in mockery of a mother's gaze upon her child. 'Let us sing him,' said one fiend to the other, 'the lullaby of Hell.'"

Blast Books; $10.95
1991; softcover; 240 pp.

## FROM CHOCOLATE TO MORPHINE:
### EVERYTHING YOU NEED TO KNOW ABOUT MIND-ALTERING DRUGS (REVISED AND UPDATED)
### by Andrew Weil, M.D., and Winfred Rosen

The second edition of this groundbreaking book presents an evenhanded look at a large number of legal and illegal drugs. It is written from a neutral viewpoint—the authors neither condone nor condemn the use of any drugs. They just want you to have accurate information regarding these substances.

The very first chapter is titled "Straight Talk from the Start." When I read it, I flashed back to my seventh-grade health class: "It is a bad idea to take drugs in school. Even if school bores you, you have to be there, and mastering classroom skills is your ticket to freedom and independence in adult life." While this may be true to a large degree, it comes across as propaganda, but fear not! The rest of the book dispenses with such moralizing and presents the good, the bad, and the ugly facts about drugs.

The authors won my trust when they defied "chemical correctness" by telling the truth about acid: "Despite loud arguments and much bad publicity about the medical dangers of LSD in the 1970s, there is no evidence that it damages chromosomes, injures the brain, or causes any other physical harm." I was surprised to learn about sniffing glue, gas, etc.: "All of the scare stories exaggerated the dangers of solvent inhalation, saying that it certainly led to brain, heart, and liver damage, destruction of the bone marrow, blindness, and death.... Young people who sniff solvents occasionally are not likely to develop serious medical problems." That word *occasionally* is extremely important. Some kids spend hours every day with their faces over cans of gas and end up dead.

The authors also give the straight dope about marijuana, cocaine, barbiturates, opium, mushrooms, amyl nitrite, tobacco, alcohol, steroids, caffeine, cough syrup, smart drugs, and many others. In separate chapters they look at why people take drugs, the problems with drugs, and alternatives to chemical highs. Figuring that if you're going to use drugs, you'd better do it the right way, the authors offer suggestions about using pot, PCP, and nitrous oxide, among others.

Houghton-Mifflin; $13.95
1993; oversize softcover; 240 pp.

*From Chocolate to Morphine by Dr. Andrew Weil & Winfred Rosen*

*Helping mother cope, with drugs.*

That "good morning" feeling... thanks to

\*

glutethimide

## FS CATALOG

Although they offer some books on privacy, revenge, 'n' such, FS Books' main focus is on drugs. Lots of books on growing/making/using drugs and some on history, ethnobotany, etc. Titles include *Cooking with Cannabis, Conquering the Urine Tests, Hallucinogens and Culture, The Mushroom Cultivator, Plants of the Gods, Recreational Drugs, Marijuana Growing Tips, FS Resource Guide, Cocaine Consumer's Handbook*, and dozens more. Orders are shipped within twenty-four hours, and they have a low-price guarantee.

FS Book Company
PO Box 417457/Sacramento, CA 95841-7457

## HIGH TIMES:
### 20 YEARS OF SMOKE IN YOUR FACE
### by the editors of *High Times*

Perhaps the only magazine devoted exclusively to illegal substances, *High Times* has been covering the cultural, political, religious, economic, medical, and practical aspects of certain drugs for twenty years. Contrary to what many people believe, *High Times* doesn't deal with all drugs. It devotes most of its attention to pot, with hallucinogens a distant second, and an occasional appearance by an unusual drug like ecstasy. It almost never discusses the "hard drugs," such as cocaine and heroin.

This big anthology collects hundreds of the best articles, essays, interviews, and cartoons from *High Times*. Twenty-four pieces are reprinted in their entirety, covering how to beat a urine test, hemp paper, marijuana myths, cloning for better pot yields, government studies that found pot to be relatively nontoxic, hemp as food, the medicinal uses of Mary Jane, and the Black Crowes. In sidebars alongside these larger articles are artwork and smaller fragments of articles. The covers of one hundred issues are reproduced, along with cartoons and pictures of drug notables. The smaller articles include snippets of interviews with Abbie Hoffman, Mick Jagger, Tommy Chong, Willie Nelson, Terence McKenna, Jerry Garcia, Wavy Gravy, and William Burroughs; articles on hemp clothing, government drug smuggling, raves, ayahuasca, LSD's fortieth birthday, Groucho Marx, JFK's dealer, and much more. Plus a center section contains full-color photos of beautiful buds and *The Fabulous Furry Freak Brothers*.

St. Martin's Press; $13.95
1994; oversize softcover; 187 pp.; heavily illus.

## HOW TO BUY ALMOST ANY DRUG LEGALLY WITHOUT A PRESCRIPTION
### by James H. Johnson

In July of 1988 the FDA put into effect a startling policy: individuals can buy prescription drugs—including those unapproved in America—from other countries and have them imported into the United States. There are several conditions and restrictions, of course. The drugs must be for personal consumption (as opposed to resale); you can only buy three months' worth at a time; and you must swear in writing that the drugs are for you and provide the name and address of the physician treating you. You cannot import restricted substances or drugs that are under import alert (meaning the FDA believes they are clearly dangerous or fraudulent).

So what are the benefits of importing foreign drugs? First of all, you save megabucks. The author buys four prescription drugs (two for hypertension, one for high cholesterol, and one for ulcers), which in America (in 1990) cost him $325 for a three-month supply. In Mexico, the same drugs cost $135. You also save money by not having to pay a doctor a visit to get a prescription.

Another advantage is that you can buy "orphan drugs," drugs that are sold in other countries but not in the United States. "Usually this is because the FDA approval process is too expensive and the potential American market too small to make it financially profitable for a company to market such a drug." There are orphan drugs that treat AIDS, heart conditions, hemorrhage, rheumatic disorders, muscle spasms, Parkinson's disease, and many rare disorders such as Lou Gehrig's disease and Tourette's syndrome.

The author does a great job covering the subject. He tells exactly how to go about getting drugs from other countries, including addresses of foreign drug companies, price lists, and a sample form you should send. Much of the book is a detailed listing of the available drugs—prescription drugs, orphan drugs, and drugs currently in the FDA approval process. The author not only tells what the drugs are for and how they work but lists recommended dosages and known side effects. He also includes a section on drugs currently under import alert.

This is one important and powerful book. The knowledge it offers will help you take control of your own body. The book's only flaw is that it came out in 1990 and is in desperate need of updating.

Avon Books; $5.99
1990; paperback; 340 pp.

## LAUGHING GAS:
### NITROUS OXIDE

### edited by Michael Sheldin and David Wallechinsky with Saunie Salyer

A reprint of the classic 1973 book on everybody's favorite dental assistant, laughing gas. The "gas of paradise" has a rich history, beginning with its discovery in 1772 by Joseph Priestley, who also discovered oxygen during the same experiments. Starting in 1899, nitrous oxide was used for fun for fifty years. It was then that a dentist named Horace Wells started using it on patients during tooth extractions. "As its use as a pain killer spread, its use as an exhilirant was driven underground, fear of pleasure being one of the major cultural traits of the past century."

Besides the history of laughing gas, this book contains historical documents on the effects of the gas, including first-hand experimentation by William James, one of the most important figures in the history of psychology. There's also a chapter on safety precautions and a four-way conversation among people zonked out on N.O. Another section of the book looks at the effects of laughing gas, such as transcendence of space and time, a sense of sacredness and unity, and positive, peaceful feelings. Say, I suddenly realized I'm overdue for a trip to the dentist....

Ronin Publishing; $12.95
1973 (1992); softcover; 96 pp.

## OPIUM FOR THE MASSES:
### A PRACTICAL GUIDE TO GROWING POPPIES AND MAKING OPIUM

### by Jim Hogshire

Although the subtitle would lead you to believe that the focus of this book is the production of opium, a little more than half the book is devoted to the history, chemistry, and effects of this drug. "Fossilized poppy seeds and other archeological evidence show the opium poppy was used by Neanderthal man as long as 30,000 years ago." From there it went to Egypt, Greece, Rome, and other hot spots of antiquity. Famous people, such as Ben Franklin and Edgar Allan Poe, were users. Despite its somewhat romantic reputation, opium can lead to a living hell of an addiction, a fact that the author expressly points out. He also examines the legal battles surrounding opium, from the Opium Wars of the mid-1800s to the strange policies surrounding it today.

Finding opium poppies is probably easier than you think: "Opium poppies are available to the general public, commonly sold in craft stores and flower shops as bunches of dried heads. Normally these are used in floral decorations but they are still chock full of opium." Instructions are given for making poppy tea, laudanum (opium booze), and smoking opium. To ensure a fresh, constant supply, the book tells you how to grow your own poppies outdoors and indoors.

Loompanics Unlimited; $14.95
1994; softcover; 112 pp.

## PILLS-A-GO-GO

This twelve-page newsletter is devoted to pills, pills, and more pills. Over-the-counter, prescription, illegal, experimental—they're all here, along with some news about drugs in nonpill form. Issue #19 has an article about pharmacists, and it isn't too flattering. Pharmacists, the author says, are untrusting people who make you feel like a junky for getting a prescription filled. This distrust arises because pharmacy students spend five years and tons of money in a very hard course of study just to become pill-counters who are disliked by doctors and patients. "Doctors prescribe ready-made medicines, often by brand name. Doctors decide if a generic can be substituted. The pharmacist just gets the right bottle of pills and starts counting. A pigeon could do the pharmacist's job." Another article decodes prescription forms that doctors write.

*Pills-a-Go-Go* also prints book reviews and lots of short news items. Among the things you'll learn:

•Dr. Richard H. Teske, head of veterinary drugs at the Food and Drug Administration, is living up to the FDA's reputation for being back-asswards. "Since 1991 he's banned so many drugs for use on animals that vets have resorted to hoarding and appealing for 'compassionate use' permission to treat suffering animals."

•"Miles Laboratories agreed to stop paying pharmacists a thirty-five dollar bounty every time they talked a patient into switching blood pressure meds...."

•"Israeli scientists have mixed the opium alkaloid papaverine into a cream that can give men a boner."

•It appears that a side effect of Pfizer's blood-pressure pill Procardia is that it makes sperm unable to penetrate an ovum. In other words, the male birth control pill may be here! What I want to know is, why hasn't such incredible news made international headlines?

Pills-a-Go-Go
1202 E. Pike Street #849/Seattle, WA 98122-3934
Single issue: $2 or will trade zines
Four-issue sub: $12

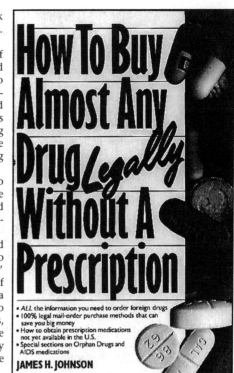

◄ *How To Buy Almost Any Drug...* by James H. Johnson

## RECEPTORS
### by Richard M. Restak, MD

*Taking control of your chemistry.*

There is a great debate raging about how much of an effect our neurochemicals have on who were are. Some people—who hate anything that smacks of biological determinism—say that they have little or no effect. Others, like the author, feel that our neurotransmitters basically *are* us. While this assumption makes me uneasy, it does lead us down an interesting path. The author examines the history of humanity's attempts to chemically alter itself. He ends up discussing what have elsewhere been called "neuromantics"—drugs that can change our mental capabilities and even our personalities to a distressing degree.

The author begins with a refresher course in the brain's structure and chemistry for those of you who slept through biology class. He briefly looks at the use of psychedelic plants through the ages. The world's first LSD trip, taken by acid inventor Albert Hofmann, is seen as a milestone in the history of neuromantics: "It was now clear that a chemical—furthermore, a chemical synthesized in a laboratory and taken in only the tiniest amounts—could exert an overwhelming effect on psychic functioning."

Antipsychotic agents were the next pre-neuromantics to come along. Lithium and chlorpromazine were found in the late 1940s to combat the effects of schizophrenia and the mania stage of manic-depression. Antidepressants and tranquilizers soon followed. The author goes on to look at the effects of the pseudo–designer drug MPPP, PCP, cocaine, opium, marijuana, nicotine, and caffeine on the brain and what these substances can tell us about ourselves.

The last part of the book looks at current and future research, showing how drugs can and will help mental disorders, memory loss, sexual functioning, hyperactivity, shyness, and that hollow, empty feeling many people experience. Finally, the author envisions the era of designer brains, when we can pick and choose the personality traits and mental abilities we want to a near-certain degree.

Bantam; $23.95
1994; hardcover; 228 pp.

# SECRETS OF METHAMPHETAMINE MANUFACTURE
## (THIRD EDITION)
### by Uncle Fester

A lot of "underground manuals" for performing illegal acts just don't stack up. They offer commonsense advice but hardly any hard-core instructions. This book is different. Uncle Fester gives detailed plans for making speed. He discusses several different ways to make it, on a small scale and on a large scale (for you entrepreneurs out there). One method involves using easily obtainable drugs—white crosses, Sudafed, and Dexatrim—as the raw materials.

Be warned, the instructions are detailed and call for a fair amount of knowledge about chemistry. Witness these steps for making phenylacetone, the precursor of meth: "Two 500 ml Erlenmeyer flasks are placed on the table, one marked A, the other marked B. The stop cock on the sep funnel is opened, and the water layer is drained into B. The top layer is poured into A. B is poured back into the sep funnel, and the 50 ml of benzene is added. The funnel is shaken for 15 seconds, then the water layer is drained back into B." Numerous diagrams of lab equipment and molecules are included. Fester makes sure to discuss the physical dangers of each chemical and the precautions you need to take to avoid getting busted.

Loompanics Unlimited; $24.95
1994; softcover; 196 pp.

# UNDERGROUND PSYCHEDELIC LIBRARY

The 1970s saw the height of drug booklet publishing. Tiny presses in California put out sixteen-page (usually) booklets with explicit instructions for making and using drugs. Ronin Publishing has gathered fourteen such booklets and one audiocassette into the Underground Psychedelic Library, yours for thirty bucks, which is only two dollars per booklet. Among the titles you will find:

•*The Marijuana Consumer's and Dealer's Guide.* Instructions for extracting lysergic acid amides from morning glory or Hawaiian wood rose seeds, making hashish from pot, converting inferior pot to supergrass, and extracting pure mescaline from peyote.

•*Dr. Atomic's Marijuana Multiplier.* Covers making pot two or three times more potent and producing hash, hash oil, and other stuff.

•*Ancient and Modern Techniques of Growing Extraordinary Marijuana.* Gives basics on cultivating wacky weed and goes on to reveal the growing secrets of India and Mexico and modern-day advances.

•*Marijuana Grower's Guide.* A sixty-minute cassette on indoor and outdoor growing from Mel Frank and Ed Rosenthal.

•*Drug Manufacture for Fun and Profit.* How to make DMT and Khala-Khij, an African aphrodisiac. Also, how to grow superior grass.

•*The Book of Acid.* How to make LSD from legal, available materials.

•*The Psilocybin Producer's Handbook.* Raising magic mushrooms in the privacy of your own home.

•*Peyote and Other Psychoactive Cacti.* How to find or raise psychedelic cacti, how to use them, how to extract mescaline, etc.

•*The Cocaine Tester's Handbook.* Explains many methods for testing the purity of cocaine and detecting the presence of various adulterants.

•*Freebase Cocaine.* Step-by-step instructions for freebasing coke.

•*Herbal Aphrodisiacs.* A guide to using herbal substances that enhance sexual performance and feelings.

•*Herbal Highs.* A guide to using natural, legal substances to get high. Covers wild cucumbers, morning glory, nutmeg, fly agaric, etc.

These titles are not available separately; they come only as a set.

Ronin Publishing; $29.95
Fourteen booklets, one cassette

Most publishers and zines in this chapter require that you be over twenty-one to buy their publications. Whenever you order anything from this chapter, send a statement that says, "I am over twenty-one years old" or "I am ___ years old" and *sign* and date it.

## SM

### BAD ATTITUDE:
#### LESBIAN EROTIC FICTION

Rude and crude leatherdykes with bad attitude! Uncompromising, yet containing a sense of fun, *Bad Attitude* confronts you with fiction like "Fucking My Bitch" by Karen Baggen and a full-page photo of a wicked-looking knife being pushed just inside a pussy (both in volume 8, issue 6). The main focus is on fiction and graphics, but there are letters, an advice column, and some nonfiction articles. "Cleaning Out My Closet: Lesbian Code" (in the above issue) is a funny article on the names lesbians have developed for themselves over the years: "She could be a...DIT, a (Dyke in Training). Or an FDA (Future Dyke of America). In any case, she's always a VT (Visual Treat) to see, especially when it's DL and DR, (Dykes to the Left and Dykes to the Right).... She speaks in tongues.... She's a Lesbyterian...." Well, I could go on forever, but you get the idea. Humor and pain mixed for an interesting treat.

Bad Attitude/PO Box 390110/Cambridge, MA 02139-0110
Single issue $6. Six-issue sub (one year) $30
Overseas 6-issue sub $50

## BOB FLANAGAN: SUPERMASOCHIST

Performance artist, poet, and supermasochist Bob Flanagan was born in 1952 with the genetic disease cystic fibrosis, which almost always causes an early death. In fact, Flanagan holds the record as the person who has lived the longest with fibrosis. During his life, as the disease has taken its toll on his body, Flanagan has decided that he's going to take his own toll on his body. He's going to push it to its outermost limits of endurance and see what lies there.

As Flanagan explains in his written piece "Why" (reprinted in this book): "Because it feels good; because it gives me an erection; because it makes me come; because I'm sick; because there was so much sickness; because I say FUCK THE SICKNESS; ...because I had awful stomach-aches and holding my penis made it feel better; because I felt like I was going to die..."

In six interviews Flanagan discusses his childhood, his disease, his body modification and manipulation, his writing and art, his philosophy on the body, pain, and death. The book contains more than one hundred photographs showing Flanagan doing some of the most extreme things imaginable to his frail body—hanging by his arms, blindfolded, gagged, with clothespins on his dick and a weight on his scrotum; pinning his scrotum to a butterfly board and inserting needles perpendicular to his urethra; hanging a ten-pound weight from his balls; nailing his dick to a board; having six needles inserted through his left nipple; and having his mouth sutured shut.

Flanagan is definitely one of the underground's more interesting inhabitants. RE/Search did a good job covering his exploits, but I wish they had included more of his writings. His books are next to impossible to get hold of.

RE/Search Publications; $14.99
1994; oversize softcover; 128 pp.; heavily illus.

### BRAT ATTACK

*Brat Attack*, "the zine for leatherdykes and other bad girlz," doesn't play nice. In "Child's Play" (issue #5), an almost too intense piece of writing, Wickie Stamps describes her brutal childhood and how it affected her sexuality. "What I Should Have Said" by Jen Johnson is a letter written by Samantha to Angela. Sammy is lusting after Angie, and fights very hard to keep her transgressive tendencies in check, but it's a lost cause: "I've wanted to tell you for so long How I've (Longed to fuck you up against the wall until those stick-in-the-ass neighbors of yours called the police and hid under their Kitchen table) wanted to get to know you better. (yeah, right.) I've always thought you deserved (TO BE TIED UP AND DRAGGED INTO MY ATTIC WHERE I CAN HAVE MY WAY WITH YOU WHETHER YOU LIKE IT OR NOT) beautiful things..." "Girls' Night Out" is a comic by Fish in which four tough grrrlz beat the shit out of men for kicks.

◄ *Bad Attitude*

*Rude and crude, yet containing a sense of fun!*

Lest you think *Brat Attack* is too rough, rest assured it does have a lot of humor. The comic "Dungeon Etiquette" has good rules for SM, such as "Be nice to your top: 'I BROUGHT YOU TWINKIES (sir)'" and "Be nice to your bottom: 'I'M GONNA BEAT YOU ANYWAY.'" There are also serious, less confrontational articles about life in women's prison, the lack of women of color in the SM scene, and experimenting with gender.

Brat Attack/PO Box 40754/San Francisco, CA 94140-0754
Current issue: $5
Three-issue sub: $12

### DIFFERENT LOVING:
#### AN EXPLORATION OF THE WORLD OF
#### EROTIC DOMINANCE AND SUBMISSION
### by Gloria G. Brame, William D. Brame, and Jon Jacobs

*Different Loving* is a detailed look at the practices involved in sadomasochism, dominance and submission, bondage and discipline, etc. Yes, it is written by outsiders, so it's not likely to be given much credence within the sexual subcultures it examines, but it is based on hundreds of interviews with practitioners. It also proves its worth by offering an unflinching, uncensored examination of what goes on, making it a good book for people who want to know more, people who might want to get involved. Of course, nothing can take the place of reading books and magazines, such as the ones in this section, that come from within the subculture itself. The problem is that these books and magazines may not cast as wide a net as this book, or they may assume a lot of prior knowledge and use slang, technical terms, and such that an outsider may not be familiar with.

The authors realize that the general vanilla population has negative stereotypes of people into SM and related activities. "Dominatrices are, for example, typically portrayed as destroyers of men... Female submissives are depicted as neurotic, self-destructive victims. And the very word sadist conjures the image of a criminal inflicting violent torture on helpless victims." The authors are intent on showing that SM is "safe, sane, and consensual." Its practitioners are as well adjusted as the population as a whole, they just have a different method of expressing their sexuality.

The initial chapters trace the development of SM as an

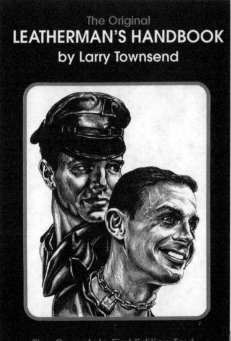

*The Original Leatherman's Handbook* ➤ by Larry Townsend

*A galvanizing force that opened up the world of leather.*

observed phenomenon, look at the formation of the leather subculture, explain some jargon, and look at basic principles. The second section of the book, "Imagination and Desire," covers power, erotic coercion, role-playing, humiliation, age-play, depersonalization, lifestyles, etc.

"The Pleasures of Discomfort" is the next section. It deals with bondage, spanking, whipping, hot wax and ash, clamps, fisting, tit torture, cock and ball torture, electricity, and more. Further sections deal with corsetting, tattooing, piercing, scarification, fetishes, erotic wrestling, transgenderism, golden showers, enemas, etc.

The book is filled with the actual words of the practitioners themselves—smaller quotes are embedded throughout the text and at least two long interviews follow every chapter. *Different Loving* is a good book to get, but it should be only a part of a balanced reading diet.

Villard (Random House); $25
1993; hardcover; 539 pp.

## LEATHERFOLK

A collection of twenty-eight essays about the gay SM and leather subculture that achieves a transcendence of sorts. The essays, taken as a whole, go beyond merely being insiders' accounts of the scene, and show the political, personal, spiritual, and—naturally—sexual aspects of SM. Samuel Steward (aka Phil Andros) reflects on his encounters with the legendary Dr. Kinsey. Arnie Kantrowitz looks at the role of the swastika in SM. Jack Fritscher examines the impact of the militant, hardcore posters of artist Chuck Arnett.

Carol Truscutt answers some basic SM questions. When discussing why people do SM in the first place, she says, "Whether we spin, ride swings, dance, receive communion, meditate, practice alpha wave control, get our tits tortured, whip ass, or fuck, the ecstasy we seek and achieve is the same kind of change of consciousness programmed into the genetic pattern of all human beings."

A groundbreaking and illuminating book.

Alyson Publications; $12.95
1991; softcover; 328 pp.; illus.

## THE MASTER'S MANUAL:
### A HANDBOOK OF EROTIC DOMINANCE
#### by Jack Rinella

A collection of Jack Rinella's columns on male leathersex. Approximately half the columns are about SM in general, and the other half are instructions for masters, although slaves would benefit from reading them, too. The author explains that SM is so wonderful because it's fun, it empowers the participants, it creates a bonding between partners, and it can lead to ecstatic experiences. "More and more, the SM experience is discussed in terms of ritual, alternate spaces, religious awakening, and bliss. How and why those spiritual events happen, and how often they happen, remains a mystery."

SM also lets us touch danger in a world that tries to repress it. "We are not allowed to feel. It is wrong to be angry. There is no space for the revelations of base instinct in today's sanitized world. But they remain there nevertheless, and they will confront us more often than we want." That's where leather comes in.

"Leather, in each of its various scenes, lets us get in touch with the primal issues of life and death, fear and bravery, violence and peace."

As far as concrete advice goes, Rinella covers safety considerations, necessary equipment (dildos, handcuffs, clothespins, catheters, etc.), larger optional equipment (cages, examination tables, etc.), dungeons, spanking, nipple torture, verbal abuse, golden showers, drugs, finding a slave, scenes that go wrong, and much more.

Daedalus Publishing Co; $14.95
1994; softcover; 199 pp.

## THE ORIGINAL LEATHERMAN'S HANDBOOK
### by Larry Townsend

*The Leatherman's Handbook* was published in 1972 by Olympia Press. It caused an immediate sensation and instantly became a classic. Back then, leather sexuality was happening in places, but it wasn't a full-fledged movement or subculture. It was a very hidden, basically invisible fringe element of gay sexuality. When Larry Townsend's book appeared on the scene, it proved to be a galvanizing force that opened up the world of leather to thousands of men. It was instrumental in the creation of the world of gay leathersex.

A second edition of *The Leatherman's Handbook* was published in 1974 and went out of print in the early 1980s. This reprint contains the complete original text of the first edition. As such, it makes no references to AIDS or safer sex, so be advised. It's also littered with expressions like "groovy" and "dig," so again, be prepared to stomach it.

The book covers bondage without SM, SM without bondage, whether to be a top or a bottom, equipment, finding a partner, motorcycles, booze and drugs, friendship, long-term relationships, gang bangs, golden showers, body shaving, long-term bondage, castration, dangers, and much more. Interspersed throughout Townsend's commentary are explicit vignettes, designed, I believe, for instruction and one-handed reading, in which Townsend's acquaintances recount their adventures.

LT Publications; $11.95
1972, 1993; softcover; 319 pp.

## THE Q LETTERS:
### TRUE STORIES OF SADOMASOCHISM
#### by Sir John

Sir John has been a dominant in the SM scene for more than two decades and, in an effort to demystify this form of sexuality, he has written his memoirs. *The Q Letters* (John's last name starts with "Q") is one of the most enlightening books on SM I've come across. Sir John reveals that there are actually several types of masochist. He's encountered several women who fall into each category, and, by telling about his adventures with each one, he sheds light on the different reasons people become submissives, as well as the reasons he became a dominant.

The "classic masochist" is someone who gets turned on and sexually gratified by pain. Paula is an example of this type. Sir John met her by answering an ad in *Confidential Flash*. When he first talked to her on the phone, she revealed her m.o.: "Most guys just want to fuck and I hate that, so I fight and fight and I only fuck the ones who beat me into it."

Karen is an example of an "O" (named after the main character of Pauline Réage's classic erotic novel, *The Story of O*): "She does not enjoy pain—she screams when she is whipped—but she knows that her Master derives pleasure from her pain and humiliation, and because she loves him, she offers him these gifts of her suffering." Karen became Sir John's twenty-four-hour-a-day slave, doing household chores with clothespins on her nipples, suspending herself naked and gagged so John would find her when he came to her apartment, performing oral sex on other men at John's command. "Being my total slave obsessed Karen.

She called me 'Sir' or 'Master' routinely, while I called her 'slave.' She would kiss my hand whenever we met in public and in private she would kneel and kiss my feet. She knelt next to me whenever I sat down, and began asking my permission to perform even the most routine acts."

Probably the most disturbing of John's liaisons was with Bonny, a "psychological masochist," who felt that she needed to be punished and humiliated. She didn't derive sexual pleasure from it, but was emotionally gratified. At her request, John would tie her up and whip her hard 150 to 200 times, during which she would pass out. She would end the session by going down on him. When John reveals the childhood incident that prompted Bonny's needs, it's pretty unsettling, but the real shocker comes when he realizes that she had only given him half the story.

Sir John also discusses the "classic submissive," the "challenger," and several women who don't fit into any category. Highly recommended.

Prometheus Books; $23.95
1993; hardcover; 198 pp.

## SENSUOUS MAGIC:
### A Guide for Adventurous Lovers
### by Pat Califia

Sensuous Magic is part manifesto, part psychological profile, and part nuts-and-bolts manual. It is directed at couples of any orientation who want to get into SM but don't really know what to do. In a very relaxed, conversational style, Califia effortlessly weaves together sections on communicating wants and needs, tying up your partner, tickling, applying pressure, delivering blows, etc., along with sections on the reasons for participating in SM, the psychology of SM scenes, safety precautions, anal and oral sex, and more. The end of the book contains a glossary, an annotated bibliography, and a resource guide for clubs, classes, videos, etc. This helpful, nonthreatening book is highly recommended to couples who are craving a sexual flavor besides vanilla.

A Richard Kasak Book; $12.95
1993; softcover; 185 pp.

## SEDUCED INTO SUBMISSION
### (VHS videocassette)

What actually happens when you have a session with a professional dominatrix? Mistress Jacqueline shows us in this video. Her client, Joseph, is a shoe salesman in a store that MJ frequents. He eventually gets up the nerve to become one of her slaves. We see them first in the lounge area discussing the basics. Joseph assures the Mistress that he wants to be her servant, and she teases him a little. The action moves to another room where Joseph, wearing only a G-string, has his hands cuffed behind his back. Jacqueline is done up in a nice leather and stud one-piece with thigh-high boots. She lays down the three rules for Joseph: 1) speak only when spoken to; 2) keep your eyes lowered—never make eye contact; and 3) never touch the Mistress in any way without permission. She then has Joseph lick and suck her boots from the toe to the top. Joe gets carried away and tries to keep going, licking Jacqueline's thigh. For this indiscretion she bends him over her knee and spanks the hell out of him.

Later, in the main dungeon, Joseph is tied up in an X-position, leaning back slightly. Jacqueline puts nipple clamps on him, tickles him with a feather, puts clothespins on his balls, and marks him up with a whip and riding crop. She unties Joseph and straps on a dildo. She makes Joe lick her ass, eat out her armpit, and suck her silicone. She moves around behind him and is about to mount him when the video ends, leaving Joseph's defloration to our imaginations.

Seduced into Submission is an authentic look at a ritual that is cloaked in secrecy. These are people who love and live what they're doing. Joseph's constant moans of ecstasy and pitiful subhuman groveling just can't be faked. The man is obviously loving every minute of it.

On the down side, the video's sound quality is pretty bad, and Mistress Jacqueline makes a mistake by *constantly* playing to the camera and looking offstage, instead of ignoring the camera and crew and going ahead as if she and Joseph were the only two there. Still, if you want to see a real-life pro dominatrix in action, and not some porno starlet pretending to be into SM, check out *Seduced*. It's the real thing.

Mistress Jacqueline; $49.95
VHS videocassette; over 60 min.

## WHIPS & KISSES:
### Parting the Leather Curtain
### by Mistress Jacqueline, as told to
### Catherine Tavel and Robert H. Rimmer

This is the autobiography of Mistress Jacqueline, star of *Seduced into Submission* (above) and allegedly the most popular dominatrix on the West Coast. She grew up as an overachieving and slightly mischievous girl in an abusive Jewish family in the Bronx. While at college, the Mistress went through her hippie period, smoking pot, engaging in free love, and protesting the Vietnam War. She describes her unsatisfying relationships with selfish guys, her being raped, and her crummy marriage.

It isn't until about page 100 that Jacqueline gets down to the nitty-gritty. She describes her newfound abandon after her divorce, and the night that changed her life. She responded to an ad in a sex paper and got spanked by Sir William. She formed a steady relationship with William, and he introduced her to the world of SM. Soon Mistress was pulling down some serious bucks working as a submissive at The Chalet, where men would pay to watch her masturbate, spank her, and tie her up. When all the dominant women quit The Chalet, Jacqueline was forced to become a dominant and discovered she was quite good at it.

During this time, she had become an alcoholic and cokehead. After getting busted for possession, she cleaned herself up and set out to become the dominant dominatrix of California. Indeed, the Mistress is proof positive that sex and capitalism were made for each other. Not only does she have a large clientele, she puts out videos, magazines, an interactive CD-ROM, and more. She also has 900-numbers and sells her worn panties. You can get her catalog from her address in Appendix B.

Prometheus Books; $23.95
1991; hardcover; 237 pp.

## TIES THAT BIND:
### The SM/Leather/Fetish Erotic Style—
### Issues, Commentary and Advice
### by Guy Baldwin, MS

Guy Baldwin is a gay leatherdude and a psychotherapist who has many clients in the SM/leather/fetish communities. In this book, mainly a collection of his columns for *Drummer*, he reflects on the needs and problems of people into radical sexuality, mainly SM. He addresses issues such as "SM correctness," discovering your needs, switching between being a top and being a bottom, group SM, relationship troubles, dealing with friends and family, practitioners who were abused as children, the needs of tops, the subtleties of consent, drugs, and the ecstatic, transcendental SM experience.

In an examination of master/slave relationships, Baldwin shows that they come in many varieties: "...I have seen a Master with several slaves. Some slaves have more than one Master. Some slaves have slaves, and some Masters are themselves slaves to yet other Masters. Another slave I know has a lover (mostly vanilla) and a Master as well—each knows and likes the other."

Baldwin discusses problems with tops. "Most dangerous are the Tops who play from an angry place. They somehow get the idea that bottoms are people whose lot in life is to be punching bags for Tops who have had a bad day at the office or a rough time on the freeway." Some bottoms can also be troubled. "Bottoms have lots of power too, and they are in danger of harm-

*Dressing for Pleasure*

*PVC, leather, Latex, Rubber— you know who you are.*

ing when they don't know it, don't acknowledge it, don't want it, or don't respect it."

Daedalus Publishing Co; $14.95
1993; softcover; 239 pp.

# CLOTHING FETISH

## DRESSING FOR PLEASURE

*Dressing* is devoted to PVC, leather, latex, rubber, and fishnet. Like its companion publication, the *Rubberist* (below), it is printed in color on slick paper and more than half the pictures come from readers, so they lack a professional quality.

Issue #23 featured a well-done photo spread of six women who are in the scene, a look at Mackintoshes (trenchcoats), an article on boots, lots of letters, news items, personals, and more.

G&M Fashions Ltd.
PO Box 42/Romford Essex RM1 2ED
ENGLAND
Single issue: UK: £10; elsewhere: £11
Four-issue sub: UK: £36; elsewhere: £40

## THE LEATHER CONTEST GUIDE:
### A HANDBOOK FOR PROMOTERS, CONTESTANTS, JUDGES, AND TITLEHOLDERS
### by Guy Baldwin

Anyone involved in any way with leather contests will find this unique guide to be extremely useful. The author, a psychotherapist and leatherman, won the titles of Mr. Leather 1989 and Mr. National Leather Association 1989, so he obviously knows what he's talking about.

The first and longest section of the book is about how to organize, promote, and pull off the contest. The first thing to do is decide what the point of your contest is. Is it an informal event designed to bring more people to your bar? Is it for charity? Is your winner going to go on to higher levels of competition? What you decide will set the tone for everything else. The author discusses location, financing, finding contestants, prizes, scripts, emcees, judges, scoring, and more.

The section on judging tells how to score interviews, casual wear segments, jockstrap/skinshow segments, fantasy segments, the full-leather segment, general etiquette, etc.

Possible contestants will want to read the chapter on how to win a leather contest. "The 'I'm hot and you're not' attitude is a quick ticket to last place. Except for the occasional fluke, muscles and shapeliness no longer make up for bad attitude, no smarts, or no social skills." Other topics include how to handle being nearly nude, your stage skills, winning the judges over, the fantasy segment, etc. When you win the contest, you can turn to the last chapter on how to be a good titleholder. You'll learn about coping with publicity, handling promoters, giving autographs, traveling, leadership, and so on.

The appendixes contains sample press releases, judging forms, scripts, etc.

Daedalus Publishing Co; $12.95
1993; softcover; 139 pp.

## RUBBERIST

If the sight of someone in a leather bodysuit and a gas mask turns you on, then this is the magazine for you. Printed in full color on slick paper, *Rubberist* publishes scads of pictures of men and women wearing a surprising variety of outfits and masks. Rubber outfits in issue #17 include French maid costumes, a nurse's outfit, skintight black bodysuits, red aprons, a thin orange bodysuit, what looks basically like a Hefty garbage bag, and lots more. The masks range from simple rubber with eye and nose holes to World War II surplus gas masks and sleek modern gas masks.

Although production values are high, quality of the photos can be quite low. The *Rubberist* apparently doesn't do much of its own shooting—it relies mainly on pictures sent in by its enthusiastic readership. These photos are sometimes blurry and lack the aesthetic appeal (form, balance, etc.) of pros' shots. Also, the people in these pictures are usually not especially attractive. I guess the point is that we're not seeing a bunch of charge-by-the-hour walking mannequins in these outfits, but rather people who are really into it, making for a more authentic glimpse at the rubber/gas mask scene.

G&M Fashions Ltd.
PO Box 42/Romford Essex RM1 2ED/ENGLAND
Single issue: UK: £10; elsewhere: £11
Four-issue sub: UK: £36; elsewhere: £40

## SKIN TWO

I had heard a lot of great things about *Skin Two* before I actually received an issue, and I have to admit that the hype was completely justified. *Skin Two* does for fetish mags what Ferrari did for cars—make everything else look lame by comparison. *ST* is an oversized, ultraglossy, full-color, coffee-table-quality magazine brimming with top-notch photography and writing. The focus is on clothing, but don't expect the same old rubber pants and lacy corselettes you've seen everywhere else. That stuff looks like church clothing compared to what's in here—mesh, chain mail, fishnet, PVC, spikes, metallic material, ceramics, rubber, lace, plastic, latex, velvet, and I-don't-know-what combined in hundreds of colors, textures, and styles to create some of the most outlandish clothes of all time. There's a wasp bodysuit, leather nun's habit, futuristic/alien outfits, and a woman with sequins attached to her flesh, all of which must be seen to be believed.

*ST* covers fashion shows and "perv" events, spotlights designers, photographers, and other artists, looks at different aspects of the scene, and provides killer review and resource sections—five pages alone list way more than a hundred mail-order clothing dealers. Plus, the ads are just as funky as the magazine itself. Get it.

Tim Woodward Publishing Ltd.
BCM Box 2071/London WC1N 3XX/ENGLAND
Single issue: £10; Subscriptions: £55 (US); £35 (UK);
£45 (Europe); Accepts checks drawn on UK banks,
Eurocheque, Visa, MasterCard, and American Express

## THE BEST OF SKIN TWO
### edited by Tim Woodward

This is a collection of the best articles to have appeared in *Skin Two* so far. Tim Burton talks about his use of fetish imagery in *Batman Returns*, Pat Califia defends lesbian SM against attackers. Others tell us about the bondage art film *Mano Destra*, the ideal mistress, SM clubs worldwide, SM and British law, Bettie Page, safe SM, and other topics that represent *Skin Two*'s eclectic focus on art, politics, psychology, and hard-edged advice. The book's biggest drawback is that it is all text—none of the magazine's trademark beautiful photography is included. Of course, when you realize that *Skin Two* is about $20 an issue, getting this collection of articles for thirteen bucks is a steal.

A Richard Kasak Book (Masquerade Books); $12.95
1993; softcover; 188 pp.

# GENDER-BENDING

### CANDY DARLING
#### by Candy Darling

A smattering of journal entries and letters written by Candy Darling, the male transvestite, from 1971 to 1973, the time in which she made several movies, including two by Andy Warhol. The entries are strange, personal, boring, and nonsensical. Taken together they paint a picture of a lonely, confused, but hopeful person. "MY 1 YEAR PLAN/It matters not what men see. For they see but what is put in front of them./I'm a thousnd [sic] different people. Every one is real." "And I know I have a look of refinement and nobility which is sometimes thought of as being angelic and athereal [sic]. Perhaps people think my touch will heal them. Why must I be deified? It is such a burden."

Hanuman Books; $5.95
1992; mini-paperback; 144 pp.

### DRAG GAGS
#### by Ralph Judd

This loving tribute to female impersonation in the movies contains sixty stills from 1914 to 1949. Each shot is accompanied by the name of the movie, the actor(s) in drag, studio, date, and a very corny caption. One shot features Stan Laurel, obviously on stilts, wearing a dress in the movie *Sugar Daddies*. The caption reads, "Who's your tailor...Omar, the tent maker?" Another shows Melvyn Douglas with his hair frizzed in *The Amazing Mr. Williams*. The caption is, "They 86'd me from Vidal Sassoon's." The back of the book contains indexes by movie and by actor.

Ralph Judd Communications; $7.95
1991; softcover; 64 pp.; heavily illus.

### DRAG GAGS RETURN
#### by Ralph Judd

Sixty more images from the rich tradition of male transvestism in the movies. Little Scotty Beckett, in a dress, is beside Mom and Dad. The caption: "I wanted a boy. You wanted a girl. Now we're both happy." Cornball humor isn't my thing, but if you like it, or if you like vintage movies, you'll groove on this book.

Ralph Judd Communications; $8.95
1992; softcover; 64 pp.; illus.

### GENDER PENDING

From the man who brought you *Drag Gags* comes this set of ten postcards showing vintage movie posters in which men and women cross-dress. Among the stars represented are Shemp Howard, Nell O'Day, Vera Reynolds, Julian Eltinge, Rosemary Thebe, Ben Turpin, and Neal Burns. The backs of the cards give the actor's name, movie title, studio, date, and a brief description.

Ralph Judd Communications; $4.95
1994; 10 postcards

### HOLLYWOOD ANDROGYNY
#### (SECOND EDITION)
#### by Rebecca Bell-Metereau

*Hollywood Androgyny* is an overview of the rich cinematic tradition of reversing or blurring sexual identities. Its most obvious form is transvestism, as in the *Crying Game*, but it can also take the form of androgyny—Sigourney Weaver in *Alien3*—or nontraditional sex roles, featured in *Three Men and a Baby*. The

author covers all this ground and more.

She takes us all the way back to 1914, when Charlie Chaplin gave perhaps the first, and one of the best, female impersonations in cinema. In *The Masquerader*, Chaplin's character is an actor who loses his job and disguises himself as a woman to get it back. "Chaplin's imitations of women are extremely convincing because of his small stature and the delicacy and beauty of his features. More important, though, is the fact that he is willing to become a woman to the best of his considerable ability. He does not hesitate to adopt female mannerisms, to wear makeup, or to flirt with the men as enthusiastically as a true coquette would do."

The author makes an interesting observation about male buddy team pictures. "When one sex is excluded from a film, often a character will take on its attributes.... In *Thunderbolt and Lightfoot* (1974), which has a minimum of women, Jeff Bridges first takes on the female role in a symbolic fashion, behaving in a supportive, submissive fashion, and later putting on women's clothes to help his friends in their scheme."

The section on *Alien* also offers some insights. Reviewers were generally hostile to the film, although, looking back on it, it's a good movie and there's really nothing to trash it for. The author thinks it has to do with the fact that gender roles were trashed, most noticeably by having a powerful female character who is smart and kicks ass. "Like the alien, half mechanical and half organic, Weaver's character is also alien to our expectations for the genre because she is not stunning, stunned, or simpering." Other gender reversals included a female computer, "Mother," with a breathy, very feminine voice and a man (played by John Hurt) "giving birth" to a baby alien.

The book covers much more, including *Dressed to Kill, The Rocky Horror Picture Show, Psycho, Tootsie, Blue Velvet, Thelma and Louise*, Betty Grable, Marlene Dietrich, Divine, and Grace Jones. Besides cataloging cinematic gender-bending, the author does a good job of interpreting the causes, meanings, and effects of this basic element of movies.

Columbia University Press; $16
1993; softcover; 345 pp.; illus.

◄ *SKIN TWO*
(See page 76)

*Does for fetish mags what Ferarri did for cars.*

### THE MORGAN MYSTIQUE:
#### MORGAN HOLLIDAY'S ESSENTIAL GUIDE TO LIVING, LOVING, AND LIP GLOSS
#### by Morgan Holliday with Peter Hawkins

Drag queen Morgan Holliday offers detailed instructions for men who want to look like women. The majority of the book is on make-up. "The face is 70% of the total illusion. You can have the best coiffed wig, a fabulous outfit and be accessorized to the hilt, but if your make-up is not up to snuff, you may as well stay home." Be warned, Holliday doesn't go for the "less is more" philosophy. "My approach to make-up combines a natural look with versatility. I don't pretend that I'm not wearing make-up." In fact he does wear too much make-up, especially rouge. He has that freshly-slapped-across-the-face look, but if that's your approach, too, you're in luck.

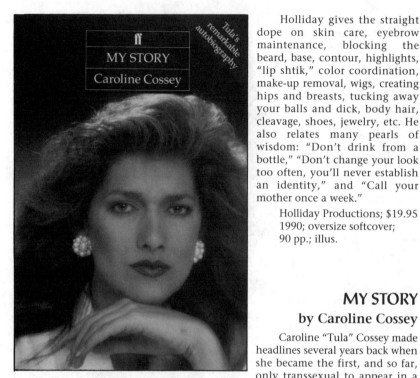

ff
MY STORY
Caroline Cossey

*Tula's remarkable autobiography*

*My Story
by Caroline
Cossey*

*Transexual
adventures of
a Bond girl.*

Holliday gives the straight dope on skin care, eyebrow maintenance, blocking the beard, base, contour, highlights, "lip shtik," color coordination, make-up removal, wigs, creating hips and breasts, tucking away your balls and dick, body hair, cleavage, shoes, jewelry, etc. He also relates many pearls of wisdom: "Don't drink from a bottle," "Don't change your look too often, you'll never establish an identity," and "Call your mother once a week."

Holliday Productions; $19.95
1990; oversize softcover;
90 pp.; illus.

## MY STORY
### by Caroline Cossey

Caroline "Tula" Cossey made headlines several years back when she became the first, and so far, only transsexual to appear in a *Playboy* pictorial. It turns out that this former man had also been the model in a Smirnoff ad and was James Bond's plaything in *For Your Eyes Only*.

In her autobiography Tula tells about her childhood and adolescence as a boy, feeling confused and isolated. By the time she was a young man, she had realized she was gay and, after moving to London, started to cross-dress, earning herself a job as a showgirl at the Latin Quarter club. Later, she was swept off her feet and into the lap of luxury by a wealthy Kuwaiti man. She eventually left him and got a sex-change operation. She started a modeling career and soon landed a job on the British show *3-2-1*, but the press got wind that Tula had once been a man and attempted to "out" her. However, they couldn't get any conclusive proof, so they backed off for the time being. They waited till Tula had landed the role of Bond's main squeeze before the *News of the World* tabloid declared "James Bond Girl Was a Boy."

Later, Tula would become involved with a man who didn't know about her past. When he proposed to her, she told him the truth. He accepted her anyway, and they married but decided not to tell his conservative Jewish family of Tula's sex change. Once again the tabloids broke the news, and Tula's in-laws freaked. Her husband left her and had their marriage annulled on the grounds that Tula was still technically considered a man. The British government dissolved the marriage, and Tula took the case to the European Court in Strasbourg, which ruled that Tula was still legally a man and that she could not be allowed to marry.

Since that experience, Tula has become an ardent supporter of transsexual rights. "I had never wanted to stand up and be counted as a transsexual, but now that everyone knew the truth, I felt I had to put in my own plea for tolerance and understanding."

Faber and Faber; $12.95
1991; softcover; 225 pp.; illus.

## TRANSFORMATION

A multifaceted, slick magazine for "men who enjoy being women." Covers all aspects of TV/TS with practical transformation tips, profiles and interviews, news and events, video reviews (mainly porn), book reviews, cartoons, and nonexplicit pictorials. Although there is some nudity, this is definitely not porn. It is a very well-done magazine for any man who crosses society's gender line.

Transformation/PO Box 459/Orange, CA 92666
Single issue: $15.50
One-year sub (4 issues): $40

## TRANSVESTITE CATALOG

Full-color, slick, forty-five-page catalog filled with clothes for the discriminating male cross-dresser. Lots of petticoats, corsets, lycra and satin dresses, bondage gear, and shoes, plus extras like medical adhesive, form-shaping undergarments, a breast-form bra, and female hormones.

Transformation/PO Box 459/Orange, CA 92666
Catalog: $25.50

## TV/TS TAPESTRY JOURNAL

A thick, well-done magazine for "all persons interested in cross-dressing & transsexualism." It's a very honest, open forum for people to express their concerns and share experiences regarding the crossing and blurring of gender. The topics covered usually relate to acceptance and nonacceptance, trying to change attitudes, legal barriers, etc. In the article "Lessons from Gender Explorers" by Rev. John Eric Gibbons (in issue #12), the author discusses how what is considered masculine changes over time: "I could never figure out that framed photograph of my father at age five, the one that shows him in a frilly white dress, page-boy haircut and more bangs than Mamie Eisenhower. Is that the same guy who ranted about manliness when I grew my hair into a ponytail down my back? We like our reality small and neat."

The *Tapestry* also contains a directory of organizations and services, ads, and personal listings. The International Foundation for Gender Education, the group that publishes *Tapestry*, also puts out a small catalog of publications that I'm sure they'd send along with an issue. I'll list the basic subscription rate. You can write if you're interested in becoming a supporter of the Foundation.

Single issue: $12
Four-issue subscription: $40 (USA and Puerto Rico); Canada, Mexico, overseas surface mail: $55; overseas air mail: $65

# PORNOGRAPHY

## ASIA BLUE

Tired of your run-of-the-mill homegrown porn. Do you have a more *internationale* taste in sleaze? Then Asia Blue is your catalog. As the name suggests, you can get hardcore videos from Japan, China, the Philippines, Thailand, Taiwan, Singapore, etc. They also carry videos from Europe—Italy, Germany, France, Hungary—as well as Brazil, Canada, and, for those of you feeling patriotic, the good ol' US of A.

The porn is all hetero except for some lesbian tapes, and there is some "specialty" stuff—pregos, pornonation, she-males, and hairy girls. Most is pro but there is a good deal of amateur.

The catalog contains hundreds of films with censored stills from each one and those ridiculous capsule descriptions you know and love.

Astral Ocean Cinema
PO Box 931753, Cherokee Avenue/Hollywood, CA 90093
Catalog: $5

## CAUGHT LOOKING:
### FEMINISM, PORNOGRAPHY, AND CENSORSHIP
### (THIRD EDITION)
### by Caught Looking, Inc.

This classic and daring collection of articles and photographs is based on the premise that pornography isn't the cause of rape, domestic violence, and the general oppression of women. On the contrary, porn can be a liberating device, allowing women to express their own sexuality. The editors want women to be "creators, explorers, and engineers in every realm of life, including the sexual."

*Caught Looking* remains the premiere feminist defense of porn because of its sheer guts. In "Among Us, Against Us" Pat Califia rails against the "new Puritans." "Material which exists for the sole or primary purpose of turning someone on is illegal. There is no freedom of sexual speech." Later she writes, "The antipornography movement espouses a very traditional role of women's sexuality. Women do not (according to them) enjoy pornography, casual sex, genital sex, or sex outside the context of a romantic relationship.... This Victorian imagery—pure women controlling the vile, lustful impulses of men—is one of the feminine stereotypes the women's movement should be working against."

Annie Sprinkle is even more blunt in her "ABC Study of Sexual Lust and Deviations." The letter S is for "Spread Shot": "We have a desire/to spread our thighs/For everyone to/cast their eyes./No one has the right/to make that taboo,/so Women Against Pornography,/fuck you!"

The book is liberally illustrated with multiple photos on every page. The sex comes in all shapes and sizes—gay, lesbian, straight, masturbation, SM, etc. And these images aren't one bit coy, baby. As often as not, they are graphic representations, including close-ups of penetration of every orifice, come shots, spread legs, and raging hard-ons.

LongRiver Books; $15.95
1986, 1992; oversize softcover; 96 pp.; heavily illus.

## COMING ATTRACTIONS:
### THE MAKING OF AN X-RATED VIDEO
### by Robert J. Stoller and I.S. Levine

This collaboration between sexologist Robert Stoller and porn creator Ira Levine is a series of interviews with the people making an adult film. Stoller and Levine pick the brains of the director, producer, writer, editor, and performers of *Stairway to Paradise*.

At one point Levine is talking about his script-writing troubles: "[Writer Jim] Holliday got so mad about one word change [made later in editing]. The line was, 'Performing sex with members of your own sex.' We changed that to 'gender.' He seized upon it as a prime example of how my Hollywood background made me unsuited to write porn scripts." Stoller: "Why?" Levine: "Because the lunchbucket audience wants to hear the word *sex* as many times in one sentence as is humanly possible."

In another interview, Stoller, Levine, and porno star Nina Hartley are watching the final cut of the movie. Hartley offers some interesting insights into the bodily aesthetics of pornography when she discusses one of her colleagues: "She also had cheek implants, and because of that, she looks really good giving head. She looks really good sucking a cock. It's amazing. The lines of her face are graphic art. She looks great with a dick in her mouth. [Laugh.] She really does. I look at her giving head, and she looks so pretty." Stoller: "That's an interesting thought." Levine: "It improves a lot of people, actually."

The conversations also cover a lot of technicalities—how to film different positions, various camera lenses, editing to cover up goofs, using stand-in penises, etc. If you've ever wondered how a skin flick really gets made, you need to get your hairy hands on this book.

Yale University Press; $32
1993; hardcover; 246 pp.

## DIRTY LOOKS:
### WOMEN • PORNOGRAPHY • POWER
### edited by Pamela Church Gibson and Roma Gibson

A collection of essays by women opposed to censorship. Quasi-academic in tone, these essays are out to prove that the issues surrounding pornography are "more complex and more interesting" than the knee-jerk antiporn crusaders would have us believe. Psychology professor Lynn Segal takes a hard look at the belief that pornography causes violence toward women. An examination of the research indicates that *violent* porn may cause *some* men *sometimes* to take a more accepting attitude toward rape. (Recent research shows most men react with anxiety, depression, and revulsion to scenes of sexual cruelty.) The research also indicates that it is probably the violence itself, and not the sexual explicitness, that is to blame for increased callousness. Further, the violence doesn't *cause* these attitudes but may exacerbate them if they're already present. Finally, just because a man answers a questionnaire in a lab that indicates an acceptance of rape doesn't mean that he would actually commit such an act. Segal concludes, "It is time for feminists, and their supporters, who want to act against men's greater use of violence and sexual coercion, and their continuing social dominance, to abandon the search for some spurious causal link with 'pornography'—however we define it."

Linda Williams, author of *Hard Core*, argues that as the definitions of "obscenity" have relaxed and hard-core porn has become common, the new enemy has become the pornography of "sexual minorities"—gays, lesbians, bisexuals, and sadomasochists. Jennifer Wicke looks at academia's newfound fascination with pornography. Erotic/fetish photographer Grace Lau talks about the meaning and the fun that lie behind her art. Other essays examine transgender porn, performance sex artist Annie Sprinkle, Asian porn, and the history of porno films.

British Film Institute; $18.95
1993; softcover; 238 pp.; illus.

## DOING RUDE THINGS:
### THE HISTORY OF THE BRITISH SEX FILM 1957–1981
### by David McGillivray

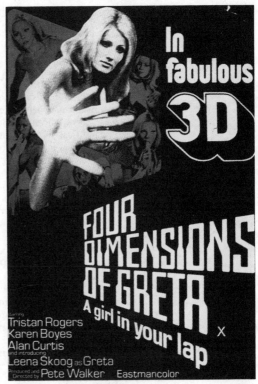

The sex film was a genre that flourished in Great Britain for about twenty-five years, starting in 1957. Such films were shown in practically every theater in Britain and became better known than musicals and Westerns. Sex films, as the term is used here, doesn't refer to hard-core porn, which was illegal at the time and is still not very common in Britain. Instead, sex films were soft-core tease-o-ramas. They showed partial or complete nudity and, later on, simulated sex. As the author freely admits, these films sucked. "They were characterised by inane writing, hack direction, amateurish performances, technical inadequacy, and a consequent deficiency of entertainment value." He lists only three sex films that could even be considered "competently made." So why write a book about them? Because they were so popular and because they represent an ignored aspect of cinema, since there had never been a book devoted to them.

The first sex film was *Nudist Paradise*, shot on location at a nudist camp. The British censorship board required that all the early sex films be shot at nudist camps to preserve the illusion that the intent was more documentary than erotic. The sex film industry moved on to dramas, comedies, and "documentaries" such as *Groupie Girl, The Wife Swappers, It Could Happen to You* (allegedly a warning to teenagers about V.D.), *London in the Raw, My Husband in Panties*, and hundreds more.

*Emmanuelle in Soho*, released in 1981, was the last sex film. By that time the genre was at the end of a slow death owing to lack of audiences and a hostile financial climate. The death blow

*Doing Rude Things* by David McGillivray

*British sex movies: Soft-core tease-o-rama!*

was given by the Conservative government, which discouraged the making of such films, shut down theaters (and the entire sex industry) in Soho, and finally withdrew government subsidies for filmmaking.

*Doing Rude Things* has an appendix containing capsule biographies/filmographies of the sixty-five most important people involved with sex films. The book is liberally illustrated with movie stills and posters containing tons of T&A.

Sun Tavern Fields; £9.95
1992; softcover; 141 pp.; heavily illus.

## THE INVENTION OF PORNOGRAPHY:
### OBSCENITY AND THE ORIGINS OF MODERNITY, 1500–1800
### edited by Lynn Hunt

Pornography—explicit visual or written sexual images designed to arouse lust—has only been considered a distinct category of art and literature since the 1800s. To be sure, there had been explicit sexual material around for centuries, but "pornography was almost always an adjunct to something else until the middle or end of the eighteenth century. In early modern Europe, that is, between 1500 and 1800, pornography was most often a vehicle for using the shock of sex to criticize religious and political authorities."

Porn came into existence as the Western world came into the modern age. It has ties to the Renaissance, the Enlightenment, and other such movements. "Writers and engravers of pornography came out of the demimonde of heretics, freethinkers, and libertines who made up the underside of those formative Western developments."

The ten essays in this book cover the materialist philosophy of porn, prostitution in porn, and the political meaning of porn in sixteenth-century Italy and seventeenth- and eighteenth-century France and England. The essays are accompanied by dozens of pornographic illustrations from the periods in question.

If you learn nothing else from this book, remember this from the essay "Obscenity and the Origins of Modernity": "Pornography was not [always] a given; it was defined over time and by the conflicts between writers, artists, and engravers on the one side and spies, policemen, clergymen, and state officials on the other. Its political and cultural meanings cannot be separated from its emergence as a category of thinking, representation, and regulation."

Zone Books (MIT Press); $26.95
1993; hardcover; 411 pp.; illus.

## THE JAGUAR AND THE ANTEATER:
### PORNOGRAPHY DEGREE ZERO
### by Bernard Arcand

A dense book that takes an unusual approach to the study of pornography. Arcand uses anthropology to examine the meaning of porn, especially as it exists today. "The work of an anthropologist generally proceeds in reverse, beginning with a case that is incontestably modern and real, and proceeding to show that the questions that underlie it have always been known and have sometimes even been answered somewhere else and often long ago." Arcand believes the South American myths involving the jaguar and the anteater provide the answer. The jaguar is seen as a hard-living, supremely sexual being, while the anteater is more content to stay away from any kind of interaction. Porn appeals to the anteater in us, the part of us that wants a comfortable isolation that entails no social obligations.

Along the way to this unique conclusion, the author offers interesting takes on the problems of defining pornography, the people who have attacked and defended it, and how it fits in our capitalist society.

Verso; $29.95
1993; hardcover; 286 pp.

## MOVIE BUFF CHECKLIST:
### A HISTORY OF MALE NUDITY IN THE MOVIES (4TH ED)
### by Marvin Jones

This book functions mainly as a guide to all the male nude scenes in mainstream movies released in the United States. The almost two thousand scenes are broken down by actor and contain the name of the movie, the nudity contained (rear, front, side, or brief), the movie's date, and an extremely brief description. For example, under Dustin Hoffman we find "*Straight Time*/Rear/1978/Prison shower scene." The entry for Cory Haim reads, "*Blown Away*/Rear/1992/Good exposure in several love scenes." In one of Robert De Niro's entries we read that he did a frontal shot in *1900* (1977) consisting of "Brief exposure in sex-play scene with prostitute." Of course, most of the actors listed aren't nearly as famous, but you get the idea.

The first part of the book contains an exhaustive history of male nudity in the movies, but the discussion expands to include all of pop culture (magazines, album covers, theater, ads, etc.). This book is profusely illustrated with uncensored rear and front pictures of actors in the buff. Some of the better-known subjects include Douglas Fairbanks Jr., Arnold Schwarzenegger, Beau and Jeff Bridges, Don Johnson, Al Pacino, Richard Gere, and Johnny Depp.

Campfire also produces several video compilations of male nudity in the movies, as well as several other nonporno videotapes devoted to nekkid dudes. Write for info.

Campfire Video; $19.95
1993; oversize softcover; 236 pp.

## MY LIFE AS A PORNOGRAPHER:
### AND OTHER INDECENT ACTS
### by John Preston

John Preston has created some of the most famous gay male erotica every written—*Mr. Benson*, the Alex Kane series, the Master series, and much more. As a pornographer dealing with gay sex and SM, he has been on the front line of the battle for sexual freedom. This book collects seventeen of his essays.

In the title essay, Preston writes, "It is much more interesting to be a pornographer than to be any other kind of writer." Why? The sex. When you turn people on with your stories, they automatically want to sleep with you. While this can be fun and interesting—like when a reporter masturbated at Preston's feet at the end of an interview—it does have its down side. People think *you* are those incredible characters that you create and are disappointed when you don't live up to their expectations. Also, Preston found out that some people will stoop to impersonation. "Someone was using my name to get laid!"

Preston's uncompromising attitude about sexuality rings out in his essay on what it means to be gay and proud: "It meant telling the truth. It meant saying that our lives were sexy and worth living. It meant we weren't going to lie anymore. It meant we weren't going to be part of the system of silence and suppression that left women and men so alone that they couldn't find a reason to go on living. It meant dressing up and flaunting it on Boylston Street and Fifth Avenue and Market Street and Santa Monica Boulevard and Main Street. It meant saying to the whole world: Fuck you. In your face. Get out of my life. Look at it and wish you had it. *That's why there's gay pride, goddamn it!*"

"A Modest Proposal for the Support of the Pornographic Arts" suggests two ways to help out pornographers. The first is to get editors and publishers to pay more: "We are grossly underpaid, and then have to live with the impression that we just do it for the money." The other suggestion is something everyone who reads porn can do: "They should put out for pornographers." After all, "The way to get better pornography is to give pornographers better sex."

Other essays sound off on race in porn, the lives of people in the sex industry, gay porn pioneer Sam Steward, men's underwear, and more.

A Richard Kasak Book (Masquerade Books); $12.95
1993; softcover; 266 pp.

## PORN:
### MYTHS OF THE TWENTIETH CENTURY
### by Robert J. Stoller, M.D.

Sexologist Robert Stoller, co-author of *Coming Attractions* (above), believes that studying the feelings and beliefs of people hired to act out a culture's fantasies can lead to important insights about that culture. Stoller focuses on heteroporn by interviewing several current and former stars and directors. The interviews are very long and have their interesting and dull moments.

Bill Margold, a porn actor, comments on the porn industry: "We're the last rebels in society. At least we're better than the stupid terrorists who go around blowing up people. No one ever died from an overdose of pornography." About porn actors, he says, "We're pieces of meat. I have referred to my cohorts as pieces of meat, and they don't like being called pieces of meat, but we are indeed pieces of meat. Because without the appendage, we are of no value whatsoever."

You might think that getting paid to boff all day in front of a camera would be the good life, but I guess it isn't that easy. In a classic moment during an interview, a female porn star named Happy and her boyfriend Jeff get into an argument. He says he has a problem with her line of work. He's jealous, not because she's banging other guys, but because she's doing what he always wanted to do—work in adult films. Happy: "What's holding you back or preventing you from taking charge of your dream [to be a porn star] and making it become a reality?" Jeff: "Because I don't have the balls for it." Happy: "Why?" Jeff: "I don't know." Happy: "Are you scared?" Jeff: "Yeah." Happy: "Don't you think I'm scared? I am, I'm terrified, I am." OK, so they're not the most eloquent orators on earth, but at least you do get some insight into the minds of porn stars.

Yale University Press; $14
1991; softcover; 228 pp.

## THE SEX PANIC:
### WOMEN, CENSORSHIP, AND "PORNOGRAPHY"

This little booklet put out by the National Coalition Against Censorship is a report on their Conference on Women, Censorship, and "Pornography" held at the City University of New York in May 1993. The women in this conference are all feminists who are against censorship of anything, including pornography. One of the main points made at the conference is that "sex panics" are nothing new. "Nor are unholy alliances between women's advocates and morality cops. And none of this has ever been good for women." Many times in the past, attention has been diverted from serious underlying problems to superficial "quick fixes." "The temperance movement turned women's anger against domestic violence to a campaign to ban alcohol. Rape and abuse went unabated." The battle against sexually explicit material is the same type of wasting of energy and resources.

Antiporn forces are really interested in "protecting" and oppressing women, not liberating them. In the 1992 Butler decision, the Canadian Supreme Court developed a new, hopelessly vague definition of obscenity that rested on notions of obscene material being that which is "degrading" or "harmful" to women. Thelma McCormack, professor of sociology at York University in Ontario, said, "The Supreme Court of Canada doesn't give a damn about gender equality. It is concerned about control and was pleased to put a feminist gloss on it."

The *Sex Panic* brings up many interesting, hard-hitting points in its twenty-four pages. It's proof that good things sometimes do come in small packages.

National Coalition Against Censorship; $5
1993; booklet; 24 pp.

## VIDEO SEX:
### CREATE EROTIC AND ROMANTIC HOME VIDEOS
### WITH YOUR CAMCORDER
### by Kevin Campbell

Amateur videos are the biggest thing to hit pornography since the come shot was invented. Do-it-yourself porn arose with the advent of relatively inexpensive home camcorders that can make almost anybody into a porn producer. This book teaches you everything you need to know to make your own sex tapes. The emphasis, though, is on using these tapes to fulfill your fantasies and entertain you and your partner(s). But should you want to sell them, that option is certainly a possibility.

"We ran out of tape the first night, it went on so long."
—Melissa, married 6 years

CREATE EROTIC
& ROMANTIC
HOME VIDEOS
WITH YOUR
CAMCORDER

KEVIN CAMPBELL

After some opening material about the need for communication between partners and getting your lover to participate, the book gets down to the nitty-gritty. It gives ideas for what to put on tape—seduction, exhibitionism, wearing sexy clothes, oral sex, shaving pubic hair, anal sex, masturbation, etc. There's also a guide to lingerie and other clothing, sex toys, and food. The section on dialogue, which you might think is basically unnecessary, provides some good advice. One technique is labeled "blathering, moaning, and grunting": "The key is to express yourself gutturally, while trying not to overdo it (overacting with moans and whimpers is common in commercial adult video).... The same words used for a loud orgasm can work: 'Oh God, oh God, oh God,' and 'Oh yes, oh yes, oh yes.'" You can also use "key love-making phrases," talk dirty, or say nothing at all.

Several chapters cover the more technical aspects of video-making, such as shooting techniques, lenses, filters, lighting (very important—this is what ruins countless amateur and "professional" porno tapes), audio, adding music, camera framing, first-person point of view, close-ups, and so on. Where you have your on-camera encounters is very important. The book tells how to handle your virtually unlimited possibilities—bedroom, bathroom, kitchen, garage, car, hotels, the office, locker rooms, outdoors. Besides sex you can film massages, sexy eating, dancing, wrestling, sun worshipping, workouts, telephone sex, and more.

For those who are really into it, the book gets into editing, postproduction, and creating elaborate features.

*Video Sex* is written in a simple, easy-to-follow manner. It's illustrated with dozens of diagrams and more than a hundred shots of beautiful lovers in action, although these pictures don't reveal anything more than breasts and butts. If you want to put your fantasies on tape, you can't go wrong with this book.

Amherst Media; $19.95
1994; oversize softcover; 218 pp.; heavily illus.

*Video Sex
by Kevin
Campbell*

*A
do-it-
yourself
guide from
cameras to
copulation.*

# FEMME PRODUCTIONS

Femme is the groundbreaking producer of "feminist pornography." Femme's chief, Candida Royalle, is a feminist, but she disagrees with the party line that says pornography is harmful and degrading. She thinks that porn can be a vehicle for the expression of female sexuality. However, most porn is made by men for men and does tend to represent the male view. In femporn there is a concentration on foreplay. Lots of kissing, stroking, and licking. The men always go down on the women. This happens sometimes in regular sex movies, but in femporn it's a requirement. As in regular porn, the women perform oral sex on the men. Finally, the most heretical aspect of femporn is that there are no come shots.

Those of you weaned on the nonstop, come-spurting spermathon of mainstream porn will find femporn to be a whole new experience. It's slower, more passionate, and more focused on the whole of sex. The bumping and grinding is there, but it's just one element instead of the whole reason for the movie's existence.

## LOVERS:
### AN INTIMATE PORTRAIT, VOLUME 1: SYDNEY AND RAY
### (VHS VIDEOCASSETTE)

In the *Lovers* series, Femme lets us in on the sex lives of various couples. In this tape, it's Sydney, twenty-five, and Ray, fifty. They talk separately for a while about how they met, their first dates, their first time. They start to talk more explicitly about sex—what they like about each other, how they do it, their fantasies and fears. Eventually, we get to see them doing all kinds of sexual things: she goes down on him, she works out in the nude, they screw on the kitchen counter, they massage each other, they have more sex, and they watch each other masturbate.

The best part is when they get to act out their deeply held fantasies for the camera. In Ray's fantasy, Sydney is a prostitute he picks up. In her fantasy, Ray is tied up and has to watch as another woman munches Sydney's muff. Syd then unties him and gives him one of the best blowjobs ever captured on film. In her second fantasy, Sydney is raped by Ray. Explosive stuff? You betcha. I was glad to see that Femme is so dedicated to honestly showing couples' fantasies that they didn't back away from such a hot potato.

Femme Productions;
1994; VHS videocassette; 70 min.

## REVELATIONS
### (VHS VIDEOCASSETTE)

Set in a sexual dystopia, *Revelations* tells the story of a woman who tries to enjoy sex, not just use it for breeding. This subversion starts when our heroine—an obedient citizen of the state—sees a man being taken from his apartment by the Gestapo-like police force. The police kicked in the door but didn't reseal it, so she goes in to snoop around. She finds a secret room lined with porno pictures and containing a VCR and skin flicks. She goes to the room several times, watches the tapes of couples having sex, and starts to masturbate. She eventually tries to enjoy herself while boffing her fascist husband, but he wigs out. In the end our sexual rebel is caught by the police while masturbating to a lesbian movie.

Besides being an excellent porno movie, *Revelations* is also a pretty good movie, period. The acting is as good as in your better B-movies, which is about twenty-five levels better than in regular porn. The direction is well done. The close-ups on the heroine's face as she recounts these incidents are especially effective. Finally, the plot is interesting and moves along quickly. When's the last time you saw that in a sex video? The sex scenes are hot, but, as in all Femme films, they are just one ingredient in the mix.

Femme Distribution; $39.95
1993; VHS videocassette; 80 min.

## SENSUAL ESCAPE

Two short films. *Fortune Smiles* stars Nina Hartley and Richard Pacheco as Yuppies in Heat. Up to this point they've only petted. We see them meet at a French restaurant, where they talk about Yupster things and try to be witty and amusing. They also grope each other under the table. Once they head back to her place, they start making out and undressing each other. While this is going on, we're hearing their thoughts. She's thinking, *I'm tired of guys who can't get it up or keep it up.* She wonders how to handle their increasingly steamy embrace. *If a woman's too passive, she's a wimp, but if she's too aggressive, she's a sexual drill sergeant.* He's wondering, *What if she's uptight about oral sex?* When she starts stroking his dick, he thinks, *I can't tell if she thinks my cock is too small or too big.* He pauses a split-second. *How could she think it's too big?* From there they move into a full-size adult bangeroo, and they realize that all their worrying was unnecessary.

*The Tunnel*, directed by Candida Royalle herself, is about a female artist who has vivid erotic dreams involving a mysterious man doing a hip-swaying quasi-dance on a stage. The beautiful set for her dreams is partly surrealistic, partly Gothic. Eventually, she meets a man who seems as though he might be the slinky dude in her wet dreams. She sees him in a weird alleyway that looks like her dreamscape. She almost wimps out and runs away, but her loins get the better of her, and she heads back to him for some good sex.

Femme Distribution; $34.95
1988; VHS videocassette; 80 min.

# OTHER SEX WORK

## DANCING NAKED IN THE MATERIAL WORLD
### by Marilyn Suriana Futterman

This book is a revealing glimpse at the human side of strippers. In it we get to see the women inside the naked bodies. Futterman got a job as a waitress in a strip club in Atlanta, and after getting to know the dancers, photographed and interviewed them. This photodocumentary consists of posed portraits as well as "action shots" of the women at work. But don't expect this to be a book-length version of your favorite skin mag, *Hot Throbbing Ultravixens*. The photographs are shot in a very stark black and white. The shots in the club itself are contrasty, with bright light illuminating the dancers and the rest of the club swimming in murkiness. There is a lot of blurred motion, and many of the early photos are grainy.

The portraits are revealing—the various women look by turns proud, tough, unsure, seductive, and tired. Also revealing are the interviews and the essays and poems the women wrote, which are published alongside the pictures. The strippers' feelings about their jobs and lives run the gamut from love to hatred, with a lot of ambivalence in between.

The message of *Dancing Naked* is stated in the foreword: "Those who frequent topless clubs should be warned that the rituals and relationships behind the windowless facades of these strip joints will never quite seem the same after a trip through this book. They will realize that they, too, have been watched and rated and, not by the 'blonde bimbos' they imagine, but by intelligent and streetwise women driven to their profession by reason and the survival instinct—not by their hormones."

Prometheus Books; $26.95
1992; oversize hardcover; 137 pp.; heavily illus.

## HUSTLING:
### A GENTLEMAN'S GUIDE TO THE
### FINE ART OF HOMOSEXUAL PROSTITUTION
### by John Preston

Just what every enterprising young man needs—a book on how to become a male prostitute. Gay porn legend John Preston has been there and done it, so the advice he offers isn't theory, it's cold, hard fact. Preston was a hustler twice in his life—for a couple of years when he was fourteen and for an unspecified amount of time when he was thirty. He says that it's a hell of a lot better than being a wage slave. "I have been a secretary. I have been a hustler. Being a hustler is better for your self-esteem. I know that for a fact."

One of the secrets of suc(k)cess that Preston divulges is that clients aren't just looking for sex. They also want intimacy and acceptance. "Any hustler who forgets that he must provide more than a hard cock and a willing ass and mouth is not going to make a go at it for long."

You don't have to be incredibly attractive to be a hustler. "There are only two absolutes about your physical reality: (1) You cannot be fat. (2) Your cock must be sufficiently large.... Your cock needn't be the Eighth Wonder of the World—though you might get rich if it is. Your penis only needs to be adequate."

Preston covers the various ways you can work as a hustler: in an agency, on the street, in malls, in bars, as a masseur, as a public or private stripper, and working the phone, his preferred method. He tells exactly how to place your ad, what it should say, where to put it, etc. You then find out what to do when you get a call from a potential client, how to handle the trick, how to set prices, what specialty services you can offer (SM, clothing fetish, etc.), modeling for gay porn, and much more.

Get your copy and start hustling today!

A Richard Kasak Book (Masquerade Books); $12.95
1994; softcover; 175 pp.

## MALE PROSTITUTION
### by Donald J. West and Buz de Villiers

This book is an academic study—the only one of its kind—on the rent boys of London. The authors conducted interviews with fifty gay male prostitutes about their childhoods, sexual experiences, entry into prostitution, exactly what they do, bad experiences with clients, unusual requests, their fears and desires, etc. Almost half the men (46 percent), when asked about their orientation said that they were predominantly or exclusively heterosexual except for their business transactions. The researchers chalk a lot of this up to macho posturing.

One of the men describes his entry into the rent scene: "Basically, I was walking around Victoria Station depressed, no money. A guy came up to me and said, 'Do you want to earn some money?' I says, 'How?' He says, 'Well, all I want you to do is wank me off, I'll wank you off.' And he offered me forty pounds. So I says, 'Yeh, fair enough!' Went into his car, drove off somewhere, done our things, he give me the forty pounds and I was happy."

Many rent boys claimed that they would refuse clients who wanted anything "kinky" or "revolting." Some are more obliging: "Caning people, tying them up. There was one had about a twelve-inch dildo, it was about three inches wide, and you have to put it inside of him—things like that." "And what about you being tied up?" "Yea, I've had that as well." "Spanked?" "Yea, and things shoved up me and weights tied to me balls and things like that."

Despite the fact that this is an academic study, the authors keep the theorizing to a minimum and include lots of excerpts from their interviews, letting the men speak for themselves.

Harrington Park Press (The Haworth Press); $19.95
1993; softcover; 358 pp.

## SOME OF MY BEST FRIENDS ARE NAKED:
### INTERVIEWS WITH SEVEN EROTIC DANCERS
### by Tim Keefe

The author interviewed seven dancers at a peep show about their experiences and attitudes regarding their work, their lives, and society. Each interview consists of more than two hundred questions, most of which are exactly the same for each woman, which makes it easy to compare the wide range of answers from the different dancers. Among the many questions that are asked: What were you told was your job? What sexual depictions do you perform on stage? Do you ever become aroused by what you are doing and what is happening around you on stage? Describe the customers. Describe your relationship with your parents. Are you a feminist? What do you think the future holds for relations between men and women?

The women's answers are as in-depth as the questioning. My favorite interviewee was Ann More, simply because of her extreme attitudes that she wasn't afraid to share. When asked to describe the customers, she said, "It reminds me of being at the Humane Society and seeing a bunch of dogs in the kennel. But these you don't want to take home. These are the ones you want to send away to be destroyed." Responding to the question, "Do you test your power to arouse?": "...I did the first year and a half. It was a trip. You want to see what you can do, and now it's been proven to me that anything with tits and a cunt can do anything to a man."

Of all the books purporting to examine the human side of sex workers, I found this one to be the most revealing. The sheer number and variety of questions, along with the women's up-front answers, provide a very rich picture of these ostracized people.

Barbary Coast Press; $12.95
1993; softcover; 378 pp.

## SWEET TALKERS
### by Kathleen K.

An insider's account of what it's like to be a phone sex worker. Kathleen runs a thriving 900-number operation and is one of the "sweet talkers," under the pseudonym Jamie. There is an art to getting men off with just your voice. "The best operator is almost telepathic: a question or two, and she is flying into the guy's head, rattling his thoughts, making his mind leap and twitch, triggering old associations and making new connections with him. She echoes in his head for days."

Operators get all sorts of clients. Some just want to talk about their lives—mainly about relationship or sex problems. They want advice. Others don't say a single word. The operator won't hear anything except heavy breathing and a few groans for several minutes, until the client hangs up. Or, "The caller may want to know the operator's history. When did she bloom? Who was the first? How was it? When did she start blowing cock, letting a man lick her? How was her premiere at an orgy? Married? Kids? Did her first gal-pal go all the way with her, or what? How many men has she had?... Who has the privilege of loving her now? Is that a long-term arrangement? What are his chances of meeting her, someone like her?"

Kathleen reveals lots of interesting juicy details. She relates how she tells off religious nuts who call and harass her. She pulls mindfucks on guys who get on the line and cop a superior intellectual attitude. And of course, she reveals what it is that her callers want. "The big surprise? Men want their butts played with. An overwhelming majority will gasp if you volunteer that detail during the re-creation of a sex act...just grabbing it while he screws is a turn-on. If you detail that you'll pry his cheeks apart to expose his asshole, he'll more often than not say 'yes, oh yes,' and once you put a finger in it, he is going to climax rapidly."

*Sweet Talkers* can be read three ways; as a firsthand report from a relatively new and unexplored aspect of sex work; as a stroke book—Kathleen prints lots of explicit dialogues between her and her callers—and finally, as a how-to book. Kathleen gives lots of tips on how to run a phone sex business and be an operator.

A Richard Kasak Book (Masquerade Books); $12.95
1994; softcover; 208 pp.

## VICE ART:
### AN ANTHOLOGY OF LONDON'S PROSTITUTE CARDS

In London, one way prostitutes advertise their wares is by sticking calling cards in telephone booths. *Vice Art* examines this neglected form of functional art by reproducing more than one hundred such cards. Most cards include a photo or illustration of a tart, some juvenile text ("Ooooh! I'm a naughty girl!"), and a phone number (every number has three digits blanked out, so you can't use this book as a directory). Despite the hokeyness and redundancy of the cards as a whole, some do stand out either because of a choice visual image or imaginative copy.

The cards are presented in sections covering straight, exotic, domination, submission, transvestite, fantasy and uniforms, and specialist services (foot worship and watersports). The book's production values are unfortunately lacking. All of the cards are reproduced as black ink printed on yellow paper. The original cards must have been scanned into a computer and then output on a low resolution device, because the quality of the images is poor and the text has a bad case of the jaggies (it's bitmapped, for all you computer jocks).

Good concept, bad execution.

Turnaround Distribution; £5
1993; softcover; 64 pp.; heavily illus.

## YOSHIWARA:
### THE PLEASURE QUARTERS OF OLD TOKYO
### by Stephen and Ethel Longstreet

*Whores in History* ➤ by Nickie Roberts

*The unrepentant whore: The most maligned woman in history.*

For more than three centuries, a sexual utopia existed in Tokyo. Yoshiwara was a walled "city within a city" where any pleasure you can name was available for a price. Filled with brothels, Yoshiwara became a mecca for hedonists, hard-ups, businessmen, artists, actors, and other bohemians and thrill-seekers.

This pleasure dome has been whispered about in the West for more than a century, achieving a semi-mythical status. In the only available book on the subject, the authors present a factual account of the founding, conditions, religion, art, literature, fashions, celebrities, activities, and eventual end of Yoshiwara.

This decadent mini-city was the brainstorm of a brothel-keeper who petitioned the shogun to create a district for whorehouses, reasoning that officials would be better able to keep an eye on crime (sexual slavery, child prostitution, and other problems) if all the houses of ill repute were in the same area. In 1617 the shogun gave the nod.

Yoshiwara eventually encompassed eighteen acres. Visitors could choose from among hundreds of establishments, from high-class centers—where the most beautiful and "talented" women would engage customers in a night of singing, dancing, drinking, drugs, and sex—to sleazy cathouses that offered quick sex with less desirable women.

Of course, not everything was perfect in this alleged paradise. Many of the women were indeed held against their will, forced to lead a miserable existence. There were also many clip joints that would use dirty tricks or violence to take some poor sap for everything he had.

It goes without saying that Yoshiwara couldn't last. Eventually, pressure from people concerned about the coercion of some of the prostitutes, and bluenoses concerned that people were having fun, proved to be too much. In 1958, Yoshiwara—by then just a shadow of its former self—

was abolished. But, as the authors point out, this move "did not do away with sex outside the home or marriage. Nor did it eliminate the prostitutes, the bathhouse girls, the bar hostesses, the night-club and gyp-joint whores or their erotic games." It only drove those things underground while abolishing the greatest pleasure center in the world. What's a libertine to do?

Yen Books (Charles E. Tuttle & Co); $12.95
1970; paperback; 225 pp.; illus.

## A VINDICATION OF THE RIGHTS OF WHORES
### edited by Gail Pheterson

Prostitutes are tired of being harassed by cops, beaten by johns, terrorized by pimps, cold-shouldered by the feminist movement, and pissed on by society in general. They feel charging for sex is a legitimate business, and they want the same rights and protections as everybody else. The wonderfully titled *A Vindication of the Rights of Whores* is a collection of documents pertaining to the prostitutes' rights movement. We get the inside story on the First World Whores' Congress, as well as the "Declaration of Independence" that was passed at this meeting—the "World Charter for Prostitutes' Rights."

Detailed proceedings from the Second World Whores' Congress are reprinted, making for especially interesting reading. Active and retired prostitutes from the Netherlands, England, Israel, West Germany, Australia, India, the United States, and other corners of the globe discussed human rights, health concerns, and feminism in their home countries.

Several essays report on repression and struggles to organize whores in Africa, Indonesia, Europe, and elsewhere. A resource section gives addresses and phone numbers for worldwide prostitutes' rights groups, including COYOTE (Call Off Your Old Tired Ethics) and England's PLAN (Prostitute Laws Are Nonsense).

This pioneering book firmly sets the political and social agenda for whores, showing that they are yet another oppressed group who are tired of being silent.

Seal Press; $16.95
1989; softcover; 296 pp.

## WHORES IN HISTORY:
### PROSTITUTION IN WESTERN SOCIETY
### by Nickie Roberts

Nickie Roberts presents a richly detailed history of whores, but it's more than a dry recitation of facts. Roberts believes in the right of a woman to sell her body if she so chooses, and she shows the constant fear, cowardice, and hypocrisy of those who would restrict this freedom. She considers the unrepentant whore to be the most maligned woman in history, and she wants to set the record straight.

Roberts begins her story with the sacred prostitutes/priestesses of ancient Egypt and Mesopotamia. Having sex with these women was a holy act of communion with the Goddess. However, this is the point at which the patriarchy took over—male priests ousted the temple whores and introduced their own gods.

Ancient Rome was a hotbed of debauchery. Besides the infamous exploits of the emperors and other male members of the ruling class, there are tales of how the royal females got their kicks—some of them willingly prostituted themselves. Julia, the daughter of Augustus, would service her clients on the platform of the Forum, the very place her father stood when making royal decrees (including his pronouncements against adultery). Messalina, the wife of Claudius, enjoyed whoring so much that she wouldn't leave the brothels when they closed for the night and had to be tossed out. "Her most famous exploit was to hire a prostitute who was well known for her sexual stamina and challenge her to a contest to see who could accommodate the greatest number of men in a single night. The empress won."

During the Middle Ages European royalty kept *gynacea*, houses full of beautiful concubines. These would often become private whorehouses for the friends of the royal families. But members of the Crown weren't the only ones seeing action. "Throughout the entire [medieval] period the men of God, even while they spouted an endless stream of anti-pleasure propaganda, were unable to control their own sexual habits...." The clergy's preference for debauchery didn't go unnoticed, though. The French writer Jean Gerson lamented that cloisters of nuns had become "brothels of harlots." Statues of the clergy's antics were actually present in many cathedrals: "In one place a monk was represented in carnal connection with a female devotee. In others were seen an abbot engaged with nuns, a naked nun worried by monkeys, youthful penitents undergoing flagellation at the hands of their confessor, lady abbesses offering hospitality to well proportioned strangers, etc., etc." In one of the ultimate examples of religious hypocrisy, the glorious cathedrals of Europe were partially funded by Church-run whorehouses.

Roberts's account of hidden whore history continues through the Renaissance and Reformation, the formation of the United States, and right up to today, with the prostitutes' rights movement and feminism's rejection of whores. Well-written, with fascinating anecdotes on every page, *Whores in History* casts a new light on the world's oldest profession.

Grafton; £7.99 ($12)
1993; softcover; 380 pp.; illus.

## WHOREZINE

News, views, and humor for prostitutes and their pals. Issue #25 had subverted ads, including Macintosh's "What's on Your Powerbook?" ad featuring Bettina Rods, a madam, and Lillith Plowright, a dominatrix. The latter's Powerbook includes Quark-Sexpress, clients' stat sheets, *Whorezine*'s address, and illustrations of sexy bald captains. There are reprints of newspaper articles dealing with prostitution in Cuba, whores in Kenya who are immune to AIDS, new prostitution laws, etc. Editor Vic St. Blaise contributes two articles on the San Francisco Taskforce on Prostitution and San Francisco's Street Survival Project. There are also reviews, a resource list, an advice column from Mistress Manners, and your monthly "whorescope."

Now that *Oldest Profession Times* has indefinitely suspended publication, *Whorezine* is the only prostitute magazine I'm aware of. A lot of its focus is on San Francisco, but even if you work someplace else, at least you know you're not alone.

Whorezine
2300 Market Street, Suite 19/San Francisco, CA 94114
Single issue: $4 cash; 12 issue sub: $40 cash

# OMNISEXUALITY

## FRIGHTEN THE HORSES:
### A DOCUMENT OF THE SEXUAL REVOLUTION

*Frighten the Horses* almost doesn't belong in the omnisexuality section, but something about it makes me put it here. Almost all of the fiction features queer sex, as does most of the artwork. But still...there's lots of articles on abortion rights (and if people are getting knocked up, some heterosex must be going on), frequent essays on where man/boy love fits into the movement, an exposé of lesbians' fantasies about guys (issue #10), and issue #12 features a taboo-smashing, explicit story about a woman making love to a man (the only catch is, the man's dead). There's also lots of body modification going on, so all in all, we do get a rainbow of flavors with vanilla nary in sight.

*Frighten* presents a good blend of fiction and nonfiction. The latter is especially wide ranging, covering sexual freedom, freedom of speech, homophobia, the pro-choice movement, etc. Issue #12 features three fascinating articles, two on the Satanic Panic sweeping America and one on how you may be unknowingly giving away your sexual preferences with the help of the shoddy state of privacy.

The significance of the name *Frighten the Horses* has eluded many people (including me), so I will now tell it. A Victorian actress named Mrs. Patrick Campbell was a member of an acting company that contained two gay lovers. When asked if she disapproved, she said, "My dear, I don't care what these affectionate people do as long as they don't do it in the street and frighten the horses."

Heat Seeking Publishing/41 Sutter Street #1108
San Francisco, CA 94104
Single issue: $6
Four-issue sub (one year): $18; Canada: $25; Foreign: $30

## LIBIDO:
### THE JOURNAL OF SEX AND SENSIBILITY

Try to explain to your average member of society that there is a magazine out there that deals with sex, but it's not a skin mag. Yes, it publishes photographs of naked people, alone and having sex, but these photographs are of supreme aesthetic quality, taken by some of the best erotic photographers in the world. Yes, it has explicit stories about sex and they often use four-letter words, yet this fiction has a refined quality about it. It even runs enlightening and often humorous nonfiction pieces about sex, but it's far from a dry academic journal. You will receive a blank look from the person who's straining to comprehend what the hell you're talking about. Such a magazine can't even be imagined. Anything that shows naked bodies and talks about fucking is pure smut, right? Not that I'm taking anything away from smut. It definitely has its own appeal. But *Libido* is different. Someone once labeled it "erotica for eggheads," which is probably the best capsule description possible.

*Libido* publishes everything from beautiful nudes to people getting it on. They aren't afraid to break taboos, either. One picture showed a woman squeezing milk from one of her breasts into a lactate-splattered glass bowl. Another photo, which violates a different set of assumptions, shows a reclined woman masturbating with one hand while blowing her nose with the other. It's an antiglamour statement. Another jolting photograph shows a lit candle lodged between a pair of buttcheeks.

*Libido*'s other main strong point is its nonfiction. The fall 1993 issue has an article on the quackish medical/sexual devices sold around 1900, like the Testone Radium Energizer, a pad that was supposed to increase virility by enveloping the testicles in the radioactive element radium. The fall 1992 issue had an article on the cross-dressing Zuni Pueblo tribesman who, in the late 1800s, fooled Washington D.C.'s high society into thinking he was a woman, despite his strapping six-foot frame.

I've listed *Libido* under omnisexuality because they make a conscious effort, through their visuals and writing, to represent men and women, same-sex and mixed-sex couples, and groups. They also include transgenderists, but to a lesser degree.

*Libido* is one of my favorite magazines.

Libido/5318 N Paulina Street/Chicago, IL 60640
Single issue: $7; Canada: $8; Europe: $12; elsewhere: $15
One-year sub (4 issues): $26; Canada: $36; Europe: $46;
elsewhere: $56

## MELTING POINTS
### by Pat Califia

A collection of short stories from SM *überdyke* Pat Califia. But, you say, why is this book in the "Omnisexuality" section? I thought Califia wrote leatherdyke fiction. Ah, how quick we are to categorize. Actually, Califia's fiction does focus on lesbians, but there are also gay men and female transgenderists inhabiting these stories. The sex is often brutal and semiconsensual. People are given what they want, even though they may not know they want it at the time.

A bar called Jax is the unforgettable setting for "Big Girl": "Shark and Chambray are locked in a hard-core carnal embrace on the dance floor. Two of the other dancers, big women with enormous tits, had taken their shirts off. At one table, a woman

*A Taste Of
Latex* ➤

*"It's what you
wanted. It's
why you're
here, where
you know
you don't
belong..."*

in a three-piece suit was getting a shotgun hit off a blimp-shaped joint from her date, who was wearing a sequined cocktail frock. At another table, three hookers in Cher wigs, halter-tops, miniskirts, fishnet hose, and high-heeled boots sat close together, kissing and fondling each other's breasts, while a fourth woman, on her knees under the table, went down on one of them. Her hands were busy underneath the other two women's skirts. Somebody in a baseball jacket was studiously cutting up coke on the jukebox."

Califia takes pride in trashing every taboo she can get her hands on, even those of lesbian erotica itself. This unrelenting set of stories will violate your every assumption.

Alyson Publications; $9.95
1993; softcover; 223 pp.

## SLIPPERY WHEN WET

A fresh, fun, "penetration-positive" zine by and for people who aren't afraid to admit they like sex. Issue #4 had articles on nonmonogamy, meeting kinky people, tips for cruising, changing the Library of Congress's antiquated system for classifying material dealing with sex, and an interview with the men behind *Monk* zine. "Even Better Than the Real Thing" is about cybersex. "Sure, technology's kinda crude right now (*bored executrix, sitting behind her desk, pager set to BUZZ between panty-hose thighs, waiting for her lover to call*), but just let those horny ol' geeks and dweebs in Silicone Valley work on it for a few more years and—ZAM!...Right now (*aside from the executrix*) things are at the asking-her-out stage—we've got quite a while to go before first, second, third base, and SCORE! (*clickity, clack on a keyboard: '<Are you naked?>' he types. '<Yeah, and my nipples are hard and my pussy's real wet>' a guy somewhere responds*)."

"Gender Bending Barbies" looks at the dissent and subversion swirling around that archetypal all-American doll. "In Florida, several Ken dolls are discovered to have been carefully dressed in outrageous drag and put back in their boxes for sale. In Ohio an anonymous maniac wanders the malls and mutilates the breasts of Barbie dolls; authorities worry it may spark 'copycat Barbie slashing.'"

There are also photos by Annie Sprinkle and Michael Rosen, dirty limericks, comix, and short stories. I think *Slippery*'s motto sums it up nicely: "Don't sweat the petty things; pet the sweaty things."

More! Productions/PO Box 3101/Berkeley, CA 94703
Single issue: $6
Four-issue sub: $20

## TASTE OF LATEX

Billing itself as "Entertainment for the Sexually Disenfranchised" and "The McPorn Alternative," *Taste of Latex* offers "all sexual flavors with no bitter after-taste of apology." (Do you think I could possibly crib more than three quotes in a single sentence?) This is high-grade, ultra-kinked sexcapades featuring men, women, gender-benders, pierced people, punks, sex workers, and anyone else who wants to get in on the fun. No one is turned away (except boring people). Each issue is a smorgasbord of fiction, poetry, black-and-white photos, practical nonfiction, rants, and reviews. Some big names regularly show up in these pages—Pat Califia, Carol A. Queen, Annie Sprinkle, Vaginal Davis, Alice Joanou, Charles Gatewood, and Rick Castro have all contributed some riot porn.

*Taste of Latex* is noted for its "transgressive" fiction. Not everybody involved is exactly willing, or are they? "You know he's following you, but you don't speed up or cross the street. You don't try to get away. He comes up beside you, wraps his arm around your shoulder, and lays the sharp point of a blade against your stomach. He whispers in your ear—*come with me...* It's what you wanted. It's why you're here, where you know you don't belong..." (from "i'm sorry" by Trish Thomas, issue #9).

Taste of Latex/PO Box 460122/San Francisco, CA 94146
Single issue: $5.95. Four-issue sub (one year): $19.95;
Canada: $24.95; Foreign: $34.95

# BISEXUALITY

## ANYTHING THAT MOVES:
### BEYOND THE MYTHS OF BISEXUALITY

Some people have been upset by this magazine's name, claiming that it perpetuates the stereotype that bisexuals will fuck anything that moves. Actually, writes the editor, "This magazine is about ANYTHING THAT MOVES: that moves us to think; that moves us to fuck (or not); that moves us to feel; that moves us to believe in ourselves—To Do It For Ourselves!"

Issue #7 is the "Spirituality and Healing" issue. The guest editor discusses his personal link between (bi)sexuality and spirituality: "I can hardly find the words to tell you how important sensual pleasure is to my spirit. I remember going through hard times and thinking after I had an orgasm, 'Now *there's* a reason to live.'"

Articles cover churches and bisexuality, concepts of gender and sexuality in various belief systems, building a national spirituality/sexuality coalition, being Jewish and bisexual, organizing queer labor, spiritual abuse, domestic violence, surviving HIV, and more. There's also poetry, fiction, reviews, an advice column, and an interview with neopagan/bisexual/healer Starhawk.

*Anything* is a wide-ranging, forthright publication that wears its heart on its sleeve. Even though I often see it considered as a regional publication (the Bay Area, to be exact), the material it publishes is of benefit to bis everywhere.

BABN/2404 California Street #24/San Francisco, CA 94115
Single issue: $6
Four-issue sub: $25; Foreign: $30

## BI ANY OTHER NAME:
### BISEXUAL PEOPLE SPEAK OUT

### edited by Loraine Hutchins and
### Lani Kaahumanu

Bisexual people have found themselves in a peculiar spot—rejected by both the straight and gay worlds, because they are of both worlds and, therefore, of neither. This has been changing recently, as many queer organizations hold gay, lesbian, and bisexual marches, among other gestures. One of the key turning points in this battle for acceptance was the publication of *Bi Any*

*Other Name*, a collection of essays, poetry, and fiction by and about bis.

Carol Queen writes in "The Queer in Me": "Nobody makes it easy; I belong to and identify with a community whose values were forged in reaction to homophobic fire—a community that, finally, could proclaim, 'Gay is good,' but that found bisexuality too difficult, too close to heterosexuality, too *confusing* to embrace." In "This Poem Can Be Put off No Longer," Susan Carlton lists the reactions she's gotten about being bi: "Yeah, I've heard that's trendy right/now. You're just trying to be cool.... You're a fence/sitter.... You just take it/wherever you can get it don't you?... Don't worry, you'll grow out of it.... You're just oversexed/desperate horny confused...." More than seventy other people contribute their thoughts about bi liberation, having a bi son, having a bi dad, the joy of bisex, monogamy, bi movies, the politics of labeling, and much more.

Alyson Publications; $11.95
1991; softcover; 379 pp.

## BISEXUALITY:
### A READER AND SOURCEBOOK
### by Thomas Geller

This book, along with *Bi Any Other Name* (above), was crucial in bringing bisexuality out of the closet in the early 1990s. Roughly the first third of the book is a collection of articles, interviews, and one song giving a general overview of the problems and hopes of bis and the bisexual movement. Anthropologist Margaret Mead is quoted: "We shall not really succeed in discarding the straitjacket of our own cultural beliefs about sexual choice if we fail to come to terms with the well-documented, normal human capacity to love members of both sexes."

The middle section of the book reprints three academic articles dealing with bisexuality, including "Normal and Atypical Gender Differentiation," which argues the biological model that says sexual orientation is basically a physical, genetic trait.

The final section lists seventy-five pages of resources. It gives addresses, phone numbers, and descriptions of bi organizations in the United States (including various state groups), Canada, England, the Netherlands, etc. There are also listings of periodicals, international films dealing with bisexuality, and a twenty-six-page bibliography.

Although *Bisexuality* was groundbreaking, it is now dated. After five years, this valuable guide deserves to be revised.

Times Change Press; $10.95
1990; small softcover; 184 pp.

## DUAL ATTRACTION:
### UNDERSTANDING BISEXUALITY
### by Martin S. Weinberg, Colin J. Williams, and Douglas W. Pryor

This book is the first major scientific study of bisexuality ever produced. During the 1980s, the authors interviewed, observed, and gave lengthy questionnaires to more than eight hundred bis, gays, lesbians, and straights. The results of their quest show that bisexuality is a quite complex subject. The differences between the sexes are interesting, if not totally unexpected: "For men it was easier to have sex with other men than to fall in love with them. For women it was easier to fall in love with other women than to have sex with them.... Both bisexual men and women, however, seemed to share the same traditional ideas about gender; for example sex with men was described as more physical, with women as more intimate."

The authors had their bisexual subjects rate themselves on three 6-point scales that measured sexual feelings, sexual behaviors, and romantic feelings. A 0 on the scale meant the person was completely heterosexual in that area, while a 6 indicated that the person was completely homosexual in that area. A 3 meant that the person felt equally strongly toward both sexes. Based on the results, they found five types of bis. The pure type scored perfect 3's on all three scales. This type accounted for only 2 percent of the men and 17 percent of the women. The mid type marked 3 on at least one section and 2 or 4 on the other sections. About a third of the men and women fell into this category. The heterosexual-leaning type marked mainly 0 to 2 on each dimension. Forty-five percent of the men and 20 percent of the women were in this category. The homosexual-leaning type, conversely, marked 4 to 6 on each section. Approximately 15 percent of the men and women were in this category. Finally, the varied type scored toward different extremes on the different scales. This type accounted for 10 percent of both genders.

The authors also examine what types of relationships their bisexual subjects found ideal. The most common ideal was to have a core homosexual relationship and a core heterosexual relationship. The second most common was to have a core heterosexual relationship with same-sex relationships on the outside. The opposite arrangement was not very popular, but when it was selected, it was wanted mainly by women. The third most common ideal situation would be some sort of communal group.

This study covers a lot more ground—transsexual bisexuals, types of sexual activity, marriage, jealousy, discrimination, the instability of sexual preference, AIDS, etc.

Oxford University Press; $27.50
1994; hardcover; 437 pp.

## LESBOMANIA!

*Black Lace* ▼

*An oppressed group within an oppressed group act out.*

## BLACK LACE

A magazine of erotic African American lesbian fiction, poetry, and photography. This oppressed group within an oppressed group doesn't get much recognition, but this magazine helps give voice to their desires. There's a truly honest feel to the work presented here, unlike the sterile niche-porn cranked out by money-hungry corporations. It's real and it's hot! "Driven by her refusals, I started hanging out wherever women could be found sweating profusely between their thighs. I joined a health club and never exercised there; I'd simply come in, right after the aerobics classes, and sit in the locker rooms. Every inch of my body, every single pore could *smell* each woman..." (from "Obsession" by Claudia Washington in issue #4).

Blk Publishing Company
PO Box 83912/Los Angeles, CA 90038-0912
Single issue: $7
Four-issue sub: $20; Foreign: $36

## DAGGER:
### ON BUTCH WOMEN
### edited by Lily Burana, Roxxie, and Linnea Due

This collection of articles, essays, comix, and photos is a loving tribute to butch dykes. In her opening essay, Carol A. Queen writes, "What is butch? Rebellion against woman's lot, against gender-role imperatives that pit boyness against girlness and then assign you-know-who the short straw. Butch is a giant *fuck YOU!* to compulsory femininity, just as lesbianism says the same to compulsory heterosexuality."

In "A Random Sampling of Butches," *Taste of Latex* editor Lily Burana asked eight butches some questions. Who's your role model? "Jean-Claude Van Damme in *Hard Target*. OK, so he's a big, greasy, macho guy, but with that haircut (spiked on top, long in the back), he looks just like a dyke." Other answers included "my dad," "faggots," and "the Fonz." Fashion musts are Levi's 501 jeans, a white T-shirt, and boxer shorts. A low point of butch life is "figuring out which public restroom is safer for me to use—the men's or the women's." A high point of butch life is "having a gay man hit on me, not realizing that I was a woman."

"Packing, Passing, and Pissing" is a guide for women who want to pass as men. It includes tips on how to stuff your pants to get that sought-after bulge effect. You can use a dildo or create your own dick with pantyhose, condoms, and hair gel. Merely having a bulge isn't always enough, though. You may want to piss standing up. Although there is no surefire method yet, the authors review several products and techniques.

Other articles discuss black bulldaggers, the women of American Gladiators, butch icons of the silver screen and comic strips, a "butchiest dyke" contest, interviews with butches, a butch sex worker, the joys of dating butch women, dyke daddies, and cruising tips for butches.

Cleis Press; $14.95
1994; oversize softcover; 229 pp.; illus.

*Girljock*

*"Dear Femme Jock..."*

## GIRLJOCK

The magazine for athletic lesbians, *Girljock* is fun, fresh, unique, and has a humor quotient that's right off the map. Issue #11 had articles on the Women's Basketball Association and women's professional beach volleyball, short blurbs on ice skating, women's soccer, and flag football; and a long section on rock climbing—how to do it, where to do it, why it's so much fun, why it's even better with a girlfriend, etc.

There are also comix, an advice column ("Dear Femme Jock"), and music and movie reviews. Strangely, the movies *Girljock* reviews are mostly mainstream drivel. They do redeem themselves by giving honest reviews and by commenting on the women in the movies. For example, they reveal *Sliver* to be the piece of shit that it is, and address Sharon Stone: "You are an amazing babe, and even though I hated this movie you still managed to hold your head up high and give us thrill after thrill of naked and semi-naked views, plus tight skirts and soft, fuzzy sweaters."

Rox-a-tronic Publishing
PO Box 882723/San Francisco, CA 94188-2723
Single issue: $5
Four-issue sub: $12

## LESBIAN NUNS: BREAKING SILENCE
### edited by Rosemary Curb and Nancy Manahan

This cult classic was the first book to peek under the nun's habit and report on what's hidden underneath. About fifty Brides of Christ tell their stories of recognizing their lesbianism, coming out, falling for other nuns, and leaving the sisterhood and the Catholic Church (except for four women who were still nuns when this book was written).

What emerges is a riveting firsthand account of the simultaneous war and partnership between religion and the flesh. Maria Cristina writes, "Pain helped us be in the presence of God..." and "The purpose of flagellation was to dominate our sexuality." It didn't always work that way. "But sometimes when I hit myself I awakened my carnal desires." Cristina would then masturbate and,

feeling ashamed, confess before everyone. She would ask for and receive extra-heavy penance. Unfortunately, "Heavy penance was self-inflicted flagellation, which sometimes aroused me again."

Many of the sisters split, not solely because of their sexuality, but because their desires made them question everything they believed. Monique DuBois states this most emphatically in her interview. Co-editor Rosemary Curb asks her: "Did awareness of your sexuality lead to your departure from religious life?" She replies: "No. Complete disillusionment and rejection of the Catholic Church and a need to preserve my psychological and emotional sanity did!"

Naiad Press; $9.95
1985; softcover; 383 pp.; illus.

## LESBOMANIA!:
### HUMOR, COMMENTARY, AND NEW EVIDENCE THAT WE ARE EVERYWHERE
### by Jorjet Harper

A collection of fifty of Jorjet Harper's humor columns, *Lesbomania!* pokes fun at heterosexuals and lesbians. Several of the columns focus on a fictitious civil war occurring in Beaver Dam, Wisconsin: "A mob of fired-up femmes, wielding farm implements purchased at a nearby feed store and tools borrowed from local gas stations, broke down the barricaded door of the Huggy-bear Lounge in an effort to regain control of the landmark role-playing bar from which they had been banned by butches."

Harper presents the theory that in the past earth was visited by ancient lesbonauts. As evidence, she offers the pyramids of Egypt: "...the pyramids are actually *giant three-dimensional vulvas aimed at outer space!*" She also points out that "in ancient Vulvanian—a lost language which was spoken in an area rich with prehistoric goddess statuary—an expression has survived that seems to be describing ancient lesbonauts: *Ugati....aliti....tiki....alura*, which some paleolinguists have translated as: 'Women who come...from the sky...and go down...on each other.'"

Other columns deal with Greta Garbo, Liberace, the horrors of love, lesbian guru Mamarama, a pair of lesbian geese at the San Francisco zoo, and much more.

New Victoria; $9.95
1994; softcover; 149 pp.; illus.

## THE PERSISTENT DESIRE:
### A FEMME-BUTCH READER
### edited by Joan Nestle

A truly groundbreaking anthology that finally gives voice to butches and femmes—their struggles, joys, feelings, and desires. Butches and femmes each have their own ecstasies and agonies. Butches deconstruct gender. Their masculine appearance and actions shatter society's notions of what a woman should be like, but this makes them the most visible target of hatred and contempt from our homophobic society. Femmes more subtly subvert gender by being lesbian but also being the absolute paragon of society's concept of female. They look nothing like the straight world's stereotype of a lesbian (read: butch). However, this often makes them the target of attacks from other lesbians, who may view them as dupes of straight society.

The more than eighty pieces in this book comprise a decades-spanning look at the femme-butch relationship. Selections include "Miss Ogilvy Finds Herself" by Radclyffe Hall, "Butch to Butch: A Love Song" by Leslie Feinberg, "Technicolor Dykes" by Judith Schwarz, "Roll Me Over and Make Me a Rose" by Scarlet Woman, "Walt Whitman: A Model Femme" by Christine Cassidy, "Stone Butch" by Lee Lynch, "Gender Fuck Gender" by Pat Califia, and "Flamingoes and Bears: A Parable" by Jewelle L. Gomez.

Alyson Publications; $14.95
1992; softcover; 503 pp.

## (SEM)EROTICS:

### THEORIZING LESBIAN : WRITING

### by Elizabeth A. Meese

You think reading French literary theory is rough going? Just wait till you read this book in which a pomo lesbo deconstructs lesbian writing. "To write lesbianism is to enter a rhetorical, that is, a metaphorical, field—a scene of 'transposition...[involving] the figure as such' and a scene of 'resemblance' (Ricouer 17). In other words, when I write (of) the lesbian, I engage the problem of speaking metaphorically about metaphor, or representationally of representation. Through resemblances, I write 'in other words' of the 'woman' and her 'lesbian'/shadow, or the 'lesbian' and her 'woman'/shadow, of 'me' and 'you.'" Are you with me so far? I didn't think so.

Meese applies the postmodernist brand of thinking to the relationship between Virgina Woolf and Vita Sackville-West, lesbian SM, Gertrude Stein, experimental lesbian texts, the connection between writers' lives and their works, reader self-presence, etc.

I may be risking my intellectual hipness by admitting this, but the deconstructionists leave me in the dark. I appreciate what they're trying to do. They say language is basically a trap—words have meanings codified by society; they're defined by other words, which have their own meanings. To find the true meaning of a text it is necessary to break down this barrier brick by brick, to see what the words are truly signifying. But pomo literary theory always degenerates into an incomprehensible mishmash of hyph-ens, slash/es, (paren)theses, and co:lons.

New York University Press; $14.95
1992; softcover; 167 pp.

## SEX VARIANT WOMEN IN LITERATURE

### Jeannette H. Foster

First published in 1956, this is the classic and definitive survey of lesbian writing and lesbian writers. The author begins, naturally, with the work of Sappho of Lesbos. It's interesting that Sappho's considerable reputation rests entirely on a few hundred lines of poetry, which is all that survives of the 12,000 lines she's believed to have written. The biblical Book of Ruth and classical mythology also provide some material for speculation about who might have been "family."

Foster examines Samuel Taylor Coleridge's famous unfinished lesbian vampire poem "Christabel." Although it is ludicrously tame by today's standards, just the implication that the innocent Christabel and the menacing Geraldine had gotten it on was enough to send critics into hysterics. The *Edinburgh Review* called it obscene and was horrified by its "implications of personal turpitude." The attacks were so venomous that Coleridge never completed his epic poem, and no other English poets dealt with homosexuality for half a century.

The author also discusses Balzac's *The Girl with the Golden Eyes*, some of Shakespeare's plays, Henry James's *The Turn of the Screw*, Charles Baudelaire, Emily Brontë, poetry and fiction in France and Germany, Emily Dickinson's relationship with a young widow, and the lesbian literary renaissance of the early twentieth century, which produced Radclyffe Hall's *The Well of Loneliness* and Virginia Woolf's *Orlando*.

Even though a lot of the material this book deals with is unquestionably queer, the best parts are the gossipy "was she or wasn't she?" sections. In fact, the author devotes a whole chapter, euphemistically titled "Conjectural Retrospect," to this literary outing.

The Naiad Press; $8.95
1956, 1985; softcover; 422 pp.

## SUSIE SEXPERT'S LESBIAN SEX WORLD

### by Susie Bright

Susie Bright has become one of the foremost advocates of the unofficial sex-positive movement. The unabashed Bright wants you to know there's nothing wrong with sex, whether lesbian (her specialty), kinky, or vanilla. If you enjoy it, then piss on what everybody else thinks.

What makes Bright such a blast to read is that she exposes the forbidden. She looks at what people are really doing between the sheets (or wherever) and reports back. She founded, and subsequently left, *On Our Backs*, the magazine for the "adventurous lesbian." This collection of her writings is her first book, and it's already become a classic.

Bright credits the women's liberation movement with helping to sexually liberate women. "In a vulva-shaped nutshell, the message was find your clit, learn to create your orgasm, express your sexual curiosity to its fullest, and don't let anyone, especially a man, tell you how or when to get off. So there!" But there's still a long way to go before women—actually before everybody—really feels comfortable with their sexuality, so Bright decided to help speed up the process. The articles and advice columns in this book tackle vaginal fisting, the fear of vibrator addiction, being attracted to straight women, home sex-toy presentations (also known as "fuckerware parties"), the joys of safe sex, road-testing sex toys, and women with AIDS. Bright also tells about her travel adventures to New Orleans, Chicago, Las Vegas, and Hollywood.

Bright offers advice for playing with the "Last Frontier"—the anus. "The main idea is that your ass actively receives and opens up to penetration through relaxation and arousal. It cannot be pushed open like a vagina, which, let's be frank, can more easily be shoved around. No, your anus must definitely make the first move." She also gives the straight skinny on getting the most out of orgies. Don't try to do everything at once. "Choose one little thing that appeals to you, like watching Deidre get her ass licked, or vibrating yourself to a porn film while Lisa sucks your toes... Ask people if you can join in. If someone invites you to sit on her face, and the act or the person doesn't attract you, consider whether you could partner with them in some other scheme that you would enjoy."

Cleis Press; $9.95
1990; softcover; 154 pp.

## SUSIE BRIGHT'S SEXUAL REALITY:

### A VIRTUAL SEX WORLD PRIMER

### by Susie Bright

In this sequel to *Susie Sexpert's Lesbian Sex World*, Susie B. continues to push the envelope. "Shiny Plastic Dildos Holding Hands" is Bright's defense of dildos against those who would degrade them. "The most common prejudice is that dildos are for old maids, lonely hearts, the hard-ups who lack a hard-on." Later, she writes, "Fucking feels good—that's the basic premise of dildo popularity—and when it comes to penetration, why NOT have it your way?"

Bright also writes about Camille Paglia, masculinity in the 1990s, Virtual Sex, sexual harassment, "men who love lesbians (who don't care for them too much)," her rabble-rousing appearance on the *Phil Donahue Show*, and more. But there are two articles that blow the others away owing to their explosive subject matter. "Rape Scenes" starts off with Bright admitting she fantasizes about being raped, but the essay quickly turns into a discussion of Nancy Friday's books and, to a lesser extent, forbidden fantasies in general. A good start in talking about a hot-button issue, but it needs to stay on track.

"Egg Sex" is about sex during pregnancy, a topic ignored by books and doctors alike. Bright wanted a daughter, so, to the horror of some lesbians, she had sex with a man instead of getting artificially inseminated. Thus, we get a groundbreaking frontline report on how being preggers affects a woman's sex drive. Bright found, to her surprise, that not only did her breasts swell, her clit and labia did, too. She also realized that labor could be a sexual experience. She masturbated with a vibrator during delivery to ease the pain. "My friend Barbara confessed to me after her first child that she had never been so turned on in her life. When the baby's head was crowning, she called out to her husband over and over, 'I want to come, touch me, please touch me!'—and he thought she was hysterical."

Cleis Press; $9.95
1992; softcover; 157 pp.

# GAY

## GAY ROOTS:
### TWENTY YEARS OF GAY SUNSHINE—AN ANTHOLOGY OF GAY HISTORY, SEX, POLITICS AND CULTURE, VOLUME 1
### edited by Winston Leyland

From 1970 to 1982, Winston Leyland published the tabloid, *Gay Sunshine*, and in 1975 he started Gay Sunshine Press, now the country's oldest continuously publishing gay press. Needless to say, over two decades of intense publishing, Leyland has amassed a staggering amount of material. This huge volume is like an encyclopedia of post-Stonewall gay thought.

There are about a hundred pages of poetry—including some by Allen Ginsberg, Rimbaud, Genet, Russian poets—and six fiction pieces. Articles and essays cover Russian gay literature from the eleventh century to the present, Native American homosexuality, gay underground resistance to the Nazis, Abraham Lincoln's homosexuality and his relationship with Walt Whitman, being gay in London in the 1720s and Harlem in the 1920s, genderfuck, ageism in the gay movement, sex in prison, promiscuity as revolution, censorship (written by John Rechy), water sports, and the infamous *Straight to Hell* magazine. Tennessee Williams writes about the role of sexual identity in his plays. Huey Newton of the Black Panthers wrote a manifesto for that revolutionary group, asking that it join with the gay and women's liberation movements. "We must gain security in ourselves and therefore have respect and feelings for all oppressed people. We must not use the racist-type attitude like the White racists use against people because they are Black and poor."

*Gay Roots* is an unparalleled and essential collection.

Gay Sunshine Press (Leyland Publications); $22.95
1991; softcover; 793 pp.; illus.

## GAY ROOTS:
### AN ANTHOLOGY OF GAY HISTORY, SEX, POLITICS, AND CULTURE, VOLUME 2
### edited by Winston Leyland

The second part of the landmark anthology of material from *Gay Sunshine* and Gay Sunshine Press isn't as humongous as its predecessor, but it still packs in a lot of important writing. This time around there's poetry by Edward A. Lacey, Jim Everhard, and more from Allen Ginsberg; the novella *Costa Brava* by Frits Bernard; and articles on the history of homophobia, sex in Mexican baths, Michelangelo's homosexuality, sports and macho men, and more.

"George Washington's Gay Mess: Was the 'Father of Our Country' a Queen?" is a controversial article that presents evidence that G.W. was gay. The evidence is strongest that Washington and the Marquis de Lafayette were lovers. "When the couple went into the field, Washington kept an anxious eye on his movements. After the Battle of Monmouth in 1778, the two spent the night inside the general's greatcoat snuggled together under a tree. By 1780, Lafayette could write the general that "my sentiment has increased to such a point, the world knows nothing" In another letter to George, written from France during furlough, Lafayette refers to himself as Washington's "sweetheart."

Gay Sunshine Press (Leyland Publishing); $19.95
1993; softcover; 319 pp.; illus.

## HIGH CAMP:
### A GAY GUIDE TO CAMP AND CULT FILMS, VOLUME 1
### by Paul Roe

"In terms of film, camp has come to mean any brazen triumph of theatrical artifice over dramatic substance. Camp is phoniness that glories in itself. More essential still, camp is funny." This book is a guide to the best and worst gay camp films and films that have attracted a gay cult following. Each of the almost two hundred movies gets its own entry. *Pink Flamingos* is John Waters's raunchy tour de force that ends with the cross-dressing Divine munching dogshit. *Glen or Glenda?* is Ed Wood's somewhat autobiographical grade-Z movie about a transvestite.

Many muscleman movies are classics. *Goliath and the Barbarians, Gladiators of Rome, The Loves of Hercules*, and others all star muscle-bound men in skimpy loincloths. "*Son of Samson* is a veritable wet dream of half-naked sadists locked in orgasmic frenzies of ancient torture, bloodlust, and cruelty."

A large number of these camp and cult classics are well-known mainstream movies, such as *Rebel Without a Cause* and *The Maltese Falcon*. Many of these famous movies star equally famous actresses. Some of them are sex kittens, such as Marilyn Monroe ("a sainted icon of fag fandom"), Mae West, and Jayne Mansfield. Others play bitch-goddesses and at times bend genders—Joan Crawford, Greta Garbo, Bette Davis, and Marlene Dietrich. Each of these women has a devoted gay following. The greatest of these films, according to the author and the publisher, is *All About Eve*, which features Bette Davis at her "best and bitchiest."

*High Camp* is illustrated with lots of photos of your favorite stars at their hunkiest and bitchiest.

Leyland Publications; $15.95
1994; softcover; 254 pp.; illus.

## HOLY TITCLAMPS

A fun, informal zine of fiction, poetry, essays, reviews, art, and comix edited by Larry-bob, compiler of *Queer Zine Explosion*. Friendly, impassioned, funny, pissed-off, it's what being a zine is all about. It offers glimpses of the agony and the ecstasy of being gay and just being *alive* in today's society. What more do you want?

Larry-bob/PO Box 591275/San Francisco, CA 94159-1275
Single issue: $3 cash; Canada: $3 plus a little extra for postage (I told you it was informal); foreign: $4
Four-issue sub: $10; Canada: again, add a little extra; foreign: $16

## MY BIGGEST O:
### GAY MEN DESCRIBE "THE BEST SEX I EVER HAD"
### by Jack Hart

In this collection, forty men describe the greatest lays of their lives. The stories are divided into several sections covering first times, one-time encounters, the beginnings of long relationships, unusual encounters, etc. One man describes the night he had his first gay encounter—with his wife's brother. "Then he put my hand on his cock. It was big and thick, much larger than mine. Without a word from him, I began to jerk him off. He stopped me and knelt near my face. 'Suck it,' he said, 'I'll be gentle.' " Their relationship has gone on for eight years. "We told my wife and she approves and participates with us."

Another dude, on the day before breaking up with his partner, discovered that he likes water sports. "...I asked him to come to the bathroom with me and pee on my face. It was the first time I had asked him to do such a thing. It tasted better than all the champagne I had drunk that night, and the warmth of this golden shower gave me the hardest hard-on I ever had."

Alyson Publications; $8.95
1993; softcover; 159 pp.

## QUEER ZINE EXPLOSION

Don't even think you can keep tabs on the queer zine scene without the *Explosion*. Larry-bob from *Holy Titclamps* gives you descriptions and addresses of hundreds of gay male, lesbian, bi, and omnisexual zines in every issue. And you sure as hell can't beat the price.

Larry-bob/PO Box 591275/San Francisco, CA 94159-1275
Single issue: two 29¢ U.S. stamps; Canada: $1;
foreign: 2 IRCs, Four-issue sub: $2; Canada: send a little bit more for postage; foreign: $4

## ROCK ON THE WILD SIDE:
### GAY MALE IMAGES IN POPULAR MUSIC OF THE ROCK ERA
### by Wayne Studer

Rock has always been concerned with sex, but when it comes to gay sex, the relationship has been a little strained. Wayne Studer examines more than two hundred rock songs that have dealt with gay men or transvestites. He finds that when a song deals with homosexuality in a positive manner, it often uses ambiguous terms that leave it open for interpretation. Then there are the songs that deal negatively with the subject. Studer covers them all.

Each song is given its own entry. The earliest queer song is Elvis Presley's 1957 hit "Jailhouse Rock." Elvis sings, "You're the cutest jailbird I ever did see." Then he implores this cute jailbird to do the "jailhouse rock with me." Prisons aren't coed, folks. The sex of the jailbird in question is pretty obvious.

When it comes to hidden meanings, things don't get much more obtuse than Paul Simon's "Me and Julio Down by the School Yard." The lyrics describe a young man whose mother sees him doing something against the law. He's arrested and his parents hate him. Eventually a radical priest gets him released and they end up on the cover of *Newsweek*. This song has always given me an opportunity to practice one of my hobbies, "lyric detective work," but I never thought of the gay angle until Studer mentioned it. He does point out that he's never heard Simon interpret this song, so he may be off base, but it makes as much sense as any other interpretation.

Some rock songs are openly gay, though. Take "Relax" by Frankie Goes to Hollywood (please). This Top Ten dance hit featured a large number of lines about coming, and a lyric about shooting off. It also had that famous sound of pissing, a reference to water sports. Studer somehow fails to mention the most sexual of all the lines: "Relax, don't do it, when you wanna suck or chew it." He probably couldn't decipher that lyric, since the last four words are said as if they're one word. How "Relax" ever got played on the radio, I'll never know.

Among the homophobic tunes Studer covers are two Public Enemy songs and Guns N Roses' infamous "One in a Million." Songs dealing with male gender-benders include "Lola" by the Kinks, "Killer Queen" by Queen, and "Dude (Looks Like a Lady)" by Aerosmith.

This book is a much-needed guide to a hidden aspect of rock and roll that deserves to be outed.

Leyland Publications; $15.95
1994; softcover; 287 pp.; illus.

## STEAM:
### A QUARTERLY JOURNAL FOR MEN

*Steam* is an unapologetically raunchy magazine for men who want to have sexual encounters with other men in public or semipublic places. This often involves casual, anonymous encounters, making *Steam* even more politically incorrect than it already is. *Steam* is almost all text, containing virtually no pictures other than those in the ads.

The articles from correspondents and readers tell about no-strings sex in bathhouses, public bathrooms, locker rooms, parks, sex clubs, etc. They discuss how good the action is at various bars, gyms, clubs, colleges, and other hot spots in various cities. Volume 2 issue #1 covered Portland, Seattle, Boston, Memphis, Edmonton, El Paso, Madrid, and many others.

*Steam* isn't afraid to publish numerous accounts of unsafe sex. For example, one correspondent reports sucking off seven guys through a gloryhole in an Arkansas bathroom with nary a condom in sight. Not everybody's playing it safe, and *Steam* doesn't mind letting you know.

There are also reviews, club listings, and dispatches from the homophobia front, including queer bashing and legal harassment. *Steam* has experienced the latter firsthand. Two members of the San Diego Police Department wrote to the magazine complaining that several people they had arrested for having sex in local parks had gotten the idea from *Steam*. They asked that *Steam* no longer print anything about San Diego and ominously threatened that they could be subject to financial liability through "the State of California and City of San Diego criminal cost recovery programs."

PDA Press/PO Box 460292/San Francisco, CA 94146
Single issue: $5.95
Four-issue sub: $21; Canada: $24; elsewhere: $36

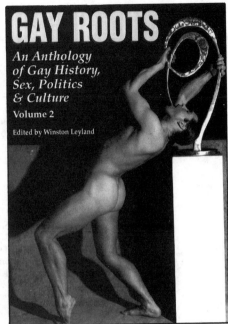

▲ *Gay Roots*
(See page 90)

*An unparalleled and essential collection. Period.*

## SACRED SEX

## FIRE ON THE MOUNTAIN:
### AN INTIMATE GUIDE TO MALE GENITAL MASSAGE (VIDEO)

This video demonstrates the techniques of Taoist erotic penis massage as practiced by Joseph Kramer. The first thing I noticed about the video was the quote on its packaging from sex guru Annie Sprinkle: "What I learned from this tape revolutionized the way I view sex!" A comment like that coming from Sprinkle is akin to Albert Einstein commenting on a physics book, "This book revolutionized the way I view physics." In other words, there's some important stuff in here.

The point is to teach you how to stroke a penis so that you stir up the powerful erotic energies in your partner. As with all sacred sex, the goal is not to cause orgasm but to unleash powerful energies. Steve Davis and Matthew Simons are the masseurs. They first warm up for the activities by facing each other naked. They go through simultaneous breathing, vocalizing, touching, stretching, drumming, body massage, and body slapping. This is to get them physically and spiritually primed, but it can cause fits of giggles in the uninitiated who are watching this video.

Then they get down to business. They alternate lying on their backs as the other one demonstrates the various strokes, rubs, and squeezes that are used—Rock Around the Clock, Gates of Consciousness, Osho's Delight, Rainbow Rub, Big U, Twist and Shout, Belly Bliss, the Juicer, Hairy Palm Sunday, Hand Jive, Carpe Diem, and several more.

After reaching a suitable point, the man being massaged performs the Big Draw by tensing every muscle in his body and lifting up his legs and head. "The Big Draw squeezes the orgasmic energy you have generated into the core of your being where it shoots up through your heart and out the top of your head—connecting your energy with all other energies, with THE energy.... After the Big Draw, most men experience a state of grace, a time of deep peace."

For an extra five dollars you can get a companion booklet that details all the warm-up and massage techniques.

EroSpirit Institute; $39.95
1992; VHS videocassette; 45 min.

## SACRED ORGASMS:
### TEACHINGS FROM THE HEART
### by Kenneth Ray Stubbs

This book, written in a flowing hybrid of poetry and prose, describes the philosophy behind sacred sex. "The paradigm in *Sacred Orgasms*/holds both the spirit and the body/as sacred." The author presents a list of ways to have out-of-the-ordinary orgasms: "while smelling a night-blooming jasmine...while taking the first bite of a peach...while videotaping a space shuttle blast-off when the rumble of the bass sound waves hit."

The author explains the gist of four major erotospiritual paths—Indian Tantra, Chinese Taoism, Native American Quodoushka, and contemporary meditation. These systems can help us integrate our seven systems—spirit body, physical body, chakras, kundalini system, light body, retrieval system, and radiance centers. An orgasm, according to Stubbs, is not the release of tension but rather the generation of energy. When it occurs, two forms of energy, such as those in the seven systems, merge to create a new energy. "With orgasm...

we can transcend our everyday mind
our everyday existence
we can become/be
our expanded self
our transcended self
we can BE."

The illustrations show mixed couples of various ages, races, and physiques in a number of sexual positions, some of which look pretty uncomfortable. This explains the disclaimer at the front of the book, which reads in part: "Some of the positions were accomplished only after years of yogic practice."

Secret Garden; $18.95
1992; oversize softcover; 80 pp.; illus.

## SACRED SEXUALITY:
### LIVING THE VISION OF THE EROTIC SPIRIT
### by Georg Feuerstein

Although monotheistic religions have ingrained in us the idea that spirituality and sex are totally, irreconcilable opposites (like God and Satan, good and evil), the concept of sacred sex says that they are completely intertwined. "When we truly understand our sexuality, we come face-to-face with the mystery of the spirit. When we truly understand the spiritual dimension of existence, we come face-to-face with the mystery of sexuality." Far from being a "sin," sexuality is a "transformative vehicle of higher human growth."

The author looks at how our society has become a "sexual wasteland" and traces the roots of our erotophobic and body-negative beliefs. He then turns to a history of sacred sexuality, covering the erotic cult of the Great Mother, phallic worship, sacred prostitutes, Dionysus, Pan, the ancient mystery religions, Tantra, Taoism, neopaganism, and the new erotic Christianity of Alan Watts, Matthew Fox, and others. The book ends with some suggestions—but not instructions—for reclaiming the sacredness of sex in today's world.

Jeremy P. Tarcher; $14.95
1992; softcover; 239 pp.

*Tantra*

*Sacred sexuality in all its variations and positions.*

## TANTRA:
### THE MAGAZINE

Tantra is the erotic path within Hinduism. This beautiful magazine offers articles, essays, and poetry dealing with not only Tantra, but other sacred sexuality systems and Hinduism in general. The articles on Tantra and related erotospiritual paths are often filled with explicit, detailed instructions and illustrations for achieving bliss and transcendence through intercourse.

However, sex is only a part of Tantric spirituality, and this magazine reflects that fact. I was prepared to encounter article after article on Tantric sex, but the majority of the articles were about other topics—myths, art, architecture, health, meditation, new physics, dance, drumming, healing, conscious dying, and so on.

Issue #9 was devoted to Kali, the head goddess of Tantric Hinduism, "The Joyous One," "The Destroyer of Time," "The Bestower of Peace and Happiness," "The Embodiment of Sensuality." Surprisingly, almost nothing in this issue deals with sex.

If you're into sacred sex, you should get *Tantra*, because it's the only magazine that deals with the subject indepth on a regular basis, although I personally wish it focused on it more. If you're a student of Eastern religion and philosophy, *Tantra* is very worth getting, because of the high quality of material devoted to a wide range of topics.

Tantra/PO Box 108/Torreon, NM 87061-0108
single issue: $4.95
4 issues: $18; Canada & Mexico: $24; Overseas: $26

# SEX TOYS AND CLOTHES

## EVE'S GARDEN

In 1974, urged by Betty Dodson, Dell Williams set up a sex-positive, feminist store to sell tools that give women sexual pleasure. Twenty years later Dell and Eve's Garden are still going strong. They carry all sorts of vibrating gizmos, dildos (including one that looks like a whale and another that looks like a giant finger with a thumb for clitoral stimulation), dildo harnesses, buttplugs, safer sex accessories, oils, balms, B&D items, and sex educational videos and books.

Eve's Garden119 W Fifty-Seventh Street, Suite 420
New York, NY 10019-2383
Catalog: $3

## GOOD VIBRATIONS:
### THE COMPLETE GUIDE TO VIBRATORS (REVISED EDITION)
### by Joani Blank

This little book will teach you how to buzz happily ever after. Sex educator Joani Blank opened Good Vibrations, the first sex shop geared for women, in 1977. Now she shares with us the knowledge she has accumulated from her experiences and those of friends and customers.

What you think of when you hear the word *vibrator*—a battery-powered phallic object—is only a small part of what Blank deals with. She pays more attention to general use vibrators that can also be used for sexual stimulation, although the manufacturers would never admit that on their packaging. Such devices include coil-operated vibrators, wand-type vibrators, double-headed vibrators, Swedish massagers, faux-penis vibrators, and novelty items like eggs and Ben-Wa balls. The first four types are generally available at drugstores, department stores, etc.

Blank gives advice on how to use your vibrator, "care and feeding," anal stimulation, using it with partners. If you've never had an orgasm or have trouble reaching orgasm, Blank shows you how to vibrate your way to multiple orgasms. Another section discusses how men can use vibrators for genital stimulation.

Down There Press; $5.50
1982, 1989; softcover; 70 pp.; illus.

### GOOD VIBRATIONS:
#### CATALOG OF TOYS

Founded in 1977 as a nonthreatening place where women (and men) could buy sexual devices, books, and videos, Good Vibrations has a sex-toy catalog offering carefully selected, high-quality vibrators, including magic wands, coil-operated vibrators, and your standard dick-shaped variety. Some of the more interesting models include a twisting vibrator, one that looks like a banana, one with a clit-tickler that looks like a kangaroo, and curved G-spot vibrators. You can also get varied shapes, sizes, and designs of buttplugs, lubes, boy toys, cock rings, harnesses, restraints, and dildos. You'll find a dildo that looks like a dolphin, one with lots of tiny bubbles just under the surface, and "Cyber," a ridged dildo that looks like a giant crinkle-cut French fry on one side.

This catalog also contains Good Vibes' video selection, from classics (*The Devil in Miss Jones*) to feminist (*Three Daughters*) to instructional (*How to Perform Fellatio*). [Good Vibrations offers another catalog, The Sexuality Library, reviewed in the "Miscellaneous" section.]

Good Vibrations
938 Howard Street #101/San Francisco, CA 94103
Catalog: $2 (or you can get this catalog and
The Sexuality Library for $3)

### LEATHER MASTERS CATALOG

An incredibly complete collection of everything you'll need for adventures in pain. Thirty-six pages of leather, leather, leather! Jackets, pants, harnesses, bras, jockstraps, G-strings, teddies, garter belts, gauntlets, collars and leashes, hoods, blindfolds, restraints, whips, crops, cock and ball restraints, all made out of leather. Plus some clamps, handcuffs, paddles, electrical toys, vibrators, and lubes. I'm impressed.

Leather Masters/969 Park Avenue/San Jose, CA 95126
Catalog: $5

### PARADISE ELECTRO STIMULATION

Are you ready for the next level in sex toys? Forget your clunky Victorian vibrator and get wired! Paradise Electro Stimulation offers a line of shocking sex toys that will give you megawatt hours of enjoyment. They carry buttplugs, cockrings, a vaginal plug, a vaginal shield, a cockhead stimulator, and an insertable sphere, all of which can be hooked up to their Electrostimulation Box.

PES
3172 N. Rainbow Boulevard, Suite 325/Las Vegas, NV 89108
Catalog: $5

### SYBIAN AND VENUS II DEMONSTRATION VIDEO

This video aquaints you with two high-end sex devices, Sybian for women and Venus II for men. They are the Rolls-Royces of vibrators and suck machines. Sybian looks like a saddle with a dildo on the top. The woman straddles it and uses the controls to adjust the speed of two *separate* movements—vibration and rotation. By adjusting each type of movement to the desired speed, from a slow comfortable screw to ride 'em cowboy, a woman can have virtually unlimited orgasms.

The video shows a couple using Sybian. First they have foreplay. Then she mounts the machine, while her partner fondles, kisses, and licks her. She proceeds to come her brains out. For those worried about getting "hooked on buzz," the video reassures you that you will not become addicted to Sybian or prefer it to real sex. In fact, it will make you more responsive to normal intercourse.

Sybian, the video reminds us, is also good for women without partners, a thought that I'm sure already occurred to many people. Reported benefits of Sybian include reduction of stress and anxiety and relief from menstrual cramps and migraine headaches.

The Venus II is demonstrated by the author of *Penis Enlargement Methods* (reviewed below). The Venus II consists of a tube with a sheath inside. The tube is connected by a hose to a motor that fits in a briefcase. The motor can be adjusted to deliver 20 to 360 strokes per minute. It's a hands-free device. Once you insert your dick, the Venus II clamps on to you and gives you the thrill of your life.

These devices come with a very high price tag, but if you want the state-of-the-art sex devices, you have to pay the price. If you buy either or both devices within a short time of receiving your video, you'll get a considerable discount. Either way, you'll also get the price of the video applied toward your purchase.

You can opt to get some printed literature for only three dollars, but, trust me, if you can't afford the video, you sure can't afford the products.

Abco; $19.95
No date; VHS videocassette; 40 min.

## MASTURBATION

### THE JOY OF SOLO SEX
#### by Dr. Harold Litten

There's nothing to jerking off, right, guys? Just bop your baloney, beat your meat, jerk your gherkin. Ha! Shows how much you know. There's an art to masturbation; there exist techniques that can make your monkey-spanking look as pitiful as your first attempt at sex with another human being. For those who want to reach the pinnacle of ecstasy by themselves, this book cannot be ignored.

Litten first discusses society's views of masturbation and the attitude you must develop if you're going to do things right. First off, you must love your body. You must realize that you're not jerking off, you're making love to yourself. Litten teaches you how to caress your body as foreplay, and how to stimulate your gland in different ways, including Shake the Head, Slapping It Silly, and the Two-Finger Down-Stroke.

There is a chapter on the use of toys and other aids. As Litten puts it, "Let's face it: It's the nature of the human male animal to insert his penis into anything that stands still long enough." Truer words were never spoken.

As things get more advanced, the good doctor tells us how to use fantasy effectively, how to have multiple orgasms, how to use abstinence to get more explosive orgasms, and how to masturbate using just your mind, never physically touching yourself. [Note: this book was originally titled *Solo Sex: Advanced Techniques*.]

Factor Press; $12.95
1993; softcover; 193 pp.

### MASTURBATION, TANTRA, AND SELF LOVE
#### by Margo Woods

This book teaches the art of sacred masturbation. The basic gist is that you masturbate until you are on the very brink of orgasm. Stop. Direct all the Tantric energy that you have stirred up into your heart. Masturbate again till you're ready to come and repeat the process. Do this as many times as you want and then have your orgasm.

The benefits of doing this are immense, according to the author. You will feel more energetic and alive. You will become more attractive to yourself and others. All this life energy in your heart will help you get over addictions and poor self-image and will help your romantic/sexual relationships with others. Plus, if you do decide to go all the way, you'll have hellacious orgasms.

Mho and Mho Works; $9.95
1981; softcover; 107pp.

## SINGULAR PLEASURES
### by Harry Matthews

This book is a collection of sixty-one very short vignettes about people masturbating. The people are of both sexes and all different ages. They're in a wide variety of settings and their methods of onanism range from the run-of-the-mill to the imaginatively bizarre. "A man of thirty-five is about to experience orgasm in one of the better condominiums in Gaza. He is masturbating, but neither hand nor object touches his taut penis: arranged in a circle, five hairblowers direct their streams of warm air toward that focal point. He has plugged his ears with balls of wax."

Another example: "A twenty-four-year-old cellist is sitting naked on a stool in her bedroom in Manila. Her legs are spread; her left hand pulls back the folds of her vulva; her right hand is drawing the tip of a cello bow over her clitoris in fluttering tremolo."

Other people in these vignettes get themselves off straddling tree trunks, while getting a foot massage from a maid, during a performance of Haydn's "Emperor" Quartet, with an electric toothbrush, while a cat watches, inside a confessional, in an overturned car, after having sex, and on a jet at 28,000 feet. Each little story is accompanied by a watercolor painting (reproduced in black and white) of a simple object, like a bat, bicycle, chair, hat, vase of flowers, etc.

Dalkey Archive Press; $19.95
1988; hardcover; 138 pp.; heavily illus.

# PRIVATE PARTS

## CIRCUMCISION:
### WHAT IT DOES
### by Billy Ray Boyd

This book explains that circumcision is an unnecessary, risky operation that is still being practiced mainly because of inertia: "...our cultural bias in favor of the procedure causes us repeatedly to misinterpret the data on circumcision and to leap prematurely to false conclusions. We seem to need to find a reason to justify something we're already in the habit of doing."

The author claims that medical circumcision started in the 1800s as a way to discourage masturbation. When doctors realized that males who had been clipped were spanking the monkey with as much gusto as those who still had all their parts, they changed their reasoning but not their practice. Penile cancer is now one of the main arguments for circumcision, but the *American Journal of Diseases in Childhood* notes that "there are more deaths each year from circumcision than from cancer of the penis."

The author is most definitely anticircumcision. He shoots holes in all the arguments for circumcision. But whether you think circumcision is right or wrong, in the end it should be the person being circumcised who makes the choice. Obviously, infants can't make this decision. Such a painful procedure being forced on a child violates U.N. international law, according to the author.

Circumcision has other effects, all duly noted: decreased sexual sensations in the penis, loss of natural lubrication, psychological scars, and we won't even mention the horror of botched circumcisions.... Basically, there's no good reason to do it. The author talks about ways of stopping this ritual mutilation and how to deal with it if it's been done to you.

C. Olson; $6.95
1990; softcover; 95 pp.

## CUNT COLORING BOOK
### by Tee Corinne

All the items that I'm telling you about have one thing in common—they expose the hidden, whether it is in the form of ideas, theories, beliefs, events, tangible items, or—in this case—body parts. Perhaps no part of the anatomy is more shrouded in mystery than the vagina, that mysterious mouth, cave, tunnel that requires the penis to enter erect and swollen but makes it leave limp and spent.

In 1975 sex educator Tee Corinne put out a revolutionary book that lifted the veil of secrecy. The *Cunt Coloring Book* is a classic collection of forty-one black-and-white line drawings of actual pussies. With this book there is nowhere to hide. You are forced to confront cunt.

Although this pioneering book is a classic, *Femalia* (below) does the same thing using actual photographs and is therefore a more powerful book.

Last Gasp; $6.95
1975; oversize softcover; 44 pp.; heavily illus.

## FEMALIA
### edited by Joani Blank

Sex educator Joani Blank has been aware that "most women...had no way of knowing what other women's genitals looked like." In fact, most women may not even know exactly what their *own* look like. In order to demystify the pussy, Blank has assembled these thirty-two color photographs from Tee A. Corinne, Michael Perry, Jill Posener, and Michael A. Rosen. Each photo is a front-and-center close-up of a vagina, mostly with the outer lips pulled apart for an unobstructed view. The women who posed represent a diversity of races, ages, and ethnicity. Some have given birth, some have shaved their pussies, and two have pierced theirs. These pictures present a gallery of vaginas, showing that they are remarkably varied though they have the same fundamental structure.

Annie Sprinkle has commented, "This book is a magic mirror letting you know exactly how you feel about female genitalia. It's a perfect coffee-table book." This last comment may seem surprising, but it's true. *Femalia* bridges the previously unrecognized gap between art and gynecological textbooks. There is nothing else like it.

Down There Press; $14.50
1993; softcover; 69 pp.; heavily illus.

## FORESKIN:
### A CLOSER LOOK
### by Bud Berkeley

Filling a gap in the history of the human race, this book presents a thorough examination of the foreskin (or lack thereof). The author is the founder of the Uncircumcised Society of America (USA). He writes of the alternating agony and ecstasy of having a foreskin. Of the pressures to get it chopped off, including almost being forced to by the army while in ROTC. The author presents a history of the attitudes toward foreskins in numerous times and cultures. There's also a question-and-answer chapter involving foreskin stretching, smegma, uncircumcising, nicknames for the old soldier's flag, etc. A selection of letters from USA publications discusses medical research, AIDS, blue balls, circumcision as punishment, hiding drugs in the snapper, and much more.

Alyson Publications; $9.95
1993; softcover; 207 pp.

## KOKIGAMI:
### THE INTIMATE ART OF THE LITTLE PAPER COSTUME
### by Heather Busch and Burton Silver

Put simply, this book contains paper costumes for your wang. Referred to as *kokigami* (or Art Dicko), it's the sexual version of the oriental art of paper-folding, origami. Now this obscure form of sexual fun dating back at least to eighth-century Japan is being brought to a Western audience.

This book contains fourteen colorful pieces of *kokigami* (*koki*) printed on thick sturdy paper. Simply cut them out, insert the tabs into the slots, and your schlong has a whole new look. Among the koki included are a pig, dragon, fire engine, space shuttle, flower, private eye (or should I say dick?), and a vintage car. There are assembly and sizing instructions, as well as suggestions for sex play. While wearing the dragon, for example, you can say, "Where are my precious jewels? My treasures? My trophies? Are they hidden there in your dark cave?" Your partner says, "Come on, hot stuff! Careful the iron gates don't snap shut and sever your burning tongue!"

Ten Speed Press; $14.95
1991; oversize softcover; 64 pp.; heavily illus.

## PENIS ENLARGEMENT METHODS:
### FACT AND PHALLUSY
### by Gary M. Griffin, MBA

This is the one book that will give you the straight dope on dick size. All of your questions will be answered here, boys and girls. What's the average size? Six inches is the average erection, with 75 percent of men falling within one inch of this measurement. How common are huge wangs? Statistics show that about one in 10,000 men has a dick ten inches or bigger, and only about 1,000 men in the entire world are a foot or longer.

How big is the biggest? Porn star John Holmes pops to mind, but his cock—reputed to be anywhere from twelve to sixteen inches—was actually just short of ten inches. Long Dong Silver is probably the best-endowed porno actor, with an estimated fifteen-inch wanker. Some doctors have reported measuring dicks around the fourteen-inch mark, and one M.D. makes the claim that he has seen the medical record of a man with eighteen inches, although he offers no substantial proof. The author himself says that he is acquainted with a man whose erection is fifteen inches long and eight inches in circumference.

What well-known men are hung? The author offers a list of about a hundred men reputed by lovers, friends, etc. to be large and in charge, including Warren Beatty, Humphrey Bogart (eight inches), Charlie Chaplin (allegedly twelve inches), Willem Dafoe (nine inches), Steve Martin (eight inches), Eddie Murphy (eight to nine inches), Tom Brokaw (eight inches), David Letterman (nine inches), President Lyndon Johnson, Lord Byron, and Jimi Hendrix.

Then, of course, there's the most crucial question of all: How do I make it bigger? The author says that the idea that there's no way to increase penis size is a myth. He details many of the most interesting, successful, and promising methods, which fall into four basic categories—manual methods, mental/visual imagery methods, genetic manipulation, and surgical methods. He claims that the simple procedure known as "milking," which you can do with your bare hands, can add half an inch to an inch if done fifteen to twenty minutes a day, five days a week, for at least six months. Also, vacuum pumps, according to the author, really do work. Surgery is the other most reliable method of dick enlargement, but it's costly and the long-term effects are not known.

This book contains lots of photos of the anatomy in question, and the bottom of each page contains a piece of penis trivia, such as: "In southern Burma, the Peguan tribe inserts tiny gold and silver bells under the skin of the penis. These can be heard tinkling as they walk."

Added Dimensions Publishing; $14.95
1993; softcover; 160 pp.; illus.

# SEXUAL FREEDOM

## JESUS ACTED UP:
### A GAY AND LESBIAN MANIFESTO
### by Robert Goss

The controversial concept behind this book is that Jesus was actually a radical, an uncompromising liberator of the oppressed. Gays and lesbians should look at him as a role model, and queer Christians should worship him as an emancipator. "For Jesus, God's reign was socially provocative and politically explosive. It was socially provocative in that its coming belonged to the least, those like children (Matt. 18:4, Mark 10:15), the destitute (Luke 6:20), the persecuted (Matt. 5:10), and outcasts (Matt. 21:31)." And let's not forget that Jesus hung out with the lepers and whores, much to the horror of his disciples. Further, "God's reign was also politically explosive. Jesus practiced liberation in his siding with the humiliated and oppressed of Jewish society."

The author attempts to build a "queer Christology" by deconstructing the orthodox Christology, showing its seams, hesitations, contradictions, and alignments with power structures. "Christianity aspires to meaning for all people at all times. Christian theology, however, is the product of people with power and privilege, influence and wealth.... This partisan bias must be unmasked."

Harper SanFrancisco (HarperCollins Publishers); $14
1993; softcover; 240 pp.

## JOURNAL OF SEXUAL LIBERTY

The *Journal* is a no-frills affair—typewriter font, almost no graphics, on nine photocopied pages stapled together. But what it lacks in production values it makes up for in information. They report news about laws and practices that are homophobic or erotophobic (afraid of sex in general). The May 1994 issue has a long article on the efforts to open a bathhouse in San Francisco. The government is trying to use safety regulations as a way to halt its opening. Short blurbs cover many other topics. "A CA Court of Appeals in LA ruled Boy Scouts do not have to accept gays as leaders. The Court says gays could be a serious disruption and that the Boy Scouts were not subject to anti-discrimination laws." On a positive note: "Minneapolis's Walker Art Gallery received NEA funding for a performance art work which included cutting a design into the back of an HIV positive man with a scalpel, tapping scalp [sic] with needles and decorating female assistants with spikes."

CPOSCL/PO Box 422385/San Francisco, CA 94142
One-year sub (12 issues): $10

## LOONY SEX LAWS:
### THAT YOU NEVER KNEW YOU WERE BREAKING
### by Robert Wayne Pelton

This book is a compendium of laws from all over the world in different time periods that regulate sexual behavior. In a way, reading this book is amusing, because most of the laws are so ridiculous that they're laughable. On the other hand, reading this book can be infuriating and discouraging when you see that authority's penchant for legislating people's private lives is a universal practice.

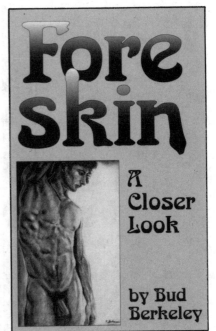

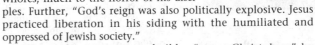

▲ *Foreskin*
*by Bud*
*Berkeley*

*A thorough*
*examination*
*of the*
*foreskin*
*(or lack*
*thereof).*

**Bad Sex** ▼
edited by John
Hoyland

*Anti-eroticism
or just a heavy
dose of reality?*

Among the hundreds of laws cited are these gems. Anal sex in Pennsylvania is punishable by a five thousand dollar fine and ten years at hard labor. Indiana and Ohio both have laws forbidding male skating instructors from having sex with their students. Violations are prosecuted as a felony. People in California can still get fifteen years in the penitentiary for performing oral sex, even if the partners are married and going at it in their own bedroom. Michigan law calls for five years in the big house for men who masturbate (You think prison overcrowding is a problem now—what if this law were enforced?). *Men* are prohibited from going topless in Ocean City, Maryland.

On the international front, in Colombia it's considered justifiable homicide for a man to shoot his wife if he catches her in bed with another man. Such cases aren't even prosecuted. Men engaging in anal sex in Peru are dragged through the streets, then hanged, and their corpses are burned. In Lebanon a man is allowed to have sex with a female animal. However, if the animal is male, the man can be put to death. An old law still on the books in Volgagrad, Russia, says that couples can only have sex in the missionary position, with the shades down, and the lights out. In turn-of-the-century Paris, waitresses working in certain cafés were required by law to actively prostitute themselves.

Walker and Company; $9.95
1992; hardcover; 190 pp.

## THE REGULATION OF DESIRE:
### SEXUALITY IN CANADA
### by Gary Kinsman

This book presents a history of gay and lesbian communities in Canada, paying special attention to their oppression by the government, the right wing, and mainstream society. The author also takes the left to task for its role in the oppression. "Some lesbians and gay men have looked to the socialist and Marxist traditions because of their promise of liberation of all the oppressed and exploited.... These ties were severed however with the establishment of the Stalinist position that homosexuality was a symptom of capitalist and fascist degeneration, and with the working class movement's defence of the heterosexual proletarian family.... Heterosexism—the ideology which claims lesbians and gay men to be 'sick' and heterosexuals to be 'normal'—has therefore been integrated into the analysis and traditions of the socialist movement."

The author's history of Canadian sexual mores and laws sounds distressingly like that of other countries. The first known trial in the French colonies for sodomy and "crimes against nature" was in 1648, when a young man was sentenced to death. In a strange twist, Montreal Jesuits opposed this harsh measure and managed to have him imprisoned instead.

In the 1890s, "Women who rode bicycles clad in pant-like bloomers were likened to prostitutes." The editor of *Dominion Medical Monthly* wrote that because of all the women riding bicycles, "Toronto's scorching thoroughfares make the streets of Sodom and Gomorrah appear as pure as Salvation Army shelters." The Canadian Immigration Act of 1952 treated gays and lesbians as "subversives" and denied them entry into the country. Currently Canadian customs is seizing massive amounts of imported homoerotic material.

The author also covers the good news, such as the courage of *Justice Weekly,* an otherwise "respectable" publication, which became the first Canadian magazine to report on the deplorable treatment of homosexuals in the 1950s. The Association for Social Knowledge, Canada's most important gay rights organization of

the time, was formed in 1964. That same year saw the start of two gay magazines. Presently, the Canadian Charter of Rights and Freedoms is offering hope for new levels of respect and rights.

Black Rose Books;
1987; softcover; 233 pp.

## SEX AND REASON
### by Richard A. Posner

U.S. Court of Appeals judge Richard Posner examines the history of sexuality from a unique perspective. He uses an economic/legal framework to look at the social controls surrounding sex and how it has affected people's behavior.

The main principle of economics is that you examine any action in terms of its cost/benefit ratio. If the potential benefits outweigh the potential costs, you do it. If they don't, you don't do it. As economists like to point out, this principle not only guides actions involving money, but any action at all, whether the action of a country or an individual. Posner applies this theory to sex, saying that we make choices on what kind of sexual activities to engage in based on risk analysis.

Possible costs of various sex acts include social diseases, pregnancy, breaking the law, being rejected by society, ruining a relationship, and—depending on the beliefs of the individual—being damned to hell. Possible benefits of sex are pleasure, pregnancy, and cementing relationships. Posner looks at how various sex acts measure up. "For example, noncontraceptive vaginal intercourse is well suited to the end of procreation, but, unless a large number of children are desired, not so well suited to the pursuit of sexual pleasure: an unwanted child is a heavy tax to pay for the pleasures of sex.... For those to whom sex is merely a matter of scratching an itch, masturbation should be an excellent substitute because it is so much cheaper in terms of time, exposure to disease, and other dimensions of cost."

The cost/benefit ratios of sex have an effect on the society as a whole. "Petting to orgasm and early marriage are more common in religious societies that discourage premarital intercourse than in permissive societies in which such intercourse is common." Also, Posner predicts that the rise of AIDS is resulting in less kids being born out of wedlock, owing to increased use of condoms.

But looking at individual rationales for sex is only part of the book; the other part looks at society's rationales for regulating sex. Such issues as freedom, privacy, religion, morality, and "the weakening of society's fabric" play a role in a society's decisions on what is acceptable/unacceptable and legal/illegal.

*Sex and Reason* is fairly dry reading, but any book that can look at the worn-out subject of sex in a new light is worth checking out.

Harvard University Press; $15.95
1992; softcover; 458 pp.

## EROTIC FICTION

### BAD SEX
### edited by John Hoyland

I thought it would be good to start the erotic fiction section with an anthology of short stories that could be defined as anti-erotic. Sex in fiction is almost always portrayed as a great, fun, easy pastime that leaves everybody happy and satisfied. These stories inject a heavy dose of reality into sexual literature. In "Grub" by Eroica Mildmay a woman agrees to go out to dinner with a man just because she's so broke, she hasn't dined out in ages. He obviously wants to bed her, and she agrees to go back to his place, even though she's not really interested in sex. Once they're at his place, she becomes so tired that she decides to sleep with him simply because she doesn't feel like having to go home in the cold. This leads to perhaps the most unsexy sex scene ever written: "When he eventually leaned forward to kiss her, she was more concerned with the wine glass that he nearly knocked over with his knee than with his kiss.... She touched him, moving her hand down along his back, to read him, not to embrace him. There was no play in her. His penis was not a friend, it was simply a member of the public. She did not seek it out."

Satan has a little chat with a missionary priest in "Believe Me" by Michael Carson. Beelzebub is tormenting the cleric because of an "indiscretion" he committed with a young man at the Mission. But it's not the sex act itself that Lucifer is berating the father for. It's the fact that the priest convinced the young man that such an act was a loving thing to do. Afterward, consumed with religiously inspired guilt, the priest told his lover that it was horribly wrong and wicked and that they must pray for forgiveness. The Prince of Darkness tells the priest of the young man's confusion, of "the desire you woke in him and then—when remorse and a certain slackening of the heart's desire hit you—tried to root out. The lad did not know anymore who he was. He still does not."

"Choosing the Incubus" by Molly Brown is a dark fantasy piece about a woman who can't get no satisfaction from her jerkface boyfriend, but finds that ecstasy can come from a supernatural source. "Morning Always Comes" by Matt Cohen earns points for having a climactic scene in which a guy barfs on his girlfriend while they're making love.

The problem with *Bad Sex* is that several of the stories are actually about Bad Relationships, with sex playing little or no role. In "The Pink Shoes" by Christopher Hope, a guy has a dead-end relationship with an uncaring, thoughtless chick. She boffs some bodybuilder in their apartment, and he kicks her out. Big deal. Sex plays even less of a role in "Do You Love Me" by Marge Piercy, a tale about two people who don't really love each other but decide to get married for the security it will bring. In the opening scene they're having sex, but it plays no role in the plot. Why is this story included?

*Bad Sex* could have been better, but seeing that there's no other anthology like it—and there probably never will be—it'll have to do.

Serpent's Tale; $12.99
1993; softcover; 249 pp.

## BANNED: CLASSICAL EROTICA
### edited by Victor Gulotta and Brandon Toropov

Over the centuries many of the greatest writers and poets have had their work censored or expurgated. This book presents these choice bits of literature, with informative introductions. Ovid's *Book of Love* has caused outrage for centuries and was seized by U.S. Customs officials as late as 1928. In the passage reprinted here we find this ancient Roman lovemaking advice: "The girl whose face is lovely should lie on her back; the one whose hindquarters are her prime asset should present that view."

Other writers whose works are represented include Chaucer, John Donne, Alexander Pope, Walt Whitman, and Shakespeare. Deleted or deliberately mistranslated parts of the Arabian Nights and the King James Bible are here also.

Many of these selections are still left out of some so-called complete collections of the authors' works and are impossible to find in older editions. The editors have done a great service by bringing this material together. For only six bucks, it's a worthy addition to your First Amendment/erotica library, and a portion of each sale goes to the American Booksellers Foundation for Free Expression.

Bob Adams, Inc; $5.95
1992; paperback; 141 pp.

## BIZARRE SEX:
### AND OTHER CRIMES OF PASSION
### edited by Stan Tal

*Bizarre Sex* is a Canadian magazine of erotic horror and dark fantasy. These twenty-one short stories expose the violent lust that lurks in the deepest, darkest regions of the heart and loins.

"Baptism at Motel 6" tells what happens when a hitchhiking Jesus freak meets a Satanist and takes a biblical verse a little too literally. In "Lady Filth," a dirtbag who runs guns, pushes drugs, and pimps thinks he can deal with filth but keep himself clean. A sex doll he gets as a gift has other ideas.

"Luck of the Draw," one of the best stories, is about a man who has a magical deck of cards. All the cards have a sex act written on them, and one is a "Rape" card. When Rake randomly chooses one from the deck, he is teleported automatically to some location where he performs the act he drew. He callously enjoys the rape card as much as the others, until he meets a woman who has a trick or two up her sleeve.

In "Metal Fatigue," another one of the best stories, a man is repeatedly abducted by hermaphrodite aliens with steel genitals. They use him mercilessly for hours at a time. But is he really experiencing intergalactic rape or is it a severe form of job stress?

A Richard Kasak Book (Masquerade Books); $12.95
1994; softcover; 211 pp.

## BLUE MOON BOOKS

Blue Moon specializes in publishing Victorian, neo-Victorian, and modern SM fiction featuring consensual, quasi-consensual, and nonconsensual encounters. Started by Barney Rossett, former publisher of the illustrious Grove Press, Blue Moon publishes well over one hundred books and is indispensable for people who thrill to the crack of the whip. Titles include *Tangerine, Shades of Singapore, Bombay Bound, Virtue's Reward,* and *Sadopaideia.* Their North Star Line imprint publishes classic works, such as *Story of O, Stirrings Still* by Samuel Beckett, and *The Olympia Reader.*

Blue Moon Books/61 Fourth Avenue/New York, NY 10003
Catalog: free

## DAUGHTERS OF DARKNESS:
### LESBIAN VAMPIRE STORIES
### edited by Pam Keesey

This powerful collection contains ten stories of lesbian vampires—nine by contemporary writers of lesbian erotica plus "Camilla," the most famous story of a sapphic bloodsucker, written in 1871 by J. Sheridan LeFanu. "Daughter of the Night" by Elaine Bergstrom is about the blood-bathing countess, Elizabeth Bathory. Elizabeth, only thirteen and already betrothed to some aristocrat, discovers that she much prefers the arms of Catherine the vampire. "Lilith" by Robbie Sommers is the hot story of a female New Orleans vampire who shows a tourist the "hidden side" of the city. In "Dracula Retold," a humorous antipatriarchal story by zana, a young homemaker is bitten by her vampiric next-door neighbor. She helps exact revenge on her domineering husband before joining a colony of female vampires.

*Daughters of Darkness* is not an excuse to dress up lesbian porn in Gothic clothing. It makes good use of the vampire element, using it to explore themes of sexuality, power, liberation, and domination. In some of the stories the eroticism is low key, while in other stories it shows up in full force. Either way, you'll be hit by love at first dyke.

Cleis Press; $10.95
1993; softcover; 247 pp.

*Daughters of Darkness* edited by Pam Keesey

*Love at first dyke.*

## DREAM MASTER:
### AND OTHER SM STORIES
### by Larry Townsend

Author of the *Leatherman's Handbooks* and gay male SM stories and novels since 1968, Larry Townsend is one of the pioneers of gay leathersex. This book is a collection of four stories and a novellete from the early and mid-1980s. In "Skin a Cat" a burglar witnesses an SM scene in a house he's broken into. He manages to escape, but the owner, a master, tracks him down and gives his ass a thrashing. Later, the burglar is arrested and the master gets him off the hook on the condition that he work in the master's stable of leathermen-for-hire. Another story is about a German man taken to a concentration camp by the Nazis because he's gay. He and the camp's sergeant develop a relationship that turns very sour.

"Dream Master" is a creative tale about a computer science researcher working on apparatus that would allow a user to communicate telepathically with a computer. He realizes that the machine he's working on has another, far more unusual use. With it, he can project his thoughts into the dreams of his rival, causing some soul-shattering nightmares. In one particularly inventive dream, our hero tortures his enemy: "First, I tied a length of leather thong around his balls, wrapping them tightly in the coils until I had driven them deeply, painfully, into the lowest extensions of his sac. I then attached a bucket to the end and left it hanging from his stretched and gleaming testicles…. A tube ran from [his mouth to a] bucket suspended from the ceiling a few inches above his head. When I loosened the clamp, a slow steady stream of water began flowing into his mouth, building up at a rate that required him to swallow every two or three minutes. 'You're going to have to piss very shortly,' I told him, 'and piss and piss, until that bucket starts to overflow. Guess how that's going to feel, pulling down on your balls, big man.'"

LT Publications; $11.95
1992; softcover; 243 pp.

## EQUINOX
### by Samuel Delany

Like *Image of the Beast* and *Pornucopia*, Samuel Delany's *Equinox* is a lost erotic classic by a big-name writer of speculative fiction. Delany was part of the New Wave movement in science fiction in the 1960s. He won several Nebula Awards for novels and short stories, including *Babel-17* and "Aye, and Gommorah." In 1973 Delany penned this radical book (which the original publisher released under the generic title *The Tides of Lust*) about the adventures of the captain of the *Equinox* and his crew, an underage boy and girl. (In an interesting move, this publisher has added one hundred years to the ages of every child in the novel, making the captain's kids 113 and 116.)

The book starts out in Delany's trademark beautiful, dense prose but, mysteriously, that style abruptly ends after chapter one, and though the rest of the book is well written, it never reaches that level again. The plot is kept to a minimum, the sex at maximum overdrive. Anybody/anything is fair game: men, women, hundred-year-old children, animals, corpses, family members, and more. *Equinox* may not excite you (then again, it may), but it's an entertaining read and a piece of porn history.

Rhino*ceros* (Masquerade Books); $6.95
1973; paperback; 173 pp.

## GAIUS VALERIUS CATULLUS'S
## COMPLETE POETIC WORKS
### translated by Jacob Rabinowitz

Gaius Valerius Catullus was a Roman rude boy who wrote lascivious poetry in the first century B.C. Ole Gaius hated authority and loved to offend as much as possible (Rome hadn't yet become a den of debauchery during Gaius's lifetime). Far from being some porno hack, Gaius was Rome's first great writer and was studied by Virgil, Horace, and Ovid. Because of his sexually frank subject matter, he's been cold-shouldered by academia. When he does show up, he's watered down by his translators. Jacob Rabinowitz has decided it's time to bring Gaius to the forefront in all his raunchy glory. These 120 poems are, in the words of William Burroughs, "the fossils of lust."

In Poem #5 (the poems are untitled) the narrator tells a friend: "I'll let you sniff that fragrance my girl gives off when she's possessed by the god of Love—/when you smell it, you'll beg the gods to turn you into a great big nose." In Poem #23 he begs a woman to let him visit her at noon and says she should be ready for "nine uninterrupted fucks." Evidently, he can't wait until noon, because at the end of the poem he writes, "In fact, why not now?/I just had lunch, I'm lolling here, gorged,/and practically punching a hole through my toga."

Gaius was in love with a woman named Lesbia. Several of his poems describe him lashing out against rivals for her affection. From Poem #61: "It pains me/that a pure girl's chaste kisses/should taste the pollution of your pissdrinking lips." One of his rivals is a (former) friend: "You stole her! Poisoner/of my life, you make friendship a disease." In another poem he says of the same person, "An unpleasant breath of rumor wafts about you like an odor—/to the effect that a wild goat lives in the valley of your armpit."

Gaius also had the hots for a fourteen-year-old boy named Juventius. He's worried that one of his friends wants Juvie, too. "It's you I'm worried about. You and your dong, a menace/to boys in general. Good lads or rotten brats—/no one's safe." In the next poem, he addresses the same person: "Think you'll get in his pants?/You'll blow me first!"

Spring Publications; $13.50
1991; softcover; 150 pp.

## THE GATES OF PARADISE:
### THE ANTHOLOGY OF EROTIC SHORT FICTION
### edited by Alberto Manguel

This anthology contains a diverse, international collection of erotic stories. They all have a literary feel to them, the kind of refined writing you find in *Yellow Silk* and *Libido*. Which isn't to say that these stories aren't hot. Some of them are, while some of them are much more subtly erotic. "Eugenia" by Sarah Sheard doesn't shy away from earthiness. A woman is remembering Eugenia, a friend from her days at school. Eugenia was quite beautiful ("Branches of forsythia foaming into blossom at her approach, dropping seed in her wake."), and the two had developed a close friendship. One night something awakened in both of them. "I began to explore her mouth as her fingers slid down my back to steady me in the narrow bed, her ass against the cool plaster wall. I palmed it, suddenly realizing I'd longed to for months—and of course had, but only through cloth, brushing her skirt smooth, not like this, my hand sliding across her cool flesh, across the small of her back, her tiny waist ebbing away below the ribcage…."

The story with undoubtedly the best title is "The Day I Sat with Jesus on the Sun Deck and a Wind Came Up and Blew My Kimono Open and He Saw My Breasts" by Gloria Sawai. Told in a humorous style, this story deals in a very restrained manner with the weird connection between religion and sex. Although the narrator and Jesus never do anything sexual, there is definitely an erotic charge in the air. When the event described in the title occurs, "I looked at Jesus. He was looking at me. And at my breasts. Looking right at them. Jesus was sitting there on the sun deck, looking at my breasts."

There are several other stories that aren't afraid to take on taboo subjects. "Jocasta" by Liliana Heker is an interior monologue in which a woman admits to her sexual feelings for her young son. Honoré de Balzac's "A Passion in the Desert" chronicles a soldier's deep, somewhat romantic love (which is never consummated) for a panther. In "What Do You Do While I'm Gone?" by Doris Dörrie a woman leaves the house for a while every so often so her husband can dress in her clothes and makeup. Of course Georges Bataille's story "The Dead Man" is one unbroken string of shattered taboos.

Although the kind of writing in *The Gates of Paradise* is considered too highfalutin by some people, it is a superb collection for people whose taste runs along such lines.

Clarkson N. Potter (Random House); $18
1993; softcover; 689 pp.

## MILKIN' THE BULLS:
### AND OTHER HOT HAZING STORIES
### by John Barton

Hazing stories are a popular subgenre of gay erotic fiction, and some of the most popular stories were written by John Barton. In the early 1980s he wrote a series of four military school stories that have become legendary. This book collects those stories plus three new ones.

The gay SM overtones of hazing in military school and frats is extremely obvious, even if it doesn't always come to its logical fruition. With Barton's stories, though, those dominance and submission rituals are nonstop orgies of merciless mansex. His four famous stories involve the Provost of Discipline at Sumpter Military Institute, a former marine whose tactics of discipline were sometimes a little too extreme for the military.

Of the new stories, two are about fraternity initiations and one is about a military school. In that story one of the upperclassmen is describing what he and his comrades did to one of the new students: "Out on the quad we made 'im sing out 'I suck big juicy dicks' till he thought he was a real cocksucker already, an' when we partied 'im we had plenty enough cock to keep 'im suckin' while we got his pussy broke in proper. We had to rack his balls some to make 'im do it at first, but it wasn't long before he was chowin' down on it like the whores down at Suzy's place. By the time we let 'im go he could take a big one right down to the balls."

Leyland Publications; $14.95
1993; softcover; 190 pp.

## NINE INCH WILL PLEASE A LADY:
### A TREASURY OF SMUT
### edited by Sir Richard Styff

This volume is a collection of bawdy and scatological poetry, much of which is purported to have been written by such famous bards as Robert Burns, John Dryden, Alexander Pope, Jonathan Swift, and Eugene Field, the creator of *Little Boy Blue*. Some of the poems are truly hilarious, some are crap. The chapter of limericks contains this gem: "There was an old hermit named Dave/Who kept a dead whore in his cave./He said, 'I'll admit/I'm a bit of a shit/But think of the money I save!'"

I have to question the authenticity of some of these poems. "Do Your Balls Hang Low?" said to have been written around 1840, contains a reference to radioactivity, which was discovered in 1896 by a French physicist (no, I didn't know that off the top of my head. I looked it up). An even more obvious anachronism occurs in the outhouse poem "Two Wives," credited to Robert Burns circa 1690. It makes reference to Charmin. Damn, Burns really was ahead of his time!

Ariel Press; $9.95
1994; softcover; 127 pp.

## THE PILLOW BOOK OF EROTICA

This slim, square-shaped book is a mixture of erotic writing and art designed to be kept bedside. Each two-page spread has a work of art (usually a photo or painting) and a brief excerpt from a poem or novel.

The book is divided into four sections devoted to the four stages of sex—desire, seduction, consummation, and afterglow. The art ranges from paintings by European masters to black-and-white photographic nudes to color pictures of Beautiful Young White People embracing. Somebody needs to call the greeting card companies and see if their stock photos for sappy romantic cards has been broken into recently.

The writing is even more eclectic than the art. There are excerpts from Emily Dickinson, Nicholson Bakers's *VOX*, Bram Stoker's *Dracula*, Amy Lowell's *The Taxi*, *The Well of Loneliness*, *Ulysses*, and Robert and Elizabeth Barrett Browning.

Aside from the blandness of some of the photos, *The Pillow Book* is a nice little treat to share with your lover.

Crown Publishers; $15
1994; small hardcover; 58 pp.; illus.

## PORNUCOPIA
### by Piers Anthony

Piers Anthony is the author of several extremely popular mainstream science fiction and fantasy series including *Xanth*, *The Apprentice Adept*, and *The Incarnations of Immortality*. But there is another Anthony that is only hinted at in the playful T&A of the Xanth novels—it is this Piers Anthony who wrote *Pornucopia*, an extremely explicit over-the-top fantasy novel. Written in the lighthearted style Anthony is best known for, *Pornucopia* will nevertheless shock even the most jaded readers.

*Pornucopia*
by Piers
Anthony

*A noted
SF master goes
over the top.*

The plot revolves around Prior Gross, who has an uncircumcised penis that measures 3.97 inches when erect. As it turns out, the smegma that Prior's penis produces has curative properties, and this makes Prior's organ the target of an underhanded abduction by a beautiful scientist named Tantamount. The rest of the novel focuses on Prior's attempts to regain his pilfered gland. Anthony has commented that when writing this book, he tried to break every taboo he could think of, even those of the erotic publishing industry itself. Indeed, *Pornucopia* deals with such verboten topics as smegma, V.D., small penis size, bestiality, circumcision, tampon insertion, and three-pronged prosthetic penises (?!). When Anthony originally submitted this book to Playboy Press, they rejected it as "too gross for words." Need I say more?

Tafford Publishing; $12.95
1993; softcover; 187 pp.

## THE ROMANCE OF CHASTISEMENT:
### OR, REVELATIONS OF SCHOOL AND BEDROOM BY AN EXPERT
### by Anonymous

One of the best Victorian erotic classics, *The Romance of Chastisement* is a collection of fiction, poetry, and anecdotes about discipline, especially flagellation, "the Victorian Englishman's favorite vice." It was first published in 1870 and reprinted in 1888, but it has been out of print ever since. Delectus Books has reprinted it in facsimile edition, retaining the quaint charm of the original.

The book is filled with saucy tales of headmistresses taking a birch to the bare backsides of schoolgirls, women whipping each other, men spanking women, an aunt whipping her nephew, and more debauched fun. An old woman tells her granddaughters, who are about to be birched for mouthing off, about the whip-

▲ *The Romance of Chastisement* by **Anonymous** (See page 99)

*"The Victorian Englishman's favorite vice."*

pings she and her friends got at school. One woman would pull down their drawers while the other would go to town on them with a rod. "In an instant the whole surface was discolored, not with a rosy blush, but with livid weals and angry blue black red. The weapon whirred, whopped on the flesh, and rose again with the force and precision of a steam hammer."

> Delectus Books; £19.95
> 1870, 1993; hardcover; 155 pp.

## SADE: A SUDDEN ABYSS
### BY ANNIE LE BRUN

This book is a translation of the introduction Annie Le Brun wrote for a new edition of Sade's complete works, to be published by J.J. Pauvert, who considers Sade "the greatest French writer." In an unusual move for a French literary theorist, Le Brun actually strips away the intellectual gobbledygook that surrounds Sade—all the ivory tower theories that see his writing as a metaphor for something else—and attempts to give a straightforward interpretation of his work. She examines what Sade was trying to tell us about the complex nature of desire and power.

When Le Brun reread all of Sade's writings (no small task) and started writing this book, she says, "I was sure of very little, except that Sade was neither the madman, revolutionary, saint, fascist, prophet, man of letters, butcher, fellow creature or even the thinker he was made out to be. I know only that he was alone, mercilessly alone, with a solitude we try to forget is possible." Her interpretation of Sade can make for some tough, and at times dull, reading. What it boils down to is that "...Sade had been demonstrating as never before the sumptuous and savage nature of desire." His books disturb us because the cruel, nihilistic debauchery he describes in detail strikes a resonant chord within us, which scares the hell out of most of us. Desire is *the* dominant force in Sade's universe, a concept that disturbs us civilized folk who are used to quashing our desires because of such concepts as guilt, sin, morality, etc. In *The 120 Days of Sodom*, Sade sums up his worldview: "Doubtless, many of the perversions you will soon see will displease you, as we realize. But there will be others that excite you to the point of costing you some sperm, and that is all we need."

> City Lights; $12.95
> 1990; softcover; 220 pp.

## THE SECRET RECORD:
### MODERN EROTIC LITERATURE
### by Michael Perkins

Poet and author Michael Perkins gives serious critical attention to the most neglected, scorned, and suppressed genre of fiction—erotic literature. Not run-of-the-mill stroke books, mind you, but writings about sex that display a high degree of literacy and talent. Hated by fundamentalists of all stripes and spit upon by academia, erotic literature is still an important subject. It has produced many outstanding works, and it can tell us a lot about ourselves. Perkins waxes philosophical: "By presenting erotic tumult, writers give form to emotions which are often unruly and sometimes anarchic. Their books are tentative maps—the rough cartography of explorers—which create order in the *terra incognita* of our psyches, and what can thus be circumscribed can be understood."

I agree with Perkins's ideas on why we are drawn to such literature: "We read what frightens us because the work confronts our deepest suspicions about life; we agree upon an objective

world we call civilization, and find in horror stories expressions of our nightmares about it. In the present some of us go to erotic literature the way our grandparents went to *Dracula* and the tales of the Brothers Grimm: for affirmation of the creative life of chaos within ourselves. We are reminded by that chaos that we have private beings which cannot be preempted by the stern demands of the world outside us."

Perkins examines Victorian erotica, early twentieth-century literature such as Georges Bataille's *Story of the Eye*, the groundbreaking publishers Olympia Press and Essex House, erotic poetry, female authors, gay male erotic fiction, and Marco Vassi, who is in a class all by himself, according to the author.

*The Secret Record* is a handy guide to the hidden literature of the past century.

> Rhino*ceros* (Masquerade Books); $6.95
> 1992; paperback; 281 pp.

## STORY OF THE EYE
### by Georges Bataille

The radical sociologist/philosopher Georges Bataille shows his fascination with transgressive sex in his first novel, one of the most shocking erotic books ever penned. It's even more amazing when you realize that this affront to all that is decent was published in 1928.

The story follows the male narrator and his girlfriend, Simone, as they have one strange sexual escapade after another. Simone, it turns out, has a thing for eggs. "She would do a headstand on the armchair in the parlor, her back against the chair's back, her legs bent towards me, while I jerked off in order to come in her face. I would put the egg right on the hole in her ass, and she would skillfully amuse herself by shaking it in the deep crack in her buttocks."

Later, during a bullfight in Spain, a rich Englishman arranges to have the testicles of the first bull to be killed brought to Simone. She takes a bite of one of the balls and stuffs the other one in her pussy. At the exact moment that the bullfighter is killed, she orgasms and sends the bull's nut shooting out.

As with most of Bataille's fiction, bodily fluids and discharge play a major role. *Story of the Eye* drips with urine, vomit, shit, jism, and blood. Also making appearances are the Bataillian themes of suicide, violent death, religion, and insanity.

Y'know, I just can't believe this book was written more than sixty-five years ago. It's so drop-dead shocking and brazenly nasty that it reads as if it were written yesterday. Bataille is yet another person obviously ahead of his time.

> City Lights; $7.95
> 1928; 1987; softcover; 103 pp.

## THONGS
### by Alexander Trocchi

The late Alexander Trocchi is one of the most famous erotic novelists to ever put pen(is) to paper. *Thongs*, originally published in 1956 by Olympia Press, is the best of his "Paris novels." It tells the story of Gertrude, a lovely young girl growing up in a poor section of Spain. Her father is Razor King, one mean SOB—kind of the Bad, Bad Leroy Brown of his neighborhood. Razor King takes women from the area to be his live-in sexual outlet for a while. One day he brings home Hazel, who secretly takes Gertrude to a mansion where she goes down on men who are being whipped and gets whipped herself. This ignites a fire in her, and she finds a local yokel—a dirty old shoesmith—to inflict loving pain on her.

She eventually goes back to the mansion and learns that the people there, including Hazel, are part of a quasi-religious secret society devoted to Pain. At the head of the Order, as it's called, is the Holy Pain Father. Under him are twelve Pain Cardinals, each of whom is over six Grand Painmasters, who in turn are each over twelve Painmasters and Painmistresses. Under them are the rank and file members of the Order.

Gertrude quickly becomes a Painmistress and finds that her local order is rife with corruption. Only a few members are still into SM; most treat their meetings as an excuse to rut like animals. Gertie quickly whips her congregation into shape, but she doesn't feel satisfied. For a while she goes to a whorehouse where she is used and abused by an uncountable number of seamen. Still, she's not happy. She realizes that her destiny is to die for Pain. She wants to be like the original Pain Virgin, voluntarily crucified as a sacrifice to Pain.

The newly appointed Holy Pain Father is glad to oblige her, but he may be doing it for personal political gain. Gertie must decide whether or not to go through with the bloody rite....

Blast Books; $9.95
1956; softcover; 172 pp.

# CIRCLET PRESS

## FELINE FETISHES:
### EROTIC TALES OF SCIENCE FICTION
### edited by Corwin

A collection of four short stories of "feline erotica." In "Divinity" by Lauren Burka a man has an encounter with an incubus in the form of a panther. Johann Sebastian Bach is the implied main character of K.A. Kristiansen's "A Persian Fancy." One night he becomes aroused by his cat, Bathsheeba, sleeping on his crotch. He wonders what she would be like as a woman, and voila!, she becomes one.

"The King's Shadow" by Mary Malmros may be the most powerful story, but there's no sex in it. It's about the relationship between a disrespectful alley cat and the snooty man who likes her but demands strict obedience from his cats. "Courtship Rites" by Reina Delacroix is a fantasy tale involving a race of catlike humans. A human prince, on the run for treason, takes refuge in their land and through a strange turn of events ends up having to marry one of the inhabitants.

Circlet Press; $5.95
1993; softcover; 69 pp.

## SEXMAGICK:
### WOMEN CONJURING TALES OF EROTIC FANTASY
### edited by Cecilia Tan

In this collection, six women contribute sexy stories set in the fantasy milieu. Try to imagine a cross between J.R.R. Tolkien and Susie Bright, and you're on the right track. "Burning at the Stake" by Reina Delacroix is one of the hottest stories in all of Circlet's books. A woman in a pagan society must willingly undergo a sexual ritual involving a priest, a tree, and dozens of men. If she can service them all, she will attain the highest rank within her society. If not, she will be sacrificed. Needless to say, our heroine passes with flying colors.

"Pipe Dreams" by S.N. Lewitt is another top-notch story. A present-day rock and roll musician dabbles in the occult, more for showmanship than actual seeking. He decides to attempt communication with his muse, Mary Shelley. Lo and behold, he reaches her and for one night they come together in painful bliss. "The razor was in his hand. Her cold fingers closed over his and she breathed in sharply. He used the razor again, her shining hands on his guiding the blade across both their bodies, pain and ecstasy burning together until the conflagration was all that was left."

Circlet Press; $5.95
1993; softcover; 71 pp.

## TECHNOSEX:
### CYBER AGE EROTICA
### edited by Cecilia Tan

Seven erotic stories with a futuristic technological twist. In "Autoerotic" by William Marden drivers are wired to their cars. They cruise the dystopian Strip looking for fights and having sex through their cars. Of course Virtual Reality sex makes an appearance. "Virtually Yours" by Dave Smed adds an interesting element as a man tries all the different virtual sex parlors in an effort to determine the best one. In "Eros the Android Love Slave," a man buys a male android for use as his sex slave. He soon realizes that his android is a special model, capable of thinking and feeling, and it wants pleasure, too. "The Intercourse Interface" by Evan Hollander is the standout piece of the collection. A married couple who are dissatisfied with their sex lives go to a sex therapist. They receive an experimental device that transfers all sensations a person is giving back to his or her own body. That way, lovers can feel exactly what their partners feel, and experience firsthand what gives the most pleasure. The device is an unqualified success. "He stuck out his tongue and fucked her with it, pushing it all the way inside her until his lips formed a tight seal around her hole. Joe felt as if his whole cock had been swallowed up by a soft, velvety sheath."

Circlet Press; $7.95
1993; softcover; 84 pp.

◄ *Story of the Eye* by Georges Bataille

*From 1928, an amazing affront to decency.*

## TELEPATHS DON'T NEED SAFEWORDS:
### AND OTHER STORIES FROM
### THE EROTIC EDGE OF SF/FANTASY
### by Cecilia Tan

Three stories by Cecilia Tan. In the title story a telepathic SM couple go to an outrageous party where masters and slaves get it on in front of everybody. Unfortunately the couple end up offending one bad motherfucker, who kidnaps the woman and has his way with her in a dungeon. "Cat Scratch Fever" is another feline fetish story. In "Heart's Desire," a lonely countess holds an SM party where she and other women whip, paddle, and just generally torture the living hell out of one of the women's "slaves." One of the most satisfying of Circlet's books.

Circlet Press; $2.95
1992; softcover; 30 pp.

# EROTIC COMIX

## BIRDLAND

Written and drawn by Gilbert Hernandez, who does the popular *Love & Rockets* comic with his brother, *Birdland* is a hardcore sex extravaganza. The convoluted plot has something to do with Mark, who's screwing Bang Bang, Inez, and his ex-wife, but not his sister-in-law Petra, who wants to screw him (and is screwing his brother), and not his wife, who won't screw him but who is screwing all of her clients (she's a psychiatrist) but won't screw Mark's brother, who wants to screw her. Confused? Don't be. Just keep your mind on the sex, which is present in spades. All the women are insatiable, and all the men are unstoppable. They fuck each other like machines and finally end up in a huge orgy with aliens aboard a spaceship (don't ask).

This comic has everything you need—humor, pathos,

▲ *Birdland*
by Gilbert
Hernandez
(See page 101)

*This comic has
everything you
need—humor,
pathos,
betrayal,
unrequited
lust, beautiful
people having
messy
nonstop sex.*

betrayal, unrequited lust, beautiful people having messy nonstop sex, and classic bits of dialogue like, "My palpitating pudenda shall forever belong to you, my love," and "Shut up and get ready because my butt's about to use your face for a trampoline."

    Eros Comics; $9.99
    1992; oversize softcover; 75 pp.; heavily illus.

## THE CHERRY COLLECTION, VOLUME III
### by Larry Welz

    *Cherry* is one of the most popular humorous sex comix around. It follows the adventures of Cherry Poptart, a leggy blonde ready to get it on at the drop of a hat. This collection contains *Cherry* issues seven through nine. The stories feature Cherry and friends discussing how they would screw their hunky science teacher, Cherry balling a truckdriver, Cherry trying on her mom's outfits (wedding dress, hippie clothes, etc.) and having a fantasy based on each one, and Ellie Dee getting trapped in cyberspace. The best stories, though, are the parodies. Cherry gets invaded by an imitation Darth Vader's "light saber" in a *Star Wars/Star Trek* satire, and she gets double-teamed by the Skipper and Gilligan in a parody of *Gilligan's Island.*

    Kitchen Sink Comix; $12.95
    1993; oversize softcover; 120 pp.; heavily illus.

## EROS COMIX

    A sister company of Fantagraphics, Eros Comix publishes and sells the best sex comix available. Their fully illustrated black-and-white catalog features Eros's own line of hard-core comix (*Karate Girl, The Young Witches, 2 Hot Girls on a Summer Night,* etc.) and loads of comix and graphic novels from other publishers. Titles include *Big Top Bondage, Stiletto-Adventures in Discipline, Ramba, 2 Live Crew Comix, The Tijuana Bibles, Soank, Alien Sex, Idol of Flesh, The Complete Crumb Comix, Bang Gang, The*

*Story of O,* and well over a hundred more.

    From vintage smut to cheesecake to XXX-rated, this is your one-stop shopping catalog for erotic comix. To protect your reputation among your nosy neighbors, Eros does business as Rose Comix (it's an anagram, get it?).

    Rose Comix/PO Box 25070/Seattle, WA 98125
    Catalog: free

## HORNY BIKER SLUTS #8

    Pure, raw, gooey sex, page after page after page. John Howard and other artists all create stories centered around big, bad, muscled, perpetually horny biker sluts who see what they want and take it. "All Knocked Up and No Place to Go" is about a pregnant woman who moves in with the biker sluts. After a hot foursome, the sluts find out that the jerk whose bun is in Pearl's oven has skipped out on her. They track him down and exact some feminist revenge.

    "Stormy Leather" is a biker slut psychosexual soap opera about a love triangle. In "Circle K Yer Fuckin' Day" biker slut Vibora Malvada is robbing a convenience store when she meets two members of the band Josie and the Pussy Farts. They go home with her, and predictable escapades ensue.

    Last Gasp; $2.95
    1994; comic; 42 pp.; heavily illus.

## MEATMEN:
### AN ANTHOLOGY OF GAY MALE COMICS, VOLUME #15
### edited by Winston Leyland

    This volume of *Meatmen* comics (the name says it all, don't you think?) has a science fiction theme. In "Out of the Blue" by Stephen Lowther, a hunky, very human, alien man crash-lands his craft in the boondocks. A hermit writer finds him and, well, interplanetary relations take a giant step forward. Drawn in a loose, doodle style, "Cryogenics" by Farraday is about a man who is cryogenically frozen for three hundred years. When he thaws out, he finds that the entire population of Earth is now gay, AIDS has been cured, and basically the only there is to do is fuck like wild animals day and night. "Time Corridor" by Osze is a wordless series of ink drawings showing a time traveler going to ancient Greece, the future, and other destinations in his quest for hugely oversize cock.

    The other eight pieces in this collection range from seriously drawn adventure stories to humorous, cartoony comics. And if you like this book, just remember there are fourteen previous volumes to collect.

    Leyland Publications; $15.95
    1993; oversized softcover; 159 pp.; heavily illus.

## WEIRD SMUT COMICS

    Crazed hard-core underground comix! Each issue features several stories or single panel artwork from a host of artists. Issue #1 has sexual dementia from S. Clay Wilson, Leslie Sternbergh, illustrations of porn stars, a disturbing comment on machismo by Seth Tobocman, and more. Issue #3, perhaps the strongest, contains Spain's character Big Bitch meeting Bettie Page, Larry Welz's comment on the hypocrisy of sexual fascism, René's take on religious misogyny, and other great work. The highlights of issue #4 are "The Lactation Contest" by Angela Bocage and another Big Bitch story. *Weird Smut* has ceased publication but you can still get these three issues while they remain (issue #2 is sold out). Besides being very good, they'll probably become collector's items.

    John A. Mozzer, Publisher; #1: $5; #3 and #4: $2.50 each
    1985, 1989, 1991; comic book; 33 pp. each

## YOUNG LUST #8

A collection of erotic comix from Ace Backwords, Angela Bocage, Charles Burns, Daniel Clowes, Spain Rodriguez, and a dozen others. "Fleshed-Out" is a typically bizarre Zippy the Pinhead story about the strangest orgy you've ever seen. In "Modern Primitive" an anthropologist and his lovely daughter explore that most dangerous of habitats—the inner city. A new Big Bitch adventure involves Vic Guano and his personalized inflatable sex dolls. Ace Backwords contributes "Love Truly Sucks," which basically speaks for itself. "Panty Raid" is an illustrated poem about a group of bulimic sorority girls who lose more than their panties when a bunch of frat boys show up.

Last Gasp; $3.95
1993; comic; 48 pp.; heavily illus.

# NBM PUBLISHING COMPANY

Nantier Beall Minoustchine Publishing Company publishes some of the highest-quality erotic comics ever produced, including many by European masters who were instrumental in developing the art form.

## THE ART OF SPANKING

### written by Jean-Pierre Enard, illustrated by Milo Manara

This is the English translation of a French work that combines prose and single panel illustrations. The plot revolves around this female gossip columnist who's riding a train from Paris to Venice (*très chic*, no?). Her compartment mate is a fellow named Donatien who happens to be writing a book called *The Art of Spanking*. Donatien explains his philosophy: "No one understands what spanking is. Some think it's a child's punishment. Others a ludicrous mania. But it's the finest form of homage to the most worthy, most refined, most generous part of a woman: her buttocks.... To spank is not to beat. It is to caress and to violate at the same time. I know of nothing more magnificent than buttocks that buck under the hand, stiffen, then reach out to beg the next blow."

Eva, the gossipmonger, looks through Donatien's manuscript, which he has illustrated. She sees a drawing of a woman Don had spanked named Gina. "If there were a contest for the most glorious ass in the world, she'd walk off with the title of Butt Beautiful. Gina's buttocks were two full, supple hemispheres; superb tender domes; firm tasty bonbons; impish melting pears.... Gina's buttocks were desires, whims, manias. Dreams you could touch, finger, weigh in the hands."

Eva reads Don's book on the train, and he tells her about some of his adventures. They play a game of seduction and rebuff until, finally, Don gives Eva a firsthand lesson in spanking on the train. The one hundred or so illustrations complement the story, showing Don and his women spanking and screwing.

NBM Publishing; $17.95
1991; oversize softcover; 88 pp.; heavily illus.

## CLICK! AND CLICK 2

### by Milo Manara

A blatantly sexist male fantasy in the form of a full-color comic. A doctor invents a remote-operated device that when inserted in the brain causes the person to become a nymphomaniac. This other doctor has the hots for the trophy wife of an old, fat, rich bastard. The problem is that she's a sexually hung-up, puritanical ice queen. So the doctor steals his rival's invention, implants it in Claudia, and has some fun. At the most inopportune moments—in a movie theater, in a store, at a swanky party—he cranks up the device and Claudia become a hot, throbbing love beast. She tears off her clothes, pulls down guys' pants, begs them to do her, etc. The ending adds an unexpected twist.

In the sequel, Claudia's got a TV show, and her estranged husband wants her ruined. He hires a James Dean lookalike named Faust to use the remote control to turn her into a raging horndog and get her fired. Faust makes her strip down to only a shirt in the TV station's men's room, then ride a bike through downtown in her exposed condition. Her rich uncle hears of this behavior and takes a belt to her butt. Faust turns on the implant, and Claudia starts enjoying her beating and molesting her uncle. In the climactic scene, Claudia loses control during her live program, so she strips and masturbates for her audience. She tries to kill herself, but Faust stops her and gives her the remote control.

NBM Publishing
#1: $9.95; #2: $12.95
1992 & 1993; oversize softcover;
46 pp. & 72 pp.; heavily illus.

*Click! & Click 2 by Milo Manara*

*A blatantly sexist male fantasy—in full color!*

## THE COUNTESS IN RED

### by Leopold von Sacher-Masoch, adapted by J.M. Lo Duca and Georges Pichard

Leopold von Sacher-Masoch was the Viennese writer whose name gave us the word *masochism*. His most famous novel is *Venus in Furs*, but he wrote a lesser-known work on Erzsebet (sometimes written "Elizabeth") of Bathory, a very real historical figure in the 1600s. The "Bloody Countess" became obsessed with maintaining her youth and her incredible beauty. To this end, she had young women killed and she bathed in their blood. She also would watch as men and women were tortured. Apparently this was just for fun and not part of any beauty regimen.

This particular telling of the tale involves a Viennese nobleman named Emmerich, who goes to visit Erzsebet for a while. He falls for the lusty countess and asks that he be sacrificed for her. She willingly grants his wish.

NBM Publishing; $9.95
1985; oversize softcover; 45 pp.; heavily illus.

## EMMANUELLE, VOLUMES 1–3

### by Guido Crepax

In this series Crepax ewinterprets the classic novel *Emmanuelle* about a sexual adventuress. In Volume 1 Emmanuelle is aboard the Concorde on a very long international flight. During the night the man next to her fingers her and she gives him a handjob. The next night, he puts some more moves on her and they head back to a little compartment and join the Mile High Club. Once in Bangkok, Emmanuelle invites a teenage girl back to her place. The girl starts reading Georges Bataille's *Story of the Eye* and masturbates in front of Emmannuelle. She then convinces Emmannuelle to rub herself while she (the girl) watches. Later Emmanuelle has sex with a countess while playing racquetball and starts seducing a gender-bender girl named Bee.

Volume 2 picks up right away with Emmanuelle and Bee taking a shower and doin' the wild thing. Emmanuelle meets up with a decadent older man who introduces her to the pleasures of group sex, including two guy/one girl threesomes, two girl/one guy threesomes, and a massive daisy chain. He also introduces her to opium and convinces her to service some of the natives.

▲
*Emmanuelle*
by Guido
Crepax

*The legendary
libertine,
lovingly
illustrated.*

In the final volume, Emmanuelle lets a thirteen-year-old Thai boy finger her, seduces a prim and proper virgin woman, takes part in an orgy with the countess, and has sex with countless strangers.

*Emmanuelle* is one of NBM's best. It's not every day you find such a well-done comic about a female libertine.

NBM Publishing; $11.95 each
1989,1989, 1990; oversize softcovers;
74 pp., 70 pp., 86 pp.; heavily
illus.

## THE ILLUSTRATED KAMA SUTRA, VOLUMES 1–2

### by Vatsyayana, illustrated by Georges Prichard

Just as Guido Crepax is Italy's pioneering master of erotic comics as an art form, Georges Prichard is France's godfather of sophisticated drawn erotica. These two volumes contain that most famous sex manual, the ancient Indian *Kama Sutra*, accompanied by scores of Prichard's illustrations.

Volume 1 contains the *Kama Sutra's* thoughts on the philosophy of sex, nonsexual skills all people should develop (singing, dancing, tattooing, etc.), socializing, the different kinds of women, genital size of men and women, kissing, scratching, biting, hitting and slapping, sexual positions, oral sex, and lovers' quarrels.

Volume 2 covers courtship, winning someone's heart, marriage, being a virtuous wife, harems, seduction, adornment, go-betweens, getting rid of a lover, reuniting with former lovers, and much more.

Each volume is filled with stylized drawings of sultry women and swarthy men having all kinds of sex—oral, anal, vaginal, group, golden showers, bondage and discipline, etc., etc.

NBM Publishing; $12.95 each
1991; oversize softcovers; 85 pp. & 96 pp.; heavily illus.

## LITTLE EGO

### by Vittorio Giardino

*Little Ego* is a full-color parody of the early twentieth century's most groundbreaking comic, *Little Nemo in Slumberland*. A young woman named Little Ego has all sorts of surrealistic, hallucinatory sexual dreams. In one, her reflections in the mirror come alive and she ends up having group sex with her many selves. Another time, she rubs some growth cream on her breasts and they balloon until each one is bigger than her torso. She also gets licked all over by a bouquet of lilies and gets laid by an alligator. About half the book is a Middle Eastern adventure in which Ego does a striptease at a cantina, becomes part of a harem, and almost drowns in milk.

A cool collection of weird sex that's not hampered by the laws of reality.

NBM Publishing; $10.95
1989; oversize softcover; 46 pp.

## THE STORY OF O, VOLUMES 1–3

### written by Pauline Réage, illustrated by Guido Crepax

*The Story of O* is one of the most famous and extreme SM novels ever published. Written by Pauline Réage in 1954, this book has become required reading for the leather set. As a gift to her lover, the heroine, named O, allows herself to be totally debased, debauched, and dominated.

In Volume 1, O goes to a mansion with René, the one she loves. René and three other men blindfold O and use her like an appliance. They shackle her hands above her head and whip the fire out of her with a cat-o'-nine-tails. After a night's rest, she is used and whipped some more. Then a large dog is made to have sex with her. Her ass is judged to be too tight, so the men make her wear a dildo strapped into her constantly. O is released and goes back to her job as a fashion photographer. René introduces O to his half brother, Sir Stephen. Since the two men share everything, O now belongs to both of them and must submit to Stephen.

In Volume 2, O gets over her fears and completely gives herself to Stephen. He and René take her to Anne-Marie's place for some rigorous torture at the hands of an old woman and three beautiful young women. Over successive days they whip her inner thighs, pierce her labia, and brand her.

The last volume goes in a completely different direction from the first two. Somehow O is involved in a scam to blackmail a banker by getting him and his family into all kinds of compromising positions and then photographing it. She even tricks the capitalist pig into screwing his own daughter. This volume isn't a part of the novel *Story of O*, and it's not nearly as compelling as the first two volumes.

NBM Publishing; $11.95 each
1990, 1991, 1991; oversize softcovers;
94 pp., 88 pp., 96 pp.; heavily illus.

## VALENTINA, VOLUMES 1&2

### by Guido Crepax

Volume 1 of Valentina follows the adventures of a cool international hipster called Neutron who fights criminals with his power temporarily to paralyze both people and mechanical devices. He's not a tights-wearing superhero, though; he's a witty, urbane, mystery man who hangs with this chick named Valentina. The book starts with a graphic interpretation of Edgar Allen Poe's "Murders in the Rue Morgue" and moves into a story about this bad guy who gets women to marry rich guys, whom he then snuffs. He and his female accomplices get the inheritance. In the last story, Neutron foils a bunch of bad guys whose act of murder had been inadvertently photographed. This volume has absolutely no sex and just a little nudity. Since it's strictly PG-rated, I'm not sure why it's part of the "Eurotica" line of comics.

Volume 2 is a whole other story. It's wall-to-wall sex featuring the slim, bob-cut Valentina. There is no dialogue and no plot, just one fantasy scene after another. In the opening scene she's in a Victorian setting. Two cruel mistress-types are bringing her to be inspected and fondled by three upper-class gentlemen. Here's where it gets really weird—they put her in a giant typewriter, hit the keys, and the letters paddle her ink-covered rear end. Then she goes aboard a spaceship, gets things going with a couple of women, and almost gets mauled by a panther.

Later she has sex with a man in front of a group of strangers, gets an enema, does some bondage, has sex with more women, spies on two sailors having sex, takes part in an all-girl orgy, rescues a man being brutalized by four women, makes love to him, and so on. Very surrealistic, demented sex. Crepax's extremely classy style of drawing takes away some of the blunt shock of what you're seeing, but it's still wild, wild stuff.

NBM Publishing; Vol. 1: $12.95; Vol. 2: $11.95
1965 & 1976; oversize softcovers;
95 pp. & 100 pp.; heavily illus.

## VENUS IN FURS

### written by Leopold von Sacher-Masoch, illustrated by Guido Crepax

This is Crepax's finely drawn version of the ultimate masochistic tale, *Venus in Furs*. There's not really a plot to speak of. Severin Sacher-Masoch loves to be dominated and abused by his wife Wanda. She treats him like a servant, making him do all kinds of drudgery and wait on her hand and foot. If he commits the slightest infraction, which he usually does on purpose, she whips him bloody. In the grand finale, Wanda ties up Severin, then invites some cruel-looking major in the German army to come over and whip him and boff him.

NBM Publishing; $11.95
1991; oversize softcover; 62 pp.; heavily illus.

## EROTIC ART

## EROTIC ART

### edited by Angelika Muthesius and Burkhard Riemschneider, text by Gilles Néret

A lot of books bill themselves as anthologies of erotic art, but they look like church hymnals compared to this titillating tome. Even though it only focuses on twentieth-century erotic art, it ranges over an enormous territory. From modern masters to underground artists, from realism to the most outrageous avant garde, from mildly suggestive to downright shocking, *Erotic Art* has all the bases covered.

Among the many works you will find:
—A plaster casting of Auguste "The Thinker" Rodin's hand holding a female torso.
—A painting by Jeff Koons of porn star and Italian parliament member Ilona Staller straddling a happy-looking man.
—Gustav Klimt's decadent but relatively tame *The Kiss*.
—Pop artist Roy Lichtenstein's cartoon-painting of a man and woman kissing.
—A disturbing pen drawing by Alfred Kubin of fornicating couples and a flying penis and vagina trapped in a gigantic spider web.
—David Hockney's self-explanatory painting *Two Men in a Shower*.
—Bruce Nauman's neon sculpture of a fourway.
—Jeff Koons's photo of a woman spreading her pussy open while a dick penetrates her anus.
—Cindy Sherman's sculpture of a female mannequin being eaten out by a disembodied head.
—Salvador Dalí's *The Great Masturbator*.
—Picasso's colored ink drawing of a mackerel performing oral sex on a woman.
—René Magritte's painting of a topless woman fondling her right breast and licking her shoulder.
There's also art work from Man Ray, Robert Mapplethorpe, Helmut Newton, Tom of Finland, Georgia O'Keeffe, and more than one hundred others. And if that ain't enough, everything is reproduced in glorious full color. This is truly a bonanza (and it's way underpriced).

Benedikt Taschen Verlag; $20
1993; oversize softcover; 200 pp.; heavily illus.

## MAN RAY

Man Ray was a true Renaissance man. He was a painter, architect, sculptor, filmmaker, goldsmith, and writer, but he is best known for his photography. Ray was a member of the dada and surrealist movements, which is reflected in his work. He pushed photography to its technical limits, pioneering and sometimes inventing many effects that are common today—

*Man Ray*

*Beautiful, provocative, realistic, abstracted, subtle and obsessive.*

solarization, granulation, negative printing, distortion, and relief processing.

Although the title of this book may lead you to believe that it's a retrospective of all facets of Ray's work, it actually focuses entirely on his erotic photos of women, nude and clothed. These fifty-five pictures show a remarkable diversity of effects, angles, and composition; they look like they're the works of several artists, not just one.

Ray has an impressive lineup of models, including Kiki de Montparnasse, the most famous model of the 1920s; Dora Maar, Picasso's female companion; artist Meret Oppenheim; photographer Lee Miller; and dancer Juliet Browner, who became Ray's wife. He has captured these women in a body of work that is beautiful, provocative, realistic, surrealistic, abstracted, subtle, and obsessive.

At a paltry ten dollars, this is definitely a book worth having.
Benedikt Taschen Verlag; $10
1992; oversize softcover; 80 pp.; heavily illus.

## MARBLE WOMAN

### by Yuri Dojc

Words cannot describe the beauty of this book. Using black-and-white infrared film, Yuri Dojc has created some of the most hauntingly beautiful, painfully exquisite, erotic photographs of women that I have ever gazed upon. Infrared film causes color shifts, making light objects extremely light and dark objects very dark. It causes Dojc's nude subjects to glow with an ethereal light, their skin becoming marble.

Dojc has a great eye for composition. Some of his images are abstract nudes, some are erotic in a disturbing way, and some are flat-out sexual. In one photo, a vampirish woman crouches in a dark area among flamingos. In one very grainy photo, a woman's face pouts at us from a large mound of paper that looks like a bean bag. In another, a short-haired brunette hunched over a mirror gazes intently at herself. One of the best images is of a statuesque blonde standing perfectly straight, gazing proudly into the camera, with a sculpture of grapes covering her pussy.

As I said before, I simple cannot convey to you the power of this book. Unfortunately, it's costly to reproduce infrared photos in a deserving manner (plus, they need to be printed on glossy coated paper). I won't even attempt to reproduce one of Dojc's pictures here, because it wouldn't do it justice. So trust me when I say that lovers of erotic imagery could not possibly be disappointed by this book. It gets my highest possible recommendation.

Firefly Books; $29.95
1993; oversize hardcover; 94 pp.; heavily illus.

## THE WOMEN:
### PHOTOGRAPHS OF THE TOP FEMALE BODYBUILDERS
### by Bill Dobbins

This book is out to challenge our ideas of female beauty. As a general rule, society prizes supple but firm female flesh with lots of soft curves. Although anorexic fashion models sometimes break with this standard, they don't come close to female bodybuilders. With these women, hardness, bulk, and lots of definition is the goal.

*The Women* contains about one hundred nude, mostly color photos of female iron pumpers. (Although there are plenty of bare breasts and buns, in all but a couple of shots pubic hair is either covered or discreetly obscured.) The women in the shots are all 100 percent buffed and ripped, but there is a wide range in their body types. At one end of the spectrum is the women who have nice definition but retain their curves (they are in the minority). At the other end are the bodybuilders who have big bunched muscles, corded tendons, and veins popping out everywhere.

These muscled beauties are presented in sharp, crisp photos posing with various props—guitars, a cow skull, chains, Greek columns—and wearing a variety of outfits—thong bikinis, skimpy armor, leather, chains, chaps, or nothing at all. Some of the women are drop-dead gorgeous, and some ain't. And, unlike most books of erotic photography, African Americans are very well represented.

*The Women* is a sumptuous challenge to the narrow definitions of female beauty.

Artisan (Workman Publishing); $25
1994; oversize hardcover; 127 pp.; heavily illus.

## BETTY PAGE CONFIDENTIAL
### by Bunny Yeager

In 1948 a voluptuous Nashvillian named Bettie (this is how she actually spelled her name) Page, after failing to break into acting in Hollywood, arrived in New York with stars in her eyes. She appeared in some summer stock theater, but she never got far, supposedly because of her thick southern accent and in-your-face sensuality, which were too limiting. Around 1952 she came to the attention of girlie exploitation kingpin Irvin Klaw, who made a series of bondage films with her. Around this time Bettie was making extra money by posing as a model for amateur camera clubs. In 1954 Bettie left the movies and met model and photographer Bunny Yeager, who shot the best-known and celebrated of the estimated half a million photographs taken of Bettie.

*Betty Page Confidential by Bunny Yeager*

*The Queen of Pinups.*

Why has Bettie become the queen of pinups? Why has an entire obsessed subculture sprung up around her, complete with zines, annuals, and tons of photographs, movies, and collectibles? A large part of it is simply her appearance—she's curvaceous, beautiful, and she just oozes with sexuality, yet still somehow manages to maintain a girl-next-door innocence, even when she's being tied up and paddled. Then there's the Bettie mystique. In 1957, Bettie simply walked away from everything. She found God, married, and became a recluse. To this day she refuses to be photographed or interviewed (with one exception).

This book contains about 125 of Bunny Yeager's photographs,

some of which appear in print for the first time. We see Bettie frolicking, posing, strutting, and being her ultra-animated self at the beach, the amusement park, and the studio. She's topless or stark raving naked in at least one-fourth of the pictures. Of course, this being done in the 1950s, she's always discreetly posed to hide her pubic hair.

Yeager and Buck Henry both provide reminiscences of Bettie. Two chapters give a bondage filmography and a listing of Bettie's magazine appearances.

St. Martin's Press; $13.95
1994; oversize softcover; 128 pp.; heavily illus.

## CASTRO
### by Rick Castro

Rick Castro uses a large pallette of styles to create an impressive body of work. He photographs mainly Adonis-like men, although a few Venus-like women are present, too. His photographs vary greatly in their presentation. All are black and white, but some are printed as blue or brown duotones. Many are sharp, but some are grainy and a few have blurred motion. Three pictures even look like scratchboard illustrations. The subjects are shown in nature or in the studio, clothed and unclothed. In short, you never know what you're going to get from Castro, except that it will defy your expectations and capture the essence of eroticism in an understated way.

Some of the best images in this book include a guy covered in dirt flexing on top of a mountain, a naked man holding a five-foot penis over his head, two blonde women in a catfight, a dude totally covered in a dark liquid drinking said liquid as it pours down from out of the picture frame (although the goop in question looks like blood, the title indicates that it's chocolate), a close-up of a woman wearing a birdcage over her head, a naked catatonic man lying across railroad tracks, and a clown with a knife.

Tom of Finland; $25
1990; oversize softcover; 117 pp.; heavily illus.

## EROTIC BY NATURE:
### A CELEBRATION OF LIFE, OF LOVE, AND OF OUR WONDERFUL BODIES
### edited by David Steinberg

This passionate anthology contains 122 black-and-white photos, 17 drawings, 15 short stories, and 38 poems that joyously celebrate the carnal pleasures. All the works display definite artistic talent and sensibilities, but that doesn't mean they're boring or coy. Some of them definitely hail from the more subtle end of the spectrum, but a lot of the writing gets down and gets funky, and many of the pictures show penetration. Nobody's shy here. And that's because there's nothing to be shy or ashamed about. *Erotic by Nature* has a very healthy sexual attitude—it's natural, it's beautiful, it's fun. All orientations and sexes are welcome.

Photographs include Charlie Clark's figure studies on entwined bodies, Michael Rosen's shots of SM practitioners, Steven Siegel's exquisite infrared nudes, and Hella Hammid's famous shot of a naked woman with a mastectomy. H.M. Ruggeri's story "Girl Next Door" is about a seventeen-year-old boy who learns about the joys of sex and the pains of love with the girl next door. James Broughton's singsongy poem "Nipples and Cocks" is a tribute to those body parts: "No need to be fancy/or unorthodox/Just try a plain diet of/nipples and cocks." Ron Koertge turns in a poetic tribute to masturbation: "...have a drink first, lay out/some poppers, open that favorite book/to the most shameful passage because/without blessed shame nothing is/as much fun."

All libraries of sexual art and fiction will be incomplete without *Erotic by Nature*.

Down There Press; $42.50
1988; oversize hardcover; 212 pp.; lavishly illus.

# THE HOMOEROTIC PHOTOGRAPH:
## MALE IMAGES FROM DURIEU/DELACROIX TO MAPPLETHORPE
### by Allen Ellenzweig

A huge, sweeping survey of erotic photographs of men taken by men. The images are presented in chronological order, starting all the way back in 1853, about fourteen years after the invention of photography. This is when Eugène Durieu, under the artistic direction of famed painter Eugène Delacroix, made pictures of a man with the classical proportions admired by the Greeks but a very French handlebar mustache. The pictures jump to the 1880s and the likes of Frank M. Sutcliffe and the American realist painter Thomas Eakins, whose photography has probably become more celebrated than his other work.

At the turn of the century Wilhelm von Gloeden took photos of men that used ancient Greek visual motifs. In the 1930s Brassaï took photos of the hidden side of Parisian nightlife. Several of his photos of gay and lesbian couples are reproduced. George Platt Lynes and Minor White were the dominant forces in male homoerotic photography at midcentury.

The 1970s brought a new breed of gay photographer, less afraid to take chances. Foremost among them was Robert Mapplethorpe, and, among the pictures included in this book are the famous *Jim and Tom, Sausalito* (one man is pissing in the other's mouth) and *Man in Polyester Suit*.

Among the contemporary artists whose work is displayed are David Lebe, who uses "painting with light" to get startling effects, and George Dureau, who takes pictures of men with physical abnormalities, such as midgets and amputees.

Allen Ellenzweig provides history, biography, and art criticism in his text, which weaves throughout the 127 duotone images. *The Homoerotic Photograph* proves that, contrary to popular belief, homoerotic photography didn't begin or end with Mapplethorpe.

Columbia University Press;
1992; greatly oversize hardcover; 230 pp.; heavily illus.

# MARQUIS DE SADE:
## ANTHOLOGIE ILLUSTRÉE
### edited by Stephano Piselli and others

A huge, shocking catalog of images based on the writings of the divine Marquis. This badass collection contains about five hundred color and black-and-white photographs, film stills, drawings, paintings, comics sequences, and movie posters depicting the brutal sexual acts that the Marquis de Sade helped to make famous. As you might imagine, women are usually the ones being targeted, but men end up on the short end of the stick also.

The book is divided into sections, including an overview, each of Sade's four major works, a filmography, and a bibliography. Although the overview and exerpts from Sade's work are printed in three languages (French, Italian, and English), the filmography, bibliography, and all the captions are only in French. I guess this doesn't matter too much, though, because images of people being sexually brutalized form a universal language.

Here are some of the many images you'll come across:
- A woman carving a bound man's butt with a dagger (line drawing).
- Naked people of both sexes who have been impaled on spears and crosses (illustration)
- A man being whipped bloody by a woman (film still)
- A woman being whipped bloody by a man (film still)
- A naked woman being forced to eat shit (film still)
- A woman's pussy being sewn up by another woman (illustration)
- A naked woman tied spread-eagle by a couple of guys in the middle of the woods (film still)
- A woman being branded on her back (illustration)
- A shackled woman awaiting her fate (film still)
- A bound woman suspended by nipple clamps being whipped by another woman (illustration)
- Women suspended from the ceiling by their feet (photo)

- A woman's ass being tortured by steel claws, spikes, candles, hot wax, and more (comic)
- A huge orgy involving a large number of people in interlocking positions (photo)
- A manacled bleeding woman being licked by another woman (book cover)
- A man with his head being pressed against a wall by someone wearing a boot (film still)

Many of these images—particularly the whippings and orgies—actually appear a number of times in different forms, since they have been present in many movies, comics, and illustrations modeled after Sade's work.

*Marquis de Sade* takes no prisoners. It is one of the most unnerving, confrontational collections of images my psyche has ever been exposed to. The Marquis would be pleased.

Glittering Images; 60,000 lira;
U.S. surface: $44; U.S. air: $50
1993; oversize softcover; 159 pp.; heavily illus.

◄ *The Homoerotic Photograph* by Allen Ellenzweig

*The definitive image of men by men.*

# PARAMOUR:
## LITERARY AND ARTISTIC EROTICA

A newcomer to the field of "egghead erotica," which has been dominated by *Yellow Silk* and *Libido*. *Paramour*, with its black-and-white nude photography and hot yet low-key fiction, is closer to *Libido*, although it lacks that magazine's great nonfiction and pervasive sense of humor. The fiction and poetry are imaginative and pretty well written. In issue #3 "Alice and the Accident" by Corwin Ericson and Amelia Copeland mixes pain and pleasure in a unique way. A couple riding a motorcycle out in the middle of nowhere take a spill. The girl's all right, but the guy's hip and leg are messed up and he's in agony. His girlfriend tends to his wounds and then tends to him. "I knew from experience how wretched my leg must have looked, and the image clashed with the sight of the lace stretched taut across Alice's full breasts. I couldn't shake the thought of her dragging the rough textured fabric across my lacerated thigh." In "Underwater Creatures" by Kristi Sprinkle, a woman finds that swimming in the sea is an erotic experience. "The water wraps around her and she becomes intensely horny feeling the saltiness of the sea in her mouth as the warm water passes around her limbs.... She forgets the things that matter and eases into the swaying motion and wetness and the soothing warmth of the ocean pressing against her flesh."

The art, mostly photography, is quite appealing. The shots of women, men, and mixed-sex couples are imaginatively done without being afraid of getting down and dirty. *Paramour* is a worthy new addition to the sexual arena.

Paramour Magazine
PO Box 949/Cambridge, MA 02140-0008
Single issue: $4.95
Four-issue sub: $18

# PRIVATE PROPERTY
### by Helmut Newton

Helmut Newton is one of the all-time masters of erotic photography. Starting as a fashion photographer for *Vogue* in 1961, Newton always pushed the limits to come up with his distinctive visual style. His sharp black-and-white photos portray a distinctively aristocratic world where, to borrow from an art

**Revelations by Housk Randall**

*Speaking for themselves in words and images.*

crit, Eros and Thanatos are constantly lurking. The women in Newton's photographs come across as cold, brittle, and totally unapproachable. They are to be admired —even gawked at—but never touched. They display their perfect bodies and perfect faces in a perfect world that we can never enter. This is why Newton is often credited with taking voyeurism to its highest aesthetic level.

*Private Property* contains forty-five of Newton's best pieces from 1972 to 1983. Besides his characteristic sexy photographs, there are about eight celebrity portraits, including Raquel Welch, David Bowie, and Sigourney Weaver.

W.W. Norton; $10.95
1990; small softcover; 110 pp.; heavily illus.

## REVELATIONS:
### CHRONICLES AND VISIONS FROM THE SEXUAL UNDERWORLD
### by Housk Randall

Photographer Housk Randall has photographed the inhabitants of London's sexual underground, of which he is a member. His more than one hundred and fifty bold black-and-white pictures, shot against a solid black background, aren't afraid to get up close and personal with their subjects, filling the entire frame with their pierced, tattooed, leathered, or otherwise modified bodies (or some portion thereof). Vein is every submissive's dream—a raven-haired beauty in a leather/fishnet/metal outfit who looks like she knows exactly what she wants to do to you. Ricky's alter ego is a campy SM dyke, although that may sound like a contradiction in terms. The close-up of him screaming at the camera is priceless. Another great shot is of Miriam in the lotus position, showing off her bizarre eye makeup, her otherwise bald head with a Hare Krishna ponytail that goes past her waist, her pierced nipple, and her V-shaped pubic hair.

Besides taking their pictures, Randall lets his subjects speak for themselves. Victoria had this to say: "When I looked up and saw this man sucking my girlfriend's nipples, I go 'Oi!' and it was Reiner and he goes 'Oh, I'm so very sorry.' Well, not too long after, we started going out together and eventually got married." Now that's something to tell your kids when they ask how you and Daddy met!

Tim Woodward Publishing; £29.95
1993; very oversize hardcover; 106 pp.; heavily illus.

## STUDIO NUDES

"Achingly beautiful" are the words that pop to mind when viewing Craig Morey's photographs of women. His work is so rich, so beautifully executed and aesthetically pleasurable, that it stirs something much deeper than just the loins, although they too will be noticeably enthusiastic. For a while I've held the theory that merely looking at something beautiful triggers certain pleasure centers in the brain. Morey's photos have convinced me that this is true. Well over half of the thirty-five pieces in this book were able to induce this slightly altered state of consciousness in me.

Morey's photos are a very soft black-and-white. It would probably be more accurate to call the pictures gray, because the extremes of total black and white are almost never present. Instead, there are hundreds of levels of rich gray. The models are all gorgeous, and their poses are graceful and elegant yet forcefully erotic. Morey has managed to mix equal parts startling sexuality and sublime beauty. Color me impressed.

Morey Studio; $29.95 (signed first edition)
1992; oversize hardcover; 75 pp.; heavily illus.

## TEASE!:
### THE MAGAZINE OF SEXY FUN

"In a world of publications that are hard-core, with nothing left to the imagination, or no-core, and not even a nipple in sight, *TEASE!* fills the void. We'll investigate human sexuality that's too tasty for your typical newsstand magazine and too tame for your average men's magazine." Created by the man who brought us *The Betty Pages*, the premiere issue of *TEASE!* covers pinups, French postcards, sexploitation movies, striptease, cheesecake, and other examples of soft- to medium-core erotica. There is an article on two forgotten glamour queens of the 1950s: the blonde, busty Sandra Giles and Juli Reding, who happened to have been close friends. There's a look at the sexploitation films of Barry Mahon, director of *White Slave Racket, Cuban Rebel Girls*, and *Hot Skin and Cold Cash*. Other articles cover pinup artists Don "Rusty" Rust and Joyce Ballantine, director John Waters, a guide to adult trading cards, Exotic World (a burlesque stripper museum) an overview of women in dinosaur movies, and more.

There are plenty of illustrations, including a color centerfold of pinup artist Olivia's latest splendiferous creation, all printed on heavy, slick paper. *TEASE!* definitely fills a gap in the erotic art scene, and it does it extremely well.

Pure Imagination
88 Lexington Avenue, Suite 2E/New York, NY 10016
Two-issue sub: $10

## YELLOW SILK:
### JOURNAL OF EROTIC ARTS

*Yellow Silk* publishes excrutiatingly subtle erotic art, fiction, and poetry. Of all the magazines into "egghead erotica"—*Libido* and *Paramour* are the others I've covered—*YS* is definitely the tamest. Actually, I'm not sure if *tame* is exactly the right word; perhaps *understated* is more accurate. *YS* seems to revel more in desire than in actual consummation. It seems to be the delicious wanting that they focus on, as opposed to the actual getting, although there are exceptions.

The art is mainly in the media of pencils, oils, scratchboard, etc.—photos are rarely used. The images are almost always somewhat abstract female nudes. The writing is generally first rate and as sublime as the art. An exception to this rule—and one of the best meldings of sex and religion—is "Speaking in Tongues" by Caron Reed. The happy couple are consummating their marriage: "Then you pulled hard at my back and fire roared down from the sky like napalm, sucking the air from my lungs and smoldering in jellied splotches on the soles of my feet. I stroked your side and buck-naked laughing seraphim appeared fluttering around me, randomly shooting morphine-dipped arrows into my butt.... And when I pulled your thighs apart the sky opened and God himself came thundering down wearing a porkpie hat with a press pass stuck in it, taking the seat at the announcer's desk of some celestial sky box, surrounded on every side by bleachers full of rowdy drunken angels."

*Yellow Silk* also offers a good selection of books, videos, and art available through mail order.

Yellow Silk/PO Box 6374/Albany, CA 94706
Single issue: $7.50
One-year sub (4 issues): $30; foreign surface: $38;
foreign airmail: $52

# MICHAEL ROSEN

Michael Rosen has been photographing sex radicals since 1982. His work has appeared in just about every sexzine you could name, he's had exhibitions, and he's self-published three books of his work. All of his books are large format, containing black-and-white photos with interspersed commentary from his subjects.

## SEXUAL MAGIC:
### THE S/M PHOTOGRAPHS
### by Michael Rosen

Michael's first book, *Sexual Magic*, contains pictures of sado-masochists in action. The photos are very grainy; there's lots of blurred motion and soft focus, giving the pictures an impressionistic quality.

The photographs show a man wearing a pig mask and nipple clamps, with his hands tied above his head, while his female captors laugh hysterically; a woman whipping another woman; a woman sucking on her partner's nipples while she tugs on the rings that are attached to them; two women chewing on the neck of their tied-up male captive; a woman throwing her head back and screaming as her nipples are yanked; a woman about to puncture her partner's cock with an X-acto knife; and a man with his hands tied over his head and a couple dozen clothespins along his armpits.

Rosen has done a superb job capturing the agony and the ecstasy experienced by sadomasochists.

Shaynew Press; $25
1986; oversize softcover; 71 pp.; heavily illus.; heavily illus.

## SEXUAL PORTRAITS:
### PHOTOGRAPHS OF RADICAL SEXUALITY
### by Michael Rosen

With his second book, Michael took a different approach. *Sexual Portraits* contains pictures of sex radicals of all stripes posing for the camera. The images are a very sharp, focused black-and-white.

Among the pictures:
- A hooded man with a combination lock hanging from his pierced foreskin
- A woman touching the erection of a man dressed like a little girl
- A woman in combat boots and lace stockings and a corset showing off the chain attached to her pussy
- Two lesbians, one wearing leather chaps and a strap-on dildo
- A man who looks just like your grandfather, except that he's wearing nipple rings (well, maybe your grandfather does have pierced nipples, I don't know)
- A woman carving the letter *M* into a man's butt with an X-acto knife
- A bald leatherdude wearing chaps and a metallic jockstrap and holding a gigantic dildo
- A woman cross-dressing as an old man
- A very pregnant Susie Bright wearing thigh-high boots and not much else
- A couple of middle-aged leathermen. One is kicking the very heavy weight that's dangling from his partner's scrotum

Shaynew Press; $25
1990; oversize softcover; 63 pp.; heavily illus.

## SEXUAL ART:
### PHOTOGRAPHS THAT TEST THE LIMITS
### by Michael Rosen

*Sexual Art by Michael Rosen*

A few years ago Michael told me that he was working on this book. He said that in it he would "test the limits," go too far, and take pictures of "nonstandard penetration." When the book came out in late 1994, I was not disappointed. In fact, I was shocked by some of the images. I knew that such things were done, of course, but *seeing* them being performed took it to another level. Like *Sexual Portraits* the photos are in sharp black-and-white. They combine posed shots with action shots.

The book opens with a bang—a picture of a man sucking himself. The next photo is one of several fist-fucking images. This one shows a man in an oxford shirt and tie sticking his hand up a man's ass. Other such photos show women fisting women, men fisting women, and a woman fisting *herself*. Dildos also play a starring role. A woman has one sticking out of her pussy headfirst. Similarly, a man has one sticking out of his keester backward. A guy is sucking the mother of all dildos, which is strapped on a woman. In the next shot, she's shoving it up his butt.

The popular sport of body modification is in full effect. There's a close-up of a bone stuck through a foreskin, pierced inner labia with the outer labia covered in clothespins, a dick with ten brass cockrings around it and the scrotum, two pierced cocks attached by a small metal object, and a chain running from one guy's hard-on to another guy's tongue.

One of the most gut-wrenching pictures shows a dominatrix crouching over the prostrate body of her slave. He is *completely* mummified in electrical tape, from the top of his head to his feet, with the sole exception of his penis, which is standing up. Underneath his head is a distressingly large pool of blood. Another picture you won't soon forget shows a smiling woman grasping a penis. Inserted into the urethra is a small American flag, like the kind people wave around at political speeches. It hurts just to look at it.

*Sexual Art* is Michael's best and most powerful work. In this age of increased sexophobia and general irrationality, he has risked a lot by publishing this book. If you only buy one of his books, make it this one.

Shaynew Press; $30
1994; oversize softcover; 63 pp.; heavily illus.

*I knew that such things were done, of course, but seeing them being performed took it to another level.*

# TOM OF FINLAND

Illustrator Tom of Finland has created the most revered and perhaps largest body of work in gay male art. His drawings portray a fantasy world of constant, easy sex among men who are all cut out of the same mold (yet somehow still distinctive from each other). They all have that ruggedly handsome look, square jaws, cartoonishly muscular bodies, and the biggest cocks the world has ever seen. To call these guys hung like horses would be an insult. The shrimpiest guys Tom ever drew have dicks the size of Arnold Schwarzenegger's forearm. The largest guys have gravity-defying equipment the size of Arnold's entire arm.

## KAKE AND THE SADISTS
### by Tom of Finland

This is said to be the most hard-core of Tom's works. In a series of one-page panels containing simple line drawings, the recurring character of Kake is sexually brutalized by a trio of horny fascists. It all starts when these guys in generic Nazi-esque uniforms grab Kake and drag him into a little building. They shackle his hands over his head and go to town. They strip him, insert a spike in his urethra, attach a cockring around his wang and nuts, stick a whip up his ass and a dildo in his mouth, and put nipple clamps on him. And that's just for starters.

Then they fist him, sit him down on a saddle outfitted with a dildo the size of a small tree, take a leak on him, and use his mouth and dick for their pleasure. Rough, rough stuff.

A shorter series in the back of the book is a silhouetted encounter between a fascist and a street punk in a doorway. This time things are nonviolent and consensual.

Tom of Finland Company; $12
No date; saddle-stitched, oversize softcover;
35 pp.; heavily illus.

## TOM OF FINLAND CATALOG

A high-quality, heavily illustrated catalog offering *beaucoup* gay male art and some fiction. Of course they offer every Tom of Finland book in print. But Tom has become a cottage industry and you can also get his art on T-shirts, portfolio sets, lithographs, greeting cards, pins, magnets, rubber stamps, calendars, videos, and more. Plus they carry *Meatmen* comics, *True Gay Encounters*, Phil Andros, Etienne, Athletic Model Guild, Colt Studio, Leyland Publications, and others.

Tom of Finland Company
PO Box 26716, Dept. RK/Los Angeles, CA 90026
Catalog: $10 (refunded with first order)

## TOM OF FINLAND RETROSPECTIVE
### by Tom of Finland

This lavish survey of Tom's work spans his whole career, from 1946 to 1988, when this book was published. The early drawings are in a distinctly different style. The men are somewhat effeminate and have normal-size cocks. During the 1950s we see Tom's style developing, and by 1960 it's in full flower.

The images include lone figures posing, two guys having all kinds of sex, and group scenes. Four of Tom's motifs are noticeable. First, men in uniform. Sailors, cops, pseudofascists, and guys in business suits abound. Second, the leather look is everywhere. Tough guys and bikers decked out in leather, denim, and chains are common. Third, rough sex. There are lots of guys tying each other up, screwing each other violently, and breaking out the whips. Fourth, rape is sometimes portrayed, as in the three-panel scene where one dude tackles another in a locker room, gives it to him hard, and then kicks him out naked into the street.

There are also a few surprises, like very un-Tom-like close-up portraits and a drawing of Michelangelo's *David* with a Tom-size tool.

Tom of Finland Company; $27.50
1988; oversize softcover; 192 pp.; heavily illus.

## TOM OF FINLAND RETROSPECTIVE II
### by Tom of Finland

Another career-spanning selection of more than two hundred of Tom's works. This collection is much more diverse than the first volume. First, besides a wide selection of the usual style of drawings, a lot of these pieces are "rough sketches." These working drawings have become very popular recently. Second, there are sixteen pages of full-color pencil drawings. Third, many of the drawings have a rough, canvaslike texture. Finally, there are reproductions of Tom's covers for twenty-five issues of *Prätkä-posti,* a Finnish biker magazine that Tom cofounded.

Once again, the full range of Tom's vision is exposed— uniformed men, biker dudes, ménages à trois, orgies, rough sex, rape, bar scenes, locker rooms, interracial sex, etc.

This is a more complete look at Tom's work than the preceding volume.

Tom of Finland Company; $27.50
1991; oversize softcover; 191 pp.; heavily illus.

# EARLY EROTIC PHOTOGRAPHY

The German publisher Benedikt Taschen Verlag GMBH specializes in books of early erotic photography of women. As surprising as it may seem, nude photography didn't begin with *Playboy* in the 1950s. In fact, you have to go back a full century before that—that's right, one hundred years—to 1847, about eight years after the first camera was created, to find the beginnings of girlie pix. In other words, pornography is nothing new. It's been with us for one and a half centuries, and civilization hasn't crumbled yet.

All four of the books have extremely high production values, yet they are shockingly inexpensive. They're truly a steal, and you'd be wise to snatch up as many as you can. You don't even have to have them sent from Germany—the Sexuality Library catalog (below) carries all of them.

## EARLY EROTIC PHOTOGRAPHY
### by Serge Nazarieff

This astounding collection contains three hundred images from the first full decade of erotic photography, the 1850s. The seven prominent photographers of the day, all French, are each given their own section. The pictures are reproduced well, especially considering how old they are. Of course, most of them are flecked with white spots and scratches, but that just gives them even more of an old-timey feel. Most of the photos were hand-colored by their creators and are remarkably bright for being so old.

What surprised me about these pictures was the fact that they are decidedly uncoy. Not only is there full frontal nudity, many of these women have their legs spread at the camera. A few are bent over, and a very few are even touching themselves, although they don't have their eyes closed and their heads thrown back in mock ecstasy like today's models. I guess that was a later invention.

The women in these shots, for the most part, don't exactly match today's ideal of female beauty. Facially, many of them are quite homely. As far as bodies go, probably half of them are quite slender, and none of them have more than a little bit of extra flesh on them. These photos aren't terribly appealing, although, from a standpoint of the hidden history of sex, they are a priceless treasure. I think the problem may be that I just can't shake the possibility that one of these women may be my great-great grandmother....

Benedikt Taschen Verlag GMBH; $19.99
1993; oversize softcover; 200 pp.; heavily illus.

## JEUX DES DAMES CRUELLES, 1850–1960
### [GAMES OF CRUEL WOMEN]
### by Serge Nazarieff

This volume collects over one hundred years' worth of erotica showing women performing dominant, humiliating, and sadistic acts on each other. This legacy of cruel women is a rich one, dating back to the very beginning of erotic photography itself. Image #3, in fact, is the earliest known whipping picture in existence, dating back to 1853. Pre-dating that is the first image (circa 1850–1852) of a woman giving another woman an enema. The rest of the pictures from the 1850–1870 period show two "nuns" in a whipping scene and a mistress switching and spanking two young women.

The next two sections contain dozens of pictures from the first decade of the 1900s. They consist mainly of a pretty young thing displaying her bum while an older woman or two, dressed in proper attire, apply a birch, cat-o'-nine-tails, switch, or hand to the area in question.

The largest portion of the book has photos from about 1930, give or take a few years. This must have been the Golden Age of cruel women. The women who delivered the punishment suddenly became much younger and less schoolmarmlike. In fact, they were indistiguishable from the women they were punishing, and they were often in various states of undress. The lesbian overtones became unmistakable during this period. The women continue to whip, flog, paddle, and smack the hell out of each other. Some of them use enemas on each other. In one series of pictures featuring three quite good-looking women, one is riding on another's back. The rider has the third woman harnessed like a horse and is taking a riding crop to her. We also see the introduction of such SM paraphernalia as chains, collars, stocks, manacles, and leather outfits.

Photos from the studio of Irving Klaw, the pathbreaking American sleazehound who produced bondage pictures and movies mainly in the 1950s, get their own section. Sharp eyes will recognize everybody's favorite sweetheart, Bettie Page, as one of the damsels in distress.

This book will certainly change your view of the past. "Age of Innocence" my butt!

Benedikt Taschen Verlag GMBH; $9.99
1992; oversize softcover; 160 pp.; heavily illus.

## PARISER PIKANTERIEN: EROTISCHE PHOTOGRAPHIEN UM 1920
### [NAUGHTY PARIS: EROTIC PHOTOGRAPHY FROM 1920]
### by Michael Koetzle and Uwe Scheid

This is the only one of the publisher's books written only in German (the others have English and French text, too), but I guess it doesn't matter that much. The pictures, not the words, are the main attraction here. As far as I can tell, based on the title, these are erotic photos from Paris around 1920. They look like the Parisian photos in the other books, except that the photographers didn't add color to them. We see women of varying degrees of beauty posing naked or having sexual encounters with each other. There are even a few shots of SM and interracial sapphic sex. The French always were ahead of their time when it came to breaking sexual taboos.

Benedikt Taschen Verlag GMBH; $9.99
1993; hardcover; 95 pp.; heavily illus.

## STEREO NUDES 1850–1930
### by Serge Nazarieff

Stereoscopic photographs are images in which two photos of one scene have been taken from slightly different angles. When viewed through special glasses, the images appear three-dimensional. Stereoscopic nudes appeared in 1850 and went through declines and resurgences in popularity before having

*Stero Nudes 1850-1930 by Serge Nazarieff*

*Naughty bits in stereo.*

one final streak of glory in the 1920s. Unfortunately, we can't see these pictures in their 3-D glory. The two plates making each composite image are shown side by side.

As with *Early Erotic Photography*, the majority of the photos were colorized, and the majority of the women aren't exactly sex goddesses by our standards. I was surprised and delighted to find image #116, which is a clear, head-on shot of a woman being penetrated by a penis. This photo dates from the late 1850s! Not only has porn been around a long time, *hard-core* porn has been around for a long time. *Sacrebleu!*

Benedikt Taschen Verlag GMBH; $9.99
1985; oversize softcover; 160 pp.; heavily illus.

# MISCELLANEOUS

## CREATIVE SCREWING:
### A WOMAN'S GUIDE TO BECOMING AN EROTIC ENCHANTRESS OF SUPERLUSTFUL SEX
### by Nannette LaRee Hernandez

Take all those retarded, adolescent "How to Make Love to a Man" books and throw them in the fire. Once you get *Creative Screwing,* you'll realize that the only good use for those other books is kindling.

Nannette LaRee Hernandez has written and published the most uncompromising, explicit, down-and-dirty, how-to-fuck book that you will ever read. Hernandez's basic philosophy is that women are way too uptight about sex. They need to let go of all the bullshit that's been programmed into them and just fuck like all hell's breaking loose. Not so that they'll please their men—although that's definitely a side effect—but because it's fun, God damn it!

Hernandez counters the idea that women who love sex are sluts with no self esteem: "The woman who lets go for a wild, lustful ride on the naked buck of a man and willingly gratifies her own carnal desires and fantasies as well as his, has more love and respect for herself wrapped up in her semen-soiled G-string than the woman who denies her sensual aches and desires for the fear of how society will label her."

Almost *ten thousand* men—and many female sex workers—were interviewed during the research for this book. Hernandez reached several conclusions, which she presents in the promotional literature accompanying her book. When it comes to prostitution, stripping, etc., "Men are the only ones who are exploited sexually in these business situations," and "Men do not keep working girls in business—wives and lovers do." More generally, "Men deeply care for their wives and lovers enough to work sixteen-hour days—but are rejected almost every time they ask for sex from the woman they love." Finally, "Men want sex above all else because they rarely get it without a quarrel, sigh, guilt trip, or demanded favor in return." After learning all this, Hernandez "wrote *Creative Screwing*—a book that tells the truth about men, explains to women the vast proportion of their power, then gives them permission to fuck like they've always wanted to—hoping to inspire at least one woman into taking control of her life."

In an even more promotional vein, the charmingly brazen Hernandez writes, "I want women to be shocked by the power of their sexuality. I want them to admit and talk about and play out and experience what's festering in the hidden closets of their minds. I want women to know that there isn't a man on earth strong enough to *control*—there NEVER was. Slide a man's cock in your mouth and down comes the Berlin Wall."

But most of *Creative Screwing* isn't about philosophy—it's about raw, juicy sex. "Few men have had the pleasure of a cremating orgasm that sends them blasting into orbit, and they don't realize how little they've enjoyed sex until they've met a woman who can drive them down the road to Sexual Insanity." You'll find out how to give your man and yourself the most incredible sex of all time in sections on "Nuclear Head," "The Fucking Menu," "The Fucking ABC's," "One Nighters," "Mastering Masturbation," and much, much more.

It would be a much happier planet if every woman (and man, for that matter) would read and put into action *Creative Screwing*.

Brilliant Creations Publishing; $21.95
1993; oversize softcover; 126 pp.; illus.

## INVESTIGATING SEX:
### SURREALIST DISCUSSIONS 1928-1932
### edited by José Pierre

Starting in 1928, the Paris surrealists conducted a series of twelve unprecedented roundtable discussions/debates on sex, which have now been translated into English for the first time. André Breton, Antonin Artaud, Max Ernst, Man Ray, Benjamin Péret, and many others offer their candid, unabashed views on sex, eroticism, and love.

The first thing I noticed was that for such a group of revolutionaries, the surrealists could often be bluenoses. Writer Pierre Unik seems the most reactionary of the group. When asked his views on gay men, he responds: "From a physical point of view, I find homosexuality as disgusting as dog excrement, and from a moral view I condemn it." On the other hand, writer Raymond Queneau appears to be the group's most outspoken defender of sexual freedom. He says, "If two men love each other, I have no objections to their physical relations." Later in the discussion the rest of the group was halfheartedly defending masturbation, implying that it's only for hard-ups. Queneau replies: "I don't believe onanism has anything to do with compensation or consolation. Onanism is as absolutely legitimate in itself as homosexuality."

About half the participants said that when making love to a woman, they always ask what she prefers (position, oral sex, anal sex, etc.). The other half—including Breton—don't ask the woman but say they don't mind if she takes the initiative and does it her way. Both Breton and Queneau admit a preference for anal sex and the 69 position when having sex with a woman.

In the second discussion, Man Ray reveals that he and his partners achieve simultaneous orgasm about 75 percent of the time, because of his "calculation and timing." Without such calculation, "I'd always come before the woman. At least the first time." When asked the parts of a woman that excite him most, Ray replied, "The breasts and armpits."

The poet and extreme left-wing militant Benjamin Péret showed the more romantic tendencies of the group when he said, "A sexual desire holds no interest for me unless it is accompanied by love, and for love I would leave everything."

In one of the most enlightening passages, the surrealists are first asked what they think of watching a woman urinate. Everyone agrees that it would be "pleasant" or "exciting," except Unik, who disingenuously says, "It's never happened to me." Next, they're asked what they think about hearing a woman fart. Prévert: "The less often the better." Breton: "Appalled by it." Painter Yves Tanguy: "I don't care." Toward the end of the session, Queneau asks, "What do you think of rape?" Breton: "Absolutely hostile to it." Queneau: "It's the only thing that appeals to me." Prévert: "I find it legitimate." Unik: "I am against it."

By turns infuriating, hilarious, revealing, boring, and always brutally honest, *Investigating Sex* sheds new light on the study of sexuality. It will probably be enjoyed most by fans of surrealism and people who are into the historical aspects of sex.

Verso; $16.95
1994; softcover; 215 pp.; lightly illus.

## PUBLIC SEX:
### THE CULTURE OF RADICAL SEX
### by Pat Califia

Erotica writer, poet, and essayist Pat Califia is the foremost spokesperson for lesbian SM. However, as this anthology of fifteen years of her essays shows, she has also been busy defending all kinds of unconventional sex, as well as sexual freedom in general. In this courageous and essential volume, she supports pornography, SM, prostitution, adult/child sex, nonmonogamy, genderbending, and sex in public. The term "radical" has become overworked and devalued, but as you can see, when applied to Califia, it still means something.

Califia trashes feminism's opposition to SM—especially lesbian SM—in "Feminism and Sadomasochism," one of the most controversial articles ever to run in *CoEvolution Quarterly* (which later became *Whole Earth Review*). "The women's movement has become a moralistic force contributing to the self-loathing and misery experienced by sexual minorities. Because sexual dissenters are already being trampled by monolithic, prudish institutions, I think it is time the women's movement started taking more radical positions on sexual issues." After all, she argues, isn't the feminist movement about helping oppressed people gain acceptance and power?

Califia looks at the issues surrounding sex in public places. "Most people who condemn public sex do not seem to know that the legal difference between public and private sex is not a simple matter of choosing either the bushes or your bedroom. There are many zones in between—a motel room, a bathhouse, a bar, an adult bookstore, a car, a public toilet, a dark and deserted alley— that are contested territory where police battle with perverts for control."

The intro to Part Three of the book, "Sluts in Utopia: The Future of Radical Sex," lists forty-two things you can do to make the future safe for sex. Among them: "When your local newspaper says police are cracking down on prostitution, call the police and tell them you don't like them spending your money to bust hookers"; "Study sex"; "Give away some pleasure"; "Write a love letter to an unlovable part of your body"; "Look at your genitals"; "Tell video stores that you enjoy being able to rent X-rated videos"; "Live a long time and make waves."

Cleis Press; $12.95
1994; softcover; 261 pp.

## THE 120 DAYS OF SODOM
### by Nick Hedges,
### adapted from the Marquis de Sade

In the Marquis de Sade's novel *The 120 Days of Sodom*, four libertines—a bishop, a duke, a banker, and a judge—take a group of young adults and four old whores to a deserted castle in Switzerland near the end of Louis XIV's reign. They engage in a four-month marathon of cruelty, debasement, and debauchery. Nick Hedges developed a highly stylized theatrical version of this tale. This book contains the dialogue and stage directions of the play, a long interview with Hedges, plus fifteen black-and-white photos from the production.

The play was staged in an eccentric, somewhat campy manner that combines Grand Guignol (theater of terror), opera, Japanese theater, and dark humor. The actors wore white face paint with bruiselike makeup around their eyes and red gashes for mouths. The eerie lighting and jarring sound effects added to the decadent, quasi-surrealistic atmosphere. Hedges makes the whole affair as unerotic and unpleasing as possible.

The libertines—all pillars of society—are shown to be immensely cruel and power-hungry.

In order to get themselves in the mood, the libertines order the whores to tell them true-life stories of their adventures. One of the women relates the time she had a special client coming over. The madam of the house forced her to eat a huge meal followed by an emetic. During her ensuing liason, "Suddenly!—at point blank and without warning!—I launched into his mouth the imperfectly digested dinner that the vomitive had fetched up from my stomach... Our man is beside himself! He rolls his eyes, pants, bolts down the steaming spew, glues his mouth to my lips and by thrusting his foul tongue into my mouth provokes a repetition!"

The four men engage in a procession of actions and story-telling that involves fist-fucking, shit-eating, father-daughter incest, branding, eye-gouging, cannibalism, bestiality, necrophilia, and so on.

At one point the judge sums up the libertine philosophy to a T: "Nothing is villainous if it causes an erection—in fact, the only villainy that exists in the world is to deny oneself anything that might produce one!"

Delectus Books; £6.95
1991; softcover; 70 pp.; illus.

## THE BREATHLESS ORGASM:
### A LOVEMAP BIOGRAPHY OF ASPHYXIOPHILIA
### by John Money, Gordon Wainwright, and David Hingsburger

Written with the help of other people, this is the autobiography of an asphyxiophiliac, someone who experiences sexual arousal and orgasm through self-strangulation. Told through narrative, poetry, and commentary, it is the only book of its kind ever written.

The problem was that Nelson Cooper didn't just use auto-erotic asphyxiation to have ultra-intense orgasms—he was obsessed by it. It gripped him and wouldn't let go. As he writes in one of his poems: "It will haunt you until you are dead/You cannot fight it; it only gets stronger/You cannot tell anyone; they won't believe you/When you speak of its strength and power/No one will see it, for it is invisible."

A crummy, abusive family, religion, the educational system, and psychiatry teamed up to screw Cooper over. He was constantly labeled "lazy and worthless" by his mother, "a sinner" by religion, "educable retarded" by the education system, and "emotionally disturbed" by psychiatry. He grew up with zero self-esteem.

In the sixth grade, Cooper started fantasizing about other students and teachers being strangled to death. Later, he would fantasize that he was being strangled. As he grew older, he started strangling himself with stockings or women's underwear while he masturbated. When he called crisis hotlines to tell about his asphyxiation fixation, he was accused of abusing the phone lines because he was just trying to scare the nurses. He went to see psychiatrists, who either became hostile or said he was lying.

Finally, he read a newspaper article about young men who had accidentally died while doing autoerotic asphyxiation. Through the article, he managed to track down Dr. John Money, a sexologist at Johns Hopkins University who is now helping Cooper overcome his obsession.

Even though *The Breathless Orgasm* was interesting, I was disappointed that it focused on asphyxiophilia as a "mental disorder" only. Cooper did seem so obsessed with it and dependent on it that it was interfering with his life. However, I'm sure there are a lot of people who engage in it every once in a while for fun. After all, it's reputed to give you orgasms that make ordinary orgasms seem about as exciting as a sneeze. I would have liked some insight into this aspect of the behavior, too.

Prometheus Books; $25.95
1991; hardcover; 178 pp.

## CENTURION-SPARTACUS CATALOG

A four-page foldout brochure of catalogs and magazines for fetishists and transgenderists. You can buy catalogs from all over the world offering discipline helmets, boots, bondage jewelry, penis restraints, armbinders, and more. They also offer magazines from England, France, Canada, and the United States.

Spartacus/PO Box 429/Orange, CA 92666
Five dollars will get you this catalog and put you on their mailing list for a year.

## CHILDREN'S SEXUAL ENCOUNTERS WITH ADULTS:
### A SCIENTIFIC STUDY
### by C.K. Li, D.J. West, and T.P. Woodhouse

When you're listing the most inflammatory topics of all time, sex with children definitely makes it into the top three, perhaps even claiming the number-one spot. Given this rating, evenhanded approaches to the topic are exceedingly rare. This book reprints two such objective examinations, a pair of recent British sociological studies.

In the first study, "Sexual Encounters Between Boys and Adults," the researchers used questionnaires and interviews to determine the childhood/adolescent sexual experiences of several hundred young men. The subjects were asked only about acts that occurred with people over eighteen years old. In the second study, "Adult Sexual Experiences with Children," the researcher interviewed twenty men who either had sex or desired to have sex with children of either sex.

The results of the studies contradict many commonly held beliefs. Based on their sample, the authors of the first study estimate that one in five men have had childhood sexual contact with an adult, with one in eight men having had contact with adult males. Almost none of the sexual contacts that were uncovered involved a family member, and almost none involved threats or "significant" violence. Also, none of the study's subjects reported extremely negative or adverse effects from their childhood sexual encounters. The researchers conclude that "most such events appear to be relatively minor episodes with no particular consequences." It should be reemphasized, though, that this study only involved males. Previous studies of females who had childhood sexual encounters with adults revealed that for them the events *were* tremendously damaging. Just what accounts for this apparent sex difference is not clear.

The author of the second study similarly concludes that while violent, brutal sexual assaults on children may grab the attention of the public, most sexual encounters between adults and children do not involve force.

Both studies are quick to point out that these controversial conclusions are not meant to condone the idea of adult-child sex but, rather, to open up the possibility that there are different kinds of adult-child sex, not all of which are forceful or damaging. As C.K. Li writes, "Rather than rejecting a priori all forms of adult-child sexual contact as abuse and hence morally wrong, it might be more fruitful to study the continuum of adult-child sexuality, bearing in mind that there is a considerable grey area in this continuum." A more heretical suggestion is almost impossible to imagine.

Prometheus Books; $39.95
1993; hardcover; 343 pp.

*The Clitoral Kiss* ▼
by Dr. Kenneth Ray Stubbs
(See page 114)

*"Fever when you kiss me..."*

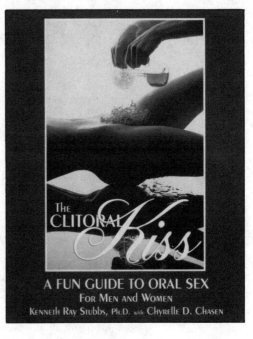

THE CLITORAL Kiss

A FUN GUIDE TO ORAL SEX
FOR MEN AND WOMEN
KENNETH RAY STUBBS, PH.D. with CHYRELLE D. CHASEN

## THE CLITORAL KISS:
### A FUN GUIDE TO ORAL SEX FOR MEN AND WOMEN
### by Kenneth Ray Stubbs, Ph.D.,
### with Chyrelle D. Chasen

A fun guide to using your mouth to give pleasure. Although the main focus of the book is using your mouth on your lover's one-eyed cobra or furburger with a side of thighs (as this book refers to them), you can also make tasty contact with the thighs, buns, breasts, back of the neck and upper shoulders, or anywhere you want for that matter.

**Dearest Pet**
by Midas
Dekkars
➤

*"The high regard in which love for animals is held is matched only by the fierceness of the taboo against having sex with them...."*

The crux of the book is the section called "Fever When You Kiss Me," which contains eighteen basic oral maneuvers. The techniques are divided into four categories depending on whether the emphasis is on the tongue, lips, teeth, or breath. The "lipstick" technique is presented: "After applying saliva to your lover's skin, moisten your own lips thoroughly. Without any suction, gently slide your lips back and forth over the skin." "Hummin'": "Place your lips on or around any part of the body and hum. Make sure the tune fits the mood."

The following section discusses which parts of the body are most receptive to which licks, sucks, etc. There are also tips for adding food—fruit, nuts, sauces, whipped cream—to your repertoire. Other sections deal with oral warm-ups (including "tongue-fu"), interesting places to do it, and the ever-present question of to swallow or not to swallow. Stubbs's advice—do what you're comfortable with, but don't be afraid to try something new. If it's the taste that bothers you, he relates a Native American recipe for a shake that makes jism more palatable.

If you delight in orality, you owe it to yourself and your partner to get this book.

Secret Garden; $16.95
1993; oversize softcover; 79 pp.; illus.

## CYBORGASM

This is a recording of erotica in 3-D sound, meaning it uses technology that makes it seem as though someone is whispering in your ear, yelling to you from another room, walking around you, etc. The sixteen tracks let you listen in on women and men having sex, talking about it, wanking off, and so on. The orientation is definitely hetero—mainly men and women boffing, with some lesbian scenes here and there.

Annie Sprinkle sets the mood with a guided erotic meditation. In "Je veux t'embrasse" we hear a woman getting off in French. I took French in college, but I don't think we learned the things she was saying. I did manage to catch *chat* (pussy). In "Absolute Sadist," the formidable Mistress Kat will whip you into a bloody pulp.

Proving that the sexual underground is nothing if not unpredictable, Susie Bright, the foremost spokeswoman for sapphic pleasure, contributes a heterosexual fantasy. "Circus Whore" is a monologue in which Bright is kept by "you" in a cage, where she is a sexual freak at your disposal. She moans, "You only let animals and the other girls lick my pussy. You never lick my pussy. You only give me your cock."

Sacred cows are ground into hamburger on "Daddy's Grrrl" and "Succubus (Wet Nightmare)." On the introduction to the former track, Susie Bright makes sure to tell us that we aren't supposed to be hearing a father and daughter having sex; we're listening to a couple playing an incest fantasy. On the latter track Diana Trimble describes a dream in which she's a succubus. She swoops into a cathedral and makes whoopee with a corpse.

On "Dirty Fare" Jon Bailiff recounts being a cabbie who gets more than a tip from one of his female fares. "Blue Light" is a humorous monologue in which Don Bajema talks about having sex with "you." The two women in "Pink Sweatboxes" start off by talking about multiple orgasms, G-spots, men who don't know how to give head, and all that other stuff women talk about when there aren't any guys around. Eventually they get so hot and bothered, they retire to the bedroom for a screaming round of sex.

*Cyborgasm* comes to a climax with "The Swing," a six-minute sexfest that is destined to be a classic piece of audio erotica. A mixed-sex group of six people have a massive orgy. At its height, there are three sex acts going on simultaneously with everybody talking dirty, moaning, screaming, and gasping at once.

Time Warner AudioBooks; $9.98 cassette & $15.98 CD
1993; 64 min.

## DEAREST PET:
### ON BESTIALITY
### by Midas Dekkers

"The high regard in which love for animals is held is matched only by the fierceness of the taboo against having sex with them.... Hence, in spite of the dangling penises and the cries of females in heat, the eroticism of our dogs and cats is completely ignored. With these darlings we adopt the role not of lover, but of master or mistress." However, the author points out, people do have sex with animals, but this act occurs most often in the realm of imagination. Thus, "it is no surprise to find art and culture permeated with physical love for animals."

In this nonexploitive yet readable and entertaining book, Danish biologist Midas Dekkers traces the history of bestiality, paying special attention to its representation in high and pop culture. He begins his survey with Greek mythology, which contains one of the most famous human-animal couplings of all time: the gorgeous Leda being ravished by Zeus in the form of a swan. "The thought of the combination of the divine swan's down and the human skin of a beautiful mortal has inspired painters and draughtsmen for twenty-five centuries." During the Romans' infamous Games, the lives of the gods were imitated for spectators. Women and girls were forced to have sex with bears, leopards, apes, giraffes, crocodiles, and snakes.

*Dearest Pet* is more of an anecdotal history of the subject than a linear history. It doesn't follow bestiality through the Middle Ages, Reformation, etc. Instead, it picks here and there, examining bestiality from psychological, legal, sociological, and anthropological angles (I know this sounds boring, but, believe me, it isn't). It also looks at human-animal sex that is either implied or graphically depicted in religion, art, literature, pornography, advertising, etc.

The book is lavishly illustrated with well over one hundred images. There aren't any photographs, but there are paintings, drawings, engravings, woodcuts, mosaics, cave art, and Greek vases. *Dearest Pet* is quite simply one of a kind. It will fill the bestiality gap in everyone's collection of sex books.

Verso; $29.95
1994; hardcover; 208 pp.; heavily illus.

## DELECTUS BOOKS

Delectus Books is Britain's leading dealer in secondhand sex books. Their catalogs are filled with many antiquarian tomes, first editions, foreign language books, etc. They carry hundreds of books ranging from relatively recent offerings to some seriously rare volumes. For example, you can get a six-volume French edition of Sade's *Juliette,* published in 1797, for six hundred and fifty pounds or the 1883 edition of *The Worship of Priapus* (only one hundred of which were printed) for ninety-five pounds.

Delectus is also a great source for rare books on the occult, weirdiana, decadent literature, and surrealism. Be sure to ask for their Decadence catalog if you're interested.

For the most part Delectus's prices are more expensive than those of Ivan Stormgart (see below), but then again, they do carry more rare books. Most prices are ten pounds and up, with twenty-five pounds a quite common price. (A rule of thumb for currency conversion is to double pounds to get the dollar equivalent. Before ordering, check your bank or CNN for exact exchange rates.) There are a decent number of books under ten pounds, but Delectus is definitely for the serious collector.

Delectus is also resurrecting lost erotic classics. And when I say "lost," I mean "lost"! They've republished *The Petticoat Dominant*, only four copies of which are known to exist. Even rarer is *A Guide to the Correction of Young Gentlemen*. All known copies were burned by court order seventy years ago, but one has recently resurfaced, allowing Delectus to bring this "flagellation cookbook" back into the world.

Delectus Books
27 Old Gloucester Street/London WC1N 3XX/ENGLAND
Erotica catalog: $5
Decadence catalog: $5
Delectus does accept U.S. checks

## EIDOS

EIDOS is an acronym for "Everyone Is Doing Outrageous Sex." This thick quarterly tabloid is devoted to the radical concept that sex is good, clean fun and we should enjoy it without guilt. *EIDOS* is very concerned with sexual freedom—they run a lot of material about "theofascists" who want to impose their sexophobic hysteria on the rest of us. They also defend numerous other types of freedom—reproduction, speech, press, religion, drugs, etc. Add to this mix a good dose of conspiracy theory, and you have a highly unusual publication.

Each issue is crammed full of original essays and rants, reprinted articles, long, detailed letters from readers, tons of reviews (*EIDOS* has one of the best review sections of any zine), personal ads, mediocre poetry from readers, art and photos of men, women, and couples, and ads, ads, and more ads. The ads alone are worth the price of the zine. Almost every zine, book publisher, mail-order catalog, and organization in the sexual underground—including dozens from outside the United States—advertise in *EIDOS*. Your most bizarre needs can probably be met within these pages.

With its blend of radical politics, guiltless love of sex, and uncompromising material, *EIDOS* achieves a unique, powerful blend.

EIDOS/PO Box 96/Boston, MA 02137
Single issue: $10
One-year sub (4 issues): $30

## EROTIC MASSAGE:
### THE TOUCH OF LOVE
### by Kenneth Ray Stubbs, Ph.D., with Louise-Andrée Saulnier

This is a clear, loving guide to performing massage, which is defined most simply as "patterned touch." Seventy-eight different strokes are covered. Each one is explained very plainly. If there's more than one step involved in a stroke, each step is spelled out separately. Every one of the strokes is accompanied by a detailed drawing showing exactly how to place your hands, fingers, and so on, and black arrows signify the direction of movement. Again, if there's more than one step in a stroke, each step will often have its own separate illustration.

The techniques you'll learn include shoulder strokes, side pulling, thumb slide, back hug, forearm stroke, palm massage, thigh kneading, moon stroke, head scratch, temple circles, eye stroke, and many others. There is a long section on male and female genital massage, covering sweet thrills, the juicer, countdown, ring around the rosy, rockin' around the clock, and several more.

*Erotic Massage* is so elegantly simple and straightforward that it can't help but heighten the eroticism between you and your lover.

Secret Garden; $16.95
1989; oversize softcover; 112 pp.; heavily illus.

## HISTORY OF SYPHILIS
### by Claude Quétel

Sex isn't all fun and games, as this book firmly reminds us. The sexually transmitted disease of syphilis has a long and interesting history. I was hoping this book would answer a burning question—if you get syph from having sex with somebody, then how did the very first person get it? Unfortunately, the answer isn't cut and dried. In Europe the new disease slammed into France first and quickly spread. Ideas about its origins were numerous and ludicrous—it was created when a knight with leprosy had sex with a courtesan, Spaniards mixed leper's blood with wine, the Italians poisoned wells, it was a new form of leprosy, it was caused by a bad alignment between Saturn and Jupiter. Two of the early theories have parallels with today's AIDS situation. Some people thought syphilis was caused by men screwing monkeys, and others said that it was God's wrath. The general concensus today is that it came from the "New World," but exactly how it started is still the center of debate.

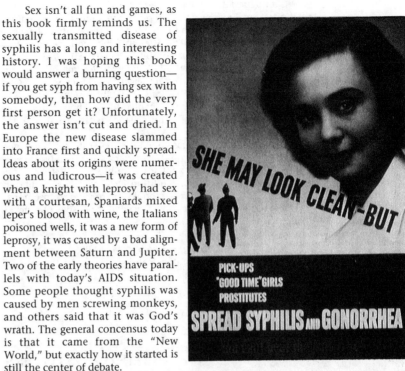

*History of Syphilis by Claude Quétel*

*The cultural history of a killjoy.*

*The History of Syphilis* is about much more than medical debates, though. Syphilis rapidly became a cultural phenomenon, affecting the arts, religion, and politics. While science was desperately trying to find a cure, it was being battled by forces that thought syph was a scourge on sinners and shouldn't be cured. The author also traces the battle fought by the government to contain the disease (and sometimes the diseased themselves), and the art and literature, such as Rabelais' *Pantagruel*, that incorporates the scourge.

As you might expect, this book is pretty dry. It gets technical in some places but not so much that it will lose your interest.

The Johns Hopkins University Press; $14.95
1986; softcover; 342 pp.; illus.

## INTIMATE TREASURES
## CATALOG OF CATALOGS

A great idea—have a catalog that offers other catalogs, as well as some magazines and videos, for sale. No more having to hunt down addresses for each company, just circle the numbers of the catalogs you want, and they're yours (for a price, of course). Intimate Treasures has catalogs of leather goods, sex toys, condoms, lingerie, software, and videos. Ah yes, the videos. No matter what your taste, there's a catalog specializing in videos about it. Choose from nude female wrestling, tease videos, raised skirts, wet T-shirts, transgender, nude bodybuilding, big busts, amateur, B&D, African-American, cartoons, and your basic porn. A must for the true connoisseur.

Intimate Treasures
PO Box 77902/San Francisco, CA 94107-0902.
Catalog: $5

## IVAN STORMGART BOOKS

Ivan Stormgart produces several catalogs offering second-hand books on sex, many of which are rare, out of print, and/or first editions.

Vintage Paperback Catalogue No. 5 is the thickest, containing hundreds of works of erotic fiction from the Marquis de Sade, Henry Miller, Phil Andros, Alexander Trocchi, Olympia Press,

Grove Press, and a host of other players, both well-known and forgotten. The prices seem pretty reasonable, most being in the five to twenty dollar range.

Catalogue #21 contains used nonfiction books—sexology, memoirs, travel guides, etc. The prices are a bit more expensive, almost all being in the two-figure range, with twenty dollars and up not being uncommon. The titles available send the mind reeling: *Sexual Slavery in America* (published in 1935!), *Gigolos, Loose Women Throughout the World*, *Voluntary Sterilization: A Decade of Achievement*, *The Dieter's Guide to Weight Loss During Sex*, and *Gary Griffin's Confidential Report on Penis Enlargement Methods*.

Special Catalogue No. 8 is devoted to used books and magazines on SM, B&D, and a few miscellaneous fetishes. Again, the prices are within reach.

The loving care that has gone into these catalogs is obvious. All the information you could ever want to know about every item is presented. Dates, publishers, publishing history, series numbers, number of pages, conditions, and contents are all duly noted. If you're into erotica/sex books, there is no excuse not to get these catalogs (well, they are somewhat expensive, but, hey, if you're serious about this...).

Ivan Stormgart Books
PO Box 470883/San Francisco, CA 94147-0883
Vintage Paperback Catalogue No. 5: $15 (applied toward first purchase)
Catalogue No. 21: $5
Special Catalogue No. 8: $10

## THE LOTUS LOVERS:
### THE COMPLETE HISTORY OF THE
### CURIOUS EROTIC CUSTOM OF FOOTBINDING IN CHINA
### by Howard S. Levy

The only book that chronicles the history of footbinding, a centuries-old Chinese practice of tightly wrapping women's feet in cloth starting when they're young girls. This caused their feet to developed into small, deformed, stumplike objects that were called "golden lotuses," reflecting the fact that men thought that such feet were beautiful.

Footbinding is probably nonexistent now, but it lasted for about one thousand years. The author's theory is that it was a fashion statement started by court dancers in the tenth century. Undoubtedly they did it lightly or it would have interfered with their movements. The fashion was imitated by the upper classes and then everybody was doing it. Somehow, the binding develop to the point that its purpose was to radically deform the foot.

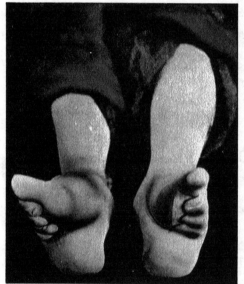

*The Lotus Lovers by Howard S. Levy*

*Small, deformed, stumplike objects also known as "golden lotuses."*

The binding would usually occur when a girl was six or seven. Her mother would bend all toes but the big one down and under the sole. A piece of cloth about two inches wide and ten feet long was wrapped very tightly in a figure eight around the whole foot. The object was to make the toes fuse into the sole and to bring the heel and the ball of the foot together. A missionary who observed this process wrote, "The flesh often became putrescent during the binding and portions sloughed off from the sole; sometimes one or more toes dropped off. The pain continued for about a year and then diminished, until at the end of two years the feet were practically dead and painless."

The reasons for this are twofold. First, when it came to feet, especially women's feet, the mo' smaller, the mo' better. The book contains writings in which praise and adoration were heaped on women's tortured tootsies. One such essay gives instructions for eighteen sexual positions that give the woman's tiny feet center stage. The second reason for footbinding was to

keep women in the house. This was seen as a surefire cure for adultery. Although it might keep the women from going out and about, there was nothing to stop amorous men from coming to the women, which must have occurred to someone over the course of a millennium. A wife's useless feet also were a status symbol for men, because it meant they were prosperous enough that their wives didn't have to work or help in the fields.

Eventually several forces brought an end to footbinding. The Manchu conquerers of China didn't like it. They thought big healthy feet were sexy. At the beginning of the 1800s, long before the West had a women's movement, influential Chinese leaders were calling for equality between the sexes, and this included an end to footbinding. Missionaries also fought against the custom on the grounds that it was "unnatural." Finally, in 1902 an imperial decree banned the torturous practice and it died out.

But lest we feel all high and mighty, the book's introduction reminds us, "...most Westerners have preferred and still prefer women with small feet; many people adore the feet of ballet dancers, which do not appear too different from the bound feet of the Chinese; millions of men enjoy seeing women in shoes with heels so high that the foot appears to be deformed and the whole movement of the body is changed. What men in the West feel when they see all the 'unnatural' female apparel is surely not too different from what a Chinese felt when seeing a bound foot."

*The Lotus Lovers* contains dozens of photographs of bound feet and firsthand accounts from women who went through this ordeal.

Prometheus Books; $31.95
1991; hardcover; 352 pp.; illus.

## LOVE WITHOUT LIMITS:
### THE QUEST FOR SUSTAINABLE INTIMATE RELATIONSHIPS
### by Dr. Deborah M. Anapol

Founded by Dr. Deborah Anapol, the Intinet Resource Center offers all kinds of information for people who want to be involved in two or more "sexualoving" relationships at once with full knowledge of everyone involved. They offer a newsletter, a retreat center, workshops, and *Love Without Limits*, which is the indispensable primer on "responsible nonmonogamy."

Responsible nonmonogamy is not a synonym for swinging. Although Anapol doesn't have anything against swinging, its main purpose is casual sex, not caring, intimate relationships. Therefore, she doesn't deal with it. Nonmonogamy can take several forms. An open marriage/relationship occurs when both partners agree that they can have outside sexualove relationships. In group marriage, three or more people are in long-term, committed, primary relationships with each other. The group marriage may be open or closed. An intimate network "is a lovestyle in which several ongoing secondary relationships exist. Sometimes all members of the group eventually become lovers."

Such relationships are fraught with difficulties. First of all, our society's idea of normal is the nuclear family, so dealing with guilt, hostility, and rejection by family members is a problem. Second, you may have to face some legal and financial hassles. Finally, there are the interpersonal struggles—jealousy, breakups, not liking a member of your relationship, etc. *Love Without Limits* discusses all of these things and gives further resources (groups, books, seminars, etc.) for dealing with them.

This book is remarkably well written and lucid. Anapol gently takes the reader through a gradual process that starts with defining nonmonogamy. She helps you decide if nonmonogamy is right for you with a discussion of the character traits you need. If you want to try it, she tells how to make the transition, find other "polys," form nonmonogamous relationships, and "come out of the closet" as a poly.

It's hard to imagine a better introduction to the subject than this book. If you're considering ditching monogamy, you've got to get it.

IntiNet; $16
1992; softcover; 180 pp.

## MALE SEXUAL ARMOR:
### EROTIC FANTASIES AND SEXUAL REALITIES OF THE COP ON THE BEAT AND THE MAN ON THE STREET
### by Patrick Suraci, Ph.D.

For this book Patrick Suraci, a clinical psychologist, interviewed policemen and men in other occupations regarding sexual feelings, fantasies, beliefs, fears, and behavior. He wanted to learn about the sex lives of one of the most "hypermasculine," or macho, segments of society and compare his findings to men in general society.

Much of Suraci's work focuses on passivity in sex. He wonders if society's repression of passiveness in men is even more prominent among cops. His overall finding is that there is a surprisingly high level of passiveness among policemen, although it's not as high as among the general population. Sixty-six percent of police reported that they were sometimes passive during sex, while 77 percent of civilians said they were.

Not all the questions bore this out, though. When asked if they would bear a child if they could, twice as many civilians as cops said yes (36 percent compared to 18 percent). The author asked the subjects if they wished their penises were larger; 55 percent of police and 36 percent of civilians said yes.

When asked, "Is sex or love more important to your lifestyle," the policemen's answers were love (64 percent), both (25 percent), and sex (11 percent). Civilians' answers were love (69 percent), both (17 percent), and sex (14 percent).

Out of the police who reported fantasizing about women, 19 percent report having rape fantasies, compared to 17 percent among the comparable civilian population. Among the cops who had the rape fantasies, 43 percent imagined themselves as the aggressor and 57 percent imagined themselves as the victim of a rape by a female. Eleven percent of the police and 8 percent of the civilians reported actually having been involved in a rape.

As far as anal sex goes, 16 percent of the police and 45 percent of the civilians claim to have "penetrated the anus of a male." However, 71 percent of the cops and 58 percent of the civilians report having anally penetrated a woman.

Other questions deal with the attractiveness of genitals, the superiority of one sex over the other, fantasies about men, foreplay, likes and dislikes about relationships, having orgasms, and more. Besides giving the results of the questions, Suraci also lets the men who were interviewed speak for themselves.

Irvington Publishers; $19.95
1993; hardcover; 323 pp.

## THE MASQUERADE EROTIC NEWSLETTER

Masquerade, the world's largest publisher of erotica and, coincidentally, the publisher of *Outposts*, puts out a thirty-two-page magazine (the word *newsletter* is something of a misnomer) covering the world of sex. It runs reprints from sex zines, new writing from Masquerade writers such as Pat Califia and Michael Perkins, book reviews, fiction, interviews with authors, and photos by Charles Gatewood, Richard Kern, and others.

Past features have included a rant against modern primitive poseurs, interviews with Andrei Codrescu and Samuel Delany, literary criticism of the pornographic genre, a history of the groundbreaking publisher Essex House, Picasso's erotic gravures, a photo-essay on peep shows, and an exerpt from Samuel Delany's novel *The Mad Man*. The Sept/Oct 1994 issue was entirely devoted to reprinting the premiere issue of the free sex zine *Porn Free* (well, it's almost free—you have to pay postage).

The last eight or so pages of each issue is a catalog of Masquerade's numerous books, including the latest ten titles that come out every two months. They always have some kind of ordering deal going, usually letting you choose a free book for every four you buy.

Masquerade Books
801 Second Avenue/New York, NY 10017
Single copy: $5
One-year sub (4 issues): $30

## PURE

*Pure* is a skin mag based on a novel idea—let women totally create the contents. The photos, the stories, the articles—everything. At first glance, it looks like most other straight porno magazines, but a closer examination reveals some differences. First of all, taboos are broken. The December 1994 issue contains "Stirrup Fun," in which Lisa Crystal Carver admits that gynecological exams get her hot. "High Heels and Hollow Points" is about the growing use of guns by women. Jane shows up at target practice in a tight silver miniskirt and three-inch black leather pumps. "She likes feeling sexy with a killing machine clenched between her manicured nails." Nadine says, "The greatest orgasms of my life have been those right after shooting practice when a gun instructor has fucked me with the barrel of a loaded .44." Each issue also features a pictorial based on the actual fantasies of a female *Pure* reader. This issue showed a woman having sex with three guys in a porno theater.

The second thing that makes *Pure* different is that photos abound. There are six pictorials per issue (compared with three in *Playboy*), and all but one of them are eight pages long. Plus, other features are illustrated with nude photos. *Pure* isn't afraid to give its readers what they want.

Finally, *Pure* is just plain hot. The photographers somehow manage to reach new levels of heat while still using the tactics of male-dominated medium-core pornography (à la *Penthouse*)—namely, spread-leg and bend-over shots. Maybe female photogs know how to capture something that lots of males miss. "The Right to Bare Arms" has a leggy blonde in an urban setting brandishing several pistols and assault rifles. Another pictorial has a curvaceous redheaded bombshell doing household chores. I know it sounds cliché as hell, but it works, dammit!

*Pure* is tough, brazen, not one bit bashful, yet it's playful and fun in places. When I started this book, I didn't think I'd be recommending a glossy, full-color skin mag, but *Pure* rocks.

PURE
9171 Wilshire Boulevard, Suite 300/Beverly Hills, CA 90210
Single issue: $4.95
Subscription address: PO Box 358/Mount Morris, IL 61054
One year sub (6 issues): $19.95

## REAL WOMEN DON'T DIET!:
### ONE MAN'S PRAISE OF LARGE WOMEN AND HIS OUTRAGE AT THE SOCIETY THAT REJECTS THEM
### by Ken Mayer

Ken Mayer, a quite muscular dude, judging from his author photo, is out to redefine the aesthetics of female beauty. To put it another way, he's pissed off at the way overweight women are viewed, and he wants it to change. There are two main components to this book. First, Mayer looks at society's narrow definition of beauty and insists that fat women should be part of a more inclusive paradigm of attractiveness. (Incidentally, Mayer uses the term "fat" frequently in an effort to reclaim it from those who use it as a pejorative epithet.) Mayer admits that he is attracted to large women, which has brought him "face-to-face with a society unconditionally at war with feminine flesh of any substantial dimensions." He tells about his life and his "search for big women." He is now a fashion photographer of large women.

His exposure to the world of glamour leads to the second main element of the book, which looks at the forces that keep women oppressed. The diet, fashion, beauty, and medical industries all promote the idea of "you can never be too thin," and, what's

*Real Women
Don't Diet!*
by Ken Mayer

*"Face-to-face
with a society
unconditionally
at war with
feminine
flesh of any
substantial
dimensions."*

more, they all benefit from this notion. Women eagerly snap up diet foods, diet pills, exercise programs, exercise machines, etc. to attain the look they're told they should have. What these industries give them in turn, says the author, is "insulting lies regarding health, a poor self-image, depression, eating disorders, feelings of isolation and frustration, a dramatic lowering of their quality of life, and sometimes even senseless death."

Men are co-conspirators in the plot. They too have accepted the idea that protruding ribs and knobby knees are attractive. This is another aspect of male domination. For an uptight and uncertain male population, "Trying to keep women physically small and feeble, uncertain about their own sexual identity, and preoccupied with their body is just what the doctor ordered."

The center photo section contains photographs of several attractive fat women, taken by the author.

Bartleby Press; $18.95
1993; hardcover; 190 pp.; illus.

## REDEEMER

Georges Bataille would have loved this magazine. Sex, death, violence, and religion are all thrown into a blender and scrambled so much that you can't tell where one ends and another begins. Issue #1 has one of the most transgressive fashion layouts of all time. While modeling Chanel clothes and jewelry, two female models get sexual and violent with each other. One photo shows the brunette model on a leash held by the blonde. In another the blonde is reaching from behind to fondle her companion's breasts. In the final shot, the blonde is holding a rather large Magnum to her head. But the most shocking picture of all is a two-page spread of the blonde shooting a hole through the bru's neck. The wall behind her is splattered in blood. The second fashion layout, almost tame by comparison, has infrared photos of babes with parts of their skeletons visible through their flesh.

The section on vampires contains articles on the bloodsucker in film and literature, accompanied by gory photos of vampire chicks. The article "Sacred Whores" overviews the movies about "bad nuns" (i.e., those who are lesbian, knocked up, sadistic, or addicted to drugs).

One of the photo spreads in issue #2 portrays several aristocratic Marie Antoinette clones armed with Uzis. They've staged their own revolution, apparently against men, whose unattached heads are all over the place. Articles cover B-movies about Nazis (for example, *Last Orgies of the Third Reich*), European Sadeian movies, American fetish artists, a history of Frankenstein movies, the do-it-yourself funeral movement, and more. All articles are accompanied by appropriately disturbing photographs.

The third issue had pictorials on the girls of *A Clockwork Orange* and an erotic interpretation of Salomé and her favorite toy, John the Baptist's head.

Each issue contains extreme book, magazine, and video reviews and an article on a B-movie actress. *Redeemer* focuses a lot of its attention on movies, and its pictorials feature all women (I'm not counting male corpses). If this sounds like your cup of tea, then this taboo-trashing magazine will delight you.

The Redeemer
PO Box 50/Stroud GL6 8YG/ENGLAND
Issues #1 and #3: UK: £5;
US & Canada: £8.50; Europe: £6.50; elsewhere: £9.50
[prices are for each issue separately]
Issue #2: subtract £1.50 from above prices
Four-issue sub: UK: £20; US & Canada: £34; Europe: £26; elsewhere: £38

## SEX DRUGS AND APHRODISIACS
### by Adam Gottlieb

This cult classic, published in 1973, is a guide to the drugs, herbs, and other substances alleged to be aphrodisiacs. "For our purposes in this book, we regard as an aphrodisiac or sex drug any substance which can be used to increase sexual energy and desire, promote and help maintain erection of the penis, delay premature ejaculation, relax inhibition without interfering with performance, serve as a tonic for the health of the sexual organs, overcome sexual lassitude and exhaustion, increase the production of sperm, augment sexual awareness, intensify orgasm, or enhance the enjoyment of sex."

Substances that are covered include absinthe, amyl nitrate, buchu leaves, DMSO, ginseng, licorice root, nutmeg, opium, pumpkin seeds, strychnine, yohimbe, and dozens of others. Most of the entries contain information on how the substance works, the optimum dosage, and the best way to take it.

Iboga is made from the root of an African forest shrub. The author and his acquaintances personally testify that Iboga works—he claims that some people, after ingesting a gram, have nonstop sex for *six to seventeen hours*. Fugu is a very popular and effective aphrodisiac in Japan. It is made from the testes of a species of poisonous pufferfish. Most of the time it acts as a potent stimulator, but sometimes it acts as a powerful poison. It claims around three hundred lives in Japan a year, and there is no known cure. The things we'll do for sex.

Ronin Publishing; $9.95
1973; paperback; 89 pp.

## SEXUAL PARADISES OF EARTH:
### A SINGLE MAN'S GUIDE TO INTERNATIONAL TRAVEL
### by Bill Bronson

At last, a travel guide that dispenses with the museums and historical sights and tells you how to find what you really want—sex, sex, and more sex. Although the author does talk a little about prostitution, the vast majority of the advice he gives is about free, easy, heterosexual sex. He also spends some time on the pursuit of love and relationships, if for some strange reason that's what you're into. You need not be a stud-muffin to make use of this knowledge—the women in these countries will very often be to be attracted to you even if you're old, fat, ugly, etc.

The three best sexual paradises on earth are Thailand, Jamaica, and the Dominican Republic. "Each of them is easy to get to, welcoming of tourists, relatively safe for the traveler, and inexpensive once you are there (for most things). They also have good food, provide easy, happy sexual experiences, and have other things to see and do as well." There are six other paradises that aren't quite as perfect as the top three, but will do quite nicely—Mexico, the Netherlands, the Philippines, Brazil, Egypt, and India.

The top three countries each get their own chapter. The author gives general info on tourist destinations, getting around, language, money, etc. But the part you're most interested in is his specific advice on where and how to get laid. For instance, in the chapter on Thailand, the author says, "Thai women are some of the most beautiful in the world." Finding a partner is easy: "In areas frequented by tourists, the number of available women is incredibly large. An unaccompanied man can expect to be followed down the street or beach by women hopeful of winning the chance to share his company." In the city of Pattaya, there are large bars that may contain forty unescorted women, all eager to be picked up by an American tourist. On the morning after, you can expect your lover to get up early and start doing chores, such as washing your clothes. Should you prove to be the sorriest guy on earth and are unable to get lucky in the sin capital of the world, don't worry. Prostitution is cheap, widespread, and, although illegal, it is unheard of for a tourist to be arrested for patronizing prostitutes.

Besides giving similar information for the other eight countries, the book covers health and safety concerns (STDs, bad water, crime), what gifts to bring, how to bring a woman back to the United States if you want a more permanent relationship, and more. There's even a chapter on special considerations for the disabled.

BB Press; $18.95
1993; softcover; 240 pp.; illus.

## THE SEXUALITY LIBRARY

A superlative catalog of books and videos about sex from your friends at Good Vibrations. The books cover a wide range: female sexuality (*The Lesbian Sex Book*), male sexuality (*Gay Sex*), family sexuality (*A Kid's First Book About Sex*), sex for one (*Solo Sex*), sex for two (*Hot Monogamy*), setting the mood (*Touching for Pleasure*), power play (*Learning the Ropes*), East meets West (*The Tao of Love and Sex*), erotic art (*Stereo Nudes*), erotic literature (*Herotica*), sex facts (*Sex in History*), and more.

This catalog also has Good Vibes' complete video selection: drama, comedy, compilations, porn noir, SM, feminist, lesbian, gay, bisexual, cult, educational, and amateur.

This is definitely a catalog worth having.

Good Vibrations
938 Howard Street #101/San Francisco, CA 94103
Catalog: $2 [you can get this catalog and Good Vibes' sex toy catalog for $3]

## STAND CORRECTED

A high-quality magazine of "spanking erotica." Lots of pictures (most in black-and-white), illustrations, and fiction featuring red-bottomed lasses getting the stuffing spanked out of them by men and women using brushes, paddles, riding crops, and hands. There are also illustrated guides to spanking in mainstream movies and in literature. There is no sex in this magazine (although there is plenty of nudity)—it's all spanking, pure and simple. *Stand Corrected* apparently isn't published on a regular basis, so there's no subscription information, but you can get the issue I've reviewed (#12).

Shadow Lane, the the company that puts out *Stand Corrected*, also has a catalog of spanking products. It's a fully illustrated, fifty-five-page guide to spanking movies, magazines, books, tapes, and paddles. And don't forget their third publication, *Scene One*, a digest of personal spanking ads from around the country.

Shadow Lane/PO Box 1910/Studio City, CA 91614-0910
Stand Corrected #12: $14.95
Catalog: $10
Scene One: $10
Be sure to include a flat fee of $3 for shipping and handling.

## SYNERGY BOOK SERVICES

Synergy puts out the *Whole Sex Catalog*, which carries a lot of material but isn't as all-inclusive as the name might lead you to believe (although with each new catalog, they are growing by leaps and bounds). They offer books, videotapes, cassettes, and reprints of magazine articles and out-of-print book chapters. Titles include *Threesomes, The Sex Maniac's Bible, The Monogamy Myth, Mystical Sex, SM 101, The Ultimate Kiss*, and some titles reviewed in this chapter. The second half of the catalog contains reviews of zines, newsletters, and catalogs. You can't buy these through Synergy, but their addresses and prices are given.

Synergy publishes several taboo-violating collections of erotic stories, including two covering bestiality and incest. They also put out *Sexual Perspectives*, a newsletter of essays, news, art, reviews, and stories of a sexual nature.

Even though the *Whole Sex Catalog* does have some good things to offer, the twenty-dollar price tag seems way too high, even if it does include a ten-dollar coupon.

Synergy Book Service/PO Box 8/Flemington, NJ 08822-0008
Catalog: $20
Four issues of *Sexual Perspectives*: $20

◄ *The Sexuality Library*

*A most excellent selection of books and videos on every sexual subject.*

## TALES OF TIMES SQUARE
### by Josh Alan Friedman

From 1978 to 1984, Josh Alan Friedman plunged into that sexual cesspool known as Times Square. His reports from Sleazetown U.S.A. have been collected into this book, first published in 1986, but out of print until now because the original publisher "didn't have the guts" to reprint it.

The world Friedman describes is populated by mondo mammary strippers, porno starlets, street kids, pushers, peep show masturbators, "a short tempered black midget" named Pee Wee, and a woman who made eighty-three men come in one night, among other debased denizens of this tawdry wasteland. The writing is superb—Friedman knows how to use just the right phrase or four-letter word to invoke the proper atmosphere. Like a slumming Mark Twain, he has a knack for capturing the dialects of the strange characters he encounters.

*Tales of Times Square* is a compulsively readable, unabashed frontline report from a small section of New York where the American libido surges unchecked.

Feral House; $12.95
1986, 1993; softcover; 201 pp.; lightly illus.

## VOYAGES

A mail-order catalog that runs the gamut. Plan how to spend your money on fantasy wear, sex toys, condoms, restraining devices, fetish mags, and a ton of hardcore vids in such categories as international, all-girl, all-guy, transgender, fetish, bondage, voyeurism, classics, etc. But the item that got my attention was the genuine ostrich feather from Africa, perfect for tickling all the right spots.

Voyages/PO Box 78550/San Francisco, CA 94107-8550
Catalog: $10

## WOMEN TALK SEX:
### AUTOBIOGRAPHICAL WRITING ON SEX, SEXUALITY, AND SEXUAL IDENTITY
### edited by Pearlie McNeill, Bea Freeman, and Jenny Newman

This book was conceived out of the idea of simply letting women talk about their sexuality—their experiences with lesbianism, bisexuality, heterosexuality, abuse, masturbation, celibacy, pregnancy, etc. They discuss their sexual awakenings and their struggles to go with their desires, no matter what form they might take. They also talk about the roles their race and class played in their sexuality.

This is not a book of sexy stories. These women matter-of-factly tell about the experiences in their lives that have shaped their sexuality. Grace Walker writes of being raped by a white man when she was eight. She still hasn't been able to come to terms with it. "I would gladly forget the whole event. But I have no control over my memory. That man has been in my bed for fourteen years and I just don't know how to get him out." This quote illustrates the most refreshing, but also disturbing, aspect of this book. Sexuality isn't presented all nice and neat with a bow on top. These women are angry and happy, confused and sure, discontented and satisfied. They haven't resolved everything and still have problems. Because of this, *Women Talk Sex* has a universal element to it. It shows you that you're not the only one dealing with shit and confused about sex and life.

Scarlet Press; $15.50
1992; softcover; 231 pp.

## THE WORLD OF HUMAN SEXUALITY:
### BEHAVIORS, CUSTOMS, AND BELIEFS
### by Edgar Gregersen, Ph.D.

This book provides a detailed, far-reaching survey of sexual practices and beliefs from all over the globe. Edgar Gregersen's approach is truly cross-cultural—from present-day Sweden to isolated Aboriginal tribes to small Russian religious sects, he ties it all together into one big, fascinating package.

You could easily get lost in this book for hours. The following is just a sampling of the many thousands of wondrous facts filling this book:

- The section on sexual mutilation assures us that excising the nipples of adolescent boys is found in only one society, the Janjero of Ethiopia. Many societies practice infibulation (sewing up) of the vagina. The Conibo Native Americans of Peru add a special touch—a clay dildo, an exact replica of the dick of the girl's fiancé, is inserted before she's sewn up. When the threads are snipped on their wedding day, she will supposedly provide a perfect fit.
- The earliest known written reference to fisting is in James Joyce's *Ulysses,* published in 1914: "Bello bares his arm and plunges it elbow deep in Bloom's vagina." There are earlier visual depictions of the act, though. Michelangelo's *Last Judgment* in the Sistine Chapel shows a demon fisting a damned man.
- In the United States, oral sex is more common among people who have been to college than people who have not.
- In some West African societies, large women are so prized that brides-to-be are sent to "fattening huts" to gain as much weight as possible before the wedding.
- "The Mormons require the faithful to wear a sacred garment at all times, even when copulating."
- In several native societies men wear "codpieces" made out of a gourd up to two feet long. The gourd is decorated with "bird feathers, beaks, animal fur or tails."
- Although mother-son incest is often cited as perhaps a universal taboo, that isn't so. To mark the beginning of the sex life of a Kubeo (South America) boy, he has sex with his mom. If a Tutsi (aka Watusi) man experiences impotence on his wedding night, one of the cures is to make it with Mom.
- Some Navajo believe that a man will get pregnant if he has sex with a woman on top.

- "Nightcrawling" is a reportedly common practice in Polynesia (it's also found in the Philippines) in which a man attempts to have sex with a sleeping woman who might otherwise be unwilling.

*The World of Human Sexuality* is an encyclopedic treasure trove that will educate you more than you thought possible, make you laugh out loud, and make you say, "Hmmm, I'd like to try that..."

Irvington Publishers; $49.95
1983, 1994; hardcover; 438 pp.; illus.

# ALTERNATIVE & FRINGE CULTURE

## UNDERGROUND OVERVIEWS

### APOCALYPSE CULTURE
#### (EXPANDED AND REVISED)
#### edited by Adam Parfrey

An underground classic, guaranteed to warp your impressionable mind. The basic idea behind *Apocalypse Culture* was to gather the most extreme documents available that prove we are very near the end of civilization as we know it. Among the many disturbing pieces here: "Latter-Day Lycanthropy"; an interview with a female necrophile; an article on the late G.G. Allin, the self-described "sickest, most decadent rocker of all time"; interviews with Psychopath Frank, publisher of the extreme zine *Livin' in a Powder Keg and Givin' Off Sparks*, and Peter Sotos, publisher of another extreme zine, *Pure*; "Love, Lithium, and the Loot of Lima," a fragment of a seven-hundred-page prose/poetic work by a schizophrenic; a look at the most revolting performance art ever perpetrated; "Surgeons and Gluttons in the House of Flesh," which concerns surgery, amputee, and obesity fetishes; "Cut It Off: A Case for Self-Castration," "Let's Do Justice for Our Comrade P-38" from the Italian terrorist group the Red Brigades; a look at the Satanic cult called The Process; "The Invisible War" by Anton LaVey; psychotic letters written to newspapers ("Hi my name is Robert and i want to get in To porno FILMS. but i dont no waer to go."); an essay by a man who has reviewed thousands of porn flicks; a look at the alleged government conspiracy to commit genocide on African-Americans; and "Vengeance in Secret Societies."

All in all, you'll have a hard time finding a more twisted collection of documents under one cover.

Feral House; $12.95
1987,1990; softcover; 362 pp.

### BENEATH THE UNDERGROUND
#### by Bob Black

Bob Black is fringe culture's combination of Andy Rooney and Jack Anderson. He comments on and reveals the machinations of various aspects of the "underground." Black isn't universally liked because he isn't afraid to express his opinions (speaking of *Factsheet Five*'s former movie reviewer Anni Ackner, he writes, "I know of no worse writer on the planet. The Internal Revenue Code sings by comparison.").

Black's critiques of his nonconformist compatriots are entertaining, even if you don't always agree with them. The whole point is that he's trying to point out blandness, hypocrisy, and lack of talent when he sees it, without trying to be nice or tactful. He absolutely torches the anarchist zine *The Match!*: "Assertedly atheist, it is bombastic in style and dogmatic in substance. Assertedly anarchist, it overtly extols—and exercises—authority even as it vilifies most of the anarchist movement, almost always for the wrong reasons. If anarchism retained any interest for the police, this is how they would want it to look."

Black slags the hell out of *Twisted Image*, a collection of Ace Backwords's anarcho-comic strip of the same name (which I happen to like). "To read him in book form is like sitting down to a multi-course banquet catered by Burger King. In a fanzine his cartoons are endurable because [they're] soon over with. Here they appear massed in their mediocrity."

Black doesn't trash everybody, though. He gives good, although far from ecstatic, reviews of Hakim Bey's *T.A.Z.* and the Loompanics catalog. It's telling to note that most of the parties who get slammed the hardest by Black are ones that have taken a dim view of him—the Church of the SubGenius, Ace Backwords, *Processed World*, and others. Could there be a little shit for shat going on here?

*Beneath the Underground* isn't a good introduction to the extreme scene. It will only have meaning and value to people who are already familiar with the subject matter.

Feral House; $10.95
1994; softcover; 190 pp.; lightly illus.

### FACTSHEET FIVE:
#### THE DEFINITIVE GUIDE TO THE ZINE REVOLUTION

*Factsheet Five* is an underground institution. It was started in 1981 by Mike Gunderloy as a one-page summary of strange amateur magazines (zines) he had stumbled across. One thing led to another, and Mike ended up publishing a thick magazine every two months for eight years. Evidently, working twelve hours a day, seven days a week, without a vacation for eight years finally got the best of Mike and he let *Factsheet Five* go. Hudson Luce volunteered to carry on the legend, but after one issue, he realized he was in over his head and abandoned ship.

Then in 1992 something miraculous happened. Amid proclamations that *FF* was dead, a new issue hit mailboxes. *Factsheet Five* was alive! A foolhardy zine publisher named Seth Friedman resurrected *FF* and made it better than ever. In its redesigned pages are bite-size reviews for well over a thousand zines in such categories as sex, food and health, personal zines, work, spirituality, humor, B-movies, fringe, grrrlz, queer, poetry, music, comix, etc. There are also reviews of loads of catalogs, music, and books. Of course, complete ordering information is given for every single item, so you can get your grubby little hands on it. To top it all off, I review several books in every issue. What more could you possibly want?

It is impossible to overstate *FF*'s importance to the alternative/underground circles. It keeps everybody abreast of what every one else is doing. If you only get one thing in this entire book, make sure it's *Factsheet Five*.

Factsheet Five Subscriptions
PO Box 170099/San
Francisco, CA 94117-0099
Single issue: $6 (US & Canada);
Europe: $8; elsewhere: $9
Six-issue sub (bulk rate): $20;
first class: $40; Canada: $35;
Europe: $45; elsewhere: $55

*KOOKS*
by Donna Kossy

### KOOKS:
#### A GUIDE TO THE OUTER LIMITS OF HUMAN BELIEF
#### by Donna Kossy

"A kook is a person stigmatized by virtue of outlandish, extreme or socially unacceptable beliefs that underpin their entire existence. Kooks usually don't keep their beliefs to themselves; they either air them constantly or create lasting monuments to them." With this definition of kooks, Donna Kossy treads where the sane fear to, looking at people who are sure that they have uncovered the secrets of the world—even of

*Outlandish, extreme or socially unacceptable behavior, lovingly collected.*

*Rapid Eye*▼
edited by
Simon Dwyer

*Straight-
forward
approach to
some very
crooked
material.*

the universe or reality itself. But while most others would enter this strange world just to bash its residents, Kossy is fascinated by the kooks and wants to present their views in a judgment-free manner.

This book presents material from Kossy's zine *Kooks* as well as new research. We get to meet the Anglo-Israelites, who believe that those of Anglo-Saxon descent are God's chosen people, and Jews are just impostors; the Nation of Yaweh, who believe that Blacks are God's chosen people; the Aggressive Christianity Missions Training Corps, who make Jehovah's Witnesses look like wimps; two people who know that Satan created the dinosaurs; trepanners, who drill holes in their heads to expand their consciousness; the Voluntary Human Extinction Movement; the Flat Earth Society; conspiracy theorist William Cooper; Steve Renstrom, who claims that the former California senator Alan Cranston is a master conspirator behind the deaths of John Belushi and JFK and the Sonic Youth Song "Kill Yr. Idols"; Bernie Bane, who says that JFK is still alive; and dozens more people who have stumbled onto the TRUTH!

The articles on each kook or kook group contain lots of excerpts from their writings. Several chapters are reprints of complete kook fliers and letters. *KOOKS* is a vast cornucopia of kookiness that no lover of lunacy can afford to be without.

Feral House; $16.95
1994; oversize softcover; 253 pp.

## LOOMPANICS' GREATEST HITS

Loompanics Unlimited's catalog features a large selection of the world's most subversive books (for more info, see Appendix A). Besides books, the Loompanics catalog and quarterly updates also feature original articles on controversial subjects. This book collects the best of the first ten years' worth of features. These inflammatory writings cover nuclear apocalypse, the truth behind the Declaration of Independence, what to do when the FBI comes, squatting, financial privacy, survivalism, tax protest, fake ID, Holocaust revisionism, the real child molesters, the sex police, autoerotic asphyxiation, gun control, conspiracy theories, computer viruses, and cold fusion. On top of that, there are comix by Ace Backwords, posters by Anti-Authoritarians Anonymous, and subverted comics by the Situationists. More than seventy-five hard-hitting articles, features, and interviews, which are now impossible to find elsewhere, make this book a valuable find.

Loompanics Unlimited; $16.95
1990; oversize softcover; 300 pp..

## RAPID EYE #2
### edited by Simon Dwyer

More linear and coherent than any of the other books in this section, *Rapid Eye #2* offers straightforward articles about all kinds of strange topics. "Nihilist Cinema" looks at the work of two of the most brutal movie directors of all time—Richard Kern, creator of *Thrust in Me, Fingered,* and *Nazi-a-go-go,* and Jörg Buttgereit, creator of the graphic necrophile movie *Nekromantic.* Another article examines whether Lobsang Rampa was real or a hoax. "Brain Dead" by Colin Wilson is about the moment of death—when it actually occurs and what happens afterward. Other articles deal with conspiracies, H.P. Lovecraft, Carlos

Castaneda, poet/performance artist Aron Williamson, outlaw publishers Savoy Books, mondo movies, and nineteenth-century woman of adventure Alexandra David-Néel.

Not quite half the book is given to Part Two of editor Simon Dwyer's *In the Jungle of the Plague Yard,* a hilarious, cynical travelogue of his journey through the United States. He travels from L.A. to Chicago to New York, hitting the highlights and lowlights, and breaking into long digressions about artists, fringe religions, and other such topics. Dwyer calls it like he sees it, referring to Jesse Helms as "a man who conveniently photographs rather like a Nazi war criminal" and Abraham Lincoln as "the nation's most revered VD-ridden hypocrite." He describes the Disneyland ride "It's a Small World": "The walls of this ride truly are worse than the characters one sees in a Hieronymous Bach [sic] painting. They consist of disgusting children, all of whom should have been murdered at birth along with their filthy parents, dressed-up in national costumes which nobody ever wears."

Creation Press; $19.50
1992; softcover; 391 pp.

## SEMIOTEXT(E) USA
### (SEMIOTEXT(E) #13)

In this edition of *Semiotex(e),* the fearless editors have attempted to create an alternative map—one that charts "areas not found on the official map of consensus perception." Although the articles and art they reprint from zines and micropresses are impressively bizarre, they are presented without any background or guidance, meaning that this book isn't really useful as a map, which locates areas in relation to other areas, but as a compilation of some of the most interesting rest stops on society's twisted mindscape.

The almost 150 comix, rants, articles, collages, stories, poems, and other goodies in this book defy explanation or categorization (or rationalization, for that matter). So lemme just throw a few titles your way to give you some idea of what you're in for: "Mormons in Space," "The Puberty of Smell," "Variations on Jesus and the Fly," "Wall, Anus, Wall, Vulva, Wall," "Killing the President (Simulated)," "Monkey Boy," "Dial-a-Rumor," "The Secret of Levitation," "Power Iz Fun, History Iz Happiness," "Barbie and Tammy: The Real Story," "Garp on Valium," and "Does God Sanction Slavery?"

Autonomedia; $12 (a steal)
1987; oversize softcover; 352 pp.

## SENSORIA FROM CENSORIUM
### VOLUME II

Promising "Low Culture, High Culture, and No Culture," this book delivers more than three hundred pages of art, film, fiction, photography, journalism, activism, theory, comix, and things that fit into no known category. A lot of this stuff defies explanation, but here is what I can decipher: an interview with J.G. Ballard, Annie Sprinkle's writings and photography, conspiracy articles from Prevailing Winds Research, a look at Bruce La Bruce's homocore movie *Super 8 1/2,* Max Allen on porn, a reprint of the *Beyond Blade Runner* pamphlet, a photo essay on bizarre dolls, antiracist demonstrations, an article on the radical Working Press, lots of material on rampant censorship in Canada, and art damage out the wazoo.

Beautifully designed in a confusing pomo kind of way, and produced on the finest of paper. Truly a fitting testament to the underground, it definitely deserves a place on everyone's bookshelves.

Mangajin Books; $21.95
1993; oversize softcover; 335 pp.

# CLOTHING

## GOTHIC

Do you long for the gothic days of the vampire—pale-skinned women in velvet dresses, men in capes, and dark castles lined with gargoyles? Now you can recapture those fun times with the funky clothes, jewelry, and props from Gothic. They offer, among other things, velvet and cotton capes, buccaneer shirts, poet shirts, crushed stretch velvet leggings, waistcoats, and a readingote, a one-piece crinkle velvet outfit with a long full skirt and Venetian point lace trim. They also carry chain mail jewelry such as chokers, bracelets, and belts. Other available items include gargoyles, iron candelabra, and satyr bookends. All items in the catalog are beautifully photographed being worn by decadent vampire babes and boys.

Gothic Ltd.
245 Eighth Avenue, Suite 395/New York, NY 10011
Catalog: $3

## NOIR LEATHER

Whether your scene is Harley-Davidson, heavy metal, SM, or just the disaffected punk act, you'll find your leather and metal gear here. Noir Leather sells all kinds of spiked bracelets, studded collars, bootstraps, charm bracelets, voodoo dolls, inverted cross pendants, glowing crucifixes, rosary beads, Viking jewelry, mandala medallions, spurs, boot tips, special safety pins, studs, T-shirts, and videos. Everything you need to make sure people avoid eye contact with you when they see you coming.

If bondage gear is what you're looking for, choose from leather handcuffs, bits, ankle restraints, leashes, surgical forceps, and more. Noir has an impressive selection and their prices seem fairly reasonable.

Noir Leather/317 S. Center Street/Royal Oak, MI 48067
Catalog: $1 bill and two 32¢ stamps; overseas: two $1 bills

## ST. MICHAEL'S EMPORIUM

Creating "leather attire for the Middle Ages through Armageddon," St. Michael's offers wearable art that you simply won't find anywhere else. Using old world, hand techniques, Michael Saint creates leather masks, collars, corsets, bras, helmets, belts, arm bracers, codpieces, chaps, and, of course, partial and full suits of armor. This stuff must be seen to be believed! Michael's creations are beautiful, intricate combinations of leather and metal that truly look at home either in the Middle Ages or the End Times. The catalog contains pictures of every piece.

Michael's customers span a wide spectrum, from Renaissance fairs and movie studios to motorcycle clubs and the leather community. The prices aren't too high considering the quality and uniqueness of the products. Some random examples: the Satyr Mask is $46.50; the pulse-quickening Mistress Corset is $190.00; the Demon's Cod Piece is $160.00; the Apocalypse Chaps are $575.00 per pair; and complete suits of armor are around $4,000. Michael also does custom work, if you have a particular need that must be fulfilled.

St. Michael's Emporium
156 E Second Street, Suite 1/New York NY 10009
Catalog: $3

## STREETSTYLE
### by Ted Polhemus

*Streetstyle* is a visual encyclopedia of the fashions of subcultures—called "styletribes" by the author—from the 1940s to today. Each of the forty groups gets its own two- to four-page section, with text and many color and black-and-white pictures. Among those covered are zooties, bikers, hip cats, beatniks, teddy boys,

rockabillies, surfers, mods, rockers, greasers, hippies, skinheads, glam, Rastafarians, headbangers, punks, New Romantics, Goths, pervs, ravers, grunge, cyberpunks, and others. It's like a who's who of cool dudes and hip chicks.

*Streetstyle by Ted Polhemus*

*A Tribe Called Style (and its sycophants).*

The accompanying text is insightful and just lightly sprinkled with cynicism. Ted Polhemus obviously enjoys and is fascinated by his subject, but he knows that people are basically lemmings who just want to follow the latest style. With the exception of the few brave souls who *start* a new trend, most members of these styletribes are unthinking clones.

The photographs are dynamite. They are visually stunning, and they capture the very essence of these subcultures. Polhemus recognizes that not every tribe is a unified whole—there are many subgroups and factions. In the section on B-Boys and Flygirls, for example, there are pictures of the early Adidas/gold chain style of Run-DMC, the bright, tight, quasi-African clothes of Salt-N-Pepa, the Afrocentric style of A Tribe Called Quest, and the militant look of Public Enemy. The section on headbangers shows the two opposing styles: "The scruffy denim look, which derives from the Hippies...[and] the sexy leather look, deriving from Glam."

*Streetstyle* contains several essays covering the street's influence on high fashion (and vice versa) and the postmodern fragmentation of youth culture. In "The Gathering of Tribes," Polhemus notes that today young people have a large variety of streetstyles to choose from, and they often mix and match styles, creating interesting hybrids. Some people are even opting to resurrect defunct streetstyles, such as New Romantic, mod, and beatnik.

Thames and Hudson; $19.95
1994; oversize softcover; 144 pp.; heavily illus.

# MISCELLANEOUS

## ALTERNATIVE PRESS REVIEW

*APR* started as a column in *Anarchy* but grew into a full-fledged magazine, the bulk of which consists of reprinted articles from a variety of alternative press sources. Issue #1 has articles on the War on (Some) Drugs, detective novels, Operation Rescue head dweeb Randal Terry, NAFTA, false memory syndrome, televangelists, fluoridation, bisexuality, and media control. There are also seven pages of capsule magazine reviews and a few book and movie reviews.

C.A.L. Press
PO Box 1446/Columbia, MO 65205-1446
Current issue: $4.95
One-year sub (4 issues): $16
(add $6 for first class);
foreign: $24 (add $8 for airmail)

*Alternative Press Review*

*Beyond mass media —offerings from the rest of the press.*

## THE ARCHIVES OF ESTHETIC NIHILISM

"A delve into the mass schizophrenic breakdown at the end of the second millennium A.D." This photocopied, stapled catalog contains videos, tapes, books, magazines, and photocopied articles having to do with the most unusual and grotesque topics of our times: Charles Manson, serial killers, Satanism, drugs/hippies, Nazis, white supremacists, Velvet Underground,

THE FACE ON MARS    PSYCHEDELIC CACTI

## CRASH COLLUSION

A Quarterly Guide to the Fringe    Issue #6  $4.00

UFO COVER-UPS • WEIRD SCIENCE
INTERVIEW WITH THOMAS LYTTLE
BLACK MAGICK • THE ULTIMATE HIGH
SAUCERS • REVIEWS AND MORE

*Crash
Collusion*
▼

*A strangely
coherent mix
of the wild and
the weird.*

bizarre film, Jim Jones, the Process Church, and more.

There are things in here that I have never, ever seen for sale anywhere else. You want a tape of the Manson Family singing Charlie's songs? It's here. Or how about a copy of the Nazis' most famous anti-Semitic film, *Jud Süss?* No problem. Maybe you want a copy of a BBC documentary on David Lynch, with two of his early short films thrown in as a bonus? Look no further. If William Burroughs is to your liking, there are twelve audio tapes of interviews, readings, etc. Wait a minute, do my eyes deceive me? Could it possibly be? Yes, the *AAN* carries the infamous, whispered-about, rarely seen Rolling Stones film *Cocksucker Blues!*

How can you live another minute without the forbidden source materials available in this twisted catalog?

Aes-Nihil Productions
7210 Jordan Avenue, #B-41/Canoga Park, CA 91303
Catalog: $8; foreign: $12 (refundable with order of $50 or more). Postal money orders only

## ARG-ZINE/ACTION RESOURCE GUIDE

*ARG-Zine* is a progressive/radical political magazine for people who are tired of being quiet. *The Action Resource Guide* is a rapid-fire network listing of zines and projects looking for submissions, people wanting to trade stuff, interesting catalogs, and more. Lots of entries on mail art, portfolios, e-mails, BBSs, stamps, pen pals, zines, and more. The 1994 *Action Resource Guide* (five dollars) also includes *ARG-Zine #5*, which lets prisoners speak their minds about prison life, the justice system, crime, etc.

The ARG people also publish *Global Mail*, a newsletter listing mail art events, archives, compilations, exchanges, and related stuff. Much like the listings in the *Action Resource Guide*, except *Global Mail* comes out three times a year instead of once.

ARG/PO Box 597996/Chicago, IL 60659
ARG-Zine/Action Resource Guide: one-year sub: $15; foreign: $17,
Global Mail: one year sub (3 issues): $8; foreign: $10
Foreign orders: add $2 to prices

## CRASH COLLUSION:
### A QUARTERLY GUIDE TO THE FRINGE

In this magazine, a number of oddly related subjects come crashing together and somehow collude into a jarring whole. The main subjects covered are UFOs, psychedelic drugs, altered consciousness, conspiracies and cover-ups, Fortean phenomena, and magick. Articles in #6 include "Paranoia, Necromancy, and Magick," "Is There Really a Cosmic Watergate?" "Modern-Day Trepanning," "Guide to Mescaline-Containing Cacti"; #7 includes "PKD [Philip K. Dick], The Unicorn and Soviet Psychotronics," "Evil in the Field of Dreams," and "Fringe Elements of the Third Reich." There are also plenty of book and video reviews in each issue. It's a fun-packed peek behind the wizard's curtain.

Crash Collusion/PO Box 49233/Austin TX 78765
Single issue: $4
Four-issue sub: $14

## EMPHERA BUTTONS

How can words express the utter coolness of the objects in this catalog? Hundreds of pin buttons and magnets containing the funniest, most anti-authoritarian, and insulting phrases you've ever heard. But let the buttons/magnets speak for themselves:

• Anybody who claims God is on their side is dangerous as hell
• Die Barney Die!
• I take drugs and I vote
• I think, therefore I'm dangerous
• Who the hell is FICA and why does he take my money?
• A man is just a big dildo with a carrying case
• That's Mister Fuckhead to you!
• Doing my part to piss off the religious right
• It takes balls to be a fairy
• I'm being paid to talk to you
• Stop staring at my tits
• Thank you for turning a simple transaction into a bizarre ritual

Of course, simply reading the phrases doesn't do the buttons justice, since they're colorful and well designed, with imaginative type and graphics. Emphera also carries a bunch of buttons with pictures of Betty Boop, Felix the Cat, Mickey Rat, and other notables, as well as symbols (Grateful Dead, pro-gay, the eye on the pyramid, pot leaf, etc.).

Emphera Buttons/PO Box 490/Phoenix, OR 97535
Catalog: four 32¢ stamps

## EYE

*EYE* is a cool newsprint zine covering drugs, the unexplained, pop culture, Big Brother, and other juicy topics. They've run articles on cremation vs. burial (#1), injectable microchips (#2 & #3), STP (#2), the *Flintstones* TV show (#2), the *Addams Family* TV show (#3), and human corpses in auto crash tests (#3).

Issue 4 had several great articles. One covered ibogaine, a substance that is extracted from an African bush. Street use and limited scientific studies have shown that ibogaine can instantly cure most users of their addiction to alcohol, heroin, and cocaine. Yet this miraculous natural substance is banned in the United States, having been put on the DEA's Schedule I list. Why? The authors surmise that the drug giants pressured the government into banning it. After all, "The last thing the health and pharmaceutical industries want is a cure for a disease [addiction] which currently is a top money maker."

Other articles examine forced electroshock therapy, the symbolism of the *Planet of the Apes*, an update on surveillance technology, and a haunted Connecticut town. Most articles are accompanied by an extensive and useful resources listing, for further studies.

EYE Publishing/Box 303/New York, NY 10009
Single issue: $3.95; overseas: $6
Four-issue sub: $14.95 (make checks or money orders payable to L. Crosby)

## HEADPRESS:
### THE JOURNAL OF SEX RELIGION DEATH

A zine that unapologetically romps through the darkest, seamiest aspects of our world. In an irreverent style, *Headpress* looks at porn, murderers, shocking art, suicide, and other morbid subjects. Issue #8 is the "Big Sexyland" issue. Features include an essay on various words for sex acts and private parts, the confessions of a masturbator, an interview with Steven E. Johnson, creator of the underground's most famous unpublished book, *My Stinking Ass* (accompanied by plenty of artwork from the book), an article on serial-killer-groupie VerLyn, a guide to public bathrooms in Manchester, an interview with Gen of the band The Genitorturers, and a look at which female porn stars have the best booties in doggie-style scenes (About Mai Lin: "When she's slung over a four-poster getting her money maker shaken, her cheeks vibrate about as rigorously as a can of paint being electronically mixed"). *Headpress* has a regular column called "It's a Mad Mad Mad Mad World," where readers write about their experiences with weirdos. A loving glimpse into the dark side.

Headpress
PO Box 160/Stockport Cheshire SK1 4ET/ENGLAND
Single issue: $7 plus $3 shipping; UK: £3.50
Four-issue sub: $40; UK: £14; Europe: £16

## THE MOORISH SCIENCE MONITOR

A small magazine from your friends in the fringe religion known as Moorish Science. Much silliness, satire, and crazy wisdom is to be found here. One article in issue #7 contains pictures of women, including, I think (the picture's a little dark), the ultimo magician's assistant Claudia Schiffer, with the caption "THESE AND OTHER SULTRY MOORISH WENCHES AWAIT YOUR LETTERS. WRITE—IF YOU WOULD PLUCK THESE BLOSSOMS OF PARADISE. WRITE—IF YOU WOULD KNOW THE PURE BLISS OF EPISTOLARY INTERCOURSE. COMING SOON: DIAL-A-HOURI." At last, a religion that's not afraid to give the people what they want!

Ziggurat/PO Box 25193/Rochester, NY 14625
Single issue: $2

## PUCK:
### THE OFFICIAL JOURNAL OF THE IRREPRESSIBLE

A kinda Generation X, kinda pomo magazine of hip fiction, essays, poetry, and reviews. Issue #10 is the "psiberPuck! issue." Stories include "Cogitor, Ergo Sum," "The Drug Dealer," "Schroedinger's Albatross," "Mutant Kabuki," and "Urban Angst at the 7-Eleven in 2019." "Edge Tutorial" asks us, "Do you wear glasses? Contact lenses? Use a hearing aid? Have an artificial limb or organ? Guess what: YOU'RE A CYBORG." In "Aliens Invade Classrooms!" McKenzie Wark discusses the situation wherein media-drenched kids are in classrooms designed for the 1800s: "The 'moral panic' frequently takes the form of a call to return to the 'Three Rs': reading, writing, and arithmetic. Why schools and universities should persist with such quaint skills is beyond me. Arithmetic is what calculators were invented for. Novels are for people too dumb to understand *Twin Peaks*. Let's face it, in today's world, arithmetic and reading are soft options for people who can't program their VCRs or figure out the manuals for their spreadsheet program."

Issue #11 will be the libertine *Puck*/sex issue, and after that will be the big tenth anniversary blowout issue. Now's a great time to *Puck yourself!*

Permeable Press
47 Noe Street, Studio 4/San Francisco, CA 94114-1017
Single issue: $6.50
One-year sub (3 issues): $17; foreign: $26

## SOUND PHOTOSYNTHESIS

It's tempting to list this catalog in the "Drugs" chapter, but that would be too limiting. Yes, this catalog of audiotaped and videotaped lectures does have a lot of hallucinogenic material on it, but it also delves into theories of reality, spirituality, New Age thinking, Buddhism, and Sufism. They have tons of lectures by Terence McKenna, John C. Lilly, Robert Anton Wilson, Colin Wilson, and other visionaries. Particularly exciting are the audio/videotapes of the 1991 Bridge Conference: Linking the Past, Present, and Future of Psychedelics. It's more than thirty tapes of prominent guest speakers discussing every imaginable aspect of hallucinogens. Luckily for those of us who don't have a lot of bucks, the tapes are available separately.

Also, look for Sound Photosynthesis to be offering CDs and Mac CD-ROMs in the future.

Sound Photosynthesis/PO Box 2111/Mill Valley, CA 94942
Catalog: $1

## THE STAKE:
### HUMOR AND HORROR FOR A DYING PLANET

This magazine from III Publishing contains stories, essays, comix, and articles that use satire as a vehicle for attacking the church, the state, and other bastions of authority. Issue #5 features a "Vatican Correspondent" fondly recalling the Inquisi-

tion and hoping for a new one, Adolf Hitler commenting that Virtual Reality and other technologies are going to be his new tool for controlling the masses; a short story, "The Trial of the Alleged Prince Alfredo Gor," where the title character is put on trial for "impersonating a wise and glorious leader of state"; and an ad for Auschwitz Temps: "Your Future Belongs to Us."

III Publishing
PO Box 1581/Gualala, CA 95445
Single issue: $3.95
Three-issue sub: $9

▲ *The Stake*

*Attacking the Church and State in a fun-to-read format.*

## TELEVISION MAGICK
### by The Temple of Psychick Youth

This little booklet discusses the power television has over us and how we can use TV for our own ends. "Walk into any room in which there is a television and you will notice that the room is set around the position of the television. It demands your attention and is the central focus. We give it this power, we allow it to manipulate our viewpoints, emotions and our lives. While the lawmakers are raising the taxes, or dumping nuclear waste near our homes, what are we doing? 20,000,000 of us are watching a Soap Opera; and we wonder where our rights/rites went."

Besides reminding us that TV manipulates us, *Television Magick* offers ways to manipulate reality with your TV. For example, one section suggests turning to a nonbroadcasting station, staring at the snow onscreen, and allowing the mind to create images. Having been a practitioner of video hallucination for years, I can attest that it is an interesting experience. Another section suggests creating a feedback loop by focusing a camcorder on a television being used as a monitor. "You will discover an astral tunnel in black and white. Now turn the camera ever so slightly and observe! With a little practice you can see every geometric pattern under the Sun—an almost infinite variety of symbols, all fluctuating, all changing constantly."

Don't smash your TV set—use it as a toy!

Temple Press; $5
1993; saddle-stitched booklet; 23 pp.

## THIS IS YOUR FINAL WARNING!
### by Thom Metzger

First of all, let's clear up some confusion—this book is by underground writer Thom Metzger, not the neo-Nazi Tom Metzger, head of the White Aryan Resistance. OK, having established that, let me say that reading this book is the literary equivalent of experiencing psychosis. Not one damn bit of it makes sense, but because of that, it all makes sense. Perfect, beautiful schizophrenic sense. (Am I making sense? Stop making sense!)

This book collects the rants, ravings, and religious tracts self-published by Metzger's Ziggurat Press. Here's an excerpt from "The Gagamon Brothers" (I know I'm presenting it out of context, but it doesn't make any more sense when it is in context): "And then the flying saucers from Planet Vem attack with the Monkey Dwarfs and the Glow In The Dark Lizards and the no-wax floors spinning around dancing with their heads cut off and everybody so happy doing latest dance craze with sexy Vampire Chickens and Have a Nice Day button spitting out fire and tongues and octopus arms and feelers like on bugs and radioactive worms wearing sunglasses."

Inflict psychic damage on yourself. Get this book.

Ziggurat; $6
1992; small softcover; 181 pp.

# CYBERCULTURE

## HACKING AND CRACKING

### THE LITTLE BLACK BOOK OF COMPUTER VIRUSES,
#### VOLUME 1: THE BASIC TECHNOLOGY
#### by Mark Ludwig

This is undoubtedly the most controversial book on viruses ever published. It caused an uproar in the computer community when it was published. There were already lots of books on the market that talked about viruses—what they are, how to protect yourself, etc. But this was the first book that actually gave the code for the viruses, meaning that anyone with basic programming knowledge can easily create these viruses. (On top of that, the publisher also sells a disk full of live, executable viruses for a mere $15.)

The author gives his rationale for this highly explosive action: "I am convinced that computer viruses are not evil and that programmers have a right to create them, possess them and experiment with them.... [This book] goes beyond a mere technical treatment, though, to defend the idea that viruses can be useful, interesting, and just plain fun." Later, he says, "The purpose of this volume is to bring them out of the closet and look at them matter-of-factly, to see them for what they are, technically speaking: computer programs." The author holds the Founding Father/cyberpunk belief that information is inherently neither good nor bad and that withholding it is wrong. He feels that we can learn a lot from the study of computer viruses, particularly because they may be a primitive form of artificial life.

*The Little Black Book* discusses what viruses are and exactly how they work. It also lists the code for TIMID, INTRUDER, KILROY, STEALTH, and other viruses. As you might expect, it's extremely technical, so don't expect a "fun read."

American Eagle Publications, Inc.; $14.95
1990; softcover; 178 pp.

### IRON FEATHER JOURNAL

A crazed journal of illicit information, whose editor seems to live a somewhat nomadic existence. Issue #13 is pure helter-skelter information overload. (It is promised that future issues will be better organized. I hope not.) Among the bits and pieces of wondrous info to be found are articles on blue box phone phreaking, making laughing gas, using ecstasy, password hacking techniques, do-it-yourself pirate radio, vending machine phun, a list of BBSs with porno GIFs, electronic zines, strange Japanese remote control toys, fuel from water, hi tek contacts, zine/catalog reviews, and more.

An article on shoplifting told of this prank, which I must pass along: "In London a group calling themselves the King Mob Group entered a Selfridges store in Oxford Street with one of their number dressed as Santa Claus. Good old Father Xmas toured the store giving away free gifts from the stock on display and wishing everyone a 'Merry Chirstmas.' Soon afterward the shoppers were witness to the edifying spectacle of policemen arresting Father Christmas and snatching back toys from small children...."

Stevyn Protheroe/PO Box 1905/Boulder, CO 80306-1905
Single issue: $4
Four-issue sub: $12

## SECRETS OF A SUPER HACKER
### by The Knightmare

This book gives fairly detailed instructions for breaking into computer systems. Although some hackers may have malicious intent, The Knightmare claims he does not. "The true hacker is motivated by her or his desire to learn, to understand, to cleverly and harmlessly outwit." In other words, this is about hacking for hacking's sake—breaking into systems just because it can be done. "Hackers hack because they are in love with the idea that any accessible computer has a secret side that can be broken into." But whether you're hacking for the fun of it or to cause trouble, this book will help you get started. I learned quite a few things from it, but I think it's way too simple for hard-core hackers.

**Fractals ▼**
**John Briggs**
(See page 128)

*The visual representations of chaos.*

The section "Before Hack" tells you how to pick your target, how to research it (going through trash, snooping, examining shots of screens in magazines, manuals, and even TV), how to determine passwords, and social engineering (fooling legitimate users into giving away information) and its counterpart, reverse social engineering. The next section, "During Hack," discusses gaining access to CD-ROM databases, public access terminals (like those at libraries and colleges), corporate and government computers, bulletin board systems (BBSs), and on-site terminals and what to do once you've gained entry. Finally, "After Hack" looks at how to avoid getting caught and the many laws regarding hacking.

There are also a glossary and appendixes of ASCII codes, commonly used passwords, default passwords, and more.

Loompanics Unlimited; $19.95
1994; oversize softcover; 205 pp.

## 2600:
### THE HACKER QUARTERLY

*2600* is the premier hacking/phreaking magazine. It relays uncensored, technical information on viruses, computer hacking, phone phreaking, and how to violate just about any electronic/mechanical system in existence. The spring 1994 issue, for example, has articles on building a DTMF decoder, a guide to the guts of the NYNEX telephone charge card, how to hack the LED display of a Stairmaster exerciser, getting cable channels you haven't paid for, a guide to CCITT International signaling (the way in which the phone system communicates with itself), and using the telex code for legit and illegit purposes. One article exposes the use of OptoComs, which are devices that sense the flashing lights of approaching emergency vehicles and change a traffic light to green, giving the vehicle a safer path. You can build your own flashing Chrome Box that will simulate an emergency vehicle's lights, triggering automatic green lights for you.

If you had any trouble understanding anything in the preceding paragraph, then *2600* probably isn't for you. The magazine is saturated with techtalk, acronyms, and slang that will leave you hopelessly confoozed unless you are already among the initiated. If you do have the basics down, then *2600* will provide you with mountains of useful info.

2600 Magazine/PO Box 752/Middle Island, NY 11953
Single issue: $4
One-year sub (4 issues): $21; overseas: $30

# RADICAL SCIENCE AND TECHNOLOGY

## FRACTALS:
### THE PATTERNS OF CHAOS—DISCOVERING A NEW AESTHETIC OF ART, SCIENCE, AND NATURE
### by John Briggs

I've been dreading reviewing this book because it means I have to try to explain fractals, not an easy task, since there is no set definition of this strange beast. At the root of fractals is a simple mathematical equation. Think of a computer screen as a plane mapping out complex numbers. Each pixel represents a number. Add zero to that number. This is the answer to the first equation. Take that answer and add it, instead of zero, to your first number. Take this new answer and feed it back into the equation. Do this about a thousand times. If the answers to the equation hover around the same value, color the pixel black. If the answer approaches infinity slowly, color the pixel with a certain color, and if it approaches infinity quickly, use another color. Different shades are used depending on the exact speed.

This seeming act of mathematical masturbation produces some of the most crushingly beautiful designs that the human race has ever seen. What's more, these fractals are visual representations of chaos, the force that shapes complex systems. According to chaos theory, everything from the world's weather to financial markets, which appear random and unpredictable, are actually governed by the sublime laws of chaos. Much of nature obeys similar hidden rules, which is why the branching of veins and vessels in your body is basically the same as the branching of rivers and tributaries on the earth.

In a clear style designed for the layperson, the author explains the nature and implications of chaos and fractals. What makes this book so great, though, are the scads of glorious full-color pictures it contains. Not only does the author include reproductions of all kinds of fractals, he graphically demonstrates the fractal designs in nature with lots of beautiful photographs of lightning, jellyfish, leaves, Jupiter's eye, forest fires, cauliflower, moss on rocks, tree branches, etc.

If you're a beginner when it comes to chaos, this is definitely the book to get. It's a treat for the mind and the eyes.

Touchstone (Simon & Schuster); $20
1992; oversize softcover; 192 pp.

## HYPERSPACE:
### A SCIENTIFIC ODYSSEY THROUGH PARALLEL UNIVERSES, TIME WARPS, AND THE 10TH DIMENSION
### by Michio Kaku

This is the first popular treatment of the theory of hyperspace, one of the theories of everything that just might explain the very core nature of reality. This theory, the best-known form of which is the superstring theory, says that there are ten dimensions. Everything we sense in our four dimensions (length, width, height, and time) are really vibrations from the higher dimensions of hyperspace. Physical phenomena that required wholly separate, incompatible formulae to be explained—light, gravity, magnetism, nuclear forces, subatomic particles—can now all be reconciled with simple, elegant formulae based on hyperspace.

Besides possibly being the Holy Grail of science, this theory raises many interesting possibilities including the existence of parallel universes, time travel, wormholes (interstellar shortcuts), and the power to completely manipulate reality. Bear in mind that this theory has a large number of adherents, including Nobel Prize–winning physicists, and has unleashed an incredible flurry of activity (more than 5000 papers and 200 international conferences so far).

The author presents this theory and its implications for the lay reader as much as is possible. Knowing something about theoretical physics and having a good imagination would help you get a lot more out of this book.

Oxford University Press; $25
1994; hardcover; 359 pp.

## OUT OF CONTROL:
### THE RISE OF NEO-BIOLOGICAL CIVILIZATION
### by Kevin Kelly

Kevin Kelly, executive editor of *Wired* and former *Whole Earth Review* editor, offers a new paradigm for understanding the natural world and the increasingly technological world. Kelly's springboard is the concept of self-organizing systems, which says that large, complex systems are created by a large number of small units spontaneously organizing. This leads to what Kelly calls the phenomenon of "something from nothing." Obviously, he doesn't literally mean nothing, but things that by themselves as units cannot even come close to performing the function of the systems they form a tiny part of. Examples of such systems are living organisms, intelligence, the economy, a beehive, a supercomputer, and evolution.

Kelly looks at how these systems spring into being and how this can apply to technology. Essentially, technology should be allowed to take on its own life and evolve as a natural biological system would. Kelly sees this as a marriage of "the made and the born": "The realm of the born—all that is nature—and the realm of the made—all that is humanly constructed—are becoming one. Machines are becoming biological and the biological is becoming engineered...the world of our own making has become so complicated that we must turn to the world of the born to understand how to manage it.... Our future is technological; but it will not be a world of gray steel. Rather our technological future is headed toward a neo-biological civilization."

Another area the book covers is using the principles of self-organizing systems in business management, graphic design, manufacturing, creating new drugs, running countries, etc. In a brilliant, hubris-filled move, Kelly lays down "The Nine Laws of God," the basic principles of "something from nothing systems." These include: control from the bottom up, maximize the fringes, honor your errors, seek persistent equilibrium, and change changes itself.

*Out of Control* presents a great new way of viewing the world.

Addison-Wesley; $28
1994; hardcover; 521 pp.

## THE RECONFIGURED EYE:
### VISUAL TRUTH IN THE POST-PHOTOGRAPHIC ERA
### by William J. Mitchell

To the general public, the media, and the courts, a photograph represents the "truth." A scene has been objectively captured on a piece of light-sensitive paper, providing proof of the scene's reality. Not so fast, pal. There have always been ways to manipulate reality with the camera. Scenes have been staged. Creative cropping can be used. Camera lenses can distort depth, making you think that the tiny bedroom in a condo is as huge as it seems in the brochure. Of course, an X-acto knife and spray mount have been in the tabloids' photographic arsenal for years, making it appear that Michael Jackson and Princess Di are getting real chummy.

Technology has taken this deception to a new level with digital manipulation techniques. Just give me a Macintosh with

*The Reconfigured Eye* ➤ by WIlliam J. Mitchell

*If Rambo and Groucho Marx had advised FDR...*

Adobe Photoshop™ (retail: $800) and I'll make it look like your mom is having an affair with Godzilla. If such a picture is done well enough, there would be no way to tell it's a fake.

This book examines the brave new world of digital imaging. The author discusses the technical aspects of filmless cameras, scanners, and imaging software. Although he doesn't provide instructions for any particular software package, he demonstrates the basic concepts of color, shading, halftones, contrast, sharpening, diffusion, filters, etc. He investigates how people who were never together can look as though they were, how people can be taken out of photographs (à la *1984*), how different heads can be put on the same body, how a person's race can be altered, and more. Not all of the uses examined are this sinister, though. Purely aesthetic processes, such as posterization and changing texture, are also discussed.

These new capabilities are bound to have a big impact on the world at large. The author looks at what digital imaging is doing and will do to photojournalism, the justice system, and society.

*The Reconfigured Eye* is thoroughly illustrated with examples of manipulated photographs. Among the images reproduced are the 1991 faked picture of three POWs and the original photo on which it was based, Rambo and Groucho Marx at the Yalta conference, Richard Nixon with a Pinocchio nose, a composite of Ronald Reagan's and Mikhail Gorbachev's faces, and the infamous *TV Guide* cover showing Oprah Winfrey's head on Ann-Margaret's body.

The MIT Press; $39.95
1992; oversize hardcover; 273 pp.

## VIRTUAL REALITY:
### THROUGH THE NEW LOOKING GLASS
### by Ken Pimentel and Kevin Teixeira

Virtual Reality—in case there is still a human being on the planet who doesn't know—is a technology that completely engulfs you in a computer-generated world. In its most common form, you put on a helmet with screens inside, which allows you to have a complete 360-degree view of the virtual world, and wired gloves that let you manipulate objects in the virtual world. In just a few years, VR has gone from a fringe technology to the Next Big Thing involving dozens of start-up companies, big boys like Sega, constant reports on CNN, and, of course, books, books, books.

There are literally scores of books now out on Virtual Reality. Many of them are primers, designed to introduce you to the basic concepts behind VR, its uses, and its ramifications. This book is one of the best I've seen, but you might want to scan the shelves in the computer section of your bookstore before you buy it. New books come out every month, and some of them are packaged with disks or CD-ROMS filled with low-end VR software.

In this well-illustrated book the authors start with a history of VR from its precursors, such as stereoscopic pictures and Sensorama, through its development by the military and NASA, to its current state in the hands of cutting-edge corporations like VPL, Sense8, and Autodesk. They look at the nuts and bolts of VR—the programs, the "engines," helmets, gloves, wands, sound devices, motion platforms, and other devices that attempt to simulate reality. The third section gives a rundown of VR's uses, such as prototyping, architectural walk-throughs, aiding surgery, physical rehabilitation, games, interactive movies, on-line museums, and new forms of art. Appendixes offer by-now-thoroughly outdated info on available VR products.

Windcrest (McGraw-Hill); $22.95
1993; softcover; 301 pp.

# MISCELLANEOUS

## bOING bOING
### A BLUEPRINT FOR THE FLIPSIDE OF SERIOS CULTURE

*bOING bOING*

A fun cyberzine with a high Generation X quotient and even higher humor factor. They snatch the flotsam and jetsam of cyber/youthculture, inject several cc's of smartass cynicism, and somehow cobble together a Frankenstein's monster of a magazine. One classic article described a trip through that kiddie wasteland, Toys R Us. (Tell me about it, pal. I worked there. Remind me to tell you sometime about the way these toys and games mindfuck kids into becoming good little capitalist citizens.) Another excursion to a wasteland of a different type (Taco Bell) is told in "Refried Brains" (issue #12).

You can also expect to find interviews with cyberpeople, comix, and reviews of software, zineware, bookware, musicware, comixware, and miscellaneous stuffware. Issue #12 has pieces on marital infidelity and the *Flintstones*, the overuse of used condom imagery in science fiction, a guide to the alternative 1970s, the nine types of assholes, and fiction. My favorite was the "Emergency Personal Life T.V." It's a miniature television that you cut out and fold. Then hold it up to your eyes, viewing what's happening around you as if it were on TV. "Instantly turns any real-life drama into a situation comedy!"

bOING bOING/544 Second Street/San Francisco, CA 94107
Single issue: $4.95
Four-issue sub: $16

*The usual suspects and several cc's of smartass cynicism.*

## CYBERIA:
### LIFE IN THE TRENCHES OF HYPERSPACE
### by Douglas Rushkoff

A guided tour of the cyberculture by one of the first journalists to bring this new terrain to the public's attention. Rushkoff says, "We may in fact be at the brink of a renaissance of unprecedented magnitude, heralded by the 1960s, potentiated by the computer and other new technologies, mapped by chaos math and quantum physics, fueled by psychedelic drugs and brain food, and manifesting right now in popular culture as new music, fiction, art, entertainment, games, philosophy, religion, sex, and lifestyle." He examines each one of these elements in turn.

With a good eye for revealing details, Rushkoff writes about hackers and crackers, LSD, ecstasy, DMT, smart drugs, chaos theory, raves, house music, neopaganism, magick, Thee Temple ov Psychick Youth, cyberpunk SF, multimedia, billboard modification, and more. Along the way we meet some of Cyberia's most famous denizens—John Barlow, Timothy Leary, Terence McKenna, Craig Neidorf, Marc Laidlaw, Earth Girl, R.U. Sirius, and many others.

If you're already a resident of Cyberia, you won't find much in this book that you don't already know or haven't already done. But if you're interested in emigrating to Cyberia or just want to know what all the racket is about, this book is an informative and entertaining travelogue.

HarperSanFrancisco (HarperCollins); $22
1994; hardcover; 250 pp.

## INCORPORATIONS (ZONE #6)

A collection of more than forty pomo essays and articles on the interface between humans and technology and the super technobiological organism that this interaction is creating. In the tradition of *Zone* anthologies, the essays here range from works of dazzling brilliance to "what in God's name are they talking about?" pieces to somewhere in between to both at the same time. "Artificiality and Enlightenment" looks at the implications of the Human Genome Initiative. "When Man™ Is on the Menu" discusses artificially created life forms, such as Du Pont's OncoMouse.™ "Nonorganic Life" discusses the implication of chaos theory. "The Living Machine" examines the fundamental flaw in psychology: "What psychology sought above all else was the identity of a being who could be represented, quantified, and, in effect, mastered."

The nature of reality is tackled in "The Construction of Perception" by Leif H. Finkel: "I will argue, that reality, as we know it, is largely an internally generated construct of the nervous system, and that once constructed it is projected back onto the world through behavioral interactions with objects in our local environments.... What we take to be the basic physical properties of our environment may reflect the structure of our brains more than the structure of the universe."

J.G. Ballard contributed "Project for the Glossary of the Twentieth Century," which contains the following definitions: "Telephone: A shrine to the desperate hope that someday the world will listen to us." "Biochemical warfare: Nerve gases—the patient and long-awaited revenge of the inorganic world against the organic." "Forensics: On the autopsy table science and pornography meet and fuse." "Body-building: Asexual masturbation, in which the entire musculature simulates a piece of erectile tissue. But orgasm seems infinitely delayed."

As dense as this veritable encyclopedia of pomo thought is, it will scramble the reality software in your head, causing you to look differently at everything around you.

The MIT Press; $34.95
1992; softcover; 633 pp.

## MONDO 2000

*Mondo 2000* is the leading voice of the cyberculture. But being the forefront magazine of such a diverse, independent group of people has its downside. *Mondo* is always the subject of controversy. It has been accused at various times of being elitist, humorless, not covering enough "hard tech," including way too much material on music, and being of poor quality. Personally, I think it's no more elitist that the cyberculture it covers, it has run some of the funniest articles I have ever read, it *has* cut back on its "nuts and bolts" articles, it—thankfully—has eased up on its incredibly overdone coverage of music, and its quality is uneven. Some issues are packed with good stuff, setting off megatons of idea bombs in my head, and other issues are so lame they can barely walk. Overall, *Mondo* does seem to have lost its "edge." I miss early articles that covered "jiggering one's own biochemistry for personal fulfillment" or theorized on the alleged cause of Jim Morrison's death—cancer of the penis.

*Mondo*'s mission is to bring together the best of the cyberculture, to let musicians, artists, fashion designers, philosophers, psychonauts, inventors, hackers, conspiracy theorists, and others express their ideas. When it finds the right mix of people and ideas, it is one of the best magazines being published. When it doesn't, it isn't.

Mondo 2000/PO Box 10171/Berkeley, CA 94709
Single issue: $7
Five-issue sub: $24; Canada: $27; others: $50

## THE NEW HACKER'S DICTIONARY
### (2ND EDITION)

The title is actually something of a sensationalistic misnomer. The word *hacker* has a negative connotation in general society, usually being applied to malicious individuals who try to get into NASA's computers and launch the space shuttle an hour early, or something like that. Technically, these people are called "crackers." A hacker, in reality, is "a person who enjoys exploring the details of programmable systems and how to stretch their capabilities...." So, while the title might imply that these terms pertain to the illegal and quasi-legal escapades of crackers, they're really used by anybody who's heavily into the digital terrain—computer geeks, keyboard cowboys, programmers, Netsurfers, and others. Much of it is humorous. Most of it will have no meaning except to residents of Cyberia.

Because new technologies involve new techniques, experiences, problems, protocols, etc., a new language grows around them. Some of it is incomprehensible technobabble, but a lot of it is street-level slang, which is where this book comes in. It contains thousands of informal terms used in cyberspace. This second edition has added 200 new entries and updated 175 others. Let's take a look: "Angry fruit salad" is "a bad visual-interface design that used too many colors." "Bit rot" is defined as "hypothetical disease the existence of which has been deduced from the observation that unused programs or features will often stop working after time has passed, even if 'nothing has changed.'" "Notwork": "A network when it is acting flaky or down. Compare nyetwork [a synonym]." "Helen Keller mode" is the "state of a hardware or software system that is deaf, dumb, and blind, i.e., accepting no input and generating no output...." The "lunatic fringe," in IBM slang, are "customers who can be relied upon to accept release 1 versions of software." A "Heisenbug": "[from Heisenberg's Uncertainty Principle in quantum physics] n. A bug that disappears or alters its behavior when one attempts to probe or isolate it." The acronym "RTFM" stands for "Read the Fucking Manual!"

The book ends with hacker folklore and a profile of "J. Random Hacker."

The MIT Press; $14.95
1993; softcover; 505 pp.

## SPASM:
### VIRTUAL REALITY, ANDROID MUSIC, AND ELECTRIC FLESH
### by Arthur Kroker

A pomo meditation on the pomo state of the world. Kroker's main thesis is that "it is no longer technology as commodity-form or as icon, but as a living species existence. That is the real meaning of virtual reality. Technology actually comes alive, actually acquires organicity. First, the animal species, then the human species, and now the technology species."

Joining Kroker in his quest to understand the merging of the human and the machine is Linda Dawn Hammond, who takes photographs of "fetish freaks and body outlaws"; David Therrien, creator of The Ice House, where machines use humans in performance art; and Steve Gibson, a musician whose digitized, sample-filled creations destroy notions of sequential, linear music. *Spasm*, the book, comes packaged with a CD of Gibson's work, also called *Spasm*.

This book/CD combo is a fine introduction to pomo thought. I'm going to have to cut this review short. Reading books by pomo philosophers always makes my head hurt.

St. Martin's Press; $19.95
1993; softcover book and CD; 177 pp.

## WHO OWNS INFORMATION?:
### FROM PRIVACY TO PUBLIC ACCESS
### by Anne Wells Branscomb

The issues surrounding the ownership of tangible items may not always be cut and dried, but they don't compare to the infinite intricacies and gray areas that come when deciding who owns information. Until recently, patents and copyrights had done a decent job in assigning ownership to intellectual property, but technology has zoomed ahead, leaving our archaic laws choking in the dust.

This book examines the most crucial issues facing us in the nebulous world where "property" becomes an abstract term. Lest you think all this talk of "information" and "intellectual property" concerns an obscure subject best left to academics and lawyers, think again. It directly concerns every one of us. The chapter "Who Owns Your Name and Address?" is about the scourge of junk mail. When you fill out a change-of-address card at the Post Office, which you have to do if you want your mail forwarded, your new address will be sold to more than twenty "list managers," who will in turn sell it to mass mailers. "The average consumer is on approximately a hundred mailing lists and in at least fifty databases." The author concludes that it is the United States Postal Service that owns your name and address.

"Who Owns Your Image?" examines the issues surrounding photography and video. Does the artist or the subject own the image? Can you stop someone from taking your picture? The author also examines the use of digital imaging to alter photographs, a common practice that becomes a hotly debated issue every once in a while, as when *National Geographic* rearranged the Egyptian pyramids on its cover.

"Who Owns Religious Information?" looks at the explosive Dead Sea Scrolls issue. For forty years a small group of religious scholars jealously guarded the scrolls as they slowly pieced them together and translated them. Outsiders were not allowed access to these extremely important documents. In 1991 the Biblical Archeology Society offered its own translation of the scrolls, based on computer deciphering of a concordance published by the "official" scroll scholars. The author examines both sides of this issue: that of the renegade scholars who broke the information monopoly on these crucial religious documents and that of the official scholars who spent forty years of their lives piecing the scrolls together only to have the rug pulled out from under them. Other chapters examine who owns your telephone number, your medical history, your e-mail, video entertainment, computer software, and government information.

Basic Books (HarperCollins); $25
1994; hardcover; 241 pp.

## WIRED

The tamest of the cyberculture rags. While *Iron Feather Journal* and *2600* break the law and *Mondo 2000* flirts with danger, *Wired* plays it safer. Although each issue usually contains some "edgy" articles on privacy, conspiracy, and the dark side of technology, most of the magazine is about the business aspects of interactivity, multimedia, high-definition TV, etc. Its main target seems to be suits who "need to keep up with today's marketplace," although its innovative graphic design, sharp writing style, and cutting-edge topics make *Wired* more interesting than wonkish computer mags. The conservative nature of many of *Wired*'s readers becomes painfully apparent whenever the magazine uses the word *fuck* in an article. Inevitably, some crybaby stuffed shirt writes in and complains.

Wired/PO Box 191826/San Francisco, CA 94119-9866
One-year sub (12 issues): $39.95; Canada/Mexico: $64; others: $79

*Wired*

*This mag gets you from the everyday world to the outskirts of cyberia.*

# EXTREMISM

## TERRORISM

### THE IRA:
#### A HISTORY
#### by Tim Pat Coogan

You couldn't ask to know more about the Irish Republican Army than what's contained in this mammoth book. The author starts with a brief history of Ireland for background and gives a thoroughly detailed look at the IRA—from its beginnings in the Easter Rising of 1916 to its rise as the best-known terrorist group in the world to its activities as of early 1993. It's all here: the assassinations, bombings, crackdowns, court cases, hunger strikes, and internal struggles. Throughout all the guns, blood, and explosions, though, the author never lets you forget the IRA's goals.

Coogan has inside connections to the IRA, which provides much interesting material. Particularly fascinating are the long excerpts from *The Green Book*,\* the IRA's instruction and philosophy manual. Coogan is also on good terms with several members of Protestant Loyalist paramilitary groups, terrorist groups who target the IRA, Sinn Féin, and other Republicans. He has uncovered evidence that some of these groups have very close ties to British intelligence.

Besides this wealth of information, *The IRA* also contains fifty-nine pictures, a glossary, and two indexes totaling eighteen pages. It's no wonder the *New York Times* has called this book "the standard reference work on the subject."

Roberts Rinehart Publishers; $27.95
1993; hardcover; 510 pp.

### PERU'S SHINING PATH:
#### ANATOMY OF A REACTIONARY SECT
#### by Martin Koppel

This booklet comes from Pathfinder Press, a very leftist publishing outfit. Many people of similar persuasion might be in danger of supporting the goals of the Shining Path of Peru, an ultraviolent terrorist group that proclaims itself of Maoist political orientation. The author shows that in actuality, the Shining Path is not a people's movement of liberation, but a reactionary sect that looks a lot like Cambodia's quasi-genocidal Pol Pot regime. "Reflecting the middle-class outlook of its leadership, the outfit is hostile to any action by workers and peasants in their own interests. It attempts to push working people out of political activity and instill fear, passivity, and dependence on a savior, namely [founder Abimael] Guzmán and his gang."

Pathfinder Press; $3.50
1993; booklet; 35 pp.

### SECURITY INTELLIGENCE REPORT:
#### EXECUTIVE REPORT ON POLITICAL AND IDEOLOGICAL VIOLENCE

First the good news: This ten-page biweekly newsletter is the unbeatable source for news on terrorism and counterterrorism. Each issue is filled with events that you'll never hear about in the press, mainstream or alternative. In just one issue I learned that the Khmer Rouge is now implementing a policy of kidnapping Americans in Cambodia, that Interpol says 5 percent of world trade is criminal, that East Germany's intelligence agency Stasi has been linked to the bombing of Pan Am 103, that an insurance company is now offering kidnap, ransom, and extortion insurance to multinationals, that the IRA has a nasty habit of shooting people in the knees, and that the government botched a case in Tucson, Arizona, against six men suspected of buying weapons for the IRA. Each issue has a bunch of small articles, a couple of longer ones, and dozens of "incident reports" on terrorist violence around the globe.

Now the bad news: You can't afford this gold mine. I'm not making fun of you. I can't afford it either, so I'll have to eat my heart out, too. This newsletter is obviously aimed at people with a professional interest in such info: security firms, corporations, government agencies, the media, etc. So unless you can cough up almost four Ben Franklins, you're S.O.L.

Interests Ltd.
8512 Cedar Street/Silver Spring, MD 20910-4347
One-year sub: $390 (no, this isn't a misprint); outside U.S., Canada, Mexico: $430

### TELEVISIONARIES:
#### THE RED ARMY FACTION STORY, 1963–1993
#### by Tom Vague

An updated, expanded version of a very long article appearing in the British anarcho-punk magazine *Vague*. *Televisionaries* chronicles the saga of the far-left German terrorist group, the Red Army Faction. In a breathless, bare-bones style, the author gives a detailed account of the RAF's history and exploits—its evolution from KOMMUNE 1, its merging with the SPK terrorist group, fatal shoot-outs with police, bombings of police and U.S. Army targets, the takeover and destruction of the West German embassy in Stockholm, the kidnapping of the head of Daimler-Benz, its ill-fated Lufthansa hijacking, and the suspicious suicide of three of its most prominent members while in prison.

*Televisionaries* is a fast, highly entertaining read and a valuable source of information about a legendary terrorist group few Americans are familiar with.

AK Press; $6.95
1994; softcover; 109 pp.

### VIOLENT PERSUASIONS:
#### THE POLITICS AND IMAGERY OF TERRORISM
#### edited by David J. Brown and Robert Merrill

One person's terrorist is another person's founding father. Just what is a terrorist? Who decides who's a terrorist and who's not? How are terrorists presented to us by the media and government? Is terrorism ever justified? How much terrorism does the United States sponsor? What role do terrorists play in the United States? These and many other questions are discussed and debated in a series of essays, discussions, and artwork presented in this challenging book.

"One of the classic examples of so-called terrorism in recent years is by any fair account a legitimate act of war. This was the bombing of the Beirut bunker in Lebanon, on October 23, 1983. Some 241 Marines died in the attack. This event is always referred to in the United States as a terrorist attack. But the target was a strictly military installation containing armed marines who were in combat supporting the minority and foreign-backed Christian government of Amin Gemayel against majority insurgent Lebanese Muslims. The fact that the bomb was delivered in a truck and was not a laser-guided "smart bomb" launched by a stealth bomber seems to be the essential factor in choosing to label the act as terrorism and not just another episode in a larger but legitimate war." This book really has the power to change how you think about terrorism.

Bay Press; $18.95
1993; softcover; 298 pp.

*Violent Persuasions edited by David J. Brown and Robert Merrill*

*"One person's terrorist is another person's founding father."*

## ZAPATISTAS:
### SPREADING HOPE FOR GRASSROOTS CHANGE STARTING FROM CHIAPAS MEXICO (OPEN MAGAZINE PAMPHLET SERIES # 30)
### by Marc Cooper

A sympathetic examination of the Zapatistas, the indigenous (Mayan) insurgency movement against the Mexican government. The Zaps are demanding more democracy and basic human rights for the poor and oppressed people of Mexico. They grabbed worldwide headlines when they seized the city hall of San Cristóbal de las Casas and government buildings in other Mexican cities. "...800 Zapatistas poured into the municipal offices here [San Cristóbal], opened the police and property archives and set them on fire, and then another thousand—maybe two thousand—of their comrades simultaneously seized five other nearby towns, opening the food warehouses to the poor, chasing out and in some cases killing the local police, dismantling another town hall stone by stone with sledgehammers, yet another with axes and saws, and then fought the Mexican Army to a standstill for a week...."

This pamphlet gives a brief history of the Zapatistas and tells of the conditions that led to their revolt (the passage of NAFTA was the spark that set off the powder keg). The second half of the pamphlet contains the Zapatistas' original declaration and several communiqués, which are great, unfiltered, source material.

Open Magazine Pamphlet Series; $4
1994; long thin pamphlet; 23 pp.

# NAZIS

## FORGOTTEN FATHERLAND:
### THE SEARCH FOR ELIZABETH NIETZSCHE
### by Ben Macintyre

The philosopher Friedrich Nietzsche is one of the most important and controversial thinkers of all time, but his sister Elizabeth is also an important figure—for different reasons. She has been undeservedly relegated to the footnotes of history. In 1886 Elizabeth, along with her husband, Bernhard Förster, a leading German anti-Semite, set up an Aryan colony in the jungles of Paraguay. *Nueva Germania*, New Germany, was to be a proto-Nazi utopia, where blond, blue-eyed Germans could build their own empire. And if that isn't strange enough, here's the kicker—New Germany still exists. The author visited it, with much difficulty, in 1991. He found many fourth-generation colonists and a few old-timers who still remember Förster from when they were young and he was old.

The book's other main focus concerns what Elizabeth did after she came back from her racial experiment. In 1893 she returned to Germany to take care of and dominate her now-insane brother until his death. The author demonstrates that it was Elizabeth who grafted her anti-Semitic, proto-Nazi views into her brother's work. She, in fact, was the principal author of *The Will to Power*, Friedrich's posthumous book. Liz organized the cult that grew around Friedrich's philosophy, and she was instrumental in convincing Hitler and the Nazis to use her brother's alleged ideas to back up their aims. The author convincingly shows that had Friedrich lived, he would have condemned the Third Reich. He often wrote of his contempt for Germany and its people, and he openly and consistently condemned his sister's anti-Semitic views and her colony.

*Forgotten Fatherland* offers a surprising reevaluation of history, the effects of which are still with us.

HarperPerennial (HarperCollins Publishers); $12
1992; softcover; 256 pp.

## THE HITLER DIARIES:
### FAKES THAT FOOLED THE WORLD
### by Charles Hamilton

In April of 1983 the world was stunned that Hitler's diaries, all sixty-two volumes of them, had been discovered. The diaries, along with two hundred watercolors by Hitler, letters, and Hitler's uniform and helmet, had been rescued from a crashed plane in 1945 and had been stored, forgotten, in a tiny village in East Germany. The diaries offered a new view of Hitler; he was a kind, peaceful man, not even aware of the Holocaust, who had been duped by the other Nazis. Handwriting experts and historians declared the diaries real. Magazines around the world got into huge bidding wars over the diaries. The only problem was, they were forgeries.

This book examines the whole sorry affair—who forged the diaries, what they said, why so many people were fooled, the role of the media, the trial of the forger, and more. The author, a handwriting expert who was the first to blow the whistle on the diaries, shows how easy it was to tell the diaries were fakes. The handwriting is so unlike Hitler's authentic penmanship that it only takes a few words to tell the diaries are crapola. The author presents examples of Hitler's handwriting along with those of the diaries, and the differences are so glaring that even I can tell they weren't written by the same person.

University Press of Kentucky; $25
1991; hardcover; 211 pp.

## THE HOLY BOOK OF ADOLPH HITLER
### by James Larratt Battersby

A strange little book, first published in 1952, claims that Hitler is a messiah, perhaps even God. "Adolf Hitler is the Heaven-sent answer to the age-long yearnings of the Germanic or Aryan soul. Prophet, Redeemer, and Leader, He has fulfilled the Divine Will of the Almighty Creator in destroying the world foundations of the system of Mammon or International Jewish Finance." As you might imagine, the author gives a completely sympathetic account of Hitler's rise to power and his leadership of Germany. He reminds us many times that the Germans are destined to rule mankind. In fact, he lays out a blueprint for a one-world government—under Aryan control, naturally.

The second part of the book presents Aryan principles as they apply to race, property, youth, women, industry, culture, education, etc. One section lists more than a hundred "Hitlerian maxims and sayings," including: "It is madness to think that suddenly a majority can take the place of a man of genius." *The Holy Book* presents an unadulterated look into the Nazi mind-set.

CPA Book Publisher, $4
1952; softcover; 93 pp.

## THE NAZI CONNECTION:
### EUGENICS, AMERICAN RACISM, AND GERMAN NATIONAL SOCIALISM
### by Stefan Kühl

Eugenics deals with ways of keeping groups of people genetically healthy, strong, and "pure." It claims that introducing other races or people with inborn disabilities into a group will degrade the gene pool and make for an inferior stock of people. The sterilization and murder programs of Nazi Germany are the most extreme example of applied eugenics the world has seen, but where did Hitler and his cronies get their ideas? From the United States. *Mein Kampf* praises a U.S. law prohibiting the immigration of people with hereditary illnesses and members of certain ethnic groups. When the Nazis came to power in 1933 they purposely based their laws regarding forced sterilization on similar U.S. laws, which called for the mandatory sterilization of the mentally retarded, insane, epileptic, criminal, blind, deaf, deformed, and others.

As a whole, American eugenicists applauded and admired Germany's efforts. Apparently, Germany was so far advanced on this front that a eugenicist in Virginia lamented, "The Germans are beating us at our own game." The Germans continued to scrutinize American eugenic studies and laws, while Americans did the same with German studies and laws. Many American scientists went to Germany to study their programs firsthand. Upon returning, they wrote laudatory articles for journals. The geneticist, T.U.H. Ellinger, after visiting with German scientists, including an SS man, "explained to readers of the *Journal of Heredity* that the treatment of Jews in Germany had nothing to do with religious persecution. Rather, it was entirely 'a large-scale breeding project, with the purpose of eliminating from the nation the hereditary attributes of the Semitic race.'" Many scientists showed off their personal notes from Hitler thanking them for their books.

One of the foremost American eugenicists, Harry Laughlin, distributed a Nazi sterilization propaganda film called *Erbkrank (Hereditary Defective)* in the United States. It was shown in a slightly altered version at churches, clubs, colleges, and high schools.

Though most elements in the American eugenics movement had wholeheartedly supported and even aided Nazi Germany's actions, including their "euthanasia" programs, once WWII ended and the full horror of the concentration camps was revealed, the movement backpedaled in a hurry. They hastened to distance themselves from the Nazis, saying that only the most radical, isolated members of their movement had supported Hitler. They now claimed that the Nazis had perverted science.

Besides showing the Nazi connection, this book also examines the history of eugenics and the present state of scientific racism, which doesn't call itself "eugenics" anymore but still espouses the same principles.

Oxford University Press; $22
1994; hardcover; 166 pp.

## SECRETS OF THE SS
### by Glenn B. Infield

A good introduction to the exploits of Hitler's elite henchmen, the SS. Although the book promises "secrets," there isn't too much here that's new. The author tells of the formation and activities of the "black shirts." Some of the more interesting topics include how the SS looted Europe's art treasures for museums that Hitler and Göring wanted to build, and the strange disappearances of two members of Hitler's inner circle, Hermann Fegelein, Hitler's brother-in-law, and Martin Bormann, Hitler's secretary. Of course, no one is actually sure what became of Hitler himself, so the author examines the conflicting evidence regarding the Führer's fate.

The post-Reich antics of the SS are covered in several chapters. In one of the most shameful episodes in U.S. history, the intelligence community hired many SS members as assets. Other SS men retired to South America, where they are pursued by Nazi-hunters. Most of the Nazis in South America have changed their names and are lying low, but those in Chile aren't: "A political party headed by Franz Pfeiffer openly featured swastikas, storm troopers in uniform, and Nazi banners. In 1968 they selected a "Miss Nazi World" and the pageant was publicized throughout South America. There is also a Chilean organization known as *Das Reich*, which is composed of German ex-military men who served in World War II."

Finally, the author brings up the possibility that the SS is still active today. He doesn't present much evidence to back up this idea, but he does show that as late as 1977, a secret organization of SS men, *Die Spinne* (The Spider), was very active and powerful in defending comrades who were being charged with war crimes.

Jove (The Berkeley Publishing Group); $4.99
1982; paperback; 256 pp.

## WHO FINANCED HITLER:
### THE SECRET FUNDING OF HITLER'S RISE TO POWER 1919–1933
### by James Pool and Suzanne Pool

Things were no different in the early twentieth century than they are now—politicians and parties need lots of money to get into power. This included Adolf Hitler and the Nazis. There had been anti-Semitic fringe groups in Germany for a long time, but it was the money brought in by Hitler that was the key ingredient in turning these outsiders into the rulers.

Hitler was a fund-raising genius, and the authors are the first to expose where he got much of his money. In the earliest days, when the National Socialist German Worker's Party (as it was called) was literally made up of a few men, local businessmen provided support. As the party grew, it gained more wealthy backers, which caused it to grow even more. A lot of money came to Hitler through Captain Ernst Röhm of the Bavarian army. Without his superiors' knowledge, Röhm funneled army money, equipment, and vehicles to the Nazis through two front corporations. Hitler was also receiving money from Germans in other countries, some German aristocrats, White Russians, and German Naval Intelligence.

Eventually, extremely wealthy citizens of other countries contributed to the Nazis. The best-known of these Nazi-backers is Henry Ford, who hated Jews. His book, *The International Jew: The World's Foremost Problem*, which was translated into dozens of languages, actually converted many Germans to Nazism. The authors trace the ways Ford funneled money to Hitler. They also examine the generous donations of Benito Mussolini, who hoped to encourage German fascism, and Grand Duchess Victoria of Russia.

*Who Financed Hitler* has shone light into one of the shadiest, most important, but least discussed aspects of Nazi Germany.

The Dial Press; $10
1978; softcover; 535 pp.

## NEO-NAZIS AND FASCISTS

## FASCIST EUROPE:
### THE RISE OF RACISM AND XENOPHOBIA
### by Glyn Ford

A reprint of a report issued by the European Parliament concerning the increase in extreme right-wing activity. The book gives a country-by-country analysis of racist and xenophobic groups, activities, and incidents, making it a great resource for hard-to-find information. For example, in the Netherlands, "The Jongeren Front is a small but highly active neo-Nazi group about fifty-strong. Its leader, Stewart Mordaunt, is also a member of Centrum Partij '86 and is a city councillor in The Hague. Members of this group have been regularly convicted for racism and illegal possession of arms and they promote their racist policies among skinheads and soccer hooligans." And in Denmark, "A new form of xenophobia with 'Christian respect for the cultures of others' (who should remain where they are), advocated by a Lutheran parish priest, Rev. Af. Søren Krarup, is gaining some ground."

*Hate on Trial*
*by Morris Dees*
*and Steve Fiffer*
(See page 136) ▼

*Tom Metzger:*
*Animal,*
*Mineral, or*
*Vegetable?*

The book also gives similar reports on Germany, Greece, France, Ireland, Italy, Portugal, Spain, Austria, the United Kingdom, and several other countries. Subsequent sections examine community efforts and governmental policies with regard to extreme rightist activity. The book concludes with fifty recommendations from the authors of the report.

Pluto Press; $19.95
1991; softcover; 216 pp.

## HATE ON TRIAL:
### THE CASE AGAINST AMERICA'S MOST DANGEROUS NEO-NAZI
### by Morris Dees and Steve Fiffer

Morris Dees has got to be one of the bravest people on the face of the earth. He sold a self-started multimillion-dollar business to create the Southern Poverty Law Center, which fights racism tooth and nail. In 1987 Dees launched a trial against the United Klans of America, holding them responsible for the lynching of an Alabama student. Dees won the trial, the fruit of which was a $7 million award that bankrupted the UKA. In this book Dees tells of his next great trial, in which he took on Tom Metzger and his group, the White Aryan Resistance, for the beating death of an Oregon student. This time he won a $10 million suit. Dees gives us a blow-by-blow account of this explosive trial.

Villard Books (Random House); $21
1993; hardcover; 280 pp.

## RELIGION AND THE RACIST RIGHT:
### THE ORIGINS OF THE CHRISTIAN IDENTITY MOVEMENT
### by Michael Barkun

Christian Identity has become the dominant religious viewpoint of the racist right, especially the most violent groups such as the Order, the Posse Comitatus, the Aryan Nations, various elements of the KKK, and the Covenant, Sword, and Arm of the Lord. It isn't a denomination as such, but a loose belief system that many white supremacists identify with.

Christian Identity has three main tenets. The first and most fundamental belief is that the "Aryan race" is descended from the lost tribes of Israel. In other words, white people are God's true chosen people. It follows, then, that the second tenet of Identity is that "Jews are not only wholly unconnected to the Israelites, but are the very children of the Devil, the literal biological offspring of a sexual dalliance between Satan and Eve in the Garden of Eden." The final main pillar of Identity is a millennial belief that there is a huge, apocalyptic showdown coming between Aryans and the Jewish conspiracy that controls the world.

This book examines the ideas, actions, writings, and leaders of Identity groups, and it looks at Identity's precursor, a nineteenth-century Anglican belief known as British Israelism. Although it gave birth to Christian Identity, British Israelism is radically different, most obviously in its attitude toward Jews. It regarded Jews as fellow Israelites who descended from different tribes. The author spends a lot of time examining how this pro-Jewish belief system metamorphosed into a violently anti-Semitic one.

In the course of tracing the history of the Identity beliefs, this book becomes a cornucopia of extremist thinking, covering David Duke, Bo Gritz, the Silver Shirts, *The Turner Diaries*, the American Nazi Party, Henry Ford, the Church of Jesus Christ Christian, the Populist Party, Christian fundamentalism, millennialism, Mormonism, and much more. It's a fascinating chronicle of a stream of thought that has received little attention but appears to be growing larger all the time.

The University of North Carolina Press; $15.95
1994; softcover; 290 pp.

## SIEGE
### by James Mason

In 1966, when he was fourteen years old, James Mason joined the American Nazi Party. Ten years later he quit the group, disgusted at its lack of accomplishments. The ANP was an aboveground organization that was using legal means in an attempt to change the system from within. Mason wanted hands-on tactics, including murder, to be incorporated into the struggle. Around the time he quit the ANP, he briefly formed the National Socialist Movement, which would attempt to unify and radicalize the Nazi movement. It was during this time that Mason put out a piece of propaganda that would alienate him from the movement and mark him as a unique extremist. He designed a leaflet containing a mugshot of Charles Manson. Under the picture was a quote from George Bernard Shaw: "Whilst we...the conventional...were wasting our time on education, agitation and organization, some independent genius has taken the matter in hand...."

In 1980 Mason started a group called the National Socialist Liberation Front and began publishing a newsletter, *SIEGE*. Mason used the newsletter to condemn the impotence of the Nazi movement, call for armed struggle, and espouse the philosophy of Charles Manson. He was in charge of every aspect of *SIEGE*—writing, typing, printing, and distributing. He abandoned the NSLF two years later, to start a new one-man operation called Universal Order (a name suggested by Manson himself). He kept publishing *SIEGE*, every month without fail, through 1986.

This book collects the best of *SIEGE*. A more radical, uncompromising vision is hard to imagine. Mason's favorite tactic is murder, because it strikes at the very heart of the "System." *SIEGE* is full of praise for serial killers and mass murderers. People who kill African-Americans and Jews are singled out for special commendation. Of James Huberty, the man who gunned down twenty-one people in a San Diego McDonald's, Mason says: "Since the killer was White and the victims mainly non-White, it must stand as a stunning victory and a landmark in itself simply by virtue of the LACK of any other really revolutionary action at present." Mason also comments on the Tylenol poisonings of the early 1980s: "The beautiful part is that it is all undetectable and uncontrollable. Welcome it but at the same time watch your own step."

Mason's basic feeling toward Manson is that he is a true revolutionary in the same way that Adolf Hitler was—he has a clear vision of what he wants and he goes about making it happen, no matter what has to be done. Manson is "personally gifted, selfless, fearless—both morally and physically—and absolutely dedicated to Life, to Earth and to Truth. What he did—in spite of a life full of the worst adversity—rather than drown in a sea of bitterness as most would have done, he established a racial-socialist colony in Death Valley, in California, in the midst of the push-shove of the 1960's, which was neither hippie nor Right Wing."

Mason sees a huge race war on the horizon, what Manson called Helter Skelter. "We can grumble and mystify at why it has taken the White Man so long to start lashing back at his mortal enemies. But it won't do any good. What is happening, or beginning to happen, will be regarded as something that is a biological, historical and worldwide phenomenon. It's keeping no set schedule.... It's a massive 'Viking berserker rage' about to explode and consume the Enemy in blood." *SIEGE* contains numerous rare pictures of Mason, Manson, American Nazi Party founder George Lincoln Rockwell, and others, plus reprints of NSLF propaganda, newspaper articles, etc.

There is nothing else out there like *SIEGE*. To twist a line from an old commercial: "It don't get no extremer than this."

STORM; $20
1992; softcover; 434 pp.

## THE TURNER DIARIES
### by Andrew Macdonald

In 1989 personal ownership of firearms was outlawed and the Gun Raids began. Earl Turner and his ultra-right-wing-patriot racist comrades in the Organization are forming an underground resistance. They start an all-out guerrilla war across the country by blowing up the FBI's national headquarters, the *Washington Post*'s press room, and killing the liberal editorial-page editor of the *Post*.

More destruction ensues, along with government crackdowns, until the Organization has taken over Southern California and deported all "non-Whites." The city streets are lined with the corpses of 55,000 "race traitors" hanging from street lights.

The Organization then uses nukes to bomb American cities. They also nuke Russia and Israel, which provokes retaliatory strikes. In the resulting anarchy, the Organization bombs the Pentagon and takes over the country. From there, they move on to take over the entire world, creating a White planet.

While *The Turner Diaries* may seem like a self-gratifying form of wish-fulfillment, some people are taking it seriously. It was allegedly the inspiration for The Order, a super-secret racist group that robbed and murdered. The FBI has declared this book to be "the bible of the racist right." The publisher claims that it is the most controversial book in America. While that bit of hyperbole isn't true—the honor would have to go to *Final Exit* or *The Myth of Heterosexual AIDS*—*The Turner Diaries* is still pretty damn scary.

National Vanguard Books; $4.95
1980; paperback; 211 pp.

# THE HOLOCAUST

## DENYING THE HOLOCAUST:
### THE GROWING ASSAULT ON TRUTH AND MEMORY
### by Deborah Lipstadt

Here is an example of why the worst thing you can do to controversial, unsettling ideas is to ignore them. For years the Jewish community and the world at large were content to cold-shoulder Holocaust revisionists, who continued working to get out their message that the Holocaust is a lie. Now Holocaust revisionism has become a full-fledged movement, and a large number of people think it's possible that the Holocaust might not have occurred.

The author examines the history, current state, and effects of Holocaust revisionism. She states that the concept that the Holocaust didn't happen is so absolutely absurd and ridiculous, it doesn't even deserve serious consideration. She has refused to appear on shows to debate revisionists because she says that there is no question that the Holocaust happened. The only question is what effects this belief is having.

The author states that Holocaust revisionism is purely a result of anti-Semitism and not a search for truth. She examines the precursors of revisionism, the first rumblings right after WWII, early revisionists, the Institute for Historical Review, *The Hoax of the Twentieth Century*, and more. She exposes the revisionists as anti-Semitic and looks at the methods they use to achieve their ends: "...deniers misstate, misquote, falsify statistics, and falsely attribute conclusions to reliable sources. They rely on books that directly contradict their arguments, quoting in a manner that completely distorts the authors' objectives."

What I found disturbing was the author's somewhat ambiguous statements about free speech. She states that although most intellectuals haven't bought into revisionism, "some have succumbed in another fashion, supporting Holocaust denial in the name of free speech, free inquiry, or intellectual freedom." Later she says, "I reiterate that I am not advocating the muzzling of the deniers. They have the right to free speech, however abhorrent. However, they are using that right not as a shield, as it was intended by the Constitution, but as a sword. There is a qualitative difference between barring someone's right to speech and providing him or her with a platform from which to deliver a message."

Plume (Penguin); $10.95
1993; softcover; 278 pp.

## AN EYE FOR AN EYE:
### THE UNTOLD STORY OF JEWISH REVENGE AGAINST GERMANS IN 1945
### by John Sack

This book brings to light a shocking aspect of history that had never before been written about. In 1945 the Soviet Union set up a de-Nazification program run by Jewish survivors of the Holocaust. The "official" aim of the program was to round up Nazis and sympathizers and try them for their actions. In reality the program imprisoned tens of thousands of German men, women, and children in many locations, including more than one thousand concentration camps. Conditions were just as miserable at the Jewish prisons and concentration camps as at the German concentration camps. Rations were starvation level, and disease was rampant. Confessions were extracted through brutal, nonstop torture.

The author examines this disturbing display of revenge mainly through the story of Lola, a Jewish woman whose mother, siblings, and baby were killed by the Nazis. She became a commandant of a prison for Germans after the war, but like many others in the de-Nazification program she agonized over what was happening. She realized that by treating the Germans inhumanely, she and the others had lowered themselves to the level of those they despised. At the trials of the Germans, very few were convicted of war crimes, and the Jewish judges let most of the people go. Eventually, most of the Jews left the program and returned to the peaceful practice of their religion.

The author gives excruciatingly detailed documentation for every claim he makes. His sources include more than three hundred hours of taped interviews with German prisoners, their Jewish captors, government officials, historians, etc., as well as source documents.

Basic Books (HarperCollins Publishers); $23
1994; hardcover; 252 pp.

THE FUTURE BELONGS TO THE FEW OF US STILL WILLING TO GET OUR HANDS DIRTY.

POLITICAL TERROR

It's the Only Thing They Understand.

Build the National Socialist Revolution through Armed Struggle.

**National Socialist Liberation Front**
Post Office Box 42    Chillicothe, Ohio 45601

Tommasi's infamous "Political Terror" flyer.

◄ *SIEGE*
by James
Mason

*More than just another sick, hate-mongering extremist.*

## THE HOAX OF THE TWENTIETH CENTURY:
### THE CASE AGAINST THE PRESUMED EXTINCTION OF THE EUROPEAN JEWRY
### by Arthur R. Butz

The most infamous of the Holocaust revisionist books. Arthur Butz, a professor of electrical engineering at Northwestern University, claims that the Holocaust didn't happen and, what's more, that Hitler never even had a plan to exterminate European Jews. He attacks the Holocaust from several angles. He uses statistics in an attempt to show that six million people didn't die in concentration camps, although he admits around one million may have. This, however, was because of bad sanitation and inadequate supplies. He maintains that the Nazis were actually horrified by the appalling death rate and worked to lower it.

Butz blasts the Nuremburg trials as a mockery. "In some cases the 'defense counsel' was an American with no legal training, who could not speak German. Competent interpreters were not provided at the trial. The 'prosecution' also lacked legal training, as did the 'court,' which consisted of ten U.S. Army officers.... While the prosecution could hunt all over Europe for witnesses and, if necessary, torture or otherwise coerce Germans in order to get 'evidence,' the accused, cut off from the outside world and without funds, were rarely able to summon anyone to their defense."

Massive amounts of Nazi documents outlining the operation of the Final Solution were presented at the trials. Butz claims that these tens of thousands of documents are forgeries, planted by a Zionist conspiracy. The Nazis at these trials who admitted their guilt were either confused or didn't see any point in denying what so many people believed, so they pled guilty to something they didn't do.

Butz also claims that the gas Zyklon-B was actually used as a delousing agent; that the stories of human lampshades and soap are lies; that SS guards didn't regularly mistreat their prisoners; that the gas chambers were actually showers and crematoria; that the media and various governments support the "Zionist propaganda" regarding the Holocaust; and more.

Get this book and see for yourself why the publisher's offices were burned to the ground.

Institute for Historical Review; $9.95
1976; softcover; 369 pp.

## THE THEORY AND PRACTICE OF HELL:
### THE GERMAN CONCENTRATION CAMPS AND THE SYSTEM BEHIND THEM
### by Eugene Kogon

*Among The Thugs* ➤
by Bill Buford

*"The thugs love lager, soccer, kicking ass, and the Queen, and hate everything else."*

Eugene Kogon spent seven years in prison camp at Buchenwald. He performed various types of labor and eventually became an assistant to SS Major Ding-Schuler, who oversaw human medical experimentation at the camp. Using his own experiences and the experiences and research of others, Kogon presents a detailed look at how the camps were run.

People sent to the concentration camps fell into one of four categories: "political opponents; members of 'inferior races'; criminals; and 'shiftless elements' (called 'asocial' by the Germans)." Each camp contained a lavish headquarters area, comprising "an administration building, barracks for the SS, fine residences with large gardens for the leading officials, and a whole series of show places, such as zoological gardens, hothouses, parks, riding academies and clubs—all carefully planned and beautifully landscaped." The zoological gardens contained wild animals in cages. Occasionally, the SS would have some fun by putting a prisoner in a cage with a bear.

Kogon takes an unflinching look at the camps' admission procedures, daily routines, discipline, food, "recreation" (the SS set up camp whorehouses filled with women from other camps), sanitation, etc. The medical experiments were a particularly gruesome part of camp life. Prisoners were infected with typhus and malaria to test possible cures. Others were put in icy rivers to see how long it would take them to die. Men would have their genitals exposed to X rays for fifteen solid minutes. A month later they would be castrated and their testicles dissected. Kogon also details the liquidation of the Jews and other groups and the disposal of the bodies.

In one of the most enlightening chapters, Kogon details the underground resistance within the camps. Prisoners attempted to demoralize their Nazi captors by sowing dissension among them, helping to corrupt them, or trying to convince them that Germany was bound to lose and when it did, they would be in deep trouble.

*The Theory and Practice* of Hell is an uncompromising account of one of the most brutal systems for human subjugation and extermination ever put into practice.

The Berkeley Publishing Group; $5.95
1950; paperback; 333 pp.

## MISCELLANEOUS

### AMONG THE THUGS
### by Bill Buford

Bill Buford, editor of the terminally hip literary journal *Granta*, risked life and limb to hang out with Britain's soccer thugs, stepping right into the pages of a real-life *Clockwork Orange*. The thugs love lager, soccer, kicking ass, and the Queen, and hate everything else. They enjoy violence, from individual beatings to full-scale riots. Buford describes these lads as "ten years younger than me and about seventy-five pounds heavier whose passion for expression seldom went beyond the simple but effectively direct (and often repeated) phrase: 'You fuckin' bastard.'"

To get a firsthand look at this subculture, he approached one of these hooligans and explained what he was doing. "He stared at me. Then he said, 'All Americans are wankers.' And paused. 'All journalists,' he added, showing, perhaps that his mind did not work along strictly nationalist lines, 'are cunts.' We had established a rapport."

Buford was able to run with the thugs, taking part in many clashes. After a violent confrontation between the English hooligans and some Italian soccer supporters, there was a charged feeling in the air. "It was an excitement that verged on being something greater, an emotion more transcendent—joy at the very least, but more like ecstasy. There was an intense energy about it; it was impossible not to feel some kind of thrill."

Buford's account, filled with humor and sick violence, of life in this brutal subculture makes for an entertaining and eye-opening read.

Vintage; $12
1991; softcover; 317 pp.

### ANGELS FROM HELL:
### THE ANGEL CHRONICLES
### by Mick Norman

Published in 1973 and 1974, *The Angel Chronicles* was made up of four volumes: *Angels from Hell, Angel Challenge, Guardian Angels*, and *Angels on My Mind*. These classic "youthsploitation novels" are set in Britain at the turn of the millennium. The Hell's Angels have been driven underground by the government, but they still manage to have fun by running over blind people and setting reporters on fire. These endearingly B-grade books follow the Last Heroes chapter of the Angels as they try to have good clean violent fun but are thwarted at every turn by police, government officials, a rival chapter known as the Ghouls, and a new brutal subculture of mod/skinhead hybrids called skulls. Through it all the Angels rape, kill, kidnap, rob banks, get laid, do drugs, and commit all kinds of sadistic acts. "With almost fanatical strength, he scrabbled at the Angel's boots, trying desperately to get to his feet. Vincent lifted one foot and stamped down, as one would on a revolting slug, cracking the skull and forcing the pulp of the nose into the gravel. Then, Tarquin screamed, once only. Vincent stamped twice more, then edged back and kicked accurately for the base of the skull. The toe of the boot seemed to dig in a dreadful distance, then cartilage and bone parted and Tarquin Wells was dead...."

Creation Books; $16.95
1973/1974 (1994); softcover; 348 pp.

### ANSWER ME!

Put out by the husband/wife team of Jim and Debbie Goad, *ANSWER Me!* is one of the most hate-filled, misanthropic, nihilistic zines ever published. The Goads hate everything and everybody, and they want to see you—yes, you specifically—on the ground, squirming in pain. What saves *AM!* from being just a pathetic, sputtering rag is that it has a pitch-black sense of humor, the writing is top-notch, and it has a plethora of gruesome visuals incorporated into a demented design scheme.

*AM!* has become the hottest zine around. What the Power Rangers are to toys, *AM!* is to zines. As soon as each new issue becomes available, it sells out, never to be reprinted. According to *Factsheet Five*, some people are selling their copies for $50.

What's all the fuss about? Let's take a look at the highlights of issue #3. It starts off with an essay by Jim in which he fantasizes about beating you almost to death. Debbie prank calls Jack Kevorkian, convincing him that she has cancer and wants him to assist her suicide. Following that are two interviews, one with Reverend Al Sharpton, and the other with a spokesman for the North American Man/Boy Love Association. Debbie supplies several rants—"The Homeless Can Eat Shit," "Music Blows," "I Hate Being a Jew," and "Nothing but Enemies." "Your Turn Me Off" is her tirade against sex: "Your sex organs are so blindingly ugly, they sting my eyeballs. Whenever I see a picture of another woman's labia I shriek with horror.... You brag that you've had a thousand women. More like two chancrous whores and nine hundred ninety-eight solo jerk-off sessions. Any slit looks good to you. Your balls hang as low as your standards."

The centerpiece of the issue is a huge, fifty-seven-page section detailing one hundred suicides and briefly mentioning about one hundred more. With tongue planted in cheek, the Goads describe (and laugh at) the *hara-kiris* of Ernest Hemingway, photographer Diane Arbus, porn actress Colleen Applegate, Adolf Hitler, Abbie Hoffman, Sylvia Plath, Sappho, Vincent van Gogh, and other less famous casualties.

Suicide #7 is about Raymond Belknap and James Vance, whose suicide pact was blamed on subliminal messages in Judas Priest's album *Stained Class*. The Goads ask, "Did the victims' parents ever consider the possibility that their sons' suicides could be blamed on factors other than alleged commands issued by a combo of aging, gaseous Brits?" Speaking about Vance, they wonder, "Did a known predilection for marijuana, cocaine, amphetamines, alcohol, heroin, LSD, barbiturates, and PCP somehow impair his judgment? What could be gleaned from the fact that at age seven, he was sent to a therapist for tying a belt around his head and pulling out clumps of his hair in class? Or that he attempted to strangle his mother a year later?... Didn't it seem odd that both boys collected guns, spoke about becoming mercenaries, and frequently talked about committing mass murder in the Reno area?"

Surely the most explosive article in the issue is "Pederastic Park?" which focuses on the rumor that Steven Spielberg has "an overweening fascination with child actors." The issue is rounded out by art from eight murderers—including Mark David Chapman, Henry Lee Lucas, Charles Manson, John Wayne Gacy, and Richard Ramirez—and a fake call to a suicide hotline.

But *AM!* #3 is a hymnal compared to issue #4, which deals with rape. Forget your dime-a-dozen white supremacist screeds and your zines with instructions for homemade bombs, this issue will go down as one of the most controversial zines *ever* published. Overall, it's an intensely nauseating document. Parts of it are destined to be misunderstood, because they satirize the mind-set that leads to rape. A perfect example is the cover illustration. A waitress in a restaurant full of wolves has a black eye and a bloody nose. She is wearing a name tag that says, "Hi! I asked for it!" But a large part of the material can only be interpreted as pro-rape (yes, you read correctly), and is therefore indefensible.

Because of *ANSWER Me!*'s unprecedented popularity, you basically don't have a chance of getting the current issue. The best thing to do is send your five bucks and an over-twenty-one age statement, ask for the current issue, and request that if it's sold out, you be sent the next one. (Helpful hint: AK Press is planning on releasing a book that collects the entire first three issues of *AM!* It should be out any day now.)

Goad to Hell Enterprises
1608 N. Cahuenga Boulevard #666/Hollywood, CA 90028
Single issue: $4 (third class), $5 (first class); overseas: $7

## BLACK MASK AND UP AGAINST THE WALL MOTHERFUCKER:
### THE INCOMPLETE WORKS OF RON HAHNE, BEN MOREA, AND THE BLACK MASK GROUP

During the late 1960s, the Black Mask was a radical left-wing organization. Their ideas, as reproduced here in their ten newsletters and four leaflets, sound extraordinarily like most other extreme left wingers: "Goddamn your culture, your science, your art. What purpose do they serve? Your mass-murder cannot be concealed. The industrialist, the banker, the bourgeoisie, with their unlimited pretense and vulgarity, continue to stockpile art while they slaughter humanity. Your lie has failed. The world is rising against your oppression...."

In a way, though, Black Mask was unique. They sympathized with the struggles of the post-Watts African-Americans and urged solidarity between radical whites and Blacks. "The assault against the black community in N.Y. has begun. They are attempting to divide in order to conquer. We in the white community must stand with our black brothers." As a result, it is said that the Black Mask were the only white people that the Black Panthers trusted and respected.

At some point Black Mask mutated into the even more extreme, violence-prone organization, Up Against the Wall Motherfucker. The Motherfuckers, as they were called, were upset with the other far-left groups of the day. "It seems the respectable far-left organizations (YSA, PLP, SDS, PFP, ISC) never tire in providing entertainment for the bourgeoisie—and worse, keep trying to rechannel any really radical energies back into their bullshit forms.... And now that Huey [Newton] is convicted, what will they do??? Sadly, we all know, they'll have another rally, they'll picket death row, they'll march on the courthouse, they'll shift from their tv armchairs to auditorium armchairs; while they sit righteously clukking like hens, disapproving of the 'terrorists and provocateurs' who are taking care of business." They took care of business, all right. Many Motherfuckers went to the big house for their activities. Although the revolutionary statements of these two groups are fun to read, they are presented in a vacuum. There is practically zero background information given. When did these groups form and who was in them (besides the few names mentioned)? Exactly what kind of stunts did the Motherfuckers pull that landed them in jail? Background info presented without source material is a common flaw of many books; source material without background info is a little better but still very frustrating.

Autonomedia; $11
1993; softcover; 140 pp.

## CPA BOOK PUBLISHER CATALOG

The catalog of the Christian Patriot Association, the same group that publishes *The Patriot Review* (reviewed in the "Freedom" chapter). Listing this group's tabloid in the chapter on freedom and listing their book catalog in the chapter on extremism may seem a little strange, so let me explain. The CPA is an ultrapatriotic white Christian right-wing organization. Their periodical covers the usual ground for such groups—exposing government abuse of power (particularly the IRS), showing that the New World Order is approaching, Christianity is under attack, a Jewish conspiracy is attempting to run everything, etc. Definitely not mainstream, but also not undeniably extreme, in my judgment. Their book catalog, however, is another story. Many of the one thousand or more books, booklets, videos, and audiotapes offered are racist, anti-Semitic, and violently homophobic: *Death Penalty for Homosexuals Is Prescribed by the Bible, Death Penalty for Race-Mixers Is Prescribed by the Bible, The Bible and Segregation, Jewish Ritual Murder, The International Jew: The World's Foremost Problem* (by Henry Ford), *White Man, Think Again!* are some examples. Although these types of books are in the minority, they do characterize this catalog as extreme.

The rest of the items deal with the IRS, the Federal Reserve, Christianity, Satanism, humanism, home schooling, alternative health, conspiracies (Jewish and otherwise), law, the New Age, Masonry, survivalism, and lots of other topics.

CPA Book Publisher
33838 SE Kelso Road, Suite 2/PO Box 596/Boring, OR 97009
Catalog: no price given but send in a buck or two.

## CRYING WOLF:
### HATE CRIME HOAXES IN AMERICA
### by Laird Wilcox

Hoo boy, talk about a powderkeg! This explosive book examines a subject nobody wants to talk about—people who fake hate crimes, such as physical attacks and the destruction or defacing of property that are alleged to be motivated by the victims' race, religion, sexual orientation, etc. Political extremism expert Laird Wilcox has collected documents on three hundred such disturbing incidents.

There is obviously no doubt that hate crimes do happen. However, the lure of media attention, increased sympathy, and possible financial gain have proven irresistible to some members of oppressed groups.

*Free the Animals!* ➤ by Ingrid Newkirk

*Putting it on the line for our brothers and sisters in the animal kingdom.*

Wilcox relates many specific examples of hoaxes. In October 1988 an African-American student at Northwest Missouri University reported that he had been the victim of a racially motivated assault and death threats. The university went into a frenzy. The FBI and a special unit of the Justice Department were called in, and the story gained national attention. Rumors started swirling that there was a Ku Klux Klavern on campus. A month later, the student who reported the alleged hate crimes admitted that he'd fabricated the whole thing.

In another incident, a Jewish woman staunchly supported desegregation at a City Council meeting in Yonkers, New York. Days later she reported receiving death threats, and she soon became a media heroine because of her perceived courage. Later that year, a camera that the FBI had installed without the woman's knowledge recorded her writing an anti-Semitic threat against herself on the wall outside her apartment door.

There are also instances of white people falsely blaming crimes on members of minority groups. In Michigan in 1989 a white woman reported being kidnapped and beaten by three baseball-bat-wielding African-American men. Police later reported that the woman had made up the story after her boyfriend had beaten her up.

Wilcox also examines related issues. For example, he provides detailed examples of how the Anti-Defamation League, Klanwatch, and other antihate groups outrageously inflate the statistics on the occurrence of hate crimes, and the number and membership of hate groups. To come up with the frequency of hate crimes, minor incidents like graffiti, verbal altercations, and telephone harassment are often lumped in with very serious crimes like brutal assaults, murder, and arson. The power of hate groups is almost always overblown. "In 1984 a terrifying right-wing Halstead, KS, organization with the creative name of 'the Farmer's Liberation Army' was finally determined to have one member, founder Keith Shive. Anti-racist groups took the organization very seriously and references to it appeared in the national press. Shive was absolutely delighted with the response."

*Crying Wolf* also contains a list of traits that may suggest a hate crime hoax, government documents, and a faked racist leaflet.

Editorial Research Service; $20
1994; oversize softcover (plastic-comb binding); 145 pp.

## DER ANTICHRIST
### by Friedrich Nietzsche

A very limited-edition printing of Nietzsche's last work, in which he severely thrashes Christianity. The Nietzster believed in the inherent goodness of strength, power, and individuality and the inherent badness of weakness and conformity. People who are weak choose to band together and promote conformity and blandness in an effort to be safe. Christianity, Nietzsche believed, is one of the prime examples of this tendency for wimps to form groups which then try to push their mediocrity on those *über-*

*menschen* who are strong and play by their own rules. "Christian, finally, is the hatred of the *spirit,* of pride, courage, freedom, liberty of the spirit; Christian is the hatred of the *senses,* of joy in the senses, of joy itself."

The publisher says that this book is "aesthetically pure," that it "flies in the face of the academicians who would reduce Nietzsche to an impotent, politically correct victim of intellectual imprisonment." This edition, published by a neo-Nazi press, contains about two dozen tipped-in works of art by Trevor Brown, all focusing on the death of Jesus. The print run was limited to five hundred, and each book is individually numbered.

STORM; $10
1888 (1988); softcover; 88 pp.

## ECO-WARRIORS:
### UNDERSTANDING THE
### RADICAL ENVIRONMENTAL MOVEMENT
### by Rik Scarce

This book presents a sympathetic treatment of the radical environmental/animal rights movement, focusing on the four most prominent groups in this movement. Earth First! is famous for its monkeywrenching techniques, such as spiking trees and destroying bulldozers. Members of Greenpeace take direct action by chaining themselves to the harpoon guns of whaling ships. The Animal Liberation Front rescues animals from labs and supply houses. The Sea Shepherds protect marine life by freeing aquatic animals and sabotaging whaling expeditions.

The author tells the histories, triumphs, and setbacks of each group. He looks at the uncompromising people who are part of these groups or who act on their own. Two members of the Sea Shepherds, for example, completely trashed a whaling station in Reykjavik and sank two whaling ships—half of Iceland's fleet.

Besides relating such extreme actions, the author looks at the philosophies and structures of the groups: "A fifth distinguishing characteristic of radical environmentalists is that they usually have but minimal hope of actually ending on their own the practices against which they protest.... In fact nearly everything environmental extremists do takes place with an eye toward how it will play in the media, their strongest weapon in the fight for the Earth."

Noble Press; $12.95
1990; softcover; 291 pp.

## THE FINAL CALL

The Final Call Publishing Company is the publishing arm of the Nation of Islam, also known as the Black Muslims, led by the highly controversial Reverend Louis Farrakhan. I got their catalog too late to order anything from it, so I'll just list the catalog itself. Actually, "catalog" isn't the right word—this is really just a stapled listing of books from Final Call and other publishers. Unfortunately, the books aren't described, but most of them are extraordinarily hard to obtain, so I'm not going to complain.

Among the titles offered are *Black Economics, Countering the Conspiracy to Destroy Black Boys, Farrakhan the Traveler, Holy Qur'an, Muslim Prayer Book, The Secret Relationship Between Blacks and Jews, Somebody's Trying to Kill You, Race First,* and more than sixty others.

FCN Publishing Co/734 W. 79th Street/Chicago, IL 60620
Catalog: $1

## FREE THE ANIMALS!:
### THE UNTOLD STORY OF THE U.S. ANIMAL LIBERATION
### FRONT AND ITS FOUNDER, "VALERIE"
### by Ingrid Newkirk

The Animal Liberation Front (ALF) is a group of people who break into laboratories, biological supply houses, and other places where animals are subjected to unbelievable, legalized cruelty, and rescue the beasts. They also smash equipment, steal research, and spray-paint slogans on the walls.

Because the ALF's activities are illegal, they are an underground group in the truest sense of the word. The federal government officially considers them to be a terrorist group. No insider has ever written about them, and no one on the outside knows enough to write a book, except Ingrid Newkirk, cofounder and national director of People for the Ethical Treatment of Animals (PeTA) (don't ask me why they don't capitalize the "e"). Newkirk knows "Valerie," the founder of the American ALF, and PeTA is the ALF's connection to the world, reporting on liberation activities.

Newkirk chronicles the adventures of this shadowy organization and shows us the people behind it (well, up to the point of exposing their identities, anyway). We get firsthand descriptions of the pain and suffering inflicted upon the animals, and exciting accounts of their rescues. To say this book reads like a suspense thriller would be a cliché, but it's true. Besides being a great read, it's also the only window into a world of humans who put everything on the line for animals.

Noble Press; $13.95
1992; softcover; 372 pp.

## FUCK!

This is truly one of the most twisted, extreme magazines ever to see the light of day. There are no articles as such, just pages of collages, artwork, rants, malformed people, accident victims, unbelievably sacrilegious images, subverted ads and Christian comics, news clippings showing just how fucked-up the human race is, and several pieces urging people to kill each other. Pure, undiluted, unadulterated hatred for the human race is acid-etched into every mind-blowing page. Randall Phillips has stripped the skin from society and exposed its raw, bleeding nerves for all to see. It ain't pretty. You've been warned.

Randall Phillips Publications
PO Box 2217/Philadelphia, PA 19103
Current issue: $3 (cash or money order only. Be sure to send an over-twenty-one age statement!)

## INTERCOURSE
### by Andrea Dworkin

The term "radical feminism," I've noticed, has been plagued with misuse. This was most evident when I read theofascist Pat Buchanan refer to Gloria Steinem's ideas as radical feminism. Now, I'm sure that to Buchanan, *any* form of feminism is radical, but Steinem is truly the most mainstream feminist in existence. She could not be more different from Andrea Dworkin, Catharine MacKinnon, and Mary Daly. These three are to feminism what the Animal Liberation Front is to animal rights. They have extreme positions and steadfastly refuse to compromise.

In this book, arguably the most radical book written by a radical feminist, Dworkin rants against sex. She feels that, no matter how willing the woman is, sexual intercourse is an act of domination. "There is never a real privacy of the body that can coexist with intercourse: with being entered. The vagina itself is muscled and the muscles have to be pushed apart. The thrusting is persistent invasion. She is opened up, split down the center. She is occupied—physically, internally, in her privacy." Later, Dworkin says, "Physically, the woman in intercourse is a space inhabited, a literal territory occupied literally: occupied even if there has been no resistance, no force; even if the occupied person said yes please, yes hurry, yes more."

Dworkin also believes that sex leads to other types of domination: "To be female in this world is having been robbed of the potential for human choice by men who love to hate us. One does not make choices in freedom. Instead, one conforms in body type and behavior and values to become an object of male sexual desire...." Sex also turns women against each other. It especially pits "collaborators" against women like Dworkin, who refuse to give in to male domination. To those women she says, "The pleasure of submission does not and cannot change the fact, the cost, the indignity, of inferiority."

The Free Press; $11.95
1987; softcover; 257 pp.

## NAZIS, COMMUNISTS, KLANSMEN, AND OTHERS ON THE FRINGE:
### POLITICAL EXTREMISM IN AMERICA
### by John George and Laird Wilcox

Until this book came out, as far as I'm aware, there had never been an objective and comprehensive look at political extremist groups from the far left and the far right. This awe-inspiring book finally brings much hard-to-find information under one cover. Written by two experts in extremism, *Nazis* starts off with a relatively brief look at American extremism from pre-Columbian days to 1960. It quickly becomes apparent that the authors are prepared to call it like they see it: "If one were to describe the American Revolution as a seditious conspiracy fomented by a band of extremists, misfits, malcontents, and troublemakers dedicated to the overthrow of recognized authority, one well might be right on the mark."

Other chapters explore the nature of extremism, why people join (and leave) such movements, and how extremists on both sides of the political spectrum view the rights of those who disagree with them. The meat of the book, though, is Parts Two and Three—an encyclopedic look at the information, activities, and fate (or current activities) of groups from the extreme left and extreme right. Far-left groups that are covered include the Communist Party USA, Students for a Democratic Society, the Black Panther Party, the Revolutionary Action Movement, and eleven others. Far-right groups that are covered include the John Birch Society, the Liberty Lobby, the Minutemen, the Jewish Defense League, neo-Nazi groups, the KKK, and twelve others. Each group gets a chapter of its own. Although the book clocks in at over five hundred pages, most of the chapters seem too short, giving at times a cursory look at events. However, this drawback can easily be excused when you look at the book's strong points: there's never a dull moment; the reader gets a strong sense of what these semimythical groups really did and what they really stood for; and the authors have a strong love of freedom of speech and belief.

The book also earns distinction in the way it shows the common threads running through all extremist groups. Namely, the groups' memberships are extremely small, despite their claims to the contrary. They generate an inordinate amount of media coverage, public apprehension, and government harassment. And, when viewed objectively, almost none of them has had any lasting impact on society.

*Nazis* ends with a bang. An appendix takes an enlightening look at a favorite tactic of extremists —attributing nonexistent quotes to famous people, and the forty-seven-page annotated bibliography lists enough books on extremism to keep you reading for years.

There has been a lot written on extremism, but little of it has been comprehensive or without bias. This book corrects this problem. It is destined to be the definitive work in the field.

Prometheus Books; $29.95
1992; hardcover; 523 pp.

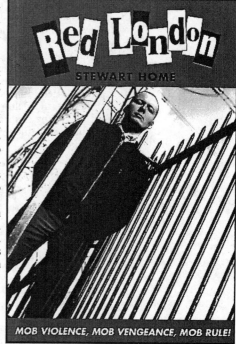

MOB VIOLENCE, MOB VENGEANCE, MOB RULE!

## RED LONDON
### by Stewart Home

Attack of the anarchist skinhead Buddhists! This ultraviolent novel tells the story of Fellatio Jones and his followers, a group of nonracist skinheads out to start a class war by killing all "rich bastards." The guiding light of their struggle is an outlawed book called *Christ, Marx, and Satan United in Struggle*. It lays down the philosophy of class war by focusing on three arche-

*Red London
by Stewart
Home*

*Attack of
the anarchist
skinhead
buddhists!*

types. Marx stands for lucidity, discipline, and struggle. Christ is duty, detachment, and mysticism. Satan represents lust, abandon, and violence. By combining these archetypes within yourself, you become a perfect human being, ready to strike down the bourgeoisie.

Taking these ideas to heart, the anti-Nazi, anticommunist, bisexual nihilists go on a rampage, snuffing millionaires, burning down posh neighborhoods, putting LSD in the water supply, and finally instigating a murderous riot in Soho. And they manage to have lots of sex while they're doing it. You might expect the sex scenes to be real cheesy, but they're actually quite original and are some of the best parts of the book. Note this scene in which a female skinhead and her prostitute friend are doing a sixty-nine: "Weird images flashed through [Cleo] Wong's mind—exploding stars, mudflats, swamps, volcanoes and surging seas. These visions were core genetic memories whose rise to the surface of Cleo's consciousness was dictated by the DNA codes that had seized control of her quivering flesh. Melody was moaning crazily as she relived a previous existence as an atom that had hurtled through hyper-space split-seconds after the big bang had spread life across this universe.... Wave after wave of pleasure broke over their twin bulks as the pair of polymorphous perverts wallowed in the accumulated ecstasy of the ages.... Simultaneously, they were able to make love as atom, amoebae, amphibian, and mammal."

> AK Press; $12.95
> 1994; softcover; 158 pp.

## SPECTRUM:
### A GUIDE TO THE INDEPENDENT PRESS AND INFORMATIVE ORGANIZATIONS, 1993 (22ND EDITION)

An address book of extremists (and not-so-extremists). This yearly guide gives addresses, phone numbers (when available), and capsule descriptions of thousands of contrary organizations. Categories of groups include anarchist, animal rights, Christian conservative, civil liberties, conspiracy theories, ethnic interests (Black, Jewish, White/Aryan, etc.), gun rights, Holocaust revisionist, Marxist, neo-Nazi, peace, pro-choice, pro-life, survivalism, tax protest, alternative health, countercult, UFO, neo-pagan, and loads more. *You must get this book.* Do you understand? Where else can you possibly find the addresses for the John Birch Society, the Communist Party USA, the Knights of the Ku Klux Klan, the Ayn Rand Institute, the Soldiers of the Cross, the Association of Clandestine Radio, the Hemp Council, the Black Panther Militia, the Nation of Islam, the Jewish Defense League, *The David Duke Report*, the Hemlock Society, Victims of Child Abuse Laws, Operation Rescue, the Cult Awareness Network, the Holy Alamo Christian Church, the Unification Church, the Peaceful Order of the Earth Mother, the Ancient Astronaut Society, etc., etc., etc.?

> Laird Wilcox Editorial Research Service; $19.95
> 1993; oversize softcover; 100 pp.

## SCUM MANIFESTO
### by Valerie Solanas

In 1968 Valerie Solanas "formed" the Society for Cutting Up Men (SCUM), a one-person organization. She had recently shot and nearly killed Andy Warhol, and she obviously felt the need to explain her violent actions. In this classic piece of hate literature, she explains why men need to be killed, blaming them for everything that's wrong with the world. *SCUM Manifesto* is well written and darkly hilarious, but what really makes it different from all other hate literature, as my sister has pointed out, is that a lot of it is true. Take the following sentences, for example: "Eaten up with guilt, shame, fears and insecurities and obtaining, if he's lucky, a barely perceptible physical feeling, the male is, nonetheless, obsessed with screwing; he'll swim a river of snot, wade nostril-deep through a mile of vomit, if he thinks there'll be a friendly pussy awaiting him. He'll screw a woman he despises, any snaggle-toothed hag, and, furthermore, pay for the opportunity. Why? Relieving physical tension isn't the answer, as masturbation suffices for that. It's not ego satisfaction; that doesn't explain screwing corpses and babies."

Later, Solanas unequivocally states: "Every man, deep down, knows he's a worthless piece of shit." She goes on to blame men for war, money, work, mental illness, suppression of individuality, lack of community, authority and government, prejudice, competition, ignorance, boredom, censorship, distrust, hate, violence, disease, death, and lots more. Her solution? Kill all men, except for those in the Men's Auxiliary of SCUM (e.g., men who kill men, gay men, and other exceptions). Then overthrow the government, eradicate the economy, and set up a feminist/anarchist utopia.

As a trip to the pop-psychology section of any bookstore will prove, "man-bashing" is the in thing right now, but Solanas did it first and she did it best.

Getting the *SCUM Manifesto* is a bit of a problem. For whatever reason, the publisher, a small British press, didn't print its address in the *Manifesto,* and I've been unable to track it down. However, some catalogs listed in Appendix A carry this masterful polemic. Specifically, I've seen it offered in AK Distribution, AMOK, and Left Bank Distribution. Also, it was reprinted in issue #8 of the omnisexual magazine *Frighten the Horses* (reviewed in the "Sex" chapter).

> Phoenix Press; £1.50
> 1968; paperback; 31 pp.

## TURNING THE TIDE:
### JOURNAL OF ANTI-RACIST ACTIVISM, RESEARCH AND EDUCATION

Put out by People Against Racist Terrorism, the tabloid *Turning the Tide* is a vital source of news and information concerning racist and antiracist action. The Jan./Feb. 1994 issue has articles on how Guns N Roses and others are idolizing Charles Manson, how multiculturalism as it is being practiced is just "a 'hip' version of cultural imperialism," the horrible treatment of inmates at a women's prison in Texas, neo-Nazi skinhead activity in Sacramento, how African-American reporter Mumia Abu-Jamal was railroaded into a death sentence for allegedly killing a cop, and more. "Update on Hate" contains small items on what white supremacists are up to. One item relates that racist literature has been planted in stores all over California: "Flyers attacking Latinos and non-whites were found stuffed inside soda six-packs at a Lucky Market and in Christmas stockings at a Sav-On in Canyon County; in children's backpacks at a Target in Valencia; in cosmetics at a Ralphs in Reseda; in 12-packs of soda and beer at Lucky's and Vons Markets in Palmdale."

*TTT* also prints a long resource listing of organizations fighting racism and oppression.

> PART/PO Box 1990/Burbank, CA 91507
> Six-issue sub: $10

## MURDER

### THE AESTHETICS OF MURDER:
#### A STUDY IN ROMANTIC LITERATURE AND CONTEMPORARY CULTURE
#### by Joel Black

This book takes on the controversial task of evaluating murder in Romantic fiction and postmodern art from an aesthetic viewpoint, as opposed to a moral or psychological one. "...[M]urder can be approached analytically from an entirely different angle. It can be subjected to the same kind of inquiry that literary historians and critics practice in the case of texts, or that art critics and historians bring to bear upon paintings and sculptures.... In this form, murder can be studied in a relatively disinterested mode as a morally neutral phenomenon..."

Among the subjects the author covers are murder as an art form, murder as an erotic act, murder while intoxicated, *Taxi Driver*, Alfred Hitchcock's *Rope*, *Dressed to Kill*, Thomas de Quincey's essays, detective fiction, the Marquis de Sade, Jean Genet, Yukio Mishima's suicide, John Lennon's murder, and Ronald Raygun's attempted assassination.

The Johns Hopkins University Press; $14.95
1991; softcover; 276 pp.

### BE YOUR OWN UNDERTAKER:
#### HOW TO DISPOSE OF A DEAD BODY
#### by A.R. Bowman

This slim book is based on the principle that one day you may need to kill in self-defense and, given a justice system with a backward sense of priorities, you may end up rotting in a jail. Of course, if you snuff somebody for revenge, money, or fun, the info in this book is useful, too, but like most books on such subjects, this one tries to play down that fact. OK, so assume some twisted scumbag does break into your home and you legitimately turn out his lights. What do you do? Bowman gives advice on whether you should even try to dispose of the body yourself or just let the police show up.

The actual advice on how to ditch your flatliner is way too sketchy to be of real value. For example, the author says, "By the way, it hardly needs saying that you should make certain the body is dead before disposing of it. Such things may seem quite comical in the movies, but real life can be a bit different." Well, how do you do that? In the movies they put a mirror under the person's nose, or maybe I should stick some needles in tender parts of the anatomy. I don't know.

When discussing disposing of the corpse in a body of water, Bowman gives us this invaluable advice: "If you're going to throw the body off a bridge, there are some things to keep in mind. First, the darker the night, the better. A stormy, rainy night is best of all, but even fog will help. Also speed is of the essence. Move quickly, even if it's late at night. Lastly, try to make certain that no one's around." Duh.

Paladin Press; $10
1992; softcover; 50 pp.

### "KILL WITHOUT JOY!":
#### THE COMPLETE HOW TO KILL BOOK
#### by John Minnery

Published from 1973 to 1984, the six slim volumes of the *How to Kill* series have been referred to as "the most controversial books ever published." Now gathered under one cover, these grisly tomes look at the myriad ways people have developed to murder other people. Reading *Kill* makes you realize the enormous amount of time and energy the human race has put into developing ways to exterminate each other.

A large part of this book is made up of illustrations and rare photos of exotic and unusual weapons, such as shoe guns, microphone cannons, and pen dart guns. It's interesting but of little practical use unless you can get your hands on a WWII belt buckle gun. However, at least two-thirds of the book gives instructions for committing murder. Minnery tells the best ways to strangle somebody, how to rig up a homemade one-shot flamethrower, the most effective way to drown someone in a bathtub, how to kill with a car, concocting and delivering poisons, how to club somebody so they'll die and you won't "jar your arm or hand" (I hate it when that happens), and dozens more ways to whack someone.

Many of Minnery's suggestions are quite ingenious. Would you have thought to electrify a urinal so that when your target takes a leak, it's his last? Minnery also recommends firing a gun filled with blanks right into the base of the skull: "Lack of evidential bullet hampers investigation and if apprehended you can claim accident or lack of malice as '...it was only loaded with blanks...'" Only once in a while does the author present the laughingly obvious, such as the "Hachet to the Medulla" technique. I think most people realize that nailing somebody in the back of the head with an axe will lead to death.

Of course, there are many other concerns besides the actual act of termination. Coping with your first kill, disposing of the body, and making the murder look like suicide are also covered. You might even want to consider the time of the month in which you are killing your target. "During a waxing moon, blood and breath circulate freely and are much enhanced. Shooting or stabbing indicated." As if you don't have enough to worry about when you're gonna put the kabosh on somebody, now you have to check the lunar phases on your calendar. Oh well, nobody ever said that killing was easy.

Paladin Press; $24.95
1992; softcover; 495 pp.

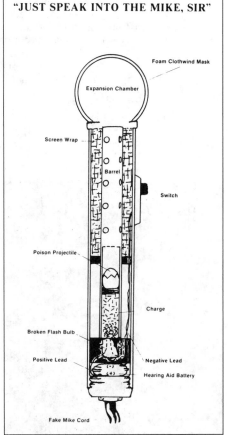

**"JUST SPEAK INTO THE MIKE, SIR"**

Foam Clothwind Mask
Expansion Chamber
Screen Wrap
Barrel
Switch
Poison Projectile
Charge
Broken Flash Bulb
Positive Lead
Negative Lead
Hearing Aid Battery
Fake Mike Cord

*Kill Without Joy*
by John Minnery

*"The most controversial books ever published."*

### MURDER CAN BE FUN

A digest-size zine that gleefully reports on the best in anti-social behavior. Editor John Marr has a cover theme in each issue, such as all the deaths that have occurred at that supposed utopia, Disneyland (issue # 13), and the murder sprees of postal workers (issue #14). We are also treated to articles on kidnapping, bizarre accidents, riots, confession magazines, and schlocky books, among others.

What makes this zine so great is Marr's hilarious cynicism. The humor is so dark you can't see your hand in front of your face. Witness selected items from the table of contents for issue #15: "The Bloody World of Mormon Cults: You live in a neighborhood of mixed religions—snake-handlers next door, Hasidim across the street, Santerias down the block. Why the Mormons in the 'hood are the most likely to slit your throat." "Ransom Kidnapping of Children: The American Top 12: Small, compact, and readily transportable, they're the most cost-effective kidnapping targets. Even if they aren't named Lindbergh." For all its lighthearted treatment of blood-drenched topics, though, *Murder Can Be Fun* contains an incredible amount of research on topics that have never before been presented in an organized, definitive manner.

Marr also publishes *(Anti) Sex Tips for Teens* ($2.50), which examines the idiotic advice that has been given to adolescents from 1897 to 1987, and a yearly date book with a morbid event commemorated on each day.

John Marr/Box 640111/San Francisco, CA 94109
Sample copies are $1.50. Subscriptions are $1.50 for each future issue. Write for back issue prices and availability.

go hunting for strangers to kill. The ones who do almost always do so with some twisted freak of a boyfriend/husband. For example, Charlene Gallego teamed up with Gerald Gallego (who "could have been a poster child for mandatory birth control") to abduct several teenage girls, whom they raped and killed.

The amount of research that went into this unique book is staggering. The information here is just not available anywhere else. Also, it's very well written, making for entertaining reading (if that's the proper word for it).

Loompanics Unlimited; $14.95
1993; oversize softcover; 195 pp.

## PICTURES AT AN EXECUTION:
### AN INQUIRY INTO THE SUBJECT OF MURDER
### by Wendy Lesser

*Bad Girls Do It!* ▼
by Michael Newton

*A colossal compendium of scary ladies.*

Murder as theater is the main subject of this book. The anchoring point is the 1991 trial in which a California public TV station sued for the right to film an execution for later broadcast. The author uses this as a springboard into the larger subject of viewing murder. "Why are we drawn to murder, as an act and as a spectacle? Who in the murder story are we drawn to—the victim, the murderer, the detective? Why, in particular, are we so interested in *seeing* murder, either enacted or caught in the act? What are the sources of pleasure in a murder story, and how do those kinds of pleasure connect with any sense of the morally suspect or reprehensible? Is it morally reprehensible to talk about such things without sounding either self-righteous or sleazy?"

To answer these questions, Lesser surveys murder in all its representations—*Macbeth, The Silence of the Lambs, The Executioner's Song* by Norman Mailer, Weegee's photographs of New York, the only photo of an electric chair execution ever published in an American newspaper, mystery novels, *Crime and Punishment* by Dostoyevsky, and more. She paints a picture of a society fascinated by murder in spite of itself.

Harvard University Press; $24.95
1993; hardcover; 270 pp.

## SERIAL KILLERS AND MASS MURDERERS

## BAD GIRLS DO IT!:
### AN ENCYCLOPEDIA OF FEMALE MURDERERS
### by Michael Newton

If you thought that Aileen Wournos, the woman who iced six men, was the "first known female serial killer in modern history," as our sensationalistic media touted her, you've got another thing coming. The hundreds of women listed here, almost all from the nineteenth and twentieth centuries, have each killed at least two people. Interestingly, the majority of these women did not kill strangers, as male serial killers are prone to do, but instead snuffed their children and/or husbands after going off the deep end. It's not unusual for other family members to get killed, too (I'm sure that this says something about patriarchal society but I haven't figured it out yet).

A lot of the other women purposely murder their successive husbands for insurance money or kill female rivals. A few women

## THE DIARY OF JACK THE RIPPER:
### THE DISCOVERY, THE INVESTIGATION, THE DEBATE
### narrative by Shirley Harrison

In 1991 Mike Barrett, a retired scrap-metal dealer, was given a book that appeared to be the diary of Jack the Ripper. The friend who gave it to him wouldn't say how he got it and later died of heart failure. Anxious to expose this possibly momentous book to the world, Barrett took it to a literary agent, who helped get it authenticated and published. Writer Shirley Harrison tells of this enigmatic diary, which was allegedly written by James Maybrick, a well-known cotton merchant in Liverpool. Maybrick died of poisoning, and his wife was found guilty of the murder in a sensationalistic trial.

Harrison relates the numerous clues that point to the author as Maybrick and Maybrick as Jack the Ripper. She also tells of the detective work that has gone into authenticating the diary. The jury is still out, and not everyone may ever agree, but so far no one has been able to disprove that it was written by Jack. Forensics experts using state-of-the-art technology haven't found anything that conclusively contradicts the theory that it was written in 1888–89. England's leading Ripperologists have been unable to come up with one damning piece of evidence, such as an error or contradiction. A report reproduced at the end of the book points out several pieces of evidence that could indicate the diary isn't genuine or at least cannot be proven genuine. Publisher Robert Smith then rebuts these arguments.

The entire diary is reproduced first in facsimile version and then typeset, to allow for easier reading (Jack may have been a wonder with the scalpel, but his penmanship leaves something to be desired). Here is a typical entry: "The head will come off next time, also the whore's hands. Shall I leave them in various places around Whitechapel? Hunt the head and hands instead of the thimble ha ha. Maybe I will take some part away with me to see if it does taste of like fresh fried bacon."

Late-Breaking News: As I move into the final stages of writing this manuscript, I read in *Fortean Times* #76 that Barrett has confessed to forging the diary. The main reason for getting this book is now gone, but at least it still has some curiosity value.

Hyperion; $21.95
1993; hardcover; 323 pp.

## A FATHER'S STORY
### by Lionel Dahmer

Imagine that you had raised a child who grew up and performed lobotomies on unwilling victims, killed them, cannibalized them, and/or raped their corpses. Well, Lionel Dahmer did raise such a child. His son Jeffrey is one of the most celebrated serial killer/cannibal/necrophiles in history. How would you cope with something like that? Would you think it's at least partly your fault?

Lionel tells the story of coming to grips with what his flesh and blood had done. At first, he went into denial. "I had leaned casually on the black table they claimed my son had used both as a dissecting table and a bizarre Satanic altar. How was it possible that all of this had been hidden from me—not only the horrible physical evidence of my son's crimes, but the dark nature of the man who had committed them, this child I had held in my arms a thousand times, and whose face, when I glimpsed it in the newspapers, looked like mine?"

Much of the book describes Jeffrey's life, from birth through childhood and adolescence to the discovery of his crimes and his sentencing to 957 years in prison. Although interesting, these events still give us no clear indication of why Jeffrey committed such heinous acts, a fact that Lionel readily admits. He can't figure out the reasons, either, but he noticed the signs early. "In a sense, his childhood no longer exists. Everything is now a part of what he did as a man. Because of that, I can no longer distinguish the ordinary from the forbidding—trivial events from ones loaded with foreboding. When he was four, and pointed to his bellybutton and asked what would happen if someone cut it out, was that merely an ordinary question from a child who had begun to explore his own body, or was it a sign of something morbid already growing in his mind?"

We may never fully understand serial killers, but books like *A Father's Story* provide invaluable clues to the mystery.

William Morrow and Company; $20
1994; hardcover; 255 pp.

## HUNTING HUMANS:
### THE ENCYCLOPEDIA OF SERIAL KILLERS, VOLUMES 1 & 2
### by Michael Newton

Together, these volumes make up a twisted treasury of scary psychopaths who slay for sport. Arranged alphabetically, the entries describe the lives and crimes of about five hundred serial killers. For some reason, each volume runs A through Z, instead of having each book cover half the alphabet.

Serial killing in the United States is largely a white male activity, according to the introduction to Volume 1: "In America, 85% are male and 8% female; sex remains undetermined in another 7% of cases, where the killers are still at large. Ethnically, 82% of American serial killers are white, 15% are black, and 2.5% are Hispanic. (Native Americans and Orientals figure in one case each, with the Oriental killer serving as an accomplice to a white man.)"

Volume 1 covers the case histories of such well-known killers as Ed "Psycho" Gein, Albert Fish, Henry Lee Lucas, Charles Manson, John Wayne Gacy, David "Son of Sam" Berkowitz, the Atlanta Child Murderer, the Zodiac Killer, the Green River Killer, Ted Bundy, and Richard "The Night Stalker" Ramirez. The second volume doesn't contain many famous murderers, but they are no less brutal.

These two books are rightly considered the definitive works on serial killers.

Avon; $5.99 each
1990; paperback; Vol. 1: 386 pp., Vol. 2: 338 pp.

## KILLER KOMIX, VOLUME 1

A collection of comix by several artists (David Kerekes, Andy Bullock, Lesley Anne Atherton, and others) dealing with Charles Manson, The Lonely Hearts Killers, Ed Gein, Jeffrey Dahmer, Richard Ramirez, David Berkowitz, the Zodiac Killer, and other endearing maniacs. The stories range from fairly straightforward accounts of the killer's exploits to more surrealistic, and at times darkly humorous, meditations on the fruitcake in question. The latter pieces help elevate this book from being merely a pictorial guide to violent death to a more intriguing examination of this morbid subject. Very well done.

Headpress; $12 (UK: £5.99)
1992; oversize softcover; 116 pp.

## RIPPERANA:
### THE JOURNAL OF RIPPEROLOGY

This interesting little magazine delves into the case of Jack the Ripper with a zeal and a penchant for obscure detail that you may have thought was only found among JFK assassination researchers. Each issue contains mentions of items relating to Jack the Ripper appearing in books, magazines, and newspapers; book reviews; and articles covering every conceivable aspect of the case. Several pages are devoted to other murders, both recent and old. Written in a very straightforward style, *Ripperana* is indispensable for true crime buffs and, of course, Ripperologists.

Ripperana
16 Costons Avenue/Greenford Middlesex
UB6 8RJ/ENGLAND
Four-issue sub (one year): £4 in the U.K.; U.S. and elsewhere: £8 U.S. subscribers must pay in cash.

## TRUE CRIME, VOLUME 2:
### SERIAL KILLERS AND MASS MURDERERS
### by Valarie Jones, Peggy Collier, and Jon Bright

Collected in book form are the trading cards that caused national hysteria. When word got out that Eclipse Books was putting out a series of cards based on killers, "10,000 pieces of hate-mail and mostly misspelled petitions and form letters from Christian groups" poured in to the publisher's offices. Attempts to ban the cards were made in several states. The city of Rosemead, California, urged the governor to ban not just the cards but all "material depicting criminals." (So not only true crime books would be banished, but any book by or about George Bush, Oliver North, or Richard Nixon would have to be yanked off the shelves.) It just goes to show, any time there is even the hint of a potential "menace," people go out of their minds with terror and immediately crumple up the Bill of Rights. Luckily, cooler heads prevailed and only Nassau County in New York passed a ban on the cards being sold to minors.

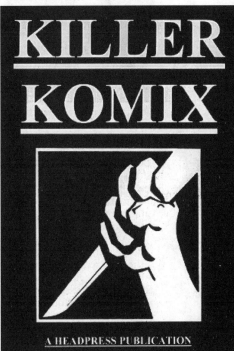

◄ *Killer Komix*

*Comic book artists and serial killers— a match made in marketing.*

This book contains color reproductions of the artwork and text of all the cards. Killers include Ted Bundy, Juan Corona, Jeffrey Dahmer, John Wayne Gacy, Ed Gein, the Zodiac Killer, Jack the Ripper, Genene Jones, Charles Manson, William Palmer, and dozens of others. The art is good, but the information is barebones, owing to the limited space on the back of the cards. The main reason to get this book is simply for its First Amendment historical value.

Eclipse Books; $4.95
1992, 1993; softcover; 61 pp.

## CAPITAL PUNISHMENT

## EXECUTION:
### TOOLS AND TECHNIQUES
### by Bart Rommel

"When an individual kills, it's murder. When the state kills, it's execution." With this definition in mind, *Execution* offers a gruesome look at the ways people are "officially" snuffed in modern times. This includes hanging, electrocution, beheading, shooting, gassing, and lethal injection. The author discusses when the methods were developed, exactly how they are administered, how they work, and gives examples from real life, including some nasty botched executions.

Other methods of execution are covered but not in much

detail. Entombment, burning to death, and crucifixion get a little attention. Ducking and disemboweling get a couple of sentences, and stoning isn't even mentioned. I hate to sound like a ghoul, but if I'm gonna get a book that purports to discuss the nitty-gritty of execution, by God, I want in-depth coverage of a large range of techniques. Don't leave anything out.

> Loompanics Unlimited; $12.95
> 1990; softcover; 119 pp.

## GUILLOTINE:
### ITS LEGEND AND LORE
### by Daniel Gerould

From its inception during the French Revolution, the guillotine has held a special place in Western society's heart. No other method of execution has inspired so much folklore, pop culture, and commentary. The author examines the introduction of the head-chopper. Adopted because it was painless and quick, its efficiency proved to be a problem. "...[I]t soon became an instrument of indiscriminate carnage.... This new technology for speeding up executions created a demand for more and more victims, and so it was that the rhythm of the guillotine imposed itself on life, effortlessly transforming it into death."

A cult immediately sprang up around the guillotine. "'Let us go see the red mass celebrated on the altar,' said one of the worshippers of the scaffold. The ritual of spurting blood was powerful and hypnotic, a sort of subverted form of Christian liturgy." Stories began circulating of heads that winked and bit each other or headless bodies that walked across the scaffold. The nature of the guillotine's victims changed over the years. The author relates the beheadings of the anarchists and the use of the guillotine by the Nazis.

Many famous writers witnessed beheadings; the accounts of Lord Byron, Charles Dickens, Leo Tolstoy, Alexander Dumas, and others are reprinted. The book goes on to examine the literature, art, and pop culture that sprang from the guillotine—cabarets, silent films, toys, cartoons, magician's props, etc. More than two hundred illustrations are included: drawings, woodcuts, photos, and film stills.

> Blast Books; $14.95
> 1992; softcover; 329 pp.

## MAY GOD HAVE MERCY ON YOUR SOUL:
### THE LAST MOMENTS OF 171 CONVICTED KILLERS WHO PAID THE ULTIMATE PRICE
### by Ed Baumann

Cook County in Chicago has executed 171 people in its history, and for the last four decades the author has seen every one of them. In this mammoth book he recounts the final moments of every single person who has been hanged or electrocuted in Cook County. Each chapter is devoted to a different person (or people if it happened to be a special two- or three-for-one deal), and the title of each chapter is a newspaper headline that reported the event. The fun begins with John Stone, hanged in July of 1840 based on circumstantial evidence that he raped and murdered a farmer's wife. The execution "was carried off with all the hoo-rah and trappings of a festive holiday." Things weren't quite so festive for Stone: "Indeed, the first public hanging was a botched affair, with the unfortunate John Stone twisting and writhing at the end of the rope, gagging and choking for several interminable minutes, while the lakefront crowd gaped in amusement."

One of the most bizarre executions to take place was that of George Painter, who was strung up for choking his fiancée. After the trapdoor of the gallows opened, Painter fell through, the rope broke, and he cracked his head open on the concrete floor. He was pronounced dead, but the law said he was to be hanged, so they put a new noose around the corpse's neck and this time it held.

Most executions aren't nearly as intriguingly strange,

though, and reading detailed accounts of 171 people getting snuffed can get a little repetitious. I think this book is useful in two ways. As a source document for people studying executions, last words, etc. Or as a good book to dip into from time to time when you feel a morbid urge.

> Bonus Books; $24.95
> 1993; hardcover; 497 pp.

# MISCELLANEOUS

## THE ART AND SCIENCE OF DUMPSTER DIVING
### by John Hoffman, illustrated by Ace Backwords

You may think dumpster diving is for desperate homeless people, but your attitude will change after reading this book because "there's gold in them thar dumpsters!" People and businesses throw away tons of perfectly good food, clothes, furniture, books, magazines, CDs, appliances, etc. In this book a veteran dumpster diver tells you how to lay claim to this booty, which you can either use yourself, convert to cash, or barter.

The author tells you what to wear and what equipment you'll need, including the "dive stick." He describes the three best dumpster sites—bakeries, grocery stores, and bookstores—and seven runners-up—discount stores, florists, residential areas, etc. Of course, the proper techniques of diving are discussed in detail, with special attention given to the various models of dumpsters that are out there. Obstacles like cops, fences, and winos are covered, too.

Reading this book brings back fond memories of my childhood dumpster diving days. Didn't find much except a bunch of porno mags, but I guess that made it worth it. The author claims you can achieve self-sufficiency through diving. I don't know about that, but you probably can pick up some cool junk.

> Loompanics Unlimited; $12.95
> 1993; oversize softcover; 152 pp.

## BREATH OF THE DRAGON:
### HOMEBUILT FLAMETHROWERS
### by Ragnar Benson

Has your Glock lost its magic? Do you find that even your illegally converted assault rifle now bores you? Well cheer up, because for about a thousand dollars you can make the ultimate weapon—your own flamethrower! Legal, except perhaps in a few local ordinances, and able to charcoal large numbers of people and vehicles, a flamethrower is a perfect addition to anyone's arsenal. Benson gives somewhat detailed instructions for constructing a dragon, but, not having tried it myself, I can't say for sure whether they're detailed enough.

Of course, once you have a flamethrower, you need something to put in it. Instructions for homebrewed napalm are included in Chapter Three. Finally, there is a listing of sources for the material you'll need to be the toast of the town.

> Paladin Press; $12
> 1990; softcover; 65 pp.

## CHEATING (AND ADVANTAGE PLAY) AT BLACKJACK
### by Dustin Marks

This hot potato of a book, written by a professional top-rank gambler and cheater, tells you exactly how to cheat casinos in blackjack. To a lesser degree, it also reveals legal and quasi-legal "advantage" playing techniques.

"The game of blackjack is a cheater's dream come true," writes the author. There are two reasons. First, the game is dealt by a human, who can make mistakes and be manipulated. Second, it's based on "dependent events," which means that all occurrences are interrelated. "The punch line is that there are so many ways to attack the game, that it is virtually impossible to circumvent all the cheating techniques without shutting down the business."

The book starts by explaining how casinos work, how blackjack is played, and the basic strategies for blackjack, which will help you whether you're going to cheat or not. There's lots of information on psyching out security, cheating in a team, dealing with detectives, etc.

Now, the fun begins. The author explains advantage play, which is legal and quasi-legal. There is one illegal move, but it is "softcore" and leaves no evidence behind. Specifically, these techniques are card counting, hole card play, cutting techniques, and "Oh, excuse me."

The hardcore scam methods are stacking the deck, performing traditional and computerized coolers (in all of these operations the dealer must be in on it), and switching cards in play.

Cheating ends with a brief chapter on how to cheat on other casino games, a glossary, and a resources section. This book is packed with diagrams and charts. Get it and start improving your odds immediately.

Index Publishing Group; $19.95
1994; softcover; 230 pp.; illus.

## THE CHRONICLE OF CRIME:
### THE INFAMOUS FELONS OF MODERN HISTORY AND THEIR HIDEOUS CRIMES
### by Martin Fido

A look at some of the most famous and horrible cases of murder, rape, cannibalism, kidnapping, extortion, assassination, and so on since 1800. From the beginning of the nineteenth century to 1860, each decade is given a two-page spread. From 1860 on, every year is given a spread with the most notorious psychos getting their own two pages. The pages are filled with killer priests, Georgia lynch mobs, failed assassinations, unsolved murders, anarchist antics, jewel thieves, wife-murderers, Mafia kingpins, soldiers who snap, thrill-killers, President Nixon, teenage sociopaths, and more.

The book is set up like a newspaper, with screaming headlines, lots of pictures, pull quotes, sidebars, etc. One to four crimes are presented on each page in bite-size chunks, making this perfect bathroom reading (except the book is too big to lay on the back of a toilet).

Carroll & Graf; $18.95
1993; oversize softcover; 320 pp.

## COUNTERFEIT CURRENCY:
### HOW TO REALLY MAKE MONEY
### by M. Thomas Collins

Just what you always wanted to know: how to make funny money. This kinda stuff will get you a room with striped sunlight, but I'm sure you'd never dream of actually using the knowledge in this book, so I'll tell you about it. The author discusses how the government prints money (both how the government *says* it prints money and how it's believed they really do it) and the safeguards they put in to foil counterfeiters.

He then discusses in detail the methods of counterfeiting, and they aren't cheap. The offset method requires a process camera (about $17,000 to $20,000), a printing press ($18,000 to $23,000), a platemaker (around $5,000), and a paper cutter ($1,500 to $3,500). Another method requires a scanner (not one of those little scanners for your computer but a high-end mother used in the printing industry costing at least $70,000) and a laser engraver (about $130,000). And these are 1990 prices! Of course, you could easily pay for all this equipment with just one good day of counterfeiting.

Finally, the author tells how to pass your newly "earned" money. Unfortunately, this book was published several years ago and could use some updating. A new form of counterfeiting has taken the country by storm recently. Color copiers are being used to duplicate money, as well as paychecks, stocks, and other valuable documents. Copy center employees have been warned about this, and companies are allegedly making copiers that can somehow recognize what is being copied and will not work if someone is trying to dupe money, checks, etc. I find this hard to believe, but who knows? Technology has helped bring counterfeiting to the masses.

Loompanics Unlimited; $15
1990; softcover; 137 pp.

## ECODEFENSE:
### A FIELD GUIDE TO MONKEYWRENCHING (THIRD EDITION)
### edited by Dave Foreman and Bill Haywood

The FBI has mounted a concerted effort to stamp out the previous editions of this book, but now it's back and better than ever in a revised, enlarged edition. You'll see why this book has had the government's panties in a wad when you thumb through it. The cofounders of Earth First! present explicit instructions, with accompanying diagrams and pictures, for spiking trees (including using ceramic pins that evade metal detectors), pulling up survey stakes, trashing powerlines, plugging waste discharge pipes, sabotaging livestock ranches, spiking roads, making tire shredders, disabling and destroying heavy equipment (bulldozers, excavators, etc.), destroying hunters' leghold traps, cutting fences, jamming locks, destroying or "modifying" billboards, and the grandaddy of them all— sinking whalers, drift netters, and other ships.

Of course, doing all this stuff is dangerous, so the editors devote more than one hundred pages to security issues—proper techniques for surveillance, camouflage, evading searches, what to do if you're caught, etc. Chances are you'll never use any of the techniques in this book, but it's so much fun just to own a book that the government would give its right arm to ban.

Abbzug Press; $20
1993; softcover; 349 pp.

*Ecodefense*
**edited by
Dave Foreman
and Bill
Haywood**

*Pissing off
the planet
killers.*

## THE EDGE COMPANY

If you're looking for a bladed weapon, you'll find it in this catalog. The Edgesters carry switchblades, butterfly knives, angel blades, stilettos, medieval daggers, bowie knives, penknives, sleeve daggers with arm holster, umbrella swords, cane swords, samurai swords, cavalry sabers, bayonets, tomahawks, straight razors, and more. I don't usually get excited about weapons, but some of these knives, such as the Raven Dagger and the pearl-handled Royal Straight, are stunning. There's also other fun stuff like blowguns, a pistol crossbow, gun lighters, stun guns, etc.

The Edge Company/PO Box 826/Brattleboro, VT 05302
Catalog: $4

## GAMBLING SCAMS:
### How They Work, How to Detect Them, How to Protect Yourself
### by Darwin Oritz

As the media have become fond of telling us, gambling is becoming a national obsession. With all this betting going on, there's a lot of opportunity to cheat, and to protect yourself you need to know how the scamsters operate. Of course, if you'd like to get in on the dirty action, this book will help you do that, too.

Oritz, "America's leading authority on crooked gambling," tells you exactly how to cheat in cards, dice, backgammon, roulette, and slot machines. He also exposes the methods behind crooked carnival games, three-card monte, con games, and bar bets. One chapter you'll want to pay close attention to reveals how casinos cheat their patrons.

Card-cheating techniques that are detailed include culling and stacking, beating the cut, the bottom deal, hand mucking, capping the deck, marking cards, and shorting pots. Dice techniques include the palm switch, tops, beards, splash moves, loading dice, the drop shot, and counter magnets. The slide shot in craps works like this: "The die to be controlled is gripped by the pinky while the other die is held loosely above it. When the dice are thrown, the freely rolling top die helps hide the fact that the bottom die only slides across the table with the same number on top throughout."

The chapter on con games ("stings") should give you all kinds of great ideas. For instance, in "The Lost Ring," an obviously rich woman pulls into a gas station, uses the bathroom, and, when she gets back to her car, realizes her unbelievably expensive diamond ring is gone. She took it off to wash her hands in the john, but she put it back on, so it has to be here somewhere. She and the station attendant look for a while, but the woman, noticing what time it is, says that she must go. She gives the attendant her name and the number of the ritzy hotel where she's staying, and says she'll pay a thousand bucks reward for the ring. Later a bum walks by the station, picks something off the ground, and starts to leave quickly. The attendant stops him and asks if he found a ring. The bum says yes, but he's keeping it. The attendant, thinking of the grand he could get, offers to pay the bum four hundred dollars for the rock. The bum agrees and leaves. The man calls the hotel, but no woman by that name is registered there. The ring is a piece of garbage. The "rich lady" and the "bum" just took him for four C-notes.

To all you young'uns out there—if you haven't decided on your future yet, this book may open up some doors for you.

Lyle Stuart (Carol Publishing Group); $11.95
1984; softcover; 262 pp.

## THE NEW IMPROVED POOR MAN'S JAMES BOND
### by Kurt Saxon

One of the undisputed champions of manuals on mayhem. This book is a grab bag of Saxon's own writings and reprints from a variety of sources, including old-time books and manuals. Some of the goodies you'll find here: recipes for prussic acid, laughing gas, poisons, and knockout drops. Instructions for firecrackers, potato masher grenades, explosives out the wazoo, tear gas, zip guns, counterfeit money. How to convert guns to full automatic. Reprints of "We Shall Fight in the Streets," "Arson by Electronics," marine and army hand-to-hand combat manuals, "Explosives, Matches, and Fireworks," and others.

Perhaps the most shocking revelation of all, though, is that Kurt Saxon, survivalist and former John Bircher, is really a pretty funny person. I love the disclaimer/explanation on the back of the book, which reads in part: "It is bad to poison your fellow man, blow him up or even shoot him or otherwise disturb his tranquillity.... But some people are just naturally crude and oafish and will, in a fit of pique, act in many ways you consider unkind. YOU, of course, are one of the Great Pumpkin's loftiest creations, so we are safe in putting this book in your hands."

Saxon has put out three other volumes and two videos in the *Poor Man's James Bond* series, each jam-packed with information on guns, silencers, explosives, mines, homemade weapons, etc. He also has two magazines going. *The Shoestring Entrepreneur* (formerly called *The Survivor*) teaches self-sufficiency skills from your grandparents' and great-grandparents' days. *U.S. Militia* contains *Poor Man's James Bond*–type material.

Atlan Formularies; $18
1988 (revised 1991); oversize softcover; 477 pp.

## PALADIN PRESS

Besides publishing many books of the type you see in this section, Paladin offers a catalog selling hundreds of books and videos on weapons, combat shooting, financial freedom, new ID, survival, sniping (for your next visit to the top of a university bell tower!), knives, silencers, special forces, police science, espionage, martial arts, locksmithing (also called "lockpicking"), action careers (bodyguards and bounty hunters), terrorism, explosives, and more. A very impressive selection.

Paladin Press/PO Box 1307/Boulder, CO 80306
Catalog: no price given but send in a couple bucks.

## PHYSICAL INTERROGATION TECHNIQUES
### by Richard W. Krousher

This book truly lives up to its reputation as one of the most disgusting books ever published. I feel unclean just touching it. I must wash my hands before approaching loved ones. But I also know my bluff has been called. I believe that information wants to be free and that every book deserves the chance to be read by as many people as possible, even a book that gives me a queasy feeling in my gizzard.

*Physical Interrogation Techniques* gives instructions for torturing people. The author, a true humanitarian, tells how to inflict maximum pain through verbal abuse, sexual violation, suspension, sensory overload and deprivation, sandpaper, clubs, whips, hot water, cigarettes, electricity, thumb screws, bonescraping, skinning, insects, etc. Despite its gruesome nature, most of this book is just common sense. And if you're such a twisted fuck that you'd actually do the things in this book, then you've probably thought up your own methods anyway.

Loompanics Unlimited; $12.95
1985; softcover; 89 pp.

## SCANNERS AND SECRET FREQUENCIES
### by Henry L. Eisenson

A great book for anyone interested in scanning. It starts out with more than fifty pages of background material on microphysics and radio principles. Another fifty pages or so discuss antennae and scanners, telling you what features to look for and what models are best (not to mention all-important instructions on modifying scanners). Next, more than one hundred pages are filled with how to listen in on the military, the government (NASA, DEA, ATF, FBI, Secret Service, etc.), Citizen's Band, emergency services, industrial radio (forestry, petroleum, telephone, motion picture production), religious groups (Jerry Falwell, the Moonies, etc.), and others. The more deviant among you will want to make special note of the information on intercepting cordless phones, cellular phones, voice beepers, and faxes. You may also want to pay attention to the full chapter devoted to the laws governing scanning (or you may not). A resources section, glossary, bibliography, and cynical sense of humor round out this book.

INDEX Publishing Group; $19.95
1993; softcover; 318 pp.

## SECRET FIGHTING TECHNIQUES OF THE WORLD
### by John F. Gilbey

John Gilbey is one bad dude. He holds a seventh *dan* in judo, a fifth *dan* in karate, and a master's certificate in Chinese boxing. He's fought some of the meanest mofos in the world, and he's delved into the secret techniques used to put people in a world of hurt. Many of Gilbey's stories may seem beyond belief, and some of his information comes second- or third-hand, but it still makes for entertaining reading, and—who knows?—it might be true.

He tells of an acquaintance who met a French judo master whose secret weapon was his breath. After years of experimentation, he had produced a combination of herbs and foods that, when he ingested it, gave him such obscenely repulsive breath that he could make his adversaries faint from as far as ten feet away outdoors. The man successfully demonstrated his killer halitosis on Gilbey's friend.

In India Gilbey encountered a master fist fighter who believed that the best offense is a good defense. He instructed Gilbey to punch him in the mouth as hard as he could. Gilbey decked him, but the master didn't even flinch. Another Indian he met had perfected the secret art of nailing people in the crotch. A third Indian he met was a member of the almost extinct Thugee cult. The Thugs were (are?) a group of assassins who worshiped Kali. Since Kali forbids the shedding of blood, because it only leads to more blood, the Thugs strangled their victims. Thugee was outlawed in 1830, and when Gilbey met this strangler in 1952, there were maybe a dozen Thugs left in India.

In probably the most hard-to-swallow but interesting of the chapters, Gilbey visits a Taiwanese master of *shaolin* (Chinese boxing), who claims to know the most feared technique in the world—the delayed death touch. The idea is based on Chinese medicine, which says that at certain times of the day, the blood circulates closer to the surface of the body in certain areas. You must know which area to strike at what time. And, of course, you have to know how to use your touch to disrupt the person's *chi* (vital energy). The master demonstrates the technique on his son, who collapses and nearly dies three days later.

Charles E. Tuttle Co; $9.95
1963; softcover; 149 pp.; illus.

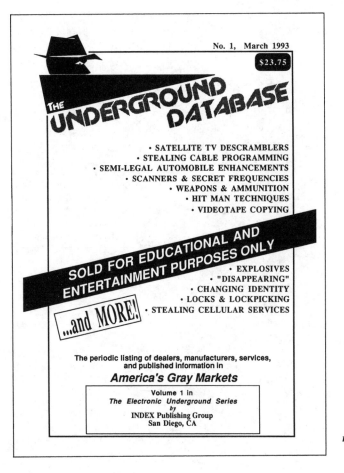

*◄ The Underground Database*

*Sends the illicit info-meter needle right off the scale.*

## THE UNDERGROUND DATABASE

This book sends the illicit info-meter needle right off the scale. It is a sourcebook/guide to America's gray markets: "Such markets are characterized by products that are legal to produce, sell, buy, and own, but that are generally used for illegal and immoral purposes. Companies that operate in these markets usually break no laws, but their products and services allow the consumer to do so."

There are three main parts to the book—"suppliers of hardware and services, publishers and sellers of literature, and the books/manuals/periodicals themselves." Categories covered are automobile "enhancement" (performance boosting and fuel economy), CB, computer hacking, credit card/ATM scams, crime and deception, explosives and fireworks, identification, lockpicking, killing, eavesdropping, revenge, revolution, scanners, smuggling, tax fraud, telephones, TV/cable/satellite, utility meter hacking, videotape copying, and weapons.

So, exactly what kind of stuff can you buy from the places listed here? A device that makes your car invisible to police radar. Cable descramblers and converters. A National Security Agency code machine! Diplomas, special weapons permits, and driver's licenses. Slim Jims, vending machine picks, etc. Nightscopes, wiretaps, long-range microphones, and spray that makes envelopes see-through. Videocipher satellite authorization codes. Caller-ID blockers. Videotape copyguard removers. Handheld rocket launchers, exploding bullets, plans to reactivate inert grenades, and more. Are you as scared as I am?

Index Publishing Group; $23.75
1993; oversize softcover; 100 pp.

# THE BODY

## AIDS

### AIDS DISSIDENTS:
#### AN ANNOTATED BIBLIOGRAPHY
#### by Ian Young

The bible of AIDS unorthodoxy! This book lists 156 books and pamphlets, 552 articles, 19 audiotapes, and 23 periodicals that offer alternative ideas and theories regarding AIDS. Every entry in the book section is accompanied by a quote from the book, a one- to two-page summary, and the address of the publisher. The audiotapes and periodicals contain brief annotations and addresses. Most of the articles listed are accompanied by a brief annotation.

Any work that challenges any aspect of orthodox AIDS thinking is included. These books, articles, and other materials offer contrary opinions on the cause and origin of AIDS, the role of HIV, how AIDS is spread, the effectiveness of AZT, the use of natural therapies, the survival of people with AIDS, the politics and economics of AIDS, the benefits of safe sex, the role of the media, and much more. Conflicting and competing theories are welcome.

The book's biggest drawback is that, although it was published in 1993, the author only includes materials issued by December 1, 1990, "though a few later items of importance have been added." He doesn't explain why he chose to disregard two to three years of material, particularly when much of it is very important. Still, *AIDS Dissidents* is invaluable for anyone serious about probing the mysteries of this disease.

Scarecrow Press; $32.50
1993; hardcover; 264 pp.

### AIDS:
#### THE MYSTERY AND THE SOLUTION
#### (SECOND EDITION)
#### by Alan Cantwell Jr., M.D.

Written in 1983 and updated in 1986, this book is an early attempt to offer an alternative explanation for AIDS. At the time, HIV had not yet been pronounced by the medical establishment as the cause of AIDS. When this book was written, cytomegalovirus and then the HTLV-3 virus were deemed the most likely suspects. Cantwell discusses these viruses, providing a snapshot of AIDS research before HIV orthodoxy set in.

Cantwell believes that a mycobacterium causes AIDS. He also advances the heretical notion that cancer is caused by a mycobacterium, perhaps the same one that causes AIDS. After presenting his own research and that of others, Cantwell presents the following hypotheses, among others: "...2) Certain kinds of cancer *and* AIDS may both be produced by the same, or similar, bacterial microbes. 3) Both cancer and AIDS may be infectious diseases. 4) On the basis of epidemiologic data, Kaposi's sarcoma may be one of the most infectious and contagious forms of cancer. 5) The *origin* of the bacteria which cause AIDS, may be either from bacteria already in the body, (endogenous infection), or by bacteria acquired from the external environment, (exogenous infection), or both."

As an aside, I have to mention something Cantwell brought up in his discussion of cancer as a bacterial disease. He presents research, which he says has been suppressed, showing that smegma may cause cervical cancer in heterosexual women.

Aries Rising Press; $9.95
1986; softcover; 210 pp.

### THE AIDS WAR:
#### PROPAGANDA, PROFITEERING AND GENOCIDE FROM THE MEDICAL-INDUSTRIAL COMPLEX
#### by John Lauritsen

Lauritsen has been on the front line of the AIDS war, throwing punches, since 1985. This book collects his writings, mostly published in the *New York Native*, from that time until 1993. Lauritsen uncompromisingly slams the hell out of the mainstream AIDS organizations ("On the whole, it would've been better if not a single AIDS organization had ever come into existence"), journalist and AIDS orthodoxist Duncan Campbell ("...his approach: fostering of fear and suspicion, character assassinations based on unsubstantiated charges, guilt-by-association, violent rhetoric, malignant innuendos, repudiation of logic"), the HIV theory ("So far, the so-called 'AIDS virus' [HIV], has ignominiously failed to fulfill even one of the bacteriologist Robert Koch's three laws for 'establishing the specificity of a pathogenic microorganism' "), AZT ("I argued that there is no scientifically credible evidence AZT has any benefits whatsoever, that AZT is a toxic drug..."), and much, much more. *AIDS War* is a veritable encyclopedia of unorthodox thinking about AIDS.

ASKLEPIOS; $20
1993; softcover; 479 pp.

*The Aids War*
*by John*
*Lauritsen*

*A veritable*
*encyclopedia*
*of unorthodox*
*thinking*
*about AIDS.*

### THE CURE FOR HIV AND AIDS
#### by Hulda Regehr Clark, Ph.D., N.D.

The author makes no bones about it: "Cure, not treatment, is the subject of this book." Dr. Clark, who has a doctorate in biophysics, claims to have discovered the exact nature of HIV and how to get rid of it. By following her instructions, she claims, you can be rid of HIV in five days, although it may take up to two years for your body to recover fully from the virus.

HIV results from the fluke family of parasites, especially *Fasciolopsis buskii*, which have heavily infested the human population. These flukes are on the upswing because they have found a biological reservoir in cattle, birds, and pets. Solvents, such as benzene, methanol, xylene, and wood alcohol, promote the growth of these microscopic pests. These solvents are now present in animal feed, accounting for the infestation of animals. On top of that, the same solvents are in practically everything we eat and drink. They allow flukes to go through an entire life cycle in our bodies.

The solvent benzene builds up in the thymus, where it attracts hordes of flukes. HIV, it turns out, is actually a parasite feeding off of *Fasciolopsis*. It needs this fluke to survive, because when the flukes in your body are killed, the HIV dies within twenty-four hours. Therefore, if you have HIV, you need to do three things: "1. Kill the intestinal fluke and all its stages." This will get rid of HIV. Then, to make sure it stays gone: "2. Rid your body of benzene. 3. Clean up your thymus gland."

Clark tells exactly how to do all of these things. She gives exact herbal recipes that will destroy *Fasciolopsis*. Keeping solvents, flukes, and other immunological stressors out of your body isn't as easy, but she gives instructions. Basically, everything around us in the modern world damages our immune systems—shampoo, soft drinks, plumbing, carpeting, dental fillings and crowns, meat, pets, and much more. You have to either get rid of these things or find safe alternatives.

As far as the AIDS-sex connection goes, Clark thinks that the fluke (and thus HIV) are in bodily fluids and can be transmitted by sex and even kissing. However, if our bodies were completely free of benzene, the fluke and HIV couldn't survive, so we couldn't get AIDS from exchanging bodily fluids or by any other means.

*The Cure* also contains the case histories of seventy people who Clark claims were cured of HIV when they followed her instructions exactly. Finally, there are instructions for creating a simple electronic device that can test for harmful substances in various elements and in your body.

If it's cancer, not AIDS, that you're fighting, the publisher also carries a companion volume—*The Cure for All Cancers* (Clark is not one for modesty)—for the same price.

ProMotion Publishing; $19.95
1993; softcover; 430 pp; illus.

# AMERICA'S BIGGEST COVER-UP:
## 50 More Things Everyone Should Know About the Chronic Fatigue Syndrome Epidemic and Its Link to AIDS
### by Neenyah Ostrom

Ostrom, a *New York Native* reporter, has been investigating chronic fatigue syndrome (CFS) for six years and has interviewed major researchers, government scientists, and patients. In this, her third book on CFS, she presents the theory that CFS and AIDS are actually both caused by the same virus, Human Herpes Virus-6. People with CFS and AIDS suffer many of the same symptoms and immunological problems. For example, Ostrom believes that the purple throat lesions found in most CFS patients are related to Kaposi's sarcoma, an AIDS-linked cancer.

The book is divided into fifty bite-size sections dealing with various aspects of Ostrom's findings. Not all of the sections deal with the CFS/AIDS connection; many concern controversial findings dealing with CFS, making it required reading for anyone concerned with CFS, as well as AIDS. (Ostrom's first two books on CFS are put out by the same publisher.)

That New Magazine, Inc; $14.95
1993; hardcover; 86 pp.

# DEADLY INNOCENCE
## by Dr. Leonard G. Horowitz

All right, the title sounds like a bad made-for-TV-movie, but don't let it fool you. This is a mind-blowing, controversial book of the first degree. It concerns Kimberly Bergalis, the young Florida woman who contracted AIDS from her dentist and became a media celebrity when she testified before Congress about the possibility of AIDS transmission from medical practitioners to patients. It also concerns Dr. Davis Acer, the dentist who infected Bergalis and five of his other patients with AIDS. But this is not a story of accidental AIDS transmission. The author claims that Acer was a psychopath who deliberately infected his patients by injecting his own blood into them.

According to the author, Acer had had sex with more than one hundred men and boys by the time he tested HIV-positive in 1986. Even though authorities knew that Acer had AIDS and was mentally unstable, he was allowed to continue his practice. During a year-and-a-half period, Acer infected six of his patients with AIDS by injecting syringes full of his blood into their mouths during operations. The Centers for Disease Control and Florida government officials investigated this cluster of dentist-to-patient AIDS transmissions and ruled them accidental, despite much evidence to the contrary, which they concealed to protect themselves from liability and embarrassment. The author methodically reveals all of this and more, including evidence

linking present attorney general Janet Reno and Hillary Rodham Clinton to the cover-up.

This is a hard-hitting book that presents evidence that was ignored by the media, which preferred to scare the hell out of people with the implausible accidental transmission theory. The author wonders how many people were so frightened by this scenario that they developed a fear of doctors and dentists and are now denying themselves necessary health treatment.

Tetrahedron Industries; $14.95
1994; softcover; 314 pp.

# THE MYTH OF HETEROSEXUAL AIDS:
## How a Tragedy Has Been Distorted by the Media and Partisan Politics
### by Michael Fumento

Is AIDS truly a democratic disease? Are the predictions of a plague sweeping the heterosexual population true? Not according to this book. Fumento gathers up research and statistics showing that AIDS is a disease that discriminates against sexually active gay men, IV drug users, and poor African-Americans and Hispanics.

*Myth* was published in 1989, and since then its central thesis has proven correct. The pandemic that was to make the Black Death look pale by comparison—predicted by Health and Human Services Secretary Otis Bowen, Surgeon General C. Everett Koop, and *U.S. News and World Report*, among others—has not come to pass. Fumento discusses the risks of heterosexual intercourse, AIDS in Africa, condoms, conservative alarmists, the media's role, and much more. This edition of the book contains two appendixes written in 1993, including one filled with statistics from medical journals and the Centers for Disease Control that support the author's thesis.

At least as interesting as the book is the absolute furor it unleashed, documented in the new introduction. Bookstores around the country refused to carry it, based partially on a letter-writing campaign that started before the book was even completed. A Seattle TV station, doing a piece on this conspiracy of silence, contacted more than eighty different stores without finding a single copy of the book. Only one store had ever even carried it. "One university book store in Seattle claimed to have over 350,000 titles, including every single AIDS title in print. Except one." Keep in mind, *Myth* was originally published by Basic Books, an imprint of the huge publishing house Harper-Collins, one of the best-distributed publishers in the country.

It gets worse, though. People checked out the book from libraries across the country and never returned it. *Forbes* magazine ran a noncommittal article about the controversy, and under pressure from ACT UP, Malcolm Forbes Sr. himself ran a retraction in the next issue, damning Fumento's views. The esteemed science journal *Nature* let a nonscientist AIDS activist trash the book in a review and then refused to run Fumento's rebuttal.

There's more, but suffice it to say that this is truly one of the most controversial and suppressed books of recent times. Whether you think it's right or not, it belongs on the bookshelves of those strange souls who want to hear all sides of every issue.

Regnery Publishing; $14.95
1993; softcover; 463 pp.

# PRAXIS:
## A Journal Exploring AIDS as Crisis in Consciousness

The aim of this journal is to "offer a fresh challenge to the dominant beliefs defining aids up to now, namely: that aids is always fatal, that it has a viral cause (hiv), that hiv inevitably leads to aids which leads to death, that azt (or anything like it) is the best hope we have for treatment, and that aids is a single (or contagious) disease, or even a sexually transmitted disease.... We embrace a multi-causal perspective on aids which opens the door to a multi-solution response.... Our work focuses on using hiv and aids as a catalyst for self transformation."

The winter 1993 issue contains an interview with molecular biologist Peter Duesberg, who rejects the HIV hypothesis, an interview with a woman who temporarily sero-converted from HIV-positive to HIV-negative, an article that questions the accuracy of HIV testing, and more. The spring 1994 issue contains "Why the Aids Numbers Don't Add Up," "The Tao of Health, Sex, and Longevity," "If It Isn't Hiv, What Is It?" and "Allowing Wellness."

CURENOW/PO Box 29386/Los Angeles, CA 90029
Single issue: $5; foreign: $7
One year sub (3 issues): $15; foreign: $25

## QUEER BLOOD:
### THE SECRET AIDS GENOCIDE PLOT
### by Alan Cantwell Jr, M.D.

In this book Cantwell argues that AIDS was created by the military and purposely introduced into the human population to obliterate the gay male population, as well as African-Americans. When I started reading this book, I was prepared for a meticulously documented argument for this theory. Instead, I found *Queer Blood* to be more of an essay and at times a rant. Information was presented in a disjointed manner, leaving me confused about several issues. Namely, exactly how was the AIDS virus engineered? How did its creators know that it would affect gays but not hets? And how was it supposed to decimate the African-American population if it was intended mainly for gay men?

Cantwell does do a good job, though, of showing that the Department of Defense was apparently working in 1969 on developing a virus that would cause AIDS. He also points out the flaws (and racism) in the official explanation of the origin and spread of AIDS. Although *Queer Blood* doesn't cohere as a unit, it does make many interesting points.

Aries Rising Press; $12.95
1993; softcover; 157 pp.

## CANCER

## CENSURED FOR CURING CANCER:
### THE AMERICAN EXPERIENCE OF DR. MAX GERSON
### by S.J. Haught

In 1959, S.J. Haught, a reporter for a New York newspaper, was preparing an attack piece on Dr. Max Gerson, who was claiming to have cured some people of cancer with a special natural diet. While researching "The Unveiling of a Quack"—interviewing Gerson and his patients, looking at X rays and medical records, writing to the AMA—Haught realized that Gerson had indeed cured cancer. He tells of how the truth became apparent during his investigation. He also claims that Gerson has also cured people of lupus and tuberculosis. Gerson had cured Albert Schweitzer's wife of TB after all traditional methods had failed.

The evidence of Gerson's success is presented clearly. So, too, is the medical establishment's resistance to his therapy. Yet another example of someone who has cured cancer and been harassed and rejected by organized medicine.

Station Hill Press; $6.95
1962; softcover; 135 pp.

## A CANCER THERAPY:
### RESULTS OF FIFTY CASES
### by Max Gerson, M.D.

For those who desire a deeper look at Max Gerson's cancer treatment than given in the above book, this book is the one in which Gerson "spills the beans." In response to the number of physicians asking for Gerson's "secret," he wrote this book

explaining his theories of cancer, disease in general, and nutrition; the exact diet his patients use; and the case histories of fifty patients who were cured.

Gerson's underlying principle is this: "A normal body has the capacity to keep all cells functioning properly. It prevents any abnormal transformation and growth. Therefore, the natural task of cancer therapy is to bring the body back to that normal physiology, or as near to it as is possible." To do this, Gerson's anticancer diet requires lots of freshly prepared juices, unpeeled fruits and vegetables, and coffee and castor oil enemas. Canned foods, tobacco, spices, chocolate, refined sugar and flour, and other fun stuff is verboten. No, it isn't the funnest regimen in the world, but has chemotherapy beat by a mile.

This is obviously *the* book to get if you're interested in trying Gerson therapy.

Station Hill Press; $14.95
1958; softcover; 434 pp.

*Sharks Don't Get Cancer* by Dr. I. William Lane and Linda Comac (See page 154) ▼

*Research showing that shark cartilage could combat cancer.*

## THE IMMORTAL CELL:
### WHY CANCER RESEARCH FAILS
### by Dr. Gerald B. Dermer

After forty fruitless years in the war against cancer, the reason the war is being lost may have been discovered. The author is a cell biologist and biochemist who studied cancer in a hospital for years by experimenting with living cancer tumors that were recently taken out of patients. When he moved to laboratory research at a med school, he noticed a fundamental difference in the way experimentation was done. The labs used cancer cells that were grown in a petri dish. These cell lines, as they are called, are used as models for human cancer cells. The only problem is, says the author, cell lines aren't anything like real human cancer cells. They live forever (hence the title of the book). All the data and findings based on these cell lines has very little to do with actual cancer. And cell lines are being used at the National Cancer Institute and most other bastions of the cancer establishment. So why use cell lines instead of the real thing? Because cell lines are convenient to store and transport, multiply quickly, and are easy to manipulate. They are based on molecular biology, the dogma of cancer researchers. And they have now become so entrenched that sheer inertia also keeps them in use. Many researchers realize the uselessness of cell cultures, but "scientists who question this model find themselves cut off from funding, removed from academic appointments, and locked out of the ivory towers of the cancer establishment."

In looking at this literally fatal error, the author examines politics, the biotechnology industry, chemotherapy and immunotherapy, breast cancer, and the promise of better cancer-cell models.

Avery Publishing Group; $11.95
1994; softcover; 212 pp.

## OPTIONS:
### THE ALTERNATIVE CANCER THERAPY BOOK
### by Richard Walters

When people get cancer, their three choices are: getting cut open (surgery), getting burned (radiation therapy), or getting poisoned (chemotherapy). Most people are unaware that there are many more choices than these. There is evidence that many of these alternative options have gotten rid of the cancer in some of the patients who tried them. Unfortunately, these

Gesundheit! ➤
by Dr. Patch
Adams

*"How to
Be a Nutty
Doctor."
A healer
with heart.*

wonderful opportunities have been hidden from us.

This incomparable book breaks the Health Police's information blackout in a big way by covering a large number of unorthodox cancer treatments/cures. It tells how each therapy works, which treatments work best on what cancers, the scientific and testimonial evidence that they work, and—most importantly—the addresses of groups who practice these therapies, so you can undergo them yourself. This book covers every alternative cancer therapy I had ever heard of and then some: Hoxsey Therapy, Gerson Therapy, Revici Therapy, hydrazine sulfate, mistletoe, macrobiotics, oxygen therapy, shark cartilage, mind/body healing, Chinese medicine, and several others. The writing is clear, in-depth, and jargon-free. *You absolutely must get this book if you or anyone you care about has cancer.*

Avery Publishing Group; $13.95
1993; softcover; 396 pp.

## SHARKS DON'T GET CANCER:
### HOW SHARK CARTILAGE COULD SAVE YOUR LIFE
### by Dr. I. William Lane and Linda Comac

Cancer tumors are nourished by a web of blood vessels that develop around the tumor. Shark cartilage contains a substance that inhibits the development of these blood vessels, thus slowing down or stopping the growth of the tumor and possibly even shrinking it. Shark cartilage might also prevent metastasis, the spread of cancer cells to other parts of the body.

The author describes the groundbreaking research that showed shark cartilage could combat cancer and looks at the successful clinical trials that have been going in Costa Rica and Mexico. He tells of his fight to make shark cartilage available (you can get it in health food stores, but it's extremely expensive). Shark cartilage may help combat other conditions, such as arthritis, blindness, and the heartbreak of psoriasis, all of which are discussed.

Avery Publishing Group; $11.95
1992; softcover; 186 pp.

# ALTERNATIVE HEALTH

## THE ANTI-AGING PLAN:
### STRATEGIES AND RECIPES FOR
### EXTENDING YOUR HEALTHY YEARS
### by Roy L. Walford, M.D., and Lisa Walford

Roy Walford was the physician for that peculiar world within a world, the Biosphere 2. During the first six months of the experiment, the Biospherians' bodies underwent amazing changes thanks to their low-calorie/high-nutrient diet. Their blood cholesterol levels went from an average of 191 to 123. Their average blood pressure fell from 110/75 to 90/58. They lost a lot of weight, and the two members with severe acne saw it clear up. The author also points to animal studies using the same type of diet, in which the animals underwent improvements in memory, sexual functioning, and appearance. This amazing diet purports to lengthen your lifespan and increase your quality of life.

"All right," you say. "I'm sold on the effects, but what kind of grub am I gonna have to eat to be a permanent lean, mean, fighting machine?" The bulk of the book is made up of more than a hundred recipes from Roy and his daughter, Lisa. Common ingredients include wild rice, buckwheat, whole-wheat flour, corn meal, black beans, soybeans, almonds, sesame seeds, seaweeds, raisins, brewer's yeast, shiitake mushrooms, tuna, corn,

peas, and all kinds of herbs and spices. The recipes really don't look too bad. Many of them include meat, although vegetarian versions of these recipes are also given. Dishes include pizza, three-bean chili, lasagna, chow mein, stuffed peppers, french toast, creole gumbo, stovetop-grilled salmon, chicken fajitas with salsa, cheese salad, spiced tomatoes, and other pretty yummy-sounding meals. The Walfords also offer tips, tricks, and shortcuts for the food preparation.

Four Walls Eight Windows; $19.95
1994; hardcover; 309 pp.

## BEES DON'T GET ARTHRITIS
### by Fred Malone

In a folksy (bordering on cutesy) style, Fred Malone tells us about his cross-country quest to find out about the curative properties of bee stings, pollen, propolis, and honey. He visited beekeepers all over the United States and found a lot of testimonials to the power of bee venom to alleviate arthritis, rheumatism, bursitis, Hodgkin's disease, and allergies. The author even used it to bring relief to his own arthritic knees.

There's a good deal of anecdotal evidence to support bee venom's powers, including the New York Cancer Institute's proclamation in 1965 that "beekeepers have the lowest incidence of cancer of all the occupations." But there's also more empirical evidence available, which the doctor relates. Many doctors have used bee venom therapy and achieved spectacular success. Of course, this doesn't prove anything to skeptics who note that every weird therapy has had doctors who claim it works. Well, chew on this—the *Annals of Internal Medicine* in 1938 and the *Nebraska Medical Journal* in 1939 both ran articles in which M.D.s performing experiments with bee venom serum achieved incredible results. The authors of the first study, running their experiment under the auspices of Cornell University, concluded: "In estimating the results obtained from this study of an injectable form of bee venom (Apicosan) for rheumatoid arthritis one is impressed with the definite improvement in the clinical symptoms... It would seem, therefore, that bee venom is worthy of further study." As we know now, the rest of the medical community didn't think it was worthy of further study, and bee venom (along with other bee products) has become yet another "quack therapy" that actually works.

Academy Books; $13.95
1979; softcover; 179 pp.

## EXPLORE MORE!

A slick magazine that covers a wide range of alternative health options. Typical topics include vitamins and minerals, cancer therapies, electromagnetic fields, menopause, body-energy healing practices, aromatherapy, toxins in our environment, etc. Good reporting from the mainstream alternative health movement (which is still pretty radical when compared with the medicofascist mind-set that dominates America).

Explore More!/PO Box 1508/Mt. Vernon, WA 98273
Single issue: $7
Six-issue sub: $39; foreign: $49 (for airmail add $10)

## EXPLORE! FOR THE PROFESSIONAL

A sibling publication of *Explore More!*, this magazine contains articles on alternative therapies written by professionals (including many M.D.s and Ph.D.s) for professionals. It presents detailed, fairly technical findings, from experiments and anecdotal evidence, plus theories, politics, legalities, and speculation. Articles in Volume 5 #1 covered motor neuron disease treated with Neurotrophin II, natural medicine for recovering addicts, color therapy, pH and electrolyte balance, the legal aspects of breast implants, and more.

Explore!/PO Box 1508/Mt. Vernon, WA 98273
Single issue: $12.50
Six-issue sub: $59 (for continental U.S.);
Hawaii, Alaska, and foreign: $75 (for airmail add $25)

## GESUNDHEIT!
### by Patch Adams, M.D.

In 1971 Dr. Patch Adams and company founded the Gesundheit Institute in West Virginia. This healing center is located on a farm. Patients stay in buildings that look like homes—because they are homes. Doctors often dress in clown costumes, and they practice complementary therapies mixed with lots of laughter and joy. Doctors and patients talk openly and discuss options. If you think this doesn't sound like any hospital you've ever been to, just wait till you find out the kicker—it's all free. Thanks to generous benefactors, the Gesundheit Institute doesn't charge for its services.

Patch presents a beautiful vision of healing that remembers that the people who are sick and even dying are still humans who want to love, laugh, and live. The techniques of person-centered healing Patch gives in this book range from the humorous to the touching. In "How to be a Nutty Doctor," he has this advice about dressing: "I love mixing colors that clash and combining stripes and checks, all surefire chuckle stealers. Hats are one of the easiest ways to have fun. Might I recommend a fire hat or a space helmet with a whirring mouthpiece?" Patch feels that dying in a hospital surrounded by strangers is unnatural. "So I encouraged patients to die at home and agreed to attend to them there. Each time I have done so, a great deal of fear has been removed from the death experience."

The Gesundheit gang is currently building a full-fledged hospital and healing community based on their unique vision of healing. It will offer free services to everyone. The struggle to construct such a visionary resource is thoroughly detailed in the last part of the book.

Inner Traditions International; $12.95
1993; softcover; 208 pp.

## THE HEALING PATH:
### A SOUL APPROACH TO ILLNESS
### by Marc Ian Barasch

Barasch was the editor of the *New Age Journal* when he found out that he had cancer. He left his job and spent seven years trying to find out, not just how to rid the body of cancer, but how such a catastrophic disease affects the entire human being—body, mind, spirit—and how the disease can be a springboard to greater personal understanding. Barasch wanted to discover "how a condition of the flesh could become an inescapable dilemma of the human spirit."

This is a somewhat hard concept for us residents of a material society to grasp, so I'll let the author explain further: "The dark labyrinth of illness does not have a simple escape route. Still, each juncture of our journey presents a choice, a turning point: whether to split ourselves off from our own experience, or make what is happening, horrific though it may be, part of our larger process of Becoming. For if we can fully inhabit our life when it is both most painfully constricted and paradoxically fraught with potential—if, even as our feet carry us into the maze, we can proceed with our eyes open rather than squeezed shut—we will inevitably discern a path of creative response.

"I do not wish to romanticize illness as some True Path to Enlightenment. There are other ways to unearth our inner treasure than to excavate it from the flesh with a backhoe."

The key is to view illness as a symptom of a deeper imbalance in and between the body and spirit. Using many people he has met as examples, the author shows how to deal with doctors, regain control, explore alternative medicine, tap the healer within, etc. Though the ideas offered are not new, they are presented with such clarity and hope that this book is well worth getting if you want an alternative perspective on life-threatening illnesses.

Putnam; $22.95
1993; hardcover; 431 pp.

## THE HEART OF HEALING
### by The Institute of Noetic Sciences
### with William Poole

This coffee-table book, a companion piece to the TBS documentary of the same name, presents a good overview of the field of mind-body medicine. It covers the role of attitude, the link between the mind and the immune system, spontaneous remission, laughter, deep relaxation, religious miracles, the placebo effect, hypnotism, shamanism, stress, crying, visualization, touch, music, and just about every other aspect of the mind/body juncture you could name. The book draws on scientific research, personal stories, sociology, and anthropology in presenting its findings.

The most interesting parts of the book relate incidents showing that there has to be something to all of this mind/body talk. Scientists can dispute medical studies of placebos all they want, but in the end there are occurrences that just plain defy the paradigm offered by modern medicine. For example, the book tells of a boy with multiple personalities. He drinks orange juice, which all but one personality is allergic to. As he slips into that personality, his rashes disappear; when that personality leaves, his rashes come back. Then there are the cases of "voodoo deaths." When some members of indigenous tribes, such as the Biami of New Guinea, learn that a sorcerer has put a death spell on them, they lie down and die within twenty-four hours. Science cannot explain the reasons, but the mind-body connection suggests that these people are so convinced they're going to die that it becomes a self-fulfilling prophecy.

Turner Publishing; $24.95
1993; oversize hardcover; 192 pp.

*The Heart Of Healing by The Institute of Noetic Sciences*

*Exploring the undeniable link between mind and body.*

## SECOND OPINION

This newsletter is from Dr. William Campbell Douglass, a renegade M.D. who tells it like it is. He advises his readers not to exercise much, not to worry about cholesterol, and to stay away from doctors, except when it's absolutely necessary. His monthly newsletter is an information-dense document crammed with findings, often from prestigious medical journals, which are ignored by mainstream medicine.

The August 1994 issue has long articles on the drug companies' fruitless battle against insomnia, the flesh-eating bacterium, and the danger of ultrasound screening. Each article ends with advice from the Doc on what you *should* do concerning each of these problems. The smaller articles covered a new study showing that antioxidants do slow aging, a new treatment for dizziness, the return of tuberculosis, a surge in the number of Germans living past one hundred, the superiority of breast milk over formula milk, and much more.

What makes *Second Opinion* even better is Doc's informal and humorous writing style, which makes his newsletter a joy to read. While bashing the rage over patches (to make you stop smoking, lose weight, etc.), he writes, "If the method would just work for curing stupidity and naiveté, then all the patch-pushers would be out of business. (There's an incongruity there but never mind.)" He also gets steamed about the American Medical Association selling mailing lists of its physician members to businesses: "I wish I was still a member of the AMA—so I could quit again!"

Second Opinion Publishing
PO Box 467939/Atlanta, GA 31146-7939
Single issue: free
One-year sub (12 issues): $49; foreign: $62

## THIRTY PLANTS THAT COULD SAVE YOUR LIFE!
### by Douglas Schar

This book is written in an extremely down-to-earth, humorous style. It's like having a friend talk to you about all these great plants and what they can do for you. The author has picked the thirty plants most used for healing worldwide. Many have been used for millennia for a large number of medicinal purposes, all of which are discussed here. Angelica, cinnamon, dandelion, echinacea, mint, and red clover are a few of the plants making an appearance. Besides relating their history and uses, Schar also gives tips for the best ways to ingest each one. At the end of the book he gives recipes for tonics for men and for women, hangovers, immunity building, colds, and more. Finally, there are addresses for herb suppliers. Well-written, lovingly designed, and practical—what more could you ask of a book?

> Elliot & Clark Publishing; $12.95
> 1993; softcover; 134 pp.

## WELL BEING JOURNAL

An extremely well-done "give-away" tabloid from Seattle that contains news and views pertinent to everybody, not just those living in the Coffee and Grunge Capital of the World. Lots of reprints, original articles, and snippets about suppressed cures, natural remedies, FDA follies, health care reform, hidden health hazards, and more. Check out this item from spring 1994: "'The American public does not have the knowledge to make wise health care decisions... FDA is the arbiter of truth... Trust us. We will tell you what's good for you.'—David Kessler, M.D., Commissioner of the Food and Drug Administration, on the *Larry King Live Show.*"

> Well Being Journal/PO Box 718/Issaquah WA 98027-0718
> Single issue: $4; Canada: $5
> Six-issue sub (one year): $18; Canada: $24.50

# MEDICAL MAYHEM

## DIRTY MEDICINE:
### SCIENCE, BIG BUSINESS AND THE ASSAULT ON NATURAL HEALTH CARE
### by Martin J. Walker

This book examines the ways in which the medical and scientific establishments, pharmaceutical companies, and the governments of England and the United States have waged a war against natural, alternative medicine. Published in Britain, this book gives a lot of good information about the War on Health on the other side of the Atlantic, something that most American readers probably aren't familiar with. But it also covers struggles in the United States in depth, making it a doubly valuable source of information.

Much attention is given to the interlocking of science, medicine, government, and nongovernmental "watchdog" agencies that are actually propaganda machines for orthodox medicine. These agencies looking out for "health fraud" work closely with the FDA and other advocates of "surgery and drug" medicine. The American Council on Science and Health, which would have you think it's an objective think tank, "is funded by many of the largest chemical companies: such as American Cyanamid, Amoco Foundation, Dow Chemicals of Canada, Hooker Chemical and Plastics Corp., Mobil Foundation, Monsanto Fund, and the Shell Companies Foundation. ACSH has published two cancer reports, both of which exonerate chemicals.... The organisation receives money from all the industrial sectors which contribute to the production of chemically-treated foodstuffs." The British Nutrition Foundation is similarly funded by multinational food, pharmaceutical, and chemical corporations.

*Dirty Medicine* tells the shameful stories of alternative health practitioners such as Dr. Jacques Benveniste, Dr. William Rea (who examines links between our environment and health), Dr. Jean Monro, nutritional doctor Stephen Davies, Patrick Holford of the Institute for Optimum Nutrition, and others who have been attacked and persecuted by organized medicine. The author also dishes out some stinging criticism of pro-science groups that attack natural medicine. Foremost among these groups is the Committee for Scientific Investigation of Claims of the Paranormal (CSICOP) and its British counterparts.

Finally, the author devotes a large part of the book to AZT and the company that invented it, the Wellcome Foundation. AZT was packaged, promoted, and hyped "like any other commodity" by PR firms and advertising agencies. It has made hundreds of millions of dollars for Wellcome, proving that AIDS is a very lucrative disease. The author sees the marketing of AZT as a symbolic turning point, during which the battle against alternative therapies became an all-out, "all's fair" war. I'm not sure how much I agree with this last point. After all, the establishment's battle against natural health care was at a fever pitch long before AZT came around. Just ask Wilhelm Reich, who had his books burned, equipment destroyed, and was thrown in jail (where he died) by the U.S. government in the 1950s, because he was curing people of cancer by natural means.

> Slingshot Publications; $24 (UK: £15)
> 1993; softcover; 729 pp.

## THE FDA FOLLIES:
### AN ALARMING LOOK AT OUR FOOD AND DRUGS IN THE 1980S
### by Herbert Burkholz

It's hard to imagine a book being more embarrassing to a government agency. *Follies* shows that the FDA is a slow, compromised, assbackwards dinosaur that doesn't know its elbow from its asshole. And we're trusting our bodies and our lives to these people? I shudder at the thought.

The Food and Drug Administration hit a new low during the Reagan-Bush years (aka the dark ages). Like the rest of the government, the FDA developed a lovey-dovey relationship with the industries it was supposed to be regulating. Remember the Dalkon Shield fiasco? It was an IUD that was infecting and even killing its users. Many women became pregnant and experienced spontaneous septic abortions. Because of public outcry, the manufacturer withdrew its "safe and effective IUD" from the market. What was the FDA's role during this mess? Nothing. Despite holding hearings and receiving requests to recall the device, the FDA didn't act.

Of course, this was during the 1970s, before the FDA had been specifically mandated to regulate medical devices, so this gives them a thin, morally weak excuse. They have no such excuse with the Bjork-Shiley 60-degree heart valve. Inherently flawed in design and improperly built, this valve was malfunctioning and killing a scary number of recipients. Despite overwhelming evidence that this device should never have been put on the marketplace, the FDA sat on its heels for years. This time it was the overwhelming number of lawsuits against the manufacturer that resulted in the valve being withdrawn from the market.

The train of travesties keeps on rolling; drug companies paying off FDA officials for speedy approval of generic drugs; the FDA's bumbling of silicone breast implants; the FDA's war on vitamins; the Chilean grape scare of 1989, in which two grapes from Chile found to contain cyanide had probably been poisoned in the FDA's own labs; how the FDA and blood banks fiddled while the blood supply became contaminated with HIV; and the FDA's failure to do anything when the Kellogg Co. began making specific health claims about its cereals, a practice that is strictly forbidden.

> Basic Books (HarperCollins); $23
> 1994; hardcover; 228 pp.

## FDA FOOD AND DRUG INSIDER REPORT

A sixteen-page newsletter giving the inside scoop on what the FDA is up to. The May 16, 1994, issue looks at a phone-in on May 6 made by alternative health supporters to the FDA. The point was to jam up lines and cripple the FDA. Although the FDA wasn't brought to its knees, the message was heard loud and clear. FDA head honcho David Kessler claimed to have gotten death threats during the phone-in, but the *FDIR* shows that the alleged threats had not been reported to officials as of May 13.

This issue also prints a transcript of the kid-gloves interview Larry King gave Kessler, a listing of FDA register notices, and articles on dietary supplement legislation in Congress, food advertising guidelines, and a lawsuit brought against an FDA-approved orthopedic device.

This is a great resource to have, but unfortunately it's aimed at organizations with a professional need to know this information. In other words, it costs an arm and a leg.

Capitol Insiders, Inc/PO Box 1846/Herndon, VA 22070
One-year sub (23 issues): $100 for individuals and nonprofits; $425 for for-profit companies

## THE GREAT WHITE LIE:
### DISHONESTY, WASTE, AND INCOMPETENCE IN THE MEDICAL COMMUNITY
### by Walt Bogdanich

An investigative report that hospitals would like to see disappear from the face of the earth. The author blows the whistle on doctor's kickbacks, billing fraud, untrained nurses, hospitals that don't tell families that loved ones have died, and doctors who are bad for their patients' health. He relates how a homeless man pretended to be a doctor at Bellevue Hospital in New York. He slept, ate, and stole at the hospital for a week and eventually committed a rape/murder—and no one realized it until the end.

Hospitals are faced with shortages of nurses, owing to low pay and bad working conditions. To fill the gaps they hire "nurse temps," some of whom are untrained, incompetent, alcoholic, and able to escape retribution because they're only temps.

The Northern Virginia Doctors Hospital let a woman's cervical cancer go undiagnosed for two years, and by then it was too late to save her life. How could this happen? The hospital had "built its Pap test program around a part-time, foreign medical graduate who had flunked her boards in clinical pathology. The hospital paid her little more than Burger King wages—$5.90 an hour—to search for cancer in her spare time. Although she held down another, full-time job, the analyst still found time to screen about twice the number of Pap slides that experts say can be accurately reviewed by a full-time worker."

After reading the roll call of horrors in this book, I can only offer this sage advice: don't get sick!

Touchstone (Simon & Schuster); $11
1991; softcover; 320 pp.

## MAKING MEDICINE, MAKING MONEY
### by Donald Drake and Marian Uhlman

This book is a gloves-off look at the ways in which the pharmaceutical industry jacks up their prices and gouges the consumer. For example, when Congress passed a law in 1990 requiring drug companies to give discounts to Medicaid, they simply raised the prices of their drugs and then gave discounts on the increased prices.

Whenever the government looks into why drug prices have risen three times faster than inflation in the last decade, the pharmaceutical industry bitches and moans about the high cost of research. In reality, the companies have found a way around this. "They buy other people's research or merge with companies that have promising drugs. They benefit from basic research done by federal or academic laboratories [your tax dollars at work!]. They get substantial tax breaks or other incentives to develop and produce many of the drugs for which they charge high prices.... They even

put premium prices on drugs they did not develop." Drug companies often boost the prices of their old drugs, long after any R&D costs have been recouped. "Decadron, an allergy medicine approved in 1958, rose 206 percent [from 1981 to 1991], to $42.50 [wholesale price for a bottle of 100 pills]." During that same ten-year period, consumer inflation rose only 50 percent.

The litany of horrors continues with many more grim facts and statistics. The book ends with an examination of how costs might be controlled.

Andrews and McMeel; $5.95
1993; softcover; 120 pp.

## THE PLAGUE MAKERS
### by Jerry A. Fisher, M.D.

Suddenly a number of infectious diseases that we thought we had licked are killing people in alarming numbers. Pneumonia, rheumatic fever, meningitis, tuberculosis, and others are back and they're badder than ever. And the chief cause is the widespread, out-of-control use of those 1950s wonder drugs, antibiotics. At first, they killed infections nicely and were hailed as a panacea. Now they're being overprescribed and the bacteria are getting wise, mutating into new strains that are resistant to antibiotics.

Fisher looks at this plague in the making. He examines how and why this has happened. In a surprise move, he implicates antibiotics in the spread of AIDS. One reason he states is that antibiotics suppress the functioning of the immune system, which may leave a person more susceptible to AIDS-causing factors. Fisher also smashes AIDS orthodoxy by relating his conversation with Dr. Luc Montagnier, the discoverer of the HIV virus. Dr. M's latest research has left him convinced that HIV is not the only organism causing AIDS. Mycoplasma is also necessary to produce AIDS, and it turns out that antibiotics can kill this type of organism at first, but the mycoplasma quickly turn to mycospheres, which cannot be killed.

This book warns that if we don't do something soon, we could face a devastating plague of untreatable killer diseases. Fisher lists fifteen things that must be done to delay or avert this catastrophe, and what you can do to help bring about each of these changes. Finally, there is a list of antibiotics (which alerts you as to which ones are the worst "plague makers") and a guide to the proper use of antibiotics for a number of ailments.

Simon & Schuster; $23
1994; hardcover; 256 pp.

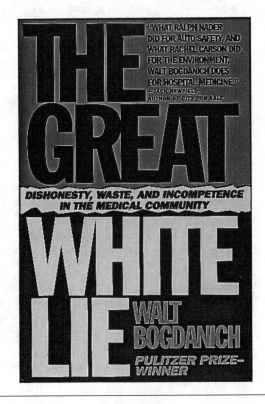

"WHAT RALPH NADER DID FOR AUTO SAFETY, AND WHAT RACHEL CARSON DID FOR THE ENVIRONMENT, WALT BOGDANICH DOES FOR HOSPITAL MEDICINE."
—JACK NEWFIELD, AUTHOR OF CITY FOR SALE

THE GREAT

DISHONESTY, WASTE, AND INCOMPETENCE IN THE MEDICAL COMMUNITY

WHITE LIE  WALT BOGDANICH

PULITZER PRIZE-WINNER

◄ *The Great White Lie* by Walt Bogdanich

*Blowing the whistle on doctor's kickbacks, billing fraud, untrained nurses and worse.*

# DEATH

## DEATH TO DUST:
### WHAT HAPPENS TO DEAD BODIES?

### by Kenneth V. Iserson, M.D.

This gigantic book takes a thorough look at the medical, physical, legal, and social aspects of what is done to corpses. Kenneth Iserson, M.D., a professor of surgery with a long medical career, could not possibly have written a more complete, straightforward book on the subject. Every question you may have regarding flatliners will be answered.

As Iserson points out, defining death is no easy task. It's a gray area that is becoming grayer as we make advances in biomedical technology. Western societies have basically settled on death as occurring when the brain dies, but, again, "brain death" isn't cut-and-dried. This ambiguity may lead to an unexpected consequence: "In the future, people may be allowed to specify under what conditions they wish to be pronounced dead: whether they want their heart to have irreversibly stopped, their entire brain to have ceased functioning, or the part of the brain that defines their identity (neocortex) to have died."

*Death to Dust*
by Kenneth V.
Iserson

*A frank look at decay that leaves nothing to the imagination.*

The author examines how physicians determine death and what happens when they misdiagnose someone who is still alive. Such cases are now exceedingly rare, but as late as June 1993, there were instances of people in the United States being incorrectly declared dead. A section that is sure to produce nightmares discusses instances of premature burial, which are now nonexistent. The stories we've all heard about corpses waking up during funerals or during grave robbery attempts are true.

Iserson is a firm believer in organ donation upon death, and he devotes a section of the book to the subject. He explains why you should do it, how to do it, how many people do it, etc. He also tells *exactly* how organs are harvested. Another option is to leave your entire body to a medical school for dissection. Other, less common, uses for corpses include crash tests, ballistics tests, and drug tests. Drug tests? Yes, science is doing amazing things with bodies nowadays. In one of the most disturbing parts of the book, Iserson describes how brain-dead cadavers are used for drug tests. "They are still connected to ventilators that 'breathe' for them and may have multiple medications being instilled to keep their blood pressure up and their other systems going. Some have suggested that these 'living cadavers' be called *'neomorts'* (newly dead) to better designate their status. As first conceived, neomorts 'would have the legal status of the dead with none of the qualities one now associates with death. They would be warm, respiring, pulsating, evacuating, and excreting bodies requiring nursing, dietary and general grooming attention—and could probably be maintained so for a period of years.'"

The descriptions of postmortem consequences and procedures leave nothing to the imagination. With the calm coolness of a true man of science, the Doc describes what insects will do to an unprotected stiff: "Insects...do not just happen upon a corpse, but appear to be attracted by a 'universal death scent.' What causes the scent has yet to be determined, but it seems to powerfully summon the insect population which can recognize microscopic quantities of odor-producing chemicals. Although people cannot detect the odor from a newly-dead body, flies, especially fleshflies (*Sarcophagidae*) and blowflies (*Calliphoridae*), swarm to the odor from as far away as two miles. In wooded areas, especially where there have been previously dead animals or humans,

they begin to land on a corpse within seconds, and in one hour some species may produce maggots."

This book covers too much ground to write about in detail. What follows is a list of some of the dozens of questions Iserson answers:

- What is a morgue and how long will my body be there?
- How is an autopsy done?
- What training do embalmers have?
- How long does it take to cremate a body?
- What are the prospects of successfully reviving a cryonically frozen body?
- How are bodies buried at sea?
- Who were some infamous body snatchers?
- What is cannibalism?
- How is a shrunken head prepared?
- What is necrophilia?
- How have corpses served as political symbols?
- What happens to bodies on the battlefield?
- What regulations govern funeral operations and costs?
- How permanent are individual graves?
- What are the differences among tombs, sepulchers, crypts, and sarcophagi?
- Can a corpse be held for nonpayment of debts?

*Death to Dust* also has a glossary, several appendixes, a seventy-page index, and a selection of poems, proverbs, and quotes about death.

If you're fascinated by death, you must save your pennies for this unparalleled trove of corpse information.

Galen Press Ltd; $38.95
1994; hardcover; 709 pp.; illus.

## ENCYCLOPEDIA OF DEATH:
### MYTH, HISTORY, PHILOSOPHY, SCIENCE—THE MANY ASPECTS OF DEATH AND DYING

### by Robert and Beatrice Kastenbaum

A cornucopia of death! The author/editors have done an admirable but not outstanding job in covering such a multifaceted topic. Entries include AIDS, autopsy, cemeteries, the death penalty, euthanasia, gallows humor, living wills, murder, near-death experiences, necrophilia, *Omega: The Journal of Death and Dying,* rigor mortis, thanatology, and zombies. Suicide and survival beliefs get several entries each. Suicide among aged adults, youth, African-Americans, Hispanics, Native Americans, and others are examined. The book also looks at the afterlife beliefs of Baptists, Buddhists, Mormons, Hindus, Jews, and other religions.

Although it covers a lot of ground, this book leaves out a number of subjects. I was surprised to find no entries for Jack Kevorkian, *Final Exit*, genocide, or pop culture examinations of death.

Avon Books; $15
1989; softcover; 295 pp.

## FINAL EXIT:
### THE PRACTICALITIES OF SELF-DELIVERANCE AND ASSISTED SUICIDE FOR THE DYING

### by Derek Humphry

The ultimate right a human can have is the right to decide when he or she wants to die. This world isn't a very fun place, and for those people who have painful, incurable diseases, it's a living hell of unimaginable depths. Choosing to die is one thing, though; actually dying is another. As Chapter Seven of this book shows, killing yourself isn't a cakewalk. It's easy to screw it up and end up worse than you were before.

What is really needed is an instruction book on the best ways to kill yourself. Enter the most controversial book of the decade (so far)—*Final Exit*, written by Hemlock Society cofounder Derek Humphry. When it first came out, it started a firestorm of a debate. Despite being roundly condemned from different sides, it briefly became the best-selling nonfiction book in the country and stayed on top of the *New York Times* "How-to" list for eighteen weeks. In *Final Exit*, Humphry gives detailed instructions for mixing surefire, lethal, chemical cocktails. He frowns on using cyanide. Reports are sketchy, but it seems that there is a great chance for violent, painful death if you down cyanide. Humphry also frowns on shooting a syringe full of air into your veins. Again, probably not a fun way to die.

The best way to die is an overdose of barbiturates or, if that's not possible, nonbarbiturates such as Valium and Darvon. On pages 120 through 126, Humphry presents a table showing the lethal dosages of eighteen prescription drugs. Chapter twenty-two presents helpful hints to make your hara-kiri go smoother. For example, eat a light meal an hour before you kill yourself, take a Dramamine so you don't throw up the pills, take the pills with alcohol, and so on.

Humphry also covers a number of related topics: legal considerations, insurance, autopsies, writing final letters, obtaining the necessary drugs, etc. The final part of the book is written especially for doctors and nurses who want to assist patients in dying.

Dell Publishing; $10
1991; softcover; 213 pp.

### HOW TO EMBALM YOUR MOTHER-IN-LAW:
#### EVERYTHING YOU EVER WANTED TO KNOW ABOUT WHAT HAPPENS BETWEEN YOUR LAST BREATH AND THE FIRST SPADEFUL
#### by Robert T. Hatch

This informal, occasionally humorous book examines how our bodies die and exactly what is done to them once they are dead. The author details the ancient method of dehydrating corpses. He notes this "method of embalming served the dead. The modern method serves the living." Because of modern open-casket funerals, it is now important for stiffs to look and smell good, but only for the few days until they're interred.

The author gives us a step-by-step account of how corpses are embalmed. He also briefly covers the ins and outs of cremation, coffins, grave digging, mausoleums, tombstones, funeral customs, and what happens to dead bodies if nothing is done to them. The author, to avoid being called a ghoul, I guess, put in a couple of chapters that don't really apply to the subject at hand—one is about his and his sister's belief about the nature of the soul and the other covers some near-death experiences. The sections on embalming cover their subject in depth, but the rest of the book is either sketchy or irrelevant. *How to Embalm* can't even begin to hold a candle to *Death to Dust* (above).

Citadel Press (Carol Publishing Group); $8.95
1981; softcover; 104 pp.

### LOOKING AT DEATH
#### by Barbara P. Norfleet

In March and April 1993, Harvard University put on a photography exhibition with death as the theme. This book collects more than one hundred of these photos for a gruesome tour de force. The black-and-white photos span one hundred and fifty years, with just a few from recent times. No famous images of death are here—no officer shooting a Viet Cong prisoner in the head, no Ruby snuffing Oswald—just a bunch of mostly anonymous people who left this vale of tears one way or another. "Death by Violence" is probably the most outright disturbing section. In it we see a young couple shot in their car, two children dead from a gas leak, revolutionaries with their heads lying beside them, and people who've killed themselves by hanging. "Death at Medical School" is filled with diseased corpses and pickled fetuses, and "Remains of Death" looks at skulls, skeletons, and mummies (once you get their bandages off, they ain't too pretty). The book's most surprisingly haunting images are from the late 1800s, when families would take pictures of departed members, usually children, in a way that made it appear that their loved ones were only sleeping.

The most unusual thing about *Looking at Death* isn't any of the images, but who published it. David R. Godine is a refined small press better known for belles lettres and books on typography than postmortem pictures. Support their bold move. Buy this book and take a look at where all of us are headed.

David R. Godine Publishers; $25
1993; oversize softcover; 140 pp.

*Looking At Death* by Barbara P. Norfleet

*A ground-breaking exhibition on where we're all headed and how we might get there.*

### ON SUICIDE:
#### GREAT WRITERS ON THE ULTIMATE QUESTION
#### edited by John Miller

This collection of twenty-two essays, poems, and fiction excerpts examines the complex issue of suicide, which Albert Camus has called "the one truly serious philosophical problem."

The acid-tongued misanthrope offers an eloquent defense of suicide: "Suicide is always courageous. We call it courage in a soldier merely to face death—say to lead a forlorn hope—although he has a chance of life and a certainty of 'glory.' But the suicide does more than face death; he incurs it, and with a certainty, not of glory, but of reproach. If that is not courage we must reform our vocabulary."

Albert Camus also steps to the plate for suicide: "In a sense, and as in melodrama, killing yourself amounts to confessing. It is confessing that life is too much for you or that you do not understand it.... Dying voluntarily implies that you have recognized, even instinctively, the ridiculous character of that habit, the absence of any profound reason for living, the insane character of that daily agitation, and the uselessness of suffering."

Poet Dorothy Parker, who tried to kill herself several times, promotes choosing life. Her defense—that killing yourself is too hard—is an intentionally weak one. "Gun's aren't lawful;/Nooses give;/Gas smells awful;/You might as well live."

Philip Loptate contributes an interesting essay about how he, other teachers, and the students at an elementary school handled the suicide of one of the teachers. Emile Durkheim, the first sociologist, offers his controversial theory that the more stable a society is, the less suicides it has. Other writers whose work is included are Plato, Sylvia Plath, Virginia Woolf, Langston Hughes, Shakespeare, Gustave Flaubert, Emily Dickinson, and Leo Tolstoy.

Chronicle Books; $10.95
1993; softcover; 271 pp.

## PRESCRIPTION:
### MEDICIDE–THE GOODNESS OF PLANNED DEATH
### by Dr. Jack Kevorkian

Surely one of the most controversial figures of the 1990s, "Dr. Death" has helped bring death out of the closet by assisting several people in killing themselves. Therefore, I was sure that Kevorkian's book would be about physician-assisted suicide. I was partially right, but the majority of *Prescription* is about an extremely controversial idea that Kevorkian has, one that I've never heard mentioned in the mainstream media. Kevorkian wants to give condemned criminals a choice—either be executed the normal way or let doctors perform medical experimentation on you (while you're completely anesthetized) and, if that doesn't kill you, they'll over-anesthetize you when they're done. Another related idea Kevorkian has is to let those on death row donate their organs to science, which they aren't currently allowed to do.

Kevorkian discusses where he got these ideas and his struggles to implement them, relating both the resistance and the support (from many condemned criminals) he has received. Along the way, he gives a gruesome history lesson in methods of execution and a history of experimentation on the condemned, and discusses why people are executed. The last part of the book gets into physician-assisted suicide and why Kevorkian believes it is the right thing to do.

Medical messiah or fascist Frankenstein? Now you can hear Kevorkian's ideas firsthand and decide for yourself.

Prometheus Books; $12.95
1991; softcover; 268 pp.

# BODY MODIFICATION

## BODY PLAY AND
## MODERN PRIMITIVES QUARTERLY

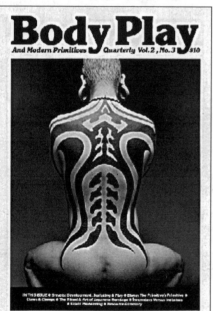

*Body Play*

*The body as canvas, fashion statement, and vessel of expression.*

Edited and published by body modifier extraordinaire, Fakir Musafar, this magazine covers the entire range of modern primitivism. Being an eclectic kind of person, I like to see people who take one area and explore it thoroughly, looking not only at the expected aspects but also the overlooked and tangentially related aspects of a subject. *Body Play* has covered branding, flesh loops, blood rites, cupping, contortionists, body painting, suspensions, small waists (as in thirteen to twenty inches), claws (ultralong toenails), surgical clamps, Japanese bondage, pierced lower lips, and more. The fall 1993 issue contained a great article on breasts covering sculpting, clamping, enlargement by pumping, augmentation, and erotic fondling and play. Each issue contains a photo essay on at least one modern primitive who has done something very special with her or his body. Wide subject range and beautiful photography make *Body Play* a terrific magazine. Its only drawback is that, although it's printed on slick paper, all the photos are black-and-white.

Insight Books/PO Box 2575/Menlo Park, CA 94026-2575
Single issue: $12 (U.S. & Canada); international: $14
One-year sub (4 issues): $45 (U.S. & Canada); international: $55

## FLASH VIDEO AND BOOKS

Flash produces and sells more than twenty videos, most of them on body modification. They show uncensored, nowhere-to-hide footage of people being pierced and tattooed on their genitals, nipples, faces, and other places, plus people showing off the results of such body artistry. Titles include "Erotic Tattooing and Body Piercing" Parts One through Five, "Painless Steel" Parts One through Three, "Body Shock," and "Tattoos for Bikers." Flash also creates the "Weird" series of shockumentaries showing the most extreme behavior imaginable. They're kind of like the *Mondo* movies, except all the footage in these is real. Titles include "Weird San Francisco," "Weird Mardi Gras," "Weird Thailand," and "Weird Amsterdam."

But videos aren't all Flash does. They've also published two high-quality books of Charles Gatewood's photographs: *Primitives* and *Charles Gatewood's Photographs: The Body and Beyond*. Their catalog is fully illustrated with stills from the videos. Be sure to include an over-twenty-one age statement.

Flash Video/PO Box 410052/San Francisco, CA 94141
Catalog: $2

## MODERN PRIMITIVES:
### AN INVESTIGATION OF CONTEMPORARY ADORNMENT
### AND RITUAL (RE/SEARCH #12)

*Modern Primitives* has come under fire from those in the body mod and SM scenes for subtly treating the book's subjects as freaks. Be that as it may, this is still one helluva book. It contains interviews with Fakir Musafar, who has performed just about every body modification and pain ritual on the face of the earth; ManWoman, who is covered in tattoos of swastikas in an effort to liberate the original spirituality of the symbol from the Nazi influence; Anton LaVey, founder of the Church of Satan; Lyle Tuttle, an American tattoo pioneer who put ink on Janis Joplin, Peter Fonda, and others; Dan Thome, who tattoos with traditional Micronesian tools; and a whole bunch of other people involved in body modification as either the artist or the easel (or both).

One of the questions that often comes up is, Why modify your body? The answers are varied and include decoration, pain gratification, achieving heightened erotic sensations, a way of claiming one's own body, and a spiritual/metaphysical act. As Ed Hardy says, "A tattoo is an affirmation: that this body is yours to have and enjoy while you're here. Nobody else can control what you do with it. That's why tattooing is such a big thing in prison: it's an expression of freedom." Fakir Musafar discusses the results of one of his early experiments: "Finally I got my body totally lashed to the wall, my arms in hooks, my head in a restraint, and I had a conscious out-of-the-body experience—and there's nothing else quite like that. You have a body but it's fluid; you can walk through walls, earth, iron...you can stay in the present or walk forward or backward in time, just like walking into another room."

*Modern Primitives* is packed with hundreds of photos showing full body tattoos, facial tattoos, pierced cocks, scrotes, labia, clits, belly buttons, needles in nipples, people hanging by flesh hooks, a woman with a thirteen-inch waist, penis weights, scarification, and even an instance of penis-splitting. A resource guide is included for those who'd like to explore further.

RE/Search Publications; $17.99
1989; oversize softcover; 205 pp.

## SKIN SHOWS III:
### THE ART OF TATTOO
### by Chris Wroblewski

Blazing full-color pictures of one hundred of the most fan-damn-tastic tattoos ever drawn on a human body. This master tat photographer has traveled the world in a search for inked flesh, and in his third installment of *Skin Shows*, he reveals what he's found.

A couple of people shown have tattoos of Joan Miró's surrealistic paintings on their backs, including a woman who has hundreds of those strange Miró-symbols and Miró-creatures winding down her back, from right shoulder to left buttcheek. Many people are displaying very striking black tattoos of traditional designs of native people all over the world.

There's no telling what subject matter people will want to cover themselves with. One dude has portraits of gangsters all over his right thigh. Jodie Foster and Anthony Hopkins from their roles in *Silence of the Lambs* adorn another person's leg. A couple of military history buffs are evident—one has Winston Churchill and bombers on his hip; the other has a scene from the American Revolution on his hip. Sherlock Holmes and Watson look for clues on yet another hip. And how would you like to have a picture of Jack the Ripper slashing a prostitute's throat on your back? Well somebody out there does.

Wroblewski has also included archival material on tattoos and pictures of various tattoo parlors, from Ricky's in Hong Kong to a little hut in Bombay.

Virgin Publishing; $19.95
1993; oversize softcover; 132 pp.; heavily illus.

## TATTOOED WOMEN

### by Chris Wroblewski

A lush, full-color collection of women with tattoos by famed body art photographer Chris Wroblewski. These hundred or so photos document "the heavily inked border between women, their flesh and their fantasies." We see female bods covered in flowers, dragons, skulls, faeries, cats, fish, rugged men, mysterious women, a Doberman, a cowboy and horse, abstract and indigenous designs, ancient symbols, leopard spots, and others.

The photographer also presents archival material dealing with tattooed women, such as German circus posters, 1950s magazine articles, and a photo of the heavily tattooed body of Yuki Desnos, wife of the surrealist poet Robert Desnos.

Virgin Publishing; $19.95
1992; oversize softcover; 127 pp.

## THE TOTAL TATTOO BOOK

### by Amy Krakow

I admit it, this book is a mainstream attempt to cash in on the modern primitives craze. The author, who organizes the Coney Island Tattoo Festival, the largest of its kind in the world, seems pretty legitimate, but because her book is being published by a huge mainstream publisher, it lacks something. For one thing, there are no genital or breast tattoos here; bare buns are as daring as it gets. Also, the word *fuck* is written "f*k." This is clearly a timid book written for outsiders looking in. This isn't to say it's all bad, though. The sixteen-page color insert contains many beautiful tattoos, and the author covers a lot of ground. She looks at the history of tattooing, describes what it's like to get a tat, profiles famous masters of the craft, lists famous people and the tats they have, examines the legal and forensic issues of tattoos, looks at the methods of removal, examines the use of tattoos as permanent eyeliner, and gives addresses for magazines, museums, conventions, and more than forty pages worth of tattoo studios in dozens of countries and every state.

Warner Books; $11.99
1994; softcover; 225 pp.

# NUDISM

## NUDE & NATURAL:
### THE QUARTERLY JOURNAL OF CLOTHES-OPTIONAL LIVING

One of the misconceptions people may have about nudist magazines is that they're exploitive. Ha! Take a look at a real nudist magazine and you'll quickly see that it's not true. The cover of *Nude & Natural* #13.3, one of the country's leading nudist magazines, contains a wizened five hundred-year-old man

standing on a cliff. Even inside, despite pictures galore, it doesn't get much racier than that, because, to tell you the truth, most people really don't look good naked. But looking good and showing pictures of hot and fancy babes isn't what true nudism is about. It's about freedom; it's about feeling good and enjoying yourself. That's exactly what *Nude & Natural* is about, too. (Actually, I'd like to qualify my statement about hot and fancy babes. Although nudist magazines today may not print such pictures, looking at the pix in the early magazines, reprinted in the books below, it's obvious that there was a somewhat prurient undercurrent present.)

Most of the articles are either about nudist events (cruises, picnics, and so on) or the problems that nudists face, such as legal harassment. There are also some looks at nudity in mainstream culture, guides to nudist spots, a resources listing, and loads of ads for resorts and vacations. Of course, there are many, many pictures in this magazine of more than one hundred pages, and they show some interesting things about nudists. The vast majority of nudists do not have perfect, sculpted bodies. Nudists run the gamut from children to young adults, middle-aged, and even the elderly, with a seemingly equal number of men and women. In the hundreds upon hundreds of people in this magazine, though, I noticed one African-American and one Hispanic. Are white people the only ones who get naked?

The Naturists, Inc/PO Box 132/Oshkosh, WI 54902
Single issue: $10
One-year sub (4 issues) without membership: $25
One-year membership (includes sub): $30

▼ *Nudist Magazines of the 50s & 60s edited by Ed Lange and Stan Sohler*

*Nostalgic looks back at the glory days of nudist magazines.*

## NUDIST MAGAZINES OF THE 50s AND 60s, VOLUMES 1&2

### edited by Ed Lange and Stan Sohler

Remember the episodes of *M\*A\*S\*H* where Hawkeye would ogle his nudist magazines? ("I only read them for the volleyball scores," he would say.) Well, now you can see material from those magazines, as well as those from the 1960s, in these nostalgic looks back at the glory days of nudist magazines. Back when there were legal battles at every turn because puritanical officials claimed that showing pubic hair in a photo made a magazine obscene and therefore not covered under the First Amendment. Back before men's skin mags forced the nudist publications out of existence during the 1970s.

The vast majority of the articles reprinted in these books come from the 1960s. In fact, each book has only one article from the 1950s, but the article in Volume One does indeed have pictures of volleyball games! This volume also contains the articles "*Sunsport*—Shrimp Boat Turned Nudist," "A Whirlwind Tour of Europe," "History's First Nudist Queen" (Nefertitti of Egypt), "The Health Kick," "The French Way," "The Private Life of a Nudist Family," and eight others. Volume Two goes *way* back, reprinting an article from *Nude Life* in 1934. It also has the features "Sunbathing Around the World," "Family Fun," "The Naked Truth About the Etruscans," "Public Protest for a City Nude Beach," "Dance Naked with Music," and nine others.

Both volumes are loaded with photos, including sixteen pages in color.

Elysium Growth Press; $18.95 each
1992; oversize softcovers; 94 pp. each

## THE SHAMELESS NUDE:
### A SELECTION OF ARTICLES AND STORIES FROM NUDE LIVING

More nude nostalgia! This book reprints twenty articles and tons of pictures from the classic nudist magazine *Nude Living*, which started publication in 1961. Articles include "The Joy of Nudism," "Would You Pose Without Clothes?" "Nudism's Fellowship with Nature," "Sex Education: The Orphan Annie of the Schools" by esteemed sexologists Phyllis and Eberhard Kronhausen, "The Joys of Sleeping Nude," "When Is a Picture Obscene?" and "Nudism in Classical Utopias." The article "Obscenity, Law and Nudism" shows that there are some enlightened government officials out there. In a ruling on the magazine *Sunshine and Health,* an Ohio judge wrote: "These front views, as well as other views, are of God's own children as he made them.... There cannot be any obscenity in God's own handiwork."

Elysium Growth Press; $24.95
1991; oversize hardcover; 136 pp.

## THERAPY, NUDITY & JOY:
### THE THERAPEUTIC USE OF NUDITY THROUGH THE AGES
### by Aileen Goodson, Ph.D.

A one-of-a-kind book that investigates the therapeutic benefits of getting naked. The author examines the nude psychotherapy movement of the 1960s and even organized a reunion of the participants. She looks at growth centers that incorporate nudity as an important part of emotional/spiritual growth—Bhagwan Shree Rajneesh's centers in India and Oregon, the Elysium Institute, and various nudist resorts. Nudity also plays a role in body work, such as Neo-Reichian therapy and Rolfing, and in sex therapy. I know that last part is kind of obvious, but nude therapy and sex therapy, including the use of sex surrogates, have a lot in common. They are principally about dealing with shame and body image and adjusting

*The Body* ➤
*edited by*
*William A.*
*Ewing*

*Examined in a stunning photographic tour-de-force.*

attitudes of self-acceptance.

The author also provides a panoramic look at nudity in history and culture. She discusses nudity in various societies and times and in art, photos, and movies. How the unclothed body is treated tells us a lot about a culture. "[The Japanese] attitude that everything natural is moral is revealed in the 'bridal books' published for hundreds of years in Japan as a means of practical sex education for young women." But in America, "The naked body is still considered unnatural."

This book has helped open my eyes. I've always felt that it is our right to be nude if we want to, but I hadn't considered the numerous psychological benefits of not wearing clothes. As Ashley Montagu says in the foreword: "Clothes put a barrier between ourselves—which are our bodies—and the rest of the world. They not only prevent us from establishing contact with others but also from contact with our selves, serving as a first layer of disguise." The solution is obvious—everybody get naked!

Elysium Growth Press; $24.95
1991; hardcover; 381 pp.

# MISCELLANEOUS

## THE BODY:
### PHOTOGRAPHS OF THE HUMAN FORM
### edited by William A. Ewing

Like it or not, we're all stuck in a bag of protoplasm during our time on earth. Fortunately, our bodies are endlessly fascinating and quite beautiful. At last there's a book that truly does justice to all aspects of this amazing creation of nature.

Packaged in a translucent slipcase, *The Body* contains more than 350 mostly black-and-white images of the human body and commentary from photography curator William A. Ewing. The photos are from all fields—anthropology, medicine, art, erotica, history, etc. Taken together, they form an astonishing examination of our corporeal nature.

The chapters explore various aspects of the body. "Fragments" contains photos of legs, breasts, torsos, ears, eyes, and feet. "Figures" looks at full-figured nudes mainly from the 1800s and early 1900s, but also includes Robert Mapplethorpe and Sally Mann. A more clinical examination of the body is offered in "Probes": pictures of brains, skeletons and bones, fetuses, cells, and people in motion. There's even an X ray and a scintigram.

"Prowess" examines the body in the peak of its form, with pictures of athletes, dancers, and contortionists. "Idols" examines the idealized body by presenting photos of bodybuilders, sex symbols, and other babes and hunks. At the opposite extreme is "Estrangement," which features pictures of deformities, disease, death, and disfigurement.

"Eros" was a disappointing chapter. It did a good job presenting sexual images from before 1920, but it totally fizzled out by showing only a few relatively tame images from the second half of the century. "Politic" contains photos illustrating the battles caused by sex, violence, and race. The last two chapters, "Metamorphosis" and "Mind," are among the best. They present imaginative photos that abstract, transform, and play with the human body.

The range of images is astonishing. All your favorite photographers are here: Man Ray, Jock Sturges, Herb Ritts, George Platt Lynes, Joel-Peter Witkin, Sally Mann, Annie Sprinkle, Edward Weston, Andres Serrano, Robert Mapplethorpe, and many others. *The Body* is an awesome achievement.

Chronicle Books; $29.95
1994; softcover in a slipcase; 432 pp; heavily illus.

## EVE'S RIB:
### SEARCHING FOR THE BIOLOGICAL ROOTS OF SEX DIFFERENCES
### by Robert Pool

The nature vs. nurture debate is one of the oldest in science. Are we who we are because of certain biological/genetic conditions or because of how our parents and society treated us? This book fired another volley in this war, this one from the biological determinism camp. The author says that we are most definitely the products of hormones that we developed while still in the womb. He posits the politically incorrect theory that men and women really are different—equal, but different.

All fetuses start out as neuters. During the eighth week, if the fetus has a Y chromosome, a "switch" is flicked, the body begins creating testosterone, and a boy develops. If the fetus has two X chromosomes, nothing happens and the fetus continues developing into a girl. "In other words, the 'default' body plan is female, and a fetus will go down this path unless diverted."

From this point on, the author contends, the sexes are irrevocably different. The brains of males and females are different in predictable ways. There are differences in all five senses. Males really are better at spatial and mathematical reasoning, and females really do have better verbal abilities. As children, boys are more easily distracted, while girls have longer attention spans. Women are more concerned with how well they do a job, and men are more concerned with how well they do compared to others.

Finally, the author discusses the philosophical questions (What do the two sexes tell us about the human race?) and the practical issues (Maybe we should teach girls and boys in different ways) of his controversial findings.

Crown Publishers; $22
1994; hardcover; 308 pp.

## THE FOURTH HORSEMAN:
### A SHORT HISTORY OF EPIDEMICS, PLAGUES, FAMINES, AND OTHER SCOURGES
### by Andrew Nikiforuk

"Of all the riders of the Apocalypse, the Fourth Horseman has been the busiest. By killing millions in a single month or year, epidemics have crumbled empires, defeated armies and forever changed the way we live and love." This book offers a glimpse at the way pestilence has run roughshod over history and medicine.

Of all the people who have ever died, half have been killed by malaria. "Until World War II it still accounted for 50 percent of the business at most cemeteries." The Black Death wiped out a third of Europe and was largely responsible for undermining feudalism. Smallpox killed about one hundred million Native Americans in one century, utterly decimating their numbers and leaving their continent ripe for the picking. Returning the favor, the New World (specifically Haiti) gave syphilis to Spanish explorers, who took it back to Europe, where it spread like wildfire.

Of course, the Fourth Horseman is still among us. There are fifteen million lepers in Africa and India today. And AIDS, the most widely feared disease on earth, "is an old-fashioned epidemic caught in the neon blare of sex, drugs, and rock and roll. Like most plagues, it is the scourge of the poor or people with poor health." This book is highly recommended, not only because of its enlightening treatment of an often overlooked aspect of history, but because the author has a very lively writing style, unlike so many other writers on medical topics. He has written a highly opinionated and, at times, darkly humorous book that will give you a grudging respect for the power of microbes.

M. Evans And Co; $18.95
1991; hardcover; 200 pp.

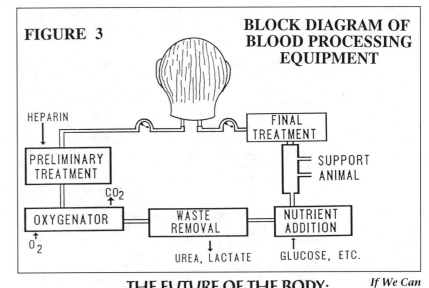

**FIGURE 3**

**BLOCK DIAGRAM OF BLOOD PROCESSING EQUIPMENT**

HEPARIN — PRELIMINARY TREATMENT — OXYGENATOR — $O_2$ — $CO_2$ — WASTE REMOVAL — UREA, LACTATE — NUTRIENT ADDITION — GLUCOSE, ETC. — FINAL TREATMENT — SUPPORT ANIMAL

## THE FUTURE OF THE BODY:
### EXPLORATIONS INTO THE FURTHER EVOLUTION OF HUMAN NATURE
### by Michael Murphy

The author believes that we all are capable of superhuman strength, agility, cognition, perception, and spiritual growth. To back this up, he examines hundreds of cases of people who have displayed metanormal abilities, such as stigmata, false pregnancy, the placebo effect, spiritual healing, hypnotic pain reduction, voluntary control of the brain's electrical activity, incredible ability in sports or martial arts, yoga, incorruptible corpses, and much more. This section of the book is incredibly thorough, covering hundreds of examples over the course of more than three hundred pages.

In the rest of the book, the author discusses the reasons we have these abilities and how to tap into them. He believes that by developing these normally latent abilities, we can bring about an upward shift in the human race's development. "Furthermore, these many extraordinary attributes exhibit an apparent continuity with features of animal nature.... I suggest that they are part of a richly complex development that began with the earliest forms of life, and that they point toward further human advance. Their cultivation, in other words, would carry forward the earth's evolutionary adventure."

Jeremy P. Tarcher; $30
1992; hardcover; 786 pp.

*If We Can Keep A Severed Head Alive... by Chet Fleming* ▼

*Get a head start on this weird technology debate.*

## IF WE CAN KEEP A SEVERED HEAD ALIVE...:
### DISCORPORATION AND U.S. PATENT 4,666,425
### by Chet Fleming

In 1987 the United States granted a patent for a device that would keep a severed head alive and conscious. The patent was issued to Fleming, who hasn't actually built the machine. He was able to convince the Patent Office, though, that such a machine could be built with already available parts, which was enough to get him the patent. His reason for getting the patent and forming a corporation based on it is to have control over this technology. "The Dis Corporation has legal standing to sue anyone who starts this type of research without permission, and the company is willing to do so if necessary to ensure that Congress and the public have a chance to consider the issues before the ball starts rolling."

The author says that it's only a matter of time before scientists keep severed heads alive and that we need to be prepared for it. There must be public debate and governmental oversight on such research or it could be a disaster. The closest anyone has come to actually keeping a head alive, that we know about, was in 1971, when "a team of neurosurgeons in Cleveland transplanted several monkey heads onto the bodies of other monkeys and then revived the transplanted heads to a state of full consciousness for up to thirty-six hours." Some people claim that certain governments have had top secret programs that actually did keep human noggins alive.

Fleming approaches this strange subject from every conceivable angle. He discusses the scientific research that has been done on isolated brains, transplanted heads, and perfused (i.e., unattached) heads; laws, regulations and agencies that will or might affect such technology; a detailed explanation of the patent; the questions of "experimental use" and "prior art" that are causing the patent to be reevaluated; what life would be like as a severed head; how living heads will affect society; religious and ethical questions; and how to control the development of this and other potentially dangerous technology.

I remember reading something that referred to this book and patent as an elaborate practical joke. It doesn't appear that way to me. Even if it's not possible to keep a cranium conscious now, given the quantum leaps that biotechnology has been making in recent years, it could be possible in the not-too-distant future. Reading this book will give you a head start on this perplexing development.

> Polinym Press; $15.95 ($11.95 if ordered directly from the publisher)
> 1988; hardcover; 461 pp.

*The Portable; Scatalog by John O. Burke* ➤

*An unrivaled classic in the annals of human waste.*

## IT'S A GAS:
### A STUDY OF FLATULENCE
### by Eric S. Rabskin, Ph.D. and Eugene M. Silverman, M.D.

Everything you ever wanted to know about farts but were afraid to ask. Every possible aspect of letting it rip is covered. The good doctors start with an entertaining look at what farts are in the form of a dialogue with a cabbie: "'...if you have floating stools you probably produce methane and there's frankly nothing you can do about it.' 'How do you know if your floating

stools come from methane?' 'Easy enough: collect your farts in a plastic bag...and then, very carefully, try to light them. If they ignite with a blue flame, it's methane.'"

There's also a look at the language of gas passing, cutting the cheese in other cultures, "famous farters of history," floating air biscuits in literature, a fart art gallery, and practical advice on how *you* can stop stinking up the place.

> Xenos Books; $9.95
> 1991; softcover; 164 pp.

## PASTEUR EXPOSED:
### THE FALSE FOUNDATIONS OF MODERN MEDICINE
### by Ethel Douglas Hume

Originally published in the 1920s, this book says that Pasteur stole the idea of microbes from fellow French scientist Antoine Béchamp. Unfortunately, Pasteur completely misunderstood the nature of bacteria. Béchamp believed that bacteria were not the cause of disease but another symptom of it. A body that is stressed and has an improper energy balance is fertile ground for bacteria. Therefore, to treat disease, you try to restore the body's balance and everything else falls into place. As a consequence of Pasteur's mistaken notions, our understanding of infection, immunity, and even genetics is wrong.

The author also believes that Pasteur screwed up in his creation of vaccines. The problem with vaccines is that they often cause illnesses and other problems. Béchamp understood this, opting for natural preventatives instead.

*Pasteur Exposed* shows the many flaws and inconsistencies in Pasteur's theories and elevates Béchamp to a higher position than medical history has given to him. This book presents a fascinating, suppressed chapter in the history of humanity's fight against disease.

> Bookreal; $18.95 (Australian dollars)
> 1923, 1989; softcover; 260 pp.

## THE PORTABLE SCATALOG
### by John G. Bourke, edited by Louis P. Kaplan

John Bourke, who lived in the second half of the 1800s, was a captain in the U.S. Cavalry and an amateur ethnologist. While stationed in New Mexico in 1881, he witnessed a purification ritual dance performed by the Zuni Indians, during which they would chug gallons of urine. This amazed and disturbed Bourke so much that he spent the next ten years gathering information about the role excrement played in the rituals and folklore of cultures around the world. His five hundred-page magnum opus, *The Scatalogic Rites of All Nations*, was published privately in 1881 in Washington, DC, and reprinted in German in the 1930s. Other than that, this book hasn't seen the light of day and has become a lost classic.

*The Scatalog* is a collection of the best and most interesting parts of the original book. It is as entertaining as you can imagine. Here are few tidbits to whet your appetite:

- "A case is given in Martin Schurig's *Chylologia* of a patient who, having once experienced the beneficial effects of mouse-dung in some complaint, became a confirmed mouse-dung eater, and was in the habit of picking it up from the floor of his house before the servants could sweep it away."
- In the 1600s the Grand Lama of Tibet's shit was dried, powdered, and sold for an arm and a leg by priests. The powder was used a condiment or a remedy for disease.
- Stercoranistes is the name given to heretics who believe that the wine and wafer of Christian communion are digested normally and become resulting "waste matter."
- Among at least some Hindus, cow urine is the equivalent of holy water.
- The ancient Romans and Egyptians "had gods of excrement, whose special function was the care of latrines and those who frequented them."
- The ancient Greek historian Herodotus claimed that Egyptian women take leaks standing up but the men do it while sitting down.

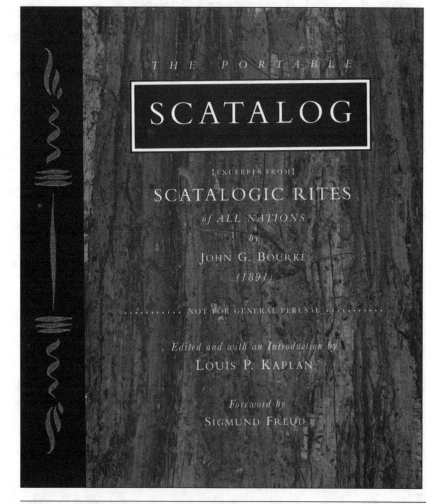

•Female urine is used for maceration (softening) in the production of cigars in Cuba.

•Urine, sweat, menstrual blood, and semen have been used as ingredients in aphrodisiacs.

This cataloging goes on and on and on, like a bad case of Montezuma's revenge. *The Scatalog* is an unrivaled classic in the annals of human waste.

William Morrow and Co; $16
1994; small hardcover; 191 pp.

## SELL YOURSELF TO SCIENCE
### by Jim Hogshire

This book caused quite a stir when it first came out and with good reason. It tells you how to make money by selling your bodily parts or secretions and being a guinea pig in medical experiments. "Our body parts have become so valuable that we might start seeing ourselves as human cash machines: containers made of flesh and bone, storing precious organs in a climate-controlled environment. This book is about how to make a withdrawal."

Part One discusses renting out your body to experimenters. You'll find out where to go, what you'll be expected to do, the different kinds of studies there are, and how much you can expect to make (up to a hundred dollars a day, plus expenses). Most such experiments involve taking new drugs, such as analgesics, hormones, and antibiotics. The author assures us that these experiments are almost always quite safe, but I still wouldn't let scientists use my body as a petri dish.

Part Two deals with selling parts of your body. Selling organs is illegal in the U.S., although it is done. It is legal in Britain, Germany, India, the Philippines, and other countries. If you'd like to take a trip there, you can come back lighter in the body but heavier in the wallet. How much heavier? A cornea can bring in four thousand dollars, bone marrow is around ten thousand dollars a cup, a kidney fetches ten to fifty thousand, and liver can pay off to the tune of one hundred-fifty grand per slice! Less lucrative but less drastic is selling your "liquid assets"—blood, sperm, and milk—and your "chunky bits"—hair and eggs. The author also discusses the highly controversial issues of selling fetal tissue and renting out your womb (carrying an infertile couple's child). Appendixes give addresses and phone numbers for test sites, organ/tissue banks, and sperm banks.

Loompanics Unlimited; $16.95
1993; softcover; 160 pp.

## THE VIRILITY FACTOR:
### MASCULINITY THROUGH TESTOSTERONE, THE MALE SEX HORMONE
### by Robert Bahr

This is the only popularly written book to deal exclusively with the hormone testosterone. The author discusses the great effect this hormone has on the physical and psychological aspects of masculinity: aggressiveness, ability to handle stress, "penile vigor," muscle development, voice tone, etc. We find out why testosterone does what it does, and what happens when the body doesn't produce enough.

For middle-aged men, a slowdown in testosterone production can cause irritability, fatigue, and a diminished sex drive. The author presents the case for taking extra testosterone and counters some of the myths surrounding this type of treatment. He also gives valuable advice on what all men can do to get their balls to create more of the stuff. Having orgasms is one way (at last, medical advice that everyone will want to follow!), eating certain nutrients, and laying off booze are other ways.

This book is an informative look at an aspect of men's health that has been all but ignored.

Factor Press; $12.95
1992; softcover; 213 pp.

*Sell Yourself ◄ to Science* by Jim Hogshire

*"We might start seeing ourselves as human cash machines."*

# THE MIND

## EXOTIC DISORDERS AND STRANGE BEHAVIORS

### BODIES UNDER SIEGE:
#### SELF-MUTILATION IN CULTURE AND PSYCHIATRY
#### by Armando R. Favazza, M.D.

The author looks at self-mutilation as it occurs in cultural rituals (such as Christian self-flagellation) and in disturbed individuals (such as gouging one's eye out). Many far-flung practices are discussed: religious mutilation, automutilation in animals, male and female circumcision, ear piercing, trephination (creating holes in the skull), autocannibalism, tongue cutting, footbinding, skin slashing, cutting off one's penis and testicles, and other things that make my skin crawl. The good doctor doesn't shy away from describing these events, so we jaded thrill seekers are in luck.

His constant comparison of ritual and clinical mutilation draws many interesting parallels that I had never thought of before. For example, in many religions, true believers beat themselves bloody as an act of devotion to God. Many mental patients mutilate themselves, very often by chopping off their penises, because "God told them to" or they knew that they had to sacrifice their sex organs to get into Heaven.

Favazza theorizes that self-mutilation of all types occurs for the same underlying reason—"to correct or prevent a pathological, destabilizing condition that threatens the community, the individual, or both.... Pathological conditions such as epidemic disease, crop failure, widespread sinfulness, enmity among group members, and the perceived sexual rapaciousness of females may threaten the stability and even the existence of the community." Individuals may engage in self-mutilation to overcome detachment, punish themselves for "bad" feelings or actions, or forestall suicide by sacrificing part of themselves instead of the whole. Disturbed adolescents who cut their skin may be intuitively trying to engage in rite-of-passage rituals like those in many indigenous societies.

In the final chapter, the author recommends methods of treatment for self-mutilators.

The Johns Hopkins University Press; $13.95
1987; softcover; 270 pp.

### THE DINOSAUR MAN:
#### TALES OF MADNESS AND ENCHANTMENT FROM THE BACK WARD
#### by Susan Baur

For nine years Susan Baur worked with schizophrenics in a psychiatry ward. Instead of detaching herself from them and teaching them how to conform to society's expectations, as other mental health workers do, she became involved in their worlds. She tried to understand the strange reality that surrounded each patient. She tells of Mr. Nouvelle, who thinks that the nightly 2:00 A.M. safety inspection is a signal for beautiful women to waft into the room and have sex with him. "There followed nightly orgies of incredible proportions, the descriptions of which sounded like the rich interleafing of a pornographic novel and a poultry breeder's manual. Sweet milk ran from wombs and penises, a son sucked his mother's zucchini, and duck eggs moved throughout the male and female anatomy as easily as one draws a breath. Soon the invisible ladies moaned in ecstasy, as Mr. Nouvelle drove his thirty-eight good dicks into their cantaloupes and streams of green beans poured from the women's fingers and out their ears." (Jeez, even SM looks boring by comparison!)

Other people whom Baur dealt with include God the Father, a man educated by aliens, a woman who dines with the president, a man who spent two and a half years "in a basket strapped to the back of Tommy Two-ton Eagle," and Jack London, who had a pres-

sure brain and a mechanical brain and who told the author, "Rest in the soft green light of the holy spirit." Baur further blurs the line between hallucination and reality by writing about some of the patients' realities in the same way she writes about consensus reality. In other words, it's up to you to decide if what she's describing is "real" or real only to one patient.

With graceful, beautiful writing, Baur takes us into the shadowiest regions of our minds. While reading her book, I felt I was being allowed access to a separate, distinct reality that exists all around us but that most of us can't see.

HarperPerennial (HarperCollins); $10
1991; softcover; 203 pp.

◄ *Bodies Under Siege by Armando R. Favazza*

*A disturbed young woman's cry for help or cultural rite-of-passage?*

### FIRE IN THE BRAIN:
#### CLINICAL TALES OF HALLUCINATION
#### by Ronald K. Siegel

In this book the author presents seventeen case studies of people who experience hallucinations caused by a variety of sources—drugs, fever delerium, mental illness, traumatic situations, etc. They make for fascinating reading. The book starts with an almost unbelievable tale involving the group of psychonauts who take hallucinogenic drugs and record in detail their visions for Siegel. All of them reported seeing a black curtain containing thirty human eyes, plus or minus one or two. Siegel saw it himself while smoking pot. Visitors from India, Japan, and England who participated, and were not aware of the consensus hallucination, reported the same thing. He eventually realized that the vision was based on an image from a slide show he gives to his group. Other drug users report talking to God while under the influence of DMT and being terrified of a giant black hole, the product of LSD flashbacks.

Some people have dreams that don't end when they wake up or have "daymares" while fully awake. The author tells of his encounter with a succubus, a father and son who were abducted by a UFO, and a sleep-deprived nurse who saw swastikas on her patients' sheets. Part Three takes a look at imaginary companions. Most kids have them, but some adults do, too. Steve's pregnant wife had died several years ago, but their unborn daughter was still his companion. Another man was visited by a childhood friend when he was caught in a hurricane while sailing. One sad case involved a man whose lover just up and left him. For five more years, he continued to live with a realistic mental construct of her, talking, making love, etc.

Finally, the author relates hallucinations that occur during times of great physical duress. To gain firsthand knowledge, he actually spent three and a half days without food or water, isolated in a Vietnam-style POW cage. During that time he carried on conversations with his only companion, a fly. He also tells of a woman who, while locked in a closet by an intruder, saw a doppelgänger, her exact double. One very unfortunate man was tortured by ex-Nazis in Bolivia. He discovered that if he screamed at a certain pitch while they were slowly peeling his skin off, he would be transported to a beautiful beach where he was free from pain.

Plume (Penguin); $10
1992; softcover; 275 pp.

## THE MAN WHO TASTED SHAPES
### by Richard E. Cytowic, M.D.

Synesthesia is a condition in which a person's senses are intertwined, instead of functioning on relatively different paths like most people's. Synesthetes can hear colors, see sounds, smell tactile sensations, and taste shapes. In 1980 the author entered this strange world when he met a man who experienced taste sensations as shapes. Embarrassed by his previously undiagnosed condition, he explained how he prepares chicken: "'Flavors have shape,' he started, frowning into the depths of the roasting pan. 'I wanted the taste of this chicken to be a pointed shape, but it came out all round.' He looked up at me, still blushing. 'Well, I mean it's nearly spherical.... I can't serve this if it doesn't have points.' "

From there, scientific detective work ensues, and we get to see Cytowic's quest to learn more about the mingling of senses. In the end, he shows that synesthesia, although it only affects one in one hundred thouand people, is relevant to all of us because it helps unlock the mysteries of the mind. The fact that synesthesia is such an immediate, unfiltered experience leads the good doctor to develop a radical new theory of the mind, one that shows that it is emotion and not reason that rules us. He then examines the implications this has for memory, creativity, spirituality, and other areas.

Anyone interested in the nature of consciousness should definitely read, smell, and/or taste this book.

Putnam; $21.95
1993; hardcover; 249 pp.

## PATIENT OR PRETENDER:
### INSIDE THE STRANGE WORLD OF FACTITIOUS DISORDERS
### by Marc D. Feldman, M.D.,
### and Charles V. Ford, M.D., with Toni Reinhold

Some people deliberately fake or even manufacture physical symptoms to get medical attention, as well as sympathy from family and friends. This is often referred to as Munchausen syndrome, although that term technically denotes only the most pathologically extreme cases of people with factitious disorders. The authors, two M.D.'s who have personally dealt with "false patients," shed light on this perplexing behavior.

One of the most incredible examples in the book is Jenny, who faked having breast cancer. She told her family and friends she had the disease, shaved her head and starved herself to simulate the side effects of chemotherapy, and even joined a cancer support group. The results were that "Jenny became an instant 'somebody,' the object of sympathy and attention from people who had never noticed her before." Eventually her lies were uncovered, and she successfully went through therapy.

Another unbelievable case history is that of a woman who came into a clinic in which one of the authors worked. She was gaunt and her skin was ashen white. She complained of feeling weak. The doctor did blood tests and found her blood count was so low that she should have been dead. After being questioned, she admitted to siphoning her own blood with a syringe. Other patients have been known to cut themselves to produce "surgery" scars, inject themselves with bacteria, and scrape their urethras to produce blood in their urine. Occasionally, the creation of such symptoms goes too far, as in the case of the nurse who had injected talc under her skin to produce lesions. Eventually the talc entered her bloodstream and formed a clot that killed her.

"The cruelest and deadliest form of the factitious disorders is Munchausen by proxy (MBP)," in which a parent—almost always the mother—creates an illness in her child. This not only fosters sympathy and gets attention, but gives the parent the chance to play "heroic caregiver" or, if the child dies, "martyred parent." Parents will temporarily smother their children to simulate sleep apnea, rub oven cleaner on their skin to produce ulcerations, or stick them with pins to cause bleeding.

The authors not only examine these disturbing behaviors but offer reasons for it. They also look at the horrible effects factitious disorders produce—family members whose lives are ruined, baffled doctors, and the squandering of medical resources.

John Wiley & Sons; $19.95
1994; hardcover; 228 pp.

## VAMPIRES, WEREWOLVES, AND DEMONS:
### TWENTIETH CENTURY REPORTS IN THE PSYCHIATRIC LITERATURE
### by Richard Noll

Definitely one of the coolest books in recent memory. Noll has gathered obscure and all but impossible-to-obtain psychiatric articles on three of the most extreme mental conditions in the world: vampirism, in which the individual gets pleasure from drinking blood; lycanthropy, in which the individual believes that he or she has become a wolf (or some other animal) and acts accordingly; and possession, in which the individual believes that a hostile spirit has entered his or her body. Each section is given a long, detailed introduction by the author.

The section on vampirism contains an article on autovampirism. "Masturbation began at age 11, and became associated with drawing his own blood and the compulsion to see it. He achieved this by puncturing his neck veins; and by performing the Valsalva maneuver, he could make his blood pour rapidly while watching in a mirror.... He discovered that by lying on his back, he could catch the spray of blood in his mouth and drink it. At times, a cup was used." Other articles discuss cannibalism and vampirism in paranoid schizophrenia, and John Haigh, the vampiric "acid bath murderer."

Part Two looks at many cases of lycanthropy, including people who "turn into" cats, dogs, rabbits, gerbils, and birds (patient behavior includes "chirping, perching, head bobbing, flapping arms"). The final section contains articles on the "cinematic neuroses" developed by four people after watching *The Exorcist*, "demon possession" in children, the use of possession as a legal defense, and a reprint of an article on "Demonomania" from an 1845 French book on insanity.

This is one of the necessary books to have in your collection on the extremes of human behavior.

Brunner/Mazel Publishers; $14.95
1992; softcover; 244 pp.

# ART AND LITERATURE BRUT

The term *art brut* (French for "raw art"), was coined by dada artist Jean Dubuffet to describe the type of art he was collecting—art created by "outsiders," principally people who were institutionalized for being mentally ill. He believed that such individuals created pure, unrestricted art that came from the depths of their beings and wasn't stifled by the "rules" of art, the quest for money, or hunger for an artistic reputation. The term *literature brut,* which I think I coined, simply refers to the written counterpart of *art brut.*

## DARKNESS VISIBLE:
### A MEMOIR OF MADNESS
### by William Styron

Technically this probably doesn't qualify as *literature brut* since it was written after the author had recovered from his condition rather than during. So, technically speaking, he wasn't "insane" when he wrote it. However, it offers a rare firsthand account of the living hell of true depression and, I think, deserves a place in the newly forming canon of "raw literature."

In 1985 the Pulitzer Prize–winning author of *Sophie's Choice* plunged into depression. Not the down-and-out feeling we all get from time to time, but the honest-to-God, bottomless pit of suffering that took the lives of Vincent van Gogh, Virginia Woolf, and countless other people. Styron discusses his downward spiral, which almost ended in suicide, while interjecting his own feelings about depression, suicide, and alcohol: "...the pain of severe depression is quite unimaginable to those who have not suffered it, and it kills in many instances because its anguish can no longer be borne." While many people do survive depression, for those who kill themselves "there should be no more reproof attached than to the victims of terminal cancer."

Right before Styron checked into a mental hospital, he had hit his low point: "I had now reached that phase of the disorder where all sense of hope had vanished, along with the idea of a futurity; my brain, in thrall to its outlaw hormones, had become less an organ of thought than an instrument of registering, minute by minute, varying degrees of its own suffering." Fortunately, Styron recovered in the hospital. This short, unassuming tale of his struggle is a scary but important portrait of a misunderstood condition.

Vintage Books (Random House); $8
1990; softcover; 84 pp.

## IN THE REALMS OF THE UNREAL:
### "INSANE" WRITINGS
### edited by John G.H. Oakes

The only anthology of its kind in the English language, this book collects prose, poetry, and unclassifiable writings from more than seventy people who are considered insane. Most of them have spent much of their lives in institutions. The majority of the writers are schizophrenic, but some have been diagnosed with manic-depression, paranoia, senile dementia, etc.

Reading this stuff can seriously mess with your own fragile grip on reality, so consider yourself warned. I feel schizophrenia creeping up on me when I read "The Little Fifty-First Psalm" by Alvin Wilson: "O, Lord in Heaven/O, Most Merciful/Slip me please/A clean shave/Or cancer." Richard Lax's "Utopian Space Bible—God (The Eternal Quest)" offers an alternative history of earth: "In the age of Space-time beginning in 1957 (A.A.—after Atom, a new age, the Space age) God's slave rigger Atom on planet Hellose conquered a mountain named Duston (Mt. Fear) at the remotest ends of the Universes full of aliens (unto themselves) and was trying to make planet Hellose (Earth) into planet Godose (a Utopian God planet) with the help of Duster—Rhiannon (Duston), and Serianna (Queen of the planet Hellose)."

This unique book is a must-have for anyone into insanity or experimental writing. James Joyce doesn't have anything on these people.

Four Walls Eight Windows; $12.95
1991; softcover; 253 pp.

## PARALLEL VISIONS:
### MODERN ARTISTS AND OUTSIDER ART

An impressive collection of *art brut* and the modern art it influenced. As it turns out, many twentieth-century artists have not only been fascinated with art created by society's outsiders, they've also adapted many of the styles, techniques, and imagery of this art, even going so far as to appropriate many of the exact images. Salvador Dalí, Jean Dubuffet, Max Ernst, André Breton, Pablo Picasso, and Jackson Pollock are some of the many artists who have purposely adopted "insane" art techniques.

This massive book contains 264 reproductions, many in color. The essays examine surrealism, expressionism, the move of *art brut* from asylums to museums, and other topics. One section contains short biographies of thirty-four outsider artists. Henry Darger spent sixty-three years working on a fifteen-volume, *fifteen thousand-page* manuscript concerning an imaginary war fought over child slavery. He illustrated the story with eighty-seven collages and sixty-seven pencil drawings. Like so may other creators of *art/literature brut*, he never sought a publisher or told anyone of his work. (A later chapter in the book examines Darger's epic in detail and presents excerpts.)

Karl Brendel, committed to an asylum because of his hallucinations, made sculptures out of chewed bread. Luckily, he was given wood to work with, from which he carved gargoylelike animals, Christ, and other figures without the use of models. Ferdinand Cheval gathered stones along his postal route. Untrained in architecture, he nonetheless spent thirty-three years putting those stones together to form *Palais idéal* (Ideal palace), an unbelievably beautiful and detailed building that incorporates "figures of antiquity, tombs, a Hindu temple, biblical scenes, models of a mosque, the White House, a medieval castle, and a Swiss chalet..."

The hallucinatory Adolf Wölfi spent twenty-two years creating his "autobiography." "The text of the fanciful autobiography, interspersed with poetry, musical composition, and three thousand illustrations, comprises more than twenty-five thousand pages. Hand bound by Wölfi and stacked in his cell, the forty-five volumes eventually reached a height of more than six feet. Intermingling reality and fiction, Wölfi's autobiography begins as an adventurous geographical world expedition, of which Doufi (Wölfi's childhood name) is the hero, and expands to a grandiose tale of cosmic war, catastrophe, and conquest, with Doufi transformed into Saint Adolf II."

*Parallel Visions* is a treasure trove of works from individuals who truly practiced art for art's sake. They did what they did only to satisfy their burning urge to create, not to teach lessons or please anyone else.

Princeton University Press; $24.95
1992; oversize softcover; 334 pp.

*Parallel Visions* by Maurice Tuchman & Carol S. Eliel

*Johann Hauser's view from the other side.*

# ANTI-PSYCHIATRY

## AGAINST THERAPY
### by Jeffrey Moussaieff Masson

Psychotherapy is inherently flawed, according to the author. It is a system in which the psychotherapist, an imperfect human being, is assigned the task of changing the patient, another imperfect human being. In this system, "The psychotherapist is superior, the patient inferior. The psychotherapist by virtue of his knowledge, training and special insight has access to truths above and beyond the capacity of the patients. The psychotherapist's truths have a higher value than the patient's truths. The psychotherapist interprets the patient's truths and tells him what they *really* mean." To put it simply, psychotherapists treat people like patients, not like human beings.

In the process of taking on psychotherapy, the author slams Freud, Jung, Carl Rogers, gestalt therapy, family therapy, feminist therapy, Ericksonian hypnotherapy, and more. In particular, he looks at Freud's theory that women's memories of being sexually abused as children are false and at Jung's kissing up to Hitler and the Nazis. He examines the incredibly cruel, but common, therapy practiced by Dr. John Rosen: "On November 6, as I continued my pressure toward reality, I called Mary's attention to the fact that in the three weeks that she was in the [mental] hospital her mother had not come to see her once. The patient fainted dead away. I should say, in all fairness, that the mother had been acting on my orders."

Common Courage Press; $15.95
1994; softcover; 340 pp.

## AND THEY CALL IT HELP:
### THE PSYCHIATRIC POLICING OF AMERICA'S CHILDREN
### by Louise Armstrong

The private multibillion-dollar child psychiatry industry has started a disturbing trend by convincing parents, social workers, and others that adolescents going through the normal phases of teenage angst and rebellion are mentally disturbed and in need of obscenely expensive treatment. You've probably seen the TV commercials for these facilities—near-hysterical parents discussing the fact that little Johnny just doesn't do what they say anymore.

He's sullen and won't talk. Well, no shit! He's a teenager, for God's sake. He's going through what several generations of teens in America and Europe have gone through, yet now it's cause for him to be committed.

It's not only "troubled teens" who are being imprisoned, though. Abused and neglected children are also grist for the mill. The author plunges into this disturbing world, reporting all the horrors she encounters. She finds unbelievable abuses—older children being allowed to hit and restrain younger children, children being forced to cut grass with scissors for up to fourteen hours, children not allowed to wear coats outside in the snow. But the blatant abuses are only part of the problem. Much more subtle and insidious is the way child psychiatry tries to eliminate individuality. The author points to the recently "discovered" Attention Deficit Disorder as an example that "brings together most of the elements currently at play in the world of kiddie psych: entrepreneurial technology (pharmaceuticals); the demand for conformity suited to the prevailing social climate; the changing roles of schools as the agents of that conformity; the shifting focus from institutional deficits to individual diseases..."

The children's movement says that the most powerless, rights-less group in the world is children. This book shows it to be undeniably true.

> Addison-Wesley; $22.95
> 1993; hardcover; 306 pp.

## BEDLAM:
### Greed, Profiteering, and Fraud in a Mental Health System Gone Crazy
### by Joe Sharkey

For more than a decade businesses have been offering more and more mental health benefits to their employees (by 1990 these benefits equaled one-quarter of all health benefits paid for by employers). Well, with all this money floating around, somebody's going to end up getting rich, right? Yessiree, and those somebodies are the for-profit psychiatric hospitals and addiction centers that use deceptive and even illegal techniques to bleed insured "patients" for all the money they can get. Amazingly, many people in these facilities are declared cured on the very day their insurance runs out. For some, it was a good thing their insurance ran out, because otherwise they might not ever have been released. You see, some facilities coerce and even force (read "kidnap") patients into being admitted. Other ways of getting "patients" include giving kickbacks to clergy members and school counselors for referrals and setting up phony 800-number "help lines" where the advice consists of "why don't you come to our facility?" I haven't even gotten to what happens once you're in one of these rip-off joints. Abuses abound. In Oklahoma City, a psychiatrist threatened to pull off a five-year-old child's fingers with a pair of rusty pliers. In another incident, a woman came to the hospital to see if she needed to be admitted. She signed papers to stay but changed her mind before being taken to the unit. The staff called security guards who told her to go to the unit or they would take her there.

These places make so much money that it's a joke. One hospital was nailing insurance companies for forty dollars a day for "relaxation therapy," which consisted of playing taped music in the hallways while the prisoners got ready for bed. A man who sent his daughter to a hospital got a $41,000 bill. On a single, typical day, the bill came to $1,045 for fifteen group-therapy sessions, three dance-therapy sessions, two counseling sessions, and one individual therapy session!

With the constant proliferation of these places (I see ads for them on TV all the time) and their continuing quest to create more patients, you really need to read this book before you go into (or are forced into) one of them.

> St. Martin's Press; $22.95
> 1994; hardcover; 294 pp.

## HOW TO BECOME A SCHIZOPHRENIC:
### The Case Against Biological Psychiatry
### by John Modrow

When the author was six years old, his mother took him to a psychiatrist who said that Modrow would be psychotic within a year. His parents didn't have him committed, but they did begin treating him as though he were crazy, and eventually he became "schizophrenic." "Psychiatry, with its pseudoscientific doctrines of inherited insanity and its incompetent practitioners with their self-fulfilling prophecies, together with my parents' gullibility and other personal limitations, had in effect driven me insane."

Drawing on his own experiences and scattered research and theories, the author forms a coherent explanation of what makes a person become schizophrenic. In Part Two, Modrow tells his personal story, from childhood to his schizophrenic episode at sixteen and his recovery. The last section of the book contains an assault on the notion that schizophrenics are biochemically or genetically different than (and inferior to) the rest of society.

> Apollyon Press; $14.95
> 1992; softcover; 291 pp.

## IDEOLOGY AND INSANITY:
### Essays on the Psychiatric Dehumanization of Man
### by Thomas Szasz

Psychiatrist Thomas Szasz is the leading light of anti-psychiatry. His works have helped bring into question the whole consept of insanity and the field that deals with it, psychiatry. This book is a collection of Szasz's seminal essays, which convey his most important ideas. Szasz believes that mental illness is a myth. To be sure, some people do act strangely, but they are not ill in any way. They merely don't act/think/perceive like most of us. Psychiatry then slaps some meaningless label on them, like "schizophrenic," and acts as if it has accomplished something.

If mental illness doesn't exist, then psychiatry is nothing but a repressive system for labeling people and a tool for creating a conformist society. Institutionalization is imprisonment. And the insanity defense lets guilty people get away with murder. All of these points and others are well argued in the essays here: "The Myth of Mental Illness," "Mental Health as Ideology," "What Psychiatry Can and Cannot Do," "The Insanity Plea and the Insanity Verdict," "Psychiatric Classification as a Strategy of Personal Constraint," and seven others.

Consider this to be a textbook on Szasz's brand of anti-psychiatry.

> Syracuse University Press; $13.95
> 1970, 1991; softcover; 265 pp.

## TALKING BACK TO PROZAC:
### What Doctors Aren't Telling You About Today's Most Controversial Drug
### by Peter R. Breggin, M.D.

Prozac has become the drug of choice for millions of Americans. Not only is it supposed to relieve depression, it also can allegedly help with obesity, PMS, shyness, and even that "blah feeling" of ennui so common in modern life. One of the greatest boosts the drug got was being the subject of a number one best-seller, an almost completely uncritical "hip hip hooray" treatment titled *Listening to Prozac.*

The drug has now reached fad status. It used to be that the in thing to do was have a therapist; now taking Prozac is the way to go. The drug's 1993 sales were almost $1.2 billion, and almost *one million* prescriptions are being written every month.

But there's trouble in the Prozac Nation. As with any alleged panacea, Prozac has a dark side. It is this hidden and ignored information that is presented in *Talking Back to Prozac.* There are an alarming number of cases of murder, suicide, and self-mutilation by people on Prozac. Among the dozens of stories related is that of a brother and sister. "Their father, a kind and gentle man who had never been suicidal or aggressive, took Prozac for stress and fatigue. According to his two children, under the drug's influence, without warning or provocation, he stabbed his wife—their mother—to death. After inflicting multiple wounds on her, he killed himself." The drug's manufacturer, Eli Lilly, is the target of hundreds of lawsuits from people claiming that Prozac caused them or their departed loved ones to go off the deep end. On top of that, a new legal maneuver for violent offenders has entered the justice system—the Prozac defense.

While violent, deadly actions are the most obviously disturbing aspects of the drug, there are other problems. The author examines the studies that were done to grant Prozac FDA approval so it could be sold. Like all such studies, it's the drug company itself, not the FDA, that does the testing. Also, no matter how many tests a drug fails (i.e., is shown to be ineffective), as long as it can be shown to be better than placebos in at least two trials, it can win approval. So how did our wonder drug do? "In its 'Summary of Basis of Approval,' dated October 3, 1988, the FDA states that fourteen protocols involving controlled studies were submitted by Lilly. Four compared Prozac to placebo, and of these, three were used by the FDA as evidence of some beneficial effect. One showed none at all. Of the remaining ten studies, eight showed Prozac to have no positive effect.... In six out of the seven studies where it was included, imipramine (Tofranil), a very old drug, did better than Prozac."

The author also examines the side effects that the FDA edited out of Prozac's prescription label, the possibilities of addiction and abuse, the parallels between Prozac and "classic stimulants," such as cocaine and amphetamines, how Eli Lilly convinces people to take Prozac, the cuddly relationship between Lilly and the government, including George Bush and Dan Quayle, and much more. If you're considering using Prozac to become a shiny, happy person, do yourself a huge favor and read this book before you make your decision.

St. Martin's Press; $19.95
1994; hardcover; 274 pp.

# MISCELLANEOUS

### ALONE:
### A Fascinating Study of Those Who Have Survived Long, Solitary Ordeals
### by Richard D. Logan, Ph.D.

What effects do long, often torturous, solitary ordeals have and how do people cope with them? These questions are the basis of this book, which is about the indomitability of the human spirit and will to survive. The author presents us with gripping real-life cases of people who, voluntarily or not, found themselves in these trying situations. Examples of voluntary ordeals include Charles Lindbergh's thirty-three-hour sleepless solo flight across the Atlantic and mountaineers climbing in the Andes and Himalayas. Involuntary ordeals include those of the eleven-year-old girl who survived four days at sea in a tiny raft after her parents were murdered and the British woman who spent *seven years* in solitary confinement at the hands of the Hungarian Communists.

The author lets these people tell their stories by republishing their accounts of their ordeals. He analyzes the many ways they coped with their extraordinary conditions and the effects these conditions had on later life. In the end, he realizes that these survivors draw upon a hidden strength and sheer will to live that is buried in each one of us. These people are not superhuman. They're human.

As a basically irrelevant aside, I'd like to point out that this book has one of the best covers I've ever seen. Hats off to the designers for their daring minimalism.

Stackpole Books; $16.95
1993; softcover; 215 pp.

### THE BELL CURVE:
### Intelligence and Class Structure in American Life
### by Richard J. Herrnstein and Charles Murray

In this powder keg of a book, the authors make a controversial claim: The great inequalities that exist in the United States are mainly due to differences in intelligence. All people are not created equal when it comes to smarts. A new "cognitive elite" is coming into control of our information-based society, leaving everybody else stuck with crummy jobs. On top of that, the authors contend that there is a high correlation between intelligence and social problems such as unemployment, crime, and children in poverty. "For most of the worst social problems of our time, the people who have the problem are heavily concentrated in the lower portion of the cognitive ability spectrum."

The book's most controversial aspect is that it openly discusses the idea that there is a difference in intelligence among the races as a whole. The authors state that this is indeed true, that hundreds of studies worldwide, known almost only to academia and other scholars, prove it. They bring these studies out into the light. The authors claim that East Asians (Chinese, Japanese, and Koreans) have higher nonverbal intelligence than European Americans (verbal intelligence is about the same or slightly lower for East Asians) and that European Americans have higher intelligence than African Americans, especially general intelligence.

Although these three groups form the bulk of research and debate, the authors do present a sidebar on the intelligence rankings of other groups. They note that Jewish people consistently test higher than any other group. Latino Americans are said to test below the national average. Women and men as groups have almost the same IQs, but women cluster at the center (average) of distribution, whereas men are more likely to be at the low and high extremes.

The authors realize that there is great controversy over how intelligence is measured, and they address such concerns as cultural bias, the validity of IQ tests, and so on. They also fully admit that the reported differences are due in part to envi-

◄ *Alone*
**by Richard D. Logan**

*May the (life) Force be with you.*

ronmental and cultural factors. However, they feel that the evidence suggests that genetics also plays a role.

Even if such differences are true, they offer no means by which to judge individual members of any group. Any given person may be at the highest percentile of a group, dwarfing the brainpower of most people in a group said to be smarter.

So what do the authors think all this means? There is no known way to quickly raise intelligence by an appreciable level, and programs that attempt to do so are going nowhere slowly and expensively. "For the forseeable future, the problems of low cognitive ability are not going to be solved by outside interventions to make children smarter."

Our schools are damaging society by ignoring gifted students and concentrating almost exclusively on below-average kids. In this decade only one-tenth of one percent of federal funds for elementary schools and colleges goes to the gifted. The authors aren't saying to forget about the below-average students, but to help the gifted ones more. The authors also trash affirmative action *as it is being implemented today*. However, they are in agreement with its principles and want it to get back to its original purpose.

Although *The Bell Curve* has just come out (I'm writing this review only a few days before my deadline), I'm predicting that it will become one of the most controversial books of the decade. Have the authors discovered an authentic phenomenon and a key to society's problems, or are they just promoting a racist and elitist ideology cloaked in false science? You make the call.

The Free Press (Simon & Schuster); $30
1994; hardcover; 845 pp.; illus.

*Madness and Modernism* by Louis A. Sass

*A schizophrenic's fragmented vision, or a revolution in flat space?*

## MADNESS AND MODERNISM:
### INSANITY IN THE LIGHT OF MODERN ART, LITERATURE, AND THOUGHT
### by Louis A. Sass

This book by clinical psychologist Louis Sass offers two revolutionary concepts. First is a new definition of schizophrenia and related mental conditions. Insanity has almost always been seen as a step down in mental functioning. It supposedly "involves a shift from human to animal, from culture to nature, from thought to emotion, from maturity to the infantile and archaic." Sass has a revolutionary notion. What if psychosis is actually a step up in mental functioning? "What if madness, in at least some of its forms, were to derive from a heightening rather than a dimming of conscious awareness, and an alienation not from reason but from the emotions, instincts, and the body?" Sass refers to psychosis as a state of ultraheightened awareness, hyper-

alertness, and acute self-consciousness.

The other main premise of this book is that schizophrenia, when viewed in this new light, has remarkable parallels with modern and postmodern art, literature, and philosophy. Sass isn't looking at insanity in creative works—he's saying that the nature of insanity is very similar to the sensibilities and structures of work by Franz Kafka, Charles Baudelaire, Samuel Beckett, Marcel Duchamp, Friedrich Nietzsche, Jean-Paul Sartre, and Jacques Derrida. Madness and modernism both display a defiance of authority and convention, an indifference to the audience's understanding, a "rage for chaos," the uncertainty or multiplicity of points of view, the understanding (perhaps not conscious) that reality is created by the observer, a resulting loss of the sense of reality, a fragmentation of the self, a nihilistic and alienated outlook, and more.

*M&M* is a long, demanding book, but the insights it gives into the nature of insanity, art, and perhaps reality itself make it worth the effort.

Basic Books (HarperCollins Publishers); $30
1992; hardcover; 595 pp.; lightly illus.

## QUANTUM CONSCIOUSNESS:
### THE GUIDE TO EXPERIENCING QUANTUM PSYCHOLOGY
### by Stephen Wolinsky

In this groundbreaking book, Wolinsky applies the principles of quantum physics to psychology. His most basic premise is based on the quantum theory that the observer changes the nature of the observed because on the most basic level of reality, the two are really one. In other words, observing is not a passive activity. You are interacting with—indeed, creating—the things you observe. Therefore, the thoughts and feelings you are having are actually being created by you. What you must do is pull back to a "no-state state" in which you can see your thoughts and feelings and see yourself creating and interacting with those thoughts and feelings.

If you don't understand what I'm getting at, don't feel bad. I'm having a hell of a time trying to explain these difficult concepts. Luckily, the author is much better at it than I am: "The point of having an experience of Quantum Consciousness is to open the doorway into a larger reality that provides a larger context in which to 'hold' our experience. Instead of experiencing pain, isolation, frustration, or separateness as absolute states unto themselves, one gains a residing sense of the larger whole, of how, in physicist David Bohm's terminology, 'everything is connected to everything else.' While the sense of being connected to, even indivisible from, the rest of creation tends to come and go—one does not experience Quantum Consciousness twenty-four hours a day—the periodic experience of it loosens the hold of previous, limited patterns of thinking and believing."

In other words, part of Quantum Psychology is learning to step back from yourself and observe your internal experiences. Another part is realizing that all thoughts, emotions, and feelings are just energy. You harness and put labels on this energy. You can learn to stop doing this, to just let the energy dissipate. You can also come to the realization that we are all made out of the same energy. The hippies were right, we are all one! I know that this may sound like airy, mystical conjecture, but the author shows how it is all firmly grounded in quantum physics. He also gives dozens of practical exercises to aid you in achieving these breakthroughs in perceiving the "implicate order" and applying them to your life.

Forgive me for using a cliché, but this is truly a book that can change the way you see things.

Bramble Books; $14.95
1993; softcover; 259 pp.

## QUANTUM PSYCHOLOGY
### by Robert Anton Wilson

Wilson aims a battering ram at all your preconceptions, cherished beliefs, and ingrained notions, and proceeds to reduce them to a pile of rubble. This book has the same basic gist as *Quantum Consciousness* (above), but while that book attempts to lay down a more solid framework for a new area of psychology, this book is more scattershot, throwing idea bombs at you from every direction.

"This book on Quantum Psychology, then, attempts to show that the Uncertainty and Indeterminancy of quantum physics has its origins in our brains and nervous systems; that all other knowledge has the same origin; and that the non-aristotelian logics invented by quantum physics describe all other efforts of human beings to know and to talk about the world of experience, on any level." To put it another way, how and why do we know what we think we know about the world and ourselves?

Wilson discusses the notion of language, particularly bad language, in one chapter: "Why are these words 'dirty' and 'vulgar' when other words, denoting the same objects or events, are not 'dirty' or 'vulgar'? Why specifically can a radio station be fined if a psychologist on a talk show says 'He was so angry he wouldn't fuck her anymore' but not fined if the psychologist says 'He was so angry he stopped having sexual intercourse with her?'"

Wilson gives an example of the slippery nature of knowledge by telling a supposedly true story about a professor in the early 1960s who told his class that the statement "John Kennedy is President of the United States" is not a certainty. It supposes that the situation hasn't changed since the students and professor started class. This class was held during the time that Kennedy was shot and Lyndon Johnson was sworn in. True or not, the story makes a good point about the assumptions we constantly make.

This book is chock full of parables, anecdotes, and ideas like these, designed to get you to think about what you think. To help you, each chapter contains "exercizes" to break you out of your reality tunnels.

New Falcon Publications; $12.95
1990; softcover; 192 pp.

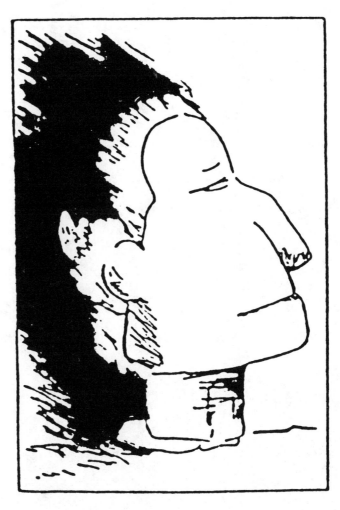

◄ *Quantum Psychology* by Robert Anton Wilson

*Down the slippery slope with the mind physicists.*

## THE TRUTH ABOUT LYING
### by Gini Graham Scott, Ph.D., J.D.

Every single one of us lies. Whether it's to save someone's feelings, get our own way, or even convince ourselves that we feel a way we really don't, we all lie like dogs. The author was lied to many times by business partners and decided to look into why we lie. The bulk of this book is devoted to cataloging the types of lies we tell: everyday social lies, lying in public, lying at work, lying in business, lying to friends and relatives, lying in romantic relationships, lying to husbands and wives, lying to parents and children, and lying to oneself. The rest of the book looks at justifications for lying, strategies for lying and perceiving lies, confronting lies, what to do if you're caught lying, and the power of telling the truth to yourself and others. A Lie-Q test at the end of the book measures your propensity to lie in different situations.

Unfortunately, this book doesn't add anything original to the field of lie-ology, but it is an entertaining overview of the large number of ways we deceive each other.

Smart Publications; $12.95
1994; softcover; 210 pp.

## NEW AGE

### BEYOND COMMON THOUGHT:
#### THE JOY OF BEING YOU
#### by Jacqueline T. Snyder

Behind this book is a very simple idea. As Valentine Michael Smith said in *Stranger in a Strange Land*: "Thou art God!" Snyder believes that we are all divine beings, but we have a tendency to forget this fact while we're stuck on this crummy planet. She writes, "This book is for all of the people who exist on our planet who want more...who through greater understanding want to reengage their enthusiasm for life and reverse some of the anesthesia they may have created in order to cope... In the tapestry of life is a thread of timeless truth and simplicity: *we exist in a supportive sea of consciousness that some call God* [ellipses are the author's]."

Snyder examines the principles of many religions, philosophies, and individual visionaries in order to find the underlying messages they contain, once you peel away all dogma, myths, rituals, politics, etc. The core beliefs of the human race are that we are all divine, that we can tap into this higher consciousness, and that we are all one. She feels that searching for answers only outside yourself is fruitless because it denies the fact that all answers are already within you.

What happens when we finally recognize our true nature? "When we learn to see the divine within, then we can also see it in one another, and then indeed we can more easily love and allow in the name of God—and thereby assist society to become one that honors the individual expression of that God within each of its members."

Windsor House Publishers; $13.95
1990; softcover; 203 pp.

### DOLPHINS, TELEPATHY AND UNDERWATER BIRTHING
#### by Timothy Wyllie

Wyllie believes that not only are dolphins intelligent creatures capable of communicating with humans through telepathy, they are actually spiritual beings who can lead us into a higher realm of consciousness. He relates numerous instances of his personal contacts with dolphins, including learning how to swim with them and communicating with them after ingesting a psychedelic.

Using dolphins as a springboard, so to speak, Wyllie travels the world exploring telepathy with Aborigines in Australia and healing with a shaman in Bali. By comparison, very little of the book deals with underwater birthing, except to say that it may help children to be more spiritual and that dolphins would like to join in the process.

Bear & Co.; $10.95
1993; softcover; 277 pp.

### HOW TO MEET AND WORK WITH SPIRIT GUIDES
#### by Ted Andrews

During my brief and ultimately unsuccessful stint selling unusual books through the mail, I probably sold more copies of this book than any other. This was pretty strange, I thought, for a catalog filled with books on sex, drugs, conspiracies, and other controversial matter. Of course, the fact that this book is dirt cheap had something to do with it, but I realized that a lot of nonconformists must be interested in this sort of thing.

This book gives step-by-step instructions for communicating with all manner of beings from other realms—angels, nature spirits, elementals, spirit totems, gods and goddesses, and dead loved ones. The nature of the spirit world is explored, and ways of perceiving the unseen are suggested. Then the author gives very specific beginning and advanced instructions for communicating with spirits.

Llewellyn Publications; $3.95
1992; paperback; 217 pp.

### INTERNATIONAL GUILD OF OCCULT SCIENCES

The IGOS is an organization that teaches courses, conducts research, and publishes books relating to occult/magick. You can join the Guild and move through the ranks, perhaps one day becoming part of the inner circle. The Guild has sorcerers who will perform magickal services for you. The Guild also publishes an amazing catalog that has everything you'll need to practice magick, Wicca, or whatever.

Reading this ninety-six-page catalog is quite a feat, since they use at least five different typefaces per page. In graphic design, this is known as "ransom note" style. But hey, it adds visual excitement, as do the numerous illustrations, so I'm not complaining. Among the hundreds of items you can get are photonic stimulators, cyborg psionic Cosimano helmets, past-life regression kits, revenge kits, rainbow pendulums, Voodoo dolls, candles, oils, incense, talismans, wands, staffs, Bigfoot powerstones, enhanced psi-ray chargers, and orgone vests.

The Guild also sells tons of books, videos, audiotapes, and photocopied info-packets on spells for all occasions, sex magick, telling the future, talking to spirits, time travel, interspecies communication, radionics, astrology, UFOs, hidden technology, healing, and much more.

IGOS
255 N. El Cielo Road, Suite 565/Palm Springs, CA 92262
Catalog: $3

**The Way a Weakened and Unbalanced Aura may Appear**

An aura (energy field) that is weakened and unbalanced is more susceptible to tearing. This leaves a hole in the field which is draining to our overall energy and enables outside energies and entities to play upon us more dynamically. Such an aura may appear to look like this.

*▲ How to Meet and Work With Spirit Guides* by Ted Andrews

*How to make friends and influence people.*

### THE INTUITIVE TAROT:
#### A METAPHYSICAL APPROACH TO READING THE TAROT CARDS
#### by Richard Gordon with Dixie Taylor

A guide to using the Tarot cards to identify negative beliefs ("I'm unworthy") that may be preventing your growth, develop positive beliefs, and see how likely a particular outcome is. The authors give spiritual and practical instructions for card reading and relate the meanings of all the major and minor arcana. Their attitude is: "This book is not intended to provide all of the answers but to assist you in your own search and to suggest some areas of focus. Look at this book as another tool to assist you in your own search for the truth."

Blue Dolphin Publishing; $11
1994; softcover; 143 pp.

### MEDIEVAL GRIMOIRE OF HONORIUS
#### by Honorius the Magus

A translation of a medieval manuscript. It consists almost entirely of detailed instructions for communicating with angels and conjuring and mastering demons. The book explains at length how to create and use the Seal of God and the Seal of Solomon. Diagrams are given for drawing the Seals, and the numerous prayers that you need to recite are related. There are also instructions for performing litany and the Beatific Visions. The steps are quite involved and time-consuming, plus you have to remain "free of sin" for the weeks that it takes to perform these rites, so you have to decide how badly you really want this. But if you want to give it a shot, be my guest.

International Guild of Occult Sciences; $25
1993; oversize hardcover; 114 pp.

## NOTHING IN THIS BOOK IS TRUE, BUT IT'S EXACTLY HOW THINGS ARE
### by Bob Frissell

How could you see a book with a title like this and not take a look at it? Bob Frissell has taken every element of the New Age you've ever heard of and put them all in a blender set to liquefy. William Cooper, Bob Lazar, Grays, Area 51, the Roswell crash, cattle mutilations, alien abductions, the face on Mars, the Philadelphia experiment, crop circles, the secret government, sacred geometry, chakras, free energy, the Great Pyramid, meditation, rebirthing, Christ consciousness, the Egyptian deity Thoth, immortality, pole shifting, interdimensional travel, Lemuria, Atlantis, and many other subjects all make appearances. Frissell attempts to tie them into one gigantic scenario.

The underlying theory of the book is your basic New Age philosophy—the human race is on the verge of an immense upward shift in consciousness. When this "unity consciousness" occurs, the planet will shift into a new dimensional level, and suddenly everyone on earth will love one another, and we'll all be holding hands and singing songs, and hatred and war and killing and bigotry and torture will be things of the past, and…well, you know the story.

*Nothing* is so far-flung and chaotic that I can't even begin to summarize it. Instead, let me give you a few quotes so you can get the flavor of this unique book. "As Lemuria sank, the poles shifted, and the land mass of Atlantis rose. The thousand or so immortal masters of the Naacal Mystery School of Lemuria went to Atlantis, specifically to one of its ten islands called Undal." "About a million years ago the race on Mars was dying from the effects of an earlier Lucifer rebellion (the third one). The planet was terminating from merkabas ["creationary patterns"] run amok." "Our mission is to wake up to our true nature so we can get on with it, so we can do what we came here to do. Our true purpose is to bring our higher dimensional light and wisdom here to co-create heaven on Earth, to assist the birth of the planet into the fourth dimension."

*Nothing* has a charm to it. It's partly Frissell's relaxed writing style and his enthusiasm for the subject matter. He also doesn't take himself too seriously, as the book's title indicates. But what makes the book so fun is his willingness to buy into almost every aspect of the New Age and try to make it all fit together. Whether you are a New Age traveller or not, Nothing is an entertaining read.

Frog, Ltd.; $12.95
1994; softcover; 230 pp; illus.

*The Black Flame* ➤

*A church that promotes the doctrine of "enlightened selfishness."*

## PSIONIC COMBAT
### by Charles Cosimano

This book is a no-holds-barred instruction manual on how to kick ass telepathically. Most books dealing with psychic warfare teach you how to defend yourself from psychic attack. This one does teach that aspect, but it devotes more space to using psychic powers to plant your ethereal boot up your enemy's ethereal rear end. "This book, properly used and studied, will equip you to deal with certain difficulties in life, difficulties which come, not from nature, but from the inconsiderate or often hostile acts of your fellow humans. If you follow the instructions given herein, you will find that you are no longer the helpless pawn of an unfeeling cosmos, beset upon all sides by relatives, neighbors, co-workers and the ubiquitous bureaucrats who infest our society like vermin in a grain bin."

The author gives beginner's tips on becoming a psychic warrior and proceeds to explain more detailed and destructive ways of attacking your opponents. He even explains how to make several devices that will increase your power. Psychic defense is covered, too, including how to deal with Psychic Vampires. To be truly effective as a warrior, you must lose your ethics, so the author gives many pep talks on how to do just that. "As you work on ridding yourself of the disease of compassion, you should also try to stop being ethical. There is a simple reason for this and that lies in the fact that most ethical principles are strictly for wimps."

What kind of things can you accomplish with these methods? You can cause injury or serious pain to your target. You can kill your target. You can attack your target's spouse and children. You can destroy your target's home. Nice.

This book is bound in black faux-leather and embossed in gold. It's quite a handsome grimoire. The only drawback is that the illustrations are the worst, most amateurish that I have ever seen in a book.

International Guild of Occult Sciences; $25
1993; oversize hardcover; 159 pp.

## SHAMAN'S DRUM:
### A JOURNAL OF EXPERIENTIAL SHAMANISM

A thick magazine with articles on shamanism, healing, psychedelic drugs, indigenous music, taking care of the earth, divination, and related topics. Most of the articles are first-hand accounts by people who actually participate in, or at least observe, shamanic rituals. Issue #33 contains articles on Korean ritual drumming, the masks of Haida artist Robert Davidson, and encounters with Fijian healers, Mayan shamans, and Tuvan mystics. There are also plenty of reviews, networking and resources, and ads for all kinds of cool musical instruments.

Shaman's Drum/PO Box 430/Willits, CA 95490
One-year sub (4 issues): $15; foreign: $19

# SATANISM

## THE BLACK FLAME:
### INTERNATIONAL FORUM OF THE CHURCH OF SATAN

Most people who read this magazine from the Church of Satan will be shocked. They will not find articles about the best ways to sacrifice puppies or how to avoid getting AIDS while drinking human blood. This is not the religion of black-robed killers or pathetic cat-killing teenage losers. Satanism, as it espoused by the Church of Satan, does not even make mention of an entity named Satan. Instead it uses Satan as a metaphor for someone who ignores all codes and restraints and lives as he or she sees fit, gaining as much pleasure as possible. I believe someone once labeled this line of thinking "enlightened selfishness."

What will be shocking is the fact that Satanism intersects and mixes with Nazism, neo-Nazism, fascism, Social Darwinism, and other "might makes right" philosophies. One of the precepts of Satanism is to give and expect no charity. Survive by your own wits. That's just natural law—the strong flourish and the weak drop like flies, so don't be a weakling. Satanism is also misanthropic, believing that most people are weak, pathetic wretches who try to ruin things for everybody. The authors of "Laugh! The Death Penalty" write: "Capitol Punishment is a euphemism for 'destroying low-life's.' If Satanists ruled the government, the degenerates [murderers] would go bound and gagged to the victim's family for them to torture, then destroy.... Since this isn't going to happen in our world just yet, let the government destroy the degenerates." The authors conclude that what we need is, "More quality people—less quantity."

Volume #4 of *The Black Flame* contains interviews with Anton LaVey and King Diamond; essays on the Satanic panic, the Temple of Set, the horrors of grocery shopping, dualism, horror fiction, Operation Rescue, and eugenics; a look at Satanic grottoes around the country; a poem titled "I Hate Everyone"; reviews; and lots of keen ads.

Hell's Kitchen Productions, Inc.
PO Box 499, Radio City Station/New York, NY 10101
Single issues are not available
Two double-issue sub: $12; foreign: $16

## THE DEVIL'S NOTEBOOK
### BY ANTON SZANDOR LAVEY

This is the first collection of essays by the founder of the Church of Satan to be published in more than twenty years. In it LaVey trashes the human race for its endless stupidity and hypocrisy and lays forth his ideas on experiencing maximum pleasure and living for yourself (which is what Satanism is all about).

This book is eminently quotable. On Satanism: "Why has Satanism succeeded? [It has?] Because from our earliest literature through the *Satanic Bible*, we have made no grandiose promises of infallible enlightenment and emphasized that each must be his or her own redeemer. That the extent of one's superiority (if any) is governed by one's human potential. That 'Satan' is a representational concept, accepted by each according to his or her needs." On misogyny: "A true misogynist is a straight man who—because he is a potential pushover for women and realizes it—resents the power a truly feminine woman yields, secretly admires this power, and seeks to capture it before it captures him." On enemies: "I defy ill wishes of my enemies by rejoicing in their discomfort.... I will never die because my death would enrich the unfit. I could never be that charitable."

While the head Satanist does have some interesting things to say, unfortunately he is sometimes terribly unoriginal. For example: "Definition of Good and Evil: Good is what you like. Evil is what you don't like." "Too much freedom is dangerous to those who cannot cope with the responsibilities that accompany independence."

Feral House; $10.95 1992; softcover; 147 pp.

## OTHER ALTARS:
### ROOTS AND REALITIES OF CULTIC AND SATANIC ABUSE AND MULTIPLE PERSONALITY DISORDER
### by Craig Lockwood

This confusing book attempts to show how ritual abusers use certain techniques to induce Multiple Personality Disorder (MPD) and dissociation in their victims. The author gives a huge history lesson, covering the history and meaning of ritual and abuse, as well as shamanism, Wicca, human sacrifice, Christianity, Gnosticism, the Knights Templar, Mormons, Freud, and much more. What the author fails to do, though, is tie all of this data together into a coherent whole that relates to his thesis.

Occasionally, he does directly address the topic at hand, as in the one-and-a-half-page section "Mind-Control Magic." He reports that some specialists in MPD are finding numerous patients who suffer from dissociation brought about by ritual abuse involving electroshock and melodic or percussive sounds. These people have been implanted with triggering mechanisms. "Therapists who have encountered this phenomenon offer clinical confirmation that certain words or phrases will produce swift behavioral changes in their patients. Well-known case studies document reactions ranging from violent abreaction to sudden and deep sleeps."

What could have been a fascinating book on a hard-to-swallow topic is instead a haphazard conglomeration of historical, psychological, and sociological bits and pieces.

CompCare Publishers; $17
1993; softcover; 273 pp.

## RAISING HELL:
### AN ENCYCLOPEDIA OF DEVIL WORSHIP AND SATANIC CRIME
### by Michael Newton

A most unusual reference book containing hundreds of entries covering crimes committed in Satan's name. Entries cover individuals, Satanic groups, and phenomena related to Satanic crime—animal killing, corpse stealing, child abuse, Dungeons and Dragons, heavy metal, etc. In the introduction, the author says that he is trying to walk the middle ground between the Christians who see Satanism as the force behind everything bad and the "apologists" who claim that Satanic violence is an urban legend. In fact, he refutes one-by-one the claims of such apologists.

The entries make for fascinating, gory reading. We learn of a group of Missouri high school cool dudes who graduated from beating kittens to death to beating a classmate to death. And of a fourteen-year-old Boy Scout who slashed his mother's throat with his Boy Scout knife, then killed himself. The word *loser* comes to mind often while reading these entries.

There are some bothersome elements to the book, though. Many of the entries don't tie the crimes to Satanism very well. Almost four pages are given to a double murder in which a psychic who channels an eighteenth-century doctor located the area where the bodies were hidden. The psychic also claimed that the murders were part of a Satanic ritual. In another entry, two Chilean tribesmen sacrificed a man to appease water gods, not Satan. Also, the link given between many "Satanic crimes" and the role-playing game Dungeons and Dragons is somewhat tenuous. The author admits this, but continues, "Enough bizarre incidents remain to warrant concern, especially where unstable players with histories of mental illness, drug abuse, or occult involvement are drawn to the game." This line of thinking crops up again when the author discusses Anton LaVey, founder of the Church of Satan, whose *Satanic Bible* has been quoted as a source of inspiration by a number of murderers. "If homicidal misfits take him literally, LaVey—like Pilate before him—is prepared to wash his hands of all responsibility." This sounds suspiciously like the "don't blame the person who committed the crime, blame the book or music that *made* him do it" mentality that is responsible for lawsuits against Ozzy Osbourne and Judas Priest and the creation of the victims of pornography legislation that would let rape victims sue porn makers for the crimes of some twisted bastard.

Overall, the book does present much interesting information. Its incredible coverage of Satanic organizations/cults alone is worth the price.

Avon; $5.99
1993; paperback; 406 pp.

## SATANIC PANIC:
### THE CREATION OF A CONTEMPORARY LEGEND
### by Jeffrey S. Victor

This book states flatly that the stories of a network of Satan worshipers who sexually abuse and torture children, sacrifice people, kill animals, deal drugs, and create pornography are groundless. "None of these claims are supported by reliable evidence," according to the author. In this lengthy book he examines the evolution of the Satanic cult legend, the social dynamics of a rumor-panic, how Satanism scares start and spread in communities, "survivor" stories (the quotes are the author's), Satanism's alleged threat to children and the real evidence, juvenile delinquents and pseudo-Satanism, the search for Satanism in schools, books, music, and games, the alleged link between multiple personality disorder and Satanic abuse, the true crises that are being faced by families, the search for scapegoats, the people who are leading the crusade against Satanism, the roles of the government, courts, and media, and the underlying dynamics of the Satanic panic.

Several appendixes present contact information for people and groups combating the Satanism scare, guidelines for dealing with Satanic rumors in a community, and synopses of Satanic scares and abuse trials across the country during the past several years.

This book presents much evidence damning the notion of an epidemic of Satanic crime and violence sweeping the country. Personally, my jury is still out on the subject till I find out more. However, as always, I feel sure the truth lies somewhere between the hysterical alarmists and the flat deniers.

Open Court; $16.95
1993; softcover; 408 pp.

# CHRISTIANITY

## SERPENT-HANDLING BELIEVERS
### by Thomas Burton

I've always thought that the small Southern churches where the believers handle venomous snakes and drank poison are among the most bizarre facets of Christianity—actually, religion in general—that I've ever come across. Imagine my bibliophilic delight, then, at finding out that the University of Tennessee was planning on publishing a book on this denomination, called Pentecostal-Holiness by its members.

I was delighted even more to find out that this book exceeded my expectations. The author visited these churches himself, got to know the people, and took photos. Everything you'd want to know is covered—exactly what they do, why they do it, how it started, who has died from it, other aspects of their belief system, and persecution they have faced.

*Serpent-Handling Believers By Thomas Burton*

The snake-handlers base their practices on the words of Jesus in the Gospel of Mark (16: 17–18): "And these signs shall follow them that believe; In my name shall they cast out devils; they shall speak with new tongues; They shall take up serpents; and if they drink any deadly thing, it shall not hurt them; they shall lay hands on the sick and they shall recover." While other Christians, such as Baptists and the Church of Christ, just give lip service to interpreting the Bible absolutely literally, these people walk it like they talk it. They hold, nuzzle, and otherwise play with rattlesnakes, cottonmouths, and other deadly snakes. They drink strychnine, lye, and Red Devil Drain Opener. A lot of them suffer no ill effects, even when bitten. However, many snake-handlers do get sick and the best estimates say that at least seventy-eight people have died from these practices.

*"They shall take up serpents," Mark 16:18. These people walk it like they talk it.*

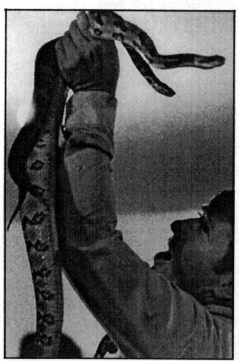

The author devotes a chapter to the persecution of the Pentecostal-Holiness by the courts. I have to have some respect for any belief system that's been persecuted and reviled as much as this one has been. I mean, if the government, society, and other Christians hate your guts that much, you must be doing *something* right.

This book contains about one hundred photographs of the snake-handlers in action, an enlightening question-and-answer section (sort of an "Everything You Ever Wanted to Know About Serpent-Handling Poison-Drinkers But Didn't Know Who to Ask"), and a twenty-two-page bibliography. Essential for your collection of books on unusual belief systems.

University of Tennessee Press; $19.95
1993; oversize softcover; 208 pp.

## WHO TAMPERED WITH THE BIBLE?
### by Pat Eddy

The problem with finding information about how the Bible has been altered and twisted through the millennia is that most of it comes from people who are obviously Bible bashers. While this may not bother you or me, it has the unfortunate side effect of weakening the information in the eyes of believers. Try showing a Christian a book that presents the contradictions and absurdities of the Bible from American Atheist Press, and they already have an escape hatch. But that won't work with this book. Winston-Derek is a Christian publisher in the buckle of the Bible Belt, Nashville, Tennessee. The author is a world-class biblical scholar whose twenty years in the intelligence community, it is claimed, have given her the ability to detect false information and ferret out what is real and what is not.

Eddy wastes no time in proclaiming that the Bible is a pastiche of misrepresentations, late additions, and outright forgeries: "...individual evangelists and sects actually altered the words of Jesus to suit their own purposes. Modern people mistakenly believe that the same attempt to record something resembling actuality, as practiced by journalists today (more or less successfully), was practiced by the ancients. Nothing could be further from reality." She goes on: "Early Christian authorities were well aware of the frequent alterations of the words of Jesus within the gospels.... The forgeries and tamperings were so numerous that determining the false from the authentic was a major duty of the first bishops. The examples of the concern expressed by the early church authorities are so numerous that one hardly knows where to begin."

Eddy proceeds to carefully dissect the Bible, focusing mainly on the Gospels but also shedding light on some Old Testament material and the Book of Revelation. She says that the Book of Deuteronomy is a complete fake, written 680 years after the death of its alleged author, Moses, in order for King Josiah to consolidate and control his kingdom. Also, the original ending of the Gospel of Mark was deleted long ago and two tamperers both wrote new endings, which are reproduced here. The book continues in this manner, mercilessly exposing not only the tampering of the Bible but the motivations of the tamperers, who were not concerned with conveying Jesus' true message but with furthering their own ends.

This book is most highly recommended.

Winston-Derek Publishing Group; $10.95
1993; softcover; 306 pp.

## THE WOMAN WITH THE ALABASTER JAR:
### MARY MAGDALENE AND THE HOLY GRAIL
### by Margaret Starbird

A fascinating glimpse of an early, suppressed version of Christianity. The author, a Roman Catholic scholar, was shaken to her core when she read the book *Holy Blood, Holy Grail*, which offered evidence that Jesus and Mary Magdalene were married and had children. She set out to disprove this shocking idea by delving into biblical scripture, European history, medieval art, Freemasonry, symbolism, heraldry, mythology, psychology, and other far-flung fields. What she came up with, she admits, is not proof that Jesus and Mary tied the knot, but proof that there is a long, rich, underground tradition that says they did.

Starbird points out that "...there were several parallel versions of Christianity from the very beginning, each with its own beliefs and interpretations of the Gospel message. Over the centuries, the message of Jesus was institutionalized. Doctrines were gradually developed that did not always reflect the faith of the early Jewish Christians of first-century Palestine." She recounts the circumstantial evidence that Jesus did indeed have a bride and shows how this tradition survived in art and stories through the ages. She also believes that this concept could help restore the feminine to Christianity and create a balance that is badly needed.

This book is a true page-turner, as secret and forbidden aspects of the world's largest religion are revealed on every page.

Bear & Company; $14.95
1993; softcover; 199 pp.

# THE DARK SIDE

### HOLY HORRORS:
#### AN ILLUSTRATED HISTORY OF
#### RELIGIOUS MURDER AND MADNESS
#### by James A. Haught

At last, there is a book that crystallizes what so many have known in their hearts: religion is an incredibly divisive, destructive force. *Holy Horrors* recounts the killings, atrocities, torturings, and genocides that have been committed in the name of God over nine centuries. The list reads like a hall of shame: the Crusades, human sacrifice, Islamic jihads, the Inquisition, witch hunts, the "hidden holocaust" in Armenia, the Holocaust, Jonestown, and more.

In 1215, a Catholic council passed the doctrine of transubstantiation, which says that during Communion, the wafer and wine literally become the body and blood of Christ. This led to Catholics starting rumors that Jews were driving nails through wafers and otherwise "killing Christ" again. "That same year [1298], a Bavarian knight named Rindfliesch led an armed brigade that stormed through defenseless Jewish towns to avenge the tortured host. He exterminated 146 communities in six months. In 1337 at Deggendorf, Bavaria, the entire Jewish population, including children, was burned after stories of host-defiling spread."

In a fascinating and sad case of hidden history, I learned that during the Black Death, many Christians blamed Jews for the plague, saying they had poisoned wells. "At Strasbourg, 2,000 Jews were herded like cattle into a large wooden barn, which was set afire. On a single day, August 24, 1349, an estimated 6,000 Jews were slaughtered by inflamed Christians at Mainz."

Of course Christians don't have a monopoly on this sort of thing. "During the first five months of 1988, [Sikh] extremists killed 1,168 in ambushes of Hindu weddings, holy festivals, and family gatherings." "In Saudi Arabia in 1977, a teen-age princess and her lover were executed in public [for having sex]."

Throughout the book are numerous woodcuts of people being tortured and executed and photos of dead bodies strewn everywhere, results of disagreements over how to worship God.

Prometheus Books; $20.95
1990; hardcover; 233 pp.

### HOLY HATRED:
#### RELIGIOUS CONFLICTS OF THE '90S
#### by James A. Haught

As we hurtle toward the end of the millennium, we find that the human race is not becoming more enlightened. Irrationality, intolerance, and violence are on the rise. Religion is fueling this horrible state of affairs. Killing in the name of God is more chic now than it ever was. In the introduction, James Haught, author of *Holy Horrors*, gives an international roll call of major religious conflict: "Christian Armenians and Muslim Azerbaijanis continue their slaughter in the Caucasus; fundamentalists who murdered a former Egyptian president now threaten his successor; Sikh militants in Punjab province kill Hindus in a drive to establish 'The Land of the Pure'; Catholic islanders of East Timor languish under occupation by Muslim Indonesia; Sudan's never-ending war between northern Muslims and Southern Christians has caused devastating famine;...black Muslims briefly shot their way to control of Trinidad..." And that's just half the list! Furthermore, those are just the largest conflicts that engulf entire nations.

The United States has so far escaped religious war on this grand scale, but it does occur. Take for instance the unrestrained terror used against abortion clinics, doctors, and workers, which reached bloodbath levels with two separate instances of cold-blooded murder. In 1992 seven leaders of the Temple of Love (located in Florida) were convicted of murdering fourteen people, including defectors. The Temple's holy man bred hatred for "white devils," and to enter the inner circle, a disciple had to kill a white person. In early 1990, police discovered the bodies of five

family members who had been sacrificed by a defrocked Mormon minister and his followers.

Some of the events in *Holy Hatred* are famous, (e.g. the storming of the Branch Davidians' compound, the bombing of the World Trade Center, and the slaughter of thirty praying Muslims in the West Bank by a Jewish doctor). Other events aren't well known. The Philippines, surprisingly, is having a horrible time with Muslim extremists, who want to overthrow the government and set up a theocracy. Muslims have kidnapped and/or slaughtered Christians and blown up Christian neighborhoods and a church. Also during the 1990s, "Iran sent assassin teams abroad to kill a dozen secularists and dissidents around Europe."

Haught's research is impressive and depressing. His chronicling of the upsurge in sacred slaughter and divine destruction should be required reading for the faithful.

Prometheus Books; $21.95
1994; hardcover; 229 pp.; illus.

◄ *Holy Horrors* by James A. Haught

*How to settle an arguement about God.*

### LEAD US NOT INTO TEMPTATION:
#### CATHOLIC PRIESTS AND THE SEXUAL ABUSE OF CHILDREN
#### by Jason Berry

So far, the Catholic Church has paid more than four hundred million dollars in legal fees, settlements, and medical costs relating to priests who molest children. It is projected that by the end of the decade, that figure could reach one billion dollars. This widespread problem was first encountered and investigated by Jason Berry, a Catholic and a reporter. In 1984 he heard that a scandal was brewing involving a priest who was sexually abusing two boys. As he dug further, he found that the problem was so widespread that four hundred priests and brothers had been fingered as pedophiles.

The results of Berry's quest are in this book, which catapulted the problem into public consciousness. Berry examines all sides: the children, the families, the priests, and the church officials. He found that instead of dismissing or defrocking the priests and offering solace to the children and families, the churches quietly transfer the priests to another diocese full of unsuspecting children and ignore the families or, when pushed into a corner, often countersue.

In an updated epilogue (1994) the author tells of what is being done and what might be done to rectify the situation, but he warns, "The Vatican thinks in terms of centuries, not in decades or even years. And today's clericalism refuses to acknowledge that the problems need a remedy."

Doubleday; $15
1992; softcover; 407 pp.

### THE STONING OF SORAYA M.
#### by Freidoune Sahebjam

"Over the past fifteen years more than one thousand women have been stoned to death in Iran." With this grim statistic in mind, the author tells the complete story of one of these women, Soraya M. But, you say, stoning a human is against the law in Iran. How can this happen? Easy. When a woman is accused of cheating on her husband, whether she has or not, she's no longer considered human. This way the law doesn't apply, and she can be brutally murdered with full consent of the government.

According to the author, Soraya's husband was looking for a way to ditch his wife, whom he had abused for years. When she started cooking for the husband of her deceased friend, her husband accused her of having an affair. When confronted with this accusation, Soraya naively defended herself by saying that she

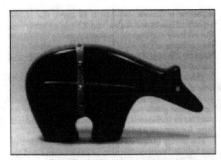

Bear spirit fetish. African wonderstone

Buffalo spirit fetish, Italian alabaster

*Breath of
the Invisible* ➤
by John Redtail
Freesoul

*"The universal
thread of all
life is breath.
Without it life
ceases."*

had done nothing and the accusations were groundless. The mayor informed her, "Soraya, you seem to be unaware of the laws of our society such as they were promulgated by our revered imam several years ago. When a man accuses his wife, she has to prove her innocence. That is the law. On the other hand, if a woman makes an accusation against her husband, she has to produce proof."

In gut-wrenching detail, the author tells of the decision to kill Soraya and of her execution, for which she was buried upright so that only her head and shoulders were showing. Her father, husband, and the rest of the villagers then threw stones at her until her head was nothing but pulp. All the while yells of "Praise Allah" and "This is God's will" rang in the air. One man actually said, "I am not the one who is throwing this stone.... It is God who is guiding my arm."

This is truly a sickening book. It presents further proof that justice is an empty, meaningless concept in this world.

Little, Brown & Co.; $15.95
1994; hardcover; 144 pp.

# MISCELLANEOUS

## AMERICAN ATHEIST PRESS CATALOG

Founded by Madalyn Murray O'Hair, American Atheist Press puts out a great catalog of books and products that promote atheism and slag religion. They offer their own books—*Atheists: The Last Minority, An Atheist Epic, The Case Against Religion, Our Pagan Christmas*, etc.—and those of other publishers. They've also got pamphlets, flyers, videos, winter solstice cards, American Atheist logo medallions, back issues of *American Atheist Magazine*, and more. Their most controversial poster is an illustration of an old white-bearded gentleman having anal sex with Uncle Sam. The top of the poster reads, "one nation under God."

AAP also carries a bunch of little stickers with quotes from famous people including some of the Founding Fathers. "What has been Christianity's fruits?—Superstition, bigotry and persecution"—James Madison. "This would be the best of all possible worlds if there were no religion in it"—John Adams.

There's also a large selection of bumper stickers:
• Atheists do it without guilt.
• Take your God and shove it!
• Jesus is Lard.
• Nothing is greater than a thinking human.
• God is just another addiction.

American Atheist Press
PO Box 140195/Austin, TX 78714-0195
Catalog: $1

## APOCALYPSE:
### ON THE PSYCHOLOGY OF FUNDAMENTALISM IN AMERICA
#### by Charles B. Strozier

Endism, as the author calls it, is the belief that the end of the world as we know it is coming. The largest and most focused group to hold this belief is the Christian fundamentalists, who are the focus of much of this book. The author spent several years going to churches, Sunday schools, and conducting interviews with a wide variety of fundamentalist Christians in New York. What he wanted to uncover was the psychology behind the belief that the world is going to be destroyed, Jesus will return, and believers will live forever.

The author sees this widespread belief as a sign of illness in our culture. In a world of random violence and the nuclear bomb, capable of unleashing an atomic apocalypse, life has become frightening and unsure. Many people take comfort in the idea that this wicked world will be flushed clean. Strozier also found out through his research that many fundies had led extremely painful lives, and they found comfort in endism.

But Christian fundamentalism isn't the only apocalyptic belief system, and the author explores alternate beliefs, such as Hopi Prophecies and the New Age. "All Hopi prophecy concerns the coming of the 'true white brother,' Pahana, the redeemer, at which time all evil will be purified and the world remade." "The apocalyptic holds center stage in the spiritual imaginations of the New Agers. The very term New Age has an apocalyptic flavor to it and implies a transformation of the world...."

This is clearly an important book and is essential reading for anyone interested in *why* so many people think the end is near.

Beacon Press; $25
1994; hardcover; 316 pp.

## THE BOOK YOUR CHURCH DOESN'T WANT YOU TO READ
### edited by Tim C. Leedom

This book claims that it isn't antireligious. By this, I think the editor means that it's not antispiritual, because it sure slams the hell out of religion, but it doesn't do so to destroy belief in God. It does so to slap people out of their deluded belief systems and allow them (perhaps force them) to think about God on their own terms, outside of organized religion.

The articles, essays, and book excerpts in *The Book* challenge all aspects of religion, particularly Christianity. Much is made over the fact that Christianity is based on paganism, Zoroastrianism, and other earlier belief systems. One excerpt lists the crucified saviors who appeared well before Christ. One of these saviors, the Oriental Virishna, was recorded in 1200 B.C. as having been born of a virgin; his parents had to flee when the land's ruler, afraid of this savior, ordered all boys under two to be killed; angels and shepherds attended his birth, where he was given frankincense and myrrh; his birth had been prophesied; he performed miracles, including healing the sick and raising the dead; he was crucified between two thieves; and he rose from the dead. Sound familiar?

Other articles cast a cold light on the Bible, atrocities committed in the name of God, the Religious Right, sex abuse in churches, circumcision, Islam, Judaism, and more. *The Book* is a helter-skelter but invaluable guide to cutting through the inanity of organized religion.

Kendall/Hunt Publishing Co.; $16.95
1993; softcover; 446 pp.

## BREATH OF THE INVISIBLE:
### THE WAY OF THE PIPE
#### by John Redtail Freesoul

If you want an honest, direct, and nonexploitive introduction to Native American spirituality, this is it. NatAm spirituality has become commodified in recent years. It's a trendy thing that whiteys get superficially involved in, and it has spawned countless New Age books. But Freesoul (don't you just love that name?) is a Cheyenne-Arapaho who speaks for the Redtail Hawk Medicine Society, an intertribal spiritual organization.

In this book he quietly explains the essence of NatAm beliefs (although not every principle applies to every tribe). He starts out with the pipe. "The universal thread of all life is breath. Without it life ceases. Animals, plants, and even rocks breathe. The winds breathe. We breathe into our pipes. In the pipe ceremony we share breath, we share smoke. The sacred smoke is the breath of life made visible, rising upward as a prayer to the Source of all breath, the Great Breath, the Great Spirit, which breathes individualized spirit as unique souls in unique creations, each unique yet all related." Breathing into the pipe reminds the smoker of what must be released or transcended. Inhaling from the pipe reminds the smoker of what must be accepted.

From there Freesoul launches into explanations of sweat

lodges, vision quests, the Medicine Wheel, the Four Directions, Native American healing, and more. In the end, he sums everything up nicely: "We are our own priests and priestesses. Only through us can the world be purified."

Quest Books; $11.95
1986; softcover; 217 pp.

## INSTITUTE OF BLINDING LIGHT CATALOG OF SACRED ITEMS

A tiny catalog offering hundreds of satirical/gag items (and a few serious ones) relating to religion. Among the items offered: Mr. Jesus Head ("Insert your own thorns and long hair. From the creators of Mr. Potato Head"), Catholic gag condom ("Jokes on them—this condom's filled with holes!"), Altar Boys of the Catholic Church Pin-Up calendar, Satan worshiper starter kit, Nintendo's Exodus Game, Dalai Lama Dolly, Jesus action figure, Circumcision Pop-Up Book, gag sour Communion wafer, *David Koresh's Best Pick-Up Lines* ("Example: Hey, I'm the savior"), Indian hand cymbals, monk robe, Christian Science medical kit ("Black medical bag—contains nothing"), *Jimmy Swaggart Guide to Hookers and Motels*, fig leaf, Styrofoam Stonehenge, *Life of Brian, Merry Christmas Charlie Brown*, and a holy lot more.

Institute of Blinding Light
1101 Clay/San Francisco CA 94102
Catalog: $3.95 plus $1.50 shipping

## MILLENNIAL PROPHECY REPORT

Published by the Millennium Watch Institute, this unique newsletter keeps tabs on the increasing number of prophecies concerning the apocalypse and other radical earth changes. Each issue summarizes and comments on pronouncements from, among others, Christian churches, Jewish sects, New Agers, Native Americans, and all sorts of fringe/extremist groups who believe that enormous, reality-changing events will happen soon. Volume 3 issue #1 looks specifically at the rapture with input from the End-Time Handmaidens, the Church of God International, Alert Americans, *UFO Magazine*, Namaste, Inc., and others.

This is how the newsletter sums up an article appearing in *End-Time Handmaidens Magazine*: "'After the Rapture!' [pp. 10–12] comes from one Olav Rodge, a Norwegian. He experienced this vision several times, to ensure that he would be able to record it properly—he was 78 when it came to him.... Panic sweeps over Oslo because so many have simply disappeared. There have been too many evanescences for the police to investigate, so they urge friends and relatives to make detailed reports of the circumstances of these vanishments. One witness recalls hearing the ephemerant saying 'Thank you, Jesus' as he faded into some sort of mist that shortly dissipated."

As an added bonus, the newsletter prints the addresses of all these contrary organizations for further contact (you'd better hurry, though!). This is an incredible resource, but like so many other specialty newsletters, it's quite costly.

Millennium Watch Institute
PO Box 34021/Philadelphia, PA 19101-4021
One-year sub (10 issues): $95; Canada and Mexico: $100; overseas: $105

## THE NAKED TRUTH:
### Exposing the Deceptions about the Origins of Modern Religions (VHS videocassette)
### hosted by Derek Partridge

Reporter and screenwriter Derek Partridge and several others present information that shows organized religion, especially Judaism and Christianity, to be nothing more than myths. Partridge starts out by noting that more people have been "killed, tortured, and mutilated" because of religion than any other force. He takes us back to the earliest days of human existence, when people had absolutely no understanding of any of the natural phenomena that were occurring around them. It was only

natural that these people should make up gods and demons to explain forces they couldn't comprehend. Isn't it time, Partridge asks, that we outgrew that mode of thinking? He sounds almost pissed off as he notes that mankind stubbornly clings to unproven and unprovable centuries-old myths. He also points out that religious leaders and military leaders often give the same type of commands—don't think for yourself, follow orders, and—often—kill your enemy.

Other experts come in to point out that Judeo-Christian belief systems are merely a Mulligan's stew of all the religions that had come before. One talking head points out, "Virtually every ancient religion had a Lamb of God who takes away the sins of the world." The numerous parallels between Horus and Jesus, Buddha and Jesus, and Krishna and Jesus are detailed. Ancient Egypt was the starting point of many Christian beliefs, including the concept that the divine pharaoh was a shepherd and the people were his flock.

A good part of the tape concerns the intriguingly weird theory that the Bible is totally based on astrology. The resident expert quotes from the Book of Job, showing that God actually mentions the zodiac. He also claims that the twelve apostles correspond to the twelve houses of the zodiac; that the name Israel is actually a contraction of the names of the gods Isis, Ra, and El; that the golden calf the Hebrews were worshiping when Moses came down from the mountain represents the sun; and other such interesting tidbits.

*The Naked Truth* may wander a bit, and it may not be visually exciting, but it does offer many worthwhile clues to the true origins of religion.

Lightworks Audio and Video; $29.95
Unknown date; VHS videocassette; 120 min.

## NEW ORLEANS HISTORIC VOODOO MUSEUM CATALOG

If you go to New Orleans, be sure to check out the Historic Voodoo Museum at 724 Dumaine. In the meantime, you can fulfill your voodoo needs with the items in this catalog. They offer T-shirts, gris-gris bags, twelve talismans, books, potions, oils, powders, more than a dozen types of voodoo dolls, alligator heads, Tarot decks, coffin kits, ritual candle kits, and more. Many of the above items—oils, gris-gris bags, etc.—are made for a single purpose, such as love, health, money, friendship, hexing, etc. If you have a purpose in mind that isn't listed, a custom item can be made for you.

NOHVM/PO Box 70725/New Orleans, LA 70172
Catalog: $1

## THE ODIN BROTHERHOOD
### by Dr. Mark L. Mirabello

Odinism is a branch of paganism that worships the "old gods" of the Vikings. Within Odinism there is a secret society known as the Odin Brotherhood. The author came into contact with members of this shadowy group while doing doctoral research at the University of Glasgow in Scotland. He relates the Brotherhood's history and beliefs in this book through an extended dialogue between himself and the Brotherhood. Although this method has some advantages, the lack of headings or even subheadings means that there are no breaks in the information flow. It's a single fifty-seven-page continuous conversation.

In 1421 a woman was burned at the stake for worshiping the old gods. She instructed her three children from beyond the grave to form a "conspiracy of equals," where every member is a leader, to worship the old gods in clandestine places, and to share knowledge only with those they trusted. The children took an oath sealed in blood, and the Brotherhood of Odin was formed. The author relates the gods and goddesses, rituals, customs, and other beliefs of this unusual group.

Holmes Publishing Group; $9.95
1992; softcover; 58 pp.

## PRINCIPIA DISCORDIA:
OR HOW I FOUND THE GODDESS AND WHAT I DID TO
HER WHEN I FOUND HER—WHEREIN IS EXPLAINED
ABSOLUTELY EVERYTHING WORTH KNOWING ABOUT
ABSOLUTELY ANYTHING

### by Malaclypse the Younger

Discordianism is one of the most successful fringe religions ever formed. It's a wacky, zany religion that parodies religion. Its followers believe that Eris, the Greek goddess of Discord, rules the universe. If this is true, then chaos is the sacred, guiding principle of all of creation. Take a good look at the world around you and tell me if this idea doesn't explain a lot of things.

*Principia Discordia* is the sacred book of Discordianism. It's a very chaotic (no surprise there) mélange of drawings, photos, rubber stamps, found images, and words of crazy wisdom. By studying this most blessed and holy book you will find out that "King Kong died for your sins." You will also learn that "in the Los Angeles suburb of Whittier there lives a bowling alley, and within this very place, in the year of Our Lady of Discord 3125 (1959), Eris revealed Herself to the Golden Apple Corps for the first time." But perhaps the most important thing you will learn is the Fifth Commandment: "A Discordian Is Prohibited of Believing What He Reads" (this includes the book you are now holding).

Loompanics Unlimited; $6.95
1970; softcover; 100 pp.

## SACRED ARCHITECTURE
### by A.T. Mann

Throughout history people all over the world have incorporated their beliefs into their buildings. They have done this in obvious and not-so-obvious ways. Many obvious ways, such as literal depictions of sacred personages, are covered here, but the main focus of the book is on the more subtle varieties of sacred architecture. Many buildings and parts of buildings were constructed based on the cosmic principles of those who did the building. For example, "Native American medicine lodges had twenty-eight poles radiating from a central pole, an *omphalos* or centre of the world. The number of poles relates to the days in the lunar month and aligns with important star orientations. A central post was placed by the Medicine Man and intersected by the four sacred paths, which converged at the pole." The Chinese have constructed many buildings based in their belief of the flow of earth energies. Buildings must be designed in a way that works with this *Feng Shui*, amplifying it instead of blocking it.

The author discusses how sacred beliefs play an integral role in temples, cathedrals, theaters, and other buildings in a variety of cultures and times. The book ends with a look at how most modern architecture has lost its sacred underpinnings.

This book is of extremely high quality. It is printed on heavy paper, and the sheer number of full-color photos, paintings, and diagrams takes the phrase "profusely illustrated" to another level.

Element Books, Inc; $19.95
1993; oversize softcover; 192 pp.

*Sacred
Architecture
by A.T. Mann*

*Incorporating beliefs into buildings.*

# THE UNEXPLAINED

## UFOS

### ABDUCTION:
#### HUMAN ENCOUNTERS WITH ALIENS
### by John E. Mack, M.D.

John Mack, a Pulitzer Prize–winning professor of psychology at Harvard Medical School, has made quite a splash by taking reports of abductions literally and offering help and support for people who think they've been abducted. You've probably seen him. Every time a news/tabloid show does a piece on abductions, they interview Mack.

When he first heard of UFO abductees, he thought they were crazy, but upon meeting them in a support group in 1980, he changed his mind. "The intensity of the energies and emotions involved as abductees relive their experiences is unlike anything I have encountered in other clinical work." He then embarked on his own quest to understand abduction. He met with abductees, discussed their experiences, and set up support groups. This process of discovering what abductions are and what they mean is one aspect of this book. Another aspect is Mack's own journey as he leaves behind his old assumptions, rejecting consensus reality for something stranger. The third facet of the book is the struggles of the abductees as they try to understand what was done to them and grow from the experiences.

*Abduction* is rich with detailed histories of the abductions of members of Mack's group. Whether you believe people are actually being kidnapped, are making everything up, or are part of some other strange phenomenon (mass hallucination, the twisting of childhood sexual abuse memories, contact with the Overmind of humanity [Terence McKenna's theory]), this book is filled with valuable source material. Although recently published, it is most likely to be considered one of the seminal works on the abduction phenomenon.

Charles Scribner's Sons (Macmillan Publishing); $22
1994; hardcover; 432 pp.

### ALIEN CONTACT:
#### TOP-SECRET UFO FILES REVEALED
### by Timothy Good

This sequel to Timothy Good's enormously successful *Above Top Secret* reveals more government UFO secrets. Good's previous book showed that the governments of many countries have been covering up their knowledge of UFOs since the 1940s. In this book, Good offers evidence of the following: "Some UFOs are indeed extraterrestrial in origin; that alien bodies have been recovered; that a few craft have been test-flown; and that contact has been established—even at an official, if restricted, level."

This book contains a wealth of information. Good has managed to dig up documents and testimony that haven't already been done to death in the UFO literature. He gives us the goods on Air Force footage of UFOs and aliens, official Russian recognition of UFOs, new evidence from the FBI linking cattle mutilations to UFOs, Area 51, encounters with several ex–intelligence officers, a possible alien base in Puerto Rico, and the extremely controversial Bob Lazar, who claims to have been a privately employed physicist sent to work on top-secret government propulsion projects.

*Alien Contact* also offers this intriguing tidbit: The late actor Jackie Gleason was extremely interested in UFOs. He had an extensive library on the subject, and he designed one of his homes to look like a flying saucer. He called it "The Mothership." "According to Beverly McKittrick, Gleason's second wife, her husband came home one night in 1973, visibly shaken. He told his wife that he had just returned from a visit to Homestead Air Force Base, Florida, where, thanks to his friend President Richard Nixon, who arranged the trip, he was shown a top-secret repository where the bodies of aliens were stored."

Quill (William Morrow & Co); $12
1991; softcover; 288 pp.

### THE CONTROLLERS:
#### THE HIDDEN RULERS OF EARTH IDENTIFIED
### by Commander X

Commander X claims to be a retired military operative (with a grandiose taste in pseudonyms). In this garish, sensationalistic book ("Warning! This book is meant for serious researchers only!"), Com X shows that we are the property of aliens. According to his version of history, up until 18,617,841 B.C., to be exact, humanity was just another animal species. In that year, Sanat Kumara (The Lord of the Flame), his four Great Lords, and one hundred assistants arrived on a spaceship from Venus. They gave higher consciousness to a human being named Adam, and they created a mate for him, Eve.

Com X is a little murky on exactly who is controlling us. Apparently there is a morally bankrupt serpentine race, originally from Venus, living beneath the surface of the earth. They are aided in their attempts to dominate the human race by the Illuminati, who are actually aliens, and the infamous Greys. Some of the aliens kidnap (abduct) humans for scientific experiments, to fill their zoos, and so on. The author claims that Jimmy Hoffa was an abductee.

From there, things get mighty confusing. Com X presents a hodgepodge of excerpts, quotes, theories, and alleged facts about AIDS, Hitler, Lyndon LaRouche, the KKK, Satanism, free energy, alien/human babies, and more weirdness. You figure it out!

Inner Light Publications; $19.95
1994; oversize softcover; 112 pp.

### THE COSMIC PULSE OF LIFE:
#### THE REVOLUTIONARY BIOLOGICAL POWER BEHIND UFOS
### by Trevor James Constable

Trevor Constable is an internationally recognized aviation expert whose four major books on the subject are universally regarded as classics. In 1958 he published *They Live in the Sky*, a classic of ufology that postulated the existence of invisible living organisms in Earth's atmosphere. In 1976, he expanded greatly on that topic with *The Cosmic Pulse of Life*, which is now published in a revised version.

*The Cosmic Pulse of Life* by Trevor James Constable

*A classic, heretical explanation of UFOs.*

Constable melds the ideas of Rudolf Steiner, Dr. Ruth Drown, and Wilhelm Reich into a theory of living energy (called orgone by Reich) and higher planes of existence that explain what UFOs are. We must drop our primitive mechanistic view of UFOs as flying machines and realize that they are powered by the "invisible" and that some of them are actually creatures living in the atmosphere. Constable presents his evidence, including more than thirty pictures of these beings taken with infrared film. Independent, substantiating research from Italy and Romania has been included in this edition. This book is a classic and offers a heretical explanation of UFOs that falls outside the thinking of the ufology establishment.

Borderlands Science Research Foundation; $24.95
1990; softcover; 488 pp.

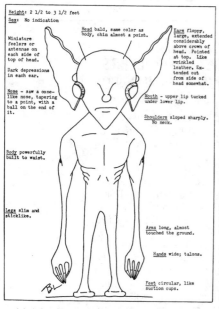

Height: 2 1/2 to 3 1/2 feet
Sex: No indication

Miniature feelers or antennae on each side of top of head.

Dark depressions in each ear.

Nose — saw a cone-like nose, tapering to a point, with a ball on the end of it.

Body powerfully built to waist.

Legs slim and sticklike.

Head bald, same color as body, chin almost a point.

Ears floppy, large, extended considerably above crown of head. Pointed at top. Like wrinkled leather. Extended out from side of head somewhat.

Mouth — upper lip tucked under lower lip.

Shoulders sloped sharply. No neck.

Arms long, almost touched the ground.

Hands wide; talons.

Feet circular, like suction cups.

A sketch of one of the goblin-like entities which besieged a farmhouse at Kelly-Hopkinsville in Kentucky in August 1955. *(Mary Evans Picture Library)*

*The UFO Encyclopedia by John Spencer* ➤

*Tiny visitors, giant crop circles, and true believers.*

## THE GODS OF EDEN
### by William Bramley

When he began researching this book in 1979, William Bramley set out to write a history of warfare that exposed the involvement of manipulative third parties in armed conflict. He wanted to show that wars are orchestrated for economic and political gain. He had never had an interest in UFOs and considered the matter unimportant, but during his research he uncovered a vast alien conspiracy. He claims that "an extraterrestrial society had come to possess Earth and sought to exploit the planet's resources. To make the exploitation easier, a work race was created: *Homo sapiens*. Humans were treated as livestock and were frequently butchered when they became too numerous or troublesome. To preserve *Homo sapiens* as a slave race and to prevent future rebellion, spiritual knowledge was repressed, human beings were scattered geographically into different linguistic groups, and conditions were created to make physical survival on Earth an all-consuming chore from birth to death."

Bramley first turns to the creation stories of various cultures to back up his theory. The Bible, he feels, is chock-full of evidence. In Genesis 3:17–19, God tells Adam that for munching on fruit from the Tree of Knowledge, he will now be mortal and will have to indulge in manual labor. This indicates "that Custodial rulers intended to make humans live their entire lives and die without ever rising above the level of arduous material existence." Furthermore, the Tower of Babel was actually a launching pad for a rocket built by the ancient Babylonians.

At this time there was a group of humans who tried to get the human race out from under the heel of the alien Custodians. The Brotherhood of the Snake, as the author calls it, spread spiritual and scientific knowledge, but it was eventually corrupted by the aliens and is now used by them as a further means of repression.

Bramley takes us on a long and winding trip through all of human history: Egypt, Mesopotamia, India, Persia, Jesus, the Book of Revelation, Mohammed, the Crusades, pre-Columbian South America, the Black Plague, the Illuminati, Freemasons, St. Germain, the American Revolution, the Mormons, Hitler, JFK's and RFK's assassinations, the New Age. All of it is reexamined through the lens of the Custodians. This massive book has become a deserved cult classic. It's not every book that attempts to rewrite all of history, especially from a "we are the slaves of aliens" angle.

Avon Books; $5.99
1989; paperback; 505 pp.

## INTERNATIONAL UFO LIBRARY MAGAZINE

A slick, professionally produced magazine written from a believer's viewpoint. It offers testimonies from abductees, UFO photos, reports from hot spots all over the world, articles on the government's cover-up, profiles of actors from science fiction TV shows (usually one of the *Star Trek* series), and a dose of New Age spirituality. Each issue also has around ten pages of UFO items available directly from the magazine. Lots of scarce books, videos of abductees telling their stories, posters, calendars, etc.

International UFO Library
PO Box 461116/Escondido, CA 92046-9892
One year sub (6 issues): $19.95

## UFO:
### A FORUM ON EXTRAORDINARY THEORIES AND PHENOMENA

A wide-ranging and thoroughly enjoyable magazine on UFOs and related matters. The editorial stance is that something funky is happening, it might be UFOs, it might be the military, it might be something else entirely, or it might be any combination thereof. The articles examine phenomena from all these aspects. A single recent issue (Vol. 9 #3) had articles on possible quantum explanations for spaceship travel, a UFO sighting in Michigan, the continuing quest for mind control, possible explanations for electrical failures during close encounters, possible Air Force connections to cattle mutilations, the Air Force's plans for the supersecret Area 51, and a look at new pictures of top-secret aerospace projects. Plus, every issue has a forum, reviews, and Mediawatch. This is the definitive UFO magazine.

UFO Magazine/PO Box 1053/Sunland, CA 91041
Single issue: $5.45
One-year sub (6 issues): $21; foreign: $28

## THE UFO ENCYCLOPEDIA:
### THE COMPLETE AND COMPREHENSIVE A TO Z GUIDE TO EXTRATERRESTRIAL PHENOMENA
### compiled and edited by John Spencer

John Spencer, vice chairman of the British UFO Research Association (BUFORA), has written more than one thousand entries for his encyclopedia on UFOs. The book's strong point is its numerous entries on people who have allegedly encountered UFOs and/or aliens. This information isn't available in one source anywhere else. Unfortunately, a lot of the entries are skimpy. "Cornfield [crop] circles" lacks many important facts, "Cattle mutilations" is vague, and "SETI (Search for Extraterrestrial Intelligence)" is downright worthless.

Besides skimping on important entries, Spencer makes the mistake of giving entries that footnote people who don't deserve it. For instance, take Ken Adams: "In 1966, in Australia, a series of 'cornfield circles' (see Circles, Cornfield) appeared. Gooloogong resident Ken Adams suggested that these were being made by a bird called the bald-headed coot. This theory has not been widely supported." Why give this idiotic, cockamamie theory its own entry instead of just mentioning it in passing in the main entry on cornfield circles?

No doubt writing an encyclopedia on such a controversial and divisive field as ufology is no picnic, but with a better set of priorities, Spencer could have put together a far superior book.

Avon; $15
1991; softcover; 340 pp.

## UFOS AND THE NEW WORLD ORDER
### (VHS VIDEO)
### by Michael Lindemann

Michael Lindemann is an investigative journalist and founder of the 2020 group, which researches human-alien contact. Presented during the 1992 Whole Life Expo, his speech contains two main points: "Aliens are here" and "Your government knows and has lied to you about it." Lindemann thinks there are at least three kinds of aliens in contact with Earth—physical beings from other planets, beings who live here on earth, and interdimensional beings living in parallel universes. They are here, he believes, to selectively harvest tissue through animal mutilations and run tests on humans.

Our government knows this and is unable to stop it. But instead of telling the people and causing a worldwide panic, the United States (and presumably other governments) lies like a dog. At first the government practiced denial, but now since the information is leaking out so fast and continuously, the secret government—those behind the New World Order—are practicing spin control to distort much of the information that gets out, causing confusion and doubt to form around the issue.

For those who are new to the idea that the government is covering up its knowledge of aliens, this video is a decent starting point, but for people already familiar with the idea, there's nothing new here.

Lightworks Audio and Video; $24.95
1992; VHS videocassette; 48 min.

## UNDERGROUND ALIEN BASES
### by Commander X

Commander X is at it again, expounding on his theory that aliens have bases inside the earth. Com X thinks the military base at Dulce, New Mexico, is a major center of alien activity: "It is at Dulce that a negative group of aliens, best known as the 'Greys' or the 'EBEs' have established a fortress, spreading out to other parts of the U.S. via means of a vast underground tunnel system that has virtually existed before recorded history, and which has been 'improved upon' by the original descendants of Atlantis, as well as other groups who now survive and go about their business unknown to the majority of us living on the Earth's surface."

Other bases exist at Mt. Shasta, California; Brown Mountain, North Carolina; Groom Lake, Nevada; Superstition Mountain Range, Arizona; the North and South Poles; the Andes mountain range; and the jungles of Brazil. Entrances to the elaborate world-wide tunnel network exist not only at these bases, but also in remote spots and major cities. "There is supposedly even an opening somewhere in New York City in the vicinity of midtown Manhattan that can be reached through an abandoned elevator shaft that only a few know about for obvious 'security' reasons." Com X goes into elaborate detail regarding the bases and the tunnels, relating the stories of abductees and explorers and the pronouncements of channeled beings.

Inner Light Publications; $15
1990; softcover; 127 pp.

## WATCH THE SKIES!:
### A CHRONICLE OF THE FLYING SAUCER MYTH
### by Curtis Peebles

We laugh at the silly Greeks and Vikings for their beliefs in Zeus, Hercules, Odin, Thor, and so on, but are we really any better? Ufologist Curtis Peebles says no. He considers the beliefs that surround flying saucers a current mythology—something that is believed at the time but is seen by future societies as a pitiful attempt to make sense of the world around us. Lightning bolts appear because Zeus is hurling them; lights in the sky appear because space aliens are flying them.

Peebles looks at the beginnings, evolution, meaning, and effects of the UFO myth. The mythology had its earliest stirrings in the "airship" sightings of 1896–97, 1909–10, and 1913. From 1933–37 "ghost airplanes" were spotted in Scandinavia.

The myth began in earnest in 1944 when the editor of the pulp magazine *Amazing Stories* began publishing the concoctions of Richard Shaver, a welder who spent up to eight years in a mental hospital, possibly for paranoid schizophrenia. Shaver's stories were presented as truth, and *Amazing Stories'* circulation went through the roof. "In September 1946, [editor] Palmer told a letter writer, 'As for space ships...we personally believe these ships do visit earth.'" Remember, this was a year before the first widely publicized saucer sighting that brought the myth into full bloom.

That sighting occurred on June 24, 1947, when Kenneth Arnold—a businessman, pilot, and former deputy federal marshal—was flying near Mt. Rainier in Washington. He saw nine flying disks that he estimated were traveling at 1,700 mph. He told a newspaper about it, the story went out on the Associated Press newswire, and the saucer myth was officially born.

Peebles traces the myth through the decades, covering famous incidents—the Roswell crash, the White Sands sightings, etc.—and showing how the various beliefs that constitute the myth have changed. In 1947 the beliefs were that people were seeing strange disk-shaped aircraft capable of very high speeds and impossible maneuvers. These craft could be U.S. or Soviet secret weapons, or they could have come from outer space. By 1950–51, the belief was that these objects were from space, that aliens were observing nuclear testing (which they considered a threat), and that the U.S. government knows about aliens but is covering up their existence to prevent a panic.

From 1953 to 1956, the "contactee myth" blossomed. It said that some humans were meeting, either physically or mentally, with "space brothers" who come from utopian societies. They are here to help us evolve, and contactees are supposed to spread the word of peace and brotherhood. It's also at this time that people started reporting "men in black," menacing figures who threaten UFO witnesses into being silent.

During the 1960s, several new beliefs were added, including the idea that UFOs may be hostile, that aliens were mutilating cattle, and that people were being abducted and medically examined. As the 1970s progressed, these beliefs gained more acceptance, and people blamed the CIA for masterminding the cover-up.

In the early 1980s people started believing that the aliens—who are short, bald, and gray—are physically weak and are therefore taking sperm and ova from earthlings to create hybrids. Also, "The aliens use implants in the noses of abductees to track and possibly control them."

From the late 1980s to the present, the "alien myth" was born, and it supplanted the flying saucer myth. The gist of the new mythology is that the groups who really run the United States and the world—MJ-12, the Trilateral Commission, etc.—have made a pact with the "Grays." They give the elite rulers advanced weapons technology, and the rulers build underground bases where the Grays can conduct their genetic programs through mutilations and abductions. Soon, MJ-12 and the Grays will take over the planet, setting up a "New World Order" dictatorship. As Peebles notes, "The alien myth is intensely political, with something for every extremist—Ultra-Right, Ultra-Left, and Nihilist."

*Watch the Skies!* is a very important book. No matter what you believe about UFOs, approaching the belief in aliens as a mythology brings a unique perspective to the whole complicated mess.

Smithsonian Institution Press;
1994; hardcover; 342 pp.

# ANOMALIES

## ANCIENT MAN:
### A HANDBOOK OF PUZZLING ARTIFACTS
### compiled by William R. Corliss

Unlike the above book, this volume of the Sourcebook Project isn't a cataloging of anomalies but a collection of articles and parts of articles on anomalies. Most of the articles come from respected journals like *Nature, American Antiquity, American Naturalist, Journal for the History of Astronomy* and others.

The theme of the book revolves around human-made objects whose existence is puzzling, given the current theories about the human race's history. The hundreds of articles cover stone circles in Europe and America, stone squares in Arizona, Stonehenge, pyramids in Polynesia, megaliths in North Africa, ancient roads in New Zealand, Mayan hydraulic systems, Roman coins found in Iceland, a huge slab of glass from ancient Galilee, the giant drawings in the sand in California, ancient North American stone carvings of elephants, fossilized technology, and more. Some articles deal with anthropological anomalies—an Indian mound containing a seven-foot, two-inch skeleton, a tribe of white Eskimos, a vanished race of red people on Madagascar, and other evidence that things are not as they seem.

The Sourcebook Project; $19.95
1978; hardcover; 786 pp.

## FORBIDDEN ARCHEOLOGY:
### THE HIDDEN HISTORY OF THE HUMAN RACE
### by Michael A. Cremo and Richard L. Thompson

In this truly massive book, the authors present loads of evidence that the scientific orthodoxy's ideas about human evolution are wrong. Humans did not appear on the scene a mere hundred thousand years ago but may have been around as long as four million years ago. As possible proof, there are accounts of scads of fossils and artifacts that refute the standard view of evolution. This evidence has been swept under the rug or offhandedly dismissed by the archeological establishment, who don't want to deal with anything that might contradict their precious theories.

In 1965 an upper arm bone was found in Kenya. Scientists judged the humerus to be more than four million years old, yet

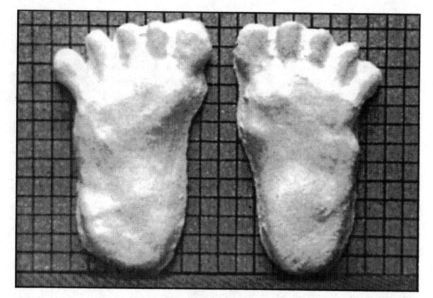

*Big Footprints* ➤ by Grover S. Krantz

*An academic on the hunt for Sasquatch.*

some scientists have also pronounced the arm to be "barely distinguishable from modern *Homo.*" As if that isn't enough to tantalize, "...in 1913 the German scientist Hans Reck found at Olduvai Gorge, Tanzania, a complete anatomically modern human skeleton in strata over one million years old, inspiring decades of controversy." If that still isn't enough, don't worry, there's plenty more where those came from. The authors explore the world to back up this radical view of human history. They look at all the controversies surrounding the fossils and artifacts, exposing the way mainstream science acts as a "knowledge filter," only allowing certain information to become part of acceptable debate and relegating other information to a kind of purgatory. Luckily, there are scientists like Cremo and Thompson who are willing to brave the abyss and bring us back the treasures they find. (Getting poetic, ain't I?)

> Govardhan Hill Publishing; $39.95
> 1993; hardcover; 914 pp.

### THE HIDDEN HISTORY OF THE HUMAN RACE

### by Michael A. Cremo and Richard L. Thompson

For those of you who don't have the time or inclination to wade through more than 900 pages of *Forbidden Archeology* (above), the publishers have kindly created this abbreviated version. At more than 350 pages it's not exactly Cliff's Notes, but it's still a much quicker read.

> Govardhan Hill Publishing; $22.95
> 1994; hardcover; 352 pp.

### LIGHTNING, AURORAS, NOCTURNAL LIGHTS, AND RELATED LUMINOUS PHENOMENA

### compiled by William R. Corliss

Here we have one of the many volumes in the Sourcebook Project, a one-person quest to catalog all the anomalies reported in science journals, as well as other sources like newspapers, Fortean magazines, and books. Most reports come from respected journals such as *Nature, Meteorological Magazine,* and *Marine Observer.*

As in all "catalog" volumes, each type of peculiar phenomenon is given its own section, complete with description, data evaluation (how likely is it that the phenomenon truly exists?), anomaly evaluation (if it does exist, how much does it violate known science?), possible explanations, similar and related phenomena, specific occurrences, and references.

Dipping into this book on light anomalies is a feast for the imagination. One of the entries is on underwater lightning (aka *te lapa*): "Streaks of light, flashes, and glowing plaques appearing

well below the surface of the ocean, apparently emanating from distant land masses." Another goodie is "lightning's pranks": "Odd, almost incomprehensible actions of lightning on people and objects. Lightning pranks range from neatly excising circles of glass from window panes to breaking every other dish in a pile." Oh, this one's just too cool—lightning figures: "Tree-like patterns or images of nearby objects appearing upon the bodies of people or animals struck or narrowly missed by lightning." Other phenomena include black auroras, ball lightning, luminous aerial bubbles, earthquake lights, mountain top glows, and more strangeness. The book ends with several indexes, arranged by date, place, subject, source, and author of article.

There are currently eighteen volumes in print in the Sourcebook Project, with more arriving at the rate of about one per year. Other volumes cover anomalies regarding humans, precipitation, visual phenomena, geology, the earth, the universe, and much more. Send a self-addressed stamped envelope for a catalog.

> The Sourcebook Project; $14.95
> 1982; hardcover; 242 pp.

# CRYPTOZOOLOGY

### BIG FOOTPRINTS:
### A SCIENTIFIC INQUIRY INTO THE REALITY OF SASQUATCH
### by Grover S. Krantz

Almost every book on Bigfoot, the Loch Ness Monster, and their ilk are classified as "New Age." Not this one. The publisher has listed it as anthropology in a bid to establish respectability for the book's treatment of what can be a hokey subject. The author is a distinguished physical anthropologist, a professor at Washington State University, and is said to be the only Bigfoot investigator with full academic qualifications.

The most abundant physical evidence for Sasquatch are footprints, and Krantz devotes seventy pages (two chapters) to examining photographs and plaster models of these impressions, concluding that some prints do indeed reveal a foot capable of supporting a thousand-pound creature. The hotly debated Patterson film of an alleged Sasquatch is examined in excruciating scientific detail. Krantz says, "No matter how the Patterson film is analyzed, its legitimacy has been repeatedly supported. The size and shape of the body cannot be duplicated by a man, its weight and movements correspond with each other and equally rule out a human subject; its anatomical details are just too good." Hair, feces, sound recordings, and other evidence are also examined. In his quest for clues, Krantz looks at the fossil record, Sasquatch-like creatures in other cultures, and the people investigating Bigfoot.

In the final analysis, Krantz concludes, "There is a considerable quantity of information indicating that a large, bipedal, wild primate is native to certain parts of North America." He speculates on the physical and mental characteristics of this creature, saying that it's only a matter of time before the legend is accepted as fact.

> Johnson Books; $14.95
> 1992; softcover; 300 pp.

### CRYPTO CHRONICLE

A smattering of reprinted and original articles on strange animals, mainly of the more famous variety such as lake monsters and Bigfoot. Issue #4 has a lot of material on the Loch Ness Monster, including the latest theory that it's a giant sturgeon. There's also a long article on the St. Augustine giant octopus controversy in the late 1800s. Other articles cover non-Nessie lake monsters, the Western Bigfoot Society, and the reappearance of bears in Britain.

Unfortunately, a confusing layout and dot-matrix printing (ugh!) lessen the enjoyability of this friendly zine.

> Craig Harris/50 Green Lane/Worcester/ENGLAND
> Single issue: $3; UK: £1.50
> One-Year sub: $10; UK: £4.50

## WONDERS:
### SEEKING THE TRUTH IN A UNIVERSE OF MYSTERIES

*Wonders* is a simply produced zine containing articles reprinted from or based on many obscure cryptozoological sources, some dating back to the 1800s. Volume 2, issue 3, contains articles on fifteen strange creatures reported in Southeast Asia, a reprint of a zoologist's explorations of the Philippines in the late nineteenth century, and an article from 1862 on strange snakes.

Mark Hall is doing a great service by bringing these old writings back to life for us. He promises that *Wonders* will be expanding by twenty-six to thirty pages; by the time you read this, that may well be the case.

MAHP/PO Box 3153, Butler Station/Minneapolis, MN 55403
Single copy: $4 (for US, Canada, and Mexico);
elsewhere: $5.50; Four-issue sub: $14.50 (for US, Canda, and Mexico); elsewhere: $20

# VAMPIRES

## THE VAMPIRE ENCYCLOPEDIA
### by Matthew Bunson

More than two thousand entries cover every aspect of bloodsuckers you could name—legends, novels, movies, and poems, how to kill vampires, powers of vampires, real-life vampires, the psychology of vampirism, and more. The focus is international: Japan, Africa, Finland, and India are a few of the places with their own vampire myths. The author points out that "...many scholars and vampirologists now believe that the vast world of the vampire began in India, in the bloody gods and legends of the ancient Indian peoples. (Some say Egypt, but other places are also suggested.) Vampires probably did start in the Indus Valley, sometime in the third millennium B.C., in the shape of deities who were often depicted as bloodthirsty and merciless embodiments of primordial fears: death, disease, nature, blood, and the night."

Entries include Lestat, Gypsies, wooden stakes, Java, exhumation, *Dark Shadows*, *Blacula*, Melrose Vampire, cats, vampirism, Elizabeth Bathory, Samuel Taylor Coleridge, and sex and love. There are also lengthy listings of vampire novels, movies, etc., sixteen pages of pictures, and addresses of more than a dozen vampiric associations.

A more comprehensive work on vampires is hard to imagine.

Crown Publishers; $16
1993; softcover; 303 pp.

## THE VAMPIRE INFORMATION EXCHANGE NEWSLETTER

A reader-driven zine for fans of vampires and people with "vampiric tendencies" (drinking blood, snoozing in coffins, sleeping all day, etc.). Issues contain news and reviews of vamp publications, classifieds, and vampire personals ("I'm into blood sucking, tantra and drinking all kinds of nectar"). There are usually one or two articles per issue, covering vampirism, *Dark Shadows*, vampire collectibles, local vampires in history, the vampire in music, Elvira, member poetry and art, and vampiric tendencies among VIE's membership. The Exchange also puts out a vampire bibliography and calendar.

Eric Held/PO Box 328/Brooklyn, NY 11229-0328
Single issue: $3.25
One-year sub (5 or 6 issues): $15; foreign: $17

## VAMPIRES OR GODS?:
### THE TRUE STORIES OF THE ANCIENT IMMORTALS
### by William Myers

A truly strange book that claims ancient divine beings were actually vampires. Isis, Dionysus, Krishna, Hercules, Quetzalcoatl, Jesus, and others are named as bloodsuckers. The author offers "proof" by way of the many vampire-like aspects of the myths surrounding these children of the night. Although there are intriguing similarities here and there, the overall evidence is scanty to say the least: "Bringing stability required that the forces of destruction be appeased. Quetzalcoatl did this by introducing human sacrifice, and in particular the heart sacrifice in which still-beating hearts were torn from the chests of the victims." "The core of Christian belief is that Jesus rose from the dead, and that his followers will do the same. This is also the core of the vampire myth."

III Publishing; $15
1993; oversize softcover; 192 pp.

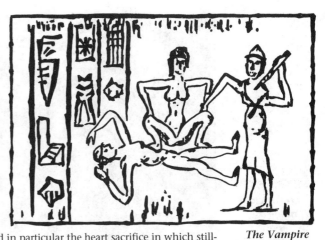

*The Vampire Encyclopedia by Matthew Bunson* ◄

*Sex, love and vampires—a combination with timeless appeal.*

# UNORTHODOX SCIENCE

## THE ANTI-GRAVITY HANDBOOK
### (EXPANDED EDITION)
### compiled by David Hatcher Childress

The quest to nullify gravity is a holy grail among fringe scientists (and probably among many governments, if the truth were known). This book is a compilation of material relating to this quest. "How to Build a Flying Saucer" discusses the obstacles to building an anti-gravity flying machine and proposes some solutions, including prototypes that have allegedly been built. The key, according to the author, is harnessing centrifugal force. "Arthur C. Clarke on Anti-Gravity" shows that that famous science fiction/science fact writer thought that eventually we would conquer gravity. W.P. Donovan offers a weighty, technical article on his ideas for anti-gravity. Another article looks at the Moller Corporation's efforts to build vertical-takeoff-and-landing aircraft that look an awful lot like UFOs.

Other articles examine what the moon tells us about gravity, the airships of ancient India, a history of people who supposedly could levitate, and more. The *Handbook* is filled with illustrations, including diagrams of several anti-grav devices. The editor of this book doesn't take things too seriously—he's also included comics, outrageous tabloid headlines, and a satirical article dealing with the topic at hand.

Adventures Unlimited; $14.95
1985, 1993; oversize softcover; 230 pp.; lavishly illus.

## BORDERLANDS

*Borderlands* has been published, under different names, since 1945 and is the *Scientific American* of fringe science. Be forewarned: *Borderlands* is not for lightweights. Most articles assume a lot of prior knowledge of both orthodox and fringe science, and, to tell you the truth, I'm left in the dark. There are lots of articles on Tesla, Lakhovsky's Multiple Wave Oscillator, ether, perpetual motion, magnetism, and other such topics. Maybe one day I'll sit down and try to figure it all out. If you're already into unorthodox science, this one's for you.

Borderland Sciences Research Foundation
PO Box 220/Bayside, CA 95524
Single issue: $6.95
Subscriptions are included as part of membership in the BSRF. One year regular membership (4 issues): $25. Other types of memberships are available.

▲
*The
Anti-Gravity
Handbook
by David
Hatcher
Childress*
(See page 187)

*The holy grail of
fringe science.*

## BORDERLANDS RESEARCH RESOURCES

A rich resource for books, including photocopies of many out-of-print sources, videotapes, and audiotapes on fringe science and related topics. Subjects include life/earth energies, Kabala, dowsing, radionics, light and color, suppressed medicine, alchemy, music, ether, Nikola Tesla, Rudolf Steiner, anomalies, lost civilizations, UFOs, anti-gravity and propulsion, and more. A very impressive collection.

Borderland Sciences Research Foundation
PO Box 220/Bayside, CA 95524
Catalog: no price is listed anywhere, but send them $2

## THE MONTAUK PROJECT:
### EXPERIMENTS IN TIME
### by Preston B. Nichols with Peter Moon

This book reads like a pure work of science fiction, but the author claims that every bit of it is true. In 1943 the infamous "Philadelphia Experiment" took place, in which the USS *Eldridge* is said to have been transported from the Philadelphia Naval Yard to Norfolk, Virginia, and back again. This was just the beginning of experiments dealing with invisibility, teleportation, and mind control. The research was carried out at an Air Force base at Montauk Point on Long Island, New York.

The author claims that he and other people he knows were manipulated into taking part in the experiments by extremely advanced mind control techniques that wiped out the memory of this part of their lives. Upon recovering their memories, they tell of the bizarre research that went on at Montauk, culminating in an experiment in which they tore a hole in space-time: "Then, something very strange happened. All of a sudden, the equipment appeared to drop into synch with something else. We didn't know what function the ship was now attuned to, but at that point, the USS *Eldridge* (the ship used for the Philadelphia Experiment) appeared through the portal. We had locked up with the *Eldridge*." Frightened by what they had done, the researchers rolled out their contingency plan. One of them visualized a monster that sprang into being and began smashing equipment on the base (yes, you are reading this correctly).

The author also addresses several other topics, including the use of mind control during the Persian Gulf War and his belief that John von Neumann, the brains behind the Philadelphia Experiment and the A-bomb, is still alive. Strange beyond belief and compulsively readable, I have to give this book two thumbs up.

Sky Books; $15.95
1992; softcover; 156 pp.

## MONTAUK REVISITED:
### ADVENTURES IN SYNCHRONICITY
### by Preston B. Nichols and Peter Moon

In this sequel to *Montauk Project* the authors offer more proof that the Montauk Project did take place, and they delve deeper into the strange occult forces that were behind the project and its manipulation of space-time. It is a gloriously wild tale involving Mars colonies, Jesus, aliens, spirit guides, Aleister Crowley, L. Ron Hubbard, the collective unconscious, Nazis, a man claiming to be Mark Hamill (Luke Skywalker of *Star Wars*), and much, much more. If it's true, your worldview has officially been trashed. If it's not true, it still makes a hell of a fun read.

Sky Books also puts out a video tour of the Montauk Base and a newsletter of the continuing developments related to Montauk, time travel, and aliens. Write for information.

Sky Books; $19.95
1994; softcover; 249 pp.

## THE ORGONE
## ACCUMULATOR HANDBOOK:
### CONSTRUCTION PLANS, EXPERIMENTAL USE
### AND PROTECTION AGAINST TOXIC ENERGY
### by James DeMeo, Ph.D.

Wilhelm Reich discovered orgone, the usually invisible natural energy that radiates from and flows through all things. The scientific establishment refuses to acknowledge orgone, even though its existence is readily provable. This book gives detailed, step-by-step plans for building various devices that will capture and concentrate orgone, including an accumulator, blanket, shooter funnel, and garden-seed-charger. There are also ideas for experiments to perform with these devices to show the existence of orgone.

The author does a good job introducing the concept of orgone and explaining Reich's research, which included using orgone to heal people, including cancer patients. This got Reich in deep doo-doo with the AMA and the FDA, and in a move that is so Nazi-like as to be unbelievable (especially since it occurred only ten years after WWII), the U.S. government burned Reich's books and destroyed his equipment with axes. It is truly one of the most shameful episodes in the history of the thought police. Luckily, we ignorant sheep are now actually allowed to read Reich's work and try to construct our own versions of his devices.

Natural Energy Works; $12.95
1989; softcover; 155 pp.

## REX RESEARCH ARCHIVE

A true godsend. Rex Research sells "infolios," collections of photocopied articles from all sorts of obscure, rare, and impossible-to-find sources. The subjects covered are mainly fringe science and suppressed inventions with some alternative health and even one sex infolio thrown in for good measure. It's truly an embarrassment of riches. Just look at these topics:

- "Automobiles—45 articles from the 1920s to date reporting major breakthroughs, improvements & innovations in automobile technology including: H. Caminez's super airplane engine (no crankshaft or gears)... Tom Ogle: No carburetor fuel system—200 mpg proven, patented!"
- "Batteries—20 Old/new designs under development or being ignored..."
- "Electric Articles—50 fascinating articles about extraordinary electrical phenomena and devices..."
- "Water Purification—16 articles about as many ways to purify water..."

Plus more articles, patents, etc. having to do with Rife's microscope, Searl's levitation disk generator, Tesla, Wilhelm Reich, cold fusion, ozone therapy, water to gasoline...

Rex Research Archive/PO Box 19250/Jean, NV 89019
Catalog: $2

# NIKOLA TESLA

## THE FANTASTIC INVENTIONS OF NIKOLA TESLA

### by Nikola Tesla with additional material by David Hatcher Childress

A compendium of patents and papers concerning Tesla's more unusual (some would say outlandish) inventions. The patent diagrams that are reproduced include an ozone generator, apparatus for producing currents of high frequency, devices for the electrical transmission of power, a lightning protector, a vertical-takeoff aircraft, lots of electromagnetic motors, and more. There is a 150-page transcript of a speech Tesla made while demonstrating various electrical experiments with alternate currents of high potential and high frequency. Also reprinted is a presentation called "The Transmission of Electrical Energy without Wires."

One of the chapters written by David Hatcher Childress concerns Tesla's "death rays." Tesla worked on a device that was to use ultrasound to disrupt mechanical devices and incapacitate or kill people. In another chapter, Childress gives a rundown of Tesla's most unusual inventions or ideas for inventions, including an electrically powered submarine, the mechanical oscillator, which compressed oxygen into liquid, the dynamo induction lamp (a light bulb said by some to be superior to today's bulbs), anti-gravity machines, a machine for photographing thoughts, and more. Tesla actually patented the first three inventions.

In a totally bizarro final chapter, Childress relates the tale that Tesla's friend Guglielmo Marconi, another supergenius scientist, took ninety-seven other renegade scientists to Venezuela with him, where they established a secret colony to work on ultra-advanced technology in peace. One of the alleged members of this colony claims that they invented a flying machine that traveled at "half a million miles per hour" and that they visited the moon and Mars. There is a story floating around that Tesla faked his death and was whisked away to Marconi's retreat in a saucer craft.

Adventures Unlimited; $16.95
1993; softcover; 351 pp.; lavishly illus.

## NIKOLA TESLA:
### FREE ENERGY AND THE WHITE DOVE
### by Commander X

While the other books in this section present straightforward accounts of Tesla's life, this book goes in the complete opposite direction, claiming that Tesla was an alien savior come to rescue mankind. He was sent to warn us about the World Wars and the birth of global communism and to present us with the liberating gifts of free energy and anti-gravity technology. Here, according to the author, is Tesla's origin: "Nikola Tesla was not an earthman. The space people have stated that a male child was born on board a space ship which was on flight from Venus to the earth in July, 1856.... The ship landed at midnight between July 9 and 10, in a remote mountain province in what is now Yugoslavia. There, according to arrangements, the child was placed in the care of a good man and his wife, the Rev. Milutin and Djouka Tesla."

Commander X goes on to discuss Tesla's advances in energy and propulsion and how they are being carried on by current inventors such as Otis T. Carr, Arthur H. Matthews, and Howard Menger. The government is also carrying on Tesla's work, the author claims, in supersecret projects being performed at the mysterious Area 51 in Nevada.

Inner Light Publications; $15.95
1992; softcover; 144 pp.

## PRODIGAL GENIUS:
### THE LIFE OF NIKOLA TESLA
### by Jon O'Neill

A well-done, straightforward (as opposed to fictionalized) biography of Tesla. No background information about the author or book is included, but apparently the author actually knew or at least spoke with Tesla. In his acknowledgments the author says that he was given access to many of Tesla's books and records. This book excerpts a lot of Tesla's own writings, including some unpublished ones. All aspects of Tesla the inventor (who created radio and refused the Nobel Prize) and Tesla the man (who could recite entire books and was sickened by the sight of pearls) are covered. Highly recommended to those who want to learn what all the fuss over Tesla is about.

Brotherhood of Life; $12
1994 (original publication date unknown but probably in the 1940s); softcover; 329 pp.

*Prodigal Genius* by Jon O'Neill

*Nikola Tesla: a brilliant, eccentric scientist or alien savior from Venus?*

## TESLA:
### A BIOGRAPHICAL NOVEL OF THE WORLD'S GREATEST INVENTOR
### by Tad Wise

Nikola Tesla is one of the greatest—some say the greatest—scientist/inventors of all time. He invented AC electricity, arc lighting, the bladeless turbine, the solar electric cell, electric refrigeration, and the speedometer, among many other creations. It is said by many (including the Supreme Court) that he is the true father of the radio. Tesla also laid down the groundwork for robotics, computers, and the "Star Wars" defense system. He is also a textbook example of the misunderstood, eccentric genius. He had many quirks, including being repelled by the thought of touching hair, and he considered it possible to photograph thoughts.

This biographical novel shows us Tesla, his employer George Westinghouse, his enemy Thomas Edison, his friend Mark Twain, and his sometime financial backer J.P. Morgan, among a host of other characters. The author paints a picture of Tesla's relentless scientific pursuits, his rise to fame and entrance into New York's aristocracy, and his last days as a pauper being hounded by the FBI. After Tesla died in a hotel room, the Office of Alien Property, acting under the authorization of the FBI, illegally confiscated Tesla's papers and other possessions, despite the fact that Tesla had become a U.S. citizen fifty-two years earlier. Apparently the FBI was taking Tesla's research into death rays and free energy much more seriously than today's scientific establishment does. Even today, much of Tesla's work remains hidden in the hands of government agencies, including the KGB.

Turner Publishing; $21.95
1994; hardcover; 381 pp.

## MISCELLANEOUS

### EXTRATERRESTRIAL ARCHEOLOGY

This fascinating book takes a look at the unusual artifacts and features on the moon and several planets in our solar system. At least half the book is devoted to the moon, and for good reason. There is evidence of obelisks, monoliths, an almost seventy-mile long wall, more than two hundred domes, a bridge-like structure, a glinting piece of "glass," a tunnel, large holes, strange lights, rays emanating from craters, pyramids, and dry riverbeds on our closest cosmic neighbor.

Mars has perhaps the most famous anomalies of all—the infamous "face," pyramids, a runway, a mound, and the much-debated canals, all of which are discussed. Lesser-known anomalies discovered by the Russian space probe *Phobos 2* are also explained, and they sure are doozies. The Reds uncovered a 230-square-mile series of parallel lines, a strange oblong shadow, a perfectly straight latticework of underground channels, and the kicker—right before *Phobos 2* suddenly stopped transmitting, it sent back a picture (reproduced in this book) of a huge cylindrical object headed either toward or away from Mars's moon Phobos.

Finally, the author looks at the evidence that Venus was once completely covered in water, strange markings on Venus and Mercury, pyramids on Mercury, cloudy wisps on Uranus's moon Dione, and the possibility that the moons of the outer planets have water and hospitable atmospheres.

This is really an exciting book. Even if you think every weird formation is just a trick of the light, it's still a valuable reference because it contains literally hundreds of photographs, drawings, and diagrams illustrating the anomalies. The photos, many of which have never been seen by the general public, come directly from NASA and the Soviet space agency.

Adventures Unlimited Press; $18.95
1994; oversize softcover; 301 pp.

### FORTEAN TIMES:
#### The Journal of Strange Phenomena

One of my favorite magazines and one of the very few that I read practically cover to cover. Several factors make *Fortean Times* one of the best magazines going. First is its wacky sense of humor, including characteristic British fondness for puns. Second, the quality of writing is excellent. Third, the layout, illustrations, and production values are top-notch. Fourth, the editors take a somewhat neutral stance. They're not true believers, although they lean in that direction, but they aren't skeptics, either, except in the cases of outright hoaxes. Finally, and most importantly, *Fortean Times* examines the entire spectrum of unusual occurrences. Not only do they cover the usual UFOs, ghosts, and monsters, they also look at exotic mental and physical disorders, bizarre religious customs, conspiracy theories, and more.

Every issue starts off with a full-page reproduction of a strange photograph. The best one so far was in issue 68, which clearly showed a frog whose eyes are on the inside of its mouth. Issue 71 was pretty cool, too, showing a Beijing boy with a snake crawling into his nostril and out his mouth. After the mind-blowing picture, *FT* prints about a dozen pages of short "News of the Weird"–type items, except these items are far more interesting than "News of the Weird." Issue 73 informs us, "In the 175 square miles of the Jharia coal fields in eastern India, there are sixty-five major subterranean fires, some of which have been burning since 1916.... Fields belch steam, with huge crevasses that glow read [sic] at night and pump out hot air like a blast furnace. Some of the ground is literally ablaze and mounds of coal simmer."

Each issue contains about a dozen articles, essays, and interviews on as diverse a group of subjects as you could imagine. Recent issues have covered real-life Rip Van Winkles, the alleged discovery of Hell in Siberia, Satanic child abuse, road ghosts, British big cats, Virgin Mary appearances, cold fusion, crop circles, red mercury, MIA photos, Munchausen syndrome, dogs that made incredibly long journeys (up to three thousand miles), disappearing trees, stigmata, false memory syndrome, cattle mutilations, unexplained submarines off Sweden's shores, separated Siamese twins, angelic intervention during wars, dinosaurs of the twentieth century, and a hell of a lot more.

Every issue also contains "Hoax!," which uncovers a bogus paranormal phenomenon, and "Diary of a Mad Planet," which documents the most extreme natural occurrences of the past two months. Issue 71 reported a swarm of locusts in Somalia that covered twenty-three thousand square miles! Of course, *FT* also contains book and zine reviews and a lively letters section. Most highly recommended.

Fortean Times
20 Paul Street/Frome, Somerset BA11 1DX/ENGLAND
One-year sub (6 issues): £12 (check/money order payable to John Brown Publishing)
U.S. subscription address: Fenner Reed & Jackson/PO Box 754/Manhasset, NY 11030
One-year sub (6 issues): $30

### GHOST TRACKERS NEWSLETTER

Published by the Ghost Research Society, this newsletter reports on all kinds of ghostly activity—poltergeists, dead loved ones, haunted houses, etc. The society takes an active role in investigating ghosts. Dale Kaczmarek, the society's president, and members visit houses, graveyards, and other locations to see or sense paranormal phenomena or capture it with recording devices. Kaczmarek claims to have filmed some strange activity.

Each issue of the newsletter reports on the society's doings and contains first- and second-hand reports of ghostly encounters from members. There are also historical articles and book reviews.

Several levels of membership are available. A regular membership gets you three issues of the newsletter, membership card, button, free psychic photo analysis, and discounts on books and the society's haunted tours and trips. A sustaining membership gets you all the above stuff plus the chance to help with research expeditions. There are many other kinds of memberships. Write if you're interested.

Ghost Research Society
PO Box 205/Oak Lawn, IL 60454-0205
Single issue: $4
Regular membership: $12
Overseas regular membership: $20
Sustaining membership: $17
Make all checks and money orders payable to Dale Kaczmarek.

### KIRLIAN PHOTOGRAPHY:
#### A Hands-on Guide
#### by John Iovine

Kirlian photography, also known as electrophotography, creates images by discharging high-voltage electricity onto film, with the subject of the photograph actually on the film itself. It produces beautiful and strange color pictures of glowing objects. Exactly how much is revealed by Kirlian photography is the subject of much debate. Some say that this method reveals mental and physical states, the presence of disease, the nutritional value of food, acupuncture points, pollution levels, and more. Skeptics say this is so much *caca*. The most famous claim of Kirlian photography is the so-called phantom-leaf phenomenon. Every once in a great while, if you photograph a leaf with a piece torn off, that piece will show up in the image as if it were still there, albeit a little weaker.

This guide gives step-by-step instructions and plans for building two types of low-cost Kirlian equipment. There are many tips on how to photograph different kinds of objects, including the famed phantom leaf. The book is illustrated with numerous Kirlian photos, some in color. Whether you're interested in electrophotography for artistic or more mystical reasons, this is definitely a book you need.

McGraw-Hill; $16.95
1994; oversize softcover; 136 pp.

## THE LOST CITIES OF CHINA, CENTRAL ASIA, AND INDIA
### by David Hatcher Childress

If you like reading true tales of adventures in faraway lands, you're in for a treat. Renegade archeologist David Hatcher Childress, called "a real-life Indiana Jones," has traveled the globe, searching for the most remote, exotic, and forgotten spots on earth. He's written books on his travels in South America, the Pacific, Africa, North America, and Central America.

This book follows his path through China, India, Mongolia, and as far west as Iran. Along the way he almost gets buried by hundreds of tons of snow during an avalanche in the Himalayas, contracts hepatitis in Kathmandu, visits a remote tribe in India, looks at the alleged tomb of Jesus in Kashmir, meets lots of strange characters, and has a pretty exciting time. Unfortunately, he never ventures into unknown, forbidden territory to uncover the ruins of a lost city or discover treasures, as the fictional Indiana Jones did. He does travel to many out-of-the-way places, though. He frequently breaks into his travelogue to write about wars, customs, secret orders, religion, mysticism, lost cities, etc. These digressions are some of the most interesting parts of the book.

Adventures Unlimited; $14.95
1991; softcover; 415 pp.; illus.

## THE LOST CONTINENT OF MU
### by Colonel James Churchward

James Churchward was a dedicated researcher who spent fifty years traveling the world, piecing together the puzzle of Mu, the lost continent of the Pacific. While he was on duty with the British army in India in 1868, Churchward became friends with a temple priest who revealed ancient stone tablets telling of the civilization of Mu, destroyed 25,000 years ago. Mu, like Atlantis, is believed by some to be the cradle of civilization that disappeared quickly owing to a natural cataclysm, leaving behind little tangible evidence that it existed. Churchward set out to prove that Mu did exist and that it provided many of the foundations for the subsequent evolution of the human race.

The detective work in this book is scholarly and well organized. Much evidence is presented to support the author's belief, including intriguing graphics, pictures, symbols, and artifacts that show connections to ancient Egypt, India, the Mayans, Easter Island, and more. Churchward presents a strong case for an ancient civilization lost in antiquity. What is missing is a more detailed account of Mu's relationship to Atlantis. The author believes Atlantis existed concurrently with Mu, but he downplays Atlantis, as if he feels that it didn't make a contribution to civilization. (Hmmm, maybe Atlantis was populated by bureaucrats....)

This book is recommended for anyone interested in exploring lost civilizations and their role in history. If you're a true-blue Muhead, you'll want to continue with the author's four other books on Mu, available from the same publisher.

Brotherhood of Life; $15.95
1959 (1987); softcover; 335 pp.

## THE ROOTS OF CONSCIOUSNESS:
### THE CLASSIC ENCYCLOPEDIA OF CONSCIOUSNESS STUDIES (REVISED AND EXPANDED EDITION)
### by Jeffrey Mishlove, Ph.D.

*The Roots of Consciousness*, originally published in 1975, became a classic work concerning the mind's hidden powers and related subjects. Now it's back and it's better than ever. It has been updated—rewritten would actually be a better word for it—to reflect all the changes, new theories, new evidence, and new challenges that have come about in the past twenty years.

This book is more than a collection of unexplained phenomena, though. It is a study of the unexplored regions of human consciousness. It investigates theories of the human mind that incorporate and explain these officially unrecognized

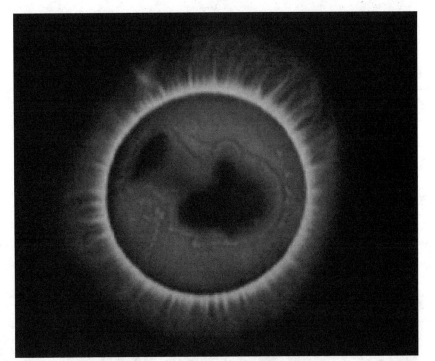

◄ *Kirlian Photography* by John Iovine

*Mystic or artistic, a step-by-step guide to electrophotography.*

powers. Section One of the book, "The History of Consciousness Exploration," examines the various explanations of the human mind that have appeared throughout the ages: shamanistic traditions, yoga in ancient India, Taoism, Pythagoras, Plato, the mystery traditions of ancient Greece, the teachings of Jesus, Hermeticism, Paracelsus, Descartes and mind-body dualism, etc.

The second section, "The Folklore of Consciousness Exploration," deals with the unexplained phenomena themselves. "Folklore" in this case just means any nonscientific, anecdotal belief or evidence in a particular area. The author takes a balanced, impartial look at astrology, out-of-body experiences, psychic surgery, healing at Lourdes, the aura, chakras, communication with higher intelligence, UFOs, life after death, near-death experiences, mind over matter, dowsing, and a whole lot more.

"The Scientific Exploration of Consciousness" is about ESP and psychokinesis experiments—problems, criticisms, exceptional experiments, methodological considerations, etc. The final section, "Theories of Consciousness," examines the theories of mind that have attempted to integrate psi phenomena from biological and quantum physics perspectives. The appendix contains a brain-crushing article entitled "Consciousness: A Hyperspace View" that is not for the mildly curious.

The book itself is coffee-table quality—oversized, heavily illustrated, well laid out, and very thick and heavy (I don't know why, but that seems to be a requirement for coffee-table books). This is the best level-headed look at psi phenomena you could possibly ask for.

Council Oak Books; $24.95
1993; oversize softcover; 416 pp.

## THE SKEPTICAL INQUIRER

Published by the Committee for the Scientific Investigation of the Claims of the Paranormal (CSICOP), *The Skeptical Inquirer* is the premier debunking publication. They cast cold, hard light on religious claims, New Age beliefs, and alternative health practices. Their articles, written by some of the world's top scientists, have taken on "recovered memories," Satanic panic, UFOs, psychics, electromagnetic fields, Bible prophecy, scientific creationism, subliminal persuasion, crop circles, near-death experiences, and practically any other unexplained or controversial phenomenon you could name.

Although CSICOP does do a good job of exposing hoaxes and taking a hard look at the real evidence for many phenomena, it has been noted (most prominently by Robert Anton Wilson in *The New Inquisition*) that scientists can be just as irrationally dogmatic as any true believer, denying any facts that don't fit into their "objective" theories. Still, to ignore what the skeptics say and be a slack-jawed believer in every phenomenon alleged to exist is no good either. As with all things, listen to what all sides have to say, then draw your own conclusions. And when it comes to skepticism, you can't do better than *The Skeptical Inquirer*.

Skeptical Inquirer/PO Box 703/Buffalo NY 14226-0703
Single issue: $6.25
One-year sub (four issues): $25. Starting in 1995, the *Inquirer* will become bimonthly. You may want to write for subscription info.

## STRANGE MAGAZINE

*Strange* Magazine

*Maybe it is, and maybe it isn't...*

Slick, professionally produced guide to the unexplained. These guys take an open-minded, maybe-it-is-maybe-it-isn't approach (à la *Fortean Times*), as opposed to the it's-absolutely-true approach of, say, *Fate Magazine*. Recurrent themes include UFOs, ghosts, and cryptozoology. Regular features include Cryptozoo News™, Alien Skies™, Strange World™ (a collection of articles and essays from readers around the world), Mixed Bag (bizarre global happenings), and reviews. Issue #13 has articles on Mars mysteries, a new alleged photo of Bigfoot (snoozing on a log, no less), first-person encounters with weirdness, a freaky sideshow, UFOs and witchcraft, the scareship sitings in Britain, and more. One of the best such magazines available.

Strange Magazine/PO Box 2246/Rockville, MD 20847
Single issue: $5.95; foreign: $7.45
Two-year sub (4 issues): $17.95; UK: £13.50; foreign: $22.95

## THRESHOLDS:
### A JOURNAL OF UFOS, SCIENCE AND EARTH MYSTERIES

An information-packed, well-designed, nonslick magazine on the unexplained, with a primary focus on UFOs. Issue #2 has a ton of material on crop circles, including an overview of 1993 formations, an assessment of real and fake circles, and a look at the mysterious lights seen in and around some crop circles. Other articles look at reports of Bigfoot on David Hill in Oregon and the much-talked-about photo of the "Beast of Bodmin Moor." As in every issue there are more than ten pages of UFO sightings from around the world, some reviews, and networking sources.

Thresholds
17320 Laverne Avenue/Cleveland, OH 44135-1940
Single issue: $5; Four-issue sub: $20; foreign: $35

## SINGLE AUTHOR WORKS

### THE DOWN AND OUT DAWG TREASURY BONANZA!!
#### by James Sturm

*The Adventures of Down and Out Dawg* is a comic strip in the student newspaper at the University of Wisconsin–Madison. The canine in question is a mangy, nappy-haired, skinny, amoral fleabag who would sell his own kid to raise money for a bet (in fact, he does). Dawg's partner in life is a grossly obese cat named Boots, the cat who lived next door to Snoopy.

Dawg's life started out on the wrong foot. He was sold to a family whose son loved to torture Dawg. So Dawg killed the brat with a large knife. Throughout his life, Dawg has many brushes with greatness—Spuds McKenzie, Underdog, Deputy Dawg, Scooby Doo, McGruff the Crime Dog, and others. Dawg ends up killing some of them, doing drugs, busting out of prison, discovering oil, becoming rich, and joining a radical left-wing student group.

Dawg's relentless nihilism, homicidal tendencies, chemical dependencies, bad hygiene, and trashing of popular culture have made him a cult hero at the U. of Wisconsin. Now we noncheese-heads have a chance to revel in the glory that is Down and Out Dawg.

Cheshire Iguana Publications; $8.95
1993; oversize softcover; 64 pp.

### FLOOD!
#### by Eric Drooker

"Written" by *World War III* veteran Eric Drooker, *Flood!* is composed entirely of scratchboard drawings, further blurring the line between comix and art. This style produces dark pictures perfectly suited to the dark tale they tell. The story concerns a nameless man living in the last days of our postmodern society. His alienation and soulless existence are loudly proclaimed on every page. The total lack of dialog or even thought balloons only heightens the profound loneliness that the book deals with. But—in the end—is our hero redeemed? Does he find love and happiness? Yeah, right. This isn't to say the ending is predictable, though. There is redemption of a sort, but it comes in a totally unexpected way. A beautifully powerful and stark work.

Four Walls Eight Windows; $15.95
1993; softcover; 160 pp.

### HATE
#### by Peter Bagge

Peter Bagge's personal comic. Issue #15 contains the story of Buddy Bradley's roommates, who include his girlfriend, ex-girlfriend, ex-roommate, and junky friend. As you can imagine, much madness ensues. A shorter piece, "Return to Hate Island," examines Bagge's desire to sell out and get rich. However, the editorial in this issue promises that huge, monstrous changes will affect *Hate*, starting with the next issue. What exactly will happen, no one knows (including Peter).

Fantagraphics Books; $2.50 per issue (plus 50¢ shipping per issue, unless you're buying a bunch of other Fantagraphics stuff. In that case, go by the shipping charges listed in the appendix.).

### HOTHEAD PAISAN:
#### HOMICIDAL LESBIAN TERRORIST
#### by Diane DiMassa

"I'M NOT YOUR FUCKIN' SPRITZ-HEAD GIRLFRIEND! I'M HOTHEAD PAISAN!" So screams the antiheroine of this extremely popular cult comic-zine, the first nine issues of which

*◄ Flood!*
*by Eric*
*Drooker*

*Stark, inky*
*visions of*
*urban*
*alienation.*

have been collected in this book. As Alison Bechdel says, "Hothead is the backlash to the backlash." HH is pissed off at being pissed on because she's a woman and because she's queer, so she does what so many people would like to do. First, she tells everyone exactly how she feels. HH's relatives: "Where's your boyfriend, dear?" HH: "UP MY ASS! Dear." Therapists: "When life gives you lemons, make lemonade." HH: "When your shrink gives you a cliché, throw a bomb at her." Priests: "COME TO CHURCH!" HH: "BURN IN PEDOPHILE HELL!"

Then she starts attacking and killing people. An arrogant SOB walking down the sidewalk gets his head blown off. Some tough guy gets "Bobbited" with an axe. A pro-life protester is crushed like a grape by a mallet-wielding Hothead. While hiding in an alley, HH jumps some guy, crotch kicks him, and shoves a log up his ass. She says to him: "So let's review! You think women like this? Hey, babe, I know ya wanted it! I could tell cause ya looked at me!"

Hothead is pure cathartic revenge fantasy. For anyone who longs to see the homophobic, dick-based patriarchy overthrown (or at least blown up), Hothead is a blessing. She's most definitely a dyke to watch out for.

You can write to Giant Ass Publishing if you'd like to get a free catalog of Hothead "crapola," including further issues of *Hothead Paisan*, T-shirts, postcards, buttons, and rubber stamps.

Cleis Press; $14.95
1993; oversize softcover; 175 pp.
Giant Ass Publishing/PO Box 214/New Haven, CT 06502
Catalog: free

### JIZZ
#### by Scott Russo

A collection of comic strips, single panels, and written pieces that are filled to the brim with anger and misanthropy. Scott holds nothing sacred: abortion, Hitler, AIDS, suicide, etc. Scott constantly exposes the stupidity of racism, sexism, and the whole human race in pieces like "Why I Hate This World, Episode 1," "The Adventures of Fetus Boy," "HIV Punch," "Secret White Man's Club," and the "Ask Isabella" column, which contains this exchange: "Q: My boyfriend has this weird habit. When he gets angry at me, he tries to give me a snap hysterectomy by tying one end of a string to my uterus, and the other end to a doorknob. Then he slams the door. I usually get dragged across the rug, and he becomes furious when the procedure fails, and beats me. A: Sounds like you two need to talk more. Many relationships suffer from lack of communication. Surveys of men who beat their spouses find overwhelmingly

THESE ARE THE VILE CONFESSIONS OF AN UNKNOWN PAINTER WHO FELL TO HELL BECAUSE OF HIS OBSESSION WITH THE EXQUISITE BEAUTY AND THE INTOXICATING SMELL OF **BLOOD**.

A PAINTER OBSESSED WITH THE COLOR OF BLOOD.

I AM A PAINTER.

*Panorama of Hell* ➤ by Hideshi Hino

Extreme manga.

that the woman just don't listen." (All of these pieces appear in issue #10)

Unfortunately, issue #10 was the last of *Jizz*. Scott says the premature end is due to creative differences with Fantagraphics and the fact that he doesn't enjoy *Jizz*ing anymore. You can still get all the back issues, though.

Fantagraphics Books; $2.50 per issue (plus 50¢ shipping per issue, unless you're buying a bunch of other Fantagraphics stuff. In that case, go by the shipping charges listed in the appendix.)

## LÈVE TA JAMBE MON POISSON EST MORT!
### by Julie Doucet

Julie Doucet's comix are a lot like life: sometimes they're funny, sometimes they're disturbing, sometimes they're pointless, and sometimes I just plain don't get it. Judging from these highly personal comix (Doucet appears in almost every frame), we're dealing with one strange woman. Who else would name her first anthology "Lift Your Leg My Fish Is Dead!"? Who else would draw comix filled with menstruation, nosepicking, farting, graphic murder and mutilation, a dog with a six-foot dick, sex with a giant talking beer bottle, levitating over a toilet, spazzing out in a theater, cannibalism, Kirk and Spock taking leaks on different planets, and other forms of sex, violence, and bodily functions? Doucet is definitely one of the most obscure, hard-to-fathom comix artists I know of. If anybody can figure her out, let me know.

Drawn and Quarterly Publications; $10.95
1993; softcover; 96 pp.

## DIRTY PLOTTE
### by Julie Doucet

Doucet's comic. Issue #6 is destined to become a classic. Within its gender-bent pages, Doucet wonders what it would be like to be a man ("I would have a girlfriend with big tits!") and tells the story of a man who has a vagina surgically implanted on his forehead. Don't count on getting this issue if you live in Canada, since it has been seized by customs officials.

Drawn and Quarterly Publications
Single issue: $2.50
Four-issue sub: $8.95; Canada: $10.95

## YUMMY FUR
### by Chester Brown

Chester Brown is one of my favorite comix artists. Ever since he short-circuited my brain with *Ed the Happy Clown* (below), I've known that he is a loose cannon and must be kept under close observation. His comic *Yummy Fur* has had at least four major story lines. The first ten issues told the story of Ed, and some of the next ones examined Brown's relationship with *Playboy* (below). Issues #26–30 are titled "Fuck" and they tell of Brown's adolescence. This series lacks the power of the first two. Now Brown is adapting the Gospel of Matthew through *Yummy Fur*'s twisted lens. The Bible is strange enough, but when you add Brown's sensibilities to the mix—look out!

Drawn and Quarterly Publications
Single issue: $2.50
Four-issue sub: $8.95; Canada: $10.95

## ED THE HAPPY CLOWN
### by Chester Brown

This outrageous, twisted, absurdist nightmare will undoubtedly go down in comic history as an undisputed classic. The basic plot involves the hapless Ed, whose penis has become Ronald Reagan owing to a bizarre interdimensional accident. This subconscious soup is a ludicrous blend of sex, violence, politics, and religion containing, among other things, a man who can't stop shitting, a janitor whose hand falls off, a vampire, vampire killers, rat-eating pygmies in the sewers, sadistic doctors, violent homophobes, "back alley" penis transplant operations, cannibalism, reincarnation, government fascists, and gun-toting grannies. This new edition contains an extra chapter and a new ending to replace the unsatisfactory ending that was the first edition's major weakness. Get it or regret it.

Vortex Comics; $12.95
1992; softcover; 215 pp.

## THE PLAYBOY
### by Chester Brown

The issues of *Yummy Fur* collected in this book recount Brown's experiences with *Playboy* magazine. He recounts the lengths he went to in order to buy issues, almost getting caught several times by people he knew. He'd be so nervous about anyone finding the *Playboy*s, he'd rip out the good parts and chuck the rest of the magazine. Several times Brown experienced guilt and turmoil over his fondness for pictures of naked women. In the last part of the book he looks at how *Playboy* affected his relationships with women. With his first girlfriend, he had to act like skin mags didn't appeal to him. While making love to his second girlfriend, he would have to fantasize about a Playmate to keep it up.

Brown's embarrassing honesty is sure to hit home with a lot of guys. Lord knows it brought back memories for me.

Drawn and Quarterly Publications; $12.95
1992; softcover; 170 pp.

## SLUTBURGER STORIES, PEEPSHOW, DANGLE, AND PALOOKAVILLE

*Drawn and Quarterly* publishes several comix besides those reviewed above. *Slutburger Stories* by Mary Fleener, "a self-deprecating beach bunny with brains and a scathing wit," is great. She tells interesting sex- and drug-filled true-life stories in a quasi-cubist style. In *Peepshow* Joe Matt tells about his aimless life with clean, simple graphics. Unclean, complicated graphics are the order of the day in Lloyd Dangle's cool comic, *Dangle*, which mixes exaggerated (I hope) real-life stories with social/political satire. *Palookaville* by Seth just bores me to tears.

Drawn and Quarterly Publications
Single issue (of each title): $2.50
Four-issue sub (of each title): $8.95; Canada: $10.95

## PANORAMA OF HELL
### by Hideshi Hino

This is surely one of the most shocking, extreme pieces of manga ever written. The narrator is an unnamed Japanese artist who paints with his own blood. He keeps pickled fetuses in his studio and paints pictures of his surroundings: a huge guillotine that chops off heads around the clock, Hell River, which is littered with trash and dead animals, a crematorium that burns huge piles of bodies, and a cemetery where headless corpses crawl out of the ground looking for their noggins (obviously this guy lives on the wrong side of the tracks). Our tortured artist is currently working on his masterpiece, a painting of a horror greater than anything the world has known.

Most of the book is spent telling us about the artist's family. We meet his kids—Krazy Girl, who draws pictures of dead puppies, and Krazy Boy, who eats pig eyeballs that he steals from the slaughterhouse. His wife runs Hell Tavern, where all the corpses meet to eat. The artist takes a trip down memory lane, introducing us to his gambling grandfather, his sadistic father, his ass-kicking brother, and his mother, who was impregnated with him by the nuclear blast on Hiroshima.

*Panorama of Hell* is an all-out assault on the senses. It contains some of the most brutal, disgusting images ever put on paper. To read it is to peer into the abyss.

Blast Books; $9.95
1982; softcover; 192 pp.

## SHE COMICS:
### AN ANTHOLOGY OF BIG BITCH
### by Spain Rodriguez

Cross Linda Lovelace with James Bond and what do you get? Big Bitch! Actually, BB isn't a spy but a globe-trotting adventurer who gets into all kinds of jams. Don't worry, though—the tall, obscenely long-legged heroine of Spain's stories kicks ass, takes names, and always ends up getting laid. In these thrilling tales she steals corporate secrets, battles antiporn forces, fights Betty Page, thwarts an apocalyptic cult, exposes an international drug and terrorist operation (run by the United States), and has more leg-spreading adventures. Filled with social and political satire, Big Bitch manages to make pointed comments about society while serving you heaping doses of sex. What more do you want?

Last Gasp; $14.95
1993; oversize softcover; 80 pp.

## SPAWN OF DYKES TO WATCH OUT FOR
### by Alison Bechdel

At the opposite end of the spectrum from Hothead Paisan is the ultrapopular *Dykes to Watch Out For* comic strip, which runs in more than forty publications. *Dykes* is a realistic, slice-of-lesbian-life strip that centers on the terminally pissed-off (but not homicidal) Mo and her politically progressive friends and lovers. There's Lois, the "sex-positive cashier" at Madwimmin Books, where Mo works. There's Sparrow, "social worker and recovering adolescent," and Ginger, "perpetual Ph.D. candidate and molder of malleable freshman minds."

In this, the fifth *Dykes* book, Mo and her love Harriet go Splitsville, and Lois hits the big 3-0. But the real crux of the collection is that Clarice and Toni do the artificial insemination thing and have a kid (hence, *spawn* of dykes to watch out for). The actual birth is recorded in a long sequence done specially for this book.

Firebrand Books; $8.95
1993; softcover; 132 pp.

## SQUEAK THE MOUSE 2
### by Mattioli

Page after page of pointless violence and sex. This isn't meant to be a condemnation—if pointless violence and sex is your thing, then this comic has your name written all over it. Imagine Tom and Jerry crossed with *The Texas Chainsaw Massacre* crossed with *Deep Throat* and you have some idea what's going on. Squeak the Mouse and an unnamed cat behead, squish, strangle, blow up, cut in half, and otherwise horribly mutilate each other and anybody else who happens to be around. What helps make the comic so amusing is that it is drawn in a very cartoony style with lots of bright colors. It looks exactly like something you'd see in the Sunday comics, except, for example, when Squeak has an explicit ménage à trois on the beach and the cat kills his partners by stabbing them with a seashell and a starfish.

NBM; $10.95
1992; oversize softcover; 41 pp.

## SUPERFLY
### by Mike Diana

Mike Diana is one of the zine world's most famous victims of the thought police. In 1993 he was arrested in Florida for producing, publishing, and distributing *Boiled Angel*, a zine filled with shocking comix and writing from Diana and others. The case centered around Diana's comix, which are some of the most brutal, extreme drawings you will *ever* see, and I'm not hyperbolizing. Murder, suicide, mutilation, child abuse (including sexual abuse), rape, bestiality, and other glimpses of hell come to life through Diana's crude "high school doodle" style of illustration. Nothing is held back.

This didn't sit well with Florida authorities, who succeeded in prosecuting Diana on obscenity charges. Luckily, Diana was given probation, but do you realize what this verdict means? The courts decided that this artwork was totally without merit and cannot be purchased by anyone, including informed adults, in the court's jurisdiction. The ramifications are staggering. This case could have a chilling effect on zine publishing and the efforts of people who want to present unpleasant views. Besides that, one of the terms of Diana's probation is sickening—he is no longer allowed to draw. Not even for his own pleasure, with no intent for publication. Further, this court-ordered criminalization of creativity is enforced with surprise police searches of Diana's premises with no warrant required. The thought police are here, baby, and they're walking right on in.

Diana isn't taking this lying down, though. During this whole mess, the first issue of *Superfly* came out. It features hideous stories about a high school kid who gets three wishes, an abused teenager who eats acid-laced candy, and a completely burned-out junkie who lives in a deserted tourist spot. It has a disgusting full-color cover of a skull with wings eating a person's innards and an interview with Diana about his legal troubles.

This publisher has also reprinted *Boiled Angel* numbers 7 and "Ate" (the issues that got Diana arrested) in limited, signed editions. Write to see if there are still some left.

Mike Hunt Comix; $4
1993; comic format; 32 pp.

## TOO MUCH COFFEE MAN
### by Shannon Wheeler

Too Much Coffee Man is addicted to caffeine and nicotine, is bulgy-eyed, paranoid, jittery, and confused, and, on top of all that, he has a huge, steaming cup of coffee on his head. In other words, he's a hero for our times. I liked TMCM the moment I saw him in *Factsheet Five*, and I'm glad to see that he has his own full-size comic now. Shannon Wheeler uses TMCM to comment on legal insanity, work, and other ridiculous aspects of our ridiculous world.

Issue #1 is a stunner. The cover, almost suitable for framing, has our caffeine-addled antihero kicking back in a huge mug of coffee, no doubt reflecting on the meaning of it all (either that, or his next cup of joe). Inside is the story "TMCM vs. TM©M" (Too Much Coffee Man vs. Trademark Copyright Man), some one-page strips, an artist's gallery, ads for TMCM T-shirts, coffee mugs, and playing cards (glory hallelujah!), and more fresh-brewed insanity. Issue #3, which should be out by the time you read this, promises to unveil the origins of Too Much Coffee Man.

Adhesive Comics/PO Box 5372/Austin, TX 78763-5372
Single issue: $3. 4-issue sub: $10

# MULTIPLE AUTHOR WORKS

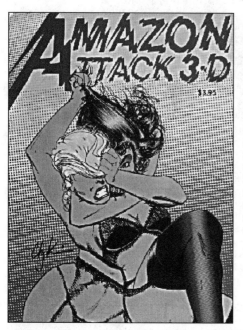

*Amazon
Attack 3-D*

*Perfect for
you fans
of female
wrestling.*

## AMAZON ATTACK 3-D

Perfect for you fans of female wrestling. This comic book contains six short (three- or four-page) stories about scantily clad women who beat the hell out of people around them. The stories mostly follow the theme of girl gets attacked, girl gets smacked around some, girl recovers and proceeds to whup up on her attacker(s). The attackers may be a man, a woman, two women, or a man and a woman. No matter what, the babes end up losing their tops, but with clever positioning there is never more than a hint of breast shown. The 3-D effects help the fight scenes leap off the page (comes with 3-D glasses).

3-D Zone; $3.95 (include over-eighteen age statement)
1990; comic book; 24 pp.

## AS-FIX-E-8
### stories by Lydia Lunch and Nick Cave,
### art by Mike Matthews

A collection of stories written by performance artist Lydia Lunch and underground musician Nick Cave. Illustrated in a dense, dark style by Mike Matthews, these depressing comix are filled with cheap, scummy sex, prison gang rape, violent intolerance, self-mutilation, cannibalism, extremely dysfunctional relationships, and corpse lovers. The character who appears at the end of "The Stoning of Ruby von Monster" does an admirable job summing up this book's theme: "Man is allowed, on occasion, to rise. But only in order that he be flung down, even harder, into his eternal lot, the trash."

Last Gasp; $6.95
1993; oversize softcover; 36 pp.

## THE BEST OF DRAWN AND QUARTERLY

A color and black-and-white collection of the best comix from *Drawn and Quarterly*'s first ten issues. Featured are "Black Cherry" by Michael Dougan, "8 Pillars of Gay Culture" by Maurice Vellekoop, "A Brief History of Civilization" by David Mazzucchelli ("Look! A woman!" "Let's fuck her!" "She's complaining." "Let's beat her." "She's gonna tell." "Let's kill her."), "Within Three Seconds" by Marti, a religious tale by Joe Matt, violent weirdness from Julie Doucet, and more. A great collection from one of comix's consistently best publishers.

Drawn and Quarterly Publications; $10.95
1993; oversize softcover; 63 pp

## BLAB! #7

A yearly collection of original underground comix. Highlights include Richard Salsa's "Psychorama," in which a shrink gives an A-to-Z of his favorite clients: "Farley was quiet, well-mannered and proper./His parents never dreamed he was the Chapel Hill Chopper.... H is for Hugo, a Peeping Tom case./He was cured of this urge by a face full of mace." "Boxcar Bertha: An Autobiography" is a prose piece accompanied by fifteen drawings by Joe Coleman. "My Mental Health??? Fine" by Gary Lieb is a somewhat disturbing work about a piglike being who can create psychosis in people. Other contributors include Josh Alan Friedman, Drew Friedman, Spain Rodriguez, Mary Fleener, and Doug Allen.

Kitchen Sink Press; $8.95
1992; softcover; 144 pp.

## COMIX COMPENDIUM

A big, fat, "pig of a book" overflowing with the best underground comix money can buy. Lots of famous names here—Seth Tobocman, Mary Fleener, Julie Doucet, Mike Diana, Ace Backwords, Cultural Jetlag, Tom Tomorrow, Joe Matt. Also, lots of not-so-famous names. But everybody in this anthology kicks ass. The range of styles and subject matter is as unbelievably huge as you could ask for. The more than one hundred pieces range from Gary Knell's dead-on parodies of mainstream comic strips to Mary Fleener's cubist look at neuroses to Fiona Smyth's goddesses and succubi to John Bergin's stark take on not speaking out to the sensory overload of Shaun Hayes Holgate to tons more stuff that I can't even describe, so I'm not gonna try. Suffice it to say that any comix library without this top-notch collection will now be considered hopelessly *incomplete*.

Mangajin Books; $18.95
1992; oversize softcover; 280 pp.

## PICTOPIA #4

The international comix here range from subversive to humorous to menacing to not making one bit of sense. "The Monkey's Paw" by W.P. Jacobs is a brooding adaptation of the famous story of the same name. "Island of Fear" by Ida Marxis is about the boogieman. "Malted Shakes -N- Shit" by Stephen Ittner is a hilarious scene involving a dumb-ass in a bar and the old boozer who sets him straight. An enjoyable anthology but by no means essential.

Fantagraphics Books; $7.95
1993; oversize softcover; 72 pp.

## SEXY STORIES FROM
## THE WORLD RELIGIONS

A collection of raunchy comix based on religion. Contributions include "Down Olecuegentile Pass with Coyote," a Native American folktale; "Let's Go to Inferno," the story of a religious man who ends up in hell because God bargained his soul for a few beers; "Holy Jizz" is about a convent full of nuns who suddenly get pregnant; and "The Adventures of Mary Baker Glover Eddy," an irreverent look at the founder of Christian Science. The best thing here is "Gods' Club" by Marcel Gotlib. Jupiter, Allah, Buddha, Wotan (Odin), Jehovah, and Jesus get together for a "guys' night out" full of drinking, dancing, and stag films.

Last Gasp; $2.95 (plus $1 shipping, unless you're buying a bunch of other Last Gasp stuff. In that case, go by the shipping charges listed in the appendix.)

## SNAKE EYES:
### PICTURES AND WORDS
### FOR GROWN-UP GENTLEMEN AND LADIES

Death, famine, racism, pedophilia, blasphemy—nope, comics sure aren't just for kids anymore! This anthology is filled to the brim with transgressive artwork and some writing. The great introduction sets the mood perfectly. While walking home, you encounter a snake that entrances you with its eyes (snake eyes, get it?), and bites you. As its venom flows, you have visions. "First you giggle as the husks of funnybook tradition—Blondie and EC and detective strips—are bodysnatched by the people your parents warned you about. Then the creatures that lurk in the everyday tromp in: child molesters, fundies, unwanted babies, crass capitalists, junkies, fools. The viper leads you through the sewer pipes of the collective unconscious, into a world of greasy cafes, boggy backlots, stale old-age homes and sticky discos. The grand carnival of ghost-gods and devils and sad-sack comedians." Stuff you'll uncover here includes "Cindy the Tattooed Sunday School Teacher," "A Snowman's Chance in Hell," "Christian Death Cult," "The Necronaut," "Famine Circus," "Bam Bam Monkey Time!" "Wasper in White Now," "Idiotland," and "A Tale of Two Shitties." Subversive to the extreme!

Fantagraphics Books; $11.95
1993; oversize softcover; 106 pp.

## TABOO #5

*Taboo* started as a collection of the most uncompromising horror and dark fantasy comix being created. Its subject matter has branched out since then, and its story lines aren't always glaringly controversial. However, *Taboo* still packs a punch with high-quality art and usually daring subject matter. This issue contains "39th and Norton" by Tom Marnick and Dennis Ellefson, a graphic examination of the cruel torture/murder of Black Dahlia; Jeff Nicholson's darkly humorous "Jar Head," about a guy who loves beer so much he wears a large pickle jar completely filled with beer over his head; "Again," Michael Zulli's graphic adaptation of Ramsey Campbell's creepy erotic horror story; and Rick Grimes's doodlish "Akimbo," about hatred and murder.

Perhaps the most extreme piece in this collection is "This Is Dynamite" by S. Clay Wilson. Wilson has created some of the most repugnant, amoral, and politically incorrect works in the history of underground comix. He has referred to "This Is Dynamite" as "the most odious, satanic, twisted commission I've ever done." It is a two-pager based on a suicide note left by a man to the younger man that he is in love/lust with. Given the fact that Wilson himself is revolted by this comic, I was expecting something brutally heinous. Alas, though controversial, it wasn't the piece of repugnant garbage I had hoped for. Maybe I've become too jaded....

Kitchen Sink Press; $14.95
1991; oversize softcover; 130 pp.

## VERRE D'EAU (WEIRDO #28)

The underground comix institution *Weirdo* returns for its last splash (probably) with a gonzo "international issue." Besides the usual American suspects, some French artists and a Serbian contribute their work. Like so many great underground comix, the ones here use the medium to comment on the "big" issues— sex, love, death, violence, fear, etc. Easily the most controversial works here (mark my words, these will be recognized as among the most controversial comix ever published) are R. Crumb's "When the Niggers Take Over America" and "When the Goddamn Jews Take Over America." Now, it pains me to have to explain this, but an alarming number of people have no clue when it comes to such advanced concepts as irony, satire, and point of view. These comix are blistering satire on racism and anti-Semitism. Crumb has taken the most ludicrous, paranoid, white supremacist fears and put them on display. It is meant as ridicule. Unfortunately, there will be a lot of people who won't get it. I've even read that some racist publication has reprinted these pieces. That's the trouble with making fun of extremist views in this manner—the extremists don't realize you're joking.

The Crumb strips alone are worth the price of admission, but you also get lots of other great comix, too.

Last Gasp; $4.95 (plus $1 shipping, unless you're buying a bunch of other stuff. In that case, go by the shipping charges listed in the appendix.)
1993; comic format; 68 pp.

## ZAP #13

The godfather of underground comix still lives! This issue contains strange metaphysical comix by Moscoso, R. Crumb's autobiographical "Dumb," several panels and a story by S. Clay Wilson, a motorcycle gang story by Spain, and "The St. Kahuna's Surfing Mysteries" by Robert Williams. As an added bonus, this issue of *ZAP* also has two stories in which all five of the demented geniuses listed above team up. Did you ever think that Big Bitch, the Checkered Demon, and Trashman would meet?

Last Gasp; $2.95
1994; comic book format; 48 pp.

## ZOMBIE 3-D

A collection of three-dimensional art and comix by Robert Williams, XNO, and the Pizz. The theme of all this madness is the undead. What makes this comic (and the others from 3-D Zone) so great is that, unlike those dorky 1950s 3-D movies, where only selected parts are in 3-D, the whole thing, from start to finish, pops out at you. The 3-D effect is quite convincing, but those glasses are making me see red and blue tints in everything. (Comes with 3-D glasses.)

The 3-D Zone; $3.95 (include over-eighteen age statement)
1992; comic book format; 24 pp.

# MISCELLANEOUS

## BUD PLANT'S INCREDIBLE CATALOG

What Bud Plant lacks in modesty (note the catalog's title), he makes up for in selection. This two hundred-page, lavishly illustrated catalog (five to eight pictures per page) is a must for anyone into comics, graphic novels, comic art, or art in general.

The first section, "Artists of the Past," contains books by realists, surrealists, Secessionists, the Art Deco and Art Nouveau crowds, and many others. The catalog's main section, "Books and Zines," has *Archie*, *Batman*, art annuals, Edgar Rice Burroughs, EC Comics, Frank Frazetta, Jack Kirby, *Prince Valiant*, tattoos, *Vampirella*, and hundreds more. Rare, out-of-print, and imported works abound.

The comics section offers current and back issues for dozens of independent comics. If you think this all sounds pretty tame so far, don't worry— there's lots of erotic art and photography, underground and adult comix, etc. featuring Olivia, Vargas, Guido Crepax, Robert Crumb, *Cherry,* and a whole section devoted to the luscious Bettie Page.

Other sections deal with Disney, instructional books, illustrated children's books, prints and posters, trading cards, and portfolios. To top it all off, there are scores of books offered at sale prices (often 50 percent or more off the retail price). Bud Plant's Catalog is, well, incredible.

Bud Plant Comic Art/PO Box 1689/Grass Valley, CA 95945
Catalog: $3 (toward first order)

*Verre D'eau*
◄ *(Weirdo)*

*When the goddamn comic book artists take over America.*

## DARK KNIGHTS:
### THE NEW COMICS IN CONTEXT
### by Greg S. McCue with Clive Bloom

Superhero comics have definitely changed since their introduction. They are no longer mindless *POW! ZAP! BAM!* stories of good guys beating up the bad guys. Superheros are shown to be people. They have dark, violent sides. They have pasts that haunt them, and they fall in and out of love. They even die of cancer. The format itself has also changed. Graphic novels, now sold in bookstores, bring art and story line to new levels of maturity.

*Dark Knights* looks at this transformation. The first half of the book traces the history of comic books from their very beginnings, through the Golden Age, the anticomics hysteria of the 1940s and 1950s, the Silver Age, and the modern age. The authors detail the increasing sophistication of comic books and the ever-present war between Marvel and DC. The second half of the book contains lengthy interviews with Stan Lee, publisher of Marvel; Tom DeFalco, editor-in-chief of Marvel; Dick Giordano, editorial VP of DC; and Dennis O'Neill, writer and editor for *Batman*.

The glaring weakness of *Dark Knights* is that it focuses all its attention on Marvel and DC while ignoring the numerous independent superhero comics who have helped revitalize the medium.

Pluto Press; $18.95
1993; softcover; 154 pp.

## A HISTORY OF UNDERGROUND COMICS
### (THIRD EDITION)
### by Mark James Estren

The essential, can't-live-with-out-it guide to underground comix. This book is so loaded down with illustrations that it almost qualifies as a huge comic itself. In fact, there are more than *one thousand* strips, single panels, and covers reprinted here. This alone would be worth the price of the book, but you also get insightful facts and commentary. The author gives a brief history of the underground, including its precursors, and takes a detailed look at several artists, including Robert Crumb, S. Clay Wilson, Jaxon, Robert Williams, Gilbert Shelton, and Denis Kitchen.

A chapter is devoted to each of underground comix's favorite themes —sex and sexism, violence, drugs, and social satire. Naturally, with such untamed subject matter, comix have run into legal trouble, as noted in the chapter "Suppression." Finally, the author shows what happens when underground meets overground: everything from museum shows and rip-off imitators to condescending magazine articles and lawsuits from Disney.

Ronin Publishing; $19.95
1993; oversize softcover; 320 pp.

*A History of Underground Comics* by Mark James Estren

*When underground meets overground.*

## MANGA! MANGA!:
### THE WORLD OF JAPANESE COMICS
### by Frederick L. Schodt

This book covers Japanese comics from fun, kooky kid stuff and social satire to serious historical adventure and depraved erotoviolent fantasies, from simple cartoony drawings to richly detailed works of art. It's all here and all of it has that deliciously warped feel to it that has made manga so successful. We get to meet Ghost Warrior, Genius Idiot, Astro Boy, Barefoot Gen, Kid Cop, and Pokochin ("Penis") the Salary-Man. The author provides a massive history of manga, touching on all the movements and genres. He devotes a chapter to analyzing the most extreme manga available, and looks at the manga industry—authors, publishers, and profits (manga is a multi-billion-dollar business). The book ends with ninety-five pages containing four works of manga (all of which are excerpts from larger works).

*Manga! Manga!* is heavily illustrated with at least one piece of art and usually more on every page. The captions are informative, and there are numerous sidebars.

Kodansha America; $19
1983; oversize softcover; 260 pp.

## THE ULTIMATE COMICS CATALOG

Fantagraphics not only publishes cutting-edge comix, they put out an incredible catalog chock-full of other publisher's comix, plus art books by quasi-comic artists like Joe Coleman and Robert Williams. Inside this sixty-three-page, full-blazing-color catalog you'll find Peter Bagge, Vaughn Bodé, Charles Burns, Guido Crepax, Robert Crumb, the Hernandez brothers, Kaz, Spain, *Raw*, and a truckload of other stuff. They also carry a lot of books of classic comics, such as *Terry and the Pirates, Li'l Abner, Prince Valiant, Tarzan, Pogo, Krazy Kat*, and *Little Nemo in Slumberland*. You can also get prints, trading cards, T-shirts, stamps, and more featuring your favorite characters.

*Understanding Comics* ➤ by Scott McCloud

*The medium is the message.*

Fantagraphics/7563 Lake City Way NE/Seattle, WA 98115
Catalog: free

## UNDERSTANDING COMICS:
### THE INVISIBLE ART
### by Scott McCloud

The book that has taken the comics scene by storm. Using comic book format, McCloud presents an examination of the medium of comics—what they are, how they work, what they do, etc. After much debate, he presents a definition of comics and a history of sequential noncomic art: the Bayeux Tapestry, Mayan petroglyphs, Max Ernst's collage novels, etc. He proceeds to examine visual processes, icons, abstraction, the love-hate relationship between words and art in comics, how different styles convey different meanings, the uses of color, the six steps of creating a comic (or any work of art), and more. One of the most enlightening and lengthiest parts of the book examines time flow in comics and what happens *between* panels (basically, our minds automatically fill in the gaps).

Writing this book about comics as a comic was a stroke of genius. Not only can the author tell us about comics, he can show us, too. A perfect example of this occurs when the narrator of the book is discussing abstraction. As he talks, he becomes more and more abstract until he is an unrecognizable group of circles, triangles, and squares. In another instance, he becomes the tortured soul who is the subject of Edvard Munch's painting *The Scream*. No true fan of comics will want to pass up this invaluable work.

Kitchen Sink Press; $19.95
1993; oversize softcover; 215 pp.

## EDGE ARTISTS

### ECSTATIC INCISIONS:
#### The Collages of Freddie Baer
#### by Freddie Baer

A collection of scores of Baer's collages, which have appeared in numerous anarchist magazines, *Factsheet Five, Science Fiction Eye, Semiotext(e) SF*, and dozens of self-produced T-shirts. Despite appearing in so many anti-authoritarian publications, these collages are for the most part surprisingly nonpolitical. They use nineteenth-century wood carvings to create surrealistic, exotic, and often gentle scenes. Women appear in one form or another in a large number of Baer's works. "Sad Eyes" is a collage of giant sunflowers with eyes watching three little girls walking on stilts. "Jason's Travels I" shows a man in a bizarre flying contraption sailing over an Arabian-looking courtyard while a sultry mystery woman stands in the foreground. In "Technological Madonna," a Venus-like statue of a woman wrapping herself in a cloth stands in front of a huge mechanical contraption of gears, cranks, and pumps. Some pieces have a more sinister quality, like "Snake Dreams," where a woman asleep in a temple (?) is being approached by several large snakes.

A few of these collages are overtly political. One shows a large, anatomically correct vagina with the caption "READ OUR LIPS! WE DEMAND CHOICE!" Several collages consist of pictures of death and destruction from the Gulf War with old-time angels flying in the scene.

*Ecstatic Incisions* also has an interview with Baer and a selection of her collaborations with several prose and poetry writers.

AK Press; $11.95
1992; oversize softcover; 73 pp.

### HARMS WAY:
#### Lust & Madness, Murder & Mayhem
#### edited by Joel-Peter Witkin

Joel-Peter Witkin, "the Photographer of the Grotesque," has put together a very special treat for us. He has combed four obscure collections of old photographs and picked out the cream of the crop. The first section of the book contains a couple dozen evidence photos of murder scenes from 1914 to 1918. These are among the most haunting images in the book, because of their spectral lighting and strange camera angles (many of the photos look straight down on the corpses from the ceiling. One particular shot of a bloody man uses a wide-angle lens up close, so the lower half of his torso is outrageously distorted, looking twice as large as the rest of him.)

The second, and most in-your-face section of the book, is made up of twenty-four medical photos from the late 1800s through early 1900s. The images include a woman with most of her nose eaten away by syphilis, a woman with lupus of the face, a baby born without a brain, a boy with alligator skin, an abused baby, a man strapped in an electric chair, and brain surgery from 1929. All of the photos in this section are annotated.

Part Three is composed of twenty-five photos from the archives of the famous Kinsey Institute for sex research. Much of this material is funny. The picture of a naked woman sticking her toe into the eye socket of a "screaming" skeleton is laugh-out-loud hilarious. You may also get a giggle out of the pictures of a woman turning away as a guy vainly tries to stick his hard-on in her face, the utterly bored woman riding a cock, or the five yokels with their dicks poking out of their flies. There are also some serious shots of SM scenes, hermaphrodites, and body modifier Fakir Musafar.

The final selection of photos is the most subtle. It shows mugshot-style pictures of the inmates of an insane asylum around 1875. You're forced to look directly into the eyes of two dozen somewhat deranged-looking people who were diagnosed with imbecility, mania, melancholia, and some ambiguous conditions. Each picture is accompanied by the original handwritten notations, recording name, diagnosis, case history, etc.

*Harms Way* is beautifully made, and the brown-tinted photos have obviously been reproduced with much care. Witkin has created a book that is beautiful in spite of itself. These photographs were not intended to be presented as art, but by looking at them in that way, we see that they transcend their original purposes to become comments on the human condition. This ties in with the book's title (the lack of apostrophe is intentional). Humans are powerless in the face of death, disease, lust, and insanity. We're all standing in harm's way.

Twin Palms Publishing; $60
1994; oversize softcover; 138 pp; heavily illus.

### HEAVY LIGHT:
#### The Art of De Es
#### by De Es Schwertberger

De Es Schwertberger explores strange and wonderful hidden dimensions in his paintings. A genius with form and color, he studied the techniques of the Old Masters to give his fantastic, surreal visions a detailed, realistic expression. The effects are stunning. *The Lesson* shows a pale, giant fetuslike being holding an old man. *Blue Forces* shows a grid formed by successive layers of blue humanoids stretching cables tied to their waists over openings in a building. Through the 1970s, stone and rock became dominant elements in De Es's work, leading to some of my favorite pieces. In *Source,* a humongous egg-shaped rock is perched on a small pile of rocks. *Light* is a picture of a Buddha-like being who's made out of rock facing the sun. In *The Joining,* dozens of rock-beings are gathered around an unseen glowing object in the middle of a field of stone.

De Es's work through the 1980s up to today has gotten much more impressionistic. Many of the paintings from this period show strange beings floating in or flying toward light. He has also created many abstract natural landscapes in this style.

The last section of the book shows the work De Es has done with sculptures of his rock-beings, which he calls Planetarians and Earthlinks.

Morpheus International; $19.95
1993; large oversize softcover; 84 pp.; heavily illus.

◄ *Harms Way* edited by Joel-Peter Witkin

*Photography that truly transcends its original purpose.*

### INCRIMINATING EVIDENCE
#### by Lydia Lunch

Spoken-word performance artist and confrontationalist Lydia Lunch offers up "RAGE, RANTS, ESSAYS, MONOLOGUES, SPEECHES, STORIES, AND RANDOM OTHER BULLSHIT IN THE HOPE THAT I'LL NEVER HAVE TO HEAR THEM AGAIN MYSELF." She spits out pure venom about her family, men, sex, censorship, blah blah blah. It's not hard to see why she's so pissed off about men when you find out about all the violent losers she's hooked up with.

Lunch's misanthropic, who-gives-a-fuck polemics do tend to wear thin fast. This is the kind of stuff that comes across better when you hear it than when you read it. On paper it seems thin, brittle, and not terribly original. Occasionally Lunch does strike a poetic nerve (all the ellipses are hers): "MY LANGUAGE IS NOT

SILENCE, MY SONG IS THE SCREAM... TERROR DWELLS IN THE SHADOW OF MY WINGS... MY HOPE IS MY FIRST BATTLE AND MY LAST GASP... I AM THE KNIFE WITH WHICH THE DEAD CRACK OPEN THE CASKET..."

Last Gasp; $12.95
1992; softcover; 184 pp.

## JOEL-PETER WITKIN:
### FORTY PHOTOGRAPHS
### by Joel-Peter Witkin

Let's get one thing straight—Witkin is one of the best edge photographers (make that, one of the best edge artists) ever to unleash his vision on an unsuspecting world, so when I tell you to buy anything with his name on it, you must heed the call. Witkin has made a mark by taking exquisite photographs of disturbing subjects. His pictures are a dark, heavy black-and-white (usually the grays are replaced by brown tints), looking more like daguerreotypes than modern photographs. Numerous scratches and creases on the pictures add to the old-time effect.

Witkin's photos are hauntingly beautiful, but they contain subjects many people wouldn't consider beautiful: corpses, detached body parts, hermaphrodites, grossly obese women, dead animals, etc. *Penitente* shows a naked, screaming man who has been crucified between two monkeys, who are also crucified (animal lovers take note: Witkin gets his subjects already dead from biological supply houses. Of course, with what I've read about supply houses, crucifixion may almost be a preferable way to die). *Mother and Child* shows a naked woman with a bird's nest for hair, goggles, braces, and those funky orthodontic devices that wrap around your head. She's holding a baby who is wearing a frilly masquerade-style mask. *Woman Breastfeeding an Eel* shows exactly what the title says.

Witkin has said that he looks forward to the day when a severed arm is considered as beautiful as a rose in a vase (I'm paraphrasing somewhat because I don't have access to the book I read this in). I'm not holding my breath, but if anyone could bring about this sort of shift, it's Joel-Peter. This book is a good introduction to his work. It contains mostly portraits of people but not much of his work with corpses and detached body parts.

Distributed Arts Publishers; $19.95
1992; oversize softcover; 46 pp.

*Support the Revolution by Wallace Berman*
▶

*Hugely influential mixtures of found art, photography and Hebrew.*

## THE MAN OF SORROWS
### by Joe Coleman

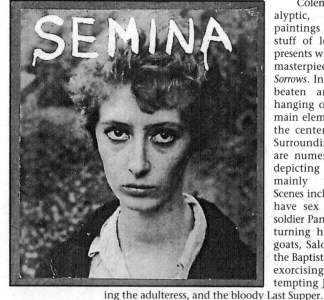

Coleman's violent, apocalyptic, brightly colored paintings have become the stuff of legend. This book presents what may well be his masterpiece, *The Man of Sorrows*. In this dense work, a beaten and bloody Jesus hanging on the cross is the main element, positioned in the center of the painting. Surrounding the crucifixion are numerous small scenes depicting biblical events, mainly involving Jesus. Scenes include Mary about to have sex with the Roman soldier Pantera, Jesus as a boy turning his playmates into goats, Salomé holding John the Baptist's nasty head, Jesus exorcising a woman, Satan tempting Jesus, Jesus forgiving the adulteress, and the bloody Last Supper.

Coleman's sources for these scenes are not only the Gospels of the New Testament, but the Apocrypha (especially the Gospel of Thomas) and Jewish and pagan writings about Jesus. For example, the scene in which Mary and Pantera embrace is based on the widespread belief during the early centuries of Christianity that Jesus was Pantera's illegitimate child.

Coleman sheds interesting lights on the "official" version of events, too. He comments about the scene "Casting out the Moneychangers": "This is not the Jesus who turns the other cheek—this is the revolutionary who advocates destruction. The repressed rage and violence has boiled to the surface."

If the life of Jesus Christ seems an unlikely subject for an artist of Coleman's—ahem—reputation, he explains that it was "Christian iconography which formed a base from which my own artistic pathology grew." He later says, "Many of my first sexual thoughts were inspired by the violent and sexy stories in the Bible. I experienced a lot of fear and confusion about the Bible, but one thing was becoming clear: there was something holy about violence and suffering."

This remarkable book is printed on black paper. The entire painting is tipped in at the front of the book, and each scene is given its own section, containing a large, full-color tip-in of that scene. Coleman's explanations and commentary on each scene are handwritten in gold ink. *The Man of Sorrows* is an essential work of fin-de-millennium art.

This book is available in two versions. The regular edition comprises two thousand numbered copies. The collector's edition is limited to one hundred signed and numbered copies and includes a linen-covered box, slipcase, wooden jigsaw puzzle of the painting, and a reliquary containing Coleman's hair and shirt fragments from one of his performance art pieces.

Gates of Heck; $40 (regular edition);
$350 (collector's edition)
1993; oversize hardcover; 31 pp.

## SHOCK TREATMENT
### by Karen Finley

Karen Finley is one of the best-known performance artists in the world. Her shocking antics, including covering her naked body in chocolate and alfalfa sprouts (representing shit and sperm), earned her the wrath of Jesse Helms and helped trigger the NEA debacle. This book collects Finley's monologues and some poems and essays. They are among the most nakedly shocking things you will ever read. "When I had a baby and it cried I killed it. I hate noise. I hate something out of control. I want a perfect baby. I want a perfect life. I didn't like the baby so I killed her. Slowly, in the water, I drowned her. Everyone kills in this world." In "The Father in All of Us" she writes, "Then I mount my own mama in the ass. That's right, I fuck my own mama in the ass 'cause I'd never fuck my mama in her snatch! She's my mama."

Finley's takes on incest, child abuse, domestic violence, prostitution, sexism, death, and censorship are uncompromising and rattling. Unfortunately, they suffer from the same fundamental problem as Lydia Lunch's work (above)—these pieces are meant to be heard, not read. The short, rapid-fire sentences and the constant repetition just don't translate very well onto the printed page. Still, Finley's works are so brutal that they must be experienced, so if you can't see her, read her.

City Lights; $6.95
1990; softcover; 145 pp.

## SUPPORT THE REVOLUTION
### by Wallace Berman

Berman was an avant-garde artist whose work involved found art, collage, photography, doodles on envelopes, mixed-media sculpture, and the Hebrew alphabet. It's a bizarre mixture of media and ideas that seeks to deconstruct and remap the visual symbols that constantly bombard us. Many of Berman's works consist of wood-stained paper and rocks on which were painted Hebrew letters. Berman also got a lot of mileage out of the basic concept of showing a hand holding a little AM/FM radio. On this radio could be any one of hundreds of pictures, including two old coins, a spider, a naked woman, a church, a football player, a Native American, a cross, a skeleton, a snake, a butterfly and a watch, a camera, ad infinitum. Anywhere from one to sixteen of the hands with radios could be on any given work, which were produced, by the way, on a primitive version of the photocopy machine.

Berman was also a pioneer of mail art. He would often draw or paste found photographs on envelopes he sent to friends and acquaintances.

Frankly, Berman's art doesn't strike me as works of pure genius, but he was hugely influential. His work from the late 1940s through 1976 was instrumental in the forming of the anti-authoritarian aesthetic of the Beat movement, avant-garde film, mail art, and more. Dennis Hopper, Miles Davis, Jim Morrison, Jasper Johns, Jack Kerouac, and many others were influenced by Berman's work.

This book contains more than two hundred illustrations, many in color, and essays on Berman's life and work by Walter Hopps, David Meltzer, Colin Gardner, et al.

Distributed Arts Publishers; $39.95
1992; hardcover; 183 pp.

## VISUAL ADDICTION
### by Robt. Williams

Williams has become a major figure in edge art as of late. He's been violating people's eyeballs for decades now. His most well known work is the painting *Appetite for Destruction,* which was used as the cover for the Guns N Roses album of the same name. (As it turned out, it was too controversial to use as the cover, so they included it as interior art and put it on their T-shirts.)

Williams paints in a dense, extremely detailed style, sometimes using a paintbrush with a single bristle to get the proper effect. Multiple scenes, juxtaposed elements, and constant violent motion make each painting a treat to be slowly savored. Williams uses ultrabright—you might even say garish—colors to help create a visual assault. His paintings contain lots of nekkid ladies, cool cars, tongues and eyeballs, clowns, devils and other imagery taken from religion, sex, and pop culture.

In the painting *Playing House Under The Tears Of The Martyr And The Slobber Of The Peephawks* a little girl in the foreground is serving tea to a doll while her puppy looks on. While this sounds peaceful enough, don't be fooled. In the sky above the girl are a voluptuous, nude, crucified woman and a squadron of menacing flying eyeballs that have wings like the "Red Baron" planes.

Sixty such paintings are reproduced in black-and-white *and* in color (don't ask me why). Williams says, "Sight is my opiate." If that's true for you too, then this book will have you higher than a kite.

Last Gasp; $24.95
1989; oversize softcover; 95 pp.

## WINDOW ON THE UNSPEAKABLE
### by Robt. Williams

A set of thirty-six trading cards containing the paintings of Robt. Williams. Works include *Nine Indo-Nostril Pickers*, an homage to nosepicking in which several strange creatures are seen rooting for boogers, and *Cowboys and Amoebas*, a Wild West scene in which cowboys on horses are shooting at rainbow-colored amoebas driving hot rods over cow skulls and through cacti. (Is Williams cool or what?)

The cards are glossy and the colors are eye-popping, but there is a disturbing lack of sharpness. The problem is that Williams's paintings are basically inappropriate for trading cards. His works are so incredibly rich and detailed that shrinking them to 2¹ᐟ² by 3 inches just doesn't work. Not that they're horrible, mind you. The cards are reasonable reproductions; they just don't do complete justice to Williams's talent.

Kitchen Sink Press; $10.95
1993; 36 trading cards

# PHOTOGRAPHY

## ANIMA
### by James Balog

James Balog is an artistic photographer whose last book, *Survivors: A New Vision of Endangered Wildlife,* got him thinking about the great apes. He realized there is a deep connection between humans and chimpanzees—a connection, like others to the natural world, that we have lost. In an effort to integrate us with our close relatives (98.4 percent of our genetic material is the same), Balog has created one of the most stunning photography books I have ever gazed upon.

*Anima* contains dozens of beautifully stylized pictures of humans and chimps interacting. Young, beautiful people, old, wrinkled people, and a pregnant woman hold hands with chimps, cradle each other in their arms, look into each other's eyes, frolic and play, sit and think. The sparse sets and solid white or black backgrounds focus all attention on the human and almost-human subjects. The similarities are overwhelming. The pictures are strangely moving and vaguely disturbing.

The text accompanying the pictures is free-form meditation on humans, what we have lost, and what we may be able to regain. The book itself is beautifully designed. It is a 10³ᐟ⁴-inch square format with one of the photos reproduced on the actual cover. The wraparound jacket is vellum and contains the title and author's name. Inside, the photos and type are printed on ultra-heavy paper.

*Anima* gets my highest recommendation. It is destined to become a classic work.

Arts Alternative Press; $29.95
1993; oversize hardcover; 62 pp.

*American Infrared Survey* by Stephen and David Paternite

*Photography is also about warping reality.*

## AMERICAN INFRARED SURVEY
### edited by Stephen Paternite and David Paternite

A lot of people think photography is just about capturing reality. Actually, it's also about warping reality. Choosing unusual lenses, filters, and films allows you to change the world around you. Infrared photography is one of the easiest and best ways to do this. By using film that picks up light at different wavelengths, you can turn even the most generic scene into a surrealistic window into another world.

Black-and-white infrared film, much more common than color infrared, causes white skin and clouds to become ghostly and glowing. The sky becomes very dark. Trees and grass also darken considerably, or they become bright if directly lit by the sun. You see a magical parallel world where objects are still recognizable but everything's color has been thrown off kilter.

The eighty photos in this book cover a wide range of subjects —a pond, eerie tree-filled landscapes, nudes, the desert, a farm, the beach, a Ferris wheel, a flower, a football game, a McDonald's sign (one of my favorite pictures), and all kinds of people. There are also several hand-tinted and color infrared shots. A superb collection.

Photo Survey Press Publishing; $21.95
1982; oversize softcover; 81 pp.

## FACES
### by Nancy Burson

With *Faces,* Nancy Burson gets her "wish to photograph people whose faces followed the exception rather than the rule." Using a cheap plastic Diana camera, she took pictures of three types of children: those with craniofacial deformities, those who had been severely burned, and those with progeria, the ultrarare condition that causes children to age prematurely, making them look like eighty-year-olds.

The Diana camera produces grainy, glowing, sometimes blurred photos that lend an ethereal quality to the subjects. The forty-five photographs capture the children playing, smiling, laughing, and interacting with loved ones. What you realize after looking at these pictures is that the children are just that—children. I hate to sound sappy, but these pictures are better than anything else I've seen in conveying that our outer packaging (the body) is meaningless when everything is said and done.

Twin Palms Publishers; $35
1993; small hardcover; 72 pp.

## GROTESQUE:
### NATURAL HISTORICAL AND FORMALDEHYDE PHOTOGRAPHY
### edited by Mirelle Thijsen

*Grotesque* is a collection of images created by photographers in natural history museums, which are always filled with the fascinating and alarming examples of nature's handiwork. Like so much other challenging art, these photographs are striving to take what is not normally considered beautiful and recreate it in a new light. The shutter-clicking couple, Akin & Ludwig, described their own reactions: "We found ourselves disturbed by these ugly yet compelling forms. Gradually we shed our feelings of revulsion and were able to perceive death, dismemberment and deformity as at once enigmatic and clear, ugly and beautiful. Once our minds had been stripped of socially conditioned responses, we could observe nature's aberrations and the grotesque side of medical dissection with new eyes."

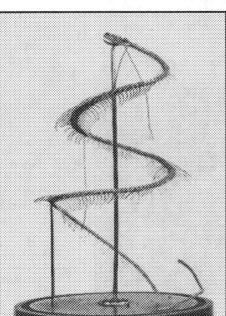

*Grotesque* edited by Mirelle Thijsen

*"Gradually we shed our feelings of revulsion and were able to perceive death, dismemberment and deformity as at once enigmatic and clear, ugly and beautiful."*

Akin & Ludwig's work in this book includes platinum prints of a tray full of pig snouts, a fetus in a jar of formaldehyde, and a preserved severed face. Joan Fontcuberta's photos show a deformed lamb with two legs growing from its back and several uncoiled snakes suspended in very tall jars. Rosamond Purcell treats us to images of shriveled corpse feet and some kind of rodent skeleton.

Joel-Peter Witkin's photos are different from the others because his natural props have been taken into his studio instead of being photographed in their museums. We are treated to pictures of a severed head being used as a vase, crucified monkeys, a woman cradling a human head, and a stillborn baby wearing some weird headgear. Olivia Parker's images are the least disturbing. She shows broken nautilus shells, a beat-up buffalo skull, and a dead butterfly.

The book also contains information on the artists' work, their books and exhibitions, and a statement from each one.

*Grotesque* is a unique visual document. Its low price (for an art book) makes it an affordable addition to your library, even though the book—and the images in it—are on the small side.

Distributed Art Publishers; $12.95
No date; paperback; 72 pp; heavily illus.

## MR. SALESMAN
### edited by Diane Keaton

Edited by actress and amateur photographer Diane Keaton, *Mr. Salesman* is a collection of photographs from a lost aspect of art history—the Jam Handy Organization. The JHO was founded in 1911 to teach door-to-door salesmen how to operate. By the mid-1950s the JHO was making instructional filmstrips with a distinct visual style. The lighting was dramatic, the sets were sparse, and the salesmen were cookie-cutter, emotionless drones. The fifty photos in this book were taken from film strips with titles like "The Man Who Sells" and "What Brings 'Em Back." Pictures include a salesman laughing as he stuffs money into his pockets, a silhouette of two figures behind an office door of frosted glass, a man looking at a row of bottles, a shadowy figure standing beside a well-lit automobile, and a salesman showing Mrs. Housewife the latest Frigidaire.

The editor of this book explains her fascination with these unusual photos: "When I think about it, these pictures are a tract, a rule book on how to lose your soul. At first glance, I thought they were funny, because the selling tools, i.e., maps, charts, briefcases, and diagrams have more personality than the men. It was only when I stopped laughing that Mr. Salesman's determined non-commitment to any emotion hit me. That's when something began to gnaw at me. That's when I got sad."

Twin Palms Publishers; $35
1993; small hardcover; 96 pp.

## OUTTAKES:
### THE PUBLICATION FOR PHOTOGRAPHERS AND THEIR FRIENDS

*Outtakes* is a tabloid printed on fairly high-quality paper, dedicated to publishing top-notch photojournalism that otherwise might not have an outlet. The photographers get to tell the stories behind the pictures.

Issue #6 contained photos from an Argentinian prison where women get to keep their children, a whaling expedition, and an AIDS facility. The pictures run the gamut from humorous to sad to chilling, but most of them have one thing in common—they're powerful as hell and won't soon be forgotten. And that's the highest praise that can be given to photojournalism.

Outtakes/PO Box 1582/Litchfield, CT 06759
Single issue: $5
Four-issue sub (1 year): $20

## RADIANT IDENTITIES
### by Jock Sturges

Photographer Jock Sturges was a target of the Thought Police, and, as such, he is an *Outposts* hero. But what makes him even greater in our book is that he refused to stop doing what he believed in.

Sturges's main area of photographic interest is "how girls become women," to use the words of internationally renowned photo critic A.D. Coleman. Sturges captures those painful and mysterious stages of life just before and during a girl's blossoming.

His pictures are soft, lush black-and-whites reminiscent of daguerreotypes. Within this dreamlike tableau are the naked bodies of men, women, and boys, but mainly angelic adolescent girls. They are on the beach, in the woods, or in their homes. In almost every shot, Sturges's subjects look boldly into the camera, not at all afraid of revealing themselves physically and psychologically.

At this point, I'm sure many of you may be wondering exactly what's going on here. Aren't nude shots of kids automatically child pornography? If you listen to the FBI, Janet Reno, conservatives, the Cincinnati Vice Squad, and a lot of other people, the answer will be yes. But if you look at Sturges's exquisite photographs for yourself, you will see the answer is no. There is nothing prurient about them. As Coleman writes, "These are reverential, even sacral images." He later points out that "the fact that he's [Sturges] willing to closely look at people this age, see them as individuals, and address the fullness of their being indicates that he's come to terms with his own sexual nature." Sturges and his subjects are honestly trying to explore the physicality and sexuality of girls on the threshold of becoming women.

But don't take my word for it, just look at Sturges's models. Instead of making them sign a blanket release, Sturges gets permission from every model every time he uses her or his picture in a book, exhibition, etc. Year after year, they grant him permission. Also, the same models pose for Sturges for years on end. In fact, because Sturges has been shooting for twenty years, some of his original models are now grown, and they bring their kids to be photographed. The ultimate proof of Sturges's integrity came after the Feds arrested him in 1990 on child porn charges and seized his life's work (he was found not guilty at the trial)—not a single one of Sturges's models stopped working with him. The photographer and his subjects continued exploring their vision together, and the results can be found in this beautiful book.

Aperture; $35
1994; oversize hardcover; 95 pp; heavily illus.

# CYBERART

## CYBERARTS:
### EXPLORING ART AND TECHNOLOGY
### edited by Linda Jacobson

A large anthology of articles exploring the intersection of technology with art, entertainment, science, education, and business. Specifically, the book covers how multimedia and virtual reality are affecting animation, music, publishing, video and film, toys and games, theaters and theme parks. All kinds of artists, computer geeks, and assorted visionaries offer views on aesthetics, human-computer interaction, hyperinstruments, 3-D audio, guerrilla video, moving holography, Expanded Books, choreography, and a whole lot more. The book is well illustrated and designed and contains a sixteen-page full-color gallery of digital art.

The articles try to strike a balance between being understandable to the layman and useful to the professional. Obviously, "The Silver Platter: A Look at CD Mastering" isn't for everybody. Most articles, though, can be understood by anyone with at least a rudimentary understanding of cyberstuff. A nice feature of the book is that terms that may be above most people's heads are printed in bold in the text and explained in the margins of the pages.

It's all very informative and exciting, but too techno-optimistic. There are a couple of pieces that address the complicated legal web being spun by this technology—copyrights, intellectual property, the First Amendment, etc.—but the other material almost always just presents the possibilities but not the problems of these new wonders. Still, if you're looking for a basic primer on the cutting edge of the arts without a detailed discussion of the implications, then this is the best book to get.

Miller Freeman; $24.95
1992; oversize softcover; 312 pp.

## ITERATIONS:
### THE NEW IMAGE
### edited by Timothy Druckey

Art is going through a rebirth, where the old media just don't apply anymore and the new media don't even have agreed-upon names yet. This book is about electronic art. The artists use video, photography, audio, laser discs, touch screens, text, and interactive installations in the wildest combinations imaginable. It's hard even to describe what the art looks like, because the images are so foreign that there's no appropriate vocabulary to work with. The five essays that make up the first half of the book attempt to remedy the situation by defining and explaining this new art.

The second half of the book contains the work of fifteen artists in full color accompanied by an essay by each of the artists. Grahame Weinbren says of his film Sonata, "In its deliberate investigation of the possibilities of interactive drama, Sonata aspires to lay the foundation for a new cinema, a cinema in which the response of the viewer affects his/her experience, a cinema of moment-by-moment collaboration between viewer and filmmaker. It opens a new dimension for the moving image, aligning the shape of the film with the shape of thought, creating a cinema that portrays the world we live in and act on, rather than a world fitted to prior conventions."

Iterations offers a mind-boggling glimpse into the potential of art in a media-saturated society. Get it or be left in the dust, wondering what happened.

The MIT Press; $39.95
1993; oversize hardcover; 199 pp.

## PIXEL VISION:
### THE COMPUTER IMAGE MAGAZINE

Beautifully printed in full color on slick paper, Pixel Vision is a guide to the latest in computer art, including animation, still art, and virtual worlds. Pixel Vision doesn't focus much on the technical aspects of cyberart, but instead profiles artists and works, prints opinions and manifestos, and acts as a gallery for some of the most beautiful, complex images being created on computer.

Every issue comes with a "Pixel Handbook" stapled inside. These handbooks often contain more technical information on producing images or on new technology (the Handbook in issue #10 is on high-definition television).

Pixel Vision
PO Box 1138, Madison Square Station/New York NY, 10159
Five-issue sub (one year): $45; foreign: $55

# CINEMA

## BEFORE MICKEY:
### THE ANIMATED FILM 1898–1928
### by Donald Crafton

Long before Mickey Mouse appeared on the screen in Steamboat Willie and proceeded to dominate the world's culture, there already existed about thirty years' worth of animated film. The author examines the "prehistory" of this medium that has recently come into its own with such landmark films as Who Framed Roger Rabbit?, Aladdin, and Tim Burton's Nightmare Before Christmas.

Filled with more than 130 illustrations, this book covers the drawn animation and stop-action animation of The Haunted Hotel, Humorous Phases of Funny Faces, Dream of a Rarebit Fiend, Dinky Doodles in the Hunt, and others. Animators who are covered include Emile Cohl, the first animator; Winsor McCay, creator of the comic strip (and film) Little Nemo in Slumberland and Gertie the Dinosaur; and Pat Sullivan and Otto Messmer, creators of the quintessential animated feline, Felix the Cat.

In the conclusion, the author draws parallels between early animation and surrealism: "Almost all the animated films discussed begin by establishing an 'alien universe' into which the spectator may project himself. Although the creators of the first animated films were not surrealists or even cognizant of that movement, they inadvertently made films that demonstrated a disregard for everyday existence, normal logic, and causality, and a propensity for dreamlike action which André Breton and his followers admired."

University of Chicago Press; $15.95
1994; softcover; 413 pp.

## BLEED PART ONE
### by Nick Zedd

An autobiography of Nick Zedd, the underground, transgressive director of such celluloid nightmares as *Whoregasm* and *Geek Maggot Bingo*. In a sparse style, he tells of his childhood, movies, and relationships with Lydia Lunch, Rick Strange, and Nazi Dick, among others. "To fulfill our desire to touch death [Lydia Lunch and I] talked about kidnapping children in some other country, killing them and filming it, then showing it in America.... If I could do that and not feel guilt I would have achieved the ultimate freedom. After thinking more about it I decided it would be a cheap way to get famous and that I had no right to do it since I didn't believe in taking someone else's life unless they deserved it."

Hanuman Books; $5.95
1992; mini-paperback; 131 pp.

## BROKEN MIRRORS BROKEN MINDS:
### THE DARK DREAMS OF DARIO ARGENTO
### by Maitland McDonagh

Dario Argento is a controversial Italian director whose films form a bridge between gore-filled horror movies and avant-garde art films. Since 1970 he has directed *The Bird With the Crystal Plumage, The Cat O' Nine Tails, Four Flies on Grey Velvet, Suspiria, Inferno, Creepers, Two Evil Eyes* (with George Romero), and others. "The world of Dario Argento is one of twisted logic, rhapsodic violence, stylized excess; it's true 20th Century Gothic with all the inversion, formal imbalance and riotous grotesquerie the term can encompass. His is a romantic vision, informed by an instinctive appreciation of the contradictory nature of erotic appeal: Argento's camera is alternately enthralled and repelled by ripe flesh and blood-drenched fantasy."

Three of Argento's films are supernatural thrillers and seven are *gialli*. *Giallo* literally means yellow, but it has a different meaning for films. What film noir is to detective thrillers, *gialli* is to mysteries. Among the typical *gialli* characters are "haunted protagonists touched by madness and irrational violence, psychopaths whose depredations are as bizarre as they are brutal, and petty criminals, perverts, and eccentrics who emerge from around every corner and beneath every metaphorical rock."

The author, a widely published American critic, meticulously analyzes all of Argento's films. Lots of stills and movie posters accompany the text. This book also contains a detailed filmography and bibliography and an interview with Argento.

Sun Tavern Fields; £9.95
1991; softcover; 293 pp.

*Screaming Mimi* ad slick exploits the traditional recourse of lurid horror pictures with reference to maturity.

*Broken Mirrors Broken Minds* by Maitland McDonagh

*"His is a romantic vision, informed by an instinctive appreciation of the contradictory nature of erotic appeal..."*

## CANYON CINEMA

An incredible catalog with more than four hundred pages of independent, avant-garde films for rent or purchase. Before you get too excited, though, let me tell you that the great majority of these films (370 pages' worth) are only on reel-to-reel tape, because Canyon Cinema's main target is small theaters, cool art houses, and the like that show films like these for a small ticket price. If you are involved with such a venture, you absolutely, positively must get this catalog. Prices of rental range mostly from ten dollars to fifty dollars. Each of the thousands of films are described and stills from some are used as illustrations. The terms of rental are that you show the film once, with no previews, and your audience must be under two hundred. For each of these conditions you must break, you pay some extra. Any way you look at it, it's a total bargain.

For individuals, there are forty-five pages of films available on VHS videocassette for sale. Prices are around thirty to seventy-five dollars for private use (prices are higher for organizations that plan on showing these tapes). Although there's not nearly as much to buy as to rent, there are some next-to-impossible-to-find gems here, such as Carol Leigh's (aka The Scarlet Harlot) documentaries on prostitution, antiwar protest, and sex freedom; performance artist Carolee Schneeman's *Viet-Flakes*; videos by the ultrastrange group The Residents; Craig Baldwin's *O No Coronado!; Where's Utopia?*, a look at successful cooperative communities; and a truckload of strange and hard-hitting films from across the spectrum.

Canyon Cinema
2325 Third Street, Suite 338/San Francisco, CA 94107
Catalog: $15

## CINEMA, CENSORSHIP, AND THE STATE
### by Nagisa Oshima

Oshima is one of Japan's most important and controversial directors. He was originally part of the Japanese New Wave and has gone on to receive international acclaim for his many films. Among his best known works are *Cruel Story of Youth, Night and Fog in Japan, Pleasure of the Flesh, Boy*, and—one of my favorite movies—*In the Realm of the Senses*.

These writings range from the mid-1950s to the mid-1980s. Oshima discusses cinematic technique, film theory, Korea and Vietnam, his feelings about his movies, etc. A large number of the essays deal with the controversy Oshima's films have produced. He is truly a renegade with a camera. His movies are often anti-authoritarian, anti-war, anti-death penalty, and/or pro-sex. Oshima doesn't shy away from showing brutality, suicide, rape, and unusual sex. Because of this, he has run into numerous problems with the Japanese government, which sometimes bans his movies and persecutes him. This was exactly the case with the erotic-asphyxiation classic *In the Realm of the Senses*, which could not be shown in Japan. Oshima was brought up on obscenity charges for, not the film itself, but the book containing the film's screenplay and several stills. In his essay "Theory of Experimental Pornographic Film" Oshima writes, "But I don't feel as if I have attained 'obscenity'.... Which leads me to think that, generally speaking, nothing that is expressed is 'obscene.' Isn't 'obscenity' contained in that which is not expressed, not seen, hidden? And in the heart of the human heart that responds to these things? I daresay that internalized taboos make for the experience of 'obscenity'.... When one feels that everything that one had wanted to see has been revealed, 'obscenity' disappears, the taboo disappears as well, and there is a certain liberation." The text of the plea Oshima enters at his trial, reprinted in this book, absolutely dissects and pulverizes the government's charges against him. It deserves to go down in history as a classic attack on the Thought Police.

The MIT Press; $14.95
1992; softcover; 308 pp.

## DAVID CRONENBERG:
### A DELICATE BALANCE
### by Peter Morris

A biography of the wonderfully demented director of *Scanners, Videodrome, The Fly, Naked Lunch*, and *M. Butterfly*. Not knowing much about Cronenberg, but having seen some of his movies, I found this bio to be interesting but extraordinarily skimpy. The author covers the first twenty years of his subject's life in eleven pages, and that's including two full-page pictures of Cronenberg's family houses. The rest of the book similarly hauls ass, giving serviceable but undernourished accounts of events that leave you wanting to know more. This book comes across more as a college report than a full-fledged biography. The lack of an index and the fact that there are no chapters, only subheadings, also make this book more of a fun read that will acquaint you with Cronenberg than a serious attempt to document his life and work.

ECW Press; $9.95
1994; softcover; 155 pp.

### DESIRE UNLIMITED:
#### THE CINEMA OF PEDRO ALMODÓVAR
#### by Paul Julian Smith

Pedro Almodóvar is the most successful Spanish director of all time. His films include *Women on the Edge of a Nervous Breakdown* and *Tie Me Up! Tie Me Down!* However, he is not often taken seriously, since his movies are often "chick flicks" (meaning their main focus is women and women's concerns) or regarded as queer kitsch. In fact, this is the first book of English-language criticism of his films.

The author examines one film per chapter, showing the contradictions and issues in Almodóvar's work. These films send strong, often conflicting signals about women, gender orientation, love, and Spain. Smith looks at how these messages are presented through plot, props, and cinematic techniques, as well as how these messages have been received by reviewers and the general public. Smith also draws on rare, revealing video and text material he obtained from Almodóvar's production company.

Verso; $17.95
1994; softcover; 162 pp.

### HOUSE OF HORROR:
#### THE COMPLETE HAMMER FILMS STORY
#### edited by Allen Eyles, Robert Adkinson, and Nicholas Fry

From the 1940s through the 1970s Hammer Films made some of the best B-grade horror and science fiction films of all time. This book presents a thorough overview of Hammer's output, first by interviewing Hammer's cofounder Michael Carreras, director Terence Fisher, and actors Christopher Lee and Peter Cushing. Then, after presenting a brief overview of Hammer's history, it delves into an illustration-drenched guide to Hammer's films. There are so many movie stills and publicity shots that probably half to two-thirds of the book is pictures. And many of the photos—this is important—are of topless vampire babes.

Hammer achieved worldwide success with *The Curse of Frankenstein* (1957) and *Dracula* (1958), both of which reinvigorated (and, in the case of Dracula, eroticized) their subgenres. In fact, Christopher Lee would become the most famous of the cinematic Draculas. Besides making many more movies on the Frank/vamp themes, Hammer also produced celluloid gems about werewolves, mummies, zombies, the abominable snowman, Dr. Jekyll and Mr. Hyde, Satanists, and psychos. Titles include *The Brides of Dracula, Taste the Blood of Dracula, Lust for a Vampire, The Curse of the Mummy's Tomb, Frankenstein Created Woman, Frankenstein and the Monster from Hell, Hands of the Ripper, She,* and *One Million Years B.C.* (which starred Raquel Welch in the role she was born to play—a bikini-clad cave-vixen).

House of Horror also looks at post-Hammer vampire cinema (paying special attention to foreign movies), contains a filmography, and has a section containing eight full-color Hammer movie posters.

Creation Books; $23
1994; oversize softcover; 175 pp.

### INCREDIBLY STRANGE FILMS
#### (RE/SEARCH #10)

A collection of interviews, articles, and essays that plum the depths of celluloid strangeness. Some of the genres that are covered include biker films, J.D. films, LSD films, women-in-prison films, mondo films, Mexican horror movies, sexploitation, industrial-jeopardy films (like *Blood on the Highway*), nudist films, and gore films.

The first part of the book contains interviews with directors Herschell Gordon Lewis (*She-Devils on Wheels* and *The Gore-Gore Girls*), Ray Dennis Steckler (*The Incredibly Strange Creatures Who Stopped Living and Became Mixed-Up Zombies*), Ted V. Mikels (*The Black Klansman* and *The Corpse Grinders*), Russ Meyer (*Faster Pussycat! Kill! Kill!*), and others. The second part gives overviews

of genres, including most of those mentioned above. A series of essays focuses on specific films. The A-to-Z directory of film personalities covers directors, producers, actors, etc. Tons of film stills, publicity shots, and movie posters abound.

If it's weird and it's on film, it's here.

RE/Search Publications; $17.99
1986; oversize softcover;
224 pp.

### THE JOE BOB REPORT

Formerly *We Are the Weird*, this sixteen-pager from Joe Bob Briggs centers on trashy movies but branches into other trashy areas of pop culture and alternative culture as well. There are movie, book, and zine reviews, rants, news, an advice column, and letters. What holds it all together is Joe Bob's great cynical sense of humor. In his review of the book *Secrets of Seduction: How to Be the Best Lover Your Woman Ever Had*, he says that it "right away gets depressing, because it implies that, if you're reading the book, you already *have* a woman. Don't they realize that only *lonely guys* read books like this?" You can even buy a special anti-Yuppie coffee mug from Joe Bobb. The front says "Cappuccino My Butt" and the back says "When did everybody go from thinking that coffee was a form of herpes to this new idea that a fourteen-dollar cup of Tahitian Vanilla-Wombat Espresso will turn you into an art director for music videos?"

The Joe Bob Report/PO Box 2002/Dallas, TX 75221
Single issue: "The newsletter that's like a drug: the first one's always free."
Six-month sub (13 issues): $19.95 (U.S. only)
One-year sub (26 issues): $35; foreign: $70

*House of Horror edited by Allen Eyles et al.* ◄

*The best grade-B horror and science fiction films of all time.*

### PIER PAOLO PASOLINI:
#### CINEMA AS HERESY
#### by Naomi Greene

Poet, novelist, essayist, and director, Pasolini is considered one of Italy's greatest modern intellectuals. This is kind of surprising when you realize that Pasolini was anti-religious, anti-authoritarian, anti-Fascist, and openly gay. His works constantly got him into trouble—he was dragged to court thirty-three times during his life and nine of his films ran the gauntlet of censorship and obscenity charges. His final film, *Salò, or The 120 Days of Sodom*, is considered by many to be the most unwatchable movie ever made.

Although he made his mark in several media, Pasolini's film work is the main focus of this book. After revealing Pasolini's early life—his father was a Fascist and his mother was anti-Fascist, which made for a volatile home life—the author launches into detailed descriptions of PPP's films and their repercussions. Pasolini's first film, *Accattone* (1961), portrayed life among Italy's ragged people—whores, thieves, and unwed mothers. This film was a harbinger: "...the sharply divided critical opinion and right-wing disturbances that greeted *Accattone* in 1961 indicated that Pasolini would probably prove even more controversial as a filmmaker than as a novelist."

In 1964 Pasolini directed *Il Vangelo second Matteo*, one of the best films of the life of Christ ever made (extremely ironic, considering Pasolini was an atheist). Both the political and mystical sides of Jesus were shown. He loves the downtrodden people and fights for social justice.

*Salò* was Pasolini's last film, and what a swan song it was. PPP purposely made his movie as extreme and uncompromising as possible. In the beginning, Fascists round up sixteen peasant teenagers and young adults and take them to a remote villa in Salò. Once there, the Fascists use the kids in the most depraved

*Pier Paolo Pasolini* by Naomi Greene

*The director of one of the most unwatchable films ever made.*

## SEX MURDER ART:
### THE FILMS OF JÖRG BUTTGEREIT
### by David Kerkes

The young German director Jörg Buttgereit has created some of the most brutal movies ever to flicker on a screen. Foremost among them is *Nekromantik*, a frank examination of a young necrophilic couple who steal a car crash victim and have a three-way with the corpse. In the film's most infamous scene, Betty (played by Beatrice M.) puts a chair leg in place of her cadaver's shriveled penis, rolls on a condom (sex doesn't get much safer than this), and proceeds to commune with the dead.

*Nekromantik 2* took the premise even further. Monika (played by Monika M.) is attracted to corpses but she pukes when she tries to have sex with them. She tries a real live boyfriend, but he brings no satisfaction. What a quandary: "She's not happy with the living and she can't make it with the dead." Monika's solution? While boffing her breathing boyfriend, she chops his head off and replaces it with the noggin of her enchanting corpse. Orgasm at last.

*Sex Murder Art* provides an in-depth look at these movies and their director, cameraperson, and co-writer/assistant director. The book also goes into detail about Buttgereit's other movies: early short films; *Schramm*, about serial killer Lothar Schramm; *Der Todesking (Deathking)*, a series of vignettes showing the suicides of seven unrelated people; and *Corpse Fucking Art*, an on-the-scene documentary about the making of several of Buttgereit's films.

Of course, *SMA* also examines the reactions to these films. They have earned their director a loyal worldwide cult following. They've also been banned all over the globe and seized by authorities. Buttgereit makes no apologies for his films. He makes movies about subjects he finds interesting, and those subjects happen to be necrophilia, suicide, and murder. Besides, as he explains, "Society gets the films it deserves."

AK Press; $19.95
1994; oversize softcover; 170 pp; heavily illus.

ways imaginable. They have feasts of piss and shit. The Fascists make their prisoners strip and bend over so that they can find out who has the most beautiful ass. They announce that the winner will be shot. The boy judged to be the winner has a gun put to his head, the trigger is pulled, and *click*—his gun's not loaded. The traumatized boy is informed that they'd never kill someone with such a beautiful ass. In the final scene, the Fascists watch through opera glasses as their prisoners torture each other in a garden. Pasolini shows this shocking violence on screen. One person is scalped. Another has her eye gouged out. One young man's penis is burned with a candle. Pasolini succeeded mightily in his goal of portraying Fascists as cruel, twisted scumbags.

Fittingly, Pasolini's life ended in a scandalously tragic fashion. He was found brutally murdered in the slums of Rome. A gay male prostitute admitted to the killing, and is generally regarded as the murderer, although some feel he either did not do it or didn't act alone.

Princeton University Press; $14.95
1990; softcover; 249 pp.

## PSYCHOTRONIC VIDEO

A quarterly guide to sexploitation, low-budget horror, grade-Z sci-fi, foreign dementia, shockumentaries, and other funky movies on videocassette. There are lots of movie reviews, including such faves as *Santa and the Ice Cream Bunny, To Sleep with a Vampire, Pig Keeper's Daughter, Female Neo Ninjas, Cat in the Brain,* and *Gorotica*. You'll also find reviews of some books, records, and zines that sometimes have to do with movies, sometimes not. There are long, detailed articles on psychotronic directors and actors, lots of pictures (with plenty of skin), and tons of ads selling what must amount to thousands of demented movies.

Psychotronic/3309 Route 97/Narrowsburg, NY 12764-6126
Single issue: $5.50; foreign: $7
Six-issue sub: $22; Canada: $24; airmail: $45;
Asia, Australia/NZ: $50

## THE SCORCHED EARTH CATALOGUE OF CULT FILMS

A collection of one thousand unusual films for your viewing pleasure. This catalog is conveniently broken down into sections on your favorite actor (Brigitte Bardot, Lon Chaney Jr., Bela Lugosi, Jayne Mansfield), director (Pasolini, Fellini, Hitchcock, Bergman, Buñuel), or category (exploitation, J.D., documentary, science fiction, underground). Plus there are trailer compilations, vintage television, and cassettes of classic radio. Every video is a mere $14.95 (except for a few films in the back of the catalog).

Scorched Earth Productions
PO Box 101083/Denver, CO 80250
Catalog: $2

## TAINTED GODDESSES:
### FEMALE FILM STARS OF THE THIRD REICH
### by Cinzia Romani

Betty Grable, Rita Hayworth, Esther Williams, Lana Turner, Olga Tschechowa, Lil Dagover, Marika Rökk, and Heidemarie Hatheyer. Recognize all the names on this list? They were all glamorous screen goddesses in the mid-1930s/early 1940s, whose audiences loved and idolized them. The first four are from the United States, and the second four are from Nazi Germany.

The movies created during the Third Reich present a hidden aspect of cinema history. Minister of Propaganda and Culture Joseph Goebbels used a heavy hand in determining the content of the more than thirteen hundred movies made in Nazi Germany. While the propaganda films are the most famous, almost half the movies were comedies, and many of the others were adventure movies or movies dealing with social and ethical problems. Of course, all films had to present Germany in a flattering light and support the principles of National Socialism. Bad reviews were not permitted by order of Goebbels.

Each chapter deals with a Nazi diva, giving a biography and going into great detail regarding her major films, including production information, cast listing, and a synopsis. *Tainted Goddesses* is lavishly illustrated with hundreds of publicity shots and film stills of the women in question, revealing that for the most part they were as glamorous and beautiful as their American counterparts.

Sarpedon Publishers; $19.95
1992; oversize softcover; 182 pp.

## WHOLE TOON CATALOG

Providing you "access to toons," this unbelievable catalog is *the* primo source for animation. They've got it all: kiddie, superhero, science fiction, Disney, Looney Toons, Nickelodeon, Dr. Seuss, silent, classic, avant-garde, Japanimation, computer animation, stop-motion animation, combo live action/animation, TV series, movies, anthologies of shorts, and more. The only thing you won't find here is pornomation, although they do carry a "sexually explicit" anthology called *Sextoons*.

Besides this unbelievable selection of videos, the toonsters carry dozens of books covering every aspect of animation. They have a free sampler catalog available, but a mere three bux will get you the full-blown, heavily illustrated catalog with more than twenty-five hundred selections (plus, the three dollars is credited toward your first order). A cartoon lover's dream come true.

Whole Toon Access/PO Box 1910/Seattle, WA 98111-1910
Catalog: $3

# MUSIC

### DIRTY LINEN:
#### FOLK, ELECTRIC FOLK, TRADITIONAL AND WORLD MUSIC

A thick, eclectic magazine that covers a wide range of music. In a given issue you might find articles on, reviews of, and ads for radical Jewish roots music, Cajun music, Irish fiddle playing, Finnish folk, accordion, dijeridoo, Russian Gypsy polkas, acoustic dance music, pop/jazz/rock, blues/rock/Native American, Celtic/Indian/R&B, and other hybrid or unclassifiable types of music. Plus, with each issue you get an insert giving tour schedules for about a hundred acts. Add to this mix strong writing and a great sense of humor (they especially love to poke fun at publicity photos), and you have an indispensable magazine.

Dirty Linen/PO Box 66600/Baltimore, MD 21239-6600
Single issue: $5; Canada: $5.50; overseas surface: $7.50; overseas air: $9.50
One-year sub (6 issues): $20 (U.S. & Canada); overseas surface: $24; overseas air: $30

### INCREDIBLY STRANGE MUSIC,
#### VOLUME 2
#### (RE/SEARCH #15)

In the relatively short history of recorded music and speech, there is an area that has gone unexplored until now. It's a vast wonderland best described as...well, incredibly strange. But not strange the way "alternative" rock tries to be strange. Strange as in people doing their own thing and not caring what it looks like.

I first encountered this world when I went through my parents' record collection from the 1950s and 1960s, but little did I realize how expansive this strange land was. Among the genres that are examined are black psychedelia, Brazilian psychedelia, antidrug records, yodeling, mood music, sitar-rock, singing truck drivers, Mad Magazine records, exotica-ploitation, and others. Albums include *Wash Your Ass* by Redd Foxx, *The Crepitation [Farting] Contest, NORAD Tracks Santa, Jesus Is a Soul Man* by The Click Kids, *LSD: Battle for the Mind, Where There Walks a Logger, There Walks a Man* by Buzz Martin, *Jungle Exotica*, etc., etc.

Interviews are conducted with collectors of this strange stuff as well as some pioneers like original bad girl Rusty Warren and synthesizer pioneer Robert Moog. They discuss the music, the artists, album covers, genres, and more. There are plenty of album covers gracing these pages, too. And, if that's not enough, you can actually hear some of this acoustic craziness on the *Incredibly Strange Music* CD ($12) or cassette ($9.99).

RE/Search Publications; $17.99
1994; oversize softcover; 220 pp.

### SECONDS

A music magazine that covers...uh...well...just what the hell do they cover? Basically anything but mainstream garbage, but whatever it is, it has to have an edge to it. No articles, just interviews. In a typical issue (#25) we see interviews with Cabaret Voltaire (industrial), Gang Starr (hip-hop), Rush (progressive rock), Liers in Wait (techno-goth), Travis Tritt (country), James Blood Ulmer (R&B), One Dove (sex rock), as well as Tool, Sisters Grimm, Gnome, Orbital, and others I won't even attempt to clas-

sify. The introductions and interviews are fun, funky, nasty, upfront, and wickedly funny. There are a lot of music mags out there, but this is one of the few that I can unhesitatingly recommend to you heretics out there who actually have an *eclectic* taste in music.

Seconds World HQ
24 Fifth Avenue, Suite 405/New York, NY 10011
Single issue: $4
One-year sub (6 issues): $18; foreign: $30

# RUBBER STAMPS

### ERASER CARVER'S QUARTERLY

A fun-to-read zine that has the author's personality stamped all over it. Articles give straightforward advice on all aspects of turning boring old erasers into works of art. Issue #18 is a particularly good one for beginners to get, since it has an article on the basics: what kind of knife and erasers to use and how to carve the image. "The Stamper's Spotlight" showcases the work of a particular artist, but the whole issue is chock-full of stamps by the editor and others. Friendly and practical, the *Eraser Carver's Quarterly* is simply a must-have for all eraserheads.

ECQ/205 Myron Road
Syracuse, NY 13219-1225
Single copy: $3.
Four-issue sub: $10.
Canada: $12. foreign: $15

◄ *Tainted Goddesses* by Cinzia Romani

*Nazi divas—as glamorous and beautiful as their American counterparts.*

### GOOD IMPRESSIONS

A collection of rubber stamps that look like illustrations from magazines in the 1800s. They have a great old-timey feel to them, but many are still bizarre enough to satisfy your twisted 1990s sensibilities. Some of the more benign designs include teddy bears, a teapot, and a crowing rooster. But get a load of the hippo in a business suit, the frog on a bike, Venus on a Half Shell, the bag of Wizard Brand Sheep Manure, and a potato with human eyes. There are also some Native Americans, pixies and gnomes, lovers, and more.

Good Impressions also puts out *The Shirley Star*, a newsletter that looks like it came straight out of the 1880s. It contains a bunch of new stamps. There's also *The Marksist Rubber Stampifesto*, a little booklet about buying bulk rubber from Good Impressions.

Good Impressions/PO Box 33/Shirley, WV 26434-0033
Catalog: $1 (refundable with first purchase)
*The Shirley Star*: $1 or free with first purchase
*The Marksist Rubber Stampifesto*: $1 or free with any unmounted stamp order.

### LOST ANGELES RUBBER WORKS

A collection of about a hundred stamps, all of which have a bizarre feel to them. Offered for your stamping pleasure are a hand with an eye in the palm, leather biker teddy bears (!), a teddy bear wearing a dildo and harness, a tattooed angel, Hawaiian petroglyphs, the radiation symbol, and a pierced tongue. If you enclose a signed statement that you're twenty-one or older, you'll get an "extra naughty flier" with stamps of a nipple ring, "winged phallus," "flaming yoni," and more.

Lost Angeles Rubber Works
PO Box 3737/Beverly Hills, CA 90212
Catalog: $1.50

## MARS TOKYO RUBBER STAMP CO.

A cool collection of stamps covering a range of almost indescribable styles. Many images are from the 1950s—Elvis, Brando, Marilyn with her dress blowing, a ray gun, and a toy robot. You can also get the pope, cabbage, a woman with two smoking guns, the fattest cat I've ever seen, an eggbeater, angels, and other assorted images from all over the map.

Mars Tokyo Rubber Stamp Co.
PO Box 65006/Baltimore, MD 21209
Catalog: $2.50 (refundable with first order)

## STAMP FRANCISCO

Stamp Francisco's catalog is definitely the Sears, Roebuck of stamps. Their one hundred plus-page catalog and supplements offer well over a thousand images, ranging from the sublime to the ridiculous. Exquisite art deco, medieval, South American, Western, Egyptian, Mexican, and Oriental are some of the more identifiable styles here. The catalog is divided into sections ranging from animals and alphabets to music and nature.

These people are serious about treating stamps as an art form. At their location in San Francisco, they not only have a retail store, but a museum containing antique and limited edition stamps and a gallery that features shows from prominent rubberists such as Stephen Kaplin and Karen Haworth.

When you order this catalog (notice I'm saying "when," not "if"), make absolutely sure you ask them to include the supplement of the Pico Sanchez Collection of Rubber Stamp Designs. They are to die for.

Stamp Francisco/466 Eighth Street/San Francisco, CA 94103
Catalog: $4

# MISCELLANEOUS

## ART? ALTERNATIVES

This magazine is the answer to the prayers of edge-art lovers. It covers the most extreme, unusual, and rule-breaking artistic terrorists currently storming our eyeballs. The February 1994 issue contained features on XNO: "King of the Monster Painters"; underground comix guru Robert Burns; J.K. Potter, who creates seamless photomontages straight from my worst nightmares; Anthony Ausgang, who paints cartoon characters on crummy paintings he picks up at flea markets; Charles Kraft, who creates "Disasterware" by painting natural and man-made disasters on plates; hallucinogenic colored-pencil artist Tony Fitzpatrick; and the art of branding.

As if this rich diversity of subjects, styles, and media weren't enough, *A?A* makes the deal sweeter by reprinting page after page of work from each artist, as opposed to the two or three works you might find accompanying such articles in other magazines. On top of that, the majority of the reproductions are in color. Plus, several of the articles list addresses where you can contact the artists in question.

In case you can't tell from my breathless gushing, I highly recommend *Art? Alternatives*.

Art? Alternatives/Subscription Dept./450 Seventh Avenue, Suite 2305/New York, NY 10123-2305
Single issue: $4.99; Canada: $5.99
One-year sub (4 issues): $19.95

## BLACK VELVET:
### THE ART WE LOVE TO HATE
### by Jennifer Heath

Black velvet paintings are among the most despised forms of art ever created. Images of flea markets and Elvis going up to the Pearly Gates spring to mind when the words are spoken. But black velvet has a long, rich tradition and the medium has produced some exceptional work. It originated in Persia more than a thousand years ago, and has been popular in Japan,

China, Europe, Mexico, and the United States. Velvet paintings hang in the Los Angeles County Museum and the National Gallery of Art, although these are quite old works. Today's velvet paintings are seen as garbage by the art world, but are bought in quantity by the plain folk, making it truly the "people's art."

The forty-three full-color, full-page reproductions range from the stunning to the stinking, from pop kitsch to religious icons to political statements. The works include Elvis (twice), the Virgin Mary (twice), John Lennon, dogs shooting pool, a crouching tiger, a naked blonde woman, Anita Hill, an African mask, a bullfight, a smurf, a skull, a Western landscape, a Native American on a horse, Geronimo, and a clown.

The one disappointing aspect of *Black Velvet* is that it only has contemporary works (with one exception). Still, it is worth having as the only available window into this neglected and offbeat genre of art.

Pomegranate Artbooks; $17.95
1994; oversize softcover; 95 pp.; heavily illus.

## CORPORAL POLITICS

This slim, oversize softcover collects the works that appeared in an exhibition put on by the MIT List Visual Arts Center. The artists' creations all deal with fragments of the human body, because, according to the introductory essay by Helaine Posner, "the body fragment [is] a highly charged metaphor for the psychological, social, political, and physical assaults on the individual." This exhibit was denied NEA money, allegedly because some of the fragmented body parts are of the type that the Christian Right wishes God had never given to humans. Robert Gober's *Male and Female Genital Wallpaper* and Kiki Smith's glass sperm are two good examples. Like many collections of cutting-edge art, *Corporal Politics* is hit-and-miss. Some of the more powerful pieces are Rona Pondick's *Little Bathers*, which look like tumors with teeth: Gober's dadaesque hairy candle; and Smith's *Bloodpool*, which appears to be an almost fully developed fetus. As always, David Wojnarowicz's text/photography/acrylic collages cut right to the bone. Because of the challenging and uneven nature of this book, I would recommend it mainly to people who are heavily into edge art. Casual observers may wish to look elsewhere.

Beacon Press; $15
1992; oversize softcover; 72 pp.

## DICTIONARY OF THE AVANT-GARDES
### by Richard Kostelanetz

With all the artists out there exploring the fringe, who can keep up? Well, this book may not provide the perfect answer, but it can help you tell your Bauhaus from your Fluxus. The *Dictionary* covers cutting-edge movements and individuals in a variety of fields: visual art (surrealism, Roy Lichtenstein, Kinetic Art), literature (*Finnegans Wake*, William Burroughs, Baudelaire), music (Velvet Underground, Igor Stravinsky, free jazz), dance (Martha Graham, Butoh, Merce Cunningham), multidiscipline (John Cage, Yoko Ono, futurism), as well as poetry, performance art, architecture, theater, theory and criticism, etc.

Far from being a staid reference work, this book contains some surprise entries, such as Ambrose Bierce and George Herriman (for his strip *Krazy Kat*). The author is not afraid to call it like he sees it, trashing performance artist Laurie Anderson and admitting that, try as he might, he can't make it through *Gravity's Rainbow* by Thomas Pynchon.

I do have some quibbles with the book's entries. First, the area of film is pitifully represented. Buster Keaton and Luis Buñuel are here, but Fellini and Pasolini are nowhere to be found. Second, photography also gets short shrift. I mean, Weegee is here but Witkin isn't. What gives? Also, there are not nearly enough illustrations representing the work being discussed. Don't get the idea that this isn't a book worth having, though. It's a good guide to the fringes of art, but it could be much better.

Chicago Review Press; $16.95
1993; oversize softcover; 246 pp.

## EMIGRE:
### GRAPHIC DESIGN INTO THE DIGITAL REALM
### by Rudy VanderLans, Zuzana Licko, and Mary E. Gray

Emigre is a graphic design studio founded in 1983 to push design to its outer limits. The next year, Apple introduced the Macintosh, and Emigre never looked back, using the new computer's power for wild experimentation. Emigre's two main projects were creating wild fonts for the Mac and publishing the avant-garde design journal *Emigre*. In these and other endeavors they have managed to piss off uncountable graphic designers but provide inspiration and hope for many others (like me). Uptight fuddy-duddies whine that Emigre's work is hard to read, anarchic, and obeys no known rules of balance, flow, proportion, blah blah blah. Good. If the invasion of the Macintosh, virtual reality, and other juggernauts of the digital culture have taught us anything, it should be that the old ways are dead. All bets are off. Long live the new flesh!

On the tenth birthday of the design industry's enfant terrible, Emigre released this hugely oversized book (11" x 15"). It contains the covers of all twenty-six issues of *Emigre,* many of the best layouts from the magazine, reproductions of all of Emigre's fonts, album covers for Emigre's music label, and promotional material. Throughout it all, the authors comment on Emigre's history and philosophies. Of course, the book was designed by the Emigre crew, so not only does it contain their work, it *is* their work.

Mr. Keedy sums it up admirably in his introductory essay. The only prerequisite for joining the Emigre crowd "is an interest in new design and an open mind. Intolerance for different ideas is the biggest obstacle in these proscribed and dogmatic times. With the mind-numbingly dull 1970s and 80s behind us, designers are waking up and starting the next millennium. Emigre is documenting where graphic design is going. And it's *going* to be interesting."

Van Nostrand Reinhold;
1993; oversize softcover; 96 pp.

## EVIL, SEXUALITY, AND DISEASE IN GRÜNEWALD'S BODY OF CHRIST
### by Eugene Monick

One of the most grotesque images of Christ's crucifixion comes to us not from Joe Coleman or Andres Serrano but from Matthias Grünewald, an early sixteenth-century German painter. He was commissioned to produce an altarpiece for a monastery that was also a hospice for terminally ill men in Isenheim, Alsace. He presented them with the most graphic depiction of the Crucifixion in premodern times and one that still inspires the willies. Nonetheless, the monastery accepted and displayed the altarpiece for centuries. It is now in Unterlinden Museum in Colmar and is considered a masterpiece of German art.

It is a twelve-panel polyptych, but the Crucifixion panel is the primary focus of this book. A pale, sickly Jesus is portrayed with various scabies, pustules, and purplish green lesions all over his body. The exact disease that afflicts Jesus has been the subject of intense debate, with several contenders being smallpox, leprosy, anthrax, bread poisoning, and syphilis.

Using a lot of Jungian analysis, the author attempts to offer a "mystical, meta-physical" frame of reference in forming hypotheses about the meaning of this unusual work of art. Some people feel that Jesus came to take on the suffering of humanity—to feel what it's like to be human. The fact that Jesus has a horrible disease, therefore, "tells me that nothing known to the human race is unknown to the Christ figure painted on the altarpiece cross." The author looks at archetypes, alchemy, gnosis, shadow, and other Jungian concepts as they relate to Grünewald's enigmatic work.

Spring Publications; $18.50
1993; softcover; 189 pp.

## HOT FLASHES FROM THE GUERRILLA GIRLS

The Guerrilla Girls is an anonymous protest group that's royally pissed about sexism, racism, and homophobia in the art world. The Girls first stormed onto the scene with their angry posters. One asked, "Do women have to be naked to get into the Met. Museum? Less than 5% of the artists in the Modern Art Sections are women, but 85% of the nudes are female."

*Hot Flashes* is a one-page, double-sided tabloid that lets the Girls air more of their feelings. The first issue trashed the *New York Times*, "the paper that's too male, too pale, too stale and too Yale!" Using pie charts, they showed how much coverage the critics gave in 1992 to white male artists (67.5%), white female artists (23.8%), male artists of color (6.6%), and female artists of color (1.9%). Graph bars reveal that practically every show reviewed took place at a museum or gallery and almost never at an alternative space, nonprofit gallery, etc.

GG also blow the whistle on apparent conflicts of interest: "No *Times* writer is allowed to accept a gift over fifteen dollars. If you've ever visited [retired chief art critic] John Russell, you may wonder how he managed to acquire his extensive art collection on a critic's salary." They also note "Sotheby's and Christie's spent over $750,000 on *NYT* ads in 1992. Is it any wonder that the *Times* created a special column just to cover auctions?"

Hot Flashes/Guerrilla Girls
532 LaGuardia Place #237/New York, NY 10012
Single issue: $3
Four-issue sub: "$9 for women and people of color, $12 for white males."

## HOWARD FINSTER:
### MAN OF VISIONS
### by Howard Finster

◄ *Black Velvet* by Jennifer Heath

*The Duke, lovingly rendered.*

Howard Finster is an eccentric Baptist preacher from Georgia. He claims to be in contact with extraterrestrials and regularly speaks to the dead, including George Washington, Shakespeare, and Hitler. He believes that man-made things are beautiful, and so has created monuments out of what most people would call junk. He's built towers of hubcaps, a small house out of Coke bottles, and a concrete fence embedded with spark plugs, plastic butterflies, a Buddhist figurine, a jar holding a pair of tonsils in alcohol, and more castoffs.

The rest of Finster's art is just as strange. He has no training and is truly creating "outsider art." He combines flat, childlike paintings, photographs, and mountains of handwritten text (all capitals, frequent spelling errors) into overwhelming multimedia creations that reflect his unique worldview based on fundamentalist Christianity and general weirdness.

This book isn't a collection of his art—it *is* his art. This is Finster's autobiography, done in the same style as the rest of his art. There are some color reproductions of his earlier work, but it's mainly Howard writing on Howard.

Finster doesn't give a damn about sequence, narration, grammar or anything uptight people worry about. He writes in his trademark crowded style (with some typewritten stuff inserted) about God, Jesus, preaching, his childhood, family, friends, art, space travel, Coca-Cola, clocks, bicycles, etc. Each page is a crazy quilt of written text, typed text, poems and songs, paintings, photos, and drawings. For instance, one page has a picture of a young Finster, a drawing of a woman's face, a typewritten poem ("Christ's Crucifixion"), a drawing of a Coca-Cola bottle, and handwritten text, which reads (in part): "HOWARD MAKES COCA COLA BOTTLE 28-IN-HIGH PAINTED ON WOOD CUTOUT.S. ON. TOP IS. EAT DRINK AND BE MERRY FOR TOMMORROW YE MAY DIE. I LIKE COLD COCA COLA. THE WAGES OF SIN IS DEATH BUT THE GIFT OF GOD IS ETURNAL LIFE."

In case you haven't guessed by now, this book is utterly cool. It's so personal, so strange, so dull, so chaotic, and so unabashedly naive that it achieves a power all its own. Do you dare to enter the Finsterian universe?

Peachtree Publishers; $14.95
1989; oversize softcover; 120 pp.; heavily illus.

*In the Spirit of Fluxus*

*Showing a healthy disregard for conventional art and podiatry.*

## IN THE SPIRIT OF FLUXUS
### organized by Elizabeth Armstrong and Joan Rothfuss

Fluxus was a loose group of artists who decided to try something different in the early 1960s through late 1970s: "They said: 'Hey! Coffee cups can be more beautiful than fancy sculptures. A kiss in the morning can be more dramatic than a drama by Mr. Fancypants. The sloshing of my boot sounds more beautiful than fancy organ music.'" Besides an attachment to the word "fancy," the Fluxists displayed a definite anti-art attitude. They were avant-garde incarnate, creating objects, music, film, and performances that challenged all notions of art. This is the kind of stuff that most people, being the sticks-in-the-mud that they are, consider to be total shit. However, if you can appreciate anything that defies convention, you'll dig Fluxus.

The *Total Art Match-Box* by Ben Vautier is a box of matches with purple heads. The box reads, in part: "USE THESE MATCHES TO DESTROY ALL ART." Performance was a large part of the Fluxists' repertoire. At Flux-Sport events, participants engaged in a one hundred-yard race while drinking vodka, "crowd-wrestling in confined spaces," and blowing Ping-Pong balls across the floor with long tubes. Another performance consists of the following: "Ask if La Monte Young is in the audience, then exit." A musical piece called *Duet for Full Bottle and Wine Glass* consists of dripping, pouring, and splashing the wine, gargling, spitting, and then breaking the glass. Fluxus's most infamous film is *No. 4* by Yoko Ono, which shows close-ups of a series of bare asses. And let's not forget *Flux Clippings*, a little plastic box filled with clipped bunions.

This book is well designed, filled with illustrations, and contains detailed history and analysis.

Walker Art Center; $35
1993; oversize softcover; 192 pp.

## KUSTOM KULTURE
### by Von Dutch, Ed "Big Daddy" Roth, Robert Williams, and others

From the 1950s through the 1970s in Southern California, especially L.A., the custom car/hot rod subculture flourished. "A hot-rodder strips this mass-produced vehicle [car] to its bare essentials, pumps the engine full of horsepower, and possibly adds a few innovative embellishments to mark it unmistakably as his hot rod... The customizer smoothes and sleekens the factory body, removes excess ornamentation—especially brand emblems (again, to personalize and mystify the car)—lowers it as much as possible, and coats it in luscious, custom-mixed paint."

*Kustom Kulture* examines the cars and art that came from this subculture, particularly that of its three pioneers: Von Dutch, Ed "Big Daddy" Roth, and Robert Williams. Von Dutch is best known for creating the flying eyeball design, Roth's most famous creation is the buggy-eyed hot-rodder Rat Fink, and Williams has become famous for his controversial paintings (see *Visual Addiction*, above). These creations and many more—cars, ads, T-shirts, models, airbrushed works, and paintings—are reproduced in color. Several essays accompany the artwork. Once again, an overlooked movement in modern art has been definitively chronicled and rescued from oblivion.

Last Gasp; $29.95
1993; oversize softcover; 96 pp.

## RATIO:3,
### VOLUME 2: TransMediators

This book contains works by three TransMediators, people who help decipher reality. "Wheels on Fire" by Z'EV is a deconstruction of *King Lear* in which the elements of myth and magick are brought to the forefront. "You Oak cleaving Lightning Bolts, singe my white head!/And you all shaking Thunder, crack Nature's moulds!/Let all sperm spill at once that makes ungrateful life!/I am more sinned against than sinning!"

"Just Because A Cat Has Her Kittens in the Oven Doesn't Make Them Biscuits" by Andrew McKenzie is set up as a thirty-one-part film narrative that peels away layers of reality to explore the nature of perception and consciousness. "The kernel of the experience as perceived can be stored within the shell of another form. A parasite dormant within foreign flesh. The organic metaphorical leech that reveals itself in its own time for what it is through the medium of that which it is not."

"To Be Ex-Dream" is a collection of writings by Genesis P-Orridge when he was with the performance art group COUM, which he founded. "Coum is a mirror ov all it coums across and all who coum across it in any ov its forms. That is why Coum can only be defined or described in thee end as thee sum total ov whoever or whatever it contains..."

Temple Press Limited; $15
1992; softcover; 110 pp.

## SEVEN DADA MANIFESTOS AND LAMPISTERIES
### by Tristan Tzara

Tzara is often considered the founder of the radical, nihilistic art movement called dada. His seven influential manifestos and a collection of writings called *Lampisteries* are reproduced in this book, complete with the typographical experimentation and whimsical doodles of the originals. The principles of dada are presented clearly and, boy, do they ever make entertaining reading. "DADA remains within the framework of European weaknesses, it's still shit but from now on we want to shit in different colours so as to adorn the zoo of art with all the flags of all the consulates." "A philosophical question: from which angle to start looking at life, god, ideas, or anything else. Everything we look at is false. I don't think the relative result is any more important than the choice of pâtisserie or cherries for dessert." "Dada is dead. Dada is absurd. Long live Dada." Amen.

Riverrun Press; $9.95
1992; softcover; 118 pp.

## THE SUBJECT OF RAPE
### from the Whitney Museum of American Art

This book is a collection of visual art, film stills, and written pieces dealing with rape. The purpose isn't to present a sanitized academic discussion of rape but to throw it in your face and make you deal with it. "[W]e have chosen to exhibit works about rape which address the issue as it is lived and represented in a variety of different voices in order to demonstrate the many ways in which one can name rape, speak about it, and reveal its impact.... We have worked to avoid reinforcing the preconception that women are victims, trying instead to indicate the ways in which this supposition is really culturally constructed." Some of the visual works presented included *Wonderful Uncle*, where a picture of a little girl against a totally black background is surrounded by swirling text describing her uncle trying to molest her and her mother's reaction: "Hush, your father won't believe you." David Wojnarowicz's *Gang Rape* depicts faceless convicts involved in a prison gang rape. Eva Rivera Castro reopened the controversy surrounding the pomo act of appropriation when she incorporated a picture by photojournalist Donna Ferrato into her collage *Untitled*.

There are also several essays and articles on rape, art, and their intersection.

Whitney Museum of American Art; $12.95
1993; softcover; 90 pp.

## WOMEN ARTISTS AND THE SURREALIST MOVEMENT
### by Whitney Chadwick

This groundbreaking book helped to set the record straight on surrealism by examining the overlooked contributions of female artists Frida Kahlo, Meret Oppenheim, Dorothea Tanning, and many others. The author communicated with most of the women in this book and gained access to previously unpublished writings and works of art.

The author writes that the role of women in surrealism has been hotly debated: "Although some have argued that woman's role as muse in Surrealism outweighs her role as artist, the fact that so many women continued active exhibition careers after leaving the Surrealist circle belies this denial of their creative lives." These women achieved artistic success in a time when "few role models existed for women in the visual arts and there was little encouragement for women to establish professional identities for themselves. Young, beautiful, and rebellious, they became an embodiment of their age and a herald of the future as they explored more fully than any group of women before them the interior sources of woman's creative imagination."

Many of the works presented rank among the best in surrealism, in my humble opinion. Kay Sage's *Small Portrait*, a deconstruction of a woman's head, Dorothea Tanning's *Eine kleine Nachtmusik*, a picture of two girls and a gigantic sunflower in a door-lined hallway, and Ithell Colquhoun's *Gouffres Amers*, a grotesque parody of a sixteenth-century male nude, show that the talent and vision that made surrealism such an important movement are in full force among its female members.

*Women Artists* contains 220 illustrations, with 20 in full color. The author's insightful commentary explores the artists' lives, imagery, influences, and legacies.

Thames and Hudson; $24.95
1985; oversize softcover; 256 pp.

# FICTION

## SPECULATIVE FICTION

### THE ATROCITY EXHIBITION
#### by J.G. Ballard

J.G. Ballard was the most experimental of the New Wave science fiction writers. In fact, his stuff was so out there that people have argued that it's not even science fiction, just straightforward experimental fiction. No matter what it is that Ballard writes, it's earned him the status of cult author.

*The Atrocity Exhibition* is one of Ballard's most extreme and, frankly, hard-to-fathom works. It's a collection of "condensed novels," which are the length of short stories. Ballard refers to them as novels, though, because they pack all the meat of a novel but without the skin and bones—dialogue, transitions, a recognizable plot, etc. Actually, there is supposed to be a plot of sorts. The series of condensed novels chronicle the mental breakdown of a doctor. They also have something to do with showing that the media landscape in which we live is a macrocosm of the human nervous system. Or something like that. Reading Ballard is hard work. I know he's saying something very important, if I could just figure out what the hell it is.

Chew on this excerpt from "The Assassination Weapon": "Captain Webster studied the documents laid out on Dr. Nathan's demonstration table. These were: (1) a spectroheliogram of the sun; (2) tarmac and takeoff checks for the B-29 Superfortress *Enola Gay*; (3) electroencephalogram of Albert Einstein; (4) transverse section through a pre-Cambrian trilobite; (5) photograph taken at noon, August 7, 1945, of the sand-sea, Qattara Depression; (6) Max Ernst's 'Garden Airplane Traps.' He turned to Dr. Nathan. 'You say these constitute an assassination weapon?'"

This book also contains three of Ballard's most infamous writings: "Plan for the Assassination of Jacqueline Kennedy," "The Assassination of John Fitzgerald Kennedy Considered as a Downhill Motor Race," and "Why I Want to Fuck Ronald Reagan," the latter story causing Doubleday to destroy its entire press run of *The Atrocity Exhibition* in 1970, which brings up another interesting point. Ballard's story was first published in 1967, when Reagan was governor of California. Reagan's becoming president only helped the story become all the more shocking.

This edition has an appendix with four stories not in the original book, including "The Secret History of World War III" and "Mae West's Reduction Mammoplasty." Also new to this edition are lengthy annotations by Ballard, which do clear up some things, and numerous complementary medical illustrations.

RE/Search Publications; $13.99
1970 (1990); oversize softcover; 127 pp.

### J.G. BALLARD
#### (RE/SEARCH #8/9)

A thorough look at the work of J.G. Ballard. Included are two interviews with Ballard, a short biography, critical essays on his work, and an excruciatingly detailed bibliography. Much of the book reprints Ballard's work. Fiction selections include "The Atrocity Exhibition," "The Index," chapter one of Ballard's brilliant novel *Crash,* and a subverted version of "Why I Want to Fuck Ronald Reagan," which was handed out at the 1980 Republican Nominating Convention. Nonfiction pieces include "Alphabets of Unreason," "Killing Time Should Be Prime Time TV," "Things I Wish I'd Known at 18," "Mythmaker of the 20th Century," and "What I Believe" ("I believe in my own obsessions, in the beauty of the car crash, in the peace of the submerged forest, in the excitements of the deserted holiday beach, in the elegance of automobile graveyards, in the mystery of multi-storey car parks, in the poetry of abandoned hotels."). Finally, there is a selection of Ballard quotations and reproductions of five of his collages.

RE/Search Publications; $11.99
1984; oversize softcover; 171 pp.

### GLOBALHEAD
#### by Bruce Sterling

A collection of short stories that shows that the label "cyberpunk" is meaningless when applied to Bruce Sterling. Although he is best known for his cyberpunk stories and novels, he is capable of much more, and this anthology shows his many hats. There's hard SF, satire, pomo, alternate future, and a bunch of stuff that doesn't fit into any category.

"Our Neural Chernobyl" is definitely ribofunk. Imaginatively written as a review of a mythical book published in the future, it tells of "gene hackers" who cause a biotechnological nightmare. "We See Things Differently" and "The Compassionate, the Digital" explore previously uncharted territory, forecasting what role Islam might play in the technological civilization of the future. In the latter story, the Muslims are the first to create an artificial person. "Dori Bangs" is a truly strange story that asks, What if rock critic Lester Bangs and underground comix artist Dori Seda had met and fallen in love? This sublime story is either a total waste of paper or it is a work of sheer genius. I haven't decided which yet.

This remarkable collection is sure to remind you why Bruce Sterling is considered one of the best speculative fiction writers in the business.

Mark V. Ziesing Books; $29.95
1992; hardcover; 301 pp.

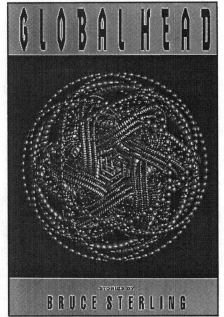

*Globalhead*
*by Bruce*
*Sterling*

*Pushing the craft of SF beyond cyberpunk.*

### THE HEAT DEATH OF THE UNIVERSE:
#### AND OTHER STORIES
#### by Pamela Zoline

Pamela Zoline was a painter who hung around with the New Wave science fiction crowd—J.G. Ballard, Michael Moorcock, Norman Spinrad, etc. One day one of them asked her to try her hand at writing a story, and she produced "The Heat Death of the Universe," one of the best writings to come out of the New Wave. It is an experimental story that follows the effects of entropy on the mind of homemaker Sarah Boyle. Each paragraph is numbered. Most of the paragraphs deal directly with the story, but others contain scientific definitions of entropy or light, and others are just factoids about turtles or love (I *told* you this is experimental). As the story progresses, we see the breakdown of Sarah's sanity. In the supermarket, "Sarah Boyle begins to pick out, methodically, deliberately and with careful ecstasy, one of every cleaning product which the store sells. Window Cleaner, Glass Cleaner, Brass Polish, Silver Polish, Steel Wool, eighteen different brands of detergent... When the same product appears in different sizes Sarah takes one of each size."

The fifty-fourth and final paragraph, in which Sarah's mind descends into complete disorder, is a mini-masterpiece. "She begins to cry. She goes to the refrigerator and takes

*The* ◄ *Atrocity Exhibition by J.G. Ballard*

*So out there, it's beyond SF.*

out a carton of eggs, white eggs, extra large. She throws them one by one onto the kitchen floor which is patterned with strawberries in squares. They break beautifully. There is a Secret Society of Dentists, all moustached, with Special Code and Magic Rings. She begins to cry."

This collection also contains Zoline's four other stories—her entire literary output (except for a children's book)—all of which are long and highly experimental. None of them hits the nail on the head the way "Heat Death" does, but they are all worth experiencing.

McPherson & Co.; $10
1988; softcover; 204 pp.

## IMAGE OF THE BEAST
### by Philip José Farmer

Philip José Farmer has written one of the most bizarre novels of all time. Farmer is best known as the author of two famous science fiction series: *Riverworld* and *Dayworld,* but in 1968 he wrote an erotic horror/SF novel that, among other things, helped to warp my sensibilities at a young age. The book opens with private detective Harold Childe and the LAPD watching a home video that was mailed to them. In it, Childe's partner, who had been missing, is shown tied down on a table. A beautiful woman "Bobbits" him, using steel fangs instead of a kitchen knife.

Childe sets out to find the people (?) who killed his partner in such a gruesome way. Of course, many shocking sexual escapades ensue, including sex with a werewolf, being raped by a hugely obese woman, and spying on a woman with a creature that lives in her vagina. Although *Image* is mind-blowingly explicit, it is more than an excuse to write sex scenes. It is truly one of Farmer's best novels.

Rhino*ceros* (Masquerade Books); $6.95
1968; paperback; 277 pp.

## IN PURSUIT OF VALIS;
### SELECTIONS FROM THE EXEGESIS
### by Philip K. Dick

Philip K. Dick was a writer best known for his science fiction novels and stories from the 1960s and 1970s dealing with exotic drugs, multiple levels of reality, and authoritarianism. During February and March 1974, Dick had strange mystical experiences in which he believed he came into direct contact with a higher wisdom/universal consciousness/Overmind that he called VALIS (Vast Active Living Intelligence System). These two months provided extremely unusual experiences that continued to a lesser degree for a year, and only sporadically thereafter. For the next eight years Dick wrote a journal about these experiences, their possible meanings, the nature of reality, how his works relate, etc.

This journal, called *Exegesis,* totaled more than eight thousand hand-written, unnumbered pages. Dick never intended it to be published, and it attained a legendary, semi-mythical status. Lawrence Sutin, Dick's biographer, finally had the stamina to sift through this colossal work and edit it down to 250 pages. It makes for some fascinating reading, but it's probably only of interest to Dickheads. Then again, it would probably be a good source document for anyone into the literature of mystical experiences and/or psychosis (which is what some people say that Dick's encounters really were). But I ask, what's the difference between the two?

Charles F. Miller, Publisher; $14.95
1991; softcover; 277 pp.

## FOR DICKHEADS ONLY

A fanzine that examines in loving detail the work and life of Philip K. Dick. Each issue is devoted mainly to a single book, although there are always other articles included. The first four issues dealt with *Clans of the Alphane Moon, The World Jones Made, The Cosmic Puppets,* and *The Solar Lottery,* respectively. The next

issue will cover *Eye in the Sky.* Dick's work is filled with symbolism, philosophy, and hidden meanings, providing enough material for decades' worth of this devoted zine.

GSM Productions,
c/o David Hyde/PO Box 112/New Haven, IN 46774
Four-issue sub: $10; foreign: same, but will trade

## INTERZONE

*Interzone,* one of Britain's leading speculative fiction magazines, publishes stories that span the entire spectrum of hard science fiction, fantasy, dark fantasy, magical realism, slipstream, and other genres. *Interzone* has gained notoriety for its willingness to publish experimental and controversial stories. It regularly publishes new work from the New Wave gang, and it was one of the breeding grounds for cyberpunk in the 1980s. Other contributors include the brightest names in subversive fiction—Paul Di Filippo, Don Webb, Michael Blumlein, Richard Kadrey, K.W. Jeter, and others.

Unfortunately, although it can be quite daring, *Interzone* publishes a lot of good but unchallenging work. They also run quite a few clunkers. Besides fiction, each issue has an interview with a big-name writer, a news/gossip column, and book and movie reviews.

If you're interested in the cutting edge of speculative fiction and you can spare fifty bucks, then, by all means, get *Interzone.*

Interzone/217 Preston Drove/Brighton BN1 6FL/UK
Single issue: £2.50; U.S.: $5; elsewhere: £2.80
One-year sub (12 issues): £28; U.S.: $52; elsewhere: £34

## SEMIOTEXT[E] SF
### edited by Rudy Rucker, Peter Lamborn Wilson, and Robert Anton Wilson

In this issue of the pomo bookzine *Semiotext[e],* the editors have sought to reinvigorate the field of science fiction with a heavy dose of sex, violence, and experimental themes and styles. "…[W]e asked for material which had been rejected by the commercial SF media for its obscenity, radicalism, or formalistic weirdness." Responses came in from members of the defunct 1960s movement known as the New Wave, the cyberpunks, and the underground SF writers. Among those who contributed original material: J.G. Ballard, Hakim Bey, Michael Blumlein, Bruce Boston, William S. Burroughs, Paul Di Filippo, Philip José Farmer, Hugh Fox, William Gibson, Marc Laidlaw, Rudy Rucker, John Shirley, and Bruce Sterling. Freddie Baer, Richard Kadrey, and James Koehnline contributed collages. All of the stories (and poems) definitely challenge convention. On the whole, though, the collection is uneven. "We See Things Differently," "America Comes," "Six Kinds of Darkness," "Shed His Grace," and "Lord of Infinite Diversions" are all great. "Vile Dry Claws of the Toucan," "Georgie and the Giant Shit," and "Frankenstein Penis" suffer from severe lameness. Overall, this is a strong collection, and it's well on its way to becoming a classic, so you must get it post haste.

Autonomedia; $10
1989; softcover; 384 pp.

## STILL DEAD
### edited by John Skipp and Craig Spector

Splatterpunk is a form of horror that knows no limits. It takes horror to its absolute extremes, using any means necessary to shock the shit out of you. Not surprisingly, Splatterpunk has led to much controversy. Critics say it's a mindless exercise in gore meant to appeal to the readers' basest instincts. Proponents say Splatterpunk simply isn't afraid to show how horrible the world can be, something that namby-pamby Gothic horror tiptoes around.

The book that sprang Splat upon the world was *The Book of the Dead,* edited by John Skipp and Phil Spector, who have coauthored several Splat novels. In this sequel they bring together nineteen more stories based on the theme of the undead. As with the first anthology, these stories are powerful, but they're not as explicitly violent and just plain gross. K.W. Jeter's "Rise Up and Walk" is about the return of Christ. Jesus is locked in a mental hospital (because he thinks he's Jesus Christ) when he raises some people from the dead. The only problem is, they don't return fully to life. They're zombies and they want to feast on the flesh of their Savior.

Two young splatter-film freaks are the subjects of "Necrophile" by Nancy Collins. They constantly court death by drinking strychnine. Mouli, the dude in the relationship, is obsessed with a beautiful woman he sees while under the influence of strychnine. He eventually finds her, but she's a little more than he bargained for. "Abed" by Elizabeth Massie will probably become a Splat classic, featuring as it does an incestuous ménage à trois involving a rotting zombie. "All she can do is feel the slopping of the trout-tongue on her cheek and taste the running, blackened brain matter as it drips to the edge of her lips. He burrows clumsily; his body wriggles as his knees work between her knees, and his sore-covered penis reaches like a dazed, half-dead snake for her center."

*Still Dead* also features corkers from Dan Simmons, Kathe Koja, Poppy Z. Brite, Nancy Holder, and Douglas E. Winter, as well as four full-color inserts of paintings by Rick Berry.

Mark V. Ziesing Books; $29.95
1992; hardcover; 276 pp.

## STORMING THE REALITY STUDIO:
### A CASEBOOK OF CYBERPUNK AND POSTMODERN FICTION
### edited by Larry McCaffrey

A mondo collection of fiction and essays focusing on cyberpunk SF and quasi-SF postmodern fiction. As the editor points out, science fiction has always been about examining the effects of technology, and now that technology has become such a dominant force—perhaps *the* dominant force—in our society and our lives, SF has more significance than ever. Cyberpunk and pomo fiction are especially important not only for the way they address technological change but how they actually reflect it in their prose style, form, and structure.

The thirty fiction pieces are by Kathy Acker, J.G. Ballard, William S. Burroughs, Pat Cadigan, Samuel Delany, William Gibson, Richard Kadrey, Marc Laidlaw, Misha, Thomas Pynchon, Rudy Rucker, John Shirley, Bruce Sterling, William Vollman, and others. All of these stories, excerpts, poems, and one comic are reprints of previously published work. The editor's aim was to bring together the best, most representative works of cyberpunk/pomo ever published. The drawback to this is that you'll already have read a lot of this stuff—Gibson's *Neuromancer*, Burroughs's *Wild Boys*, Acker's *Empire of the Senseless*, and Pynchon's *The Crying of Lot 49*. Then again, some of the stories, such as Misha's "Wire for Two Tims" and Rob Hardin's "nerve terminals," are hard to find elsewhere. The nonfiction pieces are essays on cyberpunk and postmodernism in general by Baudrillard, Derrida, Lyotard, Sterling, Tim Leary, and Takayuki Tatsumi.

This is quite simply a must-have book. It's been extremely popular, the softcover edition alone going through five printings in under three years. The folks at Duke Press must be overjoyed. University press books usually sell about as well as televisions in Amish country.

Duke University Press; $19.95
1991; softcover; 387 pp.

## TONGUING THE ZEITGEIST
### by Lance Olsen

A "post-cyberpunk" piece of brain candy in the form of a novel. Olsen's snapping, crackling prose directly stimulates pleasure centers of the brain, making you want to keep reading. The setting of the novel is America forty years in the future. Sex, violence, disease, and death have become a part of pop culture like never before. The band, Dr. Teeth, gets attacked with explosives in concert. Our hero Ben is majorly bummed, but perks up when he meets Jessika on-line. Then he finds out that two of his

own bandmates have been attacked with acid in the kitchen faucet. He meets Jessika at the Lost in Space bar, but someone (Jessika?) slips him a Mickey and abducts him, and he becomes part of a Faustian plot involving rock and roll fame.

Should I slow down and take a breath? I can't, because this book never does. It's a nonstop, manic rush of a novel that paints a strange but strangely plausible future. Slangwise, the word *ruck* has replaced *fuck*. *Nazi* is an adjective meaning cool, as in, "Dr. Teeth's concert was so nazi," and *Quayle* is the latest word meaning geek (I don't think an etymology is necessary). Styles have evolved a bit, too. Take, for instance the crowd at Dr. Teeth's concert: "The guy lapping air, diamond stud flickering on his tongue. The couple, lawyers from nine to five, sporting lilac Aramis head-injury makeup, spinning in some magical private dance down front. The woman with two black eyes, a human raccoon, hoisted between two tall, thin boys dressed as late-stage AIDS victims, laughing and rolling her gray-knit t-shirt to reveal the startling alabaster scars of her cosmetic mastectomy."

Besides having "cult classic" written all over it, *Tonguing the Zeitgeist* is a hell of a good read.

Permeable Press; $11.95
1994; softcover; 192 pp.

◄ *Still Dead*
edited by John
Skipp and
Craig Spector

*Splatterpunk:
Using any
means
necessary
to shock
the shit
out of you.*

# WILLIAM S. BURROUGHS

## NAKED LUNCH
### by William S. Burroughs

*Naked Lunch* is arguably the most famous, influential, underground novel of this century. It was written using the cut-up technique, which means there is no plot to speak of, just a series of basically random scenes involving a large number of characters. Some characters show up repeatedly, giving *Naked Lunch* perhaps its only element of consistency. As Burroughs has said, you can start reading *Naked Lunch* at any point. It really doesn't matter.

Many people have commented that Burroughs's masterpiece makes no sense. They're right, of course, if you read it expecting to find the linear, rising-action-climax-falling-action notion of plot we learned in high school. But if you read it as a series of scenes making critical and controversial comments on society and the human condition in general, you'll get more out of it. *Naked Lunch* presents all of society's ills—racism, homophobia, misogyny, violence, capital punishment—in such an extreme and unyielding manner that we're forced to confront them. For example, two detectives are discussing a case in which a father decided it was time for his son to lose his virginity. He gave him twenty bucks and told him to go to the whorehouse and ask for "a piece of ass." The boy comes back and his dad asks, "'Well, son did you get a piece of ass?' 'Yeah, this gash comes to the door, and I say I want a piece of ass and lay the double sawski [$20] on her. We go up to her trap, and she remove the dry goods. So I switch my blade and cut a big hunk off her ass, she raises a beef like I am reduce to pull off one shoe and beat her brains out. Then I hump her for kicks.'"

One of the scenes that's gotten *Naked Lunch* into trouble with the thought police is a grotesque parody of the death penalty. A man named Johnny is about to be hanged. On the scaffold, Mary wraps herself around him as they go off the platform. As so often happens to men being hanged, Johnny gets an erection. "Johnny's cock springs up and Mary guides it into her cunt, writhing against him in a fluid belly dance, groaning and shrieking with delight[...] She bites away Johnny's lips and nose and sucks out his eyes with a pop... She tears off great hunks of cheek... Now she lunches on his prick..." [Ellipses are the author's except the one in brackets.] Besides making the event as disgusting as possible, in this scene and others about hanging, Burroughs also seems to imply that people who are for the death penalty get some sort of sick sexual thrill from someone being snuffed.

Lest you think that *Naked Lunch* is too serious, rest assured that there are many darkly hilarious moments. In one scene, that redoubtable man of medicine, Dr. Benway, is talking about an operation he performed with Dr. Browbeck. Ever the professionals, Dr. Benway had a yage hangover, and Dr. Browbeck was high on oven gas and nutmeg. Browbeck started hallucinating, and "'I told him to go put his head back in the oven, whereupon he had the effrontery to push my hand, severing the patient's femoral artery. Blood spurted up and blinded the anesthetist, who ran out through the halls screaming. Browbeck tried to knee me in the groin, and I managed to hamstring him with my scalpel. He crawled about the floor, stabbing at my feet and legs. Violet, that's my baboon assistant—only woman I ever cared a damn about—really wigged.'"

If you haven't read *Naked Lunch,* you must read it immediately. If you have read it, read it again.

Grove Press; $11.95
1959; softcover; 232 pp.

## WILLIAM BURROUGHS:
### EL HOMBRE INVISIBLE
### by Barry Miles

This is at once a biography, a literary critique, and an examination of a cultural phenomenon. It explores how William Burroughs's stormy life affected his writing and how his writing affected the rest of the world.

The writing of *Naked Lunch* is one of the book's most interesting sections. During that time, Burroughs would take majoun (hashish candy) every other day, "and on the off days I would just have a bunch of big joints lined up on my desk and smoke them as I typed." Bill was also having fun in the sex department: "He had a succession of boys and even began to look favorably upon women." Ideas were coming to him so fast, he wasn't able to keep up with them. He told Allen Ginsberg, "This is almost automatic writing. I often sit high on hash for as long as six hours typing at top speed." Whenever Burroughs finished a page, he would drop it on the floor. His floor became coated with hundreds of pieces of paper covered in footprints, rat droppings, and bits of food. Eventually, Burroughs, Ginsberg, Jack Kerouac, and others assembled the manuscript, retyped it, and presented it to the legendary Olympia Press, which published it. Burroughs sent the chapters to the printers out of sequence. The printers, who couldn't read English, simply printed the chapters in the order they received them. With one small change, Burroughs left the book that way. Thus, *Naked Lunch* was born into an unsuspecting world.

Burroughs has become an icon to the disaffected. This can work against him, as the author notes: "As with Ginsberg before him, many of his fans had not read much of his work; they simply liked his image: the dead-pan expressionless businessman, neatly attired in short hair and suit, who took all manner of drugs and had ideas which made their parents froth at the mouth."

His books have become a "treasure trove of words and phrases for rock groups." Several have named themselves after Burroughsisms—Steely Dan (after a dildo in *Naked Lunch*), Dead Fingers Talk, The Naked Lunch, and Thin White Rope, which

*William Burroughs: El Hombre Invisible by Barry Miles*

*Ideas were coming to him so fast he couldn't keep up with them.*

isn't mentioned in this book. David Bowie credits Burroughs's cut-up technique in creating some of his lyrics, and the Beatles included Uncle Bill on the cover of *Sgt. Pepper's Lonely Hearts Club Band*. More recently, he collaborated with Ministry on the song and video "Just One Fix."

*William Burroughs* also explores and explains Burroughs's heroin addiction, his accidental killing of his wife, his homosexuality, the obscenity trial for *Naked Lunch*, his critical receptions, and, of course, all his books, from *Junky* through *The Western Lands*, as well as other projects. The author has done a brilliant job of shedding light on one of the most infamous subversive writers of all time.

Hyperion; $22.95
1993; hardcover; 263 pp.

## A WILLIAM BURROUGHS BIRTHDAY BOOK

On February 5, 1994, at the Phoenix Gallery in Brighton, England, a group of assorted artists, writers, astrologers, and other strange people gathered to pay tribute to the Godfather of the Strange, Uncle Bill Burroughs. Self-described revolutionary Simon Strong contributed "William Burroughs: A Biological Mistake," which looks at the three visionaries/kooks (it depends on who you ask) whose fringe science theories had the greatest effect on Burroughs—Korzybski, Wilhelm Reich, and L. Ron Hubbard. "Splinter Test: Implications ov Cut-ups & Samples as Quantum Memes" by Genesis P-Orridge philosophizes on the use of samples in cut-up works of art. "No matter how short, or apparently unrecognizable a 'sample' might be in linear TIME perception, E believe it must, inevitably, contain within it, (and accessible through it) thee sum total ov absolutely everything its original context represented, communicated, or touched in any way." In the comic "Bill Explains Aesthetics" by Caspar Williams, Burroughs explains that far from being nihilistic, his works actually try to capture the beauty in all things. "I have always written about beautiful things, such as the exquisite intelligence exhibited by multiplying cells in, say, a really interesting dermal carcinoma.... I've delighted in the seductive sheen on the plating of a good old-fashioned handgun. A simple, silly little thing, but, hell, I just like it."

Other contributions include "Nothing Is True. Everything Is Permuted: The Last Words of Hassan i Sabbah," "Pistol Poems & Shotguns," "The Temple of the Assassins," and several more. Overall, this booklet is disappointing. While there are some strong pieces, it seems that if you're mining a vein as rich as William Burroughs, surely you can come up with more treasure than is here.

Temple Press; $5
1994; saddle-stitched booklet; 43 pp.

# DENNIS COOPER

## FRISK
### by Dennis Cooper

Dennis Cooper's writing has earned comparisons to the Marquis de Sade, Georges Bataille, Baudelaire, and Edgar Allan Poe. As you can gather from that roster of names, Cooper's a literary extremist who ignores all boundaries while exploring the dark side of the human heart. Sex and murder go hand in hand in Cooper's work, including *Frisk*. The narrator, coincidentally named Dennis, becomes intrigued by a series of fake snuff photos he sees when he's thirteen. As Dennis grows up, he starts having rough sex with men and fantasizing about killing them: "I tore up his body like it was a paper bag and pulled out dripping fistfuls of veins, organs, muscles, tubes.... I drank his blood, piss, vomit. I shoved one hand down his throat, one hand up his ass, and shook hands with myself in the middle of his body, which sounds funny, but it wasn't."

Dennis moves to Holland and rents a room in an out-of-the-way windmill. There he's able to act out his fantasies. He writes letters to friends in America describing in sickening detail how he and two German psychos he met kill and dismember a bunch of men. Two of Dennis's friends think that Dennis is lying about his exploits, and they visit him in order to call his bluff....

Grove Press; $9.95
1991; softcover; 128 pp.

## JERK

### art by Nayland Blake, fiction by Dennis Cooper

This book is a collaboration between puppeteer Nayland Blake and Dennis Cooper. The story recreates a puppet show given by David Brooks, one of the accomplices of serial killer Dean Corll. David uses his puppet show to demonstrate how Dean would lure young boys to his home, where he and Wayne Henley would torture them to death while David filmed. Eventually, Wayne kills Dean and decides to do a torture-murder on his own, which doesn't end as planned.

Photos of Blake's puppets are interspersed throughout the book. Some are very plain; others are haunting. The only problem is, Blake's puppets and Cooper's story—both fine in their own right—never really intersect. They don't manage to make more than a superficial connection, meaning that the book never comes together as intended.

Artspace Books; $15
1993; small hardcover; 54 pp.

## WRONG

### by Dennis Cooper

A collection of Cooper's short stories that march right up to you and smash you in the gut with a lead pipe, then walk away totally unconcerned as you squirm on the ground clutching your stomach. The title story starts out right away with two pages of shattering, nihilistic violence. The first of the four murders described on those pages goes down this way: "Mike dragged Keith down the hall by his hair. He shit in Keith's mouth. He laid a whip on Keith's ass.... Mike kicked Keith's skull in before he came to. Brains or whatever it was gushed out. 'That's that.'"

"Dinner" is about an older man who picks up a young man in a gay bar, takes him out to his car, and fists him. Then he goes back inside. The sheer meaningless of the encounter makes for one of the bleakest comments on casual sex I've ever read. In "He Cried," a man becomes obsessed with the victims of a vicious serial killer.

Cooper has carved a unique niche for himself in contemporary fiction. Crawl in there with him if you dare.

Grove Press; $11
1992; softcover; 165 pp.

# HARLAN ELLISON

Harlan Ellison is science fiction's angry young man. Actually, he's not young anymore, but he sure as hell is still angry. Writing nonstop since the mid-1950s, Harlan's won more awards for imaginative fiction than any other living author. By my last count he had won eight Hugos, three Nebulas, the Jupiter Award (the British equivalent of the Hugo), the Bram Stoker Award for Horror, blah blah blah. OK, he's won all these awards, so you'd think he'd be universally loved. Wrongo. Ellison's writing (and to an extent the man himself) is abrasive, loud, bitter, cynical, and uncompromising. He's pissed off about everything, and, by God, he's gonna let you know it.

Harlan's output has been prodigious. He's created some of the greatest, most intense stories to come out of the New Wave and science fiction in general. He's also come up with some of the coolest story titles in the history of literature: "I Have No Mouth and I Must Scream," "'Repent, Harlequin!' Said the Ticktockman," "The Beast That Shouted Love at the Heart of the World," "Shattered Like a Glass Goblin," and "Pretty Maggie Moneyeyes." Harlan's work is notoriously uneven. When he's bad, he's terrible; but when he's good, there's no one better.

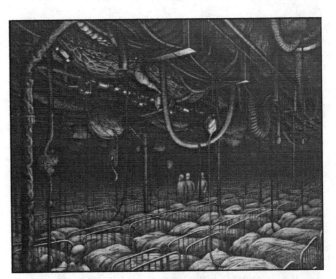

*Mind Fields* ▼
by Jacek Yerka
and Harlan
Ellison
(See page 218)

*"Establish enigmas. Not explanations."*

## DEATHBIRD STORIES

### by Harlan Ellison

Probably Harlan's most important and consistently best anthology, *Deathbird Stories* is based on the loose premise that the old gods are dead and the new gods—cars, drugs, money, violence—have taken over. Basically, it's just a good excuse to gather many of Harlan's most powerful stories under one cover.

"Paingod" is about the creature whose job it is to dispense pain to all living beings. "He was Paingod for the universes, the one who dealt out the tears and the anguish and the soul-wrenching terrors that blighted life from its first moment to its last." But the Paingod can feel no emotions, so he doesn't truly understand what he's doing. He decides to experience pain for himself by entering the body of a sculptor whose hands have been racked with trembling pain for two years. After he feels the man's agony firsthand, he changes his outlook. As he explains to his bosses, the beings who run the universe, "'I know that pain is the most important thing in the universes. Greater than survival, greater than love, greater even than the beauty it brings about.'" Asked what he will do now that he has this knowledge, the Paingod responds, "'I will send more pain than ever before. More and greater.'"

Almost all the other stories are equally uplifting. "The Whimper of Whipped Dogs" is about a woman's encounter with the god of urban violence. "On the Downhill Side" is the incredibly sad story of a New Orleans ghost and his beloved unicorn. In "Pretty Maggie Moneyeyes" a woman's soul is trapped in a slot machine. "The Deathbird," a highly experimental work, retells the story of Satan's rebellion from Satan's point of view.

Collier Books (Macmillan Publishing Co);
1975; softcover; 295 pp.

## MEFISTO IN ONYX

### by Harlan Ellison

This is Harlan's first novella in something like ten years, so it was an eagerly anticipated publishing event for me and Harlan's devoted following. You have to look no further than the acknowledgments page to see that even though Harlan has aged, he hasn't mellowed. "And finally, perversely, I owe heartfelt thanks for their rudeness, ineptitude, short-sightedness, cowardice, ignorant arrogance, and boneheaded behavior to Melissa Singer and Tom Doherty of Tor Books, and to James Frenkel. Had it not been for these three, this story would have appeared in one of their forgettable anthologies, vanished forever. And I'd be out $300,000. Thanks, y'all."

The story is about Rudy Pairis, who can "jaunt" into other people's minds and find out everything about them, an ability that has shown Rudy the dark side of human nature. "Slip into the thoughts of the best person who ever lived, even Saint Thomas Aquinas, for instance, just to pick an absolutely terrific person you'd think had a mind so clean you could eat off it (to paraphrase my mother), and when you come out—take my word for it—you'd want to take a long, intense shower in Lysol."

Rudy's only true friend in the world, whom he's actually in love with, is a deputy district attorney in Alabama. She asks Rudy to jaunt into the mind of a serial killer she convicted, because she's fallen in love with him and she now thinks he's innocent. Rudy reluctantly agrees. From there the story takes more twists and turns than the Mississippi River. The ending is so unexpected, the book should win the O. Henry Award.

Not only is the story good, but the book is a class work itself. It's exquisitely designed and features a stark wraparound cover by Frank Miller. Highly recommended.

Mark V. Ziesing Books; $16.95
1993; hardcover; 91 pp.

## MIND FIELDS:
### THE ART OF JACEK YERKA,
### THE FICTION OF HARLAN ELLISON
### by Jacek Yerka and Harlan Ellison

In this wonderful collaboration, Harlan Ellison wrote short-short stories based on each of Jacek Yerka's thirty-three paintings. Yerka's paintings are richly detailed and realistic, only their realism is jarring because the scenes aren't of a reality we're familiar with. *Eruption* is a beautiful landscape of a tiered city that's built on the outer and inner slopes of a volcano. Ellison's story for the painting concerns an old couple telling a young man about the volcano city, Yondok-Barron, and Sodom and Gomorrah. All three were destroyed at the same time, but Yondok-Barron didn't get much press.

In *The Agitators*, it's dusk, and we see five old men kneeling and standing before a tiny church in the middle of the woods. The story relates that people enter the church one at a time to complain to the altar. Then they exit the church, walk down a path through the woods, and a scream is heard. Each time someone dies, the church physically shrinks.

As with any Ellison collection, the quality is uneven. Some of these stories burn brightly. Others fizzle, and some are just plain contrived ("Please Don't Slam the Door"). Even the best stories manage to raise more questions about the paintings than they answer. It's as if Yerka is letting us peek into incomprehensible worlds, and Ellison pulls back the curtains a little farther, tantalizing us but not giving it all away. He quotes the sculptor Robert Smithson as his inspiration: "Establish enigmas. Not explanations."

Morpheus International; $24.95
1994; oversize softcover; 71 pp.

## POETRY

## AMERICAN DREAMS
### by Sapphire

By the time this book, her first collection of poetry and prose, had come out, Sapphire had already gained a huge following. She speaks angrily and beautifully, lashing out against the brutality of urban life—the hatred, the violence, broken families, struggling to rise above it all.

Sapphire isn't afraid to jump into the middle of controversy. Her poem "Strange Juice" is about Latasha Harlins, the fifteen year old African-American girl who was killed by a Korean grocer for trying to steal a bottle of juice. Speaking in Harlins's voice, Sapphire writes: "I don't remember what I did wrong./Somebody hit you, you hit 'em back./She didn't have to shoot me./I was born here/and someone can shoot me and go home/and eat Turkey on Thanksgiving—/what kinda shit is that?"

Sapphire ventured into even more dangerous territory when she wrote about the "wilding" incident in Central Park, in which a white female jogger was beaten almost to death by a group of teenagers. "Wild Thing" is written from the point of view of one of the perpetrators: "'Let's get a female jogger!'/I shout into the twilight/looking at the/middle-class-thighs /pumping past me,/cadres of bitches/who deserve to die/for thinking they're better/than me./You ain't better than/*nobody*

bitch." Sapphire's poems peer into the heart of darkness. She's unafraid to write about the shitty sides of life from the perspective of the people who are living it, and that makes for some painful reading.

High Risk Books; $10.99
1994; softcover; 175 pp.

## THE COMPLETE POEMS
## OF STEPHEN CRANE
### by Stephen Crane

Mark Twain and Ambrose Bierce are two well-known literary misanthropes, but there is a third member of this holy trinity of bitterness. Stephen Crane was a contemporary of Twain and Bierce, but he isn't nearly as well known, perhaps because he didn't leave behind a large body of work. He did what all good writers are supposed to do—he died young (at age twenty-nine, to be exact).

Crane's only famous work is *The Red Badge of Courage,* about a soldier who deserts during battle. But Crane also wrote poetry. His 134 poems, all collected here, are short, poisonous little barbs directed at the human race, God, religion, love, altruism (which Crane apparently didn't believe in), war, friendship, and so on. Here, in its entirety, is poem #96 (Crane didn't use titles): "A man said to the universe:/'Sir, I exist!'/'However,' replied the universe,/'The fact has not created in me/A sense of obligation.'"

Poem #4 runs like this: "Yes, I have a thousand tongues,/And nine and ninety-nine lie./Though I strive to use the one,/It will make no melody at my will,/But is dead in my mouth."

It's unfortunate that Crane's work is so underrecognized. His unrelentingly dark poetry earns him a prominent place in the pantheon of the great masters of cynicism and gloom.

Cornell University Press; $9.95
1972; softcover; 154 pp.

## EARTHLIGHT
### by André Breton

A collection of more than seventy of Breton's poems from 1919 to 1936, which spans his period with the dada movement and his subsequent founding of the surrealist movement. The poems cover a range of styles and subjects but all are hallucinatory and beautiful. Here are some lines from "My woman with her forest fire hair":

"My woman with her forest fire hair
With her heat-lightning thoughts
With her hourglass waist
My woman with her otter waist in the tiger's mouth...
With her tongue of polished amber and glass
My woman with her stabbed eucharist tongue...
My woman with her shoulders of champagne
And a dolphin-headed fountain under ice...
My woman with rocket legs...
My woman with her sex of seaweed and old-fashioned candies..."

I think I'm in love!

Sun&Moon Press; $12.95
1993; softcover; 213 pp.

## HAND DANCE
### by Wanda Coleman

uncapitalized (almost) unpunctuated angry poetry about sexism about racism about the underclass about inner city life about the pain of life in general

the poem that i thought made the best point in the best way is "HERITAGE" in which an african american couple and a dakota native american are at a dinner party

the husband says that his wife is part sioux but she is embarrassed "that he would tell this story to an *authentic* of tribal origin" the poem concludes with the woman saying "…i noticed his hand. look, i said, and held my hand next to his. except for color they were the same"

coleman gives us her take on love in "CONFESSIONS NOIRS": "frequently the likeness of my first husband/masks the faces of our children calling to mind/an inscription i made on a photo—some hogshit/about him being my first my last"

finally i must pass on this memorable phrase that the narrator of "BERNADETTE NEXT DOOR" uses to describe her neighbor: "the essence of fuckeduppedness"

> Black Sparrow Press; $13
> 1993; softcover; 271 pp.

## IDIOT'S DELIGHT
### by Robert Hunter

A small book of poetry from the Grateful Dead's lyricist. These are short, rapid-fire poems constituting one long, eleven-part poem that focuses on desire and appetite (in the nonphysical sense of the words). "It seems we/must learn to/value the place/of becoming;/the almost but/never quite—/the sense of/impending as/opposed to the/consummation/of any desire."

Signed copies are available from the publisher. Write for info.

> Hanuman Books; $5.95 (unsigned)
> 1992; mini-paperback; 137 pp.

## THE NEGLECTED WALT WHITMAN:
### VITAL TEXTS
### edited by Sam Abrams

Walt Whitman, writer of the groundbreaking and controversial poetry masterpiece *Leaves of Grass,* is also the creator of several poems and prose pieces that have been ignored or suppressed. Of the sixty-six writings in this book, some or most of them are left out of reader's editions of Whitman's work and *all* of them are missing from the supposedly authoritative *Complete Poetry and Collected Prose* from the Library of America.

These missing pieces show Whitman to be much more radical, subversive, and complex than is usually thought. With the addition of this book, "The reader will have full access to the two aspects of Whitman's life and work that the poet sought to conceal, or, at least, obscure: his commitment to male-male sexual love, and, most surprisingly, an intense negativity, a furious indignation, profoundly doubtful of the entire democratic experiment."

In "Calamus 9," a dejected lover's lament, Whitman writes: "Hours discouraged, distracted—for the one I cannot content myself without, soon I saw him content himself without me"; In "Repondez!" Whitman, regarded as the foremost poetic trumpeter of America and democracy, shows his anger and doubt concerning the United States: "Let the people sprawl with yearning, aimless hands! let their tongues be broken! let their eyes be discouraged! let none descend into their hearts with the fresh lusciousness of love!"

> Four Walls Eight Windows; $12.95
> 1993; softcover; 200 pp.

# ASYLUM ARTS

## ASYLUM ANNUAL 1994
### edited by Greg Boyd

The Asylum Annuals collect the best new works that incorporate the spirit of dada and surrealism. The over one hundred pieces of prose, poetry, prose poetry, drama, and art in this book manage to cover a lot of ground, from nonstop non sequiturs to stories where reality is just slightly off kilter. Richard Martin's poem "What I Am" is about being insane:

> "I like to suck my
> toes
> in front of security
> cameras
> I fondle meat in front
> of butchers
> I am coo-coo
> a strange bird
> in a foreign tree
> with vulgar song"

Judy Katz-Levine's dreamlike story "The Girl & the Sparrow" opens: "A girl was lost in the woods. She walked among ferns until she found a pool. But this pool was made of faces and blue fists. She was alone, staring into this turbulent water. A sparrow came to rest on her wrist. 'What are you looking for?'"

A high-quality collection that shows that dada and surrealism are far from dead.

> Asylum Arts; $12.95
> 1994; oversize softcover; 151 pp.

## THE BABOON IN THE NIGHTCLUB
### by Kenneth Bernhard

An explicit, scatalogical, long poem in which the narrator tells about his dreams of a baboon and a mysterious lady in white. He first encounters the two in a ritzy nightclub/restaurant. "I'm wondering about the baboon in the nightclub/he spills soup down the lady's back/and shits on someone else's table/his purple testicles terrify the young girls/and make the men tweak their moustaches/his appendage is sixteen inches long/and reaches across tables." The baboon swings on the chandeliers, pisses all over the place, masturbates, and comes on the diners. Then he has sex with the lady in white in front of the whole nightclub, including the lady's embarrassed escort.

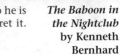

The narrator becomes obsessed with the lady in white. He longs for her, but he can never have her. Only the baboon can. Obviously, the primate represents primitive, uncivilized impulses and desires. He invades a classy nightclub, symbolizing proper society, and does as he pleases. He has unbridled sex with a member of society, and it turns out that she loves it. The narrator yearns for her, too, but she only wants the unrestrained chaos represented by the baboon. The narrator is a good family man with a wife and two kids; he could never let go enough to become like his simian rival, so he is doomed to unfulfilled desire. At least that's how I interpret it. You're welcome to take a stab at it, too.

> Asylum Arts; $8.95
> 1994; softcover; 71 pp.

*The Baboon in the Nightclub by Kenneth Bernhard*

*A long, scatalogical poem about one man's unusual fixation.*

## CARNIVAL APTITUDE
### by Greg Boyd

A collection of sixty-three pieces of short fiction and twenty-nine photomontages. The whole thing is surrealistic but not in a disturbing way, just in a weird way. The fiction comes in very small doses, often three sentences long and almost never more than a page. Here is the first half of "Autobiography": "I spent my childhood packing, then emptying out my flutecase. Between transactions, I milked the encyclopedia and nibbled on the linings of my coat." Many of the stories make comments about the human condition. One of the more lucid of these is "The Suit": "This birthday suit of mine no longer fits. Though I've altered it time and again, it still feels tight in some places, sags in others. Look closely and you'll see how the seams are coming undone…."

The photomontages are just as quirky as the stories. One shows a 1950s-looking woman peering into a glass dome containing a bunch of flies and a man firing a rifle. Another shows a couple of boys, posing for a portrait at the beach, standing in front of a field crawling with hundreds of penguins and four oil paintings of aristocrats.

Asylum Arts; $9.95
1993; softcover; 119 pp.

## CITY OF MAZES:
### AND OTHER STORIES OF OBSESSION
### by Cynthia Hendershot

A collection of twenty-nine darkly erotic, erotically violent short-short stories that deal with the pain of lost love, sexual murder, and obsessions. Each story weaves such an atmosphere of complete, unquenchable darkness that I'm amazed. It's like stepping into the hidden areas of the mind where sex and violence fuse into unspeakable desires. In "After You've Left Me to Scratch the Walls," the narrator's lover has left her. "I am pale, drained of blood by your vampire heart. When I stand I faint. My reflection glares at me from a gold-trimmed mirror. I pull out my teeth one by one. A few days later you send me a black pearl knife. I shred the clothes you left behind. I rip up photographs of you, love letters you've sent full of scrawled sentences which look like snakes ready to bite. In the yellow moonlight which stains my thin body, I puncture my eyes."

"Reflections in my ten red fingernails which I reveal to you one by one" is a series of images, including: "our underwear lying/in a corner suddenly/catching fire and burning to ashes" and "my eyes peering through/the ceiling as/she drives a nail/into your forehead."

Cynthia Hendershot is not yet a well-known writer, so I consider this pitch-black book quite a find for those whose literary tastes run along the lines of the Marquis de Sade, Georges Bataille, and Dennis Cooper.

Asylum Arts; $8.95
1993; softcover; 77 pp.

## HONORABLE MANHOOD:
### POEMS OF EROS & DUST
### by Elliot Richman

This collection of more than forty short poems tells the story of a middle-aged painter having an affair with the younger wife of an Air Force pilot who's been called to serve in the Persian Gulf War. Told from the point of view of the painter, the poems revel in the erotic and condemn the brutality of war. The two are often juxtaposed to show the ludicrousness of violence and the coolness of sex: "I slide my penis inside you. It penetrates/the wasted years in both of us,/exploding ourselves like one of your husband's/missiles making a direct hit on an enemy bunker." "Your/small breasts crushing/gray hairs on my chest/as your husband murders in a desert." The narrator laments "this sad world where we die and kill/instead of drinking hazelnut coffee/and smoking a joint/while naked/on a snowy evening/after making love."

Eventually, the war ends and the woman's husband returns. She goes back to him, even though they don't love each other and he now starts beating her. This isn't exactly a feel-good book, but it is surprisingly moving.

Asylum Arts; $8.95
1994; softcover; 71 pp.

# BLACK ICE BOOKS

## AVANT-POP:
### FICTION FOR A DAYDREAM NATION
### edited by Larry McCaffery

A collection of fiction and some graphics designed to activate your nervous system directly, bypassing the normal brain centers that are triggered when reading "normal" material. Derek Pell, Eurudice, Mark Leyner, Samuel Delany, Kathy Acker, William T. Vollman, Richard Meltzer, and eleven others attempt to short-circuit your MTV-addled neurons.

Derek Pell contributes a collage-prose piece, "The Elements of Style," as written by the Marquis de Sade. It's a guide to writing properly with examples taken from Sade's work. For example: "Quotations. When a quotation is followed by attributive phrase, the comma is enclosed with the quotation marks. 'On your knees,' the monk said to me, 'I am going to whip your titties.'"

"I'm Writing About Sally" by Mark Leyner jumps right into the thick of things: "Interestingly enough, I starred in 'South Pacific' for two years before negotiating oil rights with the Shah of Durani and then performing delicate eleventh-hour dermatological surgery upon Birgit Nilsson at Gloucester County College Hospital in Sewell, New Jersey, and now I'm writing about Sally."

"Sex Guerrillas" by Harold Jaffe is about a group of people who have sex in public places, but, of course, they are being tailed by the sex police.... In "Okay with You?" Richard Meltzer discusses the various ways you can kill him if you want to ("and I know you do"). A worthy, inexpensive addition to your library from hell.

Black Ice Books; $7
1993; paperback; 247 pp.

## DAMNED RIGHT
### by Bayard Jonson

Jack Kerouac on crack. In this hyper–road novel our hero is hauling ass from the Pacific Northwest to L.A., getting involved in bizarre, apocalyptic adventures along the way. "On the road through the mountains I keep it down to a reasonable speed. Somewhere around a hundred. 110 on the long straights. The two-lane backroads aren't where you hit 200 and beyond.... A cop sees me blur past at something over a hundred. I see his lights back there. I don't feel like stopping. If you don't feel like stopping you shouldn't stop. Some nerd in a uniform following you with flashing lights like a rolling Christmas ornament doesn't make it right."

Black Ice Books; $7
1994; paperback; 161 pp.

## DOGGY BAG
### by Ronald Sukenick

"...Doggy Bag samples advertising, the entertainment industry, and B-movie versions of ancient mythologies, splices in cryptograms, weird graphic designs, humans infected with a computer virus, conspiracy projection studios, neural image fabrication by Total Control, Inc., and gives you characters like Jim Morrison, Federico Fellini, a bird named Edgar Allen Crow, a secret sect of White Voodoo Financial Wizards, the Iron Sphincters, and Bruno the sex dog." From the book: "The Revolt of the Zombies is a situation in which everyone is carrying on his own private revolution in complete isolation from everyone else's private revolution. It's the privatization of revolution. It's revolution as free enterprise. Entrepreneurs are selling revolution as a consumer item."

Black Ice Books; $7
1994; paperback; 150 pp.

## THE ETHIOPIAN EXHIBITION
### by D.N. Stuefloten

The first part of this novel contains seventeen very short (not even two pages) chapters telling the story of a lone man crossing Ethiopia on a motorcycle. The second part of the novel is made up of commentary on the action in the first part. Through this commentary we are told the story of Ahmed, a murderer who is directing a movie about a man crossing Ethiopia on a motorcycle. "The creatures that now come forward to attack John in his weakened state are pariah dogs.... In Ethiopia the pariah dogs, although not liked, are expected to perform their role with honor. The tragedy they sometimes bring is the price one pays for being a member of the larger drama of all living things. The frenzy of the pariah dogs, when they rip into their victim, tearing off arms, chunks of flesh, scrambling amongst themselves for choice bits of entrails, liver, or spleen, is not seen as an aberration but as an example of the ferocity that exists in nature, and which thus needs expression."

Black Ice Books; $7
1994; paperback; 105 pp.

## THE KAFKA CHRONICLES
### by Mark Amerika

A rapid-fire machine-gun assault of language whose target is sex, war, politics, consumerism, and other falsehoods. "Hi I'm Cheryl. Fuck me. Fuck you. I watch TV and yes in a way I kinda get off doing it (watching TV). TV is me screaming for attention. It's when I dig pretentiousness and when I begin to see the light. Any light. The fact is that I'm horny.... Please excuse my pumped up energy but I'm currently phasing in my extra iii face. My extra iii face has three eyes. It drips come and makes you wanna see the light too and I guarantee you that you can see the light all you have to do is send $19.95 we accept Visa Mastercard Amerikan Express. I love you."

Black Ice Books; $7
1993; paperback; 189 pp.

## NEW NOIR
### by John Shirley

Angry young stories of alienation, violence, and shallow, empty lives. I don't know if Shirley would appreciate the comparison, but I think of Harlan Ellison's best work when I read these stories. Their high-octane prose, graphic imagery, themes of alienation and unconcealed rage make me think of Ellison. Then there are those two long, Ellisonian titles: "I Want to Get Married, Says the World's Smallest Man!" and "Recurrent Dreams of Nuclear War Lead B.T. Quizenbaum Into Moral Dissolution."

But while Ellison's stories usually have a science fiction element to them, Shirley's stories come straight from today's mean streets, with which, it is said, Shirley is intimately familiar. Drugs, prostitutes, guns, murder—it's all here, baby! All the stories are well-written, and most of them are extremely suspenseful. And may I add that the story "Just Like Suzie," about a woman who dies while giving a blowjob, has to be just about the most revolting piece of prose I have ever read.

Black Ice Books; $7
1993; paperback; 115 pp.

## REVELATION COUNTDOWN
### by Chris Mazza, images by Ted Orland

A collection of road stories that shows the darker side of freedom—loss of control, disorientation, and alienation. "Just down the block from the gas station phone booth, a portable sign has been wheeled to the sidewalk, an arrow of blinking lights points off the road to a small white church with a tall, needle-thin steeple. The sign's body is opaque fluorescent white, so the plastic letters are sharply conspicuous. The black letters say *Revelation Countdown*, and below that, in red, *world chaos by 7, angels 7:30, Wed. 19th, The road leads to heaven or hell, renounce sins now!*"

Black Ice Books; $7
1993; paperback; 151 pp.

# CREATION PRESS

## BLOOD & ROSES:
### THE VAMPIRE IN 19TH CENTURY LITERATURE
### edited by Adèle Olivia Gladwell and James Havoc

This anthology is the first to collect vampire stories written in the 1800s that represent all the major literary movements of the time—Gothicism, Romanticism, Symbolism, and Decadence. Special attention is paid in the selections to the sexual overtones and undertones inherent in the vampire mythos. Adèle Olivia Gladstone's introduction discusses this in detail: "A vampire's spectre augurs erotic deliria: carnal debilitation, autoerogenous metempsychosis, fetishism and lesbianism, necrophilic dementia, auto-symbolic incest, and masturbation.... The Prince of Darkness, with his waxing and waning crescent fangs, is the overriding animus of menstruation prevalent in late 19th Century and modern mythology.... He liberates his lady (his hostess). Her Victorian bustles and corsets unravel, and she swiftly cavorts in a white shroud encrimsoned with bloody maculations; utterly unhampered. Gone is her ascetic pallor as her full sexuality is embraced by her very own 'dark lover' or 'alternative husband.'"

The seventeen selections show the full range of the bloodsucker. *The Vampyre* by John Polidori, written in 1819, is the first story of the traditional vampire to appear in English. In "The Beautiful Dead" by Gautier, "Ligeia" by Edgar Allan Poe, and "The Vampire's Metamorphis" by Baudelaire, the vampires are heterosexual women. In J. Sheridan Le Fanu's "Carmilla" the vampire is a lesbian, while in "True Story of a Vampire" by Count Stenbock, the vampire is a gay man. "The First Song of Maldoror" by Lautréamont presents a sociopathic, intensely cruel vampire who feels no guilt. A similar vampire appears in an excerpt from *Là-Bas* by Joris-Karl Huysmans, except this vampire is real. He is Gilles de Rais, one-time associate of Joan of Arc and one of the most despicable humans ever to tread the earth. The collection ends with excerpts from Bram Stoker's *Dracula*, whose vampire is irresistible to women, and thus is a threat to all men and the very structure of the patriarchy.

*Blood & Roses* is a fantastic collection. It brings together vampires of various literary traditions and sexual orientations for a crimson tour de force.

Creation Books; $15.95
1992; softcover; 283 pp.

## THE GREAT GOD PAN
### by Arthur Machen

Arthur Machen was a horror/occult writer from the late 1800s/early 1900s whose work influenced H.P. Lovecraft, Peter Straub, T.E.D. Klein, and Clive Barker. His first novel, *The Great God Pan*, is a classic piece of fin-de-siècle decadence. Although it caused an uproar at the time, it is extremely tame by today's standards.

Set in Britain, the novel concerns an experiment performed by a Dr. Frankenstein type, who does some nineteenth-century brain surgery on a young woman. She sees the "Great God Pan" and goes insane with terror. Flash forward a couple of decades, to a

*◄ Relevation Countdown by Chris Mazza*

*On the road, darkly.*

wave of suicides that's sweeping London. Could there be a connection? A couple of Brits intend to find out.

*The Great God Pan* weaves a brooding, Gothic atmosphere while moving past the trappings of Gothic into somewhat more dangerous territory. *The Westminster Gazette* referred to the book when it first came out as "an incoherent nightmare of sex...," which is pretty strange considering that there is absolutely no sex in this book. None. There is, however, a very subtle erotic charge running throughout it, which must have been what the offended reviewer picked up on. *The Great God Pan* is a lost classic of death, evil, and possession that has been given a new lease on life.

Creation Press; $15.95
1894 (1993); softcover; 95 pp.

## SATANSKIN

### by James Havoc

A collection of supremely dark short-short stories from neo-Crowleyan badboy James Havoc. Among these twenty-one unrelenting nightmares of depravity is "Devil's Gold," about a man named Gillespie who uses demonic influence to become a woman. Each month he saves his shit and molds it into a baby, which he sacrifices to a demon. After the thirteenth lunar cycle, he finally becomes a woman—of sorts. Gillespie has two vaginas, and as time goes on, things get worse. "Gillespie's anus has meta-morphosed into a third vagina. The only stools that slip from its scalding lips are bloodshot, and gallows-shaped. They shriek at the first bite of cold air. Two more vulvas yawn lazily across her armpits, foaming with fried chicken bones and cigarette stubs. Thirteen nipples ooze faecal lava."

"Shadow Sickness" is about a sickening demon who has sex with a nun while his underlings search the convent for another nun to flay alive. In "Twin Stumps," a man kills and sodomizes his entire family. During the full moon, he gets out their corpses for a "family reunion." A maniac steals vaginas in "White Meat Fever." Each one he steals becomes a part of him until "mewling vaginas entrench every surface of his body. Like pets, he has named each one of them after its donor; proudly he whispers to them as he feeds them gobbets of fried chicken, eggs or walnuts. His favourite, Lydia, runs across the palm of his left hand. She hisses and pukes fish-bones."

Other stories include "Egg Cemetery," "Succubus Blues," "Syphilis Unbound," "Tongue Cathedral," and "Demon's Spice." Finally, there is a heavily reworked version of the author's first novel, *Raism: The Songs of Gilles de Rais*.

There is nothing else like *Satanskin*. It rates a perfect 10 on the extreme-o-meter.

Creation Books; $13.95
1992; softcover; 116 pp.

## THE SLAUGHTER KING

### by Simon Whitechapel

With *The Slaughter King*, Creation launches its Bad Blood imprint, "presenting transgressive art and literature for discerning readers." It's a quite an impressive debut. Whitechapel manages to take a tired plot—vicious serial killer roams the streets—and make it into something completely different. The story follows Alanna Kirk, a policewoman with a taste for violence, as she and her companion Sansiega trail the Slaughter King across Europe. Sansiega knows that the killer is basing his actions on an extremely obscure book written in Basque. Of course, *The Slaughter King* is brimming with graphic sex and violence, but they are presented in such a unique manner that even jaded readers will marvel at the newness. The violence that the Slaughter King wreaks is described in a clinical, detached way that can only be completely meaningful to people who practice medicine. During the killer's first attack, he slashes a young man across the upper thigh: "...it sliced through the rich red fibre bundles of the superficial muscles, the tensor fasciae latae, the rectus femoris, the iliacus, the psoas major, the pectineus and adductus longus, the gracilis, cutting the wet tubery of the veins and arteries..."

What makes the sex scenes so fresh isn't the language used to describe them, but the acts themselves. In an unforgettable

encounter, one woman inserts her entire foot into her lesbian lover. Another memorable scene takes place when two women start mixing it up in a freezing swimming pool. "Alanna smiled, strangely, for her lips were numbed and said something that Sansiega did not understand, and was surprised to find herself unsurprised as Alanna thrust down at her shoulders, sliding her smoothly into the freezing water, down the white cold body until the long thighs locked around her face.... Drowning, she sucked, and in the universe there was nothing but the freezing water of the pool on her body and the heat of Alanna's sex melted to her mouth."

Fifty years from now, this book will probably be referred to as a decadent fin-de-siècle classic.

Bad Blood (Creation Press); $15.95
1992; softcover; 165 pp.

# MANIC D PRESS

## GRAVEYARD GOLF:
### AND OTHER STORIES

### by Vampyre Mike Kassel

After reading fiction filled with twisted sex and gut-wrenching violence, Vampyre Mike's slice-of-weirdness stories are like a breath of fresh air. The title story must be the first ever about the underrated sport of graveyard golf. The object of graveyard golf is to hit your ball into or off of tombstones, statues, obelisks, trees, mausoleums, etc. In the story, two friends are recounting their legendary grudge match: "We hop the fence, tee up on old man Winthrope's grave and we're off. I slam my ball off the big stone angel and it goes into the rough. Bismark here hits his perfectly. It bounces off the angel's head and lines him up Vic Damone for the next shot..."

The rest of the stories are just as endearingly strange. Some of the twisted characters include two messy building painters, a herepetologist smuggling various reptiles through airport security in his pockets, a pack of homicidal Cub Scouts, a mistreated guitar named Mendel, a hoodoo man named Uncle Tuesday, a couple of guys attempting to bootleg absinthe, a Jewish blues band, and Igor, Dr. Frankenstein's lackey.

*Graveyard Golf* is truly laugh-out-loud funny. Vampyre Mike's sense of strangeness, gift for bizarre language, and absurd sense of humor add up to a first-rate collection of stories.

manic d press; $7.95
1991; softcover; 63 pp.

## MOBIUS STRIPPER

### by Bana Witt

Bana Witt has written a series of rapid-fire short-short stories about her hedonistic days during the 1970s in San Francisco. She tells about working in a Mitchell Brothers' porno movie, dabbling in SM, going to bathhouses, working in a massage parlor, doing every drug under the sun, and getting raped; describes her sexual relationship with a drag queen, and more. *Mobius Stripper* is a nonstop orgy of drug dealers, sex workers, genderbenders, cheap sex, porno movies, the backseats of cars, sleazy bars, and random violence. Ah, the good ol' days.

Here's a typical description of Witt's encounters with a doctor she went to for a thyroid test: "He came over the following night with amyl nitrate ampules (poppers), a pill bottle full of pharmaceutical cocaine, and quaaludes. I was sure I would achieve Satori, or some Far Eastern metaphor for bliss. And to top it off, he was outstanding in bed (or maybe the drugs were). It was really fun. Both of us were able to handle great quantities of drugs and vector the unleashed energy into our sex."

*Mobius Stripper* is an unapologetic look at a unique point in history—before AIDS and the War on Drugs—when, if it felt good, people did it.

manic d press; $8.95
1992; softcover; 93 pp.

## THE RISE AND FALL OF THIRD LEG
### by Jon Longhi

The tone of this short-short story collection is set nicely by the inscription in the front of the book: "Sometimes when you're driving late at night you get so tired that the white lines look like fortunes from a fortune cookie and you're tempted to pull over and read them." OK, so we know the going is getting weird.

"Slacker High Noon" is about a duel between two twentynothings trying to determine who's lazier. "We compared our extensive travels through the welfare system and low-to-no-rent housing. Our avoidance of even part-time jobs. Our lack of protestant work ethic, aspirations, consumer clout, yuppie inclinations or future goals." Generation X has never looked so bad (well, come to think of it, maybe during Woodstock '94...).

The centerpiece of the collection is the long title story about a punk band called Third Leg. One of their first big hits was "Sex Is Overrated": Sex is overrated/though no one will state it/Liz Taylor is overweighted/a new man to be traded/Reagan's crotch so hated/not even crabs invade it/Kafka masturbated/when he wrote *The Trial*." Third Leg never did manage to get anywhere, but they had fun trying. Their crowning moment came during their gig at the State Theater. After their guitar amp and drum machine gave out, and they were being pelted with food, they started lobbing Salisbury steaks into the audience and saying that they were throwing turds. Long live rock!

manic d press; $9.95
1994; softcover; 158 pp.

## SPECIMEN TANK
### by Buzz Callaway

Wally and Jane are a dysfunctional urban couple—yelling, hitting, constantly leaving each other—who answer an ad for human guinea pigs in the *Village Voice*. They get what they think will be an easy job testing cosmetics and simple drugs, but things aren't as they seem. "I mean, there I am, in a billion-dollar testing facility designed to do every conceivable type of research for governments and private corporations, but I can't get a drink of water, nobody's on duty at night, the doctors rape the nurses, the nurses rape the patients and to top it off, I run smack into doggie Auschwitz."

But that's only the beginning. Wally and Jane discover that there is much more devious and dangerous human testing going on, and they're right in the middle of it. *Specimen Tank* is a great read, a true page-turner. Plus, it has a full-color wraparound cover from Robert Williams.

manic d press; $10.95
1993; softcover; 254 pp.

# MISCELLANEOUS

## DANGER IS MY BUSINESS:
### AN ILLUSTRATED HISTORY OF THE
### FABULOUS PULP MAGAZINES: 1896–1953
### by Lee Server

During the first half of this century, magazine shelves were filled with pulps, magazines printed on cheap paper. They featured garish, outlandish covers and even more outlandish fiction inside. The pulps were the redheaded stepchildren of the slick magazines, yet they were a huge success whose influence is still being felt. The tales of strange aliens, tough private eyes, and star-crossed lovers created the markets known as genre fiction—science fiction, mystery, romance, etc. The pulps gave us such pop culture icons as Tarzan, Doc Savage, Zorro, Sam Spade, and Conan the Barbarian. Of course, the kids buying this stuff at the time didn't know they were witnessing history in the making. All they knew was that for a dime to a quarter they could get a magazine filled with weird, cheesy stories.

The pulp writers pounded away on their typewriters up to eighteen hours a day, sometimes writing two stories a day. There were no revisions—first drafts were what was published. And the writers earned about a penny per word. Not all the writers were hacks, though. Edgar Rice Burroughs, Louis L'Amour, Ray Bradbury, H.P. Lovecraft, and Raymond Chandler all got their starts in the pulps.

*Danger Is My Business* lovingly covers this era of American publishing. With full-color reproductions of more than one hundred covers and interiors, the author guides us through the worlds of horror, fantasy, adventure, private eyes, romance and sex, superheroes, science fiction, and "weird menace." He introduces us to the magazines, writers, editors, publishers, and trends of this era. To my vast delight, he peppers his narrative with unforgettable quotes from the stories. Who could forget this "love scene" from the weird menace story "Corpses on Parade"?: "In hideous nudity she advanced one step toward me. Her breasts, her hips, seemed half-decomposed. And the smell! It was like the fumes that might arise from a city's garbage lying for hours under an August sun.... Then—I've read about lips melting in an embrace, but I'll never read it again without being sick. For that is exactly what Thea's lips did. They squashed with the same plosh of rotten fruit that had marked the disintegration of Kitty's hand."

Chronicle Books; $17.95
1993; oversize softcover; 144 pp.

◄ *The Rise and Fall of Third Leg* by Jon Longhi

*Slacker punk band having fun getting nowhere, fast!*

## DROWNING IN FIRE
### by Thom Metzger

This murder thriller suspense novel by the legendary proprietor of Ziggurat, Thom Metzger, contains which of the following?
A) a serial killer
B) octogenarian gangsters
C) tri-racial isolates in the south Jersey swamps
D) the only member of a family who escaped the eugenics programs of the 1920s and 1930s
E) incest
F) hallucinogenic caustic goo
G) crypto-Egyptian hoodoo
H) spirit possession
I) strange sex
J) all of the above
    Correct answer: J

Ziggurat; $6
1992; paperback; 350 pp.

## EMPIRE OF THE SENSELESS
### by Kathy Acker

Written by pomo literary terrorist Kathy Acker, *Empire of the Senseless* is a semicyberpunk dystopian tale starring the pirate, Thivai, and Abhor, a half-robot, half-black hybrid known as a construct. The two of them are terrorists-for-hire, on a mission to find a construct called Kathy. Actually, the plot is secondary to the writing itself, which veers frequently into ruminations on death, life, sex, love, incest, murder, power, freedom, and other heavy topics.

Here are a few choice quotes. On control: "I'm not frigid because my mother used my desire to have her love me like a knotted whip over me. I'm playing with *only* my blood and shit and death because mommy ordered me to be only whatever she desired, that is, to be not possible, but it isn't possible to be and be not possible. By playing with my blood and shit and death, I'm controlling my life." On man-woman sex: "I didn't know what to do about the useless and, more than useless, virulent and destructive disease named heterosexual sexual love. I've never known." On power: "Dealers and cops always work together because they're bosses. Drugs are bad for you…only because there are bosses." On freedom (in New York City, specifically): "Liberty, shit. The liberty to starve. The liberty to speak words to which no one listens. The liberty to get diseases no doctor treats or can cure." On life: "[A terrorist says,] 'Life's a waste of booze.' I thought about dead cunts. 'Life's a waste.'"

Grove Press; $9.95
1988; softcover; 227 pp.

## FART PROUDLY:
### WRITINGS OF BENJAMIN FRANKLIN YOU NEVER READ IN SCHOOL
### edited by Carl Japikse

A collection of bawdy, irreverent writings by Benjamin Franklin. Forget the "early to bed, early to rise" rubbish, Franklin was a notorious ladies' man and a member of the Hell-Fire Club of England, known for its bacchic orgies. *Fart Proudly* lets us see the side of our Founding Father that is often lost in historical whitewash.

We read his advice in "On Choosing a Mistress": "…in all your Amours you should *prefer old Women to young ones*…. Because there is no hazard of Children, which irregularly produced may be attended with much Inconvenience…. And as in the dark all cats are grey, the Pleasure or corporal Enjoyment with an old Woman is at least equal, and frequently superior, every Knack being by Practice capable of improvement."

Bennie also enjoyed a nip or two, as evidenced by "The Antidiluvians Were All Very Sober": "Twas honest old Noah first planted the Vine,/And mended his Morals by drinking its Wine;/He justly the drinking of water decried;/For he knew that all Mankind, by drinking it, died." Other writings deal with farting, greed, governmental stupidity, and making oneself disagreeable.

Ariel Press; $7.95
1990; softcover; 128 pp.

*High Risk 2* ➤
edited by Amy Scholder, Ira Silverberg

*Sex, Death & Subversion, again.*

## HIGH RISK:
### AN ANTHOLOGY OF FORBIDDEN WRITINGS
### edited by Amy Scholder and Ira Silverberg

*High Risk* collects new and some previously published writing from some of the biggest names in subversion. These are writers who aren't afraid to jump headfirst into the darkest depths of the human heart and mind. Even though the stories in this anthology do live up to the book's title and subtitle, *High Risk* did take some slagging in some nonconformist circles for not being risky enough. I think the objections may have had more to do with the fact that it was put out by a big publisher, because any book that deals candidly and explicitly with incest, murder, self-mutilation, piss-drinking, rape, drugs, pornography, SM, prostitution, and transsexuality is pretty damn risky in my book.

"The Exemplary Life of the Slave and the Master" by Manuel Ramos Otero is a monologue by a bottom in an SM relationship. "piss on me the way that I tell you to or don't piss on me at all. hot. sun of water. hot sun of water am I. liquid sunflowers. burning petals of white light. the master urinates. his sleeping hose unwinds. he shoots jets of

solitude." In "How Dare You Even Think These Things?" gay porn writer John Preston tells about writing his first story as an adolescent. "I left my work on the table while I went to the kitchen to get a drink. When I came back to the porch, I found my grandmother reading my writing. She looked at me with fury and disgust. *'How dare you even think these things?'* she yelled at me. Then she tore my small, amateurish manuscript to shreds."

"Body" by supermasochist Bob Flanagan will make most men wince. "I nailed the head of my dick to a board, the way I saw it in a magazine the other day. I got so excited by the magazine that I had to try it myself. But while trying to drive the nail in a little farther I missed and just (I thought) tapped the tip of my poor dick. It didn't hurt (the nail was handling that job) but shit! It started swelling up immediately."

The list of other contributors reads like a *Who's Who* of the extreme scene: Gary Indiana, Pat Califia, William S. Burroughs, Dennis Cooper, Kathy Acker, Essex Hemphill, Wanda Coleman, Mary Gaitskill, Dorothy Allison, Terence Sellers, Robert Glück, David Wojnarowicz, and Karen Finley. Whew!

Plume (Penguin); $8.95
1991; softcover; 296 pp.

## HIGH RISK 2:
### WRITINGS ON SEX, DEATH, AND SUBVERSION
### edited by Amy Scholder and Ira Silverberg

Featuring an all-new cast of literary deviants, *High Risk 2* aims to pick up where *High Risk* left off. Unfortunately, it doesn't. This sequel mines almost exactly the same vein as its predecessor. I wanted it to take me deeper into the forbidden, to locate new pockets of deviance, but instead it is mostly a rehash. Not to say that it's not a good book, but I think it's like smoking crack—the second time just doesn't give you the rush of the first.

"Meet Murder, My Angel" by Rupert Adley explores the intersection of sex, violence, and murder. A lawyer picks up a young guy and takes him to his (the lawyer's) place. They get out some crystal meth and shoot up. "i straps my arm up and vein hunts—get one the first time and bang up the works in one shot

"before i get the spike out it hits me goldrush strong hot pure he pulls his needle out and looks up at me i know what he wants and i want to give it to him i smash him round the face with the back of my fist and he falls on the floor."

Suzette Partido turns in one of the most unusual stories, "A to Bee (and Back Again)," in which the female narrator admits her feelings for Aunt Bee of *The Andy Griffith Show*. As a child she would watch the show, fantasizing that she was with Aunt Bee the whole time. "Throughout the movement of the program, Beatrice and I remained together unless of course she was running food to the feeble men at the courthouse. On such occasions I darted up the stairs to her bedroom and slid ontop her single bed. Waiting for the return of her full attention, I traced the texture of her quilted spread while wishing her full weight pressing down on me, wishing never to leave."

"Dear Dead Man" by Benjamin Weissman is a series of scenes documenting different forms of violence. In the first scene, a Vietnam veteran goes crazy, murders his pets and family, and torches his neighborhood. In the second scene, a mother kills her little boy. Next, a murderer gets intimate with the unattached head of his victim. The following scene is about a depraved killer clown. Finally, in letter format, a man tells a dead car accident victim how much seeing his accident brought his family together. "The family came alive as I've never seen before…. 'I count six bodies, Daddy.' Eric noted. 'Look at that naked man,' Nina said, 'he's bright red with little black specks.'"

Other writers in *High Risk 2* include Michael Blumlein, Diamanda Galas, Stewart Home, Akilah Nayo Oliver, Sapphire, John Wynne, and over a dozen more.

Plume (Penguin); $10.95
1994; softcover; 257 pp.

## INDECENT EXPOSURES

### by Robert Bahr

This is one of the books that gave me the toughest time in terms of where to list it. At first I just assumed it would go in the Erotic Fiction section of the "Sex" chapter, but when I read it I realized that wouldn't be right. Yes, there is sex in these stories. Yes, sex is probably the most important element in these stories. But these stories don't exist to get you hot and bothered. They delve into the role sex plays in our identities and lives. Most of them deal with men and boys coming to terms (or not) with their sexuality. In "Suva Boy" a tourist has to decide whether or not to take a young Indian boy up on his offer for sex. In "The Arms of Michael" a teenager agonizes over his "sinful" sexual feelings.

Not all the stories are about sex, though. "Morningstar" deals with a girl whose grandmother dies, and "Dear and Only Friend" is the jarring story of man who loses his wife. What all the stories have in common is that they deal with the pain of being alive. Having to cope with sex and death are among the hardest things we humans have to do. Bahr takes such an honest, open look at this pain that his stories are almost unbearable. They certainly aren't enjoyable, but they hit the nail on the head so perfectly that they must be read.

Factor Press; $9.50
1993; softcover; 165 pp.

## THE LAST DAYS OF CHRIST THE VAMPIRE

### by J.G. Eccarius

"Jesus Lives—Vampires Never Die." So says the T-shirt based on this famous underground cult novel. In it we find out that Jesus is really a vampire enslaving the world through religion and direct telepathic control. It is up to Professor Holbach and a group of punks from Providence, Rhode Island, to get the world out from Jesus' heel.

Scattered throughout the book are biblical quotations that show Jesus' true vampiric nature. For example, in John 11:25 Jesus says, "I am the resurrection and the life, he who bleeds in Me shall live even if he dies." In John 1:5 Jesus is referred to as "the First Born of the Dead." Reflecting the belief that a vampire can only enter a home if invited, Jesus says in Revelation 3:20: "I stand at the door and knock. If any man hears my voice, I will come in."

*The Last Days* is simply a classic that deserves a space on your bookshelf as much as Shakespeare.

III Publishing; $7
1988; paperback; 191 pp.

## MARK V. ZIESING BOOKS CATALOG

Mark V. Ziesing Books publishes high-quality collector's editions of science fiction, fantasy, and horror, usually with an edge to it. They also put out a forty-page-or-so catalog every six weeks featuring unusual books from other publishers. Most of the books are along the lines of what Ziesing publishes—edgy, unusual, speculative fiction. But they also sell mainstream SF, avant-garde fiction, and weird nonfiction—sex, drugs, UFOs, cyberculture, etc.

Mark V. Ziesing Books/PO Box 76/Shingletown, CA 96088
Catalog: free, but be a pal and send a buck or two.

## MONKEY BRAIN SUSHI:
### NEW TASTES IN JAPANESE FICTION
### edited by Alfred Birnbaum

First off, let me nominate this book for the Best Title of the Year Award. This anthology contains eleven avant-garde Japanese stories that display the uniquely twisted Japanese sensibility you've seen in Japanimation and manga. In fact, one of the stories, "Japan's Junglest Day," is a piece of manga about two Japanese soldiers who don't realize WWII is over. The other stories are cyberpunk, erotic, surrealistic—filled with weird sex, ultraviolence, strange happenings, and delusional people.

Stories include "TV People," "Sproing!" "Kneel Down and Lick My Feet," "Peony Snowflakes of Love," and "Momotaro in a Capsule." From the last story: "Kurushima employed several techniques to protect his genitals.... In his own words: 'To protect one's genitals is to protect oneself. One's genitals are the guardians of one's identity.' An earth-shattering thesis. He also said this: 'The penis, like the tongue, nose, eyes, and ears, is a sensory organ. Its sensations are the keenest.' And: 'A penis has an outside and an inside. Men of action develop the outside. Men of thought develop the inside.'"

Kodansha America; $9.00
1991; paperback; 304 pp.

## THE NAUGHTY YARD

### by Michael Hemmingson

An evening in the life of three twentynothings. A man and two women explore sex through action and through relating past experiences. The dialogue and monologues are fast and furious. Quotation marks are scrapped and action is minimal—all attention is on the rapid-fire discussions:

"Cynthia goes to the bathroom, closes the door. We hear the water running.

Pause.

Pause.

Pause.

Kathy says I feel—I feel bad for her.

I say yes so do I.

She says I know what you are thinking.

What?

You—you want to go in there?

In?

There.

The bathroom?

Yes.

I say do you want me to?

She says I think I do. I want you to go in there. Will you please go in there? Make her feel better the way you have made me feel better."

Can life achieve meaning through sex? Does sex have a meaning? I still don't know, but for some reason this book depressed the hell out of me even though I enjoyed it.

Permeable Press; $5.95
1994; small paperback; 104 pp.

## OVER MY DEAD BODY:
### THE SENSATIONAL AGE OF THE
### AMERICAN PAPERBACK: 1945–1955

### by Lee Server

The sequel to *Danger Is My Business, Over My Dead Body* charts similarly exploitive, hedonistic territory. This time it's the early paperback novel under examination. These twenty-five cent novels offered the readers some cheap titillation. Like pulp magazines, these books can be identified by their lurid covers, which "offered endless variations on recurring motifs, namely crimson-lipped females in lingerie, granite-jawed tough guys, blazing .45s, rumpled bedsheets, neon-lit hotel rooms, a blue-gray haze of cigarette smoke, alleyways and street corners at permanent midnight." The titles ran along similar lines: *Hitch-Hike Hussy, Trailer Tramp, Love-Hungry Doctors, Teen-Age Mafia, Pure Sweet Hell, A Night for Screaming.*

*Over My Dead Body ▼
by Lee Server*

*Pure sweet pulp.*

The author charts this epochal decade in American publishing with a guided tour of the authors and publishers and about one hundred full-color reproductions of paperback covers. At first, paperbacks were reprints of hardcovers, but the new format often gave the books a new lease on life. Mickey Spillane's novels of his sadistic private eye, Mike Hammer, only sold thousands as hardcovers, but in paperback format they catapulted into the millions. The paperback publishing of Jack Kerouac's seminal novel *On the Road* helped turn it into the beatnik bible.

Soon, publishers were paying writers a pittance to churn out original paperbacks. Although a lot of what came out was hack work, some classic books did emerge from this period. John D. MacDonald, Louis L'Amour, Philip K. Dick, and Charles Willeford were all paperback writers. In fact, the legendary William Burroughs's first novel, *Junky* (published under the pseudonym William Lee), was an el cheapo paperback. The Publisher's Note to the first edition says in part: "William Lee is an unrepentant, unredeemed drug addict. His own words tell us that he is a fugitive from the law; that he had been diagnosed as schizophrenic, paranoid; that he is totally without moral values."

Of course, lack of moral values was what these books were all about. Sex, sadism, shocking violence, murder, drugs, juvenile delinquents—all were the order of the day, which was ultimately the paperback's undoing. As in the cases of the pulp magazines, comics in the 1950s, and video games in the 1990s, bluenoses and self-appointed moral watchdogs brought so much pressure on the industry, even to the point of congressional investigations, that the publishers cleaned up their acts and the Golden Age of paperbacks was over.

Chronicle Books; $16.95
1994; oversize softcover; 108 pp.

## PIMP:
### THE STORY OF MY LIFE
## by Iceberg Slim

The problem with reading outsiders' stories about the mean streets is that they haven't lived it, only glimpsed it. William Vollman (author of *Whores for Gloria*, below) has a gift for language and is to be commended for actually risking life and limb by hanging out in the Tenderloin district, but he was only slumming. No visitor can give you the real story the way a native can.

Iceberg Slim is a native of the mean streets of Chicago. He lived there for most of thirty years, running scams, doing heavy drugs, and pimping. He eventually left it all behind him, entered the "square world," married, and began to write. This book, an autobiographical novel, is about the Iceman's escapades in hell. In it, he pulls no punches. In the opening scene, 'Berg's fictional alter-ego had just picked up four of his whores in his Cadillac. They were stinking up the car, so he asked if any of them had shit themselves. "Then Rachel, my bottom whore, cracked in a pleasing, ass-kissing voice. 'Daddy Baby, that ain't no shit you smell. We been turning all night and ain't no bathrooms in those tricks' cars we been flipping out of. Daddy, we sure been humping for you, and what you smell is our nasty whore asses.'" Obviously, Iceberg was not a script consultant for *Pretty Woman*. I'd love to see Julia Roberts say those lines.

'Berg's writing is a lesson in slang: "'Sugar,' I said, 'I saw a wild vine for a bill downtown. If you laid the scratch on me, I could cop tomorrow.'" (Translation: "My love, I saw a nice suit for $100 downtown. If you give me the money, I could get it tomorrow.") Fortunately, Iceberg does provide a glossary, but it's missing an awful lot of words that he uses.

Ice has a sense of humor that pervades *Pimp*, which is pretty surprising considering its gritty, brutal subject matter. When he describes his encounter with a kinky woman who taught him lots of new tricks, he says, "If Pepper had lived in the old biblical city of Sodom, the citizens would have stoned her to death."

Iceberg's books are classics of outsider literature. They are sad, funny, violent, and chillingly honest. They simply must be read.

Holloway House Publishing Company; $4.95
1969; paperback; 317 pp.

## THE PORTABLE BEAT READER
### edited by Ann Charters

Speed, booze, grass, heroin, road trips, jazz, easy sex, Zen, living for the moment...ah, the world of the Beat generation. The Beat movement was made up of writers who rebelled against traditional, middle-class values, starting in the late 1940s. Depending on whom you listen to, the movement lasted basically until the mid-1960s, when the hippies replaced the Beats as America's counterculture.

This book is a monumental collection of stories, poems, novel excerpts, letters, and songs from this important anti-authoritarian movement. The writings of the main Beats gathered here include Jack Kerouac's *On the Road* (excerpt) and *The Dharma Bums* (excerpt), Allen Ginsberg's "Howl" and "America," William Burroughs's *Junky* (excerpt) and *Naked Lunch* (excerpt), Herbert Hunke's "Joey Martinez," John Clellon Holmes's *Go* (excerpt), and Gregory Corso's "The Mad Yak" and "Bomb." The editor also includes numerous works from a related, overlapping group, The San Francisco Renaissance poets—Kenneth Rexroth, Lawrence Ferlinghetti, Gary Snyder, et al—and people who were kinda Beat-like but not officially part of the movement—LeRoi Jones, Diane Di Prima, Bob Dylan, Frank O'Hara, and others. Other sections include memoirs of and tributes to the Beat movement from, for example, Brion Gysin and Jan Kerouac and a selection of work written by the Beats after the movement ended. If you only get one book of Beat writing, it has to be this one.

Penguin Books; $13.95
1992; softcover; 645 pp.

## SNAPSHOT POETICS:
### A PHOTOGRAPHIC MEMOIR OF THE BEAT ERA
## by Allen Ginsberg

Besides being a poet, Allen Ginsberg is also a photographer. He was snapping shots throughout the glory days of the Beat movement, and in this book he presents his best pictures. We get to see such priceless images as William Burroughs and Jack Kerouac in a mock knife fight, a shot of Kerouac looking totally cool (I'm glad the friggin' Gap didn't get its hands on this picture), Ginsberg and Gregory Corso posing nude, Ginsberg shaking hands with a monkey in India, a naked Gary Snyder with a bamboo spear, Timothy Leary and Neal Cassady on the Merry Pranksters' Bus, Lawrence Ferlinghetti and his dog Whitman, Burroughs and Norman Mailer, and dozens of others. (Interesting thing about the pictures of Burroughs: In 1953, when he was just thirty-nine years old, he already looked ancient.)

Each photo is accompanied by a lengthy caption handwritten by Ginsberg. Luckily for those of us who can't read chicken scratch, the captions are reprinted in type in the back of the book.

Chronicle Books; $12.95
1993; oversize softcover; 96 pp.

## THE RAINBOW STORIES
### by William T. Vollman

Vollman uses his hallucinatory prose style to write about the outlaws of society—whores, skinheads, winos, fetishists, religious assassins, and other underworld denizens. This book of short stories and real-life adventures covers the visible spectrum from "Red Hands" to "Yellow Rose" to "Violet Hair." Vollman's stories are surrealistic and disjointed. His true-adventure pieces are my favorites, though. Vollman does things that no one in his right mind would do and then writes about his experiences. He hung out with neo-Nazi skinheads in San Francisco for a while ("The White Knights") and trolled the nighttime streets and bars of the Tenderloin district, talking to and occasionally hiring prostitutes ("Ladies and Red Lights"): "...it is a simple matter to let a whore take you between two cars in the parking lot on Larkin and Golden Gate, and you face prudently away from the street and she kneels down and unzips your fly and puts her mouth to work and you slap her hand away when she tries to pick your pocket, and you cannot really see her face because she is looking straight at your belly, thinking no doubt thoughts which would surprise you, and after a few minutes it is all over and when she takes her mouth away you discover that sometime before you came she rolled a rubber on with her tongue and you never even felt it." Following this scene is a footnote: "This revelation cost me twenty dollars."

Penguin Books; $14
1989; softcover; 543 pp.

## WHORES FOR GLORIA
### by William T. Vollman

A sad, haunting tale of Jimmy, a Vietnam veteran and wino, who combs the streets of San Francisco's Tenderloin district looking for the love of his life, a prostitute named Gloria. The only thing is, we're not sure if Gloria actually exists. Jimmy talks for half an hour to Gloria on a broken pay phone. He tells people that he just missed seeing Gloria when she was in town a week ago, but a friend saw her. He takes pieces of whores—their hair, the stories they tell him—and pretends they're Gloria's. Wandering the streets one night, Jimmy runs into a whore: "She said doll you want a date? and Jimmy said thank you for the offer but to tell you the truth I'm looking for my friend Gloria you know the one with the big tits?—Oh that's just an excuse! sneered the whore, at which Jimmy cocked his head very wisely and said I never excuse myself except when I burp. Do you ever burp? Gloria doesn't.—Oh Christ said the whore, who was as slender and unwholesome looking as a snake, and she stalked around the corner, heels clacking angrily."

As a bonus, Vollman includes a glossary, a profile of a typical Tenderloin prostitute, and a price guide for "services."

Penguin Books; $9.95
1991; softcover; 154 pp.

## REAL GONE
### art by Jack Pierson, fiction by Jim Lewis

*Real Gone* tells the story of Jack and Jim, who went on a road trip to the land of sleaze, Las Vegas. Or does it tell their story? Is it fiction based on fact. Fact based on fiction? I don't know, but what it boils down to is this: Jim tells about their adventures, particularly those that involve an old wino named Carl. They first encountered him on the street: "As we watched he stepped back, turned, gazed up the pole of the streetlamp, and then suddenly began to shimmy up it. His knees shook as they gripped the metal, and his shoes kept slipping; he would get a few feet off the ground, slide back down, and then start to scramble up again. After three or four tries he caught us staring at him, and he shook his head as if someone else had done something stupid...." As it turns out, Carl knows a little too much about a murder that took place years ago....

Jack's colorful, often out-of-focus pictures are snapshots of the sights and sounds of Las Vegas—eighteen-wheelers, a sunbather's legs, palm trees, a Dairy Queen, a table at a greasy spoon, somebody getting busted, and of course, bright lights. A highly entertaining book, but not very nutritious.

Artspace Books; $15
1993; small hardcover; 53 pp.

## RENT BOY
### by Gary Indiana

A darkly comic tale of a young male prostitute named Danny, whose other job is waiting tables at a trendy restaurant filled with shallow, self-important celebrities, like the soft-porn writer Sandy Miller, who never tips. "Sandy whines all the time she hasn't got any money, her publishers screwed her, it seems she gets screwed on every deal she makes. Added to how much she gets screwed otherwise, Sandy's life must be one big screw."

Danny writes a series of letters to J., who is apparently a friend/lover/client(?) of Danny's. He tells J. about the tricks he

turns and how he's doing in college, where he's studying architecture. One day, Danny's best friend, Chip, latches on to a strange doctor with a Robin Hood philosophy about organ donations. Those people with two healthy organs should be forced to give one to someone who's dying. He hires Danny and Chip to help him shanghai a kidney from a rich old man with a penchant for drag queens. The only catch is, Danny learns it may be a double cross, and on the night of the kidney heist, he has a change of heart. Much madness and murder ensue.

High Risk Books; $10.99
1994; softcover; 121 pp.

## SHAMAN
### by Hugh Fox

A novel narrated by a forty-four-year-old English professor who recently came out of the closet and became a transvestite. The book follows him as he interacts with all the people in his life—friends, lovers, students, business acquaintances, his ex-wife, etc. But it's not subject matter that really makes the book unusual. It's the unique writing style of the author. Fox composes ("writes" isn't the right word) a lyrical kind of writing I'd call prosetry (prose + poetry) that piles word on top of word, image on top of image, until you may not be sure exactly what's going on plot-wise, but it sure is beautiful to read. If poets and other writers are supposed to be drunk with words, then Hugh Fox must be an alcoholic.

In this passage, Jack/Clea is in a hotel room bathroom taking a bath, shaving himself:

"all the hair off arms, chests, legs, perfume melting into the heat, so nice to get off the Shag,
     gotta watch food,
               yoga'd in her gut,
               longed for surgery,
               the excision of excess,
               Sanctity was Minimal
               Flesh, Holy Whore
               Minimalism, skin tight
               over cheekbones and jaws, ribs,
               legs,
               muscular,
               taut
               whoresaint spreadleg worship,
               taut athletic ballet bed softness..."

Permeable Press; $10.95
1993; softcover, 190 pp.

## SPEED/KENTUCKY HAM
### by William S. Burroughs Jr.

Although William S. Burroughs has been read by almost every subversive on earth, the books of the late William S. Burroughs Jr. aren't nearly as well known. Luckily for us, Overlook Press has reprinted Bill Jr.'s two books, *Speed* and *Kentucky Ham*, and combined them into one volume. Like his dad, Bill Jr. had a, shall we say, eventful life in which drugs played a big role. *Speed* tells of Little Bill running away from his grandparents' home to New York, where he became addicted to—you guessed it—speed, got arrested twice (and was bailed out by Allen Ginsberg), and eventually returned home. In *Kentucky Ham*, Bill Jr. is arrested for forging a prescription and is sentenced to detox at a Federal Narcotics Farm.

*Speed/
Kentucky
Ham*
by William S.
Burroughs Jr.

*Junior's big
adventure.*

The younger Burroughs has a wonderfully informal writing style. You feel as if he's a friend sitting next to you just talking about all the shit he's been through. His two books, especially *Kentucky Ham*, make me wish I had known him. This one-volume collection would be worth having if only because it was written by William Burroughs's son, but it's more than a literary curiosity—it's two powerful, painfully honest books that stand on their own merit.

Overlook Press; $13.95
1993; softcover; 363 pp.

*V.*
by Thomas
Pynchon ➤

*"As spread
thighs are to
the libertine,
flights of
migratory
birds to the
ornithologist,
the working
part of his tool
bit to the
production
machinist, so
was the letter
V to young
Stencil."*

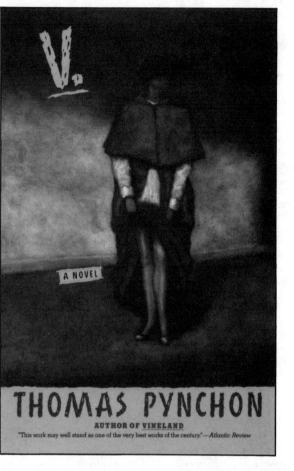

## STRIPPING AND OTHER STORIES
### by Pagan Kennedy

This collection of stories by Pagan Kennedy, pop culture commentator and Generation X nonslacker, all focus on girls and young women coming to terms with themselves at crucial points in life. In "The Dead Rabbit Pocket," a teenage girl riding a horse loses control, and her father can only watch helplessly as the horse gallops furiously around the ring. The girl realizes that what she's been through is a metaphor for growing up: "It seems to me that I'm always in that ring now, going around and around on that horse that nothing can stop.... I can see my poor father, who's driven such a long way to help me. He climbs up on the fence and calls instructions I cannot hear. He looks terrified...."

"Elvis' Bathroom" revolves around a twentysomething's visit to Graceland. "On Elvis TV specials they tell you he 'passed away,' makes it sound like he died in bed. Truth is, Elvis died on the can, then fell on the floor and curled up like a bug. Great, huh? The king of rock and roll dead on the floor with his pants around his ankles." She feels that if only she could be in the bathroom where Elvis died, she could achieve some kind of enlightenment.

Other stories include "Shrinks," "The Underwear Man," "The Black Forest," and "UFOs." Kennedy's stories are subtly powerful, but, damn, are they ever depressing. The real world isn't a nice place, which is evident in reading about these young women's initial encounters with it.

High Risk Books; $10.99
1994; softcover; 153 pp.

## THE TORTURE GARDEN
### by Octave Mirbeau

*The Torture Garden*, written in 1899, has been referred to as "the most sickening work of art of the nineteenth century." Almost one hundred years later, it's lost none of its power to disgust. The main action of the book concerns an Englishwoman named Clara and a Frenchman who discover the Chinese Torture Garden, where torture has been raised to an art form. Clara is entranced by the Garden and explores its mysteries, taking her milquetoast companion along for the ride.

Along the way, they meet a Chinese man who is well versed in the art of torture. When he says that the English suck at torturing, Clara gets offended and says, "Come now! they've made the whole world weep!" The torture artist replies, "Art does not consist in killing multitudes...in slaughtering, massacring, and exterminating men in hordes. Really, it's too easy. Art, milady, consists in knowing how to kill, according to the rites of beauty, whose divine secret we Chinese alone possess. Know how to kill! Nothing is rarer, and everything depends on that. Know how to kill! That is to say, how to work the human body like a sculptor works his clay or piece of ivory, and evoke the entire sum, every prodigy of suffering it conceals, in the depths of its shadows and its mysteries."

Besides exploring the intersection of pain, suffering, power, and pleasure, *The Torture Garden* offers savage attacks on colonialism, government bureaucracy, hypocritical bourgeois values, and sexual repression. Clearly, this book was way ahead of its time.

RE/Search Publications; $13.99
1899 (1989); oversize softcover; 115 pp.

## UNNATURAL ACTS:
### AND OTHER STORIES
### by Lucy Taylor

This collection of short stories by Lucy Taylor is a pitch-black descent into hell. The hell is known as sex. The stories are populated by people who can only get off by sexually hurting or killing their partners, but many of the other people deep down secretly get twisted pleasure from being hurt and violently violated. We're not talking about consenting SM here, but unwilling, painful rape and mutilation.

The main character in the title story is brutally attacked by one of the many brutal rapists in the book. Even though the rapist kills himself, he wins in the end because his victim willingly joins him in death. Most of the men in this book are vicious, misogynist pieces of shit, and many of them get just retribution, usually at the hands of a woman.

Taylor has an often beautiful and always unrelenting writing style. The images in her stories will sear themselves into your brain, making for some strange dreams. You'll be relieved when you wake up.

Twisted, depraved, brilliant.

A Richard Kasak Book (Masquerade Books); $12.95
1994; softcover; 190 pp.

## V.
### by Thomas Pynchon

Thomas Pynchon is a fascinating character. He's one of the only writers to have achieved massive critical acclaim, recognition in academia, and yet still retain his street credibility. His considerable reputation as one of the greatest American writers rests on four novels, his entire literary output since 1963. Further adding to the Pynchon mystique is his reclusiveness. As William Poundstone writes in *Biggest Secrets*: "There are more, and clearer, photos of Bigfoot than of Thomas Pynchon." The only decent photo of him is from his 1953 yearbook, the caption of which tells us that his ambition was to be a physicist. When his novel *The Crying of Lot 49* was first published, a black rectangle was printed where the author's picture would normally be. He doesn't give interviews or attend any writers' functions.

*V.* is Pynchon's first novel. On the surface, it seems simple enough—the book's two protagonists are Benny Profane, sort of an Everyman who goes through life letting things happen to him, and Herbert Stencil, who's on an obsessive quest to find a mysterious woman. Stencil's father, who worked for the British Foreign Office, died while investigating the June disturbances in Malta in 1919. Among his father's belongings, Stencil found a personal journal that contained the following entry: "There is more behind and inside V. than any of us has suspected. Not who, but what: what is she. God grant that I may never be called upon to write the answer, either here or in any official report." Based on this entry, Stencil combs the world looking for V. She may be his father's lover, Stencil's mother, or something else completely.

Despite such a straightforward plot, *V.* is a literary labyrinth. It twists and turns with flashbacks, digressions, subplots, and dozens of characters. Through the course of the book we meet several barmaids named Beatrice, a five-foot sailor who's filed his false teeth into sharp points, "a mad Brazilian who wants to go fight Arabs in Israel," gauchos, spies, a group of people who hunt albino alligators in the sewers, and people with names like Hiroshima, Teflon, and Mafia.

*V.* is also rife with puns and other wordplay, which made me like it even more. Check this out: "As spread thighs are to the libertine, flights of migratory birds to the ornithologist, the working part of his tool bit to the production machinist, so was the letter V to young Stencil." (If you don't get it, think of the physical shape of the letter "V".) That sentence alone should earn Pynch a hallowed place in literature.

As chocolate mousse is to desserts, so is *V.* to fiction. It's rich, dense, and filling, but it's very rewarding. It's hard to eat too much at any one time, but at least *V.* won't make you gain weight.

HarperPerennial (HarperCollins Publishers); $12
1963; softcover; 492 pp.

### WOOL GATHERING
#### by Patti Smith

A collection of reminiscences and meditations from rocker Patti Smith. Pieces include "a bidding," "cowboy truths," "indian rubies," and "art in heaven." From "the woolgatherers": "The music of the woolgatherers performing their task. Bending, extending, shaking out the air. Gathering what needs to be gathered. The discarded. The adored. Bits of human spirit that somehow got away. Caught up in an apron. Plucked by a gloved hand."

This book is available in a signed edition. Write for info.

Hanuman Books; $5.95 (unsigned)
1992; mini-paperback; 80 pp.

*Wool Gathering*
by Patti Smith

*Reminiscences and meditations from the rock diva.*

# GRAB BAG

## HUMOR

### THE ANATOMY OF A SCREAMING MAN
#### by Robert Therrien Jr, aka Badbob

A collection of single panels following Jake the Screaming Man. Jake is angry. Jake feels fear. But unlike most of us, Jake lets it all out by screaming his bloody head off. In every cartoon Jake's mouth is opened wider than his entire head and he's letting loose with a cathartic release. We see the Screaming Man's beginning in one panel: His mother is holding him (a Screaming Baby at this point), saying to the priest, "Isn't he cute?" The priest says, "He's a sinner! Let's get him baptized!"

In another panel we see the Screaming Man standing by a table in the street. Up against the table is a sign that says "Porn degrades women." One of the women present is holding up a picture of a babe in bondage. Jake asks her, "How much for that poster?"

Some of the cartoons are pure (twisted) wish fulfillment. For example, Jake launches a Stinger at a cop car and screams, "Measure the speed of this!" In another, labeled "Screaming Man Kills Significant Other," Jake is blowing a woman's head off her shoulders as he screams, "Codependent no more!"

Other people scream besides Jake, though. We see a skeleton, labeled "The Screaming Dead Man," wailing, "What was I saving all my money for?" We see Screaming Jesus on the Mount saying, "The Meek haven't got a prayer." I love this stuff—it strikes just the right nerve. I think I'll start screaming more.

LongRiver Books; $7.95
1994; softcover; 80 pp.

### ASSHOLE NO MORE:
#### A SELF-HELP GUIDE FOR RECOVERING ASSHOLES AND THEIR VICTIMS
#### by Xavier Crement, M.D.

At last, we have a book that recognizes the dreaded, universal syndrome of assholism. According to the book, it used to be that "compulsively rude treatment of others was viewed only as a character flaw, not an addiction over which the asshole has no real control. We believed that assholes were assholes because they didn't know any better." Now, however, Dr. X. Crement has officially recognized this condition and written a book for assholes who want to get better. (Of course, most assholes don't know they're assholes, so giving this book as a gift is encouraged.)

Crement gives us a history of assholism: "There have always been assholes. Now, there are more assholes than ever. This is all anyone needs to know about the history of assholism." He goes on to identify the varieties of assholes (three-piece assholes, holy assholes, New Age assholes, bureaucratic assholes, etc.), what happens when society becomes an asshole, living with assholes (working with assholes, when a friend is an asshole, adult children of asshole parents), and more.

Beware. If you buy this book for the fun of it, "you may discover you are an asshole and didn't know it. This is good.... Recognizing this gives you the chance to recover."

Ariel Press; $10.95
1990; softcover; 190 pp.

### ASSHOLES FOREVER:
#### HOW TO SPOT 'EM, HOW TO STOP 'EM
#### by Dr. Xavier Crement

In his groundbreaking book *Asshole No More*, Dr. Crement dared to expose assholism and offer help for assholes. But some people will always be assholes, and the rest of us are going to have to live with them. This book is for us.

The disclaimer for this book says it all: "If you are offended by this book, or any part of it, you are probably an asshole. If you want to stop being an asshole, please sign up for Dr. Crement's therapy. If you are comfortable being an asshole, please buy a few dozen copies of this book and pass them out to the few friends and acquaintances you have left. They will need it." Dr. Crement looks at all the tricks assholes use, such as whining, bullying, becoming a victim, and organizing into asshole groups. He also gives tips for what you can do to counter asshole techniques.

Like all true scientists, Dr. Crement calls it like he sees it, political correctness be damned. Among those targeted as assholes: the IRS, Dr. Jack Kevorkian, unrepentant Marxists, JFK conspiracy theorists, Carl Sagan, the NEA, the NRA, people who smoke, Arsenio Hall, Jehovah's Witnesses, "anyone who would rather save the life of a white rat than a human," rap singers who advocate killing, Greenpeace, and Congress. When Dr. Crement starts fingering assholes, no one is spared!

Ariel Press; $10.95
1992; softcover; 191 pp.

*The Duplex Planet*

*"What message would you send to outer space?"*

### THE DIRECTORY OF HUMOR MAGAZINES AND HUMOR ORGANIZATIONS IN AMERICA (AND CANADA)
#### (THIRD EDITION)

If you like to laugh, you're in luck. This book covers eighty-seven humor magazines/organizations, giving addresses, subscription/membership rates, and so on. They also run one-page excerpts from almost all the magazines. This book seems to be aimed mainly at libraries, since it also prints boatloads of information about each entry that you probably couldn't care less about—page size, printing method, binding, etc. There are also capsule entries for 116 more magazines/organizations, plus a writer's market guide to humor publications in case you think you're a really funny person.

Entries include the American Association for Therapeutic Humor, Capitol Comedy, Comedy Performers Association, HUMERUS, the Institute of Totally Useless Skills, International Banana Club, International Brotherhood of Old Bastards, *Journal of Nursing Jocularity*, The Marx Brotherhood, *Pun Intended, The Stark Fist of Removal*, etc. The only drawback (well, besides the price) is that this latest edition was published in 1992, so many entries are sadly out of date.

Wry-Bred Press, Inc; $34.95
1992; hardcover; 282 pp.

### THE DUPLEX PLANET

Surely one of the most prolific zines of all time (they're up to #130), *The Duplex Planet* consists of David B. Greenberger asking questions of old people and reprinting their responses. David travels to nursing homes and meal sites in New York and Massachusetts to find his participants. The answers they give him are by turns hilarious, cranky, nonsensical, touching, wise, or any combination thereof.

In issue #130 David asked, "What message would you send to outer space?" Some responses were: "JOHN CATRAMBONE: Stay out of trouble." "LEONA BELL: (WHISPERS) I need a good man!" "MARION KINNIN: Happy Day." Issue #129 had the question, "When getting into a swimming pool, do you test the water for a long time with your foot or jump right in?" "DAPHNE MATTHEWS: Well, you test the water with your foot first. It might be very cold. If you just dive right in you'll freeze your possibilities if it's cold." "VILJO LEHTO: Jump right in! Back in the twenties we didn't have no swimmin' pools, we'd just jump right in the creek. Naked, too."

*The Duplex Planet* has a quiet charm that's hard to describe. Somehow it manages to show the humanity of its interviewees without becoming patronizing. I'm just guessing, but I think people who have (or had) grandparents they're close to will get much more out of *The Duplex Planet*. I know it makes me miss mine.

The Duplex Planet
PO Box 1230/Saratoga Springs, NY 12866
Single issue: $2.50
Six-issue sub: $12. 15-issue sub: $25
Canadian subs: 5-issues: $12. 12-issues: $25
Overseas subs: 4 issues: $12. 10-issues: $25

## GETTING IN TOUCH WITH YOUR INNER BITCH
### by Elizabeth Hilts

Elizabeth Hilts is sounding the alarm—women, your days of Toxic Niceness are over. It's time to get in touch with your Inner Bitch. No more being doormats. No more giving second and third chances to guys who stand you up. No more being pushed around by bosses. The Inner Bitch stands up for herself. She's not mean and cruel, but she is firm and doesn't take any shit. "She is a part of ourselves that is smart, confident, dignified, and knows what she wants."

The main weapon in the Inner Bitch's arsenal is the simple phrase, "I don't think so." Here's an example of how to use this tactic: "The man you've been dating for a month demands in a fit of jealousy that you cancel a dinner meeting with an important client. Your response: 'I don't think so.'"

Hilts lists some icons of female power for you to use as role models: "Kara: The Valkyrie swan queen. Kara overwhelmed her enemies using only the sound of her voice. A bitch to be reckoned with, especially on the phone." "Lilith: Lilith was to be Adam's first wife, but she took one look at him and said, 'I don't think so.'"

Other chapters deal with the Inner Bitch and love, sex, food, work, daily life, politics, and more. At long last there's a self-help book that really can help you take charge of your life. And if your insecure husband or boyfriend forbids you to get this book, you know what to say. "I don't think so!"

*Hysteria*

*Feminism and humor are not mutually exclusive.*

Hysteria; $7.95
1994; softcover; 109 pp.

## HYSTERIA:
### WOMEN, HUMOR, AND SOCIAL CHANGE

There's an old joke that goes, "Q: How many feminists does it take to change a light bulb? A: That's not funny." Hysteria is here to prove that feminism and humor are not mutually exclusive. Number 6 is the "hair issue." Several articles describe the living hell that follicles can induce. Some of the steps in the "Twelve-Step Program for Bad Hair" include: "We admit that we are powerless over our hair—that our hair has become unmanageable, especially in humid weather.... We took a searching and fearless look at

our roots in bright sunlight." The steps end with the truism: "Remember, if we don't look good, we don't look good."

Other essays discuss how to get things fixed around the house when your husband "saunters off into the mist with a blonde he met in the Winn Dixie express checkout line," a woman's relationship with her cordless phone, the dangers of skinnydipping, the Zen of shopping at Kmart, being on the brink of menopause, "I Killed June Cleaver," and "PMS in a Pill."

No guy will understand this magazine, but I feel sure that every woman who reads it will be laughing and shaking her head in agreement.

Hysteria
PO Box 8581, Brewster Station/Bridgeport, CT 06605
Single issue: $4.95; foreign: $6.95
Four-issue sub: $18; foreign: $26

## THE JOURNAL OF POLYMORPHOUS PERVERSITY

OK, if you're in any aspect of the mental health field—psychology, psychiatry, social work, or teaching this stuff—you're gonna bust a gut laughing at this magazine. If you're not in the field, all you'll say is, "What's so damn funny?" *The JPP* is a parody of psychological journals. They run articles by respected members of the field who aren't afraid to laugh at themselves (and their patients) once in a while. You may run across an article on psychotherapy for the dead. Or maybe a proposal for new questions for the MMPI: "Sometimes I feel that things are real" and "I am easily awakened by the firing of cannons." You might read about "The Man Who Mistook His Wife for a Dishwasher." In "Sometimes No Heads Are Better Than One: Decapitated Programs for Mental Health Service Delivery," the authors propose a new treatment: "Unlike capitation, which sets limits on the dollar amounts allotted to treatment per patient, decapitation is a procedure resulting in the removal of the patient's head. While this may, on the face of it, appear to be a novel and radical form of cost containment, it finds ample historical precedent in the traditions of psychosurgery and insulin-coma therapy" (fall 1993 issue).

Wry-Bred Press, Inc
PO Box 1454, Madison Square Station/New York, NY 10159
Single issue: $7
One-year sub (2 issues): $14
Two-year sub (4 issues): $24

## THE REALIST

A true 1960s institution, Paul Krassner's *The Realist* made its comeback a few years ago as an eight-page newsletter. Since the beginning, the humor has been subversive and the satire acid. Krassner also reports on real stories, but as has been noted many times, he doesn't tell you what's real and what's humor, and—guess what?—it's often impossible to tell the difference! (which says something about the world we live in.) Issue #127 has articles on a urine-drinkers support group, a couple arrested for trying to ingest psychedelic toad venom, and a home for wayward clergy. *You* tell me which are real and which aren't.

Krassner plays fast and loose with libel and copyright laws with such bits as his ad for the Woody Allen movie "Honey, I Fucked the Kids" and his subverted *Peanuts* cartoon where Snoopy and cast discuss Met Life's practices. Of course, parody is supposed to be covered by the First Amendment, but since we're living in America: The Land of Litigation, I don't see how Krassner still has a shirt on his back. More power to him.

The Realist/PO Box 1230/Venice, CA 90294
Sample issue: $2
Six-issue sub: $12. 12-issue sub: $23

## SEX AS A HEAP OF MALFUNCTIONING RUBBLE:
### MORE OF THE BEST OF THE JOURNAL OF IRREPRODUCIBLE RESULTS
### edited by Marc Abrams

For almost forty years the *Journal of Irreproducible Results* has parodied scientific journals with articles written by actual scientists, doctors, psychologists, and other such life forms. The articles cover most scientific disciplines, including physics, astronomy, mathematics, sociology, psychology, biology, and medicine, as well as history and education. The complete contents of "A Briefer History of Time" is "BANG!" "The Mapletree Science Art Controversy" reprints four dirty scientific photos, like a sporozoan parasite that looks like a penis and two "dislocation pairs in silicon" (whatever that means) that look like a pair of breasts.

The uncertain future of one of nature's greatest creations is the subject of "Preserving the Grand Canyon: Final Report." Since the Grand Canyon is eroding, the author suggests a temporary solution of filling the canyon with those little foam pellets that are put in boxes during shipping. Other articles deal with the appearance of dimples on the rear ends of middle-aged women, infectious diseases in bricks, Abraham Lincoln's mustache, cats' reactions to men with beards, and the disturbing lack of arms on ancient Greek statues. If you like Stephen Hawking or *The Far Side*, this book's for you.

Workman Publishing; $9.95
1993; oversize softcover; 181 pp.

## TUNE IN TOMORROW
### by Tom Tomorrow

If you read the alternative press, especially the more leftist, progressive publications, you may be sick to death of *This Modern World*. Its overexposure (which I am helping to perpetuate) doesn't change the fact that it's a great cartoon. With its flatly drawn characters and often surrealistic backgrounds, *This Modern World* offers some of the most insightful and right-on-target social and political criticism you can get. Its politics are usually unabashedly liberal, but it isn't afraid to bash Democrats, Clinton, and the media (which is always referred to as "liberal" by conservatives but really isn't).

This collection of about a hundred strips turns its acid-tongued fury on the shallow and sensationalistic news media, corporations that manipulate us, politicians who lie, cyberculture, stupid trends, guns, tobacco, Rush Limbaugh, the war against TV and movie violence, and, of course, the sheer idiocy and complacency of most Americans.

St. Martin's Press; $8.95
1994; softcover; 120 pp.; lavishly illus.

## WEENIE-TOONS!:
### WOMEN CARTOONISTS MOCK COCKS
### edited by Roz Warren

A collection of about forty cartoons and comic strips that poke fun at that most sensitive area of male anatomy. Lynda Barry, Alison Bechdel, and Diane Dimassa are among those who give penises a pounding. I'm just guessing, but I think you have to be a woman to get the full effect of these cartoons. Some are right on target, some are just male-bashing, and some I just don't get, like the drawing of a somewhat deranged-looking woman saying, "Everything is phallic!!!" But I guess it's like the back cover says, "If you've ever laughed at a penis—This is the book for you!"

Laugh Lines Press; $4.50
1992; softcover booklet; 40 pp.

# POSTMODERN FOLKLORE

## THE BABY TRAIN:
### AND OTHER LUSTY URBAN LEGENDS
### by Jan Harold Brunvand

An urban legend is an event that is told to you as if it were true but 99.9 percent of the time it's not. The person telling it usually swears that it happened to a "friend of a friend" (abbreviated FOAF), such as my best friend's girlfriend's mom's dentist. But even if it didn't happen to a FOAF, it's often said to have happened in the city where the teller resides. However, any attempt to track down the supposed event meets a dead end.

An example of such a legend is the "broiled again" story, which I really like because it was told to me by two people who swore up and down it actually happened in our city. This high school girl was going to the prom the following evening, and she wanted a tan fast. Since tanning bed facilities have a time limit on how long you can stay in, she visited six in one day and ended up cooking her insides.

Jan Harold Brunvand is the undisputed king of urban legends. He has written five books on the subject so far, including *The Vanishing Hitchhiker* and *Curses! Broiled Again!*, which contained the above legend. In his fifth book, *The Baby Train*, he continues to relate and expose urban legends. The title refers to the story about this dorm for married people (in some versions it's a small town) that is right beside railroad tracks. The dorm has an extremely high birth rate. It turns out that every morning at 5:00 a train rolls by and wakes up everybody. Being too early to get up but too late to go back to sleep, they spend the time having sex.

A very popular legend, which I have also had told to me as if it were true, is related by the author. A woman is heard screaming for help in her apartment. Neighbors burst in to find her tied naked to the bed and her husband in a Batman outfit unconscious on the floor. They were playing sex games, and when the husband attempted to jump from the dresser to the bed, he slipped and knocked himself out. Variations of this story, which have popped up all over the country, have the husband dressed as Spiderman, Superman, or some other superhero.

Almost as entertaining as the more than seventy legends themselves is the detective work Brunvand does to get to the bottom of things. He has shone the glaring light of truth on countless supposedly true stories. He has also found germs of truth in a few, and on the rarest of occasions, a story that sounds as if it should be an urban legend turns out really to have happened. *The Baby Train* and all of Brunvand's other books are well worth seeking out.

Norton; $20.95
1993; hardcover; 367 pp.

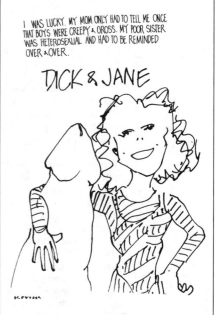

*Weenie-Toons!*
**edited by Roz Warren**
◄

*Not exactly a Girl's best friend.*

## THE BIG BOOK OF URBAN LEGENDS
### adapted from the books of Jan Harold Brunvand

This entertaining anthology collects urban legends rendered in comic form. Each of the two hundred one-page tales is by a different artist, most of whom have done work for Marvel, DC, Dark Horse, Fantagraphics, other independents, *The Ren and Stimpy Show*, *Village Voice*, *Outlaw Biker*, etc. The god of urban legends, Jan Harold Brunvand, provides an introduction and commentary at the beginning of each chapter.

All of your faves are here—the exploding toilet, the kidney thieves, the couple who get stuck while screwing in a car, the woman who purposely spreads AIDS, the finger-chopping ring thief, the bloody hook, the killer in the backseat, the vanishing hitchhiker, the experimental car that accidentally gets sold, the corpse in the hotel bed, the snake in the stomach, alligators in the sewers, the dead baby-sitter, the accidental cannibals, the Kentucky fried rat, and scads of other groovy, gruesome stories that *really* are true. I swear.

The art is top-notch, and the writing is pretty good. The problem is that since each tale is told in one page, the story line is skin and bones. For a fuller understanding, you'll want to read Brunvand's books, but this book is perfect for people who want an intro to urban legends or for us legend-mongers who want to see a new spin put on these familiar tales.

Paradox Press (DC Comics); $12.95
1994; oversize softcover; 223 pp; heavily illus.

## CRACKING JOKES:
### STUDIES OF SICK HUMOR CYCLES AND STEREOTYPES
### by Alan Dundes

Alan Dundes, one of America's foremost folklorists, has spent much of his time studying jokelore. This book collects thirteen of his articles dealing with offensive, sick, and politically incorrect joke cycles, including dead baby jokes, Jewish American Princess jokes, Auschwitz jokes, Polish Pope jokes, light bulb jokes, and the infamous reasons why cucumbers are better than men and sheep are better than women. Dundes has gotten in hot water for merely studying these jokes, but he defends his position by saying, "People only joke about what is most serious."

Dundes notes that the dead baby jokes had their heyday during the years when abortion became legal and the Pill was invented. Perhaps dead baby jokes were a way of expressing anxiety over such events. Many of the jokes do equate babies with garbage: "What's red and goes round and round? A baby in a garbage disposal."

Dundes also looks at elephant jokes, which are often sexual. For example, "Why does an elephant have four feet? It's better than six inches." "How do you tell if a woman has been raped by an elephant? She's pregnant for two years." Elephants, the author feels, may represent the white stereotypical conception of African-American males. The whispered-about consensus among whites is that Black men are hung like horses (or should I say elephants?), extraordinarily virile, sexually promiscuous, and prone toward rape. Elephant jokes came onto the scene during the civil rights movement of the 1960s. Dundes says, "The elephant may be seen as a reflection of the American black as the white sees him, and that blacks' political and social assertion has caused certain primal fears to be reactivated."

Even if Dundes's theories seem a little farfetched, he still does a great job cataloging these classic jokes. He also earns points for being unafraid to deal with even the most controversial forms of humor.

Ten Speed Press; $9.95
1987; softcover; 198 pp.

## FOAFTALE NEWS

This is the newsletter for the International Society for Contemporary Legend Research. Each issue looks at the latest urban legends, rumors, and jokelore making the rounds. Past issues have dealt with Elvis, green M&Ms, ankle slashers, Mongolian urban legends, AIDS, apocalyptic rumors, lawn ornament abductions, campus massacres, mall slashers, Desert Storm, sex in the SkyDome, snuff films, and more exciting topics. Issue #30 related several different versions of the urban legend wherein a vacationing couple return to their hotel room to find everything stolen except a toothbrush and their camera. When they develop the film days later, there is a picture of the burglar's butt with the toothbrush sticking out his anus. There's also Hurricane Andrew rumors, including one that says thousands of AIDS-infected monkeys escaped from a Florida medical research facility and are roaming the streets. In Chonqing, China, a rumor surfaced that a "'robot-zombie manufactured in America' had gone out of control in the city, and it was tracking down children dressed in

red clothing. The rumor, which had caused a full-fledged panic among both children and parents, alleged that several children had already been devoured."

Each issue also contains reviews and listings of other items of interest. The breadth of items listed is staggering—books, monographs, newsletters, videos, and articles from magazines and journals. Some of these sources are so obscure that you would never in a million years find them on your own. This feature alone is worth the cost.

The Society also publishes *Contemporary Legend,* a journal of scholarly articles. Joining for a year gets you one issue of this journal plus four issues of *FOAFtale News.*

International Society for Contemporary Legend Research/Paul Smith/Dept. of Folklore/Memorial University/St. John's, Newfoundland A1C 5S7/CANADA
One-year membership: $18; Canada: £10 (make out checks to ISCLR)
Single issue of *FOAFtale News:* $2.50 from Bill Ellis/Penn State/Hazleton Campus/Hazleton, PA 18201 (checks payable to ISCLR)

## I HEARD IT THROUGH THE GRAPEVINE:
### RUMOR IN AFRICAN-AMERICAN CULTURE
### by Patricia A. Turner

Some of the best-known, far-reaching rumors are spread among African-Americans. The author examines these rumors, which often show up at different times about different individuals, products, businesses, etc., and what their existence tells us about African-American fears and concerns. Some of the rumors covered include the following:

1) The rumor that the KKK owns Church's Fried Chicken and puts an ingredient in the food that makes African-American men sterile. This rumor has recently resurfaced but this time the sterilizer is alleged to be in Tropical Fantasy soft drinks.

2) The rumor that the Klan produces Troop, a brand of athletic clothes very popular among African-Americans.

3) The rumor that the FBI or CIA, perhaps with the help of the KKK, was responsible for the Atlanta Child Murders. The bodies were then taken to the Centers for Disease Control for medical experimentation.

4) The rumors that white supremacist groups played roles in the assassinations of JFK and Martin Luther King Jr.

5) The rumor that Reebok is owned by South Africans.

6) The rumor that AIDS was created by the government to wipe out the Black population.

7) The rumor that the U.S. government feeds crack, and sometimes guns, into poor urban areas to keep the African-American population drugged up and homicidal.

The author examines the precursors and variants of these legends. She theorizes that these rumors exist as a reaction to the racism and oppression African-Americans experience. The animosity felt toward all Blacks is translated to individual attacks on African-American bodies through a sterilizing agent, AIDS, and so on.

*I Heard It Through the Grapevine* is a much-needed study of an aspect of postmodern folklore that has not yet been given the attention it deserves.

University of California Press; $25
1993; hardcover; 260 pp.

## PILED HIGHER AND DEEPER:
### THE FOLKLORE OF CAMPUS LIFE
### by Simon J. Bronner

Universities are a whole other world. They are self-enclosed societies with their own governments, newspapers, rules, institutions, infrastructures, alliances, and rivalries. They also have their own folklore. This book examines the legends, beliefs, games, customs, slang, etc. from America's colleges. Probably the one piece of folklore that is common to almost every university is the legend that if a virgin graduates, the statue of the school's mascot/founder will come to life. So far, no university's statue has ever moved....

Many campuses also have ghost legends. "At Georgia College a woman who hanged herself in Sanford Hall is blamed for spooky lights appearing on the vacant third floor, sounds of footsteps, and warm spots in the east wing. At Coe College, a freshwoman dying of pneumonia—'Helen' as she's called—is the guilty ghost. She hangs around a grandfather clock donated to the college in her memory and kept in the drawing room of her dormitory. According to legend, Helen would appear once a year at midnight in the old clock."

Testing is an integral and rotten part of higher education, so it has spawned lots of folklore. Legend tells of a student who was obviously cheating. When he walked up to the front of the classroom to turn his test in, before his professor could stop him, he shoved his paper in the middle of all those already turned in. "Do you know who I am?" the student asks. The prof says no. The student runs out of the room. Since the professor can't identify his paper, the student ends up with a good grade.

If you went to college, you have to get this book. It had me misty-eyed for the good ol' days when my biggest worry in life was if I had memorized the new French vocabulary list. Incidentally, the title is a reference to the joke: "What do B.S., M.S., and Ph.D. stand for? BullShit and More Shit, Piled Higher and Deeper."

August House; $9.95
1990; softcover; 256 pp.

## RUMOR HAS IT:
### A CURIO OF LIES, HOAXES, AND HEARSAY
### by Bob Tamarkin

This book presents about a hundred rumors and hoaxes in one- to two-page sections. Topics include the media, politics, the military, food, death, sex, and the supernatural. I just love reading this kind of stuff, so let me share some goodies with you. In January 1992 CNN came within one second of reporting that President Bush had died. A few hours after Bush had puked on the prime minister during his trip to Japan, a man in Idaho called CNN claiming to be Bush's doctor and said that Bush had gone to the Big Iran/Contra Hearing in the Sky. Somehow this information got into CNN's central computer, and anchor Don Harrison was just beginning to report it when a supervisor yelled "Stop!" See how easy it is to hoax the media?

One strange rumor that turns out to be true concerns a phone sex operator named Raven. This comely wench was so good at giving phone that she received love letters, marriage proposals, and twenty-six calls in one day from the same man. It turns out that Raven is an ex-marine and father of four.

In a brilliant prank/hoax someone placed help-wanted ads in major newspapers across the country in 1988. The number given in the ads was the toll-free number of Michael Dukakis's campaign drive. Dukakis's staff was flooded with calls from job-seekers, and after losing an untold amount of money, they were forced to disconnect the number.

The author also relates many famous rumors concerning Paul McCartney (see below), Elvis, Procter & Gamble, Coca-Cola, UFOs, subliminal messages, Hitler's diaries, *The Education of Little Tree*, etc. There are no attempts to delve into the sociology of rumors—how and why they happen, what they tell us about ourselves. Nevertheless, this collection makes for fascinating reading.

Prentice-Hall (Simon & Schuster); $14
1993; softcover; 277 pp.

## TURN ME ON, DEAD MAN:
### THE COMPLETE STORY OF THE
### PAUL MCCARTNEY DEATH HOAX
### by Andru J. Reeve

You whippersnappers may not be aware of it, but in 1969 one of the greatest—maybe the greatest—rock and roll rumors gripped society. It was claimed that Paul McCartney had died in 1966, and not wanting to risk their fame, the Beatles kept a lid on the event and replaced Paul with a look-alike. They constantly dropped hints about this on their album covers, lyrics, and elsewhere. The author looks at this extremely popular rumor—where and how it started and spread, why so many people believed it,

what the clues were, and whether the Beatles themselves had anything to do with it.

The book gives an almost-hour-by-hour account of the four weeks when Paul-Is-Dead mania gripped the United States. The most interesting parts of the book, though, reveal the clues that the Beatles were allegedly leaking. Seventy clues are listed and commented on in an appendix, and many appear in the main text of the book. The richest piece of "evidence" is the cover of *Abbey Road*, a classic photograph that shows the Beatles walking single-file across Abbey Road. This is interpreted as Paul's funeral procession. John Lennon, in a white suit and long hair and beard, is seen as a minister (or a Christ figure); Ringo Starr, in a dark suit, is seen as the undertaker; George Harrison, in denim workclothes, is seen as the gravedigger. Paul is in a suit but wearing no shoes, which is how corpses are buried in some countries. All the other Beatles are stepping forward with their left feet, but Paul is stepping forward with his right, indicating that he is different. He is holding a cigarette in his right hand but the real Paul is left-handed. His eyes are closed, again very corpselike.

There are also allegedly hidden messages on the group's recordings. In "Revolution 9" from the *White Album*, a man repeats the phrase "Number nine." If you play these parts backward they say, "Turn me on, dead man" over and over. The author reports that this is indeed true, but it could be an aural coincidence. Also, playing the end of "I Am the Walrus" backward yields, "Ha, ha, Paul is dead." Again, the author says that this is true. The most famous musical clue can be heard forward in the coda of "Strawberry Fields Forever." John's distorted voice says, "I buried Paul." Although it sure sounds that way to me, the author assures us that on bootleg versions the voice is much clearer and can be heard saying, "Cranberry sauce."

I'm glad to see a whole book devoted to this mother of all rock and roll rumors. It's a unique source of information for all postmodern folklorists and Beatlemaniacs (or both, like me). It is marketed as a library book, though, so it comes with a hefty price tag.

Popular Culture, Ink; $40
1994; hardcover; 218 pp.

## "THE WALRUS WAS PAUL":
### THE GREAT BEATLE DEATH CLUES OF 1969
### by R. Gary Patterson

I know reviewing two books on the Paul McCartney death rumor may seem like overkill, but I found this book after I had already reviewed *Turn Me on, Dead Man*. I had to include this book, because not only is it better than the other one, it only costs half as much.

"The Walrus Was Paul" doesn't spend much time chronicling the outbreak of the rumor, which *Dead Man* does in detail. Instead, it goes album by album, revealing all the clues on the covers, in the inner artwork, in the lyrics, hidden backward in the songs, and anywhere else they might turn up. The author includes lots of quotes from the Beatles and insiders on the specific clues and the rumor in general. He also looks throughout the book at the specific scenario of Paul's "death"—dying in an early morning car crash in November 1966—to see how plausible it is.

Death clue detectives weren't the only people putting unusual interpretations on the Beatles music, though. Charles Manson "believed that the Beatles were actually angels sent by God to reveal the secrets of the terrible approaching apocalypse."

*The Walrus Was Paul* ▼
by R. Gary Patterson

*"...the Beatles were actually angels sent by God to reveal the secrets of the terrible approaching apocalypse."*

-Or not.

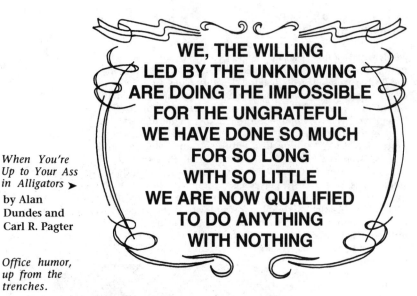

WE, THE WILLING
LED BY THE UNKNOWING
ARE DOING THE IMPOSSIBLE
FOR THE UNGRATEFUL
WE HAVE DONE SO MUCH
FOR SO LONG
WITH SO LITTLE
WE ARE NOW QUALIFIED
TO DO ANYTHING
WITH NOTHING

*When You're
Up to Your Ass
in Alligators* ➤
by Alan
Dundes and
Carl R. Pagter

*Office humor,
up from the
trenches.*

The experimental "Revolution 9" was believed by the Manson family to be the sounds of the apocalypse itself. "Helter Skelter" was seen as referring to the race war Manson thought was imminent. "In 'Don't Pass Me By,' 'Blue Jay Way,' and 'Yer Blues,' the Beatles constantly mention waiting for someone to 'arrive.' Charles Manson took this to be himself, the incarnation of Jesus Christ...." And you thought *you* came up with weird interpretations of your favorite songs.

A center photo section contains reproductions of album covers and other artwork said to contain clues.

Excursion Productions; $19.95
1994; softcover; 162 pp.; illus.

## WORK HARD AND YOU SHALL BE REWARDED:
### URBAN FOLKLORE FROM THE PAPERWORK EMPIRE
### by Alan Dundes and Carl R. Pagter

You know all those fake memos, funny hand-drawn cartoons, made-up aptitude tests, and other stuff that gets passed around your office? Well, two folklorists have collected the best of it (from the late 1960s and early 1970s) and published it in this book.

You'll laugh till you cry. I love "The Twelve Days of Christmas." It's a series of letters written by a woman whose sweetheart is sending her all the gifts mentioned in the ever-popular, repetitious-to-the-point-of-tears Christmas song we were forced to sing in grade school. The letters start off with sincere thanks, but by the seventh day this is her reaction: "Hunter: What's with you and those fucking birds??? Seven swans a-swimming. What kind of God-damned joke is this? There's bird shit all over the floor and I'm a nervous wreck, it's not funny. So stop with those fucking birds. Sincerely, Agnes." On the tenth day: "You rotten prick: Now there's ten ladies dancing. I don't know why I call those sluts ladies. They've been balling those pipers all night long. Now the cows can't sleep and they've got diarrhea. My living room is a river of shit.... Your sworn enemy, Agnes."

The New Sick Leave Policy is a fake memo expressing the policy that employers would adopt if they could get away with it: "DEATHS (Other than your own)... This is no excuse. There is nothing you can do for them, and we are sure that someone with a lesser position can attend to the arrangements.... DEATH (your own)... This will be accepted as an excuse, but we would like a two-weeks notice as we feel it is your duty to train someone else for the job."

There's also a drawing of Lucy from *Peanuts,* obviously pregnant, screaming "God damn you, Charlie Brown!"

Wayne State University Press; $14.95
1975; softcover; 223 pp.

## WHEN YOU'RE UP TO YOUR ASS IN ALLIGATORS...:
### MORE URBAN FOLKLORE FROM THE PAPERWORK EMPIRE
### by Alan Dundes and Carl R. Pagter

More office humor. This book has much more variety and more visuals than its predecessor, *Work Hard and You Shall Be Rewarded.* Pieces that are printed include "Ode to the Four-Letter Word," "How Do You Keep a Polack Occupied for a Year?" "Rejection Letter from *Playgirl,*" "Thimk, Plan Ahead, and Acurracy," "How to Write Good," "Church Bulletin Misprints," "How You Can Tell When It's Going to Be a Rotten Day," "Simplified 1040," and more than one hundred others. From "How to Write Good": "Subject and verb always has to agree. Prepositions should not be used to end a sentence with. Avoid clichés like the plague. Do not use hyperbole; not one writer in a million can use it effectively."

Wayne State University Press; $15.95
1987; softcover; 271 pp.

# LANGUAGE

## CURSING IN AMERICA
### by Timothy Jay

A psychological/linguistic study of foul language. But wait, it's not as boring as it sounds, although it does bog down here and there. Jay manages to keep things interesting and understandable, even though most academics would attempt to make this topic as sterile as possible.

In looking at the studies on frequency of use, the author finds that males swear more than females (big surprise), but both sexes do it more when around people of the same sex. *Fuck* and *damn* are the two most popular words. A 1978 study on the offensiveness of words and actions yielded strange results. Subjects were asked to rate certain words and acts on a ten-point scale as to how offensive they are to society. The word *motherfucker* was rated as being slightly more offensive than witnessing extreme violence. *Cockteaser* was more offensive than watching someone taking a dump. Strange.

The author explores many other avenues, including classification of profanity, children's use of profanity, the role of anger in cursing, free speech and censorship, and cursing in the movies. There's also a twenty-seven-page bibliography.

I'd have to recommend this fucking book only to those with a serious goddamn interest in cursing. If you're just looking for a funny-ass book full of bad words, go screw yourself, 'cause this ain't it, dipshit.

John Benjamins North America, Inc; $14.95
1992; softcover; 273 pp.

## JUBA TO JIVE:
### A DICTIONARY OF AFRICAN-AMERICAN SLANG
### edited by Clarence Major

A massive compilation of slang used by African-Americans from the days of (official) slavery up to today. The thousands of words and phrases covered include Anglo-American slang (slang originated by whites but adopted and altered by African-Americans), drug culture slang, pimp and prostitute slang, southern slang, jazz and blues slang, prison slang, youth culture slang, etc. The entries include definitions, times of usage, changes in usage, example sentences, and more.

This book is a browser's delight. "Deuce of haircuts," from the 1930s and '40s, means "two weeks." A "Devil's dick" is a crack pipe. "Fugley": "absolutely unattractive. Derived from 'fucking ugly'.... Example: 'I don't care how many generations it was handed down through, you won't catch me dead or alive in this fugley wedding dress.'" A "snag" is an ugly woman. "Un-ass" means "to give up something.... 'Hey, Betty, un-ass my scarf! You can't wear it!'#"

Penguin Books; $14.95
1994; softcover; 548 pp.

## SNAPS
### by James Percelay, Monteria Ivey, and Stephan Dweck

Snaps is the African-American art of verbal warfare. Also known as caps, signifying, or playing the dozens, it involves insulting your target in the most clever, humorous way possible. This book contains more than 450 snaps. Some of them are unbelievably lame, but others will have you rolling on the floor laughing. They're divided into seventeen sections, such as Fat Snaps: "Your mother is so fat, she uses a VCR for a beeper"; Ugly Snaps: "Your mother is so ugly, when she walks into a bank, they turn off the cameras"; House Snaps: "Your apartment is so small, the roaches are hunchbacks"; and Sex Snaps: "I heard you were getting sex all the time until your wrist got arthritis."

*Snaps* contains a foreword by Quincy Jones, a history of the dozens, and a guide to mastering the dozens. You should get this book, but I know you won't because you're so dumb, you dialed information to get the number for 911.

Quill (William Morrow & Co.); $8.95
1994; softcover; 175 pp.

## TALKING DIRTY:
### A Bawdy Compendium of Colorful Language, Humorous Insults and Wicked Jokes
### edited by Rheinhold Aman

For twenty-eight years, Dr. Rheinhold Aman has studied curse words, blasphemies, slurs, epithets, insults, offensive jokes, and the words for bodily functions, bodily parts, and sexual acts. "Every day around the world, tens of thousands of people are humiliated, fired, fined, jailed, injured, killed, or driven to suicide because of *maledicta*...Maledicta ('bad words' in Latin) cover a broad spectrum of language traditionally avoided in public by prudish professors, prim word-popes, and other properlings who none the less use many such words in private. The opposite of prayer and praise, *maledicta* are the black sheep of language that most people use but few talk or write about." If Aman sounds angry, that's because he is. He was forced to leave academia to pursue his study of foul language independently. It seems that although such language is among the most commonly used on earth and plays such an important role, the academic establishment doesn't think it's an appropriate matter for study. They would rather ponder the earth-shattering importance of how the phoneme /de/ was used in Hittite.

Aman started up his own journal, *Maledicta*, to study bad language. *Talking Dirty* collects some of the best material from this fearless publication. One article examines graffiti that alter well-known proverbs. Some examples: "A friend with weed is a friend indeed," "The best things in life are freaky," "Chastity is its own punishment," "Practice makes pervert," "Chaste makes waste," and "An orgasm in the bush is worth two in the hand." "The Poetry of Porking" lists more than 350 phrases for having sex.

One very enlightening article examines the slang medical personnel use to refer to patients. "POS" is an acronym for piece of shit: "A general term for patients medically ill because of their own failure to take care of themselves (most often alcoholics)." A "SHPOS" is a subhuman piece of shit: "A critically ill patient who, after intensive medical care and rehabilitation, fails to follow medical instructions, and is readmitted to the hospital in his previous critical condition." A "fruit salad" is a group of stroke patients. And the "International House of Pancakes" is "a neurology ward occupied by patients, often stroke victims, all of whom babble in different languages."

The dozens of other articles cover condom brand names, Italian blasphemies, euphemisms for farting, obscene Greek hand gestures, ethnic slurs, Japanese sexual maledicta, light bulb jokes, the uses of the word *shit*, ageist language, genital pet names, Iranian insults, and much more.

Carroll & Graf; $11.95
1993; softcover; 213 pp.

## COOKBOOKS

## BUCK PETERSON'S INTERNATIONAL ROAD KILL COOKBOOK
### by B.R. "Buck" Peterson

A partially tongue-in-cheek guide to living off the land. More specifically, it's about dining on road kill. Peterson's first road kill cookbook was a general introduction to the subject; this one takes a global view of the situation. The author runs down the basics of both road kill and international travel before launching into a worldwide tour of smooshed cuisine.

The tour takes us through North and South America, Asia, Europe, Oceania, Africa, and elsewhere. Recipes include Yukon Smack, Mesquite Grilled Leg of Coyote with Peyote Buttons, Björn Burger, Hungarian Gruelash, Chicken Peeloff, Chow Chow Mein, and other yummy dishes. *Bon appetit!*

Ten Speed Press; $5.95
1994; softcover; 107 pp.

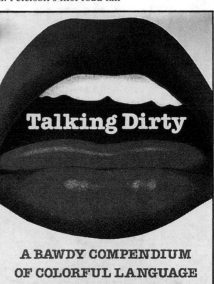

## EDIBLE FLOWERS:
### From Garden to Palate
### by Cathy Wilkinson Barash

A cookbook for making up some mean dishes using wild and domestic flowers. Cool. Now, I have to express a little disappointment in a few of the flowers that are used in this book. Some of them are not at all exotic or unusual as far as cooking goes. Chives, mint, basil, broccoli, and peas don't count as flowers in my book, and you can find a trillion cookbooks with recipes for those run-of-the-mill plants. But where the book proves its worth is in its recipes involving pansies, roses, chrysanthemums, dandelions, honeysuckle, lilacs, sunflowers, tulips, violets, and other flowers that you don't encounter in your everyday meals. You'll find recipes for pansy ravioli, rose petal sauce, potato marigold salad, dandelion wine, lilac chicken, tulip tuna, chocolate violet cake, and many, many more floral dishes.

The book itself is a first-class publication. It's printed on heavy paper, illustrated in full color. The recipes are clear, and information on the flowers is straightforward. Not being much of a cook and not being gastronomically adventurous, I can't vouch for the tastiness of the recipes, but if you're the daring type, by all means, start munching those daisies.

Fulcrum Publishing; $29.95
1993; oversize hardcover; 250 pp.

*Talking Dirty*
**edited by Rheinhold Aman**
◄

*"Every day around the world, tens of thousands of people are humiliated, fired, fined, jailed, injured, killed, or driven to suicide because of @&%#!"*

## RECIPES FOR DISASTER:
### Dinner at the Illustration Gallery
### edited by Pam Sommers

Pam Sommers owns the Illustration Gallery in New York, the only gallery devoted to the work of cutting-edge illustrators. She put out a call to her illustrator and cartoonist acquaintances for contributions to a cookbook. They could send recipes for anything they wanted, but of course it had to be done in illustration format.

In the resulting eighty-four pieces, the types of recipes vary as wildly as the styles of illustration. About half the artists turned in real recipes. Michael Bartalos offers two exotic drinks from Thailand, and David McLimans's chaotic neocubist illustration gives the recipe for Last Gasp Cookies. Other artists chose to be more conceptual. The ingredients in Melinda Beck's recipe for

Manhattan are "367,867,100 pounds of concrete, juice of discarded gum, a dash of rusty water, 56 1/2 unclaimed body parts, garnished with a rat's head." Paul Corio's directions for Squandered Youth are as follows: "Put on suit. Mix girls, drinks, smokes, pharmaceuticals, and dice. Add aspirin as necessary. Let simmer for fifteen years. Look back regretfully."

Chronicle Books; $9.95
1993; oversize softcover; 96 pp.

# MISCELLANEOUS

## ANGRY WOMEN
### (RE/SEARCH #13)

A collection of interviews with sixteen contrary women, including pomo novelist Kathy Acker, Susie "Sexpert" Bright, poets Wanda Coleman and Sapphire, performance artists Karen Finley and Carolee Schneeman, singer Diamanda Galás, theorist Avital Ronell, and sex-positive performer Annie Sprinkle. These anti-authoritarian bad girls sound off about sexism, racism, homophobia, and power structures designed to keep people down. They advocate the healing power of sex and promote a positive view of porn.

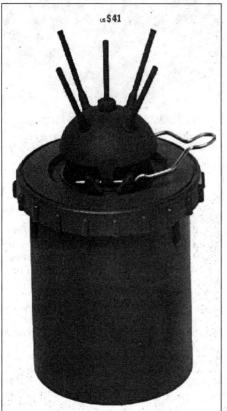

us$41

Susie Bright says, "I see that in every culture, whatever is horrifying, whatever is beyond sane social comprehension—all that is considered 'taboo' gets *eroticized*. In this country it's black-white relations, incest and rape—everything that is beyond 'typical' understanding. Any taboo subject is often a well of sexual dynamite." Commenting on society's pressures on women, Sapphire says, "When you take an individual like Twiggy and hold her up as an ideal, you're holding up death. This is not what it is to be a woman, and to hold that up for people who can never be that is to hold up hate!" Avital Ronell manages to sum up the entire book in a few words: "I believe in making trouble—if women have any *duty* at all, essentially it's to be a pain in the ass!"

RE/Search Publications; $18.99
1991; oversize softcover; 240 pp.

*Colors* ➤

*Coming soon to the Home Shopping Network.*

## CATALOG OF FOLK FLUTES, PANPIPES, AND BOOKS

A stunning array of flutes used by indigenous peoples around the world, hand-carved by Lew Paxton Price. You can get panpipes, Middle Eastern nays, Japanese shakuhachi, Keltic fifes, East Indian flutes, Chinese Ti, North and South American Indian flutes, the finger flute, and several of Price's own creations, such as the Pricepipe and the Whole Earth Forest Flute. For each type of flute, there are often several styles, colors, and musical ranges available.

Along with the detailed catalog, you get the informative *Little Book of Folk Flutes and Panpipes*, written by Price.

Lew Price/PO Box 88(K)/Garden Valley CA 95633
Catalog: $3

## COLORS:
### A MAGAZINE ABOUT THE REST OF THE WORLD

I realize I could lose my street credibility by reviewing a corporate-backed magazine, but *COLORS* is a great publication. It's informative, entertaining, smart-assed, funny, socially conscious without being sanctimonious, and gorgeous to behold. I regret that it took me so long to take a look at it. I stayed away for a long time because I had read that it was underwritten by the clothing giant, Benetton. I naturally assumed that *COLORS* was a superficial corporate rag, a thin excuse to sell sweaters. Was I ever wrong. Although I realize that in the end, Benetton does hope that this mag will move a few extra clothes, *COLORS* is quite risky. Like Benetton's controversial ads, it isn't afraid to take chances and call things like it sees them. Plus, because it has a sugar daddy, *COLORS* has very high production values, just three or four ads per issue, and it only costs $3 on the newsstand.

The "Religion Issue" (#8) is a masterpiece. Amid the glorious full-color images of snake handlers, thousands of bowing Muslims, a Mexican Catholic altar, a psychic surgeon, a Pope John Paul II bottle opener, a Russian monk, a vodoun man, a Hindu mystic with hooks in his flesh, and the Sons of God motorcycle gang, are pithy, sarcastic articles on religious hairstyles, symbols, food, clothing, miracles, cults, and Jerusalem. A giant four-page foldout chart compares sixteen individuals who are allegedly God, including Zoroaster, Jesus, Rabbi Schneerson, Reverend Moon, and David Koresh. The headline asks: "Looking for God? Choose from 16 top-selling models." Another article examines the undergarments of priests and nuns.

The "Shopping Issue" (#9) contains big color photos, prices, and descriptions of one hundred unusual, common, and/or illegal products from all over the world, including an island, a solar-powered lawnmower, a grenade, chimpanzees, a cut-rate handgun, a dog wheelchair, a purse made out of a kangaroo's scrotum, a human kidney, Snot candy, used panties, a penis enlarger, skin-whitening cream, heroin, mines, a guinea pig coffin, an abortion tool, an at-home cloning kit (I'm serious), designer water, Death Cigarettes,™ and lots of other goodies you're not likely to find at your local Wal-Mart.

Every issue contains a section in the back giving addresses and phone numbers of places that sell the (legal) items that *COLORS* writes about.

*COLORS* is bilingual, so when you order be sure to choose which language you want. One will always be English, but the other can be French, German, Italian, or Spanish.

COLORS subscriptions
Via de Ripetta, 142/Roma 00186 Italia
Single issue: $7 (available for $3 at bookstores and Benetton stores); One-year sub (4 issues): $10

## COSMIC TRIGGER, VOLUME II: DOWN TO EARTH
### by Robert Anton Wilson

This book contains about ninety short essays by Wilson covering a huge range of areas and ideas. If you've never read Wilson, this is a good a place as any to start. His main aim is to break you out of the reality tunnels you've been locked into. He wants you to reprogram your reality software. Above all, he wants you to think for your damn self! As RAW himself puts it: "What I have been saying—the important lesson of this book—can be put into two simple imperatives: 1) Never believe *totally* in anybody else's BS. 2) Never believe *totally* in your own BS." With wit, humor, cynicism, irreverence, and a total disrespect for authority, Wilson gives you clues to breaking the chains that bind you. Among the kajillions of subjects he talks about are his murdered daughter, Zen koans, the Knights of Malta, racism, God, Trotskyism, Reichian therapy, marijuana, techno-zen, and "anal-eroticism in the White House."

When you enter Wilson's world, check your reality at the door. (If you're smart, you won't pick it up again when you leave.)

New Falcon Publications; $12.95
1991; softcover; 255 pp.

## CRIP ZEN:
### A MANUAL FOR SURVIVAL
### by Lorenzo Wilson Milam

An in-your-face, politically incorrect, this-is-how-it-is guide to being disabled. Milam discusses sex, masturbation, drugs, anger, suicide, insanity, love, and hope.

On the subject of suicide, the author says, "Far be it from me to tell you not to investigate, at the very least, the options for dying. After all, what could be less dignified than the years you have faced, will continue to face in such joylessness, all the hope squeezed out of the tube—the tube itself twisted and empty? There are methods of getting out and doing it well."

About the underprescription of pain medication: "They want us to suffer with our aches. When I call my doctor for another prescription for analgesics, the messages tend to get lost. When I finally do get through, you can hear the edge in his voice. He'll write one prescription (a small one), charge $45 for it, and won't honor any further requests unless I can show a broken leg, the Yaws, or imminent death. In other words—in America (land of the free) it is immoral to avoid pain for a lifetime. We're all John Waynes, right?"

The author ends by revealing four methods that can help you cope by quieting your mind, escaping your body, and untangling the self. The methods are meditation, self-hypnosis, astral projection, and dream work.

As you can tell, this ain't a happy little "make lemonade out of lemons" manual. It's no-bullshit advice on how to attempt to cope with an intolerable situation by whatever means are necessary.

Mho & Mho Works; $12.95
1993; softcover; 255 pp.

## DIARY OF A WHACKED-OUT BITCH:
### OR, HOW TO CHANGE THE UNIVERSE STARTING WITH YOURSELF
### by Judith Heinz

*Diary* is an unassuming book written by a woman who's just trying to figure herself out. The book starts out with the maxim, "Life would not be worth living without salsa," which I mention mainly because I agree completely. We learn that Judith (if she is indeed the narrator) is a paralegal in Washington, D.C. She hates her job, though, and soon returns to her original job as a waitress at a dive called Dixie's.

Still, Judith is troubled. "I sobbed for over an hour after watching the late night news. I don't know if it was for myself I wept, or for the state of the world. At some point it all blends together into one big teardrop." Her boyfriend, Marcus (also referred to as Pondscum), no longer cares about her and she's tired of leading the same old boring existence. She tries to kill herself by overdosing on valium and tequila in Mexico, but it only ends up getting her in a psychiatric hospital in "Snob Springs, CA."

After giving the doctors hell and maybe learning something, Judith gets out of the hospital and decides to live life to the fullest. First she sails from Hawaii to California in a little sailboat with some weird captain. Then she and one of her friends, appropriately named Aimless, decide to drive all over America just for the hell of it. After reaching California, Aimless heads back home but Judith stays with her sister for a while. Then they decide, what the hell, let's travel across America, so they drive to D.C. Judith spends the summer with Aimless's family in Woods Hole, Massachusetts (Are you still following me?). Then she moves to Seattle, then Minneapolis, where she finds out she has cancer and comes to terms with herself.

*Diary of a Whacked-Out Bitch* is an honest, heartfelt look at life. Even though it occasionally veers into hokiness or sentimentality, it is an enjoyable, hilarious story.

Windbag Books; $9.95
1992; softcover; 199 pp.

## DRINKING, SMOKING, AND SCREWING:
### GREAT WRITERS ON GOOD TIMES
### edited by Sara Nicklès

This anthology of essays, fiction, and poetry is an unapologetic celebration of "vice." To these good folk, there's nothing better than a good drink, a good smoke, and a good lay (although the third one may be a bit harder to come by). Unfortunately, the crazy era we live in has spawned a hostile climate that frowns on having a good time. These writers don't give a rat's ass.

The introductory essay by "respected libertine" Bob Shaccochis deserves to go down as a classic defense of hedonism. "I've passed my HIV blood test, my most recent chest X ray reveals no horrific shadow-clump of cells, and my designated driver is out at curbside, awaiting my tipsy arrival. I know I'm not going to live forever, and neither are you, but until my furlough here on earth is revoked, I should like to elbow aside the established pieties and raise my martini glass in salute to the mortal arts of pleasure."

"When Smoke Gets in Your Eyes...Shut Them" by Fran Leibowitz, written in 1977, upholds the right to smoke and even argues that smokers aren't getting the recognition they deserve: "Smoking, in fact, is downright dangerous. Most people who smoke will eventually contract a fatal disease and die. But they don't brag about it, do they? Most people who ski, play professional football or drive race cars, will not die—at least not in the act—and yet they are the ones with the glamorous images, the expensive equipment and the mythic proportions."

L. Rust Hills, the fiction editor of *Esquire*, waxes philosophical about his obsessions: "Life is (I have been known to say) a Three-Legged Stool, supported by Booze, Coffee, and Smokes, which interdepend essentially. Kick away any leg of the stool and the whole corpus comes crashing to the kitchen floor."

Other selections include Art Buchwald on drinking wine to impress people, Henry Miller on his Parisian adventures ("Paris is like a whore"), Eve Babitz on her defloration, Corey Ford on how office Christmas parties get out of hand, and a bunch of other writings from Charles Bukowski, Spalding Gray, Erica Jong, H.L. Mencken, Anaïs Nin, Vladimir Nabokov, Mark Twain, and other people who know how to get the most out of life.

Chronicle Books; $11.95
1994; softcover; 202 pp.

*The Game of Life*
**by Timothy Leary**
(See page 240) ▼

*Classic Leary. A blueprint of reality or total crapola?*

## "FUCK, YES!":
### A GUIDE TO THE HAPPY ACCEPTANCE OF EVERYTHING
### by Reverend Wing F. Fing, M.D., Ph.D., D.D.S., L.L.D., D.V.D., and much, much more!

A unique novel/parable/self-help book that defies easy explanation. The very basic gist of the book is that *Yes* is the answer to everything. "Remember this: if you are struggling and making judgments about things then sometimes you will have to say *Yes* and sometimes you will have to say the word that some people believe is the opposite of *Yes*. However, if you stop judging, if you make up your mind to answer *Yes* to every question and request, you immediately remove struggle from your life. Confusion will be gone."

Reverend Fing goes on to reveal how saying *Yes* to various things can change your life. Chapters include "Say *Yes* to Teenage Sex," "Say *Yes* to Higher Education," "The Homosexual *Yes*," "Say *Yes* to Adultery," "Say *Yes* to Confusion," "Say *Yes* to Bruno Megasavitch," "Is *Yes* Safe?" and more.

Shepherd Books; $10.95
1988; softcover; 382 pp.

## THE GAME OF LIFE
### by Timothy Leary

Classic Leary. This book presents Uncle Tim's ideas on the nature of consciousness and the future of evolution in a rapid-fire, collagelike manner. From what I can gather (this is a book you need to read slowly at least twice to truly grasp), the basic idea is that 1) the evolution of the human race is analogous to the developmental stages of each individual human and we're heading for a major jump; and 2) we have a preprogrammed neurogenetic code that totally influences who we are. Uncle T shows that the tarot deck, the *I Ching*, and the periodic table of the elements are symbolic versions of this neurogenetic code. Every area of human knowledge and endeavor is also intimately linked with this code, since it determines what we know. Leary discusses neuropolitics, neuropsychology, neurophysics, neurogeology, and more.

Here are some random quotes: "YOU HAVE A PERPETUAL ADOLESCENT BRAIN, A SPOILED ARAB-ITALIAN PLAYGIRL-PRINCE DEMANDING TO BE ACTIVATED SO THAT YOU CAN KILL-RAPE FOR YOUR CAUSE." "Getting High—Hedonic Consumerism—is the First Step in Becoming A Post-terrestrial Divinity." "ALL PAST STATEMENTS ABOUT HUMAN NATURE (INCLUDING THE PRECEDING CHAPTERS OF THIS BOOK) ARE OUTDATED BY THE INFORMATION CONTAINED IN THE FOLLOWING CHAPTER ON EGG-WISDOM." Is it a blueprint of reality or total crapola? You make the call.

New Falcon Publications; $14.95
1979; oversized softcover; 294 pp.

## IMLAKESH

This company sells didjeridoo, the oldest known instrument in the world, used by Australia's indigenous people. A didjeridoo is a limb or trunk from a gum tree that has been hollowed out by white ants. The aborigines cut and paint them. When you send for the catalog, you will get an informative flyer and a color photograph, with prices, of the currently available didjeridoo. Some are plain wood and some have been elaborately painted. Prices range from $180 to $375, with $300 and $350 being average for a painted model.

They claim that this instrument is easy to play and, to help you out, they include an instructional cassette with every order. IMLAKESH also sells a didjeridoo musical cassette, bullroarers (another Aboriginal instrument), boomerangs, and stunning T-shirts with hand-painted Aboriginal designs.

IMLAKESH/PO Box 8237/Santa Fe, NM 87504
Catalog: free, but be a nice person and send along a buck or two.

## LETTERS AT 3 AM:
### REPORTS ON ENDARKENMENT
### by Michael Ventura

This book is a collection of essays by Michael Ventura, a social commentator for *LA Weekly*. His best essays are the ones that take bold, unusual stances on topics. "The Age of Endarkenment" looks at the extreme psychic tension of adolescence. This raw energy is nothing new, Ventura states, but our society doesn't know how to handle it. "It means that when conservatives talk of rock culture subverting the young, when others talk about the same culture liberating the young or when postmodern technologists talk of our electronic environment 'rewiring the software' of new generations—they are all making the same mistake. They fail to understand that a psychic structure that has remained constant for one hundred thousand years is not likely to be altered in a generation by stimuli that play upon its surfaces."

In "In Defense of Alcohol" Ventura writes, "Most of what you read now about alcohol and addiction leaves out how marvelous it can feel to be drunk—an omission that, as the addiction theorists would say, amounts to denial."

The problem is that much of this book is not nearly as daring or original. "Someone Is Stealing Your Life" is one of the

most articulate pieces of wage-slave rage I've read, but saying that minimum-wage work sucks isn't terribly new. Neither is writing about the takeover of our schools by fundamentalists or bemoaning the Gulf War or revealing that the American people are in terrible physical shape.

Spring Publications; $16.50
1993; softcover; 247 pp.

## LINDSAY'S TECHNICAL BOOKS

The hundreds of books in this catalog are almost all either recently written books or reprints of old books containing old-time knowledge about electricity, chemistry, explosives, alcohol manufacture, food preparation, survival skills, shortwave radio, motors, and related topics. Most of the knowledge in these books has been forgotten, shoved to the side as corporations and scientists developed faster, more complicated ways to do the same things. But newer doesn't always mean better. Lindsay's gives us old, forgotten knowledge that can still be useful—and sometimes dangerous.

Some of the titles include *Secrets of Building Electrostatic Lightning Bolt Generators, How to Make Mirrors* (1931), *Explosives for Shale and Clay Blasting* (1916), *Manufacture of Whiskey, Brandy and Cordials* (1937), and *Home Sausage Making* (yeeuuck!). There are also a few fringe science books here covering Tesla and perpetual motion.

Lindsay Publications Inc.
PO Box 538/Bradley, IL 60915-0538
Catalog: $1

## MAKE BELIEVE:
### A TRUE STORY
### by Diana Athill

Athill was an editor at the British publishing house André Deutsch when it published the autobiography of an African-American revolutionary, Hakim Jamal, in the late 1960s. Athill developed a friendship, and for a short while a sexual relationship, with Jamal. She tells the story of this interesting man, who started out as a follower of Malcolm X, seriously proclaimed himself to be God, got taken by a con man named Michael X, allowed his girlfriend (the daughter of a member of Parliament) to be murdered, and was eventually murdered himself.

It is a touching and personal account, made even more interesting by Athill's unnerving honesty: During her first meeting with Jamal/God, she recounts: "I was wearing a wool dress but could feel the coldness of his hand on my shoulder through the material, and that it was trembling very slightly. I wanted to say, 'Relax, love—I don't have to be challenged or seduced, I'd be in bed with you in a trice if you wanted it…. He struck me at once as a man who had always had any woman he wanted, but not as a particularly sensual man: it would be seducing, not fucking, that was important to him." Not exactly your stereotypical, crusty English dame!

Steerforth Press; $18
1993; hardcover; 130 pp.

## MAVERICKS OF THE MIND:
### CONVERSATIONS FOR THE NEW MILLENNIUM
### interviews by David Jay Brown and
### Rebecca McClen Novick

A collection of interviews with cutting-edge thinkers. The tone is kind of New Agey, but there's such a wide array of subjects and ideas that it transcends the New Age label. Among the hipsters interviewed are Terence McKenna, Ralph Abraham, Timothy Leary, Robert Anton Wilson, Rupert Sheldrake, Colin Wilson, John Lilly, Laura Huxley, and Allen Ginsberg. Most of the discussions focus on the expanding of consciousness and the nature of reality, with chaos theory, quantum physics, religion, and psychedelics making frequent appearances. In fact, consciousness-expanding drugs figure so prominently in these interviews that you chemical adventurers will want to pick up this book even if no other aspect of it interests you. But anybody interested in reality hacking will love this book. As Robert Anton Wilson says when asked what model he envisions to explain synchronicity: "I never have one model. I always have at least seven models for anything."

The Crossing Press; $12.95
1993; softcover; 311 pp.

## THE MOLE PEOPLE:
### LIFE IN THE TUNNELS BENEATH NEW YORK CITY
### by Jennifer Toth

Every once in a while a book comes along that offers a peek into a strange world that exists parallel to ours but which is completely unknown to us. *Mole People* is such a book. It explores the world beneath New York City—the honeycomb of subway tunnels, sewers, and water mains—and the people who live there.

Toth recounts the stories she'd heard about the underground homeless population—people who'd heard rumors, people who knew people who live underground. In fact, it sounds like an urban legend, except it's actually true. One day a police sergeant spilled the beans about "the city beneath the streets." The author followed the trail underground and met the people who live there, either alone or in small communities. One group of people who live far, far below the surface have even elected a mayor. The mole people come for different reasons. Some are postmodern hermits who reject the values of the aboveground world. Others simply want to escape the dangers of the street. But there are other dangers, as Toth realizes when she meets the underground's most infamous resident, the Dark Angel.

Like a good science fiction novel, *Mole People* is a provocative account of a previously uncharted world.

Chicago Review Press; $19.95
1993; hardcover; 267 pp.

## MOSCOW HIDE & FUR #400 LIST

With this catalog you can get basically any part of any animal that's legally obtainable (whether it's legal to possess it in your neck of the woods is another matter, though). Some of the items offered for sale: antelope horns, black bear claws, peacock feathers, skunk fur, wolf skulls, coyote's lower jaws, frozen scorpions, rattlesnake rattles, alligator teeth, boar tusks, porcupine quills, turtle shells, and other stuff that makes my skin crawl. This company offers other catalogs for leather, taxidermy, books, etc.

Moscow Hide & Fur/PO Box 8918/Moscow, ID 83843
Catalogs are free, but be a nice person and send along a buck or two.

## MOUSE TALES:
### A BEHIND-THE-EARS LOOK AT DISNEYLAND
### by David Koenig

Disneyland®©™ is a modern-day utopia, a Magical Wonderland®©™ where everything is absolutely perfect and nothing can go wrong. As David Koening writes: "From planning to performance, Disneyland is a complex show designed to manipulate guests both superficially and subconsciously. The Imagineers have created their own reality, covered by a peacefulness you can almost breathe.... The crowds can be the same people who an hour before cut you off on the freeway, yet now you feel comfortable, safe." Koenig, much to the chagrin of Disney and its mouthpieces, pulls back the curtain on this Oz and shows just how it works and how it sometimes doesn't. He reveals the army of people who run Disneyland, what it's like to work in a mouse suit, how rides break down, the underground labyrinth beneath the amusement park, lawsuits against Disneyland, employee strikes, and the trouble, including death, that has occurred in paradise.

Here are some cool factoids that you'll find. Most of them are covered in depth:

•Disneyland employs forty-eight full-time electricians. One crew's sole duty is to constantly change the 100,000 tiny light bulbs that line roof edges.

•"One man spends his entire eight-hour shift polishing the brass on the Carrousel."

•Hidden observational cameras abound. Pirates of the Caribbean has eleven, People Mover and Splash Mountain each have twelve, and the Matterhorn has two.

•To relieve monotony, the author claims employees purposely cause rides to break down. "Matterhorn attendants would put four little kids in one sled and four college football players in the next. The heavy sled would quickly catch up and trigger all the brakes."

•During a birthday party for a manager of the Matterhorn, someone spiked the punch with alcohol, the brownies with pot, and the guacamole dip with PCP! The crew munched out and then had to return to work to operate the ride.

•Once, while the wolf from Pinocchio was posing for a picture with some teenage girls, two of them pinned his arms behind him, two others grabbed his crotch, and the fifth one took his picture.

•"One night in the early 1960s, a crazed guest pulled a six-inch switchblade on Alice in Wonderland and demanded a date with her. The Mad Hatter bounded to the rescue, and the man stabbed him in his big rubber face. Fortunately, the actor was only cut on his knuckles and the White Rabbit arrived with security to apprehend the man."

•Walt Disney's private apartment is still located above the Main Street Fire Department.

•Disneyland has had problems with rats in the park. After trying several approaches, they brought in cats to hunt down the vermin. Wild cats still inhabit the park, coming out only when the crowds are gone for the day.

•At the park in 1981, a teenage boy was stabbed to death when he pinched the rear end of a girl escorted by a dude packing an eight-and-a-half-inch buck knife.

•There is a long section devoted to the "Yippie Pow Wow" at Disneyland. The counterculture group spread the word that August 6, 1970, was going to be a day of "Free love, free dope and free fun" at the park. About three hundred Yippies showed up, causing minor disturbances throughout the day. A bunch of them took over the Wilderness Fort on Tom Sawyer Island. They chased the other guests away, raised the Viet Cong flag, smoked pot, and chanted "Free Charlie Manson!" and "Legalize marijuana." Later in the evening, push came to shove and three hundred cops, riot police, and security guards rounded up the flower children. There were no major injuries and twenty-three people were arrested.

Mouse Tales is a great book. It exposes the hidden side of the Happiest Place on Earth©®™, and because of that, it is total lawsuit bait. I'm sure Disney lawyers are poring over it, trying to find one error that they can pounce on. Because there is a danger that this book would get pulled off the shelves in the event of legal action, I would recommend buying it ASAP.

Bonaventure Press; $25.95
1994; hardcover; 239 pp.; lightly illus.

*Mouse Tales*
**by David Koenig**

*The 1970 Yippie invasion of Disneyland.*

## NUCLEAR WAR SURVIVAL
### (SIXTH EDITION)
### by Duncan Long

What are *you* gonna do when the Big One drops? You think now that the Soviet Union has croaked that we're safe from a full-scale nuclear war? Think again. All those nukes are part of a huge tug-of-war game, there's lots of plutonium unaccounted for, and now we've got this mysterious red mercury on the scene, which may or may not be a way to enrich plutonium without a

*ZAP!* ➤
by Leslie
Singer

*From Buck
Rodgers to Han
Solo,
This is
hardware!*

lot of costly gigantic equipment. All in all, it wouldn't be prudent to turn your underground bunker into a rec room just yet.

If you'd like to survive a nuclear war, this book tells you everything you need to know. Personally, I think I may put on some sunblock and lounge on the veranda as the ICBMs come screaming down. Living in this world is crummy enough, never mind if it's filled with radiation, marauding mutants, *and* my cable gets knocked out. But seriously, if for some reason you do want to stay alive on a charred cinder of a planet, you must be prepared.

The author covers every crucial aspect of survival. He first dispels myths about nuclear war, a couple of which I propagated above. He says that studies of Hiroshima and Nagasaki indicate no increase in the number of babies born with genetic defects. He also says that damage from even a large nuclear bomb would be limited to ten miles, so the whole planet would not become extra crispy. Next, he discusses what to do during the actual bomb blasts and how to deal with radioactive fallout. Of course, you'll need to build a shelter, so complete instructions are given. To measure radiation levels, you're going to have to get or build a radiation meter or dosimeter. Further topics that are covered include water, food, waste disposal (something you might not think of till it's too late), tunneling, and stocking up on medical supplies, guns and ammo, etc. An appendix lists addresses for publications and sources of equipment.

J. Flores Publications; $14.95
1990; softcover; 221 pp.

## SCOUT'S HONOR:
### SEXUAL ABUSE IN AMERICA'S MOST TRUSTED INSTITUTION
### by Patrick Boyle

Any organization or institution made up of children is going to attract two kinds of adults—those that love kids and those that want to molest them. The Boy Scouts is no exception. In this daring exposé, investigative reporter Patrick Boyle traces the history of pedophiles within the Scouts. But Boyle takes an unusual tack to this inflammatory topic—he writes mainly about the perpetrators, not the victims. He rightly says, "No man in America is more despised than the man who has sex with boys...we don't want to hear him—we just want him to stop. This is understandable. His story sickens and angers us. But he doesn't stop. He is one of society's most prolific serial criminals. At the same time, he is one of the nicest guys you'll ever meet." He wants people to know how the pedophile operates, perhaps understand why he does what he does. His mission is to explain, not to excuse.

Boyle starts out by examining the sexual proclivities of the Boy Scouts' founder, Robert Baden-Powell. He presents the circumstantial evidence, arguments, and counterarguments that Baden-Powell was gay, or at least a repressed homosexual. He also notes, "Whether it was a reflection of his times or of his own desires, Baden-Powell did enjoy watching naked boys." However, "There is no evidence that Baden-Powell's admiration of boys' bodies ever went beyond looking, and no way to know if his interest was really sexual."

The book goes on to explore some of the almost two thousand known cases of scoutmasters who molest. Boyle draws on previously secret files kept by the Boy Scouts of America, court records, and interviews with victims, parents, and eight perpetrators. His interviewees include Oregon's Scouter of the Year,

who says he molested more than two hundred boys, a pedophile scoutmaster who was sexually abused by his scoutmaster, and a master who was relieved of his position, moved to another state, and headed a new troop of scouts, whom he proceeded to molest.

Prima Publishing; $22.95
1994; hardcover; 397 pp.; lightly illus.

## THE TEARS OF EROS
### by Georges Bataille

Georges Bataille was a radical philosopher, novelist, critic, and sociologist who was fascinated by the most extreme aspects of the human condition. *The Tears of Eros*, Bataille's final work, is in many ways his masterpiece. In it he shows the strange and powerful intersection of eroticism, violence, death, and the sacred.

*The Tears of Eros* is a dense, demanding work, definitely not poolside reading. "As we have seen, the probably villous Neanderthal man was aware of death. And it is out of this awareness that eroticism appeared, distinguishing the sex life of man from that of the animal.... The sexual behavior of human beings, like that of the ape in general, arises from an intense excitation, uninterrupted by any kind of seasonal rhythm; but it is also characterized by a reserve unknown in animals and which apes in particular never display. In truth, the feeling of embarrassment in regard to sexual activity recalls, in one sense at least, the feeling of embarrassment in regard to death and the dead."

Bataille goes on to make links between his thesis and war, slavery, prostitution, work, Christianity, Dionysus, the Marquis de Sade, Gilles de Rais, Goya, mannerism, and surrealism. Bataille's ideas are backed up by the hundreds of illustrations filling this book—cave paintings, drawings, vases, paintings, engravings, and some of the most shocking photographs you'll ever see, including a series showing a Chinese man being tortured to death by being cut into pieces.

City Lights Books; $14.95
1961; softcover; 213 pp.; lavishly illus.

## ZAP!: RAY GUN CLASSICS
### by Leslie Singer

A loving look at sixty years of toy ray guns. As with all of Chronicle's books on pop culture, *ZAP!* is beautifully designed and produced, containing more than one hundred large, colorful pictures on glossy paper. Pertinent information about each gun—name, manufacturer, country of origin—is given when known. The author doesn't claim that this is a comprehensive look at ray guns; instead it's a sampling of this neglected form of modern firearms.

Each chapter covers a different decade: the Art Deco look of the original 1930s ray guns, the glory days of the 1950s, and the arid wasteland of the 1970s. Guns that are covered include the Buck Rogers XZ-44 Liquid Helium Water Pistol, the Atomic Disintegrator, the Tom Corbett Atomic Pistol, the Han Solo Laser Pistol, and the Astroray Gun.

Chronicle Books; $12.95
1991 oversize softcover; 95 pp.

# APPENDIXES

## APPENDIX A: BOOK CATALOGS

This appendix lists book catalogs (as well as a video catalog and a zine catalog) that offer material on a wide range of topics. Catalogs that have a specific focus (e.g., conspiracies, sex, etc.) are listed in the appropriate chapters.

Many of the books and magazines found throughout this book are offered by one or more of these catalogs. Getting at least some of them is the best single way to keep track of what's out there. They also give you a convenient way to order books from several publishers without having to pay multiple shipping and handling fees.

Anybody who's interested enough to read this book should at the very least get the Loompanics, Flatland, and Last Gasp catalogs. If you're serious about getting strange books, it really wouldn't hurt to get all of these catalogs. It won't cost you that much, and you'll have all the bases covered. Each of these catalogs has at least some stuff the others don't.

Note: Although some of these catalogs are free, it's always nice to send a buck along to help defray the costs of printing and shipping. You can be assured that the foolhardy souls trying to make a living running these catalogs will appreciate it greatly.

### AK DISTRIBUTION

More than fifteen hundred titles with a mainly anti-authoritarian bent. Lots of stuff on anarchy, revolution, and lost rights. Some material on drugs, sex, and conspiracies. Their fiction section has groovy books from Kathy Acker, William Burroughs, Jean Genet, the Marquis de Sade, Jack London, Peter Plate, Harlan Ellison, and many others. Their comix and graphics section is 99 percent titles that I had never seen before. Plus you can get loads of magazines and journals (including one-shots), political tapes (mainly from alternative radio and the Great Atlantic Radio Conspiracy), radical music, spoken word recordings, and T-shirts. Since AK Distribution's home base is in Scotland, they have tons of otherwise unavailable material from the UK.

If you live in the British Isles, you'll want to get AK's UK catalog. It's mostly the same as the American catalog, except that you won't be paying outrageous international shipping fees. Also, you'll get access to a lot of hard-to-find American publications.

AK Press/PO Box 40682/San Francisco, CA 94140-0682
American catalog: free, but $1 for postage is
greatly appreciated
AK Retail/22 Lutton Place/Edinburgh EH8 9PE/SCOTLAND
UK catalog: free, but they do appreciate people from
Britain/Europe sending a LARGE stamped self-addressed
envelope or three International Reply Coupons. Americans
wanting the UK catalog should send $2 cash.

### AMERICA WEST

This slim tabloid offers about one hundred books and videos, including those published by America West as well as several other publishers. They carry material on conspiracies and cover-ups, alternative/suppressed science and medicine, survivalism, prophecy, spirituality (Native American, Christianity, etc.), education, growing food, Zecharia Sitchin's *Earth Chronicles* series, and UFOs. They don't have a huge selection, but most of what they do have is hard to find anywhere else.

America West Distributors
PO Box 3300/Bozeman, MT 59772
Catalog: free

### AMOK

An unbelievably huge catalog filled with thousands of the most subversive books on earth. AMOK calls their *Fourth Dispatch* a "sourcebook of the extremes of information in print" and that ain't no lie. More than any other catalog listed, AMOK believes that nothing is taboo, so in their catalog you can find Holocaust revisionism, hate literature, Tom of Finland, medical textbooks, postmortem procedures, Jack Chick, John Birch publications, Survival Research Laboratories, the *Poor Man's James Bond* series, and other incredible stuff. Of course, not everything they offer is as controversial. They've got lots of material on conspiracies, religion, sex, drugs, pop culture, art, etc. Their incredible fiction section alone is sixty-nine pages, containing books by J.G. Ballard, William Burroughs, Paul Bowles, Angela Carter, Dostoevsky, Donald Goines, Yukio Mishima, Iceberg Slim, Donald Westlake, Charles Willeford, and others.

At the end of the various sections of the catalog are subsections devoted to specific individuals. Just about every book in print by or about that person is offered. Individuals thus honored include Noam Chomsky, Malcolm X, Ted Bundy, Aleister Crowley, Timothy Leary, Wilhelm Reich, Nikola Tesla, Andy Warhol, Salvador Dalí, and John Waters.

The *Fourth Dispatch* is really a book unto itself. Almost every book is briefly described. There are many excerpts from the books being offered, and tons of photos, drawings, and other illustrations are reproduced.

What keeps this impressive sourcebook from being better is that it is at least three years old and, therefore, hopelessly out of date. Many of the books have gone out of print and many more have had price increases. But the *Fifth Dispatch* should be coming out soon. In fact, by the time this is published, you may want to check to see if the new catalog is out.

I should mention that AMOK's problems fulfilling orders have become legendary. However, they've set up an 800 number for credit card orders, so you can find out immediately if a book is in print and in stock.

AMOK/PO Box 861867, Terminal Annex
Los Angeles, CA 90086-1867
Fourth Dispatch: $10.95

### EXTREME BOOKS

Newcomers to the scene, the Extreme Books people have performed a great service by setting up an on-line bookstore. You can call up their BBS in Oregon to order books, download files, or get involved in discussions on controversial and strange topics. You can also get an electronic version of their catalog on the Internet or a printed paper version through the mail.

Since they're new, Extreme Books has a somewhat limited though respectable selection right now: books from Autonomedia, Loompanics, Blast Books, and Feral House, as well as selections on anarchy/situationism, sex, art, pomo literature, etc. I think the most valuable aspect of this venture, though, is the fact that they run a BBS. Because of this they can immediately offer a new book for sale, not having to wait until they mail out a printed update. Also, out-of-print books can be immediately taken off and price changes can be taken care of, resulting in fewer problematic orders for customers.

I wish them luck. I tried the same thing, an on-line, extreme book mail-order service called Different Drummer, from early 1992 through early 1993. It didn't do very well, but then again, I didn't have a presence on the Internet. Anyway, if you have a computer and modem, call these people up and support the cause! If you don't, get their printed catalog.

Extreme Books/PO Box 11704/Portland, OR 97211-0704
BBS Number: 503.288.3960; basic access is free
Voice Number (for questions about the BBS): 503.249.8090
Internet address for electronic catalog:
catalog@mailer.extremebooks.com
Printed catalog: $2

## FLATLAND

The Flatland catalog has always included articles, interviews and in-depth book reviews along with listings of books they sell by mail, but Jim Martin has taken this approach to the next level. Starting with issue #11, Flatland splits, becoming the Flatland catalog and *Flatland Magazine*.

The Flatland catalog is now a straight mail-order listing of books, magazines, and pamphlets on mind control, situationism, media wrenching, conspiracies, state fascism, life energy/Wilhelm Reich, UFOs, strange fiction, and more. Flatland has been in business since 1986 and offers fast, reliable service with a 100 percent money-back, no-questions-asked guarantee on everything you buy. It is one of the essential catalogs to have.

Back issues of the original Flatland magalogs are still available, including #10 (the UFO issue, $4), containing interviews with Mark Lane and Bo Gritz, articles on Blue Orgone and what aliens want with us, among others.

Flatland/PO Box 2420/Fort Bragg, CA 95437
Catalog: $2; overseas surface mail: $2; overseas airmail: $4

## LAST GASP

A thick catalog containing loads of books, magazines, and comix. Tons of books from Grove, Loompanics, RE/Search, manic d, and dozens of other small (and large) presses. Categories include sex, drugs, fiction, art, magick, women's interest, gay, movies and TV, and more.

Last Gasp is especially strong in three areas. First, their selection of comix, cartoons, and graphics is incredible. They carry every title from *all* the major independents (Fantagraphics, Kitchen Sink, NBM, Catalan) and many of the minor independents (Vortex, Knockabout, Drawn and Quarterly, etc.). A lot of the titles in this section are rare imports. Second, the music section contains books on individuals, groups, and genres including punk, pop, alternative, "classic rock," heavy metal, hip-hop, jazz, blues, reggae, and country. Plus they have dozens of songbooks. Finally, their fetish/body modification section is unmatched. They carry back issues of an international array of "perv" magazines—*Body Art, Body Play and Modern Primitives Quarterly, The Rubberist, Secret, <<O>>, Skin Two*, and *Tattootime*.

As if that weren't enough, Last Gasp also has subversive T-shirts, trading cards, buttons, Robt. Williams posters, Flash Videos, the Dealer McDope Game, and more. A treasured resource.

Last Gasp of San Francisco
777 Florida Street/San Francisco, CA 94110
Catalog: $2 (over 18 age statement required)

## LEFT BANK DISTRIBUTION

Well over one thousand radical books and zines, mainly covering anarchist, situationist, radical left-wing, monkey-wrenching, anti-authoritarian topics such as antifascism, antiracism, labor, Native Americans, gay rights, 1960s radicals, feminism, media manipulation, Marxism, terrorism, etc. Everything they carry has an uncompromising tone, and it's all from tiny, independent publishers, meaning it's quite hard to find. In fact, I was pleasantly surprised that I had never seen many of these books offered in any other catalog. Each item is accompanied by a descriptive blurb.

Left Bank also specializes in hunting down out-of-print radical books. Details are given in their catalog.

Left Bank Distribution
4142 Brooklyn Avenue NE/Seattle, WA 98105
Catalog: free, but donations of $1 in cash or stamps are appreciated.

## LOOMPANICS UNLIMITED

The godfather of all deviant catalogs. Loompanics offers a large number of books on a wide variety of subjects. One of their mottos is: "No more secrets. No more excuses. No more limits." If you're fairly new to the extreme scene, as I was when I first got this catalog, you won't believe your eyes. You would have doubted that books like this could even exist. Loompanics offers books on how to make poisons, explosives, booby traps, drugs, and gun silencers, how to convert semiautomatic guns to full auto, how to break and enter, bypass burglar alarms, pick locks, hot-wire cars, run scams, create a new identity, kill and torture, get revenge, smuggle, and make money in unusual and/or illegal ways. They also carry books on survival skills, paralegal skills, crime investigation, self-sufficiency, and self-defense.

What saves Loompanics from becoming just another outlaw survivalist catalog, besides their sense of fun, is that they carry books on other controversial but not quite so scary topics: sex, life extension, intelligence increase, outlaw history, censorship, anarchism and egoism, pop culture, reality creation, self-publishing, science and technology, etc. Another great feature of the catalog is that it includes interesting, original articles on taboo subjects.

Loompanics also publishes a large number of books on the above topics, many of which I've reviewed in this book. You can buy their catalog, but they will send a free copy with every order you place. You'll also get on their mailing list for quarterly updates. Their service is fast and dependable.

This is simply the best single subversive book catalog you can get. You'll want to get other catalogs, too, because Loompanics is by no means complete (no one catalog could be), but this is the one book source you simply can't be without.

Loompanics Unlimited
PO Box 1197/Port Townsend, WA 98368
Catalog: $5

## MYSTIC FIRE VIDEO

Mystic Fire puts out hundreds of great videos. In this full-color catalog you'll find New Age spirituality, alternative health, ancient cultures, and avant-garde film. Titles include Joseph Campbell's *Power of Myth* series, *The World Within* (rare interviews with Carl Jung), *A Change of Heart* by Ram Dass, *Arising from the Flames* by the Dalai Lama, the *Ring of Fire* series, the *Adventure* series, *Healing at the End of the Century* by Elisabeth Kübler-Ross, *The Gun Is Loaded* by Lydia Lunch, the *Beyond Hate* trilogy, *William S. Burroughs: Commissioner of Sewers, Imaginary Landscapes* by Brian Eno, *Maya Deren: Experimental Films*, and three films by Kenneth Anger. Most of the videos are $29.95, although some are less and some are more.

Mystic Fire Direct/PO Box 2249/Livonia, MI 48151
Catalog: free

## NEWSPEAK...BY MAIL

A catalog based on the radical NEWSPEAK bookstore in Rhode Island. A good source of books on conspiracies and cover-ups, hidden history, suppressed science, UFOs, drugs, sex, magick, anarchy, merry mischief, and fiction. At twenty-three digest-sized pages, this catalog doesn't have a huge selection, but it is worth having as a supplement to the larger catalogs. NEWSPEAK plans to expand to a full magazine with reviews and articles and, I am assuming, more titles. I'd say it'll be out by the time you read this.

NEWSPEAK...by Mail/5 Steeple Street/Providence, RI 02903
Catalog: $1

## QVIMBY'S QVEER STORE

A playful magalog filled with books and zines, only a surprisingly small number of which are "qveer." Filled with graphics, gossip, crazed comix, reviews, and articles, Qvimby's puts the emphasis on fun first, selling second. This can work against them because while many of the items are described/reviewed, many aren't (especially books). But their catalog is so fun, I'm willing to forgive them. They carry a varied line of goods, including many comics, trading cards, and even those insane Jack Chick religious tracts ("Get yours today or go to hell!").

Qvimby's Qveer Store
1328 N. Damen Avenue/Chicago, IL 60622
Magalog: $2

## SEE HEAR

Half of this catalog is made up of books and zines on music—every kind of cool music you could think of: jazz, blues, punk, grunge, 1960s rock, "alternative" (whatever that means), Motown, Elvis, plus assorted weirdness like Las Vegas crooning, Irish folk music, and polka. If you have an eclectic taste in music, this is the catalog for you.

The rest of the catalog contains zines and books on body modification, comix, art, Betty Page, etc. and some cool videos and spoken word recordings. Sounds like what's in all the rest of the catalogs, I know, but they do manage to come up with a good bit of stuff that I've seen nowhere else.

See Hear/59 E Seventh Street/New York, NY 10003
Catalog $2. Outside the U.S. $3

## THE USUAL SUSPECTS

An absolutely incredible catalog of zines/magazines from Xines, Inc. From the "mainstream alternative press" (*Utne Reader* and *Whole Earth Review*) to the furthest reaches of the fringe (*Jack Ruby's Slippers* and *Snake Oil: Your Guide to Kooky, Kontemporary Kristian Culture*), this is as close to one-stop shopping for magazines as you are ever going to get. Every category you could think of is represented, from sex, drugs, and conspiracies to culinary, green/eco, and travel. Each magazine is described and the covers of most of them are reproduced.

Unfortunately, you can't get specific issues of the magazines, but of course that would be a total logistical nightmare for the people who put out this catalog. Just be thankful that they're giving you access to the most current issues of these wonderful publications.

They also have an on-line presence on the Studio X BBS. Just choose Xines, Inc. at the main menu. Please note, Xines, Inc. does have a fifteen dollar minimum order requirement, but believe me, you'll have absolutely no problem meeting that minimum. The only problem you will have is staying within your budget.

Xines, Inc./1226 A Calle De Comercio/Santa Fe, NM 87505
Catalog $4 ($3.25 is refundable with your first order)
Studio X BBS: 505.438.2500

# APPENDIX B:
# PUBLISHERS' ORDERING INFORMATION

Voice and fax numbers are given for ordering only.

Abbreviations for payment methods:
- ck: personal check
- mo: money order (or cashier's check)
- MC: Mastercard
- Disc: Discover
- Amex: American Express

Phone numbers are only given for publishers who accept credit card payment.

When ordering with a credit card, be sure to include number, expiration date, and authorized signature. Give some thought before ordering with a credit card over the fax. You never know exactly where the receiving fax is or who might see your number.

Most publishers will accept cash, but sending it through the mail is a risky proposition. If it disappears en route or a publisher loses it, you're out of luck.

Shipping charges are for the United States, unless otherwise noted. Shipping charges are always given in U.S. funds.

When a shipping charge says it's so much "per order," it means that amount is the flat rate you pay no matter how many books are in your order.

Almost all publishers require that you pay sales tax when you order *if that publisher is in your state*. If they are out of your state, you generally don't have to pay tax. The exception are those publishers who have offices, distribution centers, etc., in different states. Citizens of each of those states must pay. All such cases have been noted. Also, some publishers are nonprofit, so nobody has to pay sales tax.

**Abzug Press**
PO Box 5214
Chico, CA 95927
Shipping: $2.50 per book for 1–4 books; free for 5 or more books
Payment: ck, mo

**Added Dimensions Publishing**
100 S. Sunrise Way, Suite 484
Palm Springs, CA 92263
Shipping: $2 first book, $1 each additional; Outside U.S. & Canada: $5 first book, $2 each additional
Payment: ck, mo

**Addison-Wesley**
170 5th Avenue
New York, NY 10010

**Adventures Unlimited Press**
PO Box 74, 303 Main Street
Kempton, IL 60946-0074
Voice: 815-253-6390
Fax: 815-253-6300
Shipping: $2 first book, 50¢ each additional; Canada: $3 first book, 75¢ each additional; others: $5 first book, $2 each additional
Payment: ck, mo, Visa, MC

**AK Press**
PO Box 40682/San Francisco, CA 94140-0682
European Orders: AK Distribution
22 Lutton Place/Edinburgh EH8 9PE SCOTLAND
Shipping: none in U.S.; foriegn: $4 first book, 25¢ each additional
Payment: ck, mo
*You can become a "Friend of AK Press" for $15 a month, for a minimum of three months. Your money will go completely toward publishing new books. During your term as a Friend, you will receive a copy of every book AK publishes and get 10% off all orders.*

**The Akwe:kon Press**
300 Caldwell Hall/Cornell University
Ithaca, NY 14853
Voice: 607-255-4308
Fax: 607-255-0185
Shipping: $2 per book (U.S. and foriegn)
Payment: ck, mo, Visa, MC

**Alyson Publications, Inc.**
40 Plympton Street
Boston, MA 02118

**America West Publishers**
PO Box 2208
Carson City, NV 89702
Voice: 1-800-729-4131
Shipping: $2.50 first book, 50¢ each additional; Canada/Mexico: $4 first book, $1.50 each additional; elsewhere: $6 first book, $1.75 each additional
Payment: ck, mo, Visa, MC

**American Justice Federation**
3850 S. Emerson Avenue, Suite E
Indianapolis, IN 46203
Voice: 1-800-749-9939
Shipping: $4 per order
Payment: ck, mo, Visa, MC

**Amherst Media, Inc.**
PO Box 586
Amherst, NY 14226
Voice: 716-874-4450
Fax: 716-874-4508
Shipping: $4
Payment: ck, mo, Visa, MC

**Andrews and McMeel**
PO Box 419150
Kansas City, MO 64141
Voice: 1-800-642-6480
Payment: ck, mo, Visa, MC

**Annapolis-Washington Book Publishers, Inc.**
c/o SW Orders/PO Box 545/Church Hill, MD 21690
Voice: 1-800-31-TRUTH (318-7884)/Fax: 410-758-0862
Shipping: $3 per order
Payment: ck, mo, Visa, MC

**Aperture**
20 E. 23rd Street
New York, NY 10010
Voice: 1-800-929-2323 or 212-505-5555 ext. 309
Fax: 212-979-7759
Shipping: $5 first book, $1.50 each additional; foriegn: $8
first book, $2 each additional
Payment: ck, mo, Visa, MC, Amex
Sales Tax: NY, Canada

**Apollyon Press**
order from Publishers Distribution Service

**Ariel Press**
14230 Phillips Circle
Alpharetta, GA 30201
Voice: 1-800-336-7769/Fax: 404-664-4974
Shipping: $2 for one book, $4 for more than one book;
foriegn: $7
Payment: ck, mo, Visa, MC, Disc, Amex

**Aries Rising Press**
PO Box 29532
Los Angeles, CA 90029
Shipping: $2 for one book; $3 for two or more books
Payment: ck, mo

**Arts Alternative Press**
3200 Valmont Road, Suite 7
Boulder, CO 80301
Shipping: $3.50 per book; foriegn: write for info
Payment: ck, mo

**Artspace Books**
123 S. Park
San Francisco, CA 94107
Shipping: $2.50 per book
Payment: ck, mo

**ASKLEPIOS**
c/o John Lauritsen
26 St. Mark's Place
New York, NY 10003
Shipping: free; overseas airmail: $9
Payment: ck, mo

**Asylum Arts**
PO Box 6203
Santa Maria, CA 93456
Voice: 805-928-8774
Shipping: $1.50 first book, 25¢ each additional; foriegn:
add $2 to U.S. shipping charges
Payment: ck, mo

**Atlan Formularies**
PO Box 95
Alpena, AR 72611
Voice: 501-437-2999
Shipping: $4 per order
Payment: ck, mo, Visa, MC

**Autonomedia**
55 S. 11th Street
Brooklyn, NY 11211-0568

**Avery Publishing Group**
Order Dept/120 Old Broadway
Garden City Park, NY 11040
Voice: 1-800-548-5757/Fax: 516-742-1892
Shipping: $3
Payment: ck, Visa, MC

**Bantam Books**
1540 Broadway
New York, NY 10036

**Barbary Coast Press**
PO Box 425367
San Francisco, CA 94142
Shipping: $2.45; foriegn: $3
Payment: ck, mo

**Barricade Books**
61 Fourth Avenue
New York, NY 10003
Voice: 212-228-8828/Fax: 212-673-1039

**Bartleby Press**
11141 Georgia Avenue
Silver Spring, MD 20902

**Bay Press**
115 W. Denny Way
Seattle, WA 98119-4205
Voice: 206-284-5913/Fax: 206-286-1218
Shipping: $2 first book, 50¢ each additional; foriegn:
$2.75 first book, $1 each additional
Payment: ck, mo, Visa, MC

**BB Press**
19785 W. 12 Mile Road, Suite 514CC
Southfield, MI 48076
Shipping: All countries: $3
Payment: ck, mo
*Canadians can pay Can$29.95 (postage paid) for the book,
but BB Press prefers U.S. funds if possible.*

**Beacon Press**
25 Beacon Street
Boston, MA 02108

**Benedikt Taschen Verlag GMBH**
Hohenzollernring 53/D-50672 Köln/GERMANY

**The Berkeley Publishing Group**
200 Madison Avenue
New York, NY 10016

**Berkshire House Publishers**
PO Box 297
Stockbridge, MA 01262
Voice: 1-800-321-8526/Fax: 413-298-5323
Shipping: $4
Payment: ck, mo, Visa, MC

**Big Picture Books**
PO Box 909
Carlisle, PA 17013
Payment: ck, mo

**Black Ice Books**
published by Fiction Collective Two
Unit for Contemporary Literature
109 Fairchild Hall/Illinois State University
Normal, IL 61790-4241
Shipping: $2
Payment: ck, mo

**Black Rose Books**
CP 1258, Succ Place du Parc
Montréal, Quebec H2W 2R3/CANADA
U.S. address: 340 Nagel Drive/Cheektowga, NY 14225
Shipping: $3.50 first book, $2 each additional
(when paying in U.S. dollars, please add $1.25 for bank
collection and exchange)
Payment: ck, mo

**Black Sparrow Press**
24 10th Street
Santa Rosa, CA 95401
Shipping: $2 first book, 50¢ each additional;
foriegn: $3 first book, 50¢ each additional
Payment: ck, mo

**Blast Books**
PO Box 51, Cooper Station
New York, NY 10276-0051
Shipping: $2 first book; 50¢ each additional
Payment: ck, mo

**Blue Dolphin Publishing**
PO Box 1920
Nevada City, CA 95959
Voice: 1-800-643-0765
Shipping: $3 first book, 50¢ each additional
Payment: ck, Visa, MC

**Bob Adams, Inc.**
260 Center Street
Holbrook, MA 02343
Phone: 1-800-872-5627 (in MA: 617-767-8100)
Fax: 1-800-872-5628 (in MA: 617-767-0994)
Shipping: $4.50; foriegn: billed at cost
Payment: ck, mo, Visa, MC, Amex

**Bonaventure Press**
PO Box 51961
Irvine, CA 92619-1961
Shipping: $2 first book, $1 each additional
Payment: ck, mo

**Bookreal**
8 Millar Street/Denmark, WA 6333/AUSTRALIA
Shipping: Australia: none; everywhere else: $3.50 surface
mail, $9.50 airmail
Payment: international check or money order (payable to
R. McKinnon-Lower)

**Borderland Sciences Research Foundation**
PO Box 220
Bayside, CA 95524
Voice: 707-825-7733/Fax: 707-825-7779
Shipping: $2.75 first book, $1 each additional; foriegn: $5
first book, $2 each additional
Payment: ck, mo, Visa, MC

**Bramble Books**
PO Box 209
Norfolk, CT 06058
Voice: 0-700-551-7195/Fax: 203-542-6217
Shipping: $2 first book, $1 each additional book; foriegn:
$10 first book, $3 each additional book
Payment: ck, mo, Visa, MC

**Brassey's (U.S.)**
Macmillan Distribution Center
100 Front Street
Riverside, NJ 08075
Voice: 1-800-257-5755/Fax: 1-800-562-1272
Shipping: $2 first book, 75¢ each additional
Payment: ck, mo, Visa, MC, Disc, Amex
Sales tax: all states

**Brilliant Creations**
PO BOX 833842-#193
Richardson, TX 75083-8342
Shipping: $3.95

**British Film Insititute**
order from Indiana University Press

**Brotherhood of Life**
110 Dartmouth SE
Albuquerque, NM 87106-2218
Voice: 505-873-2179/Fax: 505-873-2423
Shipping: $3.75 first book, 50¢ for second book, 25¢ each
additional book
Payment: ck, mo, Visa, MC

**Brunner/Mazel Publishers**
19 Union Square W.
New York, NY 10003
Voice: 1-800-825-3089/Fax: 212-242-6339
Shipping: $2.75 first book, $1.25 each additional; foriegn:
$4 first book, $2 each additional
Payment: ck, Visa, MC, Amex

**Campfire Video**
PO Box 44487
Panorama City, CA 91412
Shipping: $3; foriegn: $10
Payment: ck, mo

**Carroll & Graf Publishers, Inc.**
260 5th Avenue
New York, NY 10001
Voice: 212-889-8772
Shipping: $2 first book
Payment: ck, mo

**Castillo International, Inc.**
500 Greenwich Street, Suite 201
New York, NY 10013
Voice: 212-941-580/Fax: 212-941-8340
Shipping: $3 first book, $1 each additional;
foriegn: double U.S. shipping
Payment: ck, mo, Visa, MC, Amex

**Charles E. Tuttle Company, Inc.**
2-6 Suido 1-chrome, Bunkyo-ku/Tokyo 112/JAPAN
*Tuttle's Books are available at Bookstar and some other book-
stores.*

**Charles F. Miller, Publisher**
708 Westover Drive
Lancaster, PA 17601
Voice: 717-285-2255
Shipping: $2 flat rate
Payment: ck, mo, Visa, MC (credit cards are only for
orders of $25 or more)

**Chicago Review Press**
order from Independent Publishers Group

**Chronicle Books**
275 5th Street
San Francisco, CA 94103
Voice: 1-800-722-6657/Fax: 1-800-858-7787
Shipping: $3.50 for 1 or 2 books, $4.50 for 3 or 4, free for
5 or more
Payment: ck, mo, Visa, MC, Amex
Sales Tax: AZ, CA, CT, DC, HI, IL, KS, MA, MN, NE, NV, NM, WI

**City of Tribes Communications**
63 Fountain Street
San Francisco, CA 94114
Shipping: $3.50 for one tape
Payment: ck, mo

**Civilized Publications, Inc.**
2019 S. 7th Street
Philadelphia, PA 19148
Shipping: $2 per book
Payment: ck, mo, Visa, MC, Amex

**Cleis Press**
PO Box 8933
Pittsburgh, PA 15221
Voice: 412-937-1555/Fax: 412-937-1567
Shipping: 15% of order
Payment: ck, mo, Visa, MC

**Columbia University Press**
562 W. 113th Street
New York, NY 10025

**Common Courage Press**
PO Box 702
Monroe, ME 04951
Voice: 1-800-497-3207/Fax: 207-525-3068
Shipping: $2.50 first book, 50¢ each additional
Payment: ck, mo, Visa, MC

**CompCare Publishers**
3850 Annapolis Lane, Suite 100
Minneapolis, MN 55447
Voice: 1-800-328-3330

**Council Oak Books**
1350 E. 15 Street
Tulsa, OK 74120
Voice: 1-800-247-8850 or 918-587-6454/Fax: 918-583-4995
Shipping: $3 for one book
Payment: ck, mo, Visa, MC

**The Crossing Press**
PO Box 1048
Freedom, CA 95019
Voice: 1-800-777-1048/Fax: 408-722-2749
Shipping: $3 first book; 50¢ each additional book
Payment: ck, mo, Visa, MC

**Daedalus Publishing Company**
4470-107 Sunset Boulevard, Suite 375
Los Angeles, CA 90027
Shipping: $2.50 per order
Payment: ck, mo

**David R. Godine Publishers**
Horticultural Hall/300 Massachusetts Avenue
Boston, Mass 02115
Shipping: $3 flat fee
Payment: ck, mo

**Delectus Books**
27 Old Gloucester Street
London WC1N 3XX/ENGLAND
Voice: 081-963-0979/Fax: 081-963-0502
Shipping: UK: 60p; Europe: £1.20; elsewhere: £2.10
Payment: ck, mo, Visa, MC [U.S. residents can pay with
checks in dollars]

**Diablo Western Press**
PO Box 5/Alamo, CA 94507
Voice: 1-800-247-7389/Fax: 510-295-1203
Shipping: $2.50 first book, 75¢ each additional; overseas
surface: $3.50 first book, $2 each additional; overseas
airmail: $25 for one book
Payment: ck, mo, Visa, MC
Sales tax: Nevada

**The Dial Press**
1 Dag Hammarskjold Plaza
New York, NY 10017

**Distributed Art Publishers**
636 Broadway, 12th Floor
New York, NY 10012
Voice: 1-800-338-BOOK/Fax: 212-673-2887
Shipping: $3 per book
Payment: ck, mo, Visa, MC

**Down There Press**
938 Howard Street #101
San Francisco, CA 94103
Voice: 415-974-8985/Fax: 415-974-8989
Shipping: $3.75 first book, 75¢ each additional
Payment: ck, mo, Visa, MC

**Drawn and Quarterly Publications**
5550 Jeanne Mance Street #16
Montréal, Quebec H2V 4K6/CANADA
Shipping: none
Payment: ck, mo

**Duke University Press**
PO Box 90660
Durham, NC 27708-0660
Voice: 919-688-5134/Fax: 919-688-4574
Shipping: $3 first book, 95¢ each additional;
foriegn: $4 first book, $2 each additional
Payment: ck, mo, Visa, MC, Amex

**Eclipse Books**
PO Box 1099
Forestville, CA 95436

**Element Books**
Order from Penguin USA
Box 999, Dept. #17109
Bergenfield, NJ 07621
Phone: 1-800-253-6476
Shipping: $2
Payment: ck, mo, Visa, MC

**Elliott & Clark Publishing**
PO Box 21038
Washington, DC 20009-0538
Voice: 1-800-789-7733/Fax: 212-483-0355
Shipping: 1–2 books: $3, 3 or more books: $5; foriegn:
call/fax for quote
Payment: ck, mo, Visa, MC

**Elysium Growth Press**
700 Robinson Road
Topanga, CA 90290
Voice: 1-800-350-2020/Fax: 310-455-2007
Shipping: $2 first book, $1 each additional; foriegn
surface: $5 first book, $2 each additional; foriegn air: $8 first
book, $4 each additional
Payment: ck, mo, Visa, MC

**EroSpirit Research**
PO Box 3893
Oakland, CA 94609
Voice: 1-800-432-3767
Shipping: $4 per order; foriegn: $15 per order
Payment: ck, mo, Visa, MC

**Excursion Publications**
108 Randolph Road
Oak Ridge, TN 37830
Voice: 1-800-434-9440/Fax: 615-435-9444
Shipping: $3 per book; elsewhere: $8
Payment: mo, Visa, MC

**Factor Press**
PO Box 8888
Mobile, AL 36689
Voice: 1-800-304-0077/Fax: 205-380-0606
Shipping: $2 first book, $1 each additional; foriegn: $3.75
first book, $1.75 each additional
Payment: ck, mo, MC, Visa

**Feral House**
PO Box 3466
Portland, OR 97208
Shipping: $1.75 first book; $1.25 each additional
Payment: ck, mo

**Firebrand Books**
141 The Commons
Ithaca, NY 14850
Shipping: $2 first book, 50¢ each additional; foriegn: $3 first
book, $1 each additional
Payment: ck, mo

**Firefly Books, Ltd.**
250 Sparks Avenue/Willowdale, ON M2H 2S4/CANADA

**Four Walls Eight Windows**
39 W. 14th Street #503
New York, NY 10011
Voice: 1-800-626-4848
Shipping: $3.50 first book; 50¢ each additional
Payment: ck, mo, Visa, MC

**Frog, Ltd.**
c/o North Atlantic Books
PO Box 12327
Berkeley, CA 94712

**Fulcrum Publishing**
5100 Wisconsin Avenue NW, Suite 230
Washington, DC 20016

**Galen Press, Inc.**
[publishers of medicinal cannabis books]
PO Box 53318
Washington, DC 20009
Voice: 1-800-462-3080 or 202-462-3080
Shipping: $3.50 per book
Payment: ck, mo, Visa, MC

**Galen Press, Ltd**
[publishers of *Death to Dust*]
PO Box 64400
Tucson, AZ 85728-4400
Voice: 602-577-8363/Fax: 602-529-6459
Shipping: $3 per book
Payment: ck, mo, Visa, MC

**Gates of Heck**
5301 Brook Road
Richmond, VA 23227-2401
Voice: 804-266-9422/Fax: same
Shipping: $3 for up to five books
Payment: ck, mo

**Glittering Images/Edizioni D'essai**
Via Giovanni da Montorsoli 37-39/50142 Firenze/ITALY
Shipping: included in price
Payment: international money order

**Grafton**
c/o HarperCollins Publishers
77-85 Fulham Palace Road
Hammersmith, London W6 8JB/ENGLAND

**Hanuman Books**
PO Box 1070, Old Chelsea Station
New York, NY 10113
Shipping: $1 for 1–5 books; foriegn: $1.48
Payment: ck, mo

**Harvard University Press**
Customer Service/79 Garden Street
Cambridge, MA 02138
Voice: 1-800-448-2242 or 617-495-2480
Fax: 1-800-962-4983 or 617-495-8924
Shipping: $3.50 per order
Payment: ck, mo, Visa, MC

**The Haworth Press, Inc.**
10 Alice Street
Binghamton, NY 13904-1580
Shipping: $2.75 first book, $1 each additional; Canada, UK, Japan: $3.75 first book, $1 each additional; elsewhere: 15% of total
Sales tax: NY, Canada
Payment: ck, mo

**Headpress**
PO Box 160/Stockport, Cheshire SK1 4ET/ENGLAND
Shipping: $5; UK: none
Payment: International money order, Eurocheque in pounds sterling or dollars

**Holliday Productions**
238 Davenport Road, Suite 275
Toronto, Ontario M5R 1J6/CANADA

**Holloway House Publishing Company**
8060 Melrose Avenue
Los Angeles, CA 90046
Shipping: $1 per book
Payment: ck, mo

**Holmes Publishing Group**
PO Box 623
Edmonds, WA 98020
Voice: 206-771-2701
Shipping: $3 for one book
Payment: ck, mo, Visa, MC

**Hyperion**
114 5th Avenue
New York, NY 10011

**Hysteria**
PO Box 8581, Brewster Station
Bridgeport, CT 06605
Shipping: $1 per book
Payment: ck, mo

**ICS Press**
Order Dept/720 Market Street
San Francisco, CA 94102
Voice: 1-800-326-0263/Fax: 415-986-4878
Payment: ck, mo, Visa, MC

**III Publishing**
PO Box 1581
Gualala, CA 95445
Shipping: none; foreign: $2 per book
Payment: ck, mo
Sales tax: III Publishing does not collect sales tax. They believe that sales tax on books and magazines is an abridgment of freedom of the press and is therefore unconstitutional.

**Independent Publishers Group**
814 N. Franklin Street
Chicago, IL 60610
Voice: 1-800-888-4741/Fax: 312-337-5985
Shipping: $4 first book; 50¢ each additional
Payment: ck, mo, Visa, MC

**Index Publishing Group, Inc.**
3368 Governor Drive, Suite 273F
San Diego, CA 92122
Voice: 1-800-546-6707/Fax: 619-281-0547
Shipping: $3 first book, $2 each additional; foriegn: $8
Payment: ck, mo, Visa, MC, Amex

**Indiana University Press**
601 N. Morton Street
Bloomington, IN 47404

**Inner Traditions International, Inc.**
One Park Street
Rochester, VT 05767

**Institute for Policy Studies**
1601 Connecticut Avenue NW
Washington, DC 20009

**International Guild of Occult Sciences**
255 N. El Cielo Road, Suite 565
Palm Springs, CA 92262
Voice: 619-327-7355/Fax: same
Shipping: $3 first book, $2 each additional
Payment: ck, mo, Visa, MC, Amex

**IntiNet**
PO Box 4322-M
San Rafael, CA 94913
Shipping: $3 first, $1 each additional (U.S. & Canada); foriegn airmail: $10 first book, $1 each additional
Payment: ck, mo
*By joining IntiNet you can get Love Without Limits at half price. You also get discounts on conferences and workshops, and you'll receive their quarterly newsletter. Membership is $30 per person per year.*

**Irvington Publishers**
Lower Mill Road
N. Stratford, NH 03590
Voice: 603-922-5105/Fax: 603-922-8316
Shipping: $3 per order; foriegn: 10% of order
Payment: ck, mo, Visa, MC
Sales tax: NY

**Irwin Professional Publishing**
1333 Burr Ridge Parkway
Burr Ridge, IL 60521
Voice: 1-800-634-3966; Canada: 416-293-8141
Fax: 800-926-9495; Canada: 416-293-0846
Payment: ck, mo, Visa, MC, Amex
Sales Tax: every state EXCEPT AK, AR, DE, IA, ID, MS, ND, NH, NV, OR, SD, WY

**ISHK Book Service**
PO Box 381062
Cambridge, MA 02238-1062
Voice: 1-800-222-4745/Fax: 1-800-223-4200
Shipping: $4.50 for one book; foriegn: $9 for one book
Payment: ck, mo, Visa, MC

**J. Flores Publications**
PO Box 163001
Miami, FL 33116

**John Benjamins North America, Inc.**
821 Bethlehem Pike
Philadelphia, PA 19118
Voice: 1-800-562-5666/Fax: 215-836-1204
Shipping: $3 first book, $1 each additional
Payment: ck, mo, Visa, MC, Amex

**Johns Hopkins University Press**
Hampden Station
Baltimore, MD 21211-4319
Phone: 800-537-5487/Fax: 410-516-6998
Shipping: $3 first book, 50¢ each additional
Payment: ck, mo, Visa, MC

**Johnson Books**
1880 S. 57th Court
Boulder, CO 80301
Voice: 1-800-258-5830/Fax: 303-443-1679
Shipping: $3
Payment: ck, mo, Visa, MC

**Kendall/Hunt Publishing Company**
4050 Westmark Drive, PO Box 1840
Dubuque, IA 52004-1840
Voice: 1-800-228-0810
Fax: 1-800-772-9165
Shipping: $3 first book; 50¢ each additional
Payment: ck, mo; for telephone orders: MC, Visa
Sales tax: NY, KY, CA, LA, IA

**Kitchen Sink Press**
320 Riverside Drive
Northampton, MA 01060
Voice: 1-800-365-SINK(7465) or 413-586-7822
Fax: 413-586-7040
Shipping: $5 for under $50, 10% of order for over $50;
Canada: $10 for under $50, 20% of order for over $50;
International: $15 for under $50, 30% for order of $50
Payment: ck, mo, Visa, MC

**Kodansha America**
c/o Putnam Publishing Group
390 Murray Hill Pkwy
East Rutheford, NJ 07073
Voice: 1-800-788-6262/Fax: 212-727-9177
Shipping: $3.50 for orders up to $10; $4.25 for $10.01 to
$25; $5 for $25.01 to $50
Payment: ck, mo, Visa, MC, Amex

**Laird Wilcox Editorial Research Service**
PO Box 2047
Olathe, KS 66061
Shipping: none
Payment: ck, mo
Sales Tax: none

**Last Gasp**
777 Florida Street
San Francisco, CA 94110
Voice: 415-824-6636/Fax: 415-824-1836
Shipping: $5.50 for 1–3 books, $6.50 for 4–6 books, $1.50
per book thereafter; foriegn: $12 for 1–3 books, $18.50 for
4–6 books
Payment: ck, mo, Visa, MC

**Laugh Lines Press**
PO Box 259
Bala Cynwyd, PA 19004
Shipping: 75¢ per book
Payment: ck, mo (payable to Rosalind Warren)

**Legendary Publishing Company**
PO Box 7706
Boise, ID 83707-1706
Voice: 1-800-358-1929
Shipping: $2.50 per book
Payment: ck, mo, Visa, MC

**Leyland Publications**
PO Box 410690
San Francisco, CA 94141
Shipping: $2 per book; overseas: $5 per book
Payment: ck, mo

**Light Technology**
PO Box 1495
Sedona, AZ 86336

**Lightworks Audio and Video**
PO Box 661593
Los Angeles, CA 90066
Voice: 310-398-4949/Fax: 310-397-4401
Shipping: $4 first item, $1 each additional; Hawaii,
Alaska, Canada: add $2 to regular shipping
Payment: ck, mo, Visa, MC, Disc

**Little, Brown & Co.**
200 West Street
Waltham, MA 02154
Voice: 1-800-759-0190/Fax: 617-890-0875
Shipping: none if paying by check or money order; other-
wise $2 first book, $1 each additional book
Payment: ck, mo, Visa, MC, Amex

**Llewellyn Publications**
PO Box 64383
St. Paul, MN 55164
Voice: 1-800-843-6666; outside U.S.: 612-291-1970
Fax: 612-291-1808
Shipping: $3 for order under $10; $4 for order over $10
Payment: ck, mo, Visa, MC, Amex

**Long River Books**
division of Inland Book Co.
140 Commerce Street
East Haven, CT 06512
Voice: 1-800-243-0138

**Loompanics Unlimited**
PO Box 1197
Port Townsend, WA 98368
Voice: 206-385-2230
Shipping: $4 for 1-3 books, $6 for 4 or more books; foriegn: 12% of your order total plus regular shipping charges
Payment: ck, mo, Visa, MC (minimum order for credit cards is $50)

**LT Publications**
PO Box 302
Beverly Hills, CA 90213-0302
Fax: 213-655-7314
Shipping: $2.25 per book (maximum $9.50); Europe: $4.95 per item
Payment: ck, mo, Visa, MC

**M. Evans and Co.**
216 E. 49th Street
New York, NY 10017

**Mangajin Books**
Box 489, Station P/Toronto, Ontario M5S 2T1/ENGLAND
Shipping: none
Payment: ck, mo

**Mark V. Ziesing Books**
PO Box 76
Shingletown, CA 96088
Voice: 916-474-1580/Fax: 916-474-1580
Shipping: $3 (up to $30), $4 ($30.01-$60), free over $60; foriegn: exact charges will be billed to credit card
Payment: ck, mo, Visa, MC

**Masquerade Books**
801 Second Avenue
New York, NY 10017
Voice: 1-800-375-2356/Fax: 212-986-7355
Shipping: $1.50 for one book, 75c for each additional; Canada: $2 for one book, $1.25 for each additional; foreign: $4 for one book, $2 for each additional
Payment: ck, mo, MC, Visa

**McGraw-Hill, Inc.**
Order Services
13311 Monterey Avenue
Blue Ridge Summit, PA 17294-0850
Voice: 1-800-822-8158/Fax: 1-800-932-0183
Shipping: $3 per order; foriegn: $5 per order
Payment: ck, mo, Visa, MC, Amex

**McPherson & Company**
PO Box 1126
Kingston, NY 12401

**Medio Multimedia, Inc.**
PO Box 10844
Salinas, CA 93912
Voice: 1-800-788-3866/Fax: 408-655-6071
Payment: ck, mo, Visa, MC

**Mercury House**
201 Filbert Street #400
San Francisco, CA 94133
Voice: 1-800-998-9129/Fax: 415-392-3041
Shipping: $2 first book; 50¢ each additional
Payment: ck, mo, Visa, MC

**Mho and Mho Works**
PO Box 33135
San Diego, CA 92163
Shipping: $2 first book; $1 each additional
Payment: ck, mo

**Mike Hunt Comix**
PO Box 226
Bensenville, IL 60106
Shipping: none
Payment: ck, mo

**Miller Freeman Books**
6600 Siiacci Way
Gilroy, CA 95020
Voice: 1-800-848-5594/Fax: 408-848-5784
Shipping: $5; Canada: $8.50; overseas airmail: $15
Payment: ck, mo, Visa, MC, Disc, Amex
Sales Tax: CA, GA, IL, NY, TX, Canada (GST)

**The MIT Press**
55 Hayward Street
Cambridge, MA 02142
Voice: 1-800-356-0343/Fax: 617-625-6660
Shipping: $3
Payment: ck, mo, Visa, MC
Sales Tax: none

**Morey Studio**
314 The Besler Building
4053 Harlan Street
Emeryville, CA 94608
Shipping: $3.50 per book
Payment: ck, mo

**Morpheus International**
PO Box 7246
Beverly Hills, CA 90212

**Na Kane O Ka Malo Press**
PO Box 970
Waipahu, HI 96797
Shipping: $2.50 per book
Payment: ck

**National Coalition Against Censorship**
275 7th Avenue
New York, NY 10001
Shipping: none
Payment: ck, mo

**National Vanguard Books**
PO Box 330
Hillsboro, WV 24946
Shipping: $1 first book, 25¢ each additional

**Natural Energy Works**
PO Box 864
El Cerrito, CA 94530
Voice: 510-526-5978/Fax: 510-526-5978
Shipping: $2; overseas surface mail: $5; overseas airmail: $7
Payment: ck, mo

**NBM Publishing Company**
185 Madison Avenue, Suite 1504
New York, NY 10016
Voice: 1-800-886-1223/Fax: 212-545-1227
Shipping: $2 first book, $1 each additional (up to $5
maximum); foriegn: $4 first item, $1 each additional
Payment: ck, mo, Visa, MC

**New Amsterdam Books**
PO Box C
Franklin, NY 13775
Voice: 1-800-944-4040/Fax: 607-829-2057
Shipping: $3
Payment: ck, mo, Visa, MC

**New Falcon Publications**
1739 E. Broadway Road, Suite 1-277
Tempe, AZ 85822
Shipping: $2 first book, $1 each additional; foriegn: $4
first book, $2 each additional
Payment: ck, mo

**New Society Publishers**
4527 Springfield Avenue
Philadelphia, PA 19143
Voice: 1-800-333-9093/Fax: 215-222-1993
Shipping: $2.50 first book, 75¢ each additional book
Payment: ck, mo, Visa, MC, Amex

**New Victoria**
PO Box 27
Norwich, VT 05055
Voice: 1-800-326-5297/Fax: 1-800-326-5297
Shipping: $1.50 first book, 25¢ each additional
Payment: ck, mo, Visa, MC

**New York University Press**
Attn: Orders
70 Washington Sq S.
New York, NY 10012
Voice: 1-800-996-NYUP/Fax: 212-995-3833
Shipping: $3 first book, $1 each additional
Payment: ck, Visa, MC
Sales tax: CA, Canada

**Noble Press**
213 W. Institute Place, Suite 508
Chicago, IL 60610
Shipping: $3
Payment: ck, mo

**Odonian Press**
PO Box 7776
Berkeley, CA 94707
Shipping: $2 flat fee
Payment: ck, mo

**C. Olson**
PO Box 5100-MB
Santa Cruz, CA 95063-5100
Shipping: $1.50 for one book
Payment: ck, mo

**Open Court Publishing Co.**
Genral Book Division
PO Box 599
Peni, IL 61354
Voice: 800-435-6850/Fax: 815-223-1350
Shipping: $3 first book, $1 each additional
Payment: ck, mo, Visa, MC, Amex
Sales Tax: CA, IL, WA

**Open Magazine Pamphlet Series**
PO Box 2726
Westfield, NJ 07091
Shipping: none; foriegn: $2 per order
Payment: ck, mo
*You can subscribe to the pamphlet series. The next ten
pamphlets are $35; foriegn: $45*

**Overlook Press**
Lewis Hollow Road
Woodstock, NY 12498

**Paladin Press**
PO Box 1307
Boulder, CO 80306
Voice: 303-443-7250
(credit card users call 1-800-392-2400)/Fax: 303-442-8741
Shipping: $4; foriegn: $6 for surface mail; call for airmail
Payment: ck, mo, Visa, MC, Disc

**Pathfinder Press**
410 West Street
New York, NY 10014
Voice: 212-741-0690/Fax: 212-727-0150
Shipping: $3 first book; 50¢ each additional
Payment: ck, mo, Visa, MC ($30 minimum for credit card
orders)

**Permeable Press**
47 Noe Street #4
San Francisco, CA 94114-1017
Shipping: $1.50 first book, 50¢ each additional; foriegn:
$5 first book, $2 each additional
Payment: ck, mo

**Photo Survey Press Publishing**
c/o Stephen Paternite
611 Mull Avenue
Akron, OH 44313
Shipping: $2.50 for one book; foriegn: add 20%
Payment: mo (payable to Stephen Paternite)

**Pluto Press**
c/o Westview Press
Customer Service Dept./5500 Central Avenue
Boulder, CO 80301
Voice: 303-444-3541/Fax: 303-449-3356
Shipping: $3 first book, 75¢ second book, 50¢ each addi-
tional
Payment: ck, mo, Visa, MC

**PM&E Publishing Group**
PO Box 4465
Boynton Beach, FL 33424
Shipping: none; overseas: $5
Payment: ck, mo

**Polinym Press**
10028 Manchester, Suite 202
St. Louis, MO 63122
Voice: 314-968-0986/Fax: same
Shipping: $1.50 for one book; Canada: $2; elsewhere: $3
Payment: ck, mo

**Pomegranate Artbooks**
PO Box 6099
Rohnnett Park, CA 94927

**Popular Culture, Ink**
PO Box 1839
Ann Arbor, MI 48106
Voice: 1-800-678-8828
Fax: 313-761-4301
Shipping: $4.75 for one or two books
Payment: ck, mo, Visa, MC

**Prelude Press**
8159 Santa Monica Boulevard
Los Angeles, CA 90046
Voice: 1-800-LIFE-101

**Prima Publishing**
PO Box 1260
Rocklin, CA 95677-1260

**Princeton University Press**
41 William Street
Princeton, NJ 08540-5237

**Prometheus Books**
59 John Glenn Drive
Amherst, NY 14228
Voice: 1-800-421-0351/Fax: 716-691-0137
Shipping: $3.95 first book; $1.95 each additional
Payment: ck, mo, Visa, MC

**ProMotion Publishing**
10387 Friars Road, Suite 231
San Diego, CA 92120

**Publishers Distribution Service**
6893 Sullivan Road
Grawn, MI 49637
Voice: 1-800-507-2665/Fax: 616-276-5197
Shipping: $3.50 per book
Payment: ck, mo, Visa, MC, Disc, Amex

**Publius Press**
3100 S. Philamena Place
Tucson, AZ 85730
Shipping: $1.45; foriegn: $2.30
Payment: ck, mo

**Quest Books**
306 W. Geneva Road
Wheaton, IL 60187

**Quick Trading Company**
PO Box 429477
San Francisco, CA 94142-9477
Voice: 1-800-428-7825, ext. 102/Fax: 510-533-4911
Shipping: for UPS $5, for PO Box $7; Canada, Central and South America: $10 first book, $3 each additional; elsewhere: $10 first book, $8 each additional
Payment: ck, mo, Visa, MC

**Ralph Judd Communications**
1330 Bush Street #4H
San Francisco, CA 94109
Voice: 1-800-637-2256
Shipping: $2 per book; $1 per postcard set
Payment: ck, mo, Visa, MC

**Red Sea Press**
11-D Princess Road
Lawrenceville, NJ 08648
Voice: 609-844-9583/Fax: 609-844-0198
Shipping: $3 first book; 50¢ each additional
Payment: ck, mo, Visa, MC, Amex

**Regnery Publishing**
422 First Street SE, Suite 300
Washington, DC 20003
Voice: 202-546-5005/Fax: 202-546-8759
Shipping: $4 first book; $1 each additional
Payment: ck, mo, Visa, MC, Amex
Sales tax: DC, MD

**Riverrun Press**
1170 Broadway, Suite 807
New York, NY 10001
Shipping: $2.50 first book; 50¢ each additional
Payment: ck, mo
foriegn orders: Calder Publications
9-15 Neal Street/London WC2 H9TU/ENGLAND

**Roberts Rinehart Publishers**
PO Box 666
Niwot, CO 80544
Voice: 1-800-352-1985/Fax: 303-652-3923
Shipping: mail: $3 first book, 50¢ each additional book; foriegn: call
Payment: ck, mo, Visa, MC

**Ronin Publishing**
PO Box 1035
Berkeley, CA 94701
Voice: 510-548-2124/Fax: 510-548-7326
Shipping: $4 first book, $1 each additional; Canada and Mexico: double the shipping charge
Payment: ck, mo, Visa, MC

**Sarpedon Publishers**
Order from EHQ/Emperor's Press
5744 W. Irving Park Road
Chicago, IL 60634
Voice: 312-777-7307/Fax: 312-777-4828
Shipping: $3 first book; 50¢ each additional
Payment: ck, mo, Visa, MC

**Scarecrow Press**
52 Liberty Street, PO Box 4167
Metuchen, NJ 08840
Voice: 1-800-537-7107 or 908-548-8600/Fax: 908-548-5767
Shipping: $2.50 first book, 50¢ each additional; foriegn:
$3.50 first book, $1 each additional
Payment: ck, mo, Visa, MC
Sales tax: CT, NJ

**Schiller Institute, Inc.**
PO Box 20244
Washington, DC 20041-0244
Shipping: $3.50 first book, 50¢ each additional
Payment: ck, mo
Sales tax: Virginia

**Seal Press**
3131 Western Avenue #410
Seattle, WA 98121-1028

**Secrecy Oversight Council**
HCR Box 38
Rachel, NV 89001
Shipping: $3.50 for one book; Canada/Mexico: $4.50 for
one book; overseas: $10 for one book
Payment: ck, mo

**Secret Garden**
1352 Yukon Way, Suite 20
Novato, CA 94947
Voice: 415-898-6430/Fax: 1-800-869-6888
Shipping: $3 for one book, $6 for two or more; Canada:
$10 for one book, $13 for two or more
Payment: ck, mo

**The Secret Information Network**
PO Box 3185
West Sedona, AZ 86340
Shipping: free in U.S.; foriegn: 10% of order
Payment: ck, mo

**Shaynew Press**
PO Box 425221
San Francisco, CA 94142
Shipping: $5 per order
Payment: ck, mo
*If you order two books, you get a $5 discount. Order three
books and get a $10 discount.*

**Shepherd Books**
PO Box 2290
Redmond, WA 98073
Shipping: none for book rate, $2.50 per book for airmail
Payment: ck, mo

**Sheridan Square Press**
145 W. 4th Street
New York, NY 10012
Shipping: U.S., Canada & Mexico: $2.50 first book, 50¢
each additional; other foreign surface: $4 first book, $2
each additional; other foreign airmail: $9 first book, $4
each additional
Payment: ck, mo (U.S. funds payable in U.S. or Canada)

**The Shoppe Press**
PO Box 2741
Monroe, LA 71207-2741
Voice: 318-322-4081
Shipping: $4; overseas surface mail: $10
Payment: ck, mo, Visa, MC

**Sky Books**
PO Box 769
Westbury. NY 11590-0104
Shipping: $3 (orders under $30), $4 ($30.01–$60), $6 (over
$60); foriegn: $8 (orders under $30); $9 ($30.01–$60), $11
(over $60)
Payment: ck, mo

**Slingshot Publications**
BM Box 8314/London WC1N 3XX/ENGLAND
In the U.S. order from: Amy Chidester
602 Hamilton Street, Suite 120/Somerset, NJ 08873
Shipping: 10% of order
Payment: ck, mo
Sales Tax: NJ

**Smart Publications**
PO Box 4667
Petaluma, CA 94955

**Smithsonian Institute Press**
470 L'Enfant Plaza, Suite 7100
Washington, DC 20560

**The Sourcebook Project**
PO Box 107
Glen Arm, MD 21057
Shipping: $1 for orders under $30; foriegn: $1.50 per book
Payment: ck, mo

**Spring Publications**
c/o Publisher's Resources, Inc.
1224 Heil Quaker Boulevard
La Vergne, TN 37086
Voice: 1-800-937-5557/Fax: 1-615-793-3915
Shipping: $3 first book; $1 each addtional
Payment: ck, mo, Visa, MC

**Stackpole Books**
5067 Ritter Road
Mechanicsburg, PA 17055
Voice: 1-800-732-3669/Fax: 717-796-0412
Shipping: $3 first book; $1 each additional
Payment: ck, mo, Visa, MC, Amex

**Station Hill Press**
Barrytown, NY 12507
Voice: 1-800-342-1993
Shipping: $3 first book, 50¢ each additional; Canada: $3 first
book, $1.50 each additional; foriegn surface mail: $3.50 first
book, $1.50 each additional; foriegn airmail: $12 first book,
$7 each additional
Payment: ck, mo, Visa, MC (credit cards accepted by
phone only)

**Steerforth Press**
PO Box 70
South Royalton, VT 05068
Voice: 1-800-444-2524, ext. 262/Fax: 802-763-2818
Shipping: $3 first book; $1 each additional (U.S. and
foriegn orders)
Payment: ck, mo, Visa, MC, and for phone orders only:
Disc, Amex

**STORM**
PO Box 18009
Denver, CO 80218
Shipping: $2.50 for 1–3 books, 75¢ thereafter; foriegn
surface mail: $3 per book
Payment: ck, mo
*"STORM is not responsible for items seized by customs or
government agenices!"*

**Sun & Moon Press**
6026 Wilshire Boulevard
Los Angeles, CA 90036

**Sun Tavern Fields**
PO Box 982/London E1 9EQ/ENGLAND
Shipping: £5.00 each (U.S. airmail); £1.50 each
(UK/Europe)
Payment: mo (in £ sterling)

**Syracuse University Press**
1600 Jamesville Avenue
Syracuse, NY 13244-5160
Voice: 1-800-365-8929/Fax: 315-443-5545
Shipping: $3 first book, 75¢ each additional; foriegn: $4
first book, $1 each additional
Payment: ck, mo, MC, Visa

**Tafford Publishing**
PO Box 271804
Houston, TX 77277
Shipping: $2; overseas surface mail: $3 per book; overseas
airmail: $5 per book
Payment: ck, mo

**Temple Press Limited**
PO Box 227/Brighton Sussex BN2 3GL/ENGLAND
Shipping: surface to U.S.: $3 per book, air to U.S.: $6 per book
Payment: ck, mo (checks and money orders in U.S.
dollars are OK)

**Ten Speed Press**
PO Box 7123
Berkeley, CA 94707
Voice: 1-800-841-2665/Fax: 510-524-4588

**Tetrahedron Industries, Inc.**
10B Drumlin Road
Rockport, MA 01966
Voice: 1-800-336-9266/Fax: 508-546-9226
Shipping: $3.50
Payment: ck, mo, MC, Visa, Amex

**Thames and Hudson**
500 5th Avenue
New York, NY 10110

**The 3-D Zone**
PO Box 741159
Los Angeles, CA 90004
Shipping: $2 first book, $1 each additional up to $10
maximum; international: double U.S. postage
Payment: ck, mo

**Timber Press, Inc.**
The Haseltine Bldg/133 SW 2nd Avenue, Suite 450
Portland, OR 97204-3527
Voice: 1-800-327-5680/Fax: 503-227-3070
Shipping: $5.95 for orders $35.01–$50; foriegn surface
mail: $6 first book; Europe airmail: 25% of order; else-
where by airmail: 35% of order.
Payment: ck, mo, Visa, MC, Disc, Amex
Sales tax: none

**Times Change Press**
c/o Publishers Services/Po Box 2510
Novato, CA 94948
Voice: 1-800-488-8595
Shipping: $1.50 first book, 75¢ each additional; foriegn:
add 30% and round to the nearest dollar
Payment: ck, mo, Visa, MC

**Tom of Finland Company**
PO Box 26716, Dept. RK
Los Angeles, CA 90026
Voice: 1-800-3-FINLAND/Fax: 213-481-2092
Shipping: $5 per book; foriegn: $8 per book
Payment: ck, mo, Visa, MC

**Transform Press**
PO Box 13675
Berkeley, CA 94712
Shipping: $4 first book, $1 each additional; foriegn: $8
first book, $2 each additional
Payment: ck, mo

**Turnaround Distribution**
27, Horsell Road/London N5 1XL/ENGLAND
Voice: 0-171-609-7836/Fax: 0-171-700-1205
Shipping: £2
Payment: ck, mo, Visa, MC (payment must be in sterling)

**Twin Palms Publishers**
401 Paseo de Peralta
Santa Fe, NM 87010
Voice: 505-988-5717/Fax: 505-988-7011
Shipping: $3 first book, $1 each additional
Payment: ck, mo, Visa, MC

**Universal Electronics, Inc.**
4555 Groves Road, Suite 12
Columbus, OH 43232
Voice: 614-866-4605/Fax: 614-866-1201
Shipping: $4 per book (Priority Mail); write for foriegn orders
Payment: ck, mo, Visa, MC

**University of Oklahoma Press**
PO Box 787
Norman, OK 73070-0787
Voice: 1-800-627-7377/Fax: 405-364-5798
Shipping: $2.50 first book, 50¢ each additional; Canada:
$3 first book, $1 each additional plus 7% GST tax.
Payment: ck, mo, Visa, MC, Amex

**University of South Carolina Press**
205 Pickens Street
Columbia, SC 29208
Voice: 1-800-768-2500/Fax: 1-800-848-0740
Shipping: $3.50 first book, 50¢ each additional
Payment: ck, mo, Visa, MC

**University of Tennessee Press**
Chicago Distribution Center/11030 S. Langeley
Chicago, IL 60628
Voice: 1-800-621-2736
Shipping: $3.50 first book, 75¢ each additional; foriegn:
$4.50 first book, $1 each additional
Payment: ck, mo, Visa, MC

**University Press of America**
4720 Boston Way
Lanham, MD 20706
Voice: 1-800-462-6420/Fax: 301-459-2118
Shipping: $3 first book; 75¢ each additional
Payment: ck, mo, Visa, MC

**University Press of Kentucky**
Marketing and Sales
663 S. Limestone Street
Lexington, KY 40508-4008
Voice: 1-800-666-2211/Fax: 606-323-4981
Shipping: $3 first book, 50¢ each additional (U.S. and
Canada); foriegn: $4 first book, $1 each additional
Payment: ck, mo, Visa, MC, Disc, Amex

**Van Nostrand Reinhold**
115 5th Avenue
New York, NY 10003

**Victoria House Press**
67 Wall Street, Suite 2411
New York, NY 10004
Voice: 1-800-888-9999/Fax: 212-809-9087
Shipping: free
Payment: ck, mo, Visa, MC, Disc, Amex

**Vortex Comics**
PO Box 173
Sanborn, NY 14132-0173

**Walker Art Center**
Center Bookshop/Vineland Place.
Minneapolis, MN 55403
Voice: 612-375-7633/Fax: 612-375-7565
Shipping: $7 for orders $25.01-$45;$8 for $50.01-$75
Payment: ck, mo, Visa, MC, Amex

**Wayne State University Press**
Attn: Order Dept/Leonard N. Simons Bldg
5959 Woodward Avenue
Detroit, MI 48202
Voice: 1-800-WSU-READ or 313-577-6120/Fax: 313-577-6131
Shipping: $2.50 first book, 50¢ each additional; foriegn:
$3.50 first book, $1 each additional
Payment: ck, mo, Visa, MC

**Whitney Museum of American Art**
c/o Sales Dept
945 Madison Avenue
New York, NY 10021
Voice: 212-570-3614/Fax: 212-570-1807 (Attn: Sales Dept.)
Shipping: $4 first book; $1 each additional
Payment: ck, mo, Visa, MC, Amex

**Windsor House Publishers**
1420 NW Gilman Boulevard, Suite 2152
Issaquah, WA 98027
Shipping: $2.50 for 1–5 books
Payment: ck, mo

**Winston-Derek Publishing Group**
PO Box 90883
Nashville, TN 37209
Voice: 1-800-826-1888/Fax: 615-329-4824
Shipping: $1.80 first book, 50¢ each additional; Canada:
$3.12 for one book, $4.32 for two books
Payment: ck, mo, Visa, MC, Disc, Amex

**Workman Publishing Company**
708 Broadway
New York, NY 10003

**Wry-Bred Press, Inc.**
PO Box 1454, Madison Square Station
New York, NY 10159-1454
Voice: 212-689-5473/Fax: 212-689-6859
Shipping: $3.50 (U.S. or foriegn)
Payment: ck, Visa, MC, Amex

**Xenos Books**
c/o Eugene Silverman
3644 Creekside Drive
Ann Arbor, MI 48105
Shipping: $1.50 first book; 50¢ each additional; Canada:
$2 first book; 75¢ each additional
Payment: ck, mo (payable to Eugene Silverman)

**Yale University Press**
PO Box 209040
New Haven, CT 06520-9040

**Ziggurat**
PO Box 25193/Rochester, NY 14625
Shipping: no charges
Payment: ck